Development in Infancy

AN INTRODUCTION

Development in Infancy

AN INTRODUCTION

— ❖ —

FOURTH EDITION

Michael E. Lamb
Marc H. Bornstein
Douglas M. Teti

LEA
2002 LAWRENCE ERLBAUM ASSOCIATES, PUBLISHERS
Mahwah, New Jersey   London

Editor:	Bill Webber
Editorial Assistant:	Erica Kica
Cover Photograph:	Alisa Murray
Cover Design:	Kathryn Houghtaling Lacey
Textbook Production Manager:	Paul Smolenski
Full-Service Compositor:	TechBooks
Text and Cover Printer:	Hamilton Printing Company

This book was typeset in 10/12 Palatino, Italic, Bold, Bold Italic.
The heads were typeset in Minion.

Lawrence Erlbaum Associates, Inc., Publishers
10 Industrial Avenue
Mahwah, New Jersey 07430

Library of Congress Cataloging-in-Publication Data

Lamb, Michael E.
   Development in infancy : an introduction / Michael E. Lamb, Marc H. Bornstein,
   Douglas M. Teti—4th ed.
      p. cm.
   Includes bibliographical references and index.
   ISBN 0-8058-3563-6 (hb : alk. paper)
   1. Infants—Development.   2. Infant psychology.   I. Lamb, Michael E., 1953–
II. Bornstein, Marc H.   III. Title.

RJ134 .B67   2002
305.232—dc21   2002024258

To the memory of three great scientists who did so much to advance our understanding of development in infancy: Mary Ainsworth, William Kessen, and Hanuš Papoušek

Contents

— ❖ —

Preface

❖

Philosophers since Plato had speculated about the importance of infancy, but it was not until the late nineteenth and early twentieth centuries that scientific observations of infants and theoretical speculations about infants began in earnest. Charles Darwin and Sigmund Freud were largely responsible for these initiatives. Not until the middle of the twentieth century did the scientific study of infancy elicit widespread attention, although infancy has since become one of the most stimulating areas of research in the biological, behavioral, and social sciences. Researchers have come to appreciate how much the study of infancy contributes to our knowledge of developmental processes and the role early experience plays in shaping those processes. Scientific interest in infant development has also expanded during this time, in part because of the emergence of some remarkably influential theories and in part because technological advances rendered infants accessible to empirical inquiry. As a result of this intensified scrutiny, our understanding of infancy itself has increased dramatically in the last 3 decades.

This fourth edition of *Development in Infancy* reflects the enormous changes still taking place in our understanding of infants and their place in human development. Since the publication of the third edition, students of infancy have continued to creatively exploit all the methodological techniques available to them. As a result, we have rewritten each chapter to take into account the results of new research. We have reorganized chapters, restructured contents, and revised our discussions where necessary to reflect current thinking and research in the field.

This edition of *Development in Infancy* is yet more comprehensive and current than previous ones, paying thorough attention to all major aspects of infant development—contextual, methodological, neurological, physical, perceptual, cognitive, communicative, emotional, and social. Former citations have been replaced by references to more recent studies that subsume and extend early reports. With the exception of classic references, we have concentrated on the most recent articles and books and, as a result, emphasize studies published since the late 1990s. In this new edition, we have also endeavored to maintain the readability that has marked *Development in Infancy* in the past. This edition is designed for use as a textbook in classes at all levels, undergraduate and graduate, as well as in various disciplinary contexts—psychology, education, child development, nursing, and social work, for example.

Our goal in revising *Development in Infancy* has been to provide a coherent overview of infant development with a strong theoretical and research base. We have been selective rather than encyclopedic in our discussions of the literature, citing studies only where they help to elucidate critical issues in this complex and exciting field. Throughout, our strategy has been to integrate research and theory so as to introduce readers to conceptually important and descriptively valuable information. Readers should obtain a clear understanding of infant development and of key issues and problems likely to be the focus of significant research in the years ahead. Overall, readers familiar with prior editions of *Development in Infancy* will observe a number of improvements:

- The literature review has been thoroughly updated to reflect the results of new research.

- New figures have been provided to better explain important concepts and the results of recent studies.

- Implications for practical application and social policy have been emphasized throughout.

- The writing style has been revised to make the book attractive to students from diverse academic backgrounds.

- Orienting questions have been provided at the beginning of each chapter to facilitate understanding and learning.

Many researchers and theorists have shaped our understanding and contributed to our own fascination with infancy. We are indebted to them, hopeful that our integrative efforts will serve them as well as their students. We are particularly grateful and dedicate this book to three distinguished scholars who profoundly shaped our own intellectual development and died while we were working on this revision. To *William Kessen*, who pioneered scientific research on infant perception and fostered links between the clinical and basic research branches of psychology. To *Hanuš Papoušek*, who brought to bear the perspectives of a pediatrician and keen student of early learning processes. To *Mary Ainsworth*, who articulated many of the questions that animate studies of infancy today. Kessen's, Papoušek's, and Ainsworth's contributions to the study of infancy were profound and enduring.

We also would like to thank the colleagues who helped us locate new materials and provided generous feedback on our drafts. In particular, we wish to acknowledge Ross A. Thompson and Daniel Swingley.

Our editorial team at Lawrence Erlbaum Associates, ably led by Bill Webber, provided the organizational and material support needed to keep this complex process on track. Finally, we thank Drs. Owen M. Rennert and Duane F. Alexander of the National Institute of Child Health and Human Development for continuing support of research and understanding into all facets of infant development.

Michael E. Lamb
Marc H. Bornstein
Douglas M. Teti

About the Authors

❖

MICHAEL E. LAMB received his Ph.D. in developmental psychology from Yale University in 1976 and an honorary doctorate in the Social Sciences from the University of Goteborg, Sweden, in 1995. Between 1980 and 1987 he was Professor of Psychology, Pediatrics and Psychiatry at the University of Utah in Salt Lake City and he has been head of the Section on Social and Emotional Development at the National Institute of Child Health and Human Development since 1987. His research is concerned with social and emotional development, especially in infancy and early childhood; parent-child relationships; the determinants and consequences of adaptive and maladaptive parental behavior, including child abuse; children's testimony; and the interface of psychology and biology. Dr. Lamb is the co-author of *Socialization and Personality Development* (1982), *Infant-Mother Attachment* (1985), *Child Psychology Today* (1982, 1986), and *Investigative Interviews of Children* (1998). He has edited several books on fathers and father-child relationships, including *The Role of the Father in Child Development* (1976, 1981, 1997, in press), founded and co-edited *Advances in Developmental Psychology*, as well as *Developmental Psychology: An Advanced Textbook* (1984, 1988, 1992, 1999), and has edited other books on various aspects of child development, including day care, infant social cognition, social and personality development, sibling influences, social policy, and parent-child relationships. Dr. Lamb is the proud father of five children.

MARC H. BORNSTEIN is Senior Investigator and Head of Child and Family Research at the National Institute of Child Health and Human Development. He holds a B.A. from Columbia College and M.S. and Ph.D. degrees from Yale University. Bornstein was a J. S. Guggenheim Foundation Fellow, and he received a Research Career Development Award from the National Institute of Child Health and Human Development. He also received the C. S. Ford Cross-Cultural Research Award from the Human Relations Area Files, the B. R. McCandless Young Scientist Award from the American Psychological Association, a United States PHS Superior Service Award from the National Institutes of Health, two Japan Society for the Promotion of Science Fellowships, two Awards for Excellence from the American Mensa Education and Research Foundation, and the Arnold Gesell Prize from the Theodor Hellbrügge Foundation. Bornstein has held faculty positions at Princeton University and New York University as well as academic appointments as Visiting Scientist at the Max-Planck-Institut für Psychiatrie in Munich, Visiting Fellow at University College London, Professeur

Invité at the Laboratoire de Psychologie Expérimentale at the Université René Descartes in Paris, Child Clinical Fellow at the Institute for Behavior Therapy in New York, Visiting Professor at the University of Tokyo, Professeur Invité at the Laboratoire de Psychologie du Développement et de l'Éducation de l'Enfant at the Sorbonne in Paris, and Visiting Fellow of the British Psychological Society. Bornstein is coauthor of *Development in Infancy* (4 editions) and *Perceiving Similarity and Comprehending Metaphor*. He is general editor of *The Crosscurrents in Contemporary Psychology Series*, including *Psychological Development from Infancy, Comparative Methods in Psychology, Psychology and Its Allied Disciplines* (Vols. I–III), *Sensitive Periods in Development, Interaction in Human Development, Cultural Approaches to Parenting, Child Development and Behavioral Pediatrics*, and *Well-Being: Positive Development Across the Life Course*, and he is general editor of the *Monographs in Parenting* series, including *Socioeconomic Status, Parenting, and Child Development* and *Parenting: Essential Readings*. He also edited *Maternal Responsiveness: Characteristics and Consequences* and the *Handbook of Parenting* (Vols. I–V, 2 editions), and he coedited *Developmental Psychology: An Advanced Textbook* (4 editions), *Stability and Continuity in Mental Development, Contemporary Constructions of the Child, Early Child Development in the French Tradition*, and *The Role of Play in the Development of Thought*. He is author of several children's books and puzzles in *The Child's World* series. He has administered both Federal and Foundation grants, sits on the editorial boards of several professional journals, is a member of scholarly societies in a variety of disciplines, and consults for governments, foundations, universities, publishers, scientific journals, the media, and UNICEF. Bornstein is Editor Emeritus of *Child Development* and founding Editor of *Parenting: Science and Practice*. He has contributed scientific experimental, methodological, comparative, developmental, cross-cultural, neuroscientific, pediatric, and aesthetic papers.

DOUGLAS M. TETI, is a developmental psychologist and Professor of Psychology in the Department of Psychology at the University of Maryland, Baltimore County (UMBC). He received his Bachelor of Science in Psychology from St. Joseph's College in 1980, his Master of Science in general experimental psychology from Villanova University in 1984, and his Ph.D. in general psychology (with specialization in developmental psychology) from the University of Vermont in 1984. He was awarded an NIMH post-doctoral fellowship in 1984–86 at the University of Utah, under the direction of Michael Lamb and Donna Gelfand. He is a member of the Society for Research in Child Development, the American Psychological Association, and the International Society for Infant Studies. Teti's research has spanned basic and applied topics, including the assessment, caregiving antecedents, and developmental sequelae of early attachments; intervention with clinically depressed mothers of infants; the development and significance of early sibling relations; and parental, familial, and psychosocial predictors of parent–infant outcomes among families with preterm infants. He has been the principal and co-investigator of two multi-year NIMH grants examining, respectively, early attachments and sibling relationships (ADAMHA First Award), and early intervention and socio-emotional and intellectual development among infants and toddlers of clinically depressed mothers (in collaboration with Donna Gelfand). He has most recently been awarded (August, 2001) a multi-year grant from the National Institute of Child Health and Human Development to study parenting and early intervention processes among preterm infants and their single, urban-dwelling mothers and fathers. A faculty member of the Applied Developmental Psychology Ph.D. program at UMBC, he has chaired seven Ph.D. dissertations and numerous masters theses, is serving or has served on the editorial boards of *Child Development*, *Developmental Psychology*, and *Early Education and Development*. Dr. Teti is currently serving as an Associate Editor of *Developmental Psychology* and is currently directing UMBC's Ph.D. program in Applied Developmental Psychology. He served as an editor of *Infant Assessment: A Guide for Early Intervention Professionals* (Paul H. Brookes, publisher), and is currently editor of the forthcoming *Handbook of Research Methods in Developmental Psychology* (Blackwell Publishers).

Development
in Infancy

AN INTRODUCTION

1

Introduction

❖

- How do our biological endowment and our experiences codetermine our development?
- How important are early experiences in shaping later development?
- Does understanding normative development elucidate the development of individual differences—and vice versa?
- Compare main effects, interactional, and transactional developmental processes.
- In what ways does experience affect development?
- What are developmental stages, and how do they help us understand infancy?
- Distinguish between stability and continuity.

Why We Study Infants

By definition, infancy is the period of life between birth and the emergence of language roughly one and one half to two years later and thus encompasses only about 2% of the average person's life expectancy.

Why write a whole book about so brief a period of the life span? Why have philosophers, psychologists, and physicians paid so much attention to infancy? In fact, infants have been of great interest to specialists in many fields, and we introduce *Development in Infancy* by summarizing some of the chief reasons in order to make clear what motivates professionals like us to pay so much attention to infants.

There are three general reasons for studying infancy scientifically: philosophical questions, parental investment, and applied concerns. Infancy has long fascinated philosophers because it offers the opportunity for human beings to study themselves and to do so from as early in the life cycle as we are accessible to observation. As we look at the people we know and consider the range of capacities and tendencies they exhibit, it is difficult *not* to wonder how people can be so similar and yet so different.

How much do we reflect our genetic endowment, and how are we shaped by the experiences we have? Musings of these sorts have guided philosophers and scientists for centuries.

Whereas philosophers have been attracted by the opportunity to understand the infant origins of adult life, parents are heavily invested in infants, their survival, and their socialization and education. Likewise, parents are perennially fascinated by the dramatic ways in which the incredibly helpless and apparently disorganized newborn human baby transforms, as if overnight, into the remarkably competent and curious, frustrating and frustrated, child. For everyone concerned with them, infants instill endless curiosity.

How much do babies see, hear, feel, and understand? Just what can they do? What accounts for the striking changes that occur in infancy? How do infants in the same culture vary, and how do infants in different cultures vary?

Some professionals are also driven to understand infancy by the need to respond to urgent social, medical, and biological problems. In the 1950s, for example, the development of obstetric technologies led to an increase in the number of preterm infants who could survive. What quality of life could they expect? Some babies developed extremely well, whereas others became casualties. What accounted for the differences in outcome? Similar reasoning impels the study of infancy by researchers eager to address today's applied problems. Large numbers of infants are being born, sometimes prematurely, to mothers who have used illicit substances. For example, particular concern is being expressed about the effects of crack cocaine. The babies born to drug-abusing mothers face an uncertain future.

Are these infants neurologically compromised by damage done to their brains in the months before they are born? Do they have the capacity and plasticity to adapt successfully to life? Surely, if infancy were better understood, we would be in a position to promote the development of infants whose potential appears to have been compromised. But the quest of applied developmental scientists is quite broad. What can professionals do to enhance the chances that infants generally will live and thrive, actualizing their fullest potential? How significantly do experiences and activities in infancy shape development in later life?

Within the scope of these three global motivations to study babies, *Development in Infancy* examines the scientific progress being made in the study of infants. Along the way, moreover, our text speaks to both lay curiosity and applied concerns. The goal of this chapter is to introduce our readers to the major theoretical and practical points that contrive to make infancy so fascinating a focus of research. First, we turn our attention to the developmental significance of infancy, or more specifically to relations between infancy and later phases of the lifespan, focusing on the debate between those who believe that infancy is part of a seamless or continuous lifeline and those who describe major discontinuities between infancy and later childhood or adolescence. We then address a core issue for developmentalists, the nature versus nurture debate, beginning with a discussion of long-established philosophical viewpoints on this issue and moving to various models of nature–nurture effects that have guided research and thinking about development in infancy. Thereafter, we discuss stability and continuity in infant development, taking note of the fact that these two terms do not mean the same thing, and relating the concepts of stability and continuity to questions about whether or not infant development proceeds in clear-cut stages. We next describe some of the applied issues and questions that make the study of infancy important to those whose chief interests are the psychological, educational, public policy, and medical implications of variations in modern life, and then discuss interrelations among multiple aspects of development and the questions they provoke. Finally, we outline the contents of this book.

The Significance of Infancy

There has been considerable debate about the long-term significance of development in infancy. Two extreme points of view vie for adherents. Proponents of one view believe that infancy is not particularly important because experiences in infancy have little (if any) long-term predictive significance. Others argue that the experiences and behavior patterns developed in infancy are important in themselves and are of crucial importance to later life. Social orientations, motivations, and intellectual predilections established in infancy set lifelong patterns.

Proponents of the Importance of Early Experience

From the time of Plato (ca. 350 B.C.), philosophers as well as students of human and animal psychology and ethology have considered infancy to be uniquely significant. The rationales that underpin this classical position are based on common sense: The immature nervous system is thought to be especially plastic; neoteny (the prolongation of infancy, especially in human beings) is thought to have tremendous adaptive significance; the infant is thought to possess an extraordinary facility for learning and has few competing responses. All of these factors imply that early experiences should disproportionately affect the course of subsequent development. Indeed, even folk wisdom and poetry have expressed the conviction that infancy and experiences in early life are singularly important:

> The child is father to the man.
> As the twig is bent, so grows the tree.

Arguments for the special importance of early experiences and early development were popular throughout the first half of the twentieth century and derived from a diverse array of theoretical starting points. Freud (1949) was by far the most prominent and vocal advocate of this position. He was the first major theorist to focus attention on infancy, and he justified this focus by suggesting that the ways babies are treated establish lifelong orientations and personality traits. Freud proposed that there are critical phases in development during which certain sorts of experience—affecting specific types of traits—are of special significance. Infancy falls within Freud's *oral phase* of development, during which feeding experiences and other activities centered on the mouth are particularly prominent. If the baby's needs for oral gratification are overindulged or underindulged early in the oral stage, Freud believed, the baby grew into an adult who continually seeks oral gratification—through overeating, loquaciousness, smoking, chewing gum, and so on. If, by contrast, the baby's oral needs are frustrated or excessively gratified in the oral stage (after the eruption of teeth), the baby might exhibit hostile oral behavior in adulthood. Toward the end of infancy, Freud continued, the oral phase yields to the *anal phase*. During this period parent–infant interactions center on toilet training; long-term personality consequences associated with this phase are likely to involve stubbornness and obsessiveness. However smoothly things go in this phase, though, it is never possible to override the oral tendencies established earlier: Difficulties can only be overcome by "reliving" earlier experiences through lengthy psychotherapy.

Erikson, one of Freud's followers, portrayed early experiences and their effects differently, but he too believed that early experience is extremely influential. From early feeding experiences, he suggested, children develop a degree of trust or mistrust in the caregiver rather than concrete oral traits. He also believed that the harmoniousness of early interactions (i.e., whether the infant develops "basic trust") has implications for the way the infant negotiates the next stage of development, in which the key issue is establishing autonomy or shame. With respect to toilet training, therefore, Erikson emphasized not the anal organs, but the status of toilet training as a battleground of wills as the child tries to exert initial control (by determining when to give the parent the prize he or she seeks). Erikson described eight developmental stages, each marked by a crucial issue: Basic trust or mistrust is at issue in the first stage, whereas autonomy/shame is at issue in the second.

Erikson's view of how early experiences affect the child's later personality substantially improved on Freud's in two major respects. First, Erikson portrayed the lessons learned in each phase in more abstract, general terms (e.g., trust and autonomy) than did Freud (e.g., orality and anality), and the psychological issues described indeed seem pertinent to the stages concerned. Second, Erikson explicitly proposed that the ways in which different stages are resolved are somewhat interrelated. From Erikson's perspective, how much the infant trusts the caregiver may affect the infant's willingness to cooperate in toilet training and other matters. Thus, initial mistrust may yield not only a mistrustful adult but one plagued by unsuccessful resolution of later developmental issues as well. Looking at an adult, it is not obvious that problems over independence issues (i.e., products of problems in the resolution of Stage 2) stem originally from a failure to develop basic trust in Stage 1.

Unfortunately, the ideas of Freud and his followers, including Erikson, were phrased in mentalistic terms that did not lend themselves to empirical evaluation. Behaviorists and learning theorists like Watson, Hull, and Miller dominated developmental psychology from the second to the sixth decade of the twentieth century. Like the psychoanalysts, these theorists stressed the importance of infant experiences, and Miller even attempted to rephrase many of Freud's ideas in terms compatible with behaviorism (Dollard & Miller, 1950). Unlike Freud and Erikson, behaviorists eschewed the notions of stages and phases of development. For learning theorists, early experiences are important because they are first, have no competing propensities to replace, and thus yield easy and rapid learning. Moreover, early behavior patterns are believed to establish more complex behavior patterns such as personality traits.

A third group of theorists, most of them ethologists, students of animal behavior, or embryologists studying prenatal physiology, also emphasized the special role of early experiences (Lorenz, 1935/1970; Tinbergen, 1951, 1963). The ethologists and embryologists argue that there are predetermined periods in the maturation of organisms during which development is maximally susceptible to influence by specific types of experiences (see Bornstein, 1989). Just as Freud spoke of an oral phase during which feeding experiences have the greatest impact on the developing personality, the ethologists spoke of a critical or *sensitive period* for imprinting and for various other behavioral tendencies. During such periods, lessons are learned more easily and endure longer than any that follow. Likewise, studies of embryological development have shown that some experiences will have no impact at one point, but devastating impact at another time. Such demonstrations of sensitive periods accord biological and scientific credibility to Freud's model, and the notion was later integrated into theories of attachment and language development. The sensitive-periods concept assigns great importance to early experiences because experiences occurring in infancy are likely to have long-lasting influence and because, once a particular period had passed, it is no longer possible for specific experiences to shape the developing organism.

Although this diverse group of theorists similarly but separately asserted the importance of early experiences for later development, popular commitment to the proposition developed as a result of some dramatic empirical observations published between 1930 and 1950. At that time, reports that children who were reared in impersonal institutions emerged psychologically stunted led to the widespread belief that children needed close relationships in infancy, and that the denial of such relationships would jeopardize their mental health (Bowlby, 1951; Rutter, 2002). An additional perspective on the continuing importance of infancy was offered by students of cognitive and intellectual development. Piaget theorized that all intellectual capacities are built on the simple developments that take place very early in life, and thus that early experiences are of fundamental importance. Again, however, it was a quantitative (although incorrect) assertion that won more popular belief in the importance of early experience than Piaget's theory. Researchers found a very high degree of association between IQ scores obtained at 5 years of age and scores attained in adulthood. Because those results implied that a significant proportion of mature intelligence may be predictable from early measures of intelligence, Bloom (1964) made the widely publicized claim that about half of an individual's intelligence is established in the first few years of life. This claim is incorrect for a number of reasons; for example, correlations quantify the accuracy of prediction, not the amount of intelligence that has developed. Nevertheless, the claim that experiences in infancy have a major impact on functioning in adulthood was convincing.

By the early 1960s, hardly anyone doubted that early experiences hold a special place in development. Two trends resulted: a massive increase in the amount of research on infancy and the first attempts to engineer enriching experiences for deprived children. By capitalizing on the special sensitivity of the very young, politicians proposed to "immunize" children against the debilitating effects of later deprivation. More than anything else, the apparent failure of these interventions triggered a decline of confidence in the notion that early experiences were especially influential. Most would agree that this failure was more apparent then real. Many researchers reported that the effects of educational interventions on IQ scores were short-lived. There was an initial rise in IQ scores, but the experimental children's scores later dropped back to the level of control children once an intervention program ended. Critics like Jensen (1969) thus argued that intervention programs had no sustainable benefits.

Early enrichment programs were not failures, however. Rather, it seems that the timing of intervention, the nature of intervention, and the selection of outcome variables are all important (Guralnick, 1997a, 1997b; Hess, in press; Lamb, 1998). This conclusion emerges from long-term prospective studies of children who had either been enrolled in special enrichment programs or assigned to control groups as infants or preschoolers. The outcomes measured in these studies included later school competence, and the results were quite impressive: Children in the experimental groups were less likely to be held back in school than controls, and they were less likely to need special education classes. What exact factors may have mediated these long-term effects are not fully clear, but developmental scientists would stress the impact of the experimental enrichment programs on both the children and their families. Once they are sensitized to the importance of helping their children succeed in preschool, for example, parents may maintain the impetus through the grade school and high school years.

Proponents of Discontinuity

Other theorists have, with equally compelling arguments, propounded an opposite view, namely that experiences in infancy are peripheral or ephemeral, in the sense that they have little or no enduring effect on development. Instead, these individuals attribute the engine and controls of early development to biology and maturation. Gesell (1954) and Waddington (1972), for example, believed that, like anatomy, the psychology of the individual unfolds on the basis of a maturing biological program undeflected by experience.

One of the most vocal opponents of the overemphasis on early experiences is Kagan (1994a, 1994b; Kagan, Kearsley, & Zelazo, 1978), who had earlier studied the impact of social experiences in infancy and early childhood (Kagan & Moss, 1962). Kagan came to argue that maturation—the unfolding of genetically determined capacities and individual differences—had been undervalued, pointing to research indicating that major differences in rearing environments had little apparent effect on the way children develop. For example, he argued that daycare and home care have remarkably similar effects on developing infants (Kagan et al., 1978) and that even the extreme impoverishment (of, say, a rural Guatemalan environment) does not retard intellectual development (Kagan & Klein, 1973).

Kagan's arguments have been criticized by psychologists who counterargue that the measures may not be sensitive and that the discrepancy may therefore lie in the assessment, not in the concept, of experiential influence. Kagan is not alone, however, in criticizing belief in the special formative importance of early experiences (e.g., Clarke & Clarke, 2000).

Claims that there is little continuity from early development and that behavior patterns developed in infancy are unlikely to have predictable long-term consequences have attracted a great deal of attention. In our view, such conclusions were inevitable, if erroneous, responses to earlier simplistic notions about the formative importance of infant experiences and inadequate attention to the potential for remediation. The major difficulty lies in overreliance on linear models of development holding that early experiences have obvious and direct short- and long-term effects. Freud's psychoanalytic model exemplifies such linear associations between early experiences and later outcomes, with breast-feeding expected to affect oral personality characteristics directly. However, simple linear relations between early experiences and later development are seldom substantiated empirically (see Sroufe, 2000; Thompson, 1999).

The Transactional View

The linear model is inadequate, therefore, not the notion that experiences (whether early or late) affect later development. In place of the linear model, Sameroff and Chandler (1975) proposed a *transactional model* of development. The transactional view states that both child and parent bring distinctive characteristics to every interaction and are believed to be changed as a result; both then enter the next round of interaction as different individuals. From this perspective, it is naive to expect any single experience to have direct long-term effects, for its impact will be diffuse, triggering indirect effects (e.g., also changing the parent's behavior). Nevertheless, events in infancy are important because they initiate multiple developmental processes.

Consider the concrete example that Sameroff and Chandler (1975) articulated when proposing this model. Years of research on prematurity showed that only a minority of preterm babies develop abnormally even though initially they may be indistinguishable from preterm infants who later develop quite adequately. Prematurity per se does not necessarily have ill effects, Sameroff and Chandler argued, but parents cope with atypical babies in different ways. Some fail to provide the types of experiences that preterm children need in order to offset their potential for developmental delay, and preterm infants are at risk over the long term only if they are reared in such environments. Since linear models typically focus on main effects or individual factors (such as prematurity), it is not surprising that their predictive power is poor. For this reason, it is unlikely that researchers will be able to identify specific early experiences that directly shape later characteristics. In making predictions about long-term effects, the strategy must be to identify immediate effects and then determine how these changes affect the child's later experiences and their effects—both directly and indirectly.

In our opinion, the transactional model is greatly superior to the linear effects model, and for this reason (among others) we believe that it is important to study development in infancy. Grossmann and Grossmann (1986) illustrated transactional processes using data gathered in their longitudinal study of infant–mother attachment. During the first 2 weeks after birth, infants were tested for orienting three times using the Brazelton Scale (Neonatal Behavioral Assessment Scale [NBAS]—see Chapter 5). Grossmann and Grossmann found that neonatal performance on the NBAS was stable from day to day and that it was possible to divide their sample into "good" and "bad" orienters. The good orienters were those who were attentive to both social (i.e., face and voice) and physical (i.e., ball and rattle) stimuli during the NBAS tests. Subsequent observations of the mothers and infants at home allowed the Grossmanns to assess the quality of the mothers' parenting by rating the contingency and appropriateness of their behavior toward their infants, as suggested by Ainsworth (see Chapter 11), and by categorizing the mothers' vocal or conversational styles when talking to their babies.

All of the babies who were good orienters *and* had "tender-talking" sensitive mothers later developed secure attachment relationships, but only one third of the poor orienters with tender and sensitive mothers did so. Good orienters with sober-talking and less sensitive mothers had only a 38% chance of being securely attached, whereas only 13% of the babies who were poor orienters and whose mothers were insensitive developed secure attachments. Viewed together, these findings suggest that the characteristics of the baby and the characteristics of the mother jointly determined what sort of relationship they formed, just as Sameroff and Chandler predicted. Of course, the Grossmanns' small sample makes it imperative to replicate their findings independently, but they do constitute an evocative illustration of the transactional model. Support is also provided by demonstrations that children who are at risk for developmental delay develop poorly if their home environment is unstimulating, but develop normally if they have enriching and stimulating homes (Gottfried, Fleming, & Gottfried, 1998).

Interactions between parents and children always take place in a social context, framed by the community and network of relationships described in

Chapter 2. The social context, broadly defined in this way, naturally influences formative transactional processes, and this raises important questions about continuity and prediction. For example, there is growing evidence that warm, nurturant, attentive, stimulating, and nonrestrictive mothers tend to have babies who at 1 year of age display behavior that Ainsworth (see Chapter 11) identified as secure (i.e., after a brief separation, they greet their mother on reunion, seek her out, soothe quickly on pickup, and interact with her in a friendly way). Secure babies at 1 year of age are subsequently more likely to be friendly with strange children and strange adults as well as more independent, persistent, and socially competent (Teti & Teti, 1996; Thompson, 1999). As Lamb, Thompson, and their colleagues (1985; Thompson, 1998) pointed out, however, this consistency is preserved only when there is also consistency in the family's socioeconomic circumstances and childrearing conditions. This fact raises questions about the nature of consistency and prediction from infancy. Specifically, if secure infants constantly receive high quality care from their parents, the quality of care may be the real determinant of long-term prediction, not the security of early infant–mother attachment.

Direct predictions do exist too, however. Researchers initially studied cognitive stability by examining statistical associations between scores on standardized tests of infant development (mostly comprising sensorimotor items) and standardized tests of cognitive performance in childhood. No stability was found, and it was often concluded that one could not predict levels of later performance from measures of cognitive functioning in infancy. As Bornstein (1998) showed, however, measures of infant habituation (the rate of response decrement following repeated presentations of a stimulus) and recovery of attention to a new stimulus uniquely predict scores on intelligence tests in childhood moderately well, even with the contributions of the intervening experiences statistically controlled for. Infants who show efficient decrement or recovery of attention in the first 6 months of life later (between 2 and 12 years of age) perform better on traditional assessments of cognitive competence, including measures of language ability and standardized psychometric tests of intelligence. This stability has been reported by many different researchers using different measures of different sensory modalities, so it appears to be a robust pattern. In short, there is clear evidence of consistency from infancy in cognitive as well as socioemotional spheres of life.

In sum, by studying infancy we learn about processes and experiences that have long-term implications for development. Infancy is the first phase of our lives, and the characteristics we develop and acquire then are fundamental; they are the characteristics that endure and those that later experiences build on or modify. Infancy is only one phase in the lifespan, however, and so our cognitive competencies, social styles, and personalities are also shaped by our experiences and development after infancy. The start does not fix the course or outcome of development, but it clearly exerts an impact on both.

Heredity and Experience

Traditionally, theory and research in infancy are designed to evaluate when a structure or function emerges, the course of its development (that is, whether and how it changes with age), and what factors influence its development. Thus, the key research questions turn on *status*, *origins*, and *process* in the development of structure and function. Certain overriding philosophical issues concerning the origins of knowledge and the course of development also recur, however, and we now turn to them.

Past, Present, and Future

Historically, the study of development in infancy has been driven by questions concerning the roles of heredity and experience. This debate pitted against one another two groups of philosophers who were interested in *epistemology*, understanding where knowledge comes from and how it grows. Extreme views were put forward by *nativists* on the one hand and by *empiricists* on the other; these two positions define the classic confrontation between proponents of nature and proponents of nurture. The debate is age-old, but it experienced a striking philosophical upsurge in the seventeenth century.

Empiricists asserted that there is no endowed knowledge at birth, that all knowledge comes through the senses, and that mental development reflects learned associations. They argued that external stimuli naturally provoke bodily "sensations," and that through association, separate raw sensations fuse into meaningful perceptions. The empiricists' view of the mind early in life was fostered by two separate but coordinated schools of thought. One derived from John Locke (1632–1704), who is reputed to have described the infant mind as a tabula rasa, or "blank slate." A slightly different empiricist view is attributed to William James (1842–1910), who wrote that the world of the infant is a "blooming, buzzing confusion" out of which, presumably, infants' experiences help them to organize and to create mental order. Empiricism is an inherently developmental point of view because it contrasts the naiveté of infancy with the perceptual and cognitive sophistication of maturity.

The belief that human beings begin life "empty headed" was considered both philosophically intolerable and logically indefensible by nativists, who argued both that God would not create mindless creatures in His image and that an awareness of good and evil must be inherent because it could not be learned in so short a span of time as childhood. As a consequence, nativist philosophers like Rene Descartes (1596–1650) and Immanuel Kant (1724–1804) proposed that humans were endowed at birth with ideas or "categories of knowledge" to assist the infant in understanding the world. Against the empiricists, nativists asserted that the mind naturally, and from the beginning of life, imposes order on sensory input, automatically transforming raw sensations into meaningful perceptions. According to nativists, infants and adults share the same perceptual capacities and therefore perceive the world in much the same way. Because nativist theory postulates that many such abilities are present at birth it is not particularly developmental, although it does acknowledge that certain abilities take time to mature.

Although the nature–nurture debate is centuries old, its central issues have remained basic to the study of infancy into our own time. Observing the status and origins of behavior and the dramatic developmental processes that occur in infancy motivates scholars to ask about the sources of change, and attempts at answers inevitably lead to speculations about heredity and experience, nature and nurture. It seems reasonable in this connection to let more modern American theorists speak for themselves, for they give us the best flavor of their views on the origins and determinants of life in infancy. Thus, Gesell (1954, p. 354), the intellectual founder of the nativist movement in America, maturationism, wrote that

> the original impulse to growth . . . is endogenous rather than exogenous. The so-called environment, whether internal or external, does not generate the progression of development. Environmental factors support, inflect, and specify, but they do not engender the basic forms and sequences of ontogenesis.

Interest in innate biological motives and constraints on infant development continues today in many quarters (e.g., Emde & Hewitt, 2001; Haith, 1999; Price et al., 2000).

By contrast, America's premier environmentalist emphasized the infinite malleability of human beings from infancy. Watson (1924/1970, p. 104) wrote:

> Give me a dozen healthy infants, well-formed, and my own specified world to bring them up in, and I'll guarantee to take any one at random and train him to become any type of specialist I might select—doctor, lawyer, artist, merchant-chief and yes, even beggarman and thief, regardless of his talents, penchants, tendencies, abilities, vocations, race of his ancestors.

Many scientists still believe that the environment is the principal determinant of development from infancy (e.g., Gewirtz & Pelaez-Nogueras, 2000; Riviere, Darcheville, & Clement, 2000; Weir, Soule, Bacchus, Rael, & Schneider, 2000), and the nature–nurture controversy remains central to the theme and content of this book.

In the debates among the early philosophers and developmental scientists, a "main effects" model applied: Either constitution or environment was considered to be central (see Figure 1.1). The left half of Figure 1.1A shows that, in the nativist view, if the constitution of the organism was good then the outcome would be good, regardless of whether the environment was good or bad. Similarly, if the constitution of the organism was bad, the outcome would be bad, regardless

A. MAIN EFFECT MODEL

NATIVIST VIEW

NURTURIST VIEW

B. INTERACTIONAL MODEL

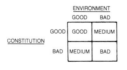

C. TRANSACTIONAL MODEL

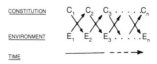

FIGURE 1.1

Three views of the importance of constitution and environment in infant development. (*A*) In the main effects model, either constitution or environment is influential. (*B*) In the interactional model, the two are believed to work together in a simple additive fashion. (*C*) In the transactional model, constitution and environment are believed to influence each other in a continual process of development and change. (After Sameroff, 1975. © 1975 by *Merrill-Palmer Quarterly*, reprinted by permission.)

of the environment. By contrast, the nurturist main effects model predicts that, if the environment is good, the outcome will be good, regardless of the constitution.

In more contemporary times, a gradual shift in orientation can be discerned in the skirmishes between those who emphasized biological, endogenous, or maturationist determinants of development on the one hand and those who emphasized experiential, exogenous, or environmental determinants on the other. In the middle of the twentieth century an "interactional" model of development achieved acceptance (Anastasi, 1958; Piaget & Inhelder, 1967). Unlike main effects proponents, interactionists offered an additive view, in which nature and nurture were believed to interact together to shape development. Thus, as shown in Figure 1.1B, a good constitution and a good environment combine to yield a good outcome, and a bad constitution and a bad environment combine to yield a bad outcome; but a good constitution in combination with a bad environment, or a bad constitution in combination with a good environment, both yield medium outcomes. Piaget (1983), for example, emphasized such interactions between heritability and maturationism on the one hand and experience and environmentalism on the other.

Although vastly different, we can see that Gesell, Watson, and Piaget all conceived of development as a static interaction between two life forces—heredity and experience. The transactional model of development (Sameroff, 1983; Sameroff & Chandler, 1975) we introduced in the previous section provides a different take on the interaction between constitution and environment—one that is inherently developmental in nature because it adds time and a dynamic component to the equation. Many early developmental scientists (particularly those in psychobiology and ethology) argued that inherited constitution and experienced environment mutually influence one another during the course of development (see Gottlieb, 1997; Hinde, 1997). Sameroff and Chandler (1975) recognized that inherent characteristics are shaped by experience and vice versa, and that a constant process of mutual influence between heredity and experience continues throughout infancy, and indeed the lifespan. Figure 1.1C portrays this transaction between constitution and environment through time. This was a very important advance, for it opened up the probability of *epigenesis*, the hypothesis that new phenomena not present in the original fertilized egg can emerge over the course of development through the interaction of preexisting elements with environmental influences.

The transactional view is now widely adopted in infancy research. It holds that at any point in infancy the effects of an experience depend on the nature of the specific experience *and* the constitutional endowment of the infant. Similarly, the individual's contribution to his or her own development at any point reflects endogenous characteristics in combination with aspects of that individual's life history. If a particular child's early experiences were pathogenic, a positive new experience may be able to reverse some adverse effects, but the child may still be worse off than another child whose early experiences were benign and who later encountered the same positive new experience. Infancy is therefore important to those interested in long-term prediction, even if the effects of experiences in infancy are neither obvious nor direct. We will return to this issue in our discussion of the debate between the proponents of continuity and discontinuity in development.

Like most contemporary students of development in infancy, our own perspective is one that emphasizes the ways in which heredity and experience codetermine the development of the individual. This leads us to stress repeatedly that biologically based propensities—nature—and individual experiences—nurture—mutually influence the life course. Infants are born with simple yet important behavioral proclivities; these innate tendencies help to direct early development by delimiting the potential for behavior change through experience. Babies who are congenitally distractible, for example, are likely to learn slowly about objects they see or hear because they are unable to attend to or to concentrate on them for long periods. Patient parenting may help offset this tendency. On the other hand, infants are born into worlds that meet their needs and provide influential experiences; these external possibilities also help to direct early development. A baby who is congenitally attentive is likely to learn slowly if reared in a stark and solitary environment. A change in environment may help to overcome this disadvantage.

Neither biological predispositions nor experiences alone determine the course, direction, termination, or final resting level of development; rather, these life forces influence one another as development proceeds. As will become clear in this text, we are interested in learning which experiences affect what aspects of development when and how, the ways in which individual children are so affected, as well as the ways in which individual children affect their own development.

Some Specific Mechanisms of Heredity and Experience

Two kinds of biologically based tendencies figure prominently in our discussions. *Species-typical* tendencies are those that all humans share. These include, for example, predispositions to cry when distressed and to respond to others' cries so as to alleviate them, to attend to novel sounds, smells, or sights, and to ignore those that have become boringly familiar. By contrast, *heritable influences* are those that distinguish one person's tendencies from another's, and they are the basis of genetically rooted individual differences. Just as some of us have blue eyes and others have green eyes, so some infants seem to be inherently more irritable (i.e., cranky or easily distressed) or more distractible (i.e., less able to concentrate on one thing for long) than others. Both species-typical and heritable tendencies exert important influences on development.

The fact that infants are genetically biased to behave in certain ways means that the paths along which they develop are not exclusively determined by the experiences others provide for them. Indeed, infants are active and contribute to their own development. Their characteristics and propensities can influence the experiences they will be exposed to and the ways in which those experiences affect them. This view is an essential component of the transactional approach. In addition, most developmental scientists now believe that the ways in which different individuals understand the world represent an important subjective or phenomenological synthesis of what they learn from their unique interactions and experiences. This approach therefore places additional stress on the individual's tendencies and capacities, rather than on the inherent informativeness of the stimuli sensed. For example, students of cognitive development propose that infants develop an understanding of the world by interpreting their perceptions and the effects of their own actions.

Unfortunately, there is often some confusion about these biological influences. Three false beliefs are especially common: One is the notion that behaviors with a biological origin are fixed and thus cannot be affected by experience. This notion runs counter to all major theories of development and is contradicted by many everyday observations. The ability to cry, for example, is biologically determined, yet the amount an infant cries may vary depending on the environmental consequences of the infant's cries. The second issue is the belief that biologically determined propensities must be present at birth. To discount this belief we need simply point to biologically determined events that directly and indirectly affect psychological development, yet do not occur until many years after birth. Puberty, for example, is a major milestone in biological and psychosocial development, yet it typically begins a decade after birth. The third myth is the assumption that biologically based behaviors must remain stable over time and are not susceptible to change. In fact, some proclivities or tendencies change in childhood, either in response to particular experiences or as a result of genetically preprogrammed variations. Thus, both heritable and species-typical traits can be shaped by experience.

As far as experiential or environmental influences are concerned, there are several key facets to which developmentalists must attend: They include source, action, and timing. Behavioral geneticists such as Plomin (1999) and Turkheimer and Waldron (2000) have identified several sources of environmental experience, distinguishing the shared from the nonshared environment. The shared environment is clear; the nonshared environment consists of environmental differences acting on individuals in the same situation or setting. In their view, the nonshared environment may be nonsystematic, or it may be systematic. Nonsystematic events include accidents, illness, or other chance circumstances that contribute to individual differences and that influence individual development. By contrast, systematic nonshared influences include gender differences, birth order, differential treatment by family, and similar family or social factors.

Second, Gottlieb (1997) suggests a useful distinction among several different *actions of experience*. Figure 1.2 illustrates these effects using perceptual development as a model. Induction is the most dramatic form of influence. It occurs when a particular experience or set of experiences completely determines whether a structure or function emerges. Without the experience, there will be no emergence or development of the structure or function. Attunement or facilitation occurs when certain experiences speed up or slow down the development of structures or functions. Finally, maintenance describes a situation in which experience preserves already partially or fully developed structures or functions. In the case of partial or full development, the absence of experience will result in loss of the structure or function.

In addition to source and action, the *timing of experience* appears to be important. By way of example, consider two models of how caregiving may affect development. In one model, an experience provided by the caregiver uniquely affects the infant at a particular time point, with effects that endure independent of later experiences or events. This model is consonant with a sensitive-period interpretation of experience effects (e.g., Bornstein, 1989; Dawson, Ashman, & Carver, 2000; Murray, Sinclair, Cooper, Ducournau, & Turner, 1999). A given experience may exert no influence on development at one time; at another it may exert a profound effect; and at a third again no effect. Alternatively, the caregiving experience may influence development only because it is consistent and thus has a cumulative impact (e.g., Thompson, 1998). Of course, there is nothing to prevent both the sensitive period and cumulative impact interpretations from operating in different spheres of infant development.

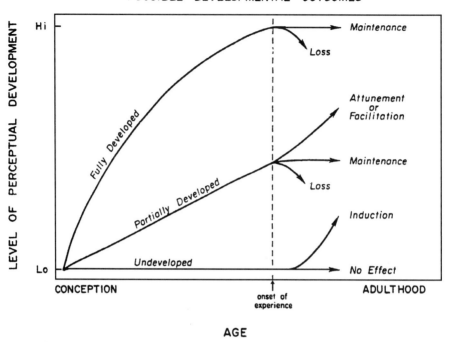

FIGURE 1.2

Possible developmental outcomes given different levels of perceptual development before the onset of experience and different experiences afterward. If a structure or function is undeveloped at the time of the onset of experience, experience may induce the structure or function; without experience, the structure or function will not develop. If a structure or function is only partially developed, experience may maintain the structure or function at that level or attune or facilitate its further development. If the structure or function is fully developed, experience would serve to maintain it. In the case of partially or fully developed structure or function, the lack of experience could eventuate in loss of structure or function. (After Aslin, 1981b. © 1981, Academic Press, reprinted by permission.)

In Chapter 3, concerned with methods, we discuss strategies and techniques developmental scientists use to understand and differentiate hereditary and experiential influences on development in infancy. One such strategy pits infants born at term with those born preterm, because one is then able to compare differential development in the context of equivalent postnatal experience. That is, babies can be matched for conceptional age but contrasted in terms of postnatal experience (Matthews, Ellis, & Nelson, 1996). A second strategy, one which we highlight in all parts of *Development in Infancy*, is cross-cultural comparison. The reasons to conduct cross-cultural developmental research with infants are many. People are perennially curious about infant development in other cultures, and social anthropological inquiry has almost always, as a matter of course, included reports of infant life. Insofar as cross-cultural descriptions of infancy attempt to encompass the widest spectrum of human variation, they are the most comprehensive, and they are therefore vital to delimiting the full range of human experience and establishing valid developmental norms. Cross-cultural developmental inquiry provides natural tests of the universality of certain scientific constructs. Theoretically, however, crossing cultures can aid in the quest for understanding life forces at work in development, because this perspective can be exploited to expose variables that may be operational in development but are "invisible" when a single culture is studied. In particular, this approach helps us understand the parts played by culture-dependent and culture-independent forces in shaping the origins, status, and development of diverse structures and functions through development (see Bornstein, 2000b; Cole, 1999). Clearly, many of the reasons that motivate cross-cultural developmental research with infants are descriptive, but cross-cultural studies also affect the development of theory.

Stability and Continuity

Beyond questions of heredity and experience, developmental scientists often ask about the extent to which infant behavior and development are consistent and stable over time. The term *stability* is used to describe consistency over time in the relative ranking of individuals in a group on some dimension or aspect of development. Activity level in infants would be stable, for example, if some infants are more active than others when they are young and continue to be more active than others when they are older. A related but separate concept is continuity. The term *continuity* is used to describe consistency in average group score on some dimension over time. Thus, for example, activity level would be deemed to show continuity if a group of infants were approximately as active when they were young and when they were older. Strictly speaking, therefore, stability refers to individual levels whereas continuity refers to group levels, and the two are independent of one another (Bornstein, Tamis-LeMonda, & Haynes, 1999).

An additional concrete example may help to illustrate these points. Bornstein and Tamis-LeMonda (1990) examined stability and continuity in the activities of mothers toward their firstborn infants between the time their babies were 2 months and 5 months of age. Their study focused on two ways in which mothers encouraged attention, two kinds of maternal speech, and maternal bids for social play in relation to the infants' exploration and vocalization. A majority of maternal activities were stable, some maternal activities showed continuity, whereas some increased and others decreased over time. Table 1.1 provides a conceptual summary of the findings for mothers, distinguishing between activities that are stable and unstable (in terms of individual differences) as well as between those that are continuous and discontinuous (in terms of absolute group level). Interestingly, every cell in the table mentions a significant maternal activity. Some maternal activities, like total maternal speech, proved stable *and* continuous. Between the times when the infants were 2 and 5 months of age, Table 1.1 shows that their mothers spoke to them in total approximately the same amount, and mothers who spoke more when their infants were 2 months old

TABLE 1.1 DEVELOPMENTAL STABILITY AND CONTINUITY IN MATERNAL ACTIVITIES FROM 2 TO 5 MONTHS

| Developmental Stability | Developmental Continuity | | |
| | Yes | No | |
		Increase	Decrease
Stable	Speech	Didactic	Infant register
Unstable	Social play	Conversational tones	Social

spoke more when their infants were 5 months old, just as those mothers who spoke less when their infants were 2 months old spoke less when their infants were 5 months old. Other maternal activities were stable and discontinuous, showing either general developmental increases (e.g., didactic stimulation) or decreases (e.g., speech in infant register). Some maternal activities were unstable and continuous (e.g., social play), whereas others were unstable and discontinuous, showing either general developmental increases (e.g., speech in adult conversational tones) or decreases (e.g., social stimulation).

Unfortunately, development often makes it difficult to tell whether fundamental change has occurred in an underlying construct (such as attachment, imitation, or fear), or whether there is simply some superficial change in the way in which an unchanging construct is expressed. Again, the distinction is best illustrated by example. Fear may look the same in the faces of 6-month-olds and 18-month-olds, and thus we may use the same scoring technique to assess fear at these two ages in order to determine whether there is temporal stability in levels of fearfulness (Haynie & Lamb, 1995). By contrast, 9-month-olds may express affection for their parents by clinging, crying, and asking to be held; one year later, signals like talking and smiling may have become more common ways to express attachment; and fifteen years later, letters may be used. These developmental changes do not necessarily mean that attachments have changed in strength; they may simply indicate that different means have been found to mediate emotional relationships.

We can distinguish among types of stability or continuity more formally by describing three models of the possible association among variables. One model describes a *homotypic stability* of the same underlying aspect of development. Child performance on behavior "A" (e.g., productive vocabulary size) at Time 1 is related to performance on the identical behavior "A" at Time 2. Another model describes *heterotypic stability* as expressed in physically different but conceptually similar dimensions. Child level of behavior "A" (e.g., productive vocabulary size) at Time 1 relates to the level of behavior "B" (e.g., symbolic play) at either Time 1 or Time 2. Heterotypic associations may be concurrent or lagged. Models of heterotypic association typically postulate that a shared component "C" in the child underlies the association between behaviors "A" and "B". A third model shows that stability between "A" and "A" or prediction between "A" and "B" is explained by a mediating variable "X" that is *not* in the child but remote from the observed variables. For example, infant behavior "A" (e.g., language) at Time 1 relates to infant behavior "B" (e.g., symbolic play) at Time 1 because of some maternal characteristic "X" (e.g., mothers who stimulate language also stimulate play). This model predicts that, once the exogenous contribution of "X" is removed, within-infant stability will be reduced or eliminated.

Individual Variation and Normative Development

Two broad classes of questions arise in connection with issues of stability and continuity in infancy. One asks about normative development, attempting to discern and describe aspects of development in all babies at specific ages or in specific circumstances. The other focuses on individual variation in levels of structure or function, attempting to discern, describe, and perhaps explain the differences among individuals. These two perspectives on consistency and change in all aspects of development reflect two recurring concerns—focus on

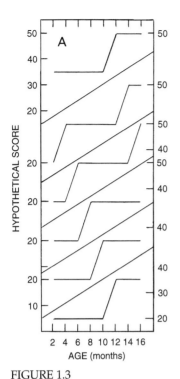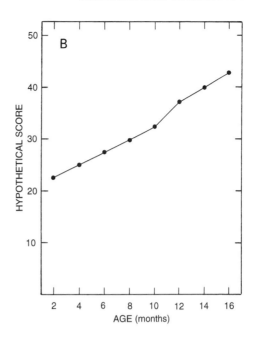

FIGURE 1.3

Individual variation and general developmental functions for language acquisition. (A) Developmental functions for six individual infants; as can be seen, each infant develops in a stepwise fashion. (B) A continuous function is created by averaging the six individual functions. Often, continuous developmental functions accurately represent the group as well as individual data. Here, however, averaging across individuals yields a deceptively continuous group function.

so-called developmental functions as opposed to focus on individual variation. A *developmental function* reflects the changing value of a group on a given attribute across age. This function defines species-typical development without regard to individual differences, and may be continuous or discontinuous (that is, stage-like). By contrast, a study of *individual variation* seeks to ascertain information about differences at any one age and to determine whether those differences among individuals in a group remain ordered in the course of development.

The general developmental function and individual functions in development should articulate with one another. The potential for disjunction between the two is ever present, however, as illustrated in Figure 1.3. Figure 1.3A depicts the times when six individual infants, followed longitudinally, begin to speak. As is clear, each infant shows a stepwise developmental path, not speaking up to a certain point and speaking afterward. Averaging across the six infants at each age, however, generates the continuous developmental curve for language acquisition shown in Figure 1.3B. Notice that this group curve portrays a growth pattern quite unlike any of the individual growth functions. Such a summary portrayal of language acquisition data could be misleading.

Questions about the developmental function and questions about individual variation are both of crucial importance in coming to understand development in infancy. In each of the chapters in this book we discuss normative development, but each child is different from every other at birth—and, of course, even before—and each remains an individual throughout development. Most parents are particularly interested in knowing how their children develop individually characteristic personalities and intellectual capacities. Scientists, too, find questions concerning the origins and growth of individual differences especially appealing, both in their own right as well as for the light they throw on general developmental trends. In *Development in Infancy*, we review and integrate normative data and larger developmental trends as well as research on individual variation.

Stages

In any discussion of stability and continuity in development, the issue of *stages* is unavoidable, and in considering infancy this is especially true. A stage is thought to represent a complex pattern of interrelated characteristics that undergo a period of formation to reach a period of attainment. First, there is the question of partitioning the life cycle so as to segregate infancy as a separate stage of life at all. Dividing the life cycle into stages, ages, or phases is complex and subtle, with both theoretical and historical currents tugging at professional and popular opinion. Biology certainly exerts a considerable influence. Self-evident physical, motor, and cognitive components of development have led to long-held and universally recognized positions about infancy as a separate stage of growth. Infants creep and crawl, whereas the young and the old walk and run; infants do not speak, whereas the young and old do. Coextant with entrenched biological views, social convention has had important things to say about infancy as a stage in life. We believe that infancy is a definable stage of life, based on biological and cognitive data as well as social convention. Harkness and Super (1983, p. 223) have suggested that "a primary function of culture in shaping human experience is the division of the continuum of human development into meaningful segments, or 'stages.' . . . All cultures, so far as we know, recognize infancy as a stage of human development." Thus, partitioning the life cycle appears to reflect a complex interaction between phases of biological maturation and sociocultural conditions. Infancy is one.

The question of stages also speaks to the existence and sources of continuity versus discontinuity in development. Stage and transition are not synonymous. As Cole (1999, p. 107) points out, "A *stage* is a more or less stable, patterned, and enduring system of interactions between the organism and the environment; a *transition* is a period of flux, when the 'ensemble of the whole' that makes up one stage has disintegrated and a new stage is not firmly in place."

Theoretical positions in the natural and social sciences have legitimately questioned whether the developmental course of the life trajectory is marked by discontinuous stages at all. Alternative views assert that development unfolds as a series of gradual and continuous transitions. Do human beings develop in the way an acorn becomes an oak, or as a caterpillar becomes a butterfly? For most developmentalists, of course, the answer is a question of emphasis. Certainly, structure and function in infants transit discrete changes over the life course, but even in these changes the new integrates the old, and so human development seems much less dramatic than, say, larval metamorphosis. The concept of life stages constitutes a kind of organizing principle that is used conventionally to compare and contrast assorted aspects of development, at one period or between periods. Stages help make sense of life. They indicate that there are developments and experiences that merit attention in their own right and in terms of their contributions to subsequent development. On such arguments, many famous developmental theorists—Freud, Piaget, Erikson, and Werner—have championed stage theories.

Is development within infancy continuous or discontinuous and stage-like? Development may involve parallel biological, psychological, and/or sociological events. The characteristics of one stage differentiate it from preceding and succeeding stages, yet the accomplishments of earlier stages are carried into and mesh with new elements that are indigenous to later ones. The American philosopher and psychologist James (1890, p. 237) wrote that development is continuous, "without break, crack, or division." Yet infancy itself has been divided and subdivided into stages. Perhaps the best known are those Piaget described (see Chapter 7), but many others have hypothesized "bio-behavioral shifts," "psychic organizations," "developmental crises," and the like, all characteristic of infancy (e.g., Erikson, 1950; Fisher & Silvern, 1985; Kagan, 1984; McCall et al., 1977; Spitz, 1965; Trevarthen, 1988).

Theorists vary in their opinions about the usefulness of the stage concept for studying development. Critics note that stage theories are descriptive rather than explanatory; they downplay differences among people and may not contribute to understanding individual development. Stages are often general and idealistic, where life is filled with variation and inconsistency, and so a stage view oversimplifies the true status of development.

Typically, stage theories of development also have a maturationist flavor as well as several other distinctive characteristics. For example, stage theories are focused on internal change, unidirectional in time, irreversible in sequence, universal, and goal directed. (In these senses, stage theories of development can be seen to have their roots in the "progressiveness" of nineteenth-century evolutionary biological thinking.) However, development need not (necessarily) entail progression toward a given "end goal." Contrasting environmentalistic perspectives do not include comparable directional assumptions. Moreover, development may be nonlinear in nature, stalling and even of regressing at times (Stern, 1998; Vaal, van Soest, & Hopkins, 2000). When we discuss imitation in Chapter 7, we suggest that neonates may be capable of certain rudimentary types of imitating, but that capacity appears to go away temporarily, only to reemerge as a much more robust dynamic capacity later in infancy and toddlerhood (Maratsos, 1998). In short, it may not be entirely correct to conceive of infancy (as theorists typically do) in terms of positive changes or singularly ordered gains.

Parental Curiosity and Applied Imperatives

Philosophical and theoretical issues aside, there are compelling practical reasons to study infancy. For many parents and professionals, the pervasiveness, rapidity, and clarity of developmental change in infancy by themselves impel a fascination with this stage of life (Bornstein, 2002). The developmental changes that take place during the two and one half years after conception—roughly, the prenatal period and infancy—are more dramatic than any others in the human lifespan. The most remarkable of these involve the shape and capacity of the body and its muscles, the complexity of the nervous system, the growth of sensory and perceptual capacity, the ability to make sense of, understand, and master objects and things in the world, the acquisition of communication, the formation of specific social bonds, and the emergence of characteristic personal and social styles. At no other time do such thoroughgoing developments occur in so many different aspects of life so quickly. Though many of these developmental changes begin during the 9 prenatal months, most continue through, or occur during, the first 2 postnatal years.

By studying infants we are often reminded of just how complicated some of the "simple" behaviors are that we take for granted. As adults, we sit up and walk without effort or a second thought, but watching a young baby's repeated failures to accomplish so simple a feat forces us to admit just how much sensorimotor coordination is involved. Many of the behavioral skills we employ in our daily lives are automatic; we gain a new appreciation of their complexity and the processes through which they develop by studying their emergence in infancy.

The desire to improve the lives of infants whose development may be compromised has also motivated a great deal of interest, and the challenges posed by infants born preterm are exemplary in this regard. The ability to intervene medically during the perinatal and neonatal development of the infant improved dramatically three decades ago, when advances in the design of incubators and respirators made it possible to keep alive preterm babies who formerly would have died at birth. Unfortunately, however, advances sometimes have unexpected consequences. For example, certain anesthetics and analgesics used to help mothers through labor were found to depress the physiological, perceptual, and learning functions of newborn infants for days and even weeks (Brackbill, 1979). Because of experiences such as these, obstetricians, pediatricians, and psychologists allied themselves in the tasks of identifying and preventing potentially harmful psychological consequences of medical interventions. As a result, parents are now able to choose more humane forms of childbearing and can deliver with less medication (if any) in more home-like birthing rooms.

Other political, social, and economic motives also conspired to increase interest in infancy. The 1960s saw the beginning of the "War on Poverty" in the United States and the introduction of interventions designed to provide children from deprived and underprivileged backgrounds with a "Head Start" during the preschool years so as to prevent later school failure (Consortium for Longitudinal Studies, 1983; Lamb, 1998; Zigler & Finn-Stevenson, 1999). By 1968 it was widely believed that these programs had failed (Jensen, 1969), and in response to this apparent failure, attempts were made to initiate educational interventions at earlier ages. The result was a proliferation of books and pamphlets designed to help parents enrich their infants' cognitive and social development. Where young infants formerly would have played contentedly with rattles, mirrors, or even scraps of paper, their parents now showered them with "creative playthings"—mobiles, busy boxes, even crib bumpers filled with goldfish!—in hopes of accelerating development (see Figure 1.4).

Applied and theoretical concerns articulate with one another. The proliferation of intervention studies with infants born preterm, and so "at risk," reflects a lack of support for strict biological determinism in development and have shown how the environment can affect outcomes (Hess, in press). For example, the Infant Health and Development Program (Bradley, Burchinal, & Casey, 2001; Hollomon & Scott, 1998; McCormick, McCarton, Brooks-Gunn, Belt, & Gross, 1998) involved an early intervention in the lives of 985 preterm infants born in eight distinct geographical and demographic sites around the United States at an average gestational age of less than 37 weeks (i.e., these babies were born less than 37 weeks after conception) weighing less than 5.5 pounds at birth. The sample was divided into an intervention group and a control group. Infants in

FIGURE 1.4
A baby fascinated with a "busy box."

the intervention group were given quality pediatric care, and their homes were visited weekly by trained caseworkers in the first year and biweekly in the second and third years. Their parents were given instructions in how to care for and enhance the development of their babies, and also had the opportunity to attend professionally led support groups. During the children's second year, they themselves attended child development centers whose staff was specially trained. Children in the control group received only pediatric care during the same period. Normally, infants born preterm show a variety of neurological and sensorimotor, feeding and sleep dysfunctions, and they experience numerous problems that make their day-to-day care more difficult. In this study, however, infants in the intervention group had significantly higher mean IQ scores than the control group at 3 years, and their mothers reported significantly fewer behavioral problems than did the mothers of control-group infants. Thus, environmental supports were shown to mitigate biological vulnerabilities and disadvantages.

The 1960s also saw the emergence of the women's liberation movement. Many popular writers encouraged women to actualize their full intellectual, social, and economic potential, and these admonishments led to a reevaluation of the former equation of femininity with motherhood. In prior decades, many people believed that only full-time mothers could provide young children with the care they needed in order to thrive, and these beliefs were fostered by extensive literature on the adverse effects of maternal deprivation (Bowlby, 1951). Since the 1960s, however, social critics have argued that high-quality daycare centers can provide good out-of-home care and thus relieve employed mothers of full-time childcare responsibilities (Lamb, 1998). For example, the quality of children's emotional attachments appears to depend not on the absolute amount of time that parents spend with their infants, but on the quality of parents' interactions with them (Lamb, Hwang, Ketterlinus, & Fracasso, 1999). These developments in turn raise several questions: What constitutes quality interaction between parents and infants? What are the long-term effects of daycare? What difference would it make if fathers rather than mothers took primary responsibility for childcare? The political and social climate for research in infancy thus became highly supportive as parents and policymakers turned to researchers for answers to such questions.

Scientific Infancy Studies

Systems

Despite the keen observations of both parents and scientists, and although today more than enough is known to permit the compilation of volumes much lengthier than ours, we remain grossly ignorant about many aspects of development in infancy. Our goals in this book are not to review every study and every theory about infants, but to summarize the most salient information available and to provide a coherent picture of development in infancy. To this end, theoretical perspectives and themes will be emphasized and described in each chapter, along with the results of recent relevant research.

The organization of our book is topical, with each chapter focused on a different aspect or outcome in development, rather than on superordinate processes or categories of influence. This organization has the distinct benefit of permitting a clear focus on the status, origins, and process of development in each aspect of development. When books are organized in this way, however, it is easy to lose sight of the fact that these different facets of development are intimately interrelated—that they are different aspects of the same single coherent organism. Before outlining the structures and functions that we examine, therefore, we first illustrate how they are interrelated.

In recent years, developmentalists, particularly those who study infancy, have begun to explore *systems models* of early development. In a systems model, the central issues are emergent properties, multicausality, autonomy, and indeterminacy (Thelen, 2001). Development in the systems-model perspective is dynamic in the sense that the organization of the system as a whole changes as the infant matures and acquires new experiences. As one subsystem emerges, that change brings with it a host of new experiences that influence and are influenced by changes in related component processes. Thus, change is not only dynamic but also thoroughgoing, taking place at many levels in the system at the same time.

These are abstract and difficult-to-grasp principles in and of themselves. Bertenthal and Campos (1990) provide an extended discussion of the systems approach using the infant's development of self-produced locomotion as a concrete example. Specifically, these investigators identify several component processes involved in and affected by the onsets of crawling and walking, structures and functions as far flung as visual–vestibular adaptation, visual attention to changes in the environment, social referencing, and the differentiation of emotions. Bertenthal and Campos then showed that higher level behavioral organization in the infant emerges from the coordination of these component processes, and that the emergence of self-produced locomotion (a change in a single process) affects a diverse set of psychological skills including fear of

A   B

FIGURE 1.5
An illustration of the significantly different perspectives infants have of their visual world
(A) before and (B) after they achieve upright locomotion. (© 1981 by Leonard Speier.)

heights, the spatial localization of hidden objects, concept formation, and social
referencing.

Indeed, we can see reverberations in development beyond even these functions. Most babies learn to pull themselves to a standing position and to walk
at around 11 to 15 months of age. Diverse aspects of cognitive or social development appear to underlie this change in motor ability, and learning to walk
has major implications for both social and cognitive development. Before standing upright, the infant viewed the world from a supine position, or from 6 to
8 inches above the ground while creeping or crawling. Suddenly, the baby can
view the world from a height of 2 feet (see Figure 1.5). A dramatic change in
perspective results: A whole new array of objects can be approached, explored,
manipulated, and mastered. These new experiences in turn facilitate cognitive
development. After being totally dependent on adults for stimulation, the infant
rapidly acquires the abilities to explore and to find stimulation independently.
As far as social development is concerned, the ability to stand, like the ability to
crawl, signals significant changes of a different sort in the infant's role vis-à-vis
adults. Standing infants seem more grown-up to adults, who in turn treat them
differently. Consider the effects that the infant's newfound ability to walk has on
parents. They must now be vigilant about the possibility that the child may fall
down steps, accidentally knock over something heavy, or munch on a dangerous house plant. Much more than before, parents must communicate to infants,
primarily through their faces, voices, and gestures, nonverbal messages that
help children to regulate their own behavior and to learn—not through "hard

knocks" but through the parents' emotional messages—what to approach and what to avoid.

Alternatively, consider the development of language as it illustrates how a variety of independent developments converge to make verbal communication possible. In infancy, the anatomical structures that speech requires must mature, as must the advanced cognitive capacity to use symbols (words) to refer to things, and the social awareness and emotional relationships that provide the motivation to engage in more sophisticated interaction and verbally communicate with others. Thus language development depends on anatomical and physiological as well as on cognitive, social, and emotional advances. All of these are crucial, for without them the capacity to speak would not develop. Moreover, the acquisition of speech has profound and obvious ramifications for all other aspects of development.

In summary, we can see that all of these aspects of development in infant life are embedded in one another insofar as they exist at multiple levels—"the inner-biological, individual–psychological, dyadic, social network, community, societal, cultural, outer-ecological, and historical" (Dixon & Lerner, 1999, p. 32). At a given point in development, variables from any and all of these levels contribute to the status of a structure or function. Moreover, these multiple levels do not function independently of one another; rather, they interpenetrate and mutually influence one another.

Challenges

As the Nobel laureate Tinbergen (1963) once pointed out, there are four questions about *why* a certain behavior occurs. First, there are questions about ultimate function: What survival value (if any) does the behavior have? Second, there are questions about causation: What internal and external stimuli or cues elicit or control the behavior? Third, there are questions about ontogenetic development: Why did this child come to behave in this fashion? Last, there are questions about evolutionary history: What aspects of the species' history led members of the species to behave in this way? All four of these questions are legitimate, and answers to them are informative. They lead toward complementary rather than competing sorts of information that advance our understanding. In *Development in Infancy*, accordingly, we try to address all four types of questions, although much of our emphasis is on causation and development because these considerations have been of greatest interest to psychologists. We strongly believe, however, that evolutionary biology provides a valuable complementary perspective on development in infancy.

To address these questions about infant development is not easy, and what we know now has been learned slowly. In large part, this halting progress can be attributed to the enormous practical and logistical problems encountered in studying young infants. Perhaps the major problem faced by students of both cognitive and social development in infancy is that, at base, they are trying to determine what is "inside the baby's head"—what infants know and feel about the people and things around them, and whether they understand the effects of those people and things. However, researchers must often make inferences about these capacities from apparently unrelated behavioral responses. First and foremost, infants are unable either to understand or to answer researchers' questions unambiguously and reliably. Those who study older children or adults can question their research participants verbally, but infants can neither understand verbal questions nor respond verbally. In addition, infants are notoriously uncooperative, because unlike adults they are not motivated to perform for researchers. Other problems that vex investigators are infants' limited attention spans, their limited response repertoires, and the variability inherent in most infant behaviors. Finally, measurement of any aspect of infant function as well as the ascription of valid behavior to the infants' repertoire is highly dependent on infant state.

To assess the capacities of infants in any given domain of development, researchers are forced to design ingenious procedures to elicit a response that is within the infant's capability. When infants do not respond as expected, substantial problems remain. Researchers have to decide whether the infants did not respond because they: (1) did not understand the question, (2) are incapable of performing the task, (3) are incapable of emitting the response, (4) are not paying attention, or (5) are not motivated to respond. Although these problems are not unique to studies of infancy, they are endemic in this field. Most important, researchers must constantly avoid reaching conclusions about the lack of certain capabilities in infancy based only on the failure of infants to behave in an expected way.

Outline of This Book

The major facets of development in infancy—physical, neurological, perceptual, cognitive, linguistic, emotional, and social—are considered serially in the chapters that follow this introduction. In order to place our study of infancy in context, we step back in Chapter 2 from the scientific study of infants and attempt to describe the "real-world" contexts in which babies grow. Infants do not develop in a vacuum; rather, their arrival and presence profoundly shape and are in turn influenced by family members and other people and institutions with whom their families come into contact. Infancy is a phase of the life cycle when adult caregiving could exert extremely salient influences. Not only does caregiving occur at its most intense levels in this period, but infants are thought to be particularly susceptible and responsive to external experiences for reasons described earlier. In this chapter, we discuss parenting and family relationships, with particular focus on the ways in which mothers and fathers and the spousal relationship influence interactions with infants. We then consider the development of infant relationships with siblings and peers—the other children who bridge the gap between the intra- and extrafamilial social worlds. Many infants today also spend time in nonparental care facilities, and thus we also describe the ways in which early development may be affected by various patterns of nonparental nonfamilial care. We end the chapter with a consideration of subcultural, social class, and cultural variations in the contexts of parenting and infant care.

In Chapter 3, we review research methods, describing in some detail the ways investigators today ask questions of young infants. We start by discussing the logic of empirical investigation, including the strengths and limitations of the various types of designs that can be used to study status, origins, and developmental processes associated with different structures and functions. We then turn from the logic to techniques, and the characteristics of procedures ranging from biographical descriptions and case studies, through naturalistic observations and observations in structured settings, to the recording of psychophysiological and behavioral activities in increasingly structured ways. The chapter concludes with discussions of the scientific method and the ethics of research with infants. Experimental and naturalistic studies carried out in homes and in laboratories underpin our growing understanding of infant development, and it is to substantive aspects of development that our attention then turns.

Infancy is characterized by remarkable physical and physiological changes, many of which are evident even on casual observation because of their magnitude and scope. Within the first year after birth the child's weight triples and the child changes from an immature being unable to move his or her limbs in a coordinated manner to one who can purposefully control the complicated sequence of muscle contractions and flections necessary to walk or reach and grasp. It is clear that these developments do not simply involve changes in size; they depend on marked physiological maturation, as we make evident in Chapters 4 and 5, where we describe early physical, motor, neural, and psychophysiological development. Growth of the central nervous system relates to changes noted in many of these spheres of development. Even when explicit references of this kind are absent, it is important to bear in mind the patterns of physiological and neural development that parallel cognitive and social development. Aspects of both pre- and postnatal growth are reviewed in these chapters, for there is good reason to view development across these early months as a continuous process on which birth has a rather modest impact.

Until the 1930s, the brain of the newborn was believed to be so immature that researchers doubted whether the cortex functioned at all until well into postnatal life. Since the cortex is the part of the brain responsible for neural coordination and integrating information, scientists questioned whether young infants were capable of any psychologically interesting processes or performance. Few people would defend this notion today, but none would question the relative immaturity of the newborn's brain. As we show in Chapter 5, the cells in the brain and the brain itself change dramatically early in development. Among the central changes occurring are the development of myelin sheaths on the axa of neural cells, a change that facilitates the cellular transmission of information. We assume that this change is involved in a plethora of advancing abilities in infancy. Increases in the number of associations among cells also facilitate communication among cells. Likewise, physiological changes seem to underlie a shift from the infants' subjugation to unpredictable changes in state and irregular cycles of sleeping and waking to the emergence of self-regulation.

It is easy to overlook these biological changes when seeking to determine what factors account for the more directly observable changes in cognitive, social, and emotional behavior, but the role of physical change in development is probably major. Whatever the case, little is known about the neuroanatomical aspects of early human development, and even less is known about relations between structural changes in the brain and changes in the child's functional capacities, or about the effects of structural and functional neural growth on behavioral development. With so many aspects of the baby's body changing so rapidly, it becomes difficult to determine whether any one development (e.g., myelination) is responsible for any particular behavioral change.

At birth, all sensory channels operate. Newborns even seem to seek out information in the environment, although they do not appear very capable of making fine differentiations. Thus, for example, newborn babies will look at a pattern and systematically explore it with their eyes as if trying to learn as much as possible about it. Newborn visual acuity is poor, however, and the newborn may be unable to focus on specific targets. During infancy the capacities to take in information through the five major sensory channels (vision, hearing, touch, taste, and smell) and to attribute meaning to that information improve dramatically. These advances have important implications for perception, cognition, social, and emotional growth—that is, for the infant's increasing capacity to make sense of the environment—and the stage is set for this development in Chapter 5. Being able to see does not necessarily mean that babies can perceive perspective and depth in their world, or even that they can differentiate between a figure and the background against which that figure appears. These capacities are necessary before the baby can recognize specific objects or persons. Only when infants gain the ability to recognize objects and observe the manner in which objects behave in relation to one another can they start learning the laws that govern activity in the physical world.

Perceptual development is discussed in Chapter 6, where we review the major issues that have dominated theorizing on this topic. The best-studied perceptual modality is vision, and our chapter reviews such issues as: what babies are capable of seeing, how they behave when shown visual stimuli, and how they integrate visual information into a coherent view of the world. Unfortunately, less is known about hearing and the other senses than about vision, with the exception of research on speech perception. It is in the study of visual perception, however, that the age-old battle between nativists and empiricists has been joined with greatest fervor, as we recount in our introduction to the chapter.

Perceptual development represents the first phase in a process of extracting information from the avalanche of sensations that the baby experiences. Cognitive development begins with primitive realizations that specific objects have an independent and permanent existence, and that acting on objects yields predictable but differing effects depending on whether the object is a table, a rattle, or a cat. Understanding these laws in turn makes it possible for the baby to act intentionally on the environment. Major cognitive theorists have viewed conscious intentionality as a critical feature of intelligent behavior.

In Chapter 7, we describe the growth of cognitive and intellectual abilities in infancy. A qualitative approach, pioneered by Piaget, emphasizes the changing ways in which infants actively attempt to interpret or make sense of their experiences, whereas a quantitative approach addresses what infants know and how they get to know it. The former approach thus promotes a stage-based view of development in which discrete phases can be discerned, whereas the latter places greater stress on measuring individual competencies in order to permit assessment of developmental change as well as comparisons among individuals. Cognition involves understanding the "laws" that govern relations among objects in the environment—particularly laws that relate one's own actions to objects and their resulting behavior (e.g., "When I push something, it moves").

Among the issues of interest to students of cognitive development, none has excited more attention recently than questions concerning individual differences: Can individual differences in infant mental life be measured reliably? Do they tell us anything about the child's later intellectual potential? In Chapter 7, we also describe various attempts to develop standardized measures of cognitive development and the generally disappointing status of longitudinal research with those measures. However, researchers have been excited to find that newer measures of very basic cognitive processes in infancy *do* predict individual differences in cognitive performance in later childhood. In addition, we discuss research on how the social contexts in which infants develop influence cognition and its development.

More specialized aspects of infant cognition are the focus of Chapter 8. Here we describe the infant's changing ability to represent events and experiences, to remember them, and to use them in ever more sophisticated ways. Since we now know that infants can learn, researchers have turned their attention to understanding how they categorize stimuli and events so as to abstract memorable lessons from them. Categorization and representation are surely essential to the organization of learning and memory, and also play a crucial role in permitting the use of symbols—a basic prerequisite for language development. As we show in Chapter 8, categorization and representation are also central aspects of both social and object-mediated play. Representation thus serves as an important bridge permitting babies to communicate with increasing precision about their thoughts, intentions, and feelings.

Socioemotional and cognitive development are integrally related phenomena, even though scholars tend to specialize in the study of one or the other. Communication and interaction are two concepts that help to explain the overlap between the two. Communication refers to the exchange of information between individuals. Early in life, the infant communicates with others by means of emotional expressions, which function as prepotent communicative signals; an example is nonverbal signals of distress, like crying. The baby also has the capacity to organize speech sounds, and in remarkably short order the baby's own repertoire of communicative tokens expands to include various gestures and a growing range of social signals, culminating in language. The comprehension of speech combined with the generation of unique utterances rank among the major cognitive goals of the infancy period—perhaps its crowning achievement—but the motivation to acquire language is surely social. Language is probably the most important medium of social interaction from infancy onward; as such, it stands squarely at the interface of cognitive and social development.

By definition, infancy ends when language begins, but it is increasingly evident that language does not suddenly emerge late in the second year of life. Rather, the use of language depends on the ability to segment and process visual and auditory information (Chapter 6), the ability to develop concepts and to represent them symbolically (Chapters 7 and 8), the formation of social relationships and motivations and recognition of the reciprocal basis of social interaction and internalization of the elementary rules of turn taking and communication (Chapter 11). Language development, our topic in Chapter 9, is driven by all of these features of infant life. In addition, the input necessary to learn language is itself a component of social interaction. Language development is also predicated on the child's innate ability and urge to make sense of linguistic experience— itself a complex cognitive task. The relative balance of interactional experience and native competency in the diverse processes of language acquisition remains unclear, and as a result this topic constitutes a second continuing battleground in the nature–nurture debate.

Communication is, of course, hardly a one-way street. Indeed, from very early in life, children learn to integrate their communicative activities, utterances, and expressions into the stream of interaction where rules of reciprocity or turn taking help to organize events and people in the world. For example, through interaction, children may come to view themselves as more effective individuals, come to see others as reliable, and more generally come to see the world as explicable and organized. Furthermore, to the extent that their interactions are patterned and their communications effective, the exchange of knowledge will be enhanced as well.

After discussing the origins of language development, we turn our attention in Chapter 10 to the development of emotions and temperament. Here we describe the communicative functions of emotions and explore both the origins and developmental significance of individual differences in emotionality and temperament. Emotions and affects permit infants to read others' appraisals and intentions, and they enable infants to communicate their own appraisals to others. Emotions also play a major role in organizing behavior within an individual. In turn, individual differences in emotionality constitute the core of temperament, commonly defined as a constitutionally based source of individual differences in personality. Temperamental variation is already evident early in infancy, and individual differences in temperament are significant because of their potential for influencing infants' cognitive and social interactions. Because of their broad implications, studies of the emotions and of temperament in infancy are currently experiencing a resurgence of interest.

Gaining the ability to differentiate between people and background is a perceptual capacity that constitutes the first step toward understanding the social environment. We discuss these social processes more fully in Chapter 11. Newborn babies certainly affect their social environment—their cries are extremely potent, eliciting prompt responses from most people who hear them—but newborns probably do not understand the potential meaning of the signals to which adults readily attach social and communicative significance. Later, infants learn that their cries have predictable effects on others, and later still, they may cry in order to have a desired effect. During infancy, we witness a gradual dawning of social awareness and a steady shift from adult to infant in responsibility for maintaining sequences of social interaction.

Another major step in socioemotional development is defined by the formation of attachments, that is, enduring relationships with specific individuals, especially parents. In Chapter 11, we also discuss the cognitive prerequisites for forming attachments, whom babies become attached to and why, and how adult activities affect the types of relationships established between infants and adults. Throughout these chapters on social and emotional development, our emphasis is on the manner in which interactions with others affect the development of a baby's characteristic social style and how that style influences later interactions and experience. Although classical theories—notably psychoanalytic and social learning—are described, our discussion of the processes involved in the formation of social relationships emphasizes an ethological theory of social development.

Throughout this book we repeatedly stress interrelations among various aspects of development. Chapter 12 is designed to underscore the importance of this perspective by discussing the early development of social cognition—infants' learning about specific people and the way they tend to behave. Our goal is to illustrate that the development of this capacity depends on the elaboration of several basic cognitive capacities (attention and memory, for example) as well as more complex cognitive competencies (e.g., the development of intentionality and the object concept), all of which relate to physiological development and perceptual accomplishments. Social experiences also play crucial roles in these developmental processes, and it is to the understanding of people and their behavior that social cognition applies. Finally, phases of emotional or affective development are integrally related to stages of social and cognitive development as well as to social cognition. Social cognition thus exemplifies interdependencies among lines of development that, for purposes of examination, are artificially separated for discussion in Chapters 4 through 11.

Summary

Because of the range, the magnitude, and the implications of the developmental changes that occur early in life, infancy is a fascinating and appealing phase of the life cycle. Some of the key issues in developmental study—those having to do with the relative importance of nature and nurture, for example, or with the interrelations among diverse aspects of development—are rendered in sharpest relief when the focus is on infancy. Thus, studying babies tells us about general developmental phenomena as well as infancy as a particular stage of the life cycle.

Patterns of development are inherently complex; infants' experiences appear to be important, but later experiences often interact with the effects of earlier ones to shape final developmental outcomes. In addition, not all infant experiences are equivalently meaningful, and certain aspects of development are more susceptible to experience than others. Stability and continuity are significant issues as well. Many theorists have asserted—and many have questioned—the status of infancy as a separate stage in the life cycle as well as the possibility of stages of development within infancy itself.

In the remaining chapters of the book, we review our current understanding of each of the major structures and functions of development in infancy and discuss these issues in detail, for they continue to frame much of the contemporary research on and theorizing about infant development. Focusing on each aspect in turn, we describe significant findings and interpret their meaning. Our review is selective rather than exhaustive, for we want our readers to know and understand meaningful perspectives and facts. In addition, we attempt to highlight the basic findings and key issues with which investigators in each area must grapple, and we relate these issues and findings to the broader questions that guide research on infant development more generally. Whenever possible, we point to connections among different facets of development.

2

The Social Ecology
of Infancy

❖

- In what direct and indirect ways do parents influence their infants' development?
- How do siblings contribute to infant development, and how do other family characteristics affect the infant's developmental processes?
- How are the qualities of infant–parent, –sibling, and –peer relationships inter-related?
- In what ways does regular nonparental care—daycare—affect development in infancy?
- Compare the ways in which the quality of parenting and the quality of child care have been conceptualized and measured?
- In what ways do early social experiences vary across economic strata, ethnic groups, and cultures? How do these variations shape infant development?

Family, Daycare, Class, and Culture

This book is about infants and the processes that define development in infancy. Our search for understanding begins with the straightforward assertion that infants do not grow up in isolation. Human beings are intensely social creatures, and researchers who ignore the multiple social contexts of infant development do so at the peril of failing to understand infancy (Bronfenbrenner, 1999). In this chapter, we discuss the several ecologies in which infants develop so that we can better understand how the different contexts of development influence infancy, as well as the diverse cognitive and social experiences they provide.

In Western industrialized cultures, parents typically play the major role in providing infants' experiences, and consequently parent–child relationships constitute the first focus in this chapter. (We return to other aspects of social development in Chapter 11.) However, highlighting dyadic relationships involving infants and their parents can disguise the extent to which infant–parent relationships are embedded in a broader social context like the family; the family shapes and is shaped by component relationships as well as by the community in which it is embedded. In the first two parts of this chapter, therefore, we discuss the nuclear family, focusing on the ways in which mothers, fathers, siblings, and infants interrelate and influence one another. The evidence we present amply demonstrates that families provide a richly textured array of relationships to young infants from the beginning of life. The patterns of influence are complex, however, because changing family dynamics shape the style and significance of each relationship. Families take different forms, and in this chapter we address infant development not only in two-parent but also in single-parent families.

Of course, nuclear families represent only one of a variety of distinct social ecologies experienced by most infants. In addition to frequent opportunities to interact with peers from early in infancy, young infants in many cultures are tended by a variety of nonparental careproviders, whether in family daycare, daycare centers, villages, or fields. We discuss the large literature on the effects of nonparental care on infant development in the third section of the chapter.

Situations like daycare represent one of the ways in which people outside the family affect infants' development in meaningful ways. The larger society in which the family is embedded is also influential in more indirect ways. Social classes and cultures vary with respect to the patterns of interaction they encourage and support. Some ensure that infants are reared in intimate extended families in which care is provided by many relatives; others isolate mothers and babies from almost all social contexts. Some treat fathers as irrelevant social objects; others assign complex and intimate responsibilities to fathers. Cultural prescriptions determine, to a great extent, the immediate social contexts experienced by infants, the short- and long-term goals parents have for their children, and the practices used by parents in attempting to meet those goals. In short, class and culture play major roles in shaping the ecology of infancy. The child-rearing practices of one's own culture may seem "natural," but some practices are actually rather unusual in an absolute sense. Furthermore, few nations in the world are characterized by cultural homogeneity; ethnic and social class differences within Western industrialized countries color childrearing practices just as surely as cultural differences do. Some effects of social class and culture are thus explored in the fourth section of this chapter.

Infant, Mother, and Father

It has been said that parents largely "create" persons (Kaye, 1982; Watson, 1928) because mothers and fathers influence the development of their infants in many ways. *Direct effects* are most obvious. Parents contribute directly to the genetic makeup of their children and directly shape their children's experiences; parents also serve as their children's social partners. We begin this chapter, then, with a general discussion of parenting.

In the natural course of things, the two sorts of direct effects are confounded: The parents who endow the infant genetically also structure their infant's world and experiences. Can we disentangle heritable from experiential influences on the status, origins, and development of infant structures and functions? Can we tell when one or both are influential in development? To isolate heritable and experiential direct effects, we can appeal to so-called natural experiments where these two sources of variation in the individual can be distinguished, at least to a degree.

Direct Effects—Heritability

Mothers and fathers directly contribute to the development of their infants by passing on their genes, and behavior geneticists attempt to assess the relative contributions of genetics (nature) and environment (nurture) to individual characteristics such as physical growth, intelligence, personality traits, and even occupation and leisure activities. Two research paradigms—involving twins and adoptees, respectively—are commonly used to study the importance of heredity. Twins born from the same egg and fertilized by a single sperm are *monozygotic*, and they share 100% of their genetic inheritance; twins born from different eggs fertilized by different sperm are *dizygotic*, and they share approximately 50% of genetic inheritance, just as other siblings do. The typical twin study (e.g., Saudino et al., 1999; Segal, 1997) involves assessing the extent to which certain characteristics are shared, or not shared, by identical twins either reared together or apart, or by monozygotic and dizygotic twins. Alternatively, behavior geneticists use adoption designs (e.g., Deater-Deckard & Plomin, 1999; Devlin, Fienberg, Resnick, & Roeder, 1995) to examine the degree to which adopted children share traits with both their adoptive and biological parents. Reviews of behavioral genetics studies indicate a high degree of genetic heritability for a surprising range of individual characteristics (e.g., Rowe, 1997). There are, of course, many ways in which genetic inheritance may manifest itself, including effects on the events actually experienced by the infant (Scarr, 1993; Scarr & McCartney, 1983). In addition, the strength of the contribution of genetic inheritance for a particular characteristic may depend on the environmental "niche" in which the infant is reared. Clearly, however, parents significantly affect their children's developmental trajectories and outcomes by endowing them genetically, just as they shape their development by providing formative experiences.

Direct Effects—Parenting

Evidence for heritability does not negate or even diminish equally compelling evidence for the direct (and indirect) effects of parental behavior on infants (Collins, Maccoby, Steinberg, Hetherington, & Bornstein, 2000). To cite even the most obvious and trivial example, genes must contribute to making siblings very much alike, but (as we all know) siblings are still very different, and it is widely held that siblings' different experiences contribute to making them distinctive individuals (Dunn & Plomin, 1991; Kowal & Kramer, 1997). Thus, even within the same family, parents (and others) create different environments for their children. In addition, there is much evidence that warm, attentive, stimulating, responsive, and nonrestrictive parental activities promote intellectual and social competencies in infants as well as older children (Bornstein, Tamis-LeMonda & Haynes, 1999; Cole, Michel, & Teti, 1994; Grolnick, Kurowski, McMenamy, Rivkin, & Bridges, 1998; Lamb, Hwang, Ketterlinus, & Fracasso, 1999; Pettit, Bates, & Dodge, 1997; Reese & Cox, 1999; Teti, in press), and most developmentalists believe that parents exert their most important influences on infant development (e.g., Cole, Michel, & Teti, 1994; Guralnick, 1997a). Although infancy is a comparatively brief period in the lifespan, no other period of life demands more parental time and investment. Infants are wholly dependent on caregiving to survive. Furthermore, adults seem to find infants especially

FIGURE 2.1
Nurturant, responsive mother–infant interaction is critically important for promoting social, emotional, and intellectual development in infancy.

appealing. Adults "melt" in response to an infant smile, find babies fun to play with and talk to, and are fascinated by how rapidly babies grow from being totally helpless at birth to developing unique personalities by age 2. It is no surprise, given how dependent infants are on adults and how much energy parents devote to infants, that infants are considered more responsive to parental input than children in any other developmental period. As a result, developmental scientists have devoted themselves to documenting how parents shape the physical, cognitive, verbal, and social development of infants.

Bornstein (2002) distinguishes among four major domains of parenting: *Nurturant caregiving*, aimed at promoting infants' basic survival (e.g., providing protection, supervision, and sustenance); *material caregiving*, involving the manner in which parents structure infants' physical environments (e.g., provision of toys and books and restrictions on physical freedom); *social caregiving*, having to do with parental efforts to involve infants in interpersonal exchanges (e.g., soothing, touching, smiling, and vocalizing); and *didactic caregiving*, pertaining to how parents facilitate infants' understanding of the world around them (e.g., directing babies' attention to and interpreting external events, and providing opportunities to learn). These domains are not mutually exclusive, and it is quite typical for two or more parenting domains to occur simultaneously as, for example, when a parent attempts to get an infant to eat (nurturant caregiving) by involving the infant in an interpersonal game (social caregiving).

Bornstein (2002) also proposes that parents can affect infants directly through two basic interactional mechanisms. One of these, the *specificity principle*, states that specific parental behaviors at specific times shape specific infant abilities in specific ways. Bornstein et al. (1999), for example, found that increases in mothers' verbal responsiveness to infant vocal or exploratory behavior from 13 to 20 months of age predicted infants' vocabulary levels at 20 months. By contrast, levels of maternal vocabulary used when speaking to infants did not predict infant vocabulary levels. These results support the specificity principle in that infant vocabulary levels were specifically sensitive to maternal verbal responsivity, not to how many different words mothers used during mother–infant exchanges. The second interactional mechanism is the *transactional principle*, which states that infants both shape and are shaped by their experiences with parents in a reciprocal manner. Students of infant temperament (see Putnam, Sanson, & Rothbart, 2002; Vaughn & Bost, 1999, for reviews), for example, propose that the extent to which an infant is perceived as temperamentally "easy" or "difficult" may influence the manner in which parents respond to the infant. The quality of the parents' response, in turn, further shapes the infant's behavior.

Thus, even with infants, parenting cuts across several functional domains and shapes infant development through specific, parent-to-child pathways as well as through reciprocal transactional mechanisms. In recognition of the fact that mothers have traditionally assumed primary, if not exclusive, responsibility for childcare, theorists and researchers have been much more concerned with the mothering rather than the fathering of infants. Research and theory about infancy are influenced by cultural assumptions about the centrality of the mother–infant relationship and the importance of mother-provided early experiences to the child's later development. Indeed, to this day, many societies, including ours, place a very strong emphasis on the mother–infant relationship (Bornstein & Tamis-LeMonda, 1989). It is important to point out, however, that fathers interact with and care for their children as well, and frequently in ways that are distinctly different from those of mothers (Lamb, in press; Lamb et al., 1999; Parke, 2002). The rising scientific and popular interest in fathers in the past two decades (Lamb et al., 1999; Lamb, 2000b, in press) reflects social changes in family structure and functioning that have led fathers to become more involved in the care and nurturance of their infants. The nature of mother– and father–infant relationships and the unique influences of mothers and fathers on infant development will be further explored in Chapter 11.

Parents' direct influences on infants can thus be a function of genetic inheritance or parental behavior. Importantly, maternal and paternal caregiving are not static phenomena. They are constantly changing, and as we explore in this chapter (and Chapter 11), reflect many sources of influence; some arise from within the individuals, whereas others are elicited and shaped by the infant. Both the most obvious and the most subtle infant characteristics can affect parents' behavior toward their infants as well.

Indirect Effects

The infant's growing awareness of other individuals predicates a series of stages through which relationships—often called *attachments*—are established with the parents. The formation of attachment reflects the convergence of built-in tendencies in infants and the propensities of adults to respond in certain ways to infants' needs and cues, and the ways in which individual adults respond vary depending on several factors, including infants' gender, their personalities, their current social, emotional, and economic circumstances, their infants' characteristics, their own life histories, and their ideologies (we discuss these more in Chapter 11). Perhaps as much as any of these factors, however, parental

FIGURE 2.2
A father and his infant play together.

behavior depends on the current status of other relationships within the family. Not only do infants experience multiple formative relationships, but so too do their mothers, fathers, and siblings. As a result, parents and siblings influence infants not only by virtue of interactions with them—direct effects—but also by virtue of each party's influence on others—*indirect effects*. Because students of infancy have come to recognize multiple social influences on infant development—maternal, paternal, and sibling—they have come to appreciate that many influences are indirectly mediated through complex paths and networks (Lamb, 1997). Lewis, Feiring, and Weinraub (1981), for example, suggested that many paternal influences on infant development are indirectly mediated through the father's impact on the mother. In other words, even if the mother has the major direct influence on infant development in a "traditional family" (in which the mother stays at home to care for and socialize her children while the father is a breadwinner), the father may have important indirect influences.

One way in which fathers may indirectly affect their children's development, even when their breadwinning responsibilities limit the opportunities for interaction, was long ago described by Bowlby (1951, p. 13):

> Fathers . . . provide for their wives to enable them to devote themselves unrestrictedly to the care of the infant and toddler [and] by providing love and companionship, they support her emotionally and help her maintain that harmonious contented mood in the aura of which the infant thrives.

In many studies since, researchers have observed that parents are indeed more attentive and sensitive to their infants when the relationship between the parents is warm and supportive (e.g., Burchinal, Follmer, & Bryant, 1996; Davies &

Cummings, 1998; Lamb, 1997; McHale & Rasmussen, 1998; Parks, Lenz, & Jenkins, 1992).

Maternal supportiveness has a greater effect on paternal behavior than paternal supportiveness has on maternal behavior, suggesting that fathers are even more susceptible than mothers to indirect influences on their interactions with children (Belsky, Gilstrap, & Rovine, 1984; Lamb & Elster, 1985). Perhaps this is because conventional social expectations give fathers greater leeway to choose whether and how to be involved in their children's lives (Bronstein & Cowan, 1988; Lamb, 1986). Mothers are expected to be committed and involved, regardless of their psychological state (Birns & Hay, 1988).

Although the quality of mothering and fathering is affected by spousal supportiveness, support appears to be especially important when families are under stress for one reason or another. For example, Crockenberg (1988) found that the amount of support received by young mothers had a much greater impact on maternal behavior when mothering was made stressful by the infant's fussiness and irritability. In addition to the infant's characteristics, the family's economic circumstances can also be a major source of stress. Many studies conducted over the last four decades confirm that economic circumstances have a major impact on the quality of relationships between parents and on the quality of their parenting, and that poverty and economic failure are associated with punitive parenting and increased child abuse and neglect (Garrett, Ng'andu, & Ferron, 1994; McLoyd, 1998; Watson, Kirby, Kelleher, & Bradley, 1996). Poverty and economic hardship are often the focus of arguments between parents that set the wrong tone and detract from the parents' ability to care for their children optimally. Stress thus not only affects each parent's behavior directly, it also reduces mutual supportiveness and adversely affects the quality of the partner's behavior (Ketterlinus, Lamb, & Nitz, 1991).

Indirect influences such as the quality of social support from other significant adults appears to be as important to infants and mothers in low-income, single-parent households as to their counterparts in middle-income, two-parent households (Weinraub, Horvath, & Gringlas, 2002). Many infants of adolescent mothers, for example, are part of three-generation families (infant–mother–grandmother) in which parental responsibilities are shared by the mother and grandmother. Apfel and Seitz (1991) found that adolescent mothering in three-generation households was best fostered when grandmother involvement was neither too low nor too high, and when the grandmother modeled competent parenting practices that the adolescent mother learned from and then used. Later, Wakschlag, Chase-Lansdale, and Brooks-Gunn (1996) found that, when the adolescent mother established some independence from, and good communication with, the grandmother, the adolescent mother's parenting was of better quality than when the adolescent mother–grandmother relationship was characterized by role confusion and conflict.

To understand fully the effects of family climate on infant–parent relationships and other aspects of infant development requires multiple types of data representing multiple levels of analysis (Parke, 1979). Information about parents' attitudes, values, perceptions, and beliefs helps to explain when and why parents behave as they do. Likewise, observations of parenting in multiple caregiving situations are required to tell the full scope of how parents behave.

Parents can thus affect infant development directly through parent–infant interaction. In addition, infant development can be affected indirectly by social–environmental supports and stressors that influence parent behavior. Concern with the impact of stress, supportiveness, and other relationships is intrinsic to ecological and contextually appropriate approaches to the study of development, which emphasize that development does not take place in a social vacuum (Dixon & Lerner, 1999). Advocates of the contextual approach also caution that relationships, like individuals, change over time. As the dynamics of the family change, changes in relationships between the two parents, and between each of the parents and the infant, can be expected to change.

Some of the most dramatic changes in family dynamics occur when a new baby is born into the family, as several researchers have noted (Cowan & Cowan, 1992; Goldstein, Diener, & Mangelsdorf, 1996). Such an event alters the roles of each family member and consequently affects the ways in which each interacts with all other family members. In many cases, the effects are so dramatic that major differences can be observed between the quality and style of parent–child interaction before as opposed to after the birth of a second child (Baydar, Greek, & Brooks-Gunn, 1997; Teti, Sakin, Kucera, Corns, & Eiden, 1996). Indeed, much interesting recent work on the dynamics of family relationships focuses on sibling relationships.

Infants, Siblings, and Peers

Parents play an especially important role in development. Through interaction with their parents—perhaps particularly with their mothers—babies develop confidence in their own effectance, trust in others, and an awareness of the reciprocal nature of social interaction. The content of parent–infant interactions may also provide the context within which the first steps in the acquisition of sex-typed behavior proceeds. Meanwhile, experience interacting with a variety of other children and adults may facilitate the development of a sophisticated and flexible repertoire of social skills by providing exposure to different individuals who have different behavioral styles and provide contrasting patterns of reinforcement.

We know relatively little about the formative significance of infants' interactions with other children, however, even though many infants grow up with older siblings. In rhesus monkeys, Harlow (1960) found that peer interactions were critical to many aspects of normal development (Figure 2.3). By interacting with their peers, infant monkeys learn how to play, how to fight, how to relate to members of the opposite sex, and how to communicate with other monkeys. When deprived of these interactions with peers, monkeys become socially incompetent adults even when they have experienced good quality care from their mothers. These findings led developmental scientists to investigate sibling and peer relationships in human infants. These relationships constitute a bridge between intrafamilial relationships and relationships beyond the home.

Sibling Relationships

Siblings in many non-Western nonindustrialized countries assume a major responsibility for childcare (Zukow-Goldring, 2002) (Figure 2.4). These siblings spend relatively little time playing with the infants; most of their interactions,

FIGURE 2.3
Rhesus monkey peers in play. Such interactions are important in the social development of monkeys. Peers are important to human infants as well. (Courtesy of S. J. Suomi.)

FIGURE 2.4
She is only 7 years old herself, but this young Kenyan girl is responsible each day for the care of her infant brother and often for her cousins as well. (Courtesy of T. S. Weisner.)

like those of Western parents, involve protection or caregiving. In Western industrialized society, by contrast, siblings seldom assume any responsibility for caregiving, and sibling relationships appear to incorporate features of both the infant–adult and infant–peer systems (Teti, 2002). On the one hand, sibling dyads share common interests and have more similar behavioral repertoires than do infant–adult dyads. On the other hand, sibling pairs resemble infant–adult pairs to the extent that they differ in experience and levels of both cognitive and social ability.

These discrepancies often lead to differences in the ways younger and older siblings relate to each other, differences which, by and large, distinguish them from the infant–peer system (see below). When siblings interact, for example, consistent asymmetries emerge between the roles assumed by preschoolers and their 1-year-old siblings (Abramovitch, Corter, & Lando, 1979; Lamb, 1978a, 1978b; Teti, Bond, & Gibbs, 1986). Older siblings tend to "lead" interactions: They engage in more dominant, assertive, and directing behaviors than their younger siblings. Infants, meanwhile, appear inordinately interested in what their siblings are doing; they follow them around, attempting to imitate or explore the toys just abandoned by the older children. This is, of course, a strategy that maximizes the amount the baby can learn about the environment from the older child. In a variety of studies, researchers have observed that older siblings spend at least some of the time teaching object-related and social skills to their younger siblings (including infants) and that the amount of teaching increases with the age of the older child (Teti, 2002). These studies, along with the findings that infants monitor and imitate their older siblings, corroborate the assertion that older siblings may influence the cognitive and social skills of infants through some combination of teaching and modeling (Zajonc, 1983).

Most researchers concerned with sibling interaction have aimed to describe the relationships and assess their impact on social development. In an early short-term longitudinal study, Lamb (1978a) found remarkable stability across time in the amount of interaction engaged in by infants and their preschool-age siblings. Furthermore, the pattern of correlations suggested that the sociability of the younger babies determined the amount of attention they received from their siblings rather than that attention from older siblings helped babies become more sociable. Individual differences in the quality of sibling relationships were also the focus of a longitudinal study conducted in England by Dunn and Kendrick (1980, 1981, 1982a). They found that same-sex siblings got along better than different-sex siblings, a finding that Kier and Lewis (1998) replicated particularly for girl–girl infant–sibling dyads. In addition, siblings interacted more poorly when mothers and firstborn girls had very positive relationships before and immediately after the birth of the second child, and when there was frequent interaction and play between the siblings and their mothers. These findings suggest that competition and envy may have an important influence on the mutual affective involvement of siblings even in infancy, as parents and other observers of the family scene have long suspected.

On the other hand, Teti and Ablard (1989) found that infants who had close, trusting, and well-meshed relationships with their mothers (secure attachments, in the terminology we explain more fully in Chapter 11) protested less and were less aggressive when their mothers played only with their older siblings (Figure 2.5). For their part, preschoolers who were securely attached to their mothers were more likely to respond to the distress of their infant siblings nurturantly than were less securely attached older siblings. Volling and Belsky (1993)

FIGURE 2.5
Nurturance is an important (and often overlooked) dimension of infant–sibling relationships and appears to be linked to the quality of children's relationships with parents.

reported similar links between warm, nurturant infant–mother relationships and low levels of sibling conflict later in childhood. Furthermore, siblings were more prosocial toward each other when the children had nurturant relationships with their fathers. In addition, Teti, Sakin, Kucera, Corns, and Eiden (1996) found that the quality of relationships between preschool-age firstborns and their mothers shortly after the birth of a secondborn was predicted by both the quality of marriage and the mothers' nurturant, supportive behavior toward the firstborn before the baby's birth.

These results indicate that qualitative aspects of sibling relationships must be considered in the context of children's relationships with parents and the broader family constellation. Indeed, Furman and Giberson (1995) noted that sibling relationships are more prosocial and less agonistic when parent–child relationships and parents' marriages are good, and when parents avoid treating siblings differently and allow (within reason) the siblings to settle their disputes themselves. Although studies of differential parental treatment of siblings typically target older children (e.g., Brody, Stoneman, & McCoy, 1994; Kowal & Kramer, 1997), the differential treatment of infants by their mothers can occur as early as 2 months of age (Moore, Cohn, & Campbell, 1998).

In summary, we know that siblings play a very salient role in infants' social worlds from early in life, offering degrees of stimulation and entertainment that vary depending on a variety of factors, include age, gender, age gap, the quality of the children's relationships with parents, and family functioning as a whole. Early sibling relationships can have permanent effects on infants' development. In addition, several studies of older children suggest that siblings may be important socialization agents in their own right, shaping both prosocial and aggressive behavior in younger siblings (Garcia, Shaw, Winslow, & Yaggi, 1997; Stormshak, Bellanti, & Bierman, 1996; Teti, Bradley, Hastings, & Zahn-Waxler, 1999; Youngblade & Dunn, 1995).

Developing Relationships with Other Children

For babies who do not have older siblings, interaction with other children usually does not begin until the child is enrolled in an alternative care setting, an informal play group, or a nursery school program. Research on relationships that develop among unrelated children has blossomed in the last two decades, largely because changes in the rates of maternal employment have led increasing numbers of infants to spend time with other children. This development surely increased the formative importance of peer relationships in infants' lives.

Using various methodologies, researchers have described a series of stages in the development of infant–peer relationships. As Rubin, Coplan, Cheah, and Lagace-Sequin (1999) concluded, social interaction between infants is not frequent in the first year, and it is not sustained very long when it does occur. However, even very young infants show an interest in peers, and although early infant–peer interactions appear simple and fleeting they develop rather quickly. Peer influences on infants are seen as early as the newborn period. Newborns respond to the cries of other infants by becoming distressed themselves. This apparent "obligatory" distress in response to the cries of other infants decreases over time, and by 6 months of age infants pay attention to crying peers but become distressed themselves when the distress is prolonged. Very young infants' responsivity to peers, however, is not limited to peer distress. As early as 2 months of age, infants' levels of arousal appear to be heightened in the presence of peers, accompanied by brief bouts of mutual gaze. By 6 months, infants interact in more complex ways—initiating exchanges and responding to one another's social overtures with combinations of looks, smiles, and vocalizations. Their sensitivity to social cries from peers is also evident in a tendency to continue interactions when their partners are responsive, whereas they cease their social bids when their partners are unresponsive. Over the next 6 months, overall levels of infant–peer interaction increase, with responsivity to peer overtures and imitation becoming increasingly common and interaction involving physical contact occurring less frequently. The onset of imitation as a form of responsivity may be the developmental precursor of more advanced forms of shared meaning that are important for sustaining the social play of peers later in childhood. The structural complexity of social interaction also grows over this period, and infants begin to behave differently with familiar and unfamiliar peers, generally preferring to interact with familiar peers and engage in more socially complex interactions with them. Over the course of the second year the complexity and degree of elaboration of peer play continue to grow, although coordinated interaction cannot be sustained until the second year of life (Figure 2.6). Complementary and reciprocal play then becomes prominent and predictable, with cooperative social pretend play (dominated by the shared understanding of nonliteral meaning) coming to characterize play in the later toddler period, beginning around 24 months of age.

There is no consensus regarding the origins of individual differences in the quality of early peer relationships, but many researchers have examined the associations between characteristics of infant–mother relationships (see Chapter 11)

FIGURE 2.6
Toddlers playing together.

and infants' social competence in interaction with peers. Sroufe and Fleeson (1986) proposed that infants develop "internal working models" (mental representations) of relationships with their parents that incorporate both sides of the parent–child relationship, and that these representations shape the relationships they establish with peers. If true, then children who enjoy warm, nurturant relationships with their parents would be expected to be more empathic, nurturant, and socially competent with peers than would children whose parents are rejecting, inconsistently responsive, or abusive, and this pattern has been reported (Belsky & Cassidy, 1995; Rose-Krasnor, Rubin, Booth, & Coplan, 1996). The quality of children's relationships with consistent, out-of-home caregivers also appears to be important to the development of peer relationships. Howes, Galluzzo, Hamilton, Matheson, and Rodning (1989) showed that relationships between infants and their care providers were better predictors of later social skills than were relationships between infants and mothers—a finding similar to that reported by Oppenheim, Sagi, and Lamb (1988) in a study of children on Israeli kibbutzim, where children of all ages received much of their daily care from nonfamilial caregivers.

Nonetheless, the notion that the ability to relate to peers emerges strictly from an earlier-developed ability to interact with parents has also been questioned. For example, Lamb and Nash (1989) suggested that sociability with others may be a generalized temperamental trait that underlies an infant's developing relationships with all social partners, including both parents and peers. Furthermore, Kagan (1997) proposed that shyness may be rooted in a temperamental predisposition to be fearful of unfamiliar stimuli, and that the degree to which children become shy depends on how well parents shape and organize their children's experiences to overcome such predispositions. As Rubin et al. (1999) noted, relatively little is known about the role of temperamental dispositional factors such as emotional reactivity and emotion regulation in shaping peer relationships.

Although peer– and adult–infant interactions differ in many respects, there are continuities across various parts of the infant's social world such that the characteristics of interaction with either peers or parents are likely to carry over to the interactions infants have with the other class of social partners. One school of thought suggests that infants develop characteristic social styles and orientations toward people from interactions with their parents. These styles may affect the infants' willingness and ability to engage in interactions with siblings and peers as well as the likelihood that they will benefit from those interactions. The underlying developmental processes for such mechanisms are still unclear. It could be that the quality of parent–infant relationships shapes relationships with others (Sroufe & Fleeson, 1986). It is also possible, though, that sociability develops in a general fashion—across social partners—in infancy and toddlerhood, without any one class of relationships playing a unique, exclusive, or determinative role (Lamb & Nash, 1989). Finally, sociability could be a complex function of temperamental predispositions interacting with parental socialization pressures, a position consistent with the transaction principle discussed earlier. Whichever approach is correct, many theorists agree that siblings and peers play important roles in the social ecology of infancy.

Nonparental Care of Infants

So far, we have seen how a greater understanding of infants must acknowledge the complexity of their early experiences. If anything, however, we have underestimated this complexity because we have limited this discussion to relationships with family members, siblings, and peers. We have considered extrafamilial factors (e.g., stress, poverty, and social support) only to the extent that they affect parental behavior and thus affect infants indirectly. Increasing numbers of infants today encounter a social world that extends well beyond the family, however. In fact, the majority of children in the United States are now cared for by someone other than a parent on a regular basis, beginning in the first year of life (Casper, 1997; Lamb, 1998).

Because infant daycare practices contrast with traditional cultural conceptions (Lamb, 1998), there has recently been heated controversy about the various forms of daycare and their effects on children's development. This controversy has featured prominently in the popular media and has thus engendered a great deal of concern among parents. Meanwhile, many professionals have questioned the ways in which scientific data that bear on this issue have been evaluated and presented to the public.

Daycare was often viewed as a service utilized primarily by single mothers and disadvantaged families (Phillips, 1991). Recent statistics illustrate that this view is inaccurate: Families of all kinds need supplementary care for their infants, and these needs are most often driven by economic concerns in families across all socioeconomic groups (Lamb, 1998). Put simply, the rise in the use of out-of-home care in the United States can be attributed to the need and/or desire for women to enter the workforce to help support their families.

In addition, commentators and politicians commonly oversimplify the wide variety of nonparental care arrangements referred to as daycare. Clarke-Stewart and Allhusen (2002) reported that, among infants of working parents as of 1998, 23% had been placed in a daycare center, 18% in family daycare, 6% in their own home (with a "nanny"), and 29% with another relative. Only 24% were being reared by their own parents. None of these types of care should be viewed as homogeneous "treatments," of course, as there are wide variations in the nature and quality of care provided across any group of centers, homes, or baby-sitters. Unfortunately, the quality of care often remains unmeasured, even though the *quality* rather than the *type* of care appears to have the greatest impact on children's adjustment (Lamb, 1996, 1998, 2000a; Zigler & Finn-Stevenson, 1999). Because the variation in quality within any type of care is often greater than the variation across types of care, however, it is often difficult to evaluate this finding.

Generalizations about daycare are further imperiled by the tendency of researchers to act as though children were randomly assigned to daycare and exclusive parental care groups. When they fail to take into account possible differences in the values and practices of parents who do or do not enroll their children in daycare, researchers run the risk of attributing group differences to daycare when any differences might be attributed (at least in part) to variation in the values and behaviors of the parents and the communities in which they live. Likewise, to ensure that later differences can be viewed solely as the effects of daycare researchers seldom assess the comparability of children and families prior to their assignment to various care arrangements. In all, a thorough understanding of the effects of daycare requires attention to both the background and needs of parents and children, as well as the characteristics of their care arrangements (e.g., quality, extent, and type).

Because so many infants and young children have been placed in out-of-home care, the past decade has witnessed a dramatic increase in efforts to conceptualize and measure the quality of infant care (Figure 2.7). The National Center for Infants, Toddlers, and Families has identified eight criteria that need to be achieved to ensure high-quality care (Fenichel, Lurie-Hurvitz, & Griffin, 1999). These include (1) health and safety, (2) maintaining small groups (e.g., no more than three-four children per caregiver), (3) assigning each infant to a primary caregiver, (4) ensuring continuity in care, (5) providing responsive caregiving, (6) meeting individual needs in the context of the larger group, (7) ensuring cultural and linguistic continuity, and (8) providing a stimulating physical environment. Measures of quality typically fall into two types: *structural* (e.g, group size, teacher–child ratios, and teacher training), which assess broad markers of

FIGURE 2.7
Children in a family daycare share a meal.

the social and physical environment that bear a straightforward relation to a child's interactions in the setting, and *process* (e.g., language–reasoning experiences, caregivers' interactional competence with the children, and the breadth and diversity of the learning curriculum), which assess the actual quality of care experienced by the children. Even though structural measures of quality tend to focus on gross environmental markers, they appear to be associated with process measures: higher staff-to-child ratios and better training correlate positively with caregiver–child interaction and the frequency of parent–caregiver communication (Cost, Quality, and Child Outcomes in Child Care Centers, 1995; Galinsky, Howes, Kontos, & Shinn, 1994; NICHD Early Child Care Research Network, 1996). Infants appear to form attachment-like relationships to daycare providers who offer stable, consistent care (Ahnert & Lamb, 2001; Howes & Smith, 1995; Seltenheim, Ahnert, Rickert, & Lamb, 1997), and secure infant–careprovider relationships (i.e., those characterized by warmth, nurturance, and trust) appear to promote more advanced, complex peer play (Howes, 1997). More broadly, quality of daycare has proved to be a critical determinant of development among infants enrolled in out-of-home care, with high-quality care predicting social competence with caregivers and peers (Brooks-Gunn, Klebanov, Liaw, & Spiker, 1993; Howes & Smith, 1995; Volling & Feagans, 1995) and language and intellectual skills, especially among infants from economically disadvantaged backgrounds (Burchinal, Roberts, Nabors, & Bryant, 1996; Cost, Quality, and Child Outcomes in Child Care Centers, 1995; NICHD Early Child Care Research Network, 1997c).

After more than two decades of research on the effects of daycare, we are moving away from asking questions such as "Is daycare bad for children?", to asking more meaningful questions about the manner in which daycare affects children's development and what can be done to optimize the development of infants in out-of-home care. Daycare has myriad incarnations and may have a broad range of effects, both positive and negative. We know that daycare, by itself, has no direct effects on the quality of infant–mother relationships and becomes linked to problematic relationships only in the context of other risk factors (NICHD Early Child Research Network, 1997). It is important that the effects of a particular daycare experience also be viewed in the context of other events and experiences in the infants' lives. Just as there is great variation in the quality of family environments, so there is great variation in the quality of daycare environments experienced by infants. For an infant in daycare, both the family and the daycare environment will likely make independent and inter-dependent contributions to development, and both somehow need to be taken into account in any effort to understand infant development. Indeed, no single factor (such as the quality of out-of-home care) can reasonably be expected to account for the differences observed in child adjustment among children in day-care, although policymakers persist in their search for single-factor models of development (Lamb, 2000a).

Socioeconomic Class and Culture

Today, extensive efforts are being made to understand the impact of society and culture on infant development. It is still the case, however, that much of what is known about infant development derives from studies of infants from middle-SES families living in modern industrialized and Western countries, particularly the United States. One implication of this is that developmental scientists often assume a limited single socioeconomic class or monocultural perspective. In fact, differences among socioeconomic classes and cultures are always impressive, whether observed among different groups in the United States or around the world (Harwood, Schölmerich, Schulze, & Gonzalez, 1999; Hewlett, Lamb, Shannon, Leyendecker, & Schölmerich, 1998). In this section, we bring socioeconomic class and culture, significant "macro" ecologies, into our analysis of infant development, showing that almost all structures or functions can be affected.

Socioeconomic Class and Infancy

Because most social scientists come from, or were trained in, middle-SES Western backgrounds, it is not surprising that they have focused their attention on the childrearing practices of people like themselves. This focus can lead to a tendency to view as deficient, rather than just different, the behaviors, practices, and experiences of those from other social backgrounds. Such an emphasis can also lead to the design of interventions to alleviate deficiencies without first un-derstanding the unique strengths and limitations of individuals from different ethnic and socioeconomic backgrounds. The shortsightedness of an ethnocen-tric perspective was illustrated long ago by Bronfenbrenner (1961) in examining SES differences of different eras. As Bronfenbrenner pointed out, middle-SES researchers consistently found ways to portray middle-SES values and practices as more desirable and appropriate than those of the lower SES, even though the values of both the middle-SES and lower-SES parents changed over time. Thus, when the same values were held at different times by middle- and lower-SES parents—say, a preference for bottle or breast-feeding—they were positively evaluated when held by middle-SES parents and denigrated when adopted by lower-SES parents. In this instance, the positive and negative evaluations clearly said more about researchers and theorists than about objective appraisals of the effects on children.

In general, social status in the United States is indexed by quantitative factors having to do with the infant's parents (Bornstein, Hahn, Suwalsky, & Haynes, 2002; Entwisle & Astone, 1994; Hernandez, 1997; Hoff, Laursen, & Tardif, 2002). A socioeconomic status index is computed using measures of the parents' educational achievement, income, and occupational status. As Gottfried, Gottfried, and Bathurst (2002) have shown, social status can often have a substantial impact.

A fruitful way of examining social-status differences in early development was advanced by Kohn (1987), who suggested that both within and across cultures parents try to inculcate values that will maximize their children's chances of success in the social station in which they are likely to find themselves as mature adults. For example, middle- and upper-SES parents in Western industrialized societies expect that their children will hold positions of leadership and professional responsibility; they are thus prone to emphasize self-reliance, independence, autonomy, creativity, and curiosity. Hoff et al. (2002) noted that middle-SES parents expect their children to show an early mastery of academic-related skills. By contrast, lower-SES parents expect their children to have as little opportunity for self-actualization and leadership as they themselves had, and hence tend to emphasize obedience and conformity, values that will maximize their children's chances of success in the roles they are expected to fill in society.

The few published studies of class differences in the treatment of infants reveal differences consistent with Kohn's predictions. Tulkin (1977) showed that middle-SES American mothers talk to their babies more than lower-SES mothers, even when the infants are as young as 10 months of age and are thus not yet talking themselves. These patterns were confirmed by Hoff (2002) in a study of infants averaging 21 months of age. At that stage, middle-SES mothers talked more in total, talked more per unit of time, and sustained longer bouts of interaction. Perhaps more importantly, there were also social status differences in the functional, discourse, and lexical properties of maternal language. Functionally, lower-SES mothers limited their utterances to directions and corrections, instead of acknowledging their children's actions or attempting to engage them in conversation. As far as discourse relations were concerned, lower-SES children were less likely than middle-SES children to receive topic-continuing replies to their utterances. Thus, in a variety of ways, middle-SES mothers encouraged their toddlers to converse and to expand their communicative abilities. Similar social-status differences in maternal speech to infants were observed in Israel, where lower-SES mothers talked, labeled, and asked "what" questions less often than upper-middle-SES mothers did (Ninio, 1980). Such encouragement of verbal communication by middle-SES mothers undoubtedly facilitates self-expression and also may help account for higher scores on tests of verbal ability in later childhood and adulthood. Lower-status mothers are also more restrictive socially—a tendency that may well increase obedience and conformity while inhibiting curiosity and mastery (Feagans & Farran, 1982). By contrast, middle-SES mothers tend to be less punitive and tolerate more intrusive interruptions from their children.

Of course, extreme economic disadvantage is likely to affect infant development in ways that go beyond maternal speech patterns, values, and expectations. Doubtless because a large and growing number of children live in poverty (25% in 1995), there has been a dramatic increase in research devoted to understanding the extent to which living in poverty influences child development (McLoyd, 1998). Compared to infants in middle-SES environments, infants living in poverty experience lower levels of emotional and verbal responsivity in mothers, fewer opportunities for variety in daily stimulation, fewer appropriate play materials, and more chaotic, disorganized, and unstructured environments (Bradley et al., 1994; Garrett et al., 1994; Hart & Risley, 1992). Poverty is also associated with reduced intellectual functioning in young children, and with oppositional, antisocial behavior that increases in frequency from the preschool years onward (Duncan, Brooks-Gunn, & Klebanov, 1994; Korenman, Miller, & Sjaastad, 1995; McLoyd, Ceballo, & Mangelsdorf, 1996).

In summary, social-status exerts direct and indirect influences on infant development. Social status affects mothers' conceptions of the complexity of development (Sameroff & Feil, 1985), and the undue hardships and stress created by extreme economic disadvantage are likely to diminish parents' ability to respond effectively to their infants, structure and organize their environment, and provide them with even the minimal levels of stimulation needed to support development (Magnusson & Duncan, 2002).

Culture and Infancy

As we wrote in Chapter 1, many reasons have been offered to justify cross-cultural developmental research (Bornstein, 1991, 1995; Cole, 1999; Harkness & Super, 2002). First, people are always curious about development in foreign cultures, and social anthropologists have almost always studied childhood and childcare in the cultures they study. Awareness of alternative modes of development sharpens perceptions and enhances understanding of our own culture. Second, to the extent that cross-cultural developmentalists attempt to describe the widest spectrum of human variation, their accounts are the most comprehensive available. They play an essential role in documenting the full range of human experience and in establishing valid developmental norms while permitting an unconfounding of variables thought to influence human behavior. Third, the examination of other cultures uniquely facilitates the quest to understand forces at work in development by exposing variables that are highly influential but "invisible" from a monocultural perspective. Fourth, cross-cultural research permits natural tests of the universality of psychological constructs.

Clearly, many of the reasons that motivate cross-cultural developmental research are descriptive, but some salient ones concern developmental processes. According to Werner (1988, p. 97):

> The yeoman's service that a cross-cultural perspective can provide for . . . researchers is to encourage them to take a systematic look at contextual parameters that vary *across* and *within* cultures and that are often restricted and/or confounded in the settings and samples they choose to study. Investigators who observe [child] behaviors in [other countries] find there is a wider range of biological and psychological factors that influence the development of infants than in industrialized countries.

One of the reasons why the effects of daycare has been such a controversial and heavily researched topic is that nonparental care was believed by influential Europeans and North Americans in the mid–twentieth century to be unnatural—to represent a break with traditional childcare practices—even though, historically, aristocratic and affluent Europeans and North Americans had long depended on wet nurses, nannies, and governesses to care for their children. The existence of such powerful ideological beliefs underscores the importance of social and cultural factors in shaping the social ecology of infancy. There are many societies in which both nonmaternal care practices and maternal employment are normative; citizens of these societies would be amazed to find that there exist cultures in which mothers are expected to devote themselves extensively to childcare, risking criticism for deviating from this pattern (Lamb & Sternberg, 1992).

Cultures help to "construct" children by influencing parental beliefs about childrearing and attributions about the developmental capacities of infants, which in turn influence parents' actions (Bornstein, 1991; Cole, 1999; McGillicuddy-De Lisi & Subramanian, 1996). After studying developmental timetables in two groups of Australian mothers (Australian born and Lebanese born), for example, Goodnow, Cashmore, Cotton, and Knight (1984) found that ethnic differences influenced developmental expectations of children much more than SES, gender, or birth order. According to these investigators, the assessment of parental beliefs (which we discuss in Chapter 11) represents an important approach to describing cultural settings and concretizing the goals of development for that culture.

Parents' ideas about child development and childrearing are thought to serve many functions: They may determine parental behavior or mediate their effectiveness. They may help to organize the world of parenting because ideas affect parents' sense of self and competence in their role, and, in a larger sense, they may contribute to the "continuity of culture" by helping to define culture and the transmission of cultural information across generations. In a study of mothers of 20-month-olds in seven countries (Argentina, Belgium, France, Israel, Italy, Japan, and the United States), for example, mothers evaluated their competence, satisfaction, investment, and role balance in parenting and attributed their successes and failures in parenting to ability, effort, mood, parenting task difficulty, or child behavior (Bornstein et al., 1998). Systematic country differences for both self-evaluations and attributions emerged that were interpretable in terms of cultural proclivities and emphases. For example, Argentinian mothers in this study rated themselves relatively low in parental competence and satisfaction, and blamed parenting failures on lack of ability. Their insecurity about mothering appeared to be consistent with the relative lack of supports, particularly the help and advice about childrearing provided to Argentine mothers. By contrast, Belgian mothers in this study rated themselves as quite satisfied with mothering, which might be expected in light of Belgium's strong childcare supports provided to parents (e.g., by offering periodicals, consultancies, home visits, health care information workshops, and parenting demonstration sessions).

Recognizing the pervasiveness of cultural influences on infant development, Harkness and Super (2002) have argued that the development of every infant must be viewed in the context of the "niche" in which the infant is reared. There are three ways in which niches vary: physically, ideologically, and in custom. Variations in physical circumstances are readily apparent. Consider two infants: One is born into a group of nomadic hunter-gatherers, living in temporary homes, and spending much of each day in large multiage groups obtaining food. The other is born into a modern Western culture, isolated at home with a single adult, whose food is purchased rather than hunted or gathered, and who comes into contact with a smorgasbord of individuals, few of whom are seen frequently or show much interest in the child's welfare. Cultural differences in ideology influence such factors as the frequency with which the infant is cared for by children or unrelated adults, the extent to which the infant is extended freedom to explore, and the extent to which the infant's experiences are nurturant or restrictive, among other things (Hewlett et al., 1998). From an early age, for instance, Japanese infants are indulged but gently prepared for compliance with the exacting demands of the educational system (White & Levine, 1986). Harkness and Super (2002) illustrated customary dimensions with infant–mother sleeping arrangements that result in very different expectations about such "norms" as sleeping through the night. Sleeping through the night without waking is a developmental milestone anxiously awaited by Western parents eager to avoid the disrupted sleep patterns brought about by the need to retrieve, feed, change, and put their infants back to bed, while persistent night waking is a source of great anxiety (Scott & Richards, 1990). This is not the case, however, in cultures in which infants and young children routinely sleep with their parents (see Figure 2.8, Morelli, Rogoff, Oppenheim, & Goldsmith, 1992).

An informative example of the pitfalls attending an ethnocentric view of development is provided by examining the literature on motor development in infancy. A pioneer in this area was Gesell (1945), who set himself the goal of documenting early physical (and psychological) development. On the basis of extensive and careful research, Gesell constructed detailed "cinematic atlases" of "normal development" and confidently offered developmental diagnoses of the progress and prognosis of normal and abnormal infant development. Gesell assumed that he had discovered universal developmental sequences, for he worked with such young infants and on behaviors thought to be almost wholly under biological control (Ball, 1977; Bornstein, 2001). The regularity of motor development that he observed in babies no doubt reinforced this belief.

Only later in the twentieth century did infant testing reach beyond the middle- and upper-SES European American society that it served. The results of cross-cultural surveys, first among American Hopi Indians and later among peoples in Bali and Africa, undermined many of Gesell's assumptions. These studies showed that babies often deviate from the accepted norms for European American babies with respect to both the stages and the timing of motor development in the first 2 years. Hopi infants begin to walk alone late (Dennis & Dennis, 1940); Balinese infants follow a different set of stages on their way to walking (Mead & MacGregor, 1951); and African Ganda and Wolof infants tend to be more advanced in sensory, psychological, and motor development than European American age norms would predict (Ainsworth, 1967; Geber, 1956, 1958; Lusk & Lewis, 1972). Indeed, the findings of some 50 studies point to a generalized accelerated psychomotor development among non-Western infants (Werner, 1972; but see Warren, 1972, for a critique).

What is the source of these developmental differences? As we read in Chapter 1, Gesell (Gesell & Amatruda, 1945) believed that early development was ballistic and largely unfolds under genetic control. In fact, some data on motor development support a hypothesis that favors genetic differences among babies. Nine-hour-old Gandan neonates are advanced in neuromuscular status (Geber & Dean, 1957a, 1957b), and native Africans are advanced beyond European Americans in skeletal maturation and ossification at birth (Tanner, 1970).

However, the majority of investigators have come to favor an environmentalist position on psychomotor development. Dennis and Dennis (1940) suggested that Hopi locomotor retardation reflected Hopi babies' traditional early

FIGURE 2.8
Like many infants around the world, this infant remains strapped to her mother's back except at night, when she sleeps in her mother's bed. (Courtesy of C. Super.)

constriction on the cradle board; Mead and McGregor (1951) proposed that the manner in which Balinese mothers habitually carried their infants promoted the babies' unique motor performance; and Ainsworth (1967) attributed advanced Ganda motor abilities to a nurturing climate of physical freedom.

The environmentalist interpretation gains more credence when one examines the evidence and the babies more closely, as Super (1976) did. Super found advanced sitting, standing, and walking among Kenyan Kipsigis babies, but retarded head lifting, crawling, and turning over. In the absence of a "generalized precocity" among these infants, Super was led to study Kipsigis mothers, over 80% of whom deliberately taught their infants to sit, stand, and walk. Super further ascertained that these practices were widespread among native Africans, thus providing a rationale for the general findings of previous investigators. In the same vein, Hopkins and Westra (1988, 1990) surveyed multiparous English, Jamaican, and Indian mothers living in the same English city and found that the Jamaican mothers expected their infants to sit and to walk much earlier, whereas the Indian mothers expected their infants to crawl later. In each case, the infants performed in accordance with their mothers' expectations, and the researchers were able to trace the precocity of the Jamaican infants to a pattern of care termed formal handling, which involved passive stretching movements and massage from birth, and to the introduction of practice stepping from about the third month. Manipulative and natural experiments further confirm the environmentalist interpretation. Zelazo, Zelazo, and Kolb (1972) showed that an early start and extra practice walking could accelerate development in otherwise "normal" European American infants. Furthermore, Super (1976) found that African Kipsigis infants who are reared in the tradition of European babies lose the advantage that their traditionally reared, genetically similar compatriots maintain.

Of course, innate differences in infant psychomotor abilities still may exist, and prenatal factors, such as maternal nutrition, activity, or anxiety level, could influence fetal development (Chisholm, 1989). However, the cross-cultural data show that psychomotor differences among infants can reflect the influence of childrearing practice. Bloch (1989) has pointed out that the long-term consequences of early motor precocity are unknown: Indeed, many would argue that there are no long-term benefits of being taught to sit or walk early.

The research on cultural differences in psychomotor development illustrates some of the problems that arise when researchers attempt to discern the origins of cultural differences. Other, more subtle problems also bedevil meaningful cross-cultural comparisons. For example, the distinction between private and public life, rules regarding the treatment of visitors, varying sizes of homes, or differences within culture often severely limit the ability of investigators to obtain representative, valid, naturalistic accounts of infant life that can be compared cross-culturally. For example, social scientists and psychiatrists have long argued about the potential effects of the communal childrearing practices employed on Israeli kibbutzim (e.g., Beit-Halachmi & Rabin, 1977; Bettelheim, 1969; Spiro, 1958). Bornstein, Maital, and Tal (1997) compared caregiving activities of kibbutz mothers and the professional nonfamilial metaplot with whom mothers share responsibilities for childrearing according to formalized social norms; this study also included homemaker mothers from urban nuclear families as a comparison. Importantly, kibbutz mothers and metaplot engaged in different levels of caregiving with the same baby: Kibbutz mothers provided more social stimulation than did the metaplot. In line with their "job descriptions," the metaplot provided infants more teaching than social experiences. Moreover, the metaplot provided infants with many more opportunities to explore visually or tactually by themselves than did kibbutz mothers. Urban and kibbutz mothers actively directed infants' attention similarly to objects in their environment and to the mothers' themselves. The kibbutz-mother/metaplot contrast suggests that mothers and their babies' daycare providers may provide infants with different kinds of experiences, which may in turn promote different developmental competencies.

Differences in cultural ideology also make for subtle, but potentially meaningful, differences in patterns of infant–parent interaction. Harwood et al. (1999) found that Anglo (White, non–Hispanic American) mothers of 12- to 15-month-old infants emphasized the development of individual autonomy, whereas Puerto Rican mothers focused on maternal–infant interdependence and connectedness. These differences were related to the mothers' actual behavior, with Anglo mothers using suggestions (rather than commands) and other indirect means of structuring their infants' behavior, and Puerto Rican mothers using more direct means of structuring, such as commands, physical positioning and restraints, and direct attempts to get their infants' attention. These observations are consistent with a variety of reports emphasizing the "interdependent/sociocentric" orientation of Latino families as opposed to the "individual/independent" orientation of European American families (Leyendecker & Lamb, 1999). Leyendecker, Lamb, Schölmerich, and Fracasso (1995) provided further evidence for the family-centered, sociocentric orientation of Latino families in a study of the everyday experiences of infants of Central American families who recently migrated to the United States and infants from middle-SES, European American families. Central American infants participated more frequently in family contexts in which there were multiple social partners, whereas European American infants more often experienced contexts with fewer social partners and more opportunities for dyadic interaction. The distinction between interdependent/sociocentric versus individual/independent childrearing ideologies is also illustrated in the work of Bornstein and his colleagues in studies of Japanese and American mothers and their 5-month-olds (Bornstein, Tal, & Tamis-LeMonda, 1991; Bornstein, Azuma, Tamis-LeMonda, & Ogino, 1990; Bornstein, Toda, Azuma, Tamis-LeMonda, & Ogino, 1990). American mothers respond more to their infants' orienting to the environment relative to their infants' social orientation, whereas Japanese mothers respond more to their infants' social than environmental orientation. When responding to their infants, Japanese mothers tend to direct their infants' attention to themselves, whereas American mothers tend to direct their infants' attention away from themselves and to the environment. Viewing their own findings in the context of earlier research (Befu, 1986; Hess et al., 1986; Kojima, 1986a, 1986b), Bornstein and his colleagues (1990, p. 290) concluded:

> Mothers in these two cultures have been thought to follow different rules of interaction with their infants. In general, Japanese mothers are believed to organise their interactions so as to consolidate interdependence and strengthen the mother–infant bond, whereas American mothers are believed to organise their interactions so as to foster physical and verbal independence in their infants.

Cross-cultural differences in parenting appear to persist even among parents born and reared in one culture but who then moved and lived in another culture with different childrearing norms. In studies of Japanese American and South American families who had moved to and been living in the United States for approximately 8 years, for example, Bornstein and Cote (2000, 2001; Cote & Bornstein, 2000a, 2000b, 2001) reported that South American mothers engaged in more social behavior, talked to their infants more, and provided more auditory stimulation in their infants' environment than did Japanese American mothers. Like their mothers, South American infants engaged in more social behaviors than did Japanese American infants, even when the behavior of their mothers was controlled. These differences reflected the South American mothers' higher levels of collectivism and the Japanese American mothers' emphasis on nonverbal rather than verbal interaction. No cultural differences emerged in the mothers' nurturing encouragement of infant locomotor development or in their teaching behavior, suggesting that mothers in these two cultural groups fostered their children's physical and cognitive growth based on the infants' developmental needs rather than on cultural proscriptions. Mothers reported that they engaged in more social behavior than teaching behavior with their infants (consistent with the proscriptions of both South American and Japanese culture), but when actually observed mothers engaged in more teaching than social behavior (consistent with U.S.-based parenting norms). This contradiction between what mothers believed they did and what they actually did suggests that parenting behaviors may acculturate more quickly or readily than parenting beliefs.

Distinctive childrearing beliefs and practices are not limited to comparisons between European American and non–European American families, however. Substantial differences in parenting practices toward infants can be found even between preindustrial, non-Western "small-scale" cultures. In their study of the nomadic hunter–gatherer Aka and the Ngandu farming cultures in central Africa, Hewlett et al. (1998) observed that 3- to 4-month-old Aka infants experienced a more "proximal" relationship with their caregivers (i.e., they were more likely to be held and fed) than were same-age Ngandu infants, who were more likely than Aka infants to be left alone, fuss, smile, vocalize, and play. The Aka and Ngandu cultures have similarly high levels of infant mortality, equivalently hazardous living conditions, equally healthy infants, and comparable maternal workloads, and thus these sociodemographic factors could not explain differences in the infant parenting practices of the two cultures. Hewlett et al. speculated that Aka parents stayed closer to their infants because of their frequent moves from one location to the next in search of food. Aka parents are always less familiar with their home surroundings than are Ngandu parents, who live a comparatively sedentary existence, and thus Aka parents may feel more inclined to stay in closer proximity to their infants to better protect them in unfamiliar environments.

Finally, we note that considerable overlap in parenting practices can also exist between families in different cultures (Fracasso, Lamb, Schölmerich, & Leyendecker, 1997; Schölmerich, Lamb, Leyendecker, & Fracasso, 1997), and one of the challenges facing infancy research is determining which aspects of parenting and infant development are culture specific and which may be culturally universal. It is also important to acknowledge that considerable variation in parenting exists within a given culture. A fuller discussion of these characteristics and their impact is provided in Chapter 11.

These few examples illustrate how cultural ideology shapes infant development and infant care patterns in profound ways; of course, other examples abound. Perhaps heredity and experience do not act on individual development directly or even in interaction, but rather have their effects mediated by culture. It is important also to keep in mind the cultural relativity of much of our thinking and knowledge about infants, because it may set limits on the generalizability of our findings.

Summary

We cannot fathom infancy or infant development fully unless we know more about the multiple ecologies in which infants develop. Within-family experiences may have the major impact during the first years of an infant's life but they are subject to diverse influences, and in this chapter we addressed four general questions: To what extent do members of the family and characteristics of its social and economic ecology influence infant development? What are the characteristics of the peer culture in infancy? What are the effects of nonparental care arrangements? How do social status and cultural factors affect the ways in which infants are reared?

The family network constitutes the primary context within which infants establish relationships with their parents and siblings. Today, increasing numbers of infants have significant experiences outside the family, often through enrollment in alternative care settings, like family daycare homes or daycare centers. The effects of out-of-home care vary depending on its type and quality, as well as on characteristics of infants and their families. Social status and cultural variations in patterns of childrearing also exert important influences on the ways in which infants are reared and what may be expected of them as they grow up. These variations deserve study because they illustrate the limits on much of what we know about development in infancy, because they serve to highlight the narrow perspective researchers often bring to their studies, and because they identify the importance of factors that are often discounted or overlooked completely.

3

Methods of Research
in Infancy

❖

- What are the strengths and weaknesses of longitudinal and cross-sectional research designs in infant research?
- In what ways do biographies or case studies, systematic observations in naturalistic and standardized situations, interviews or questionnaires, structured tests, and experiments contribute to our understanding of infancy?
- Think of examples of studies using natural preferences, conditioning, habituation, novelty preference, and norm-referenced and criterion-referenced tests.
- Why have measures of the autonomic nervous system been more useful so far to infancy researchers than measures of the central nervous system?
- How does behavioral state affect the discrepancy between performance and competence?
- Compare the ways in which reliability, validity, causality, and correlation affect the value of a study of infants.

Logic, Design, Procedures, Techniques, and Measurement

Our goal in this book is to examine development and developmental processes in the earliest part of life. For this reason, most of the chapters concentrate on the "whats" and the "whys" of infant development. The story would be far from complete, however, without describing "how" a growing understanding of infancy has been attained. The chief purpose of this chapter is to provide an introduction to both specific and general issues encountered by developmentalists in their efforts to ask "questions" of and to obtain "answers" from infants. Several key aspects of research with infants are explored with this purpose in mind. Some echo general developmental considerations; others are uniquely relevant to research on infancy because infants constitute such an unusual group of research participants.

Infants are by definition nonverbal, and they are also, especially in the earlier months, motorically incompetent and readily subject to state changes. Specific and detailed strategies of experimentation with infants geared to meet and overcome these limitations constitute the main procedures and techniques of infancy research. How much we have learned about infant behavior and development, mostly in the last half of the twentieth century, is testimony to the ingenuity and persistence of researchers in meeting and overcoming the challenges posed by infants themselves.

We begin this chapter with a discussion of the central goals of most infancy research, because the goals of a research question guide investigators to adopt one or another research paradigm. We describe the research designs, controls, and methodologies associated with different general goals. Then, we turn our attention to observational, experimental, and psychophysiological techniques used to expand our knowledge of physical, perceptual, cognitive, communicative, emotional, and social development in the first years of life. Next, we elaborate on questions of interpretation and measurement. Finally, we take up some overarching methodological considerations that are special to research in infancy, like context, state, point of view, age, performance versus competence, and ethics.

Logic and Design in Infancy Research: Status, Process, and Origins

Why study infants? Infancy research is largely concerned with delineating the status of different structures (e.g., physical features of the brain, such as the visual or auditory cortex) at different points early in life, and with the functions (e.g., visual or auditory perception). Focusing on status and processes so close to the beginning of life, students of development in infancy are also naturally concerned with the origins of those phenomena. Each of these concerns has engendered specific methodologies, which must all be understood clearly in order to grasp the nature, as well as the limits, of the contribution of research to our knowledge of infancy. In this section, we consider the logic and design of studies organized to address questions of status, process, and origins.

Longitudinal and Cross-Sectional Designs

Several research strategies have been commonly adopted to examine the existence and nature of different structures or functions at different ages, and to identify factors that affect their development. Students of development in infancy typically use either longitudinal or cross-sectional designs to gain access to information about status and process (e.g., Duncan, Duncan, & Hops, 1996; Gjerde, 1996; Hartmann & George, 1999; Saxon, Frick, & Colombo, 1997). Various advantages and disadvantages are associated with these methods and their derivatives.

Longitudinal studies involve repeated measurement of the same participants over time and constitute a principal method of assessing development. For example, the longitudinal design provides the only means of evaluating stability or change in infants over time. Thus, developmental sequences or stages in infancy can only be studied longitudinally; dynamic relations in development across different domains and cause–effect relations between early experiences and later outcomes can only be studied in this way as well. When Haynie and Lamb (1995) wished to investigate early developmental dimensions of emotional expressiveness, for example, they observed 59 infants in a variety of emotion-eliciting situations at 7, 10, and 13 months of age. They found that positive facial expressions (joy/enjoyment) and negative facial expressions (fear, anger, or disgust) were quite distinct and that individual differences in the amounts of positive and negative stimuli were consistent across time. Such consistency suggests that infants' emotional responses are stable traits, perhaps rooted in endogenous temperamental dimensions.

Longitudinal designs make possible the study of the two distinct types of consistency over time that we introduced in Chapter 1: *stability* and *continuity* (Bornstein, 1998; Bornstein & Suess, 2000a). Stability refers to consistency in the relative ranks of individuals in a group with regard to a particular ability over time. Haynie and Lamb demonstrated stability in infants' positive and negative expressions, in that infants tended to maintain their relative standing in these behaviors over time. Continuity, by contrast, refers to consistency over time in the absolute level of an ability in a group. Continuity would be exemplified by a group of infants performing at the same level across time. Stability and continuity are independent of each other. For example, individuals in a group may maintain their rank order on a particular ability (showing high stability), but the group mean on this ability may significantly increase or decrease over time (demonstrating low continuity).

Although longitudinal designs have advantages that make developmental conclusions like this possible, they have a number of prominent and troubling disadvantages as well. First, it is often difficult to guarantee the cooperation of children, especially babies, over long periods of time, so attrition (i.e., dropout) is a common problem in longitudinal designs. Second, where attrition is systematic, as when stressed families are more likely to drop out of a study over time than less stressed families, there is a threat of systematic bias in the findings: The participants who remain in the study may not be representative of all those who began it months or years earlier. Third, repeated testing can affect performance: Performance can improve with practice, or earlier test performance can interfere with later test performance. Fourth, the duration of longitudinal studies (even in infancy) makes them extremely expensive in terms of time, resources, and cost, requiring extended commitment from investigators as well as from their participants. Finally, the slow course of human development may pose additional problems: An investigator interested in infant attachment before and after the onset of stranger wariness, for example, must wait a year before the 6-month-olds who participated in the first phase of the study reach the follow-up phase at 18 months of age.

For these reasons, most developmental studies involve *cross-sectional designs*, in which investigators test groups of participants of different ages more or less simultaneously in order to determine whether and how structure and function vary depending on the age of the participants being tested. This strategy has a number of advantages. First, a researcher can obtain developmental answers relatively quickly. It is possible to determine whether stranger wariness changes between 6 and 18 months by comparing wariness in 6- and 18-month-old infants without waiting a year for the 6-month-olds to grow up. Second, repetition effects (like adjustment to a strange experimenter) can be avoided because each infant is tested at only one age. Third, no participants are lost because they were unable to attend testing sessions at every age.

Cross-sectional designs are not without their own shortcomings, however. First, the origins and consequences of individual differences and their stability over time cannot be investigated cross-sectionally: Haynie and Lamb (1995) could have identified patterns of positive and negative response at each age, but they could not have determined that these traits were stable over time had they adopted a cross-sectional methodology. Cross-sectional studies only reveal age differences and do not help to identify developmental processes, fluctuations in development, or individual differences in development. Second, when children of different ages respond differently on a given test, investigators usually infer that time or development is the cause without relying on longitudinal evidence; that is, in adopting the cross-sectional approach, investigators assume that their younger participants are essentially like their older participants, except that they are younger. *Cohort effects* threaten this assumption, as when children in two groups have experiences that render the two groups different. Suppose that most of the 18-month-olds in our hypothetical study of stranger wariness had been cared for at home by a parent, whereas most of the 6-month-olds' mothers and fathers went to work right after the babies were born, placing those babies in the primary care of others. Clearly, the different formative experiences of the 6- and 18-month-olds could influence their responses to strangers. Cohort effects pose knotty problems because they may confound or obscure the developmental phenomena of greatest interest to the researcher, and they may limit the generalizability of findings.

Although longitudinal and cross-sectional approaches to developmental study have both advantages and disadvantages, researchers usually assume that the two designs will yield basically similar results. Very few investigators have tested this assumption directly, but some studies show the expected convergence. For example, Colombo and his associates (Colombo, Mitchell, O'Brien, & Horowitz, 1987) wondered about the early ontogeny of "habituation," the decline in the amount of attention babies pay to a stimulus that they see repeatedly and thus remember. (Later in this chapter we discuss habituation more.) The researchers studied the ontogeny of habituation using a design that allowed for the simultaneous comparison of cross-sectional and longitudinal strategies of data collection. One group of infants was tested longitudinally at 3, 4, 7, and 9 months of age, and independent samples of infants were tested cross-sectionally at the same four ages. In each test, babies were habituated to color photographs of faces, and the researchers measured the total amount of time they looked at the stimuli until they habituated. The two experimental approaches yielded basically similar results—and support similar conclusions—about habituation. Figure 3.1 plots total accumulated looking time by age for infants in each of the experimental designs. The main methodological results can be summarized generally as follows: In both designs, babies of a given age habituated in approximately the same amount of time, older babies habituated more quickly than younger babies, and the greatest decline in accumulated looking time occurred between 4 and 7 months of age.

Regardless of the study design, researchers who measure development at two or more time points confront a fundamental measurement "problem": Change occurs rapidly during infancy, and the same structure or function can take different forms at different ages. For example, fear may look different in 6-month-olds and in 18-month-olds (i.e., the surface expression may consist of crying at 6 months and behavioral inhibition at 18 months), but the underlying source (i.e., fear) may be the same. As a consequence, no matter what developmental design a researcher adopts, she or he must be acutely aware of this age-construct issue and can choose between two strategies for dealing with it:

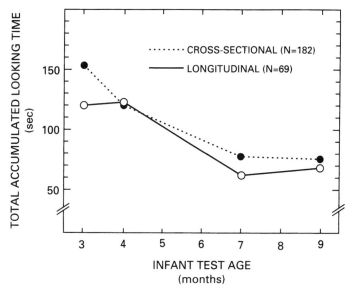

FIGURE 3.1
Developmental changes in accumulated looking time to meet a habituation criterion in the infant-control procedure. The cross-sectional curve represents independent samples for each age group; the longitudinal curve represents the same sample of infants tested at each age. (After Colombo & Mitchell, 1990.)

using the same items for different ages or using different items on the grounds that a single source construct is manifest by different surface characteristics in different developmental periods. Clearly, 6- and 18-month-olds are sufficiently different that different behaviors may be needed to reflect the one underlying construct.

Natural Experiments, Twin, and Adoption Designs

Beyond characterizing developmental status and process, students of infancy often attempt to identify (at least to some degree) genetic and environmental influences on them. To do this, researchers have often appealed to different kinds of *natural experiments*. Several are prominent. In developmental research, comparisons are often made between infants who are not assigned randomly to different groups (as is the case in true experiments) but still experience different "treatments" in the course of growing up. It is obviously not possible or ethical to assign children randomly to normal and deprived experiences, for example, so the long-term effects of institutionalization in early infancy must be studied in experiments found in nature. To assess influences on emotional development, therefore, the happiness and sadness of children reared in intact families might be compared with those of children reared in socially depriving institutions. Members of the English and Romanian Adoptees (ERA) Study Team (Rutter, 1998) described the results of such a natural experiment involving Romanian children adopted in the United Kingdom prior to 2 years of age. These infants were severely developmentally delayed when they first entered the United Kingdom, with one half of them falling below the third percentile in weight, height, and performance on standardized tests of intelligence. By the age of 4 years, however, Romanian children adopted in the United Kingdom before 6 months of age appeared to have caught up when compared to a group of 4-year-old U.K. children adopted before 6 months of age. Furthermore, catch-up was evident, albeit less complete, among Romanian children placed into adoptive homes in the United Kingdom after 6 months. Thus, although early global deprivation in infancy debilitates physical and intellectual development, these effects can be reversed by placement in more enriched environments by 2 years of age.

The dangers inherent in natural experiments are many, not the least of which is the possibility that children in the groups being compared are not the same at the outset. For example, children from disadvantaged backgrounds may be more likely than children from advantaged backgrounds to be placed in institutions. As a result, differences between children in the two groups might be accounted for by institutionalization, prior disadvantaged backgrounds, or the combined influence of these two factors.

Other kinds of natural experiments are the twin study method and the adoption study method (which we discussed in Chapter 2). Both are geared to address much the same sorts of questions. Twin studies are rare and difficult to do, but can be especially rewarding. The twin methodology is theoretically appealing when researchers want to assess the relative impact of genetic and experiential influences on development. Monozygotic (MZ) twins share 100% of their genes, whereas dizygotic (DZ) twins share only about 50% on the average. If a structure or function has genetic origins, therefore, MZ twins ought to be more alike than are DZ twins. In a review of the twin study method in which MZ and DZ twins reared together or apart were compared, Bouchard (1997) found that MZ twins reared apart were as similar in IQ as MZ twins reared together, and that MZ twins were more alike than the DZ twins. The twin methodology is not perfect, however, because experiences can also foster similarity or differences between twins, contriving to make MZ twins more similar to one another and DZ twins more different from one another. So-called assimilation effects help to make twins more alike as well, as when parents respond to their MZ twins in the same manner, whereas so-called contrast effects work to distinguish DZ twins as when parents respond to DZ twins in different ways. These effects may operate even when twins are reared apart because separated twins are often adopted into different parts of the same family, or into similar families. Nonetheless, the twin technique provides a powerful means by which the magnitude of heredity and experiential influences on the origins of behavior can be estimated (Cherney, Fulker, & Hewitt, 1997; Reznick, 1997).

Comparisons between children with biological backgrounds that differ from those of their adopting families provide another powerful means of evaluating the impact of heredity and experience on infants' development (Loehlin, Horn, & Willerman, 1997). In these comparisons, researchers ask whether a child behaves more like the biological parent, with whom the child shares genes but not environment, or more like the adoptive parent, with whom the child shares a home environment but no genes. For example, Hardy-Brown and Plomin (Hardy-Brown, 1983; Hardy-Brown & Plomin, 1985; Hardy-Brown, Plomin, & DeFries, 1981) studied the development of communicative competence and cognitive abilities in one hundred and fifty 1-year-olds, their biological parents, and their adoptive parents. They found that the rate of development of infant communicative competence related to the general intelligence of babies' biological mothers and that the behavior of the adoptive mothers (imitating and responding contingently to infant vocalization) was also related to measures of infant communicative development. These results point to roles for both heredity and experience in infant communicative development.

Specialized Developmental Designs

Additional specialized designs are often used to address other questions about status, process, and origins in infancy. The *age-held-constant paradigm*, for example, is used to assess the influence of variables other than age on the development of a structure or function, because all infants are tested at the same age. For example, Ramsay (1980) observed that at 11 months of age some infants begin using more complex verbal expressions (e.g., "daddy" rather than "dada," "cookie" rather than "kiki"), and at the same time achieve a new level of bimanual handedness (e.g., using one hand to hold an object and the other to manipulate it). To determine whether these developments were meaningfully related, Ramsay assessed language production in two groups of 11-month-olds: infants who had already developed bimanual dexterity and infants who had not yet done so. Babies with advanced bimanual skills also developed the more complex manner of speaking, whereas those who had not yet attained the more advanced form of handedness vocalized less maturely. This finding suggested to Ramsay that the developmental correspondence of the two activities was not accidental. Perhaps the two developments were attributable to a common third factor (e.g., brain organization or function) that controlled both handedness and articulation.

The *ability-held-constant design* allows investigators to assess the relative importance of maturation and specific experiences. For example, Bertenthal and Campos (1990) evaluated the determinants of depth perception and the emergence of fear in response to depth. Infants begin to avoid heights and show fear of depth late in the first year of life, which is about the time that they become mobile. Postulating that changing responses to depth cues are related to the emergence of self-produced locomotion rather than being manifestations of a maturational timetable, Bertenthal and Campos compared infants who locomoted by crawling with infants who got around using walkers. The responses to depth were similar among infants in these two groups, suggesting that self-produced locomotion, rather than an endogenous developmental timetable, was critical. The same conclusion was suggested by the fact that infants who were immobilized by body casts did not perceive and respond to depth like younger infants who were capable of self-produced locomotion.

Similar questions can be addressed when researchers compare structure or function in groups of infants matched for either *maturational age* or *experiential age*. The first comparison group uses infants who were conceived at the same time and so are of the same conceptional age; the second comparison group uses infants who are all tested the same amount of time after birth and thus have the same chronological or postnatal age. Age correction among infants has been controversial (Brandt & Sticker, 1991; DiPietro & Allen, 1991; Ross & Lawson, 1997) because of concerns about mistakenly overcorrecting and arriving at inaccurate estimates of corrected age due to imprecise measures of when conception occurred. Most researchers who study preterm infants, however, favor some form of age correction to help determine whether some aspect of development is under maturational control or is susceptible to the effects of extrauterine experience. For example, Siegel (1983, 1989) conducted a longitudinal study in which preterm and term infants were repeatedly assessed over the first 5 years of life. Examining correlations between later cognitive status and measures of both the infants' corrected and uncorrected age, she found that age correction was appropriate in the early months but not later, suggesting that environmental influences became increasingly important. Siegel's results are consistent with later recommendations for either full or half correction for prematurity during the first 2 years of life, but no correction thereafter (Blasco, 1989; Brandt & Sticker, 1991).

In summary, students of infant development have adopted a variety of research strategies to identify and describe the status, process, and origins of diverse aspects of development. These strategies all have advantages and disadvantages associated with them. The choice of strategy depends on the specific question being asked.

Procedures and Techniques in Infancy Research

Infancy studies had their formal beginnings in attempts by parents to do systematically what parents around the world do naturally—simply observe their babies. The first psychological studies of children were descriptions of infants in their natural settings by their own parents—baby biographies (Prochner & Doyon, 1997; Wallace, Franklin, & Keegan, 1994). Over time, observation systems have become much more sophisticated and informative. Today, much of what we know derives from systematic progressive experimentation.

In this section of the chapter, we lay out a taxonomy of procedures and techniques, discussing general approaches to observation and experimentation with infants. Our methodological taxonomy is organized to reflect different strategies for asking questions of infants and to underscore the fact that different methodologies require different degrees of inference on the part of investigators. To concretize the discussion, we draw on examples from various realms of study, spanning aspects of perceptual, cognitive, communicative, emotional, and social development. As we refer to particular studies throughout this book, of course, we allude to and expand on the procedures and techniques introduced in the next pages; in addition, we detail specific new ones geared to address particular experimental questions.

What is the world like to an infant? Certainly, this is an attractive question to ask, especially because it can have so many interesting ramifications. But how the baby perceives, feels, and thinks are basically private. There is no way for us to know, say, what the baby's perceptions of red, C-sharp, sweet, pungent, or soft are like, much less what the baby may be thinking or feeling. Normally, we infer the perceptions of others from their reports or from their behaviors. From a developmental point of view, the study of perception in children, adolescents, adults, or the elderly is relatively simple, because individuals of these ages can be instructed to report verbally about their perceptions or to behave in interpretable ways with respect to their perceptions. By contrast, the absence of language and the motoric incompetence of infants force us to gain an understanding of infant perception by inference from immature behaviors. How accurate, reliable, and credible that knowledge is, therefore, depends on many factors.

Some of the methods adopted by developmentalists to overcome the difficulties of studying infants—whether observing them or testing them—yield only very weak inferences about infants' perceptions; other methods yield stronger inferences. For example, if a sound produces a regular pattern of electrical responses in the brain, we can feel certain that at least some internal connections between the peripheral sensory system (the ear) and the central nervous system (the brain) are present. Unfortunately, however, regularity of brain response tells us nothing about how or even whether the infant actually perceives the auditory stimulus, and thus electrophysiological data support only weak inferences about perception. Even if two different stimuli gave rise to two distinctly different patterns of electrical activity in the brain, we still would not know whether the infant perceived either or both of the two stimuli, or whether the infant perceived the two to be different. If we were able to instruct or train the infant to respond in one way to one sound and in another way to another sound, however, our inference would be so strong that, barring artifact, we would possess incontrovertible evidence of auditory perception and discrimination. Nonetheless, even though these methods allow us to get to the infant's discriminative capacities (e.g., Field, Pickens, Fox, Gonzalez, & Nawrocki, 1998), they still fall short of allowing us to infer anything about the infant's experience of the perception. Each of the methods tells us something about what the infant experiences. In this section of the chapter, we discuss some standard observational and experimental techniques used to understand the infant's experiences.

Baby Biographies and Case Studies

Where did the idea of studying children come from? How did it develop? As the Enlightenment proceeded in eighteenth-century Europe, it brought with it a revolutionary increase in concern with understanding individuals. Jean-Jacques Rousseau's (1781) autobiography, *Confessions*, exemplified a movement historians of psychology have called the "new literature" of self-examination. Rousseau expressed interest in child development; 20 years earlier he had written a novel called *Emile* in which he expounded a theory that education ought not to involve imparting knowledge but, rather, it should strive to draw out what is already in the child. Thus, Rousseau was among the first to write about the integrity of childhood as a separate stage of life. A short while later, Tiedemann (1787) wrote a psychological diary of the growth of a young child, in other words a *baby biography*.

Wallace et al. (1994) identified three types of baby diaries that have been produced throughout history. *Domestic diaries*, which are the oldest of the three types, were typically written by mothers for the personal satisfaction of the diarist and provided insights into parental philosophies about the nature of childhood and how children should be disciplined. *Educational diaries* were written to explore the impact of educational or childrearing practices on children's development and behavior. Finally, *scientific diaries* were written for the purpose of contributing to scientific knowledge about child behavior and development.

Both educational and scientific diaries came into their own by the second half of the nineteenth century, which witnessed an intensification of focus on evolution and development (Dixon & Lerner, 1999). In *On Intelligence*, Taine (1889) looked to early childhood for the origins of human intellect. Shortly thereafter, Taine published some notes on language acquisition, and, by way of response to Taine, Charles Darwin, the founder of evolutionary theory with *The Origins of Species* (1859), assembled for publication observations he himself had made in the early 1840s on his firstborn son William Erasmus, nicknamed Doddy (Conrad, 1998, see Figure 3.2).

FIGURE 3.2
Charles Darwin, age 33, with his eldest child, William.

Darwin's publication of "A Biographical Sketch of an Infant" simultaneously in the German journal *Kosmos* and in the influential English journal *Mind* in 1877 gave great impetus to the study of infancy. Darwin specifically recounted sensory, intellectual, and emotional development in Doddy's first year. Excerpts from Darwin's diary are reproduced in Box 3.1.

Darwin was the intellectual giant of nineteenth-century science. His emphasis on *comparison* and *development* as general sources of knowledge set the stage for the emergence of developmental science as a formal subdiscipline, with infancy viewed as a significant period in the life cycle (Cairns, 1998; Dixon & Lerner, 1999). In succeeding years, baby biographies grew in popularity around the world (Prochner & Doyon, 1997) and are still popular today (e.g., Stern, 1990). For example, Preyer's (1881) detailed description of the first 3 years of his son's life set the model for a formal system of developmental examination. Preyer's biography divided child study into categories—sensation, motor activity, expression, and intelligence—that have informed the study of development ever since. Perhaps the greatest of the modern baby biographers, however, was Jean Piaget (Cairns, 1998), most of whose writing and theorizing refers to observations of his own young children. In part because of Darwin, therefore, scholars came to believe that adult human beings could be better understood with reference to their origins—in nature, in the species, and in childhood.

Baby biographies served valuable functions. However, they have also proved somewhat problematic. In his informative historical record *The Child*, Kessen (1965, p. 117) wrote:

> Darwin shows in brief compass the attraction and the problems of the baby biographer. No one can know as well as the attentive parent the subtle and cumulative changes that take place in the world of the child and in his behavior but, on the other hand, no one can distort as convincingly as a loving parent.

The strengths and weaknesses of baby biographies can be compared quite easily. On the positive side, attention by important figures like Darwin clearly excited a more general interest not only in children but in the study of children. These talented authors also made exceptional observers. In addition, the first child biographers documented basic information about development; Count Philippe de Montbeillard's (see Tanner, 1978) close analysis of physical growth in his own son between 1759 and 1777 exemplifies a database valuable both for the historical record and as a model for early child study (see Chapter 4). Finally, on the basis of their observations, the first baby biographers generated numerous novel and important hypotheses about infant and child development.

On the negative side, the informativeness of baby biographies is limited for a variety of reasons. In methodological terms, baby biographers most frequently observed only single children, usually their own. These children could hardly have been representative of the population at large and, perhaps like their parents, they were exceptional. Biographers were not concerned with comparison groups, and their observations were not always systematic. Further, some baby biographers recorded their observations contemporaneously, but others employed a more problematic "retrospective" methodology, trying to recall what the child's early life was like from some later vantage point. Baby biographers were also subject to bias in their observations; frequently, these diarists were women and men with strong theoretical points of view who tended to report the anecdotes and data that supported their theories. On balance, however, baby biographies initiated child study in spirit and in fact, and for this reason they constitute an important historical source.

Consider, too, insights obtained from a related source, *case histories*. The close focus on single individuals helps to document events that are otherwise hard to observe, and they are especially valuable theoretically when they reveal capacities that are supposed to be absent at the age in question. For example, psychoanalysts assert that infants cannot experience the emotion of sadness before 6 to 8 months of age. However, Gaensbauer (1980; Gaensbauer & Hiatt, 1984) observed sadness in a 3-month-old baby who had been abused and neglected by her father. Independent raters who knew nothing about the baby confirmed the presence of sadness, as did an objective analysis of facial muscle movements. This one case report, which clearly demonstrated something that was considered impossible, attains theoretical importance because it challenges strict psychoanalytic predictions about the origins and nature of an important basic emotion.

Case studies can be informative, but we never know about the generalizability of what is observed and often cannot determine the extent to which an

---

BOX 3.1

A Biographical Sketch of an Infant

Charles Darwin

During the first seven days various reflex actions, namely sneezing, hickuping, yawning, stretching, and of course sucking and screaming, were well performed by my infant. On the seventh day, I touched the naked sole of his foot with a bit of paper, and he jerked it away, curling at the same time his toes, like a much older child when tickled. The perfection of these reflex movements shows that the extreme imperfection of the voluntary ones is not due to the state of the muscles or of the coordinating centers, but to that of the seat of the will. At this time, though so early, it seemed clear to me that a warm soft hand applied to his face excited a wish to suck. This must be considered as a reflex or an instinctive action, for it is impossible to believe that experience and association with the touch of his mother's breast could so soon have come into play. During the first fortnight he often started on hearing any sudden sound, and blinked his eyes.... At the age of 32 days he perceived his mother's bosom when three or four inches from it, as was shown by the protrusion of his lips and his eyes becoming fixed; but I much doubt whether this had any connection with vision; he certainly had not touched the bosom. Whether he was guided through smell or the sensation of warmth or through association with the position in which he was held, I do not at all know.

Anger. It was difficult to decide at how early an age anger was felt; on his eighth day he frowned and wrinkled the skin round his eyes before a crying fit, but this may have been due to pain or distress, and not to anger. When about ten weeks old, he was given some rather cold milk and he kept a slight frown on his forehead all the time that he was sucking, so that he looked like a grown-up person made cross from being compelled to do something which he did not like. When nearly four months old, and perhaps much earlier, there could be no doubt, from the manner in which the blood rushed into his whole face and scalp, that he easily got into a violent passion....

Fear. This feeling probably is one of the earliest which is experienced by infants, as shown by their starting at any sudden sound when only a few weeks old, followed by crying. [...When he was $4\frac{1}{2}$ months old] I one day made a loud snoring noise which I had never done before; he instantly looked grave and then burst out crying. Two or three days afterwards, I made through forgetfulness the same noise with the same result. May we not suspect that the vague but very real fears of children, which are quite independent of experience, are the inherited effects of real dangers and abject superstitions during ancient savage times?...

---

observed behavior or capacity is limited to either a specific situational circumstance or to a specific child. In addition, as we have seen, baby biographies are limited by uncertainties concerning the objectivity of the reporter.

Systematic Observations

As child study developed into a scientific discipline, researchers came to place less reliance on baby biographies and case studies and instead embraced systematic observation and experimentation as the principal means of learning about children's tendencies and capacities. For example, researchers today aim to conduct studies in which systematic observational techniques are used to gather information about larger numbers of children.

BOX 3.1 (Continued)

Pleasurable Sensations. It may be presumed that infants feel pleasure while sucking, and the expression of their swimming eyes seems to show that this is the case. This infant smiled when 45 days, a second infant when 46 days old; and these were true smiles, indicative of pleasure, for their eyes brightened and eyelids slightly closed. The smiles arose chiefly when looking at their mother, and were therefore probably of mental origin....

Affection. This probably arose very early in life, if we may judge by his smiling at those who had charge of him when under two months old; though I had no distinct evidence of his distinguishing and recognising anyone, until he was nearly four months old. When nearly five months old, he plainly showed his wish to go to his nurse. With respect to the allied feeling of sympathy, this was clearly shown at 6 months and 11 days by his melancholy face, with the corners of his mouth well depressed, when his nurse pretended to cry. Jealousy was plainly exhibited when I fondled a large doll, and when I weighed his infant sister, he being then $152\frac{1}{2}$ months old.

Association of Ideas, Reason, etc. When four and a half months old, he repeatedly smiled at my image and his own in a mirror, and no doubt mistook them for real objects; but he showed sense in being evidently surprised at my voice coming from behind him. Like all infants he much enjoyed thus looking at himself, and in less than two months perfectly understood that it was an image; for if I made quite silently an odd grimace, he would suddenly turn round to look at me.... When five months old, associated ideas arising independently of any instruction became fixed in his mind; thus as soon as his hat and cloak were put on, he was very cross if he was not immediately taken out of doors....

Means of Communication. The noise of crying...is of course uttered in an instinctive manner, but serves to show that there is suffering. After a time the sound differs according to the cause, such as hunger or pain.... When 46 days old, he first made little noises without any meaning to please himself, and these soon became varied. An incipient laugh was observed on the 113th day. When five and half months old, he uttered an articulate sound "da" but without any meaning attached to it. When a little over a year old, he used gestures to explain his wishes:... At exactly the age of a year, he made the great step of inventing a word for food, namely, mum, but what led him to it I did not discover.... Before he was a year old, he understood intonations and gestures, as well as several words and short sentences. He understood one word, namely, his nurse's name, exactly five months before he invented his first mum; and this is what might have been expected, as we know that the lower animals easily learn to understand spoken words.

In conducting such observations, researchers must first address some basic strategic questions. Should children be observed in naturalistic or standardized contexts? Should the researcher aim to observe and record whatever children choose to do during the observation session, or should the researcher make an effort to ensure that each child is observed in a context that places similar demands on each? Who should do the observing: mother, father, careprovider, or researcher? When should the observations take place: at random times or on a schedule? At any time of the day or at an optimal time of the day? Answers to these questions can have clear implications for the results obtained, whether in language performance, emotional expressiveness, or social interaction. Although the naturalistic strategy would appear to be preferable because it provides a picture of typical behavior or capacity, it is potentially problematic in that the various infants in the study might be observed in very different situations, and this would make comparison among them difficult (Leyendecker, Lamb, & Schölmerich, 1997). In addition, because researchers can usually sample only a very small slice of the child's everyday life, pictures of child life based on naturalistic sampling can be misleading, particularly when they might not include behavior in situations that are deemed to be of special significance. In the study of infant–mother attachment, for example, attachment theory suggests that we should look most closely at those situations in which the child really needs maternal attention and care (see Chapter 11). Consequently, researchers today often standardize situations and their psychological demands, choosing to study babies only when they will be awake and alert, at play, or under stress. Naturalistic and semistructured observations are common, and more or less structured or standardized observations are increasingly the rule.

Having decided on the situation in which children will be observed, researchers must determine whether or not they will attempt to obtain a description of the events observed (either by using a checklist, event recorder, or notebook) in real time or whether some kind of electronic device (e.g., video recorder or computer) will be used to record the sequence of behavior so that it can be reviewed and analyzed in greater detail at a later time. Video records have a venerable history in infancy studies. Between 1910 and 1940, Arnold Gesell developed a photographic technique to provide a permanent and detailed record of the infant's developing psychological capacities (Bornstein, 2001). In the past 30 years, videotaped records have become extremely common because they permit researchers to gather records that can be reviewed to obtain finer-grained information and to assess agreement in the accounts provided by different observers viewing the same sequences of behavior.

The decision on whether or not to prepare a reviewable videotaped record has major implications for the level of detail that can be recorded. Using computerized event recorders, it is possible for researchers to note when behaviors or events occur relative to one another, just as they can with videotaped records, but unless investigators can review the sequence on multiple occasions they are limited to relatively crude descriptive categories of behaviors. By contrast, when a video- or audiotaped record is available, it is possible to make repeated passes through the record in order to obtain a much more finely grained understanding of what happened. For example, in the research conducted by Papoušek and Papoušek (1995), videotaped records of the face-to-face interaction between parents and babies were later scrutinized in great detail in slow motion in order to understand and describe the underlying tendencies of mothers and babies. These researchers were particularly interested in what they call intuitive parenting programs, that is, parental behaviors that occur too fast to be the product of conscious decisions (see Chapter 11). The rapidity with which these behaviors occur makes it necessary for researchers to review videotapes in slow motion in order to examine relations between infants' and parents' behaviors. To study such phenomena, therefore, researchers need to record not only the behaviors of individuals but also the times at which they occur so that it is possible to look at contingencies between various behaviors, such as the child's frown and the parent's touch (see Figure 3.3).

Such *time-based records* allow researchers to construct two sorts of measures: Simple indices of the frequency and duration with which certain behaviors occur and more complex measures of the contingency between the behaviors of two parties in an interaction. For example, Bornstein, Haynes, Pascual, Painter, and Galperin (1999) videotaped mothers and their 20-month-old infants in collaborative play, from which they coded both the frequency and duration of

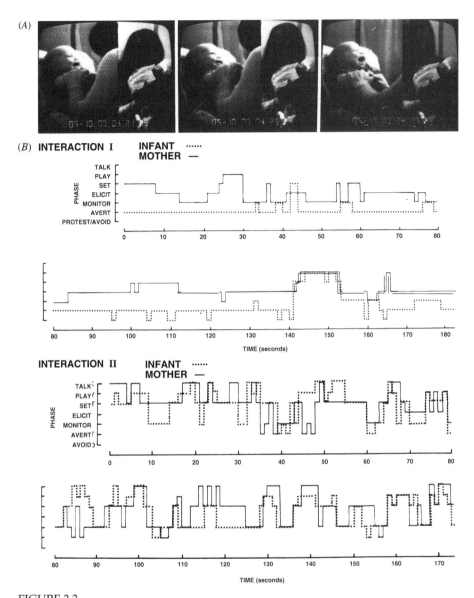

FIGURE 3.3

(A) Split-screen technology is used to obtain videotaped records that can be recoded time and again at slow speed to describe the synchronization of infant and parental behavior. (B) In order to perform sequential analyses, it is necessary to examine relations between the timing of interactants' behaviors. In this figure, the infant's and mother's behaviors are both displayed, so that their synchrony and asynchrony are clear.

maternal social play, physical affection, and verbal praise directed toward the infant. Time-based recordings of interaction also enable researchers to examine the degree to which one individual's behavior is contingent on the behavior of another. For example, Goldberg, MacKay-Soroka, and Rochester (1994) observed maternal responsiveness to different affective displays (positive, neutral, and negative) of 1-year-old infants. For some research questions, frequency counts are more useful than estimates of the likelihood of certain stimulus–response contingencies; for other questions, contingencies are more appropriate. Researchers appropriately choose their measures depending on the specific questions that are of interest.

In more rigidly standardized situations, babies are filmed as they respond to one or several stimuli or probe events. For example, Haynie and Lamb (1995) filmed babies' faces when they were presented with a series of emotion-eliciting stimuli. Puppets, masks, stomach tickling, suddenly opening umbrellas, and peekaboo are examples of the situations that the babies confronted. By coding the babies' facial expressions from the videotapes, Haynie and Lamb were later able to show that individual babies responded to these emotion-eliciting stimuli quite consistently over time and across situations. Stated differently, babies who responded rapidly and intensely to a stimulus designed to elicit positive emotions were likely to respond strongly and promptly to any other stimulus of the same sort, suggesting that responsiveness to positive emotional stimuli is a reliable characteristic of infants in the second half of the first year of life. Responsiveness to negative emotional stimuli was also stable. Likewise, Kagan (1997) and Schölmerich, Broberg, and Lamb (2000) used a series of emotion-eliciting stimuli—many of them potentially fear-provoking—in order to classify children as either inhibited or uninhibited on the basis of their tendency to respond in a consistent fashion to different situations. Standardized probes were used to subject a variety of children to the same situations so that the researchers could understand differences and similarities among the children, knowing that each of the children in the study was experiencing essentially the same situation. Such classifications or decisions could obviously not be made had researchers observed children using naturalistic or natural situations that would have varied from child to child.

Detailed standardized observations are not only useful for studies of emotional or social development. For example, researchers study infants' developing memory by examining their eye movements and search strategies. In a particularly common situation derived from Piaget's (1952) observations of his own children, researchers hid toys under a cover and allowed 6- to 10-month-old infants to uncover and find them. After several experiences of this sort, researchers hid the toys as before and then, in full view, moved the objects from their hiding place to a second location. Infants of this age are likely to persist in looking for the object under the first cover even after they have seen it being hidden under the second. This is the so-called A-not-B error (discussed more fully in Chapter 7). This error is frequently studied as a way of demonstrating deficiencies in infants' memory capacities and their understanding of the existence of objects. Variations in the length of time between the hiding and the initiation of the search has a major influence on children's success. As described in Chapter 5, furthermore, the electroencephalographic (EEG) recordings of 10-month-old infants demonstrate the role of the frontal cortex in infants' attempts to solve memory problems like this (Bell, 1998).

Nonobjective Observations

To find out what they want to know about babies, researchers can also ask questions of those who know them best. The advantage of observations using systematic techniques, in semistandardized or standardized situations, is that researchers are able to obtain an objective account of the behavior of infants—and their parents. Such observations are undoubtedly useful for learning what children and their parents do. Another possibility is to interview or question the parents. Interviews and questionnaires can provide rich sources of information not readily available in observation, revealing patterns of behavior. This is important, because the presence of other people can dramatically affect young children's social behavior.

Interview and questionnaire techniques suffer from some of the same distorting influences that beset baby biographies, but they play a valuable role in helping researchers address the problem of representativeness. As objective observational techniques have become more popular, developmental scientists have sometimes come to question the representativeness of what they observe. Representativeness may not be important when researchers are simply trying to define infant capacities, such as the ability to find a hidden object, or when researchers are able to show the validity of their observations by means of significant associations with other events or capacities with which they ought to be related. In some studies, however, it may be extremely important to establish the representativeness of observations. As a result, many researchers now use questionnaires and interviews to gain information about the representativeness of what they observe and to supplement their observations.

Nonobjective techniques, such as interviews and questionnaires, and direct observations of behavior can be used to complement one another and converge on a set of findings. For example, in a study designed to describe differences in the ways infants from different cultures were reared, Leyendecker, Lamb, Schölmerich, and Fracasso (1995) trained interviewers to conduct "time-budget interviews" with Latino and European American mothers to document cultural differences in the social contexts and activities in which first-year infants participated (see Figure 3.4). These time diaries provided important contextual information about the infants' daily lives that would have been more difficult, and more costly, to obtain from direct observation. Contextual information of this kind can help researchers better interpret the meaning and significance of information obtained through more focused, direct observation of infant

FIGURE 3.4
Infants' cycles: wake–sleep, presence of father, play, and feeding.

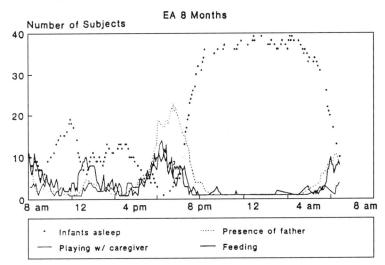

behavior. Indeed, nonobjective interview and questionnaire techniques may be very useful for understanding not *what* people do, but *why* they behave in specific ways. Thus, one can observe parent–infant interactions and then ask parents to explain their motivations. By observing and asking questions about childrearing ideologies and beliefs, one may understand how and why parents behave in the ways they do (Bornstein et al., 1998; Bornstein, Tamis-LeMonda, Pascual, & Haynes, 1996; Harkness & Super, 1996; Harwood, Miller, & Irizarry, 1995; Leyendecker, Lamb, Schölmerich, & Fricke, 1997). Interviews may also be helpful in understanding specific behaviors, as Russell and Russell (1989) demonstrated in research on mother–father–child interaction. In his technique, observers first conducted an observation of parents and children and then discussed the events with the parents and children—asking the parents to describe, explain, and interpret specific behavioral sequences that had been observed.

In addition, some interview protocols and questionnaires may be helpful in obtaining or systematizing the knowledge of individuals who are much more familiar with their own tendencies or those of their children than professional observers usually would be. Because these accounts are parental reports and can be somewhat distorted, they are best used in combination with objective reports and descriptions by disinterested observers to construct a more coherent and presumably more valid account of infant development. In this regard, the Q-sort technique pioneered by Block and Block (1980) has been particularly helpful. In the Q-sort, observers (such as parents) are forced to classify only a certain proportion of some items as "very descriptive of a child," a similar prespecified proportion as "somewhat descriptive," the same number as "not characteristic," others as "extremely uncharacteristic," and so on. Respondents cannot just give socially desirable responses (because they are forced to conform to a prespecified distribution), and this requirement seems to enhance the reliability and validity of their reports. Q-sorts have been used effectively in studies of social and personality characteristics and parent–infant attachments (Hastings & Rubin, 1999; Pederson & Moran, 1995; Teti & Ablard, 1989; Teti et al., 1996).

In summary, instead of attempting to use interviews and questionnaires in place of observations, researchers now attempt to use nonobjective techniques to supplement more objective techniques in order to obtain more comprehensive data about infants from multiple sources.

Structured Test Situations

For many problems, useful data can only be obtained if infants are tested in highly structured settings. In response, researchers have developed an impressive variety of behavioral techniques to assess diverse aspects of structure and function near the beginning of life. Wise investigators try to capitalize as much as possible on the most developed response capacities of infants in doing so. Presumably, these are those over which the infant has the best control. Because gross motor development and organization generally proceed cephalocaudally (from the head downward) and proximodistally (from the center of the body outward), the eye, mouth, and neck regions of the body are advanced earliest in ontogenesis (Chapter 4). Consequently, many of the behavioral response procedures used in infancy measure looking, orienting, or sucking. Among these procedures, the most prominent kinds yield evidence of infants' natural preferences and different kinds of learning. Again, we have ordered the discussion that follows according to the approximate strength of inference that each paradigm commands.

Natural Preference

Babies are particularly clear about their likes and dislikes, so to assess early sensitivity and capacity, researchers have often simply recorded infants' expressed preferences. In the early 1890s, James Mark Baldwin observed that his infant daughter Helen would consistently reach for a yellow cube rather than a blue one, and noted that she preferred one to the other whenever the two cubes were offered. From this, Baldwin deduced that Helen must perceive colors because her preferential reaching showed that she discriminated yellow from blue. In the late 1950s, Robert Fantz revived Baldwin's argument. Fantz argued that if babies look preferentially at one of two stimuli regardless of the spatial location of the two, their preference reveals a capacity to discriminate the two stimuli. When we discuss perceptual development in Chapter 6, we will see how much knowledge about infants the simple preference technique has yielded.

Langlois and her colleagues (Langlois et al., 1987; Rubenstein, Kalakanis, & Langlois, 1999), for example, have conducted research on infant preferences for different human faces. Langlois et al. (1987) demonstrated that 6-month-old infants looked longer at pictures of young adults who had been independently rated as physically attractive than at pictures of adults rated as unattractive. Infants' preferences for attractive faces were similar to those shown by adults; however, these findings were especially interesting because, unlike adults, 6-month-old infants have had little exposure to culturally prescribed standards of beauty or attractiveness, yet like adults they preferred attractive over unattractive faces. Rubenstein et al. (1999) suggest that preferences for attractive faces may be partially independent of cultural and socialization influences because attractive faces represent the prototypical, or "average," of the ranges of facial configurations that exist naturally in the general population, and the tendency to prefer stimuli that are prototypes of a population may be basic to human nature. In support of this hypothesis, Rubenstein et al. (1999) observed that 6-month-old infants looked longer at an "averaged" face, derived from a computer composite of 32 actual faces, than at individual faces of low attractiveness. Furthermore, the infants appeared capable of forming facial prototypes on their own, suggesting that such "cognitive averaging" information-processing capacities are innate.

Preference tests are not limited to studies of vision. Steiner (1977, 1979) used facial reactions successfully to investigate infant taste and smell. He gave newborns sweet, sour, or bitter substances to taste, and vanilla or raw fish to smell, while he photographed their "gustofacial" and "nasofacial" expressions—all prior to the first time these neonates had ever eaten. Figure 3.5 shows his results. By their preference reactions, newborns made clear that they had impressive senses of smell and taste.

Demonstrable preference offers good evidence for function, but the preference paradigm suffers from a major shortcoming: The failure to demonstrate a preference is fundamentally ambiguous. For example, an infant may look to mother and stranger equally, but still be able to tell them apart and prefer one under some but not other circumstances. This is an important methodological drawback of preference studies, and thus many investigators have turned

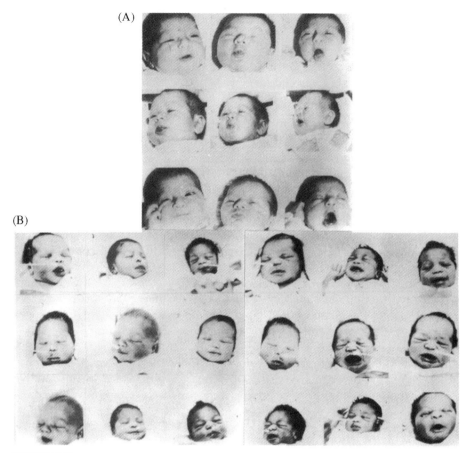

FIGURE 3.5

(*A*) Infants' "gustofacial" response to the taste of sweet (left column), sour (middle column), and bitter (right column). (*B*) Infants' "nasofacial" response to the smell of vanilla (left panel) and raw fish (right panel).

to paradigms that depend on more active infant behaviors. Among the most prominent today are conditioning and habituation.

Conditioning

Like all living organisms, infants can learn. As a consequence, it is possible for infants to develop discriminative control over some of their behaviors and subsequently to use those behaviors in answering questions. In operant conditioning, the reinforcement of voluntarily controlled behaviors leads them to be repeated. A wide variety of both simple and complex behaviors in infants has been conditioned using operant methods, including reflex-like behaviors such as rooting, simple behaviors such as head turning or foot kicking, as well as more complex response patterns such as separation protest (Weisberg & Rovee-Collier, 1998).

In a head-turning paradigm, for example, the baby might sit on a parent's lap, otherwise unencumbered, with a loudspeaker to one side. When a sound (a tone or speech syllable, for example) is played through the loudspeaker and the baby responds by orienting to it, the baby is rewarded by activation of a colorful mechanical toy located just above the speaker. Infants quickly learn to orient to

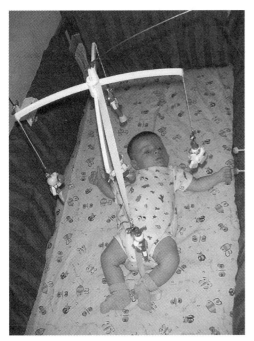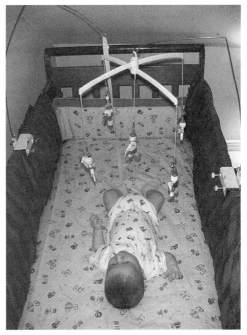

(A)   (B)

FIGURE 3.6

The experimental arrangement for mobile conjugate reinforcement used with 2- and 3-month-olds. (*A*) A nonreinforcement phase (baseline, extinction); (*B*) a reinforcement phase (acquisition).

the sound, and experimenters may then manipulate it. By varying the physical intensity and frequency of test tones, developmental psychoacousticians have acquired basic data about hearing, such as how loud sounds have to be for infants to hear. As an example of the operant conditioning of foot kicking, a ribbon connects the baby's foot to a mobile mounted over the crib so that the mobile moves when the baby kicks (see Figure 3.6). The more vigorously the infant kicks, the more the mobile moves. Using this procedure, Weisberg and Rovee-Collier (1998) have repeatedly shown robust learning and memory in infants.

As Weisberg and Rovee-Collier (1998) note, operant conditioning of infant behavior can occur with a wide variety of reinforcers, such as mother's voice, music, motion pictures, movement of a mobile, visual patterns, and squirts of milk. Indeed, the type of reinforcer is less important to operant conditioning than is the infant's ability to perceive a contingency between her or his behavior and an environmental event. Put more simply, the mere perception of environmental control may be sufficient to reinforce infant behavior.

Habituation and Novelty

Conditioning techniques provide reasonably clear data about infant capacities because babies respond actively, voluntarily, and definitively—clearly "communicating" about their functional abilities. However, some forms of conditioning take time and may be difficult to institute; moreover, only a limited number of responses can be studied using operant techniques. Novelty

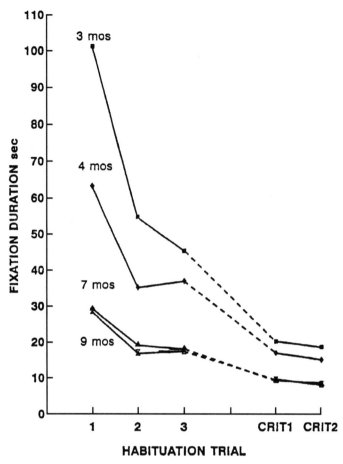

FIGURE 3.7

Developmental data showing changes in infant visual habituation, taken from the cross-sectional database reported on by Colombo, Mitchell, et al. (1987) and in Colombo and Mitchell (1990). Infants were habituated to a photograph of a face in an infant-controlled paradigm using a 50% decrement criterion. The plot shows the first three fixations and the two criterion fixations from the habituation sequence; because infants were free to vary in the number of trials they took to meet the habituation criterion, any number of other trials may have occurred between the third one and the first criterion look, and so these are signified by dashed lines. Note that the most obvious age differences are in the duration of infants' initial fixations.

and habituation represent alternative, equally rewarding, but often more readily instituted techniques.

When placed in an otherwise homogeneous environment, an infant will typically orient and attend to a novel stimulus, but if the stimulus remains visible or is presented repeatedly, the infant's attention to it will diminish or *habituate* (see Figure 3.7). After habituation, the infant can be tested with the familiar stimulus paired with another novel stimulus. *Novelty reaction* is calculated as the relative amount the infant looks at the novel stimulus following familiarization with an habituation stimulus (see Figure 3.8). Clearly, if the infant's looking at the familiar stimulus is depressed because she or he recognizes its familiarity, the infant ought to look more at the novel stimulus (Bornstein, 1985b).

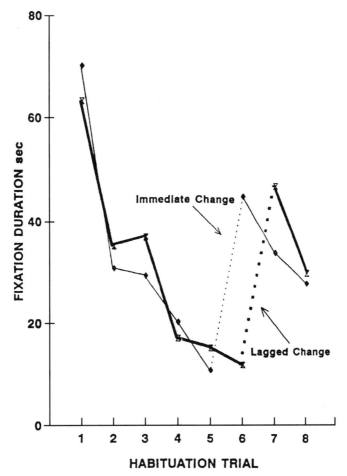

FIGURE 3.8
Schematic representation of infant responses to novelty within the habituation paradigm. One group of infants received stimulus change immediately on attainment of habituation criterion (thin line), whereas the other received one additional trial with habituated-to stimulus (thick line). Both groups attained the habituation criterion on Trial 5. Comparison of groups on Trial 6 yielded evidence that infants recover (dotted lines) as a function of novel stimulus.

Habituation and novelty have proved to be easy, versatile, and fruitful research techniques, providing the wherewithal to assess myriad aspects of perception and cognition, including detection and discrimination, categorization, recognition memory, and conceptual abilities (Bahrick, Hernandez-Reif, & Pickens, 1997; Bornstein, 1998; Colombo, Frick, & Gorman, 1997; Quinn & Bhatt, 1998; Slater, Brown, Mattock, & Bornstein, 1996; Younger & Fearing, 1999). But it should be recognized that habituation has its drawbacks as well: An habituated baby is often temporarily unhappy with the boredom, looking at a stimulus does not necessarily mean that it is perceived, and various factors make the failure to dishabituate (a novelty response) ambiguous. (These capacities are detailed in many of the chapters to follow.)

Preference, conditioning, and habituation and novelty are discrimination methods. Other procedures use *adaptive responses* in infants. Adaptive responses include blinking, reaching, and crawling (see Chapter 6).

Norm- and Criterion-Referenced Tests

A final class of highly structured settings uses *norm-referenced* or *criterion-referenced tests* that include large numbers of related items, and the infant receives a score based on the number of items completed successfully. Norm-referenced tests are so named because they have undergone standardization on a carefully chosen, typically large reference group that represents the population of infants to be assessed by the test. Examples of norm-referenced infant assessments are the Bayley Scales of Infant Development (Bayley, 1993) and the Battelle Developmental Inventory (Newborg, Stock, Wnek, Guidubaldi, & Svinick, 1984). Both of these tests have age-based norms that begin early in infancy and continue into later childhood. Children's raw scores on these examinations are compared to a distribution of raw scores obtained from their same-age standardization group, and standardized scores are then derived based on whatever part of the standardized distribution the raw scores fall. Criterion-referenced assessments, by contrast, provide information about how a child performs on a logically ordered series of items without reference to a standardization group. An example of a criterion-referenced infant assessment is the Užgiris-Hunt Ordinal Scales of Psychological Development (Užgiris & Hunt, 1975), which assesses infant performance on a variety of Piagetian-based tasks. The infant's performance presumably reflects her or his level of sensorimotor functioning, as conceptualized by Piaget (1952).

Psychophysiological Assessments

Psychophysiological assessments have been used to evaluate structure or function in both the central nervous system (CNS) and autonomic nervous system (ANS) in infants. We discuss common procedures in each.

Central Nervous System

Most research tapping the central nervous system (brain and spinal cord) to index infant development has been directed at understanding neurological anatomy or gross cortical electrical activity. Studies focused on anatomical development usually ask questions about the early ontogeny of anatomical structures and then proceed to make inferences about function. This research strategy thus involves the presumption that structure (e.g., the anatomy of the visual system) naturally precedes function (e.g., visual perception): Infants must have eyes before they can see. Using this approach, our understanding of function is inevitably constrained by knowledge of the development and status of underlying structure. However, structure is a necessary but not a sufficient condition for function: Newborns have legs but do not walk. So far as inferences about function are concerned, therefore, evidence based on neuroanatomical structure alone is very weak.

The second kind of research into central nervous system activity assesses functional development in the intact human infant through the use of electrophysiological or neuroimaging techniques. The principal electrophysiological technique has involved the cortical event-related potential (ERP), which reflects the complex sequence of electrical currents that are normally developed in the cerebral cortex and can be seen in the EEG. When a stimulus is presented to the eye or ear, for example, tiny but consistent electrical changes in the brain can be recorded from electrodes placed on the scalp over appropriate areas. These responses are individually weak and rapid; moreover, many presentations of the same stimulus must be administered and the responses averaged before the event related potential can be distinguished from the background of ongoing spontaneous brain waves (see Figure 3.9). Using such procedures, Karrer, Karrer, Bloom, Chaney, and Davis (1998) found that, in comparison to normal 6-month-old infants, 6-month-olds with Down syndrome showed slower decreases over time in ERPs recorded from the frontal and parietal lobes of the brain in response to repeated presentations of visual stimuli, presumably indicative of slower habituation and less efficient information processing. Slower habituation rate in early infancy is associated with lower scores on standardized IQ tests given as late as 12 years of age (Bornstein, 1998).

Whereas electrophysiological measures such as the ERP can be used to document when brain activity takes place, neuroimaging techniques are especially useful in documenting where brain activity occurs. Neurimaging makes use of changes in neural metabolism to pinpoint specific central nervous system regions that underlie a specific motor (such as moving a limb) or mental activity (such as attending to a visual display). Researchers using positron emission tomography (PET), for example, measure the release of positrons that results from the decay of radioactive glucose or oxygen previously injected into the bloodstream. Higher levels of positron emission take place in brain regions where higher levels of brain activity are occurring. PET is thus dependent on very expensive equipment (e.g., a cyclotron is needed to make the radioactive agents) and on radioactive injections, which raises ethical considerations, especially when one wishes to conduct research with children (Nelson & Bloom, 1997).

Functional Magnetic Resonance Imaging (fMRI) avoids these problems and also provides excellent spatial resolution and a more accurate localization of specific brain activity than does PET. fMRI identifies regions of activity by electronically scanning slices of the brain in different orientations and measuring subtle, ongoing changes in oxygen usage. fMRI has proved to be extremely useful in mapping the human visual system and in identifying specific areas of the frontal cortex and cerebellum underlying, respectively, nonspatial working memory and problem solving (see Figure 3.10). Because fMRI is relatively noninvasive and its accuracy is so great, it is increasingly used in research on brain–behavior relations (Nelson & Bloom, 1997).

Autonomic Nervous System

A second widely applied psychophysiological approach to investigating infant capacity involves monitoring the responses of the autonomic nervous system (the parts of the nervous system concerned with the involuntary control of internal organs, including the heart, lungs, and digestive tract). Orienting reflexes, respiration, and heart rate can be measured even in the youngest infants. Heart rate has proved to be an especially sensitive and productive index of infant capacity (e.g., Bornstein & Suess, 2000a, 2000b; Doussard-Roosevelt & Porges, 1999; Richards, 1997). For example, heart rate indicates whether an infant is simply staring blankly at a stimulus (heart rate is stable) or is actually attending to and processing the stimulus (heart rate slows during periods of concentration). Heart rate does not depend on infant motor skills such as reaching or crawling; it reflects infant state and thus can tell researchers whether infants are about to

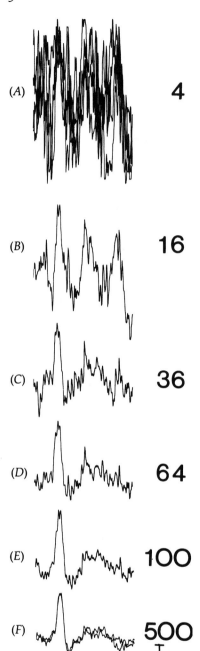

FIGURE 3.9

The improvement in signal-to-noise ratio as the averaging process of the event-related potential proceeds. (*A*) 4 trials averaged, 4 repeats superimposed. (*B–F*) 16, 36, 64, 100, 500 trials averaged. Two repeats are superimposed in *F*. (After Regan, 1972. © 1972 by Elsevier. Reprinted by permission.)

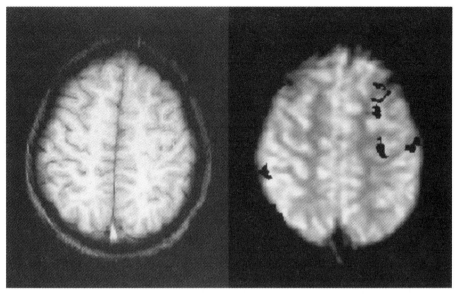

FIGURE 3.10

The image on the left side of the figure represents an anatomic (structural) view of the brain of a normal, healthy 10-year-old girl; the right side represents the functional image superimposed on the structural image. By "functional" we mean the areas of the brain that show activation (increases in oxygen consumption). Here we see regions of the motor strip (specifically the hand—see middle right portion of functional image) lighting up, as well as areas of the prefrontal cortex (see upper right portion of functional image). The former is activated because the child was pushing a button during the task, whereas the latter was activated because the task involved spatial working memory, a higher cognitive function involving the prefrontal cortex.

become drowsy or fussy. It is also remarkably sensitive, with changes of up to 25 beats per minute occurring even when behavioral changes are not observable.

Researchers have used heart rate changes to explore the development of complex affective reactions in babies. For example, in the research on depth perception described earlier, Bertenthal and Campos (1990) recorded heart rate to index fearfulness. When 4-month-olds are lowered over a height their heart rate declines, reflecting interest; when older, mobile infants are suspended in the same way their facial expressions become increasingly negative (changing from frown to whimper to cry); concomitantly, their heart rates first decelerate from resting level and then accelerate during distress. Thus, heart rate changes accompany variations in affect and provide a converging "objective" measure of emotion. Heart rate changes during infant exploration also appear to indicate infant-focused attention. Lansink and Richards (1997), for example, observed that it was more difficult to distract infants from attending to a toy during heart rate decelerations than during heart rate accelerations. They suggested that information processing in infants may be most efficient when attention to a stimulus or event co-occurs with a decrease in heart rate.

One aspect of heart rate variability that has served researchers well is the index of *vagal tone*. It reflects heart rate changes mediated by the vagus nerve and controlled by the parasympathetic branch of the autonomic nervous system (Porges, Doussard-Roosevelt, Portales, & Greenspan, 1996). Respiratory control centers in the brainstem modulate vagal nerve influences on the heart, producing rhythmic increases and decreases in heart rate, and in this way it is possible to identify a respiratory rhythm in the heart rate pattern. This heart rate oscillation is often called respiratory sinus arrhythmia, and the amplitude of this rhythm is a measure of cardiac vagal tone (Bornstein & Suess, 2000a, 2000b). As we have seen, heart rate patterns are complicated and reflect changing neural and extraneural influences. Vagal tone is consistently greater in full term and healthy infants than in high-risk infants, and vagal tone during the neonatal period predicts subsequent development. When an infant is severely stressed, either by physiological compromise due to fever or increased intracranial pressure, the vagal influences to the heart are reduced. Vagal tone varies within samples of infants at risk, however, and the higher the vagal tone the better the developmental outcome. In a longitudinal study of 41 very low birthweight infants (less than 1,500 grams at birth), Doussard-Roosevelt, Porges, Scanlon, Alemi, and Scanlon (1997) found that higher cardiac vagal tone between 33 and 35 weeks gestational age predicted more favorable social, motor, and mental processing scores at 3 years of age, especially among infants with birthweights under 1,000 grams. Bornstein and Suess (2000b) also demonstrated that high resting vagal tone and the ability to suppress vagal tone in response to visual stimuli were associated with more efficient habituation in infants, implicating the role of vagal regulation in the efficiency of information processing.

Psychophysiologists also measure neuroendocrines and hormones in an attempt to map development in infancy. The development of a procedure for measuring levels of *cortisol* has been especially popular among those interested in understanding infants' responses to stress (Lewis & Ramsay, 1999). Cortisol is a substance secreted by the body at times of stress, such as when infants are frightened or separated from their parents. Whereas heart rate responds almost immediately to such incidents, accelerated cortisol secretion is measurable in saliva 15 to 45 minutes afterward. Measures of cortisol and heart rate thus provide different information about responses to stimuli and events.

In young infants, psychophysiological indices can be more objective and sensitive than behavioral measures. Psychophysiological approaches also prove valuable in studies of atypical development. For example, the event-related potential can help in the diagnosis of deafness: If the infant does not or cannot respond behaviorally to sound, the evoked potential can at least help to tell whether or not basic brain pathways are intact.

A word of caution regarding the use of psychophysiological measures is in order, however. A basic principle of psychophysiology is that many factors determine responses, and thus there is never an exact one-to-one correspondence between a physiological index (such as heart rate acceleration or cortisol level) and a psychological state (such as fear). A sigh, a momentary dozing off, or a bodily movement can produce decelerations of heart rate, and many other factors can produce accelerations. Hence, it is incorrect to assume, without corroborating behavioral evidence, that a particular physiological index conclusively demonstrates the existence of a particular psychological state. Despite many virtues, the contributions of psychophysiology to our understanding of infancy are therefore limited by the large amount of inference involved in interpreting physiological responses, and because many factors other than those of interest to researchers may influence psychophysiological responses. The fact that a stimulus creates an identifiable pattern of activity in the brain does not mean that the stimulus is registered in perceptually meaningful and functional ways. Some autonomic system measures fare better in this regard, but they still do not conclusively demonstrate conscious function because the body may respond in the absence of awareness. To study conscious function, behavioral data are required.

In summary, measures like pupillary constriction tell us about infant sensitivity to light, head rotation indicates infant attraction to an external stimulus, and vocalization (or its inhibition) signals infant interest. Investigators have come far in overcoming the major impediment infants present to research—their inability to speak—by establishing many active forms of communication with infants that use a variety of ingenious techniques. Some have relied on observations, some on behavioral measures of preference and learning, and others on psychophysiological measurements of the central and autonomic nervous systems. In doing so, modern investigations have unearthed important information about development near the beginning of life.

Interpretation and Measurement Issues in Developmental Research

Having discussed issues of logic and design as well as the chief procedures and techniques, we briefly review in this section some more general issues in developmental and infancy research having to do with measurement and the interpretation of research results. We focus on correlation and causality, reliability and validity, and multiple assessment and converging operations.

Correlation and Causality

The study of infant development implies the evaluation of stability and change over time. Two general approaches have evolved to address these questions. One is descriptive and looks for lawful relations between the growth of a structure or function and the child's age. This approach is *correlational*. A high positive correlation indicates that a high score on one variable is associated with a high score on the other variable. Figure 3.11 shows, for example, that the weight and length of the fetus increase regularly over the course of prenatal development. This simple relation between growth and age yields direct information about normative development. Deviation from this course would alert parents and health providers about potential fetal difficulty.

The fact that growth and time are correlated, however, does not mean that growth is a function of time or that growth is "caused" by time. Correlational studies can yield important information about development, but they provide no evidence of causal relations in development. To evaluate causality, experiments are best. In the traditional experiment, participants are randomly assigned to experimental treatment and no-treatment or control groups; any differences between groups can therefore be attributed to the differing experiences in the groups (see, for example, our discussion of intervention for preterm infants in Chapter 1).

Sometimes, experiments on particularly important phenomena are not possible. For example, if researchers limited some rat pups to an inadequate and impoverished diet, they would soon find these pups becoming lighter and smaller than rat pups offered unlimited quantities of nutritionally balanced food. Such an experiment using human infants would not be permissible, of course, although

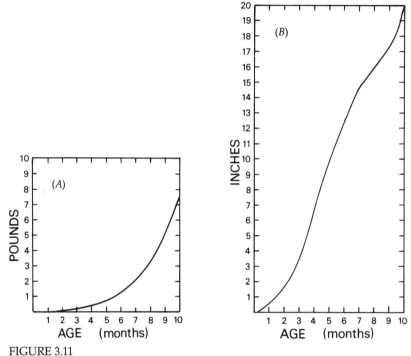

FIGURE 3.11

Continuous growth in prenatal development. (*A*) Growth in weight.
(*B*) Growth in length. With respect to both weight and length, development is
a continuous function of age.

comparable data might be obtained in a *natural experiment* or *quasi-experiment*.
For example, in the fall of 1944, the Axis halted all food supplies to western
Holland, which by the end of the year suffered from severe famine. It was not
liberated until the spring of 1945. During the famine, the number of Dutch births
in that region fell by half, and the average weight of babies declined by 10%. This
experience, unique for the fixed onset and offset of the famine, provided Stein,
Susser, Saenger, and Marolla (1975) an opportunity to assess the long-term effects of fetal and infant malnutrition on intellectual development. Surprisingly,
a massive sample of Dutch men and women surviving that famine showed no
seriously deleterious long-term mental or physical outcomes.

Correlational studies are often used in an exploratory fashion to identify
variables that may affect development; subsequently, those variables can be manipulated experimentally to confirm their role in development. For example,
Belsky and his coworkers (1980) hypothesized that, at least to some degree, parents can influence the extent to which their infants explore the environment,
and so they conducted two studies, the first correlational and the second experimental. In Study 1, the investigators saw separate groups of infants at each of
four ages—9, 12, 15, and 18 months. Mothers and infants were observed at home
twice. During those observations, the investigators systematically counted how
frequently mothers stimulated their infants either by physically pointing to or
highlighting things in the environment, or by verbally instructing or naming.
On the basis of their observations, the investigators assigned mothers scores for
"stimulation." At the same time, Belsky and his colleagues observed infants' manipulation and play, and on this basis independently assigned the infants scores

for "exploratory competence." In accordance with their hypothesis, measures of maternal stimulation and infant exploratory competence correlated with one another at each age and across all four ages; that is, mothers who stimulated their babies more had babies who explored their environments more competently. These results were only correlational, however, and so are subject to various interpretations. For example, it could be that stimulating mothers provoke their infants to explore the environment more competently *or* that more competent infants elicit more stimulation from their mothers.

To determine which interpretation was correct, Belsky and his colleagues designed Study 2, an experiment in which a sample of l-year-olds was divided randomly into experimental and control groups. The investigators visited each mother–infant dyad in the two groups weekly. The first visit involved a maternal interview; the second and third visits involved observations of mother–infant interaction like those conducted in Study l; the fourth, fifth, and sixth visits involved interventions for dyads in the experimental group and continued observations for those in the control group; the seventh visit comprised observations of interaction for dyads in both groups, as did the last visit, which took place two months later. In the intervention, the investigators surreptitiously rewarded maternal attempts to stimulate their babies. These rewards worked, and, as a consequence, mothers in the experimental group were stimulating their babies more by the seventh session than were mothers in the control group. Importantly, in the seventh and eighth sessions, infants in the experimental (mother-rewarded) group received higher scores for exploratory competence than did infants in the control (mother-not-rewarded) group.

By following the exploratory correlational study with an experimental manipulation, these investigators were able to identify maternal activities relevant to the development of exploratory competence and to specify causal relations among mother and infant variables. Belsky and his coworkers showed that maternal stimulation could facilitate at least one aspect of infant cognitive development. Of course, infants may well influence their mothers as well.

Reliability and Validity, Multiple Assessment, and Converging Operations

No matter what the experimental design, both logic and practice dictate adherence to certain general step-by-step requirements in studying structure and function in infancy. These include evaluations of the reliability and validity of measures, and the need for multiple assessments and converging operations. These criteria are especially important in studies of infants, in which alternative sources of variation (like state) are likely to compromise the quality of data.

Reliability and Validity

Infancy is a fast-developing and highly variable point in the life cycle. As a consequence, infants frequently prove to be rather poor psychological participants, especially as far as their consistency is concerned, and *reliability* of measurement is a particularly important concern. To be valuable and meaningful, a structure or function observed in an infant one day ought to be similar to that observed in the same infant on the next day, or the structure or function would not be a reliable index of the infant. For example, Bornstein, Gaughran, and Seguí (1991) evaluated the reliability of infants' temperament through semistructured observations of ten activities exhibited by 5-month-olds in four different situations. On two home visits spaced 6 days apart, observers recorded the infant behaviors in a series of situations. Not only did babies show individual variation in the rates of different activities, they showed short-term reliability across varying situations as well as between the same situations on different days.

Note that the inherently volatile nature of infancy can undermine reliability, however. Not only does the trajectory of infancy hamper the researcher's ability to distinguish reliable from unreliable phenomena, it makes it difficult to determine which performance should be deemed representative of the baby: the baby's optimal performance, the baby's average performance, or the baby's worst performance. Arguments can be made for the representativeness and desirability of each.

In addition, measurements need to have *validity*, in the sense that they measure what they are supposed to measure. First, assessments must contain items, tasks, or tests that themselves bear at least some *face validity* (relevance to the subject at hand). That is, measures should have an obvious, commonsense association with what they are supposed to measure. Furthermore, measures should have *predictive validity*. Infants who score better on intelligence tests should in general do better in real-life activities that require intelligence (e.g., they should solve math problems better); otherwise we could not trust that the original assessment was a valid measure of intelligence. Researchers have to be aware of both internal validity (i.e., the validity of any given measure) and external validity (i.e., that constructs investigated in one situation relate in a theoretically meaningful way to constructs assessed in another situation and perhaps at another age). For example, ostensible measures of the security of infant–parent attachment are validated by studies showing associations between attachment security and measures of infant–parent interaction (Belsky, 1999; Lamb, Thompson, et al., 1985; Teti & Teti, 1996; Weinfield, Sroufe, Egeland, & Carlson, 1999). Likewise, the construct of attachment security gains importance from the demonstration that individual differences in the security of infant–parent attachment predict the infants' friendliness with strange adults, their persistence in problem-solving situations, and their social competence with peers (e.g., Lamb, 1987; Thompson, 1999).

Reliability and validity typically are measured in terms of correlations. If Infant A does well, Infant B moderately, and Infant C poorly in some assessment on one day, and each infant scores similarly on the next day, the assessments made of these children would have good reliability. And if their scores on the assessment were highly correlated with their scores on some other measure of the same or a related construct, the original assessment would show good validity.

Multiple Assessment and Converging Research Strategies

Despite widespread fascination and decades of intensive research, what we know about infants has been learned slowly and arduously. Infants are notoriously uncooperative, are not motivated to perform for researchers, may be unable either to understand or to answer questions unambiguously and reliably, have limited attention spans and limited response repertoires, and show variability in most measures of performance. To assess infants in any given domain, as we have seen, researchers must design ingenious procedures to elicit responses that are within the infants' capabilities. When infants do not respond as expected, researchers have to decide whether the infants did not understand the question, were incapable of performing the task or of emitting the response, were not paying attention, or were not motivated to respond. In short, because infants fail to behave in a desired way indicates nothing about their capabilities. As we have recounted, researchers must often make inferences about what is "inside the baby's head" from impoverished, varied, and sometimes unreliable behavioral responses.

Indirect measures often provide only ambiguous information. Therefore, in studying infancy it is wise to use several different items (multiple assessments) and to employ several different strategies to assess the same phenomenon (converging operations). For example, intelligence is too complex and multidimensional to be represented by a single question or two, although single items may be very representative. Hence the need for *multiple assessments*. Moreover, multiple lengthy assessments, especially in diverse contexts, represent individuals better than do single brief assessments (Leyendecker, Lamb, & Schölmerich, 1997). Thus, a good assessment of infant activity level will have different aspects of infant activity observed in different contexts and on different days, rather than simply one aspect in one context at one time. For example, in their study of infant temperament, Bornstein, Gaughran, and Segui (1991) measured and compared infant activity level in terms of reaching, kicking, and other motor behaviors, and they did so with infants when alone, when with their mothers, and when with an observer on two different days.

Sometimes infants fail to exhibit some capacity or tendency when tested one way, yet reveal the same capacity when tested using an alternative technique. On other occasions, alternative explanations of the observed behavior are equally plausible. *Converging operations* consist of two or more experimental strategies that permit the selection or elimination of alternative hypotheses or concepts that could explain an experimental result. Converging operations are often necessary to show that the infants' responses indeed reveal the inferred capacity, and that their apparent successes are not simply artifacts of a given testing procedure. In the same study mentioned above, Bornstein et al. (1991) asked both mothers and observers to rate infant activity on different occasions and in different situations. They found that mother–observer agreement for assessments based on the home visits was significant but only moderate in size.

There are no rigid guidelines about how to do research with infants, and results obtained with any one method should not be considered definitive. A method that is suitable for asking one type of question at a given age may be inappropriate for the same or other questions at other ages. Conversely, methods that are not appropriate in one situation can yield invaluable information in another. Without careful thought, even well-established methods can yield misleading conclusions.

Research Issues with Infants

Research with infants can be special in many ways. In this final section of our chapter on research methods, we discuss some broader issues. As will be clear, these additional issues concerning context, state, point of view, age comparisons, performance versus competence, and ethics are especially important in research with young infants.

Context, State, Point of View, Age, and Performance versus Competence in Infancy Research

In 1975, Bronfenbrenner assailed developmental scientists with the assertion that "developmental psychology is the science of the strange behavior of a child in a strange situation with a strange adult" (p. 8). Because findings obtained in traditional research often lacked "ecological validity," he continued, researchers need to pay attention to the contexts in which children are reared and studied.

As we discussed in Chapter 2, the social and cultural context help to determine infants' experiences and limit the generalizability of findings about them. Moreover, infancy research is conducted in laboratories as well as in homes, and location can also be an important variable. Laboratory studies are valuable because the testing context can be controlled. However, questions often arise concerning the generalizability of laboratory-based findings and principles. Laboratory studies can show that some capacity or performance is possible, but they do not show whether the capacity or performance concerned is typical. Furthermore, infancy is a highly reactive stage of life (see below), and infants may perform differently at home and in strange laboratory situations. By contrast, because the home is comfortable and secure, a researcher may tap the infant's naturalistic performance there, but the research also risks uncontrolled factors (like the unexpected ring of a telephone) that may in the end undermine the goal of an observation.

Of course, the significance of the home-versus-laboratory distinction will depend on the methods, strategies, and purposes of the particular research. The distinction is presumably less important in studies that attempt to demonstrate the existence of specific infant capacities, such as language or play. For example, Bornstein and his colleagues found no home–laboratory differences in levels of infant symbolic play (Bornstein, Haynes, Legler, O'Reilly, & Painter, 1997) or the frequency and duration of infants' utterances (Bornstein, Haynes, Painter, & Genevro, 2000). In the case of attachment, however, an infant may show an especially adverse or atypical reaction to the unfamiliar laboratory that would not be observed at home. In that case, laboratory and home evaluations might not be comparable. One might need to conduct observations in both contexts, perhaps assessing parental behaviors in the laboratory first and then conducting naturalistic observations in the home, or else assessing social attraction and withdrawal in everyday contexts and then using laboratory experiments with specific stimuli to assess their effectiveness. Clearly, interchange between laboratory and field under these circumstances is desirable.

One of the most important and ever present influences on infant performance is *behavioral state of arousal*. Newborns and infants often shift rapidly and unpredictably from one state to another and may remain in a state of attentive alertness only for brief periods of time (see Chapter 5). Even when necessary capacities are present and a task is well designed, state may facilitate or inhibit infant performance. If state is not accounted for when assessing performance then the baby's opportunities to perform may be unfairly or incorrectly evaluated. A baby who is awake, sated, and attentive ought to have a better chance to perform well or participate more sensitively than one who is drowsy, hungry, and inattentive. Infant state also plays a central role in understanding the reliability of infant performance. Unless the infant's state is the same in both the test and retest assessments, reliability should not be expected. Failures to find reliability in infant behavior do not tell us which testing session truly represents the infant's capacities.

We see the world—literally and figuratively—through adult eyes. Infants do not. They see the world through infant eyes. What looks like one thing to us may look quite differently to a baby, and it can be a mistake to misattribute our perspective to the baby. As a consequence, research in infancy needs to be especially sensitive to the infant's point of view. To take a simple example, the "complexity" of a visual stimulus may be at one level for an adult but at quite another for a baby. An adult might see a 2″ × 2″ checkerboard as "simpler" than, say, a 24″ × 24″ checkerboard. However, when confronted with a 24″ × 24″ board, an infant may only look at one square or along one border. Consequently, the 2″ × 2″ and 24″ × 24″ boards might be perceptually similar and equally simple structures for the infant.

Although it seems almost trivial and transparent to say, one of the major factors affecting infant performance is age. Infancy is a most volatile and unstable period in the life cycle. Everything seems to be and may be changing everyday. As a consequence, investigators need to choose the ages of their research participants carefully, and they need to be sure that they keep the dispersion of the ages of infants in experimental groups they see under strict control. If we want to know the status of a structure or a function in infancy, we may very well be asking too broad a question, because the status of a structure or function may vary greatly between 1 and 3, 4 and 6, 7 and 9, or 10 and 12 months. By the same token, if we want to compare the abilities of 4- and 6-month-olds, it will defeat the purpose of the age comparison if the group of 4-month-olds contains some babies who are 3 months old and some who are already 5 months old.

Finally, in considering infancy studies and their findings, it is critical to distinguish between performance and competence. *Performance* concerns what infants do under certain conditions in certain contexts. Clearly, it is important to know what infants will do given different circumstances. However, such information does not tell us what infants can do. *Competence* defines the infant's potential ability at a given state or stage. Competence is often inferred from performance, but it is not necessarily the case that performance accurately indexes competence; competence may far exceed performance. Obviously, all of the different methods that we have discussed in this chapter need to be qualified by whether they reveal infant performance or infant competence.

Ethics

The subject of infant age brings us to a last, but by no means least, important consideration of infancy research, namely the ethics of enlisting in research babies so young and helpless that they cannot understand what is happening to them, much less render their own (informed) consent to participate in research. The discussion of research methods with infants would be incomplete without formal consideration of the central issues related to harm, deception, confidentiality, and consent (American Psychological Association, 1992; Fisher, Hatashita-Wong, & Greene, 1999; Koocher & Keith-Spiegel, 1990). Human beings who participate in research are not "guinea pigs" with whom experimenters may do what they want. Dennis and Dennis (1940) reported a "study" conducted in the 1930s in which twin infant girls were reared in a single room—rarely spoken to or played with—in order to see if the girls would develop normally despite these deprivations. Such a study is totally unethical by any standard today and would not be permitted. For such obvious reasons, infant researchers have turned to the natural experiments we described earlier in this chapter.

Much developmental research is worthwhile, and places research participants—even infants—at little or no risk. Still, the benefits of research always have to be weighed against the potential risks. Clearly, society can benefit from the knowledge provided by developmental science, but it must judge that benefit against the cost to the individuals who participate. When children, especially infants, participate in research, special ethical problems arise. Normal infants may be particularly vulnerable, for example, and in some situations may be harmed more extensively than children or adults by any negative effects of experimentation, and at-risk infants may be differently affected by the same research situations (Eckerman & Oehler, 1992). Of course, infants are also unable to judge the risks of and benefits flowing from their participation in a study. Because there are no easy answers to these problems, all research conducted today must be approved by special institutional ethics committees.

In order to offset potential risks to infant participants or to their families, researchers must satisfy certain criteria. These include the following:

1. The research must be scientifically sound and significant. If the research is not worth doing, it is not worth placing babies and their families at risk.

2. Any risk must be justifiable. If the risks are minimal (no greater than might be encountered in everyday life), then a research project may be easily justifiable. If the research entails greater risk, then the offsetting benefit must be greater in order to justify the risk.

3. Participants must be informed about what will happen to them during the study, and their consent must be obtained. In the case of infants, such informed consent must be provided by the parent or legal guardian.

4. The responsible individual (or the parent) normally has the right to withdraw from participation in a study at any time.

5. Privacy or anonymity is important, for individuals have a right to protection from the consequences of assessments of themselves.

6. Justice demands that infants not be selected as participants in experiments more than other groups of people in society simply because they are weak or vulnerable (as, for example, in the testing of vaccines).

In the end, it is the responsibility of the researcher to minimize the risk and maximize the benefit of the research.

Summary

Babies are particularly difficult research participants. They are mute, motorically inept, and subject to state fluctuations. They are also attractive to study, however, for a host of reasons. The impediments infants present have challenged and stimulated researchers to break the communication barrier that separates the two. Our goal in this chapter has been to introduce the "hows" of infancy research; in succeeding chapters, we turn attention to the "whats" and "whys" of infant development.

Most infancy studies are concerned with the status, process, and origins of structure and function. In this chapter we have discussed general design issues in studies of infants. Investigators usually employ longitudinal or cross-sectional designs in efforts to describe and understand development in infancy. We also described techniques used in different kinds of studies, noting the shift from reliance on baby biographies—a research strategy initiated a century ago—long before the systematic study of infant (or, for that matter adult) psychology led to reliance on systematic observation and experimental research. Many different techniques have been used to record and to quantify structure and function in infancy—observational, behavioral, and psychophysiological. Next, we reviewed issues about interpretation and measurement in infancy studies. Correlational studies abound in infancy research; they help to reveal associations among variables, but causality is usually identified by experimentation. Furthermore, research in infancy (as in any science) needs to meet canons of reliability and validity, and with infants multiple assessments and converging operations are required. Infant behavior reflects the physical and social context, state, point of view, and age of the infant. Finally, we reviewed the ethical considerations that guide research in infancy.

4

Physical Development
in Infancy

———— ❖ ————

- How are the stages of prenatal development defined?
- What prenatal experiences and factors shape infant development?
- What factors occurring between fertilization and birth influence sexual differentiation?
- How does preterm birth affect development?
- How can we assess the newborn baby's capacity and individuality?
- What basic principles best describe physical and motor development?

Influence Before Birth, Birth, and Growth After Birth

Infancy is a time of rapid physical and nervous system growth and development, and the study of these aspects of infancy is important for many reasons. First, principles of physical and nervous system development provide metaphors for other aspects of psychological development. For example, an important distinction in infancy studies is that between innate and congenital. The term *innate* applies to structures or functions that are attributed to heredity even though they may not appear full-blown at birth; they may also be influenced by prenatal experience. By contrast, *congenital* applies to structures or functions that are present at the time of birth but are not acquired by heredity. Thus, many secondary characteristics related to gender are innate but not congenital because they emerge years later, at the time of puberty. By analogy, it could be that certain cognitive abilities and socioemotional propensities are also innate but not congenital. Thus, the study of physical and nervous system development may facilitate our understanding of them.

The study of physical and nervous system development has a second set of implications for understanding infancy as well: Development in these very basic spheres of life sets the stage for and often influences development in other spheres of life. Consider two examples, one specialized, the other more general. The young infant cannot counterposition thumb and forefinger to hold an object, but must instead use a palmar grasp. It takes about 14 months until the average infant can hold an object in the more mature fashion, and the advent of this physical ability is accompanied by major changes in the infant's tactile and visual inspection of objects. This development in turn may have important implications for cognitive growth: Influential theorists like Piaget emphasized the importance of action in infant learning about and achieving mastery over their environment (Chapter 7), and thus improvements in grasping capacity should enhance cognitive development. As another example, consider the eagerness with which all parents await their child's first step. This achievement signifies an important stage in infant independence, permitting new means of exploring the surroundings and of determining when and how much time infants spend near their parents. By walking, the baby asserts individuality, maturity, and self-mindedness. These changes in turn affect the ways in which parents treat the young child: What parents leave around the house, and even how they speak to the walking, as opposed to the crawling, baby differ substantially. In short, researchers recognize both that motor and neurological development are interesting in their own right and that these developments have major implications for diverse aspects of infants' cognitive and social development.

This chapter and the next address physical and nervous system development in infancy. Birth occurs during an ongoing developmental process—it neither terminates nor initiates development. Consequently, postnatal development must be considered against the backdrop of prenatal development: Our goal here is to focus attention on those issues that may help us understand infancy after birth. In this chapter, we discuss genetics, anatomical changes before and just after birth, the birth process and neonatology, physical growth, and motor development. In Chapter 5 we discuss sleep cycles, states of arousal, the autonomic nervous system, as well as cellular, brain, and sensory system growth in the central nervous system. Each of these topics could warrant chapters in and of themselves, so our treatment is necessarily selective. We review research findings and highlight central principles in the discussion of each topic.

Genetics and Prenatal Development

Much is now known about the biology of conception and prenatal development. Development begins long before birth, so here we consider prenatal influences on the growth of both structure and function. Not long ago it was believed that the organism-to-be was "preformed" in the mother's egg waiting to be released, or in the father's sperm waiting for a medium in which to grow. Modern biology tells a different story.

Genetic Endowment

Figure 4.1 shows the process of *meiosis*, which involves complex changes in the reproductive cells (gametes) of each parent that split so as to retain half the number of chromosomes present in the original cell. An unfertilized ovum is released by the ovaries and descends down the fallopian tube. Membranes of the fallopian tube secrete enzymes that loosen the envelope surrounding the ovum, and this permits a single sperm to meet and fertilize the egg. The resulting 23 pairs of chromosomes compose the genetic makeup of the individual, with one

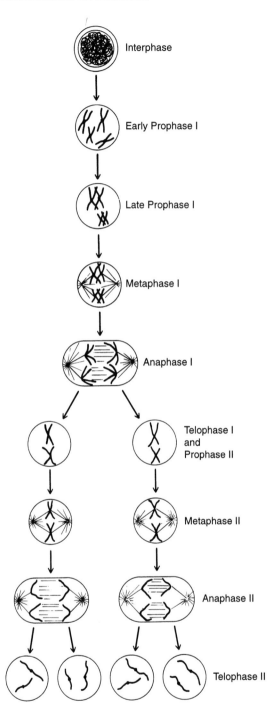

FIGURE 4.1

Each parent cell splits and contributes to the genetic makeup of the conceptus through a process of reduction called *meiosis*. In meiosis, complex nuclear changes ensure that the original cell splits into two halves, each containing half the number of chromosomes present in the original cell. These gametes lead, through fusion of the ovum and sperm, to the emergence of a single zygote.

member of each pair contributed by each parent. Chromosomes contain genes that themselves are composed of chemical codes of DNA that guide development of structure and function.

The endowment of parental chromosomes is the first critically important event in the life of a child. However, no one today argues that the *genotype* (the genetic makeup of the individual) exactly predicts the *phenotype* (the observed characteristics of the individual). Clearly, different people with different genetic endowments sometimes look or behave similarly, just as identical twins with exactly the same genetic endowment may look or behave differently. There are clear and demonstrative genetic contributions to many aspects of development. The phenotypic variability we see all around us, however, springs from several sources, because genetic endowment and experience transact over the life cycle to shape the behavior and characteristics of individuals.

The chromosomal structure of a fetus is evaluated using procedures like *amniocentesis*. In this technique, amniotic fluid is drawn off through the abdominal wall of the mother. Fetal cells are then cultivated and swelled chemically so that they can be observed individually by light microscopy. An example of the resultant distribution of chromosomes is shown in Figure 4.2A, and a

FIGURE 4.2
(*A*) The raw distribution of chromosomes drawn from the amniocentesis and analysis of fetal cells. (*B*) The ordering of pairs of chromosomes by size in a karyotype.

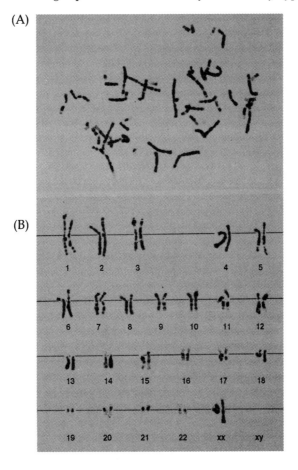

karyotype (the ordering of pairs of chromosomes by size) is shown in Figure 4.2B. Note that the XX pairing foretells a baby girl.

Amniocentesis is often employed to permit genetic testing when a pregnancy is considered to be "at risk," as, for example, when there is a history of genetic anomaly. The procedure is typically done about halfway through pregnancy in about the fourth month after conception. Analysis itself takes about 3 to 4 weeks. Even for many who approve of elective abortion, the termination of a pregnancy so long after conception is a cause of emotional and moral concern. Newer techniques for early chromosomal assessment, including *chorionic villi sampling* (CVS), have since been developed. Villi, which also contain fetal tissue, are protrusions of the chorion membrane that surrounds the fetus and later becomes the placenta. CVS can be done in the middle of the third month, and this procedure yields preliminary findings in 2 weeks. Both amniocentesis and CVS are associated with some risk, with a 1 in 150 chance of spontaneous abortion following amniocentesis and a 1 in 50 chance after CVS (Green & Statham, 1996). In addition, CVS has been linked to slightly elevated rates of limb deficiencies, with risk rates estimated between 1 in 3,000 to 1 in 1,000 (Centers for Disease Control and Prevention, 1995). Physicians and genetic counselors are ethically obligated to discuss these risks as well as the benefits of amniocentesis and CVS with all women who are considering such procedures (Punales-Morejon, 1997).

Both amniocentesis and CVS can be used to diagnose chromosomal, metabolic, and blood-borne conditions, identify congenital defects (like muscular dystrophy), assess levels of alpha fetoprotein that indicate neural tube defects such as spina bifida, and screen the fetal DNA for telltale signs of sickle cell anemia (Green & Statham, 1996; Robinson & Wisner, 1993). These procedures make valuable genetic counseling possible.

Some birth disorders are inherited, whereas others are caused by malformations of the genetic material. The latter are typically attributable to spontaneous mutations or to incompatibility of the parents' genes. They may be caused by a single gene or by many genes, and they may be transmitted by one parent or by both. In 1959, Lejeune discovered that children with Down syndrome have 47 chromosomes rather than 46. Having an extra chromosome is one of the most common chromosomal disorders. Trisomy-21, or Down syndrome (shown in Figure 4.3), occurs in slightly fewer than 1 out of every 1,000 live births. Its prevalence decreased from a rate of 1.33 per 1,000 births in the 1970s, the likely result of increased availability and use of prenatal testing (Centers for Disease Control and Prevention, 1994). Down syndrome birth rates vary with the age of the parents, with a 1 in 2,000 rate among 20-year-old women but a 1 in 20 rate among 45-year-old women (Roizen, 1997). Men with Klinefelter's syndrome have two or more X chromosomes and a Y chromosome; this problem occurs in about 1 male out of every 1,000 live births. Males with Klinefelter's syndrome have genitalia and secondary sexual characteristics that are underdeveloped, and average to low-average IQs (Batshaw, 1997). One in every 2,500 female births has Turner syndrome, an X with no second X; prevalence rate estimates for Turner syndrome range from 1 in 2,500 to 1 in 10,000 births (Jorde, Carey, & White, 1995). Turner syndrome females are short, with webbed necks, broad chests, and nonfunctional ovaries. Although they have typical intelligence, they are prone to learning disabilities because of visual–perceptual impairments (Batshaw, 1997).

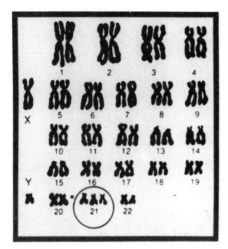 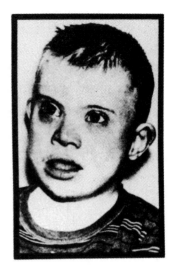

FIGURE 4.3

The karyotype of a Down syndrome child. Down syndrome is also known as trisomy-21 after the triplet of chromosomes that appears in position 21. Down syndrome is associated with a variety of identifiable physical characteristics, as shown in the picture, and with mental retardation.

Early Stages of Development

Developmentalists often describe growth in terms of stages, and three main stages of prenatal development have been distinguished: The period of the zygote (approximately conception to 2 weeks), the period of the embryo (approximately 2 weeks to 8 weeks), and the period of the fetus (approximately 8 to 40 weeks). Counting conventionally starts from the mother's last menstrual period rather than the time of conception, about 2 weeks later.

The *zygote* is the initial union of ovum and sperm, the fertilized egg. This first stage lasts from the moment of conception through the time that the new organism (sometimes referred to as a blastocyst) travels toward the *uterus*, where it implants itself (within weeks) in the *endometrium*, or nutrient-rich lining of the uterus. Multiplication of cells proceeds with extraordinary rapidity during this period. By the end of this very brief first phase, human cells have already begun to differentiate, that is, to assume specialized roles depending on their location. A fuller flowering of this differentiation emerges during the period of the embryo. Simultaneously, other parts of the blastocyst develop into support systems for the fetus, most notably the placenta. The *placenta* connects the body of the developing child to the body of the mother, and permits the exchange of sugar, fat, and waste via channels in the thick, tough, tubular *umbilical cord*.

The period of the *embryo*, the second stage of life, by definition begins when hairlike structures on the blastocyst, the villi, anchor the blastocyst to the uterine wall. The first 2 months of embryogenesis are critically important for morphological development, that is, for the differentiation of organs, limbs, and physiological systems. Even by the time of implantation, it is possible to distinguish three layers: the *ectoderm* (from the outer layer of the blastocyst), which will form skin, sense organs, and central nervous system structures of the brain and spinal

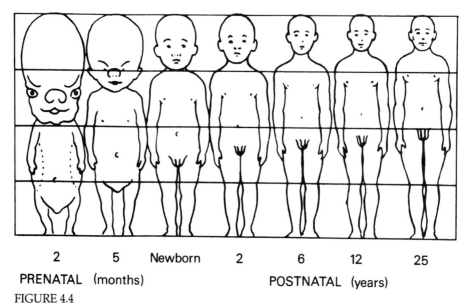

2   5   Newborn   2   6   12   25

PRENATAL (months)   **POSTNATAL** (years)

FIGURE 4.4

Proportional growth of the human between the second fetal month and maturity. This
figure shows the principle of cephalocaudal development: Half of the 2-month fetus is
represented by the head, but this proportion shrinks to one eighth by maturity.

cord; the *mesoderm* (from the middle layer), which will form muscles, blood, and
the circulatory system; and the *endoderm* (from the inner layer), which will form
digestive, respiratory, and internal organs. Particularly notable by the fourteenth
day is the appearance of the "primitive streak," which is the first overt stage in
the development of the central nervous system.

By 3 months after conception, the human embryo is little more than 1 inch
long but has many morphological characteristics similar to those recognizable
in the mature organism. All of the organs are differentiated from one another
although they are not fully developed. The embryo is strangely proportioned:
the head, for example, constitutes a much larger portion of total body size than it
will at any other time in life, between one third and one half of the entire length
of the embryo (see Figure 4.4). Large eyes are obvious. Less clearly visible but
no less remarkable are the tongue and teeth buds. Arms and legs, although
tiny, are recognizable as well; there are even fingers and toes. The embryonic
stomach produces digestive juices, its kidneys filter blood, and its heart beats.
Perhaps the least developed organs are those that constitute the respiratory
system, probably because they are not functional as long as the embryo remains
in the fluid environment of the womb. The respiratory system could not sustain
life prior to 6 months after conception.

Embryos have been made amenable to study in a number of ways. Perhaps
as many as one half of all conceptuses (i.e., blastocyst, embryo, or fetus) are
spontaneously aborted or miscarried, presumably because developmental
anomalies render these organisms incapable of survival. In addition, embryos
are often removed from the uterus in elective abortions. Modern technology
has also developed ways of recording intrauterine development. Figures 4.5A
and B show glimpses of the prenatal world obtained via *ultrasound imaging*.
In this now common procedure, sounds are sent into the pregnant woman's

(A)   (B)

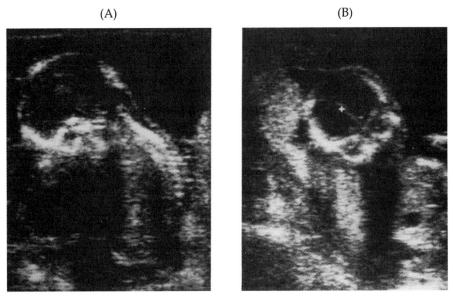

FIGURE 4.5

Two ultrasound recordings of a fetus 4 months after conception. (*A*) The profile view
shows the skull and ossification of the spinal column. (*B*) The frontal view shows the
skull and eye sockets. (The plus sign shows the fissure between the two cerebral
hemispheres.)

body from a probe applied to the abdominal skin. A computer analyzes pulses
that are reflected back and uses these to map structures within the body (Levi &
Chervenak, 1998). Figure 4.5A shows a profile view in which the bony structures
of the skull and spinal column are clear; Figure 4.5B provides a top-down view
of the skull in which the eye sockets are visible.

Ultrasound imaging reveals both structure and behavior: Observers have
witnessed fetuses suck their thumbs, blink, and even yawn. Fetuses at 6 months
also show rapid eye movements, characteristic of dreaming in adults (see
Chapter 5), and ultrasound has been used to monitor the development of the
nervous system. It is also used during amniocentesis and chorionic villi sampling
to locate the fetus to avoid damaging it. Ultrasound has become widely and routinely used to scan for fetal anomalies and appears to pose no ill effects on the
fetus (Chervenak & McCullough, 1998; Garmel & D'Alton, 1994).

The period of the *fetus* begins when the differentiation of major organs is
complete, around 2 months after conception. This is a time of increasing function
and great change in bodily proportions (Figure 4.4). Growth and development
are incredibly rapid during embryogenesis, but the organs existing at the beginning of the fetal stage only crudely resemble the forms they will later take. On
a structural level, cellular differentiation and organization during ontogenesis
dramatically alter the functional capacity of the organs. In addition, the connections among different organs take shape during the fetal period, so a more
integrated and coherent functional entity emerges. We can see arm buds in the
embryo, for example, but during the fetal period the arms lengthen, joints develop, fingers separate and grow nails, a complex network of veins develops to
nourish the cells while a network of muscle connections lays the groundwork

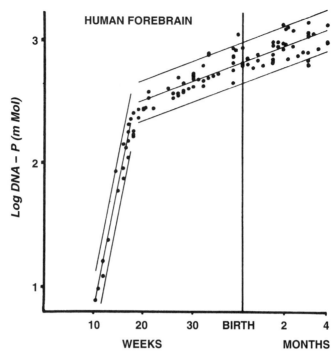

FIGURE 4.6

Total DNA-P, equivalent to total cell number, in the human forebrain from 10 gestational weeks to 4 postnatal months, showing the two-phase characteristic of prenatal cell multiplication. (After Dobbing & Sands, 1973. © by *Archives of Disease in Childhood*, 1973. Reprinted by permission.)

for the fine coordinated movements of which the arm will later be capable. Figure 4.6 shows that there are two phases of cell growth during fetogenesis; a first phase of very rapid growth until about 4½ months after conception, followed by a second phase of more gradual but steady growth.

Functional capacity increases steadily during the fetal stage as well. After 3 months, the fetus begins to swallow and urinate, and various reflex behaviors emerge (see below). By 4 months, fetuses are felt to move in utero (quickening); by 6 months, the fetus is capable of breathing and crying; and by 7 months, fetuses may survive in the extrauterine environment (viability). These are significant markers, both in the life of the child and the lives of the child's parents. Figure 4.7 shows the onset and development of fetal movements over the last half of pregnancy. Whereas movement initially occurs infrequently and randomly, movement accelerates and maintains a relatively high frequency in the last trimester of pregnancy, with a decline just before birth.

So many critically important events occur during pregnancy that volumes have been devoted to the study of prenatal development (e.g., Eliot, 1999; Nathanielsz, 1999; Nelson, 2000). It is not possible for us to review all of this material, and so we have selected two illustrative issues to explore in some detail. Both *prenatal experiences* and *sexual differentiation* represent events before birth that may have far-reaching consequences for psychological growth in the human infant and adult after birth, although we hasten to note that the impact of discrete events at any point in development may be modified by later events, in keeping with a transactional perspective on development.

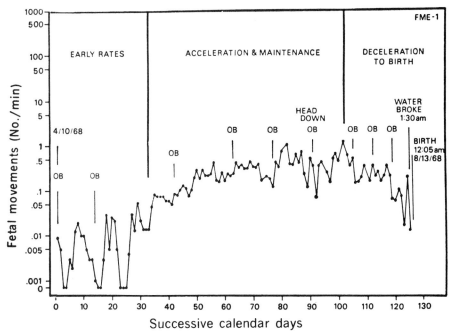

FIGURE 4.7

A graphic representation of the time course of fetal movements during prenatal development. (After Edwards & Edwards, 1970. © 1970 by the American Association for the Advancement of Science. Reprinted by permission.)

Prenatal Experience

The time before birth is a period of rapid and extensive development, as well as one of enhanced tenuousness and susceptibility. Some theorists, like Gesell, argued that biology and maturation are the prime movers of development, but research shows that experiences from outside the organism, as well as experiences produced by the organism itself during early gestation, influence prenatal development. Indeed, since the late 1970s, an important focus of developmental psychobiology has been the study of fetal motor, sensory, perceptual, and learning capabilities, how the development of specific systems in the fetus are affected by intra- and extrauterine experiences, and how fetal developments contribute to the development of the central nervous system (Lecanuet, Fifer, Krasnegor, & Smotherman, 1995).

What experiences are important in prenatal development? How do they exert their effects and when? In Chapter 1 we discussed several roles of experience in development, including induction, facilitation or attunement, and maintenance. Even embryonic behavior appears to play an important role in development: Chick embryos that are immobilized suffer muscle and joint abnormalities, perhaps because their own movements help determine which neuronal connections will grow and which will die in the course of prenatal development. Human fetuses are extremely active: Spontaneous motor activity occurs in cycles of about 1 to 4 minutes, begins early in the second trimester of pregnancy, and remains quite stable up to and shortly after birth (Robertson & Bacher, 1995). Although the origin and function of spontaneous motor activity remain unknown, Robertson and Bacher (1992) found an inverse relation between rates of spontaneous movement and rates of visual exploration in 2- to 3-month-old infants and speculated that spontaneous cyclical movement in the early postnatal period plays a role in regulating infants' visual exploration of the environment shortly after birth.

A host of external factors may influence the course and quality of prenatal development; their effects vary from positive to negative depending on the nature of the experience. They include maternal characteristics (e.g., age, diet, and stress) as well as the contraction of diseases, ingestion of drugs, and exposure to environmental toxins. During intrauterine life, the fetus is protected from many such insults by a placenta that filters such *teratogens* and prevents some, but not all, from entering the baby's system; some still pass the placental barrier. Diseases, drugs, and environmental toxins pose particular threats to the integrity of the fetus (Field, 1998; Kopera-Frye & Arendt, 1999; Needleman & Bellinger, 1994; Olson, 1998).

Bornstein, DiPietro, and their colleagues have explored the possible predictive meaning of fetal heart rate and movement for infant development. In one study, fetal cardiac function was measured at 24, 30, and 36 weeks gestation and quantified in terms of heart rate, variability, and episodic accelerations. The same children's representational capacity was evaluated at 27 months after their birth in terms of language and play. Fetuses that exhibited a more precipitous increase in heart-rate variability and acceleration over gestation achieved higher levels of language competence. Fetuses with higher heart-rate variability and accelerations, and steeper growth trajectories over gestation, achieved higher levels of symbolic play (Bornstein, DiPietro, Hahn, Painter, Haynes, & Costigan, 2002). Apparently cardiac patterning during gestation reflects an underlying neural substrate that persists through early childhood: Individual variation in rate of development could be stable, or efficient cardiac function could positively influence the underlying neural substrate to enhance cognitive performance. In a related report, the same authors found that motor activity prior to birth is predictive of motor behavior and temperament after birth. Three measures of fetal motor activity (activity level, amplitude, and number of movements) were collected at 24, 30, and 36 weeks gestation, and postnatal data collection included a neurobehavioral assessment at 2 weeks postpartum and laboratory based assessments at 1 and 2 years of age. Significant positive associations were detected between motor behavior at 36 weeks and neonatal irritability and motor development. Temperament attributes, including distress to limitations at one year and behavioral inhibition at 2 years were consistently and negatively related to fetal movement measures across gestation, and maternally reported toddler activity level was positively associated with fetal activity level at 36 weeks (DiPietro, Bornstein, Costigan, Pressman, Hahn, Painter, Smith, & Yi, 2002). Despite antenatal stability, large intra-fetal variability in motor behavior predicts temperament at later ages.

Maternal Characteristics

Maternal age is one important characteristic: Younger and older women are at increased risk for birth complications. In a study of 3,917 patients, for example, women who were 35 years of age or older were slightly more likely to have a low birth-weight infant than were women between 20 and 35 years old (Berkowitz & Skovron, 1990). Even after controlling for sociodemographic and medical risk factors, women who were 35 or older were significantly more likely to experience complications, and those who were 30 or older were significantly more likely to have both cesarean sections and infants who were admitted to the newborn intensive care unit. However, although older primiparous women are more likely to have complicated pregnancies and deliveries, their risk of a poor neonatal outcome was not appreciably higher in this study, although other researchers have shown that mothers over 30 are more likely to experience miscarriage, stillbirths, high blood pressure, and even death during delivery than are mothers under 30 years of age (Fretts, Schmittdiel, McLean, Usher, & Goldman, 1995; Hoyert, 1996; McFalls, 1990; Peipert & Bracken, 1993). Very young mothers are similarly at risk. Fraser and Brockert (1995) found significantly higher rates of preterm, low birth-weight births among mothers who were 17 years old or younger than among 20- to 24-year-old mothers, even after controlling statistically for mothers' ethnicity, income, and marital status.

Diet is another maternal characteristic that affects the developing fetus. Women whose diets are rich in protein experience fewer complications during pregnancy, have shorter labors, and bear healthier babies (Georgieff, 1994). That is why the national Women, Infants, and Children (WIC) program endeavors to supply dairy products to pregnant women and their young children. In particular, malnutrition during pregnancy, especially deficiencies in protein, zinc, and folic acid, have been linked to central nervous dysfunction, neural tube defects, prematurity, and birth defects (Keen, Bendich, & Willhite, 1993). The timing of malnutrition during pregnancy also appears to affect the type and degree of ill effects obtained. More severe consequences (e.g., neural tube defects and hydrocephalus) are associated with severe malnutrition that begins early in pregnancy, whereas prenatal malnutrition that begins later is typically associated with low birth weight (Metcoff, 1994). Maternal malnutrition is a subject of much study today because infants born in many regions of the world are likely to experience some degree of malnutrition. Clearly, maternal malnutrition in pregnancy is perilous because nutrients constitute the elements of life, they are the fuel by which development is propelled, and they nourish the placenta that provides oxygen to the fetus.

Barring the development of severe congenital anomalies or brain damage, the long-term prognosis for infants chronically malnourished in utero need not be entirely bleak, especially when remedial countermeasures are offered. Recall the results of the unfortunate 1944–1945 famine in western Holland (Smith, 1947). Stein and her colleagues (1975) assessed the long-term effects of early malnutrition, and found that men and women who survived the famine in utero suffered no serious long-term physical or mental disabilities. Zeskind and Ramey (1981) followed 42 fetally malnourished infants and their controls through 36 months of age. The babies were assigned to two environments that differed in their intellectually supportive characteristics. This investigation found continuing detrimental effects on intellectual, behavioral, and social development in children reared in the nonsupportive caregiving environment, but a comparative recovery in children reared in the supportive environment. Thus, it appears that subsequent remediation can compensate for early dietary deprivation, although the long-term effects of prenatal malnutrition are far from clear. Using the Dutch famine data, for example, Hoek, Brown, and Susser (1999) found elevated rates of schizophrenia among adults who had experienced prenatal malnutrition, compared to baseline rates in nonmalnourished cohorts. This suggests that severe prenatal malnutrition may affect central nervous system functioning in ways that facilitate maladaptations such as schizophrenia under predisposing environmental conditions (see Chapter 1). Such findings must be viewed with caution, however, because in the natural order of things, maternal malnutrition during pregnancy is often accompanied by the compounding effects of poverty, inadequate medical care, disease, postnatal malnutrition, and poor education.

Other psychological, familial, and sociological factors influence prenatal development. For example, maternal *distress* affects maternal hormones, which in turn affect the fetus. Chronic distress during pregnancy in Rhesus monkeys, for example, is associated with lower birth weights and maturational delays in the central nervous system (Schneider, 1992). Chronic prenatal stress is also associated with premature labor and birthing complications (Paarlberg, Vingerhoets, Passchier, Dekker, & Van Geijn, 1995). Because social status is associated with factors such as poor nutrition, high life stress, and inadequate medical care, impoverished women have poorer outcomes in their children (McLoyd, 1998). However, large-scale studies show that the health of neonates and fetuses can be promoted by good antenatal care (e.g., Fullilove, 1993).

Disease

Sexually transmitted diseases, smallpox, and measles cross the placental barrier and affect fetal development. For example, women who contract German measles (rubella) during the first trimester of pregnancy (when central nervous system structures like the eyes and ears are differentiating) have a 50% risk of bearing infants who have cataracts or are deaf. Various other long-term abnormalities attend rubella; brain damage and mental retardation are notable among them (Moore & Persaud, 1993).

We know, too, that the Human Immunodeficiency Virus (HIV), which produces Acquired Immunodeficiency Syndrome (AIDS), also passes the placental barrier to infect the developing fetus. The first cases of AIDS in children were reported only in 1982, yet the U.S. Department of Health and Human Services (1999, Sept.) estimated that, as of December 1998, there were about 8,500 HIV-infected children under 13 years of age in the United States. In the vast majority of these cases, HIV is acquired from an infected mother during pregnancy, labor, and delivery, or through breast-feeding (Centers for Disease Control and Prevention, 1999, August). Although this number is alarmingly high, it actually reflects a 66% decrease between 1992 and 1997 in the incidence of pediatric AIDS cases caused by mother-to-child transmission. This decline is the welcome result of widespread public health service efforts since 1994 to obtain routine, voluntary testing of pregnant women for HIV and to provide zidovudine (AZT) to infected women during pregnancy and delivery and to infants of infected women after birth. Without AZT, the mother-to-infant transmission rate of HIV is about 25%. When infected pregnant mothers are given AZT, HIV transmission rates drop by between one half and one third (Fiscus et al., 1996; Centers for Disease Control and Prevention, 1999, August).

Pediatric AIDS typically progresses along one of two developmental tracks. About 25% of HIV-infected infants will be seriously symptomatic (e.g., delayed physical growth; opportunistic bacterial infections such as pneumonias, internal organ abscesses, and meningitis; delays in normative developmental achievements) by the end of the first year and are not likely to survive past 5 years of age. It is likely that this group became infected during pregnancy before the development of a functional immune system. The remaining infants, for whom infection probably occurred at birth, may not present with HIV-related symptoms until about 5 years of age, with a life expectancy that can extend into adolescence. In addition to opportunistic infections, pediatric AIDS is associated with progressive neurological, heart, and kidney disease, cytomegalovirus of the eye, anemia, and lymphomas. Between 10% and 20% of infected infants experience a progressive encephalopathy that underlies developmental declines, motor tremors, cortical atrophy, and lack of head growth. Even among infants without progressive encephalopathy, physical and cognitive developmental delays are still evident during the first 2 years of life (Rutstein, Conlon, & Batshaw, 1997). Importantly, medical and developmental prognoses for infants with HIV infection can improve dramatically with antiretroviral therapy, aimed at blocking HIV replication. Such drugs include AZT, dideoxyinosine (ddl), and protease inhibitors, which when used in combination can suppress HIV activity completely for more than a year (Kline, Fletcher, Federici, et al., 1996; Centers for Disease Control and Prevention, 1998; Rutstein et al., 1997).

Drugs

It is well established that many common legal and illicit drugs may compromise that fetus. Nicotine from cigarette smoking is believed to constrict placental blood vessels, temporarily depriving the developing fetal brain of oxygen, stimulating the cardiovascular system and depressing the respiratory system. Women who smoke have a higher incidence of spontaneous abortions, preterm deliveries, low birth weight, and intrauterine growth retardation (Fried, 1993; Wheeler, 1993). Whether or not smoking during pregnancy places a child at risk for cognitive, linguistic, or socioemotional developmental delays is not clear (Cornelius, Day, Richardson, & Taylor, 1999). Caffeine, a commonly ingested drug found in coffee, tea, and soft drinks, has not been associated with birth defects or central nervous system dysfunction (Nehlig & Debry, 1997), but prenatal caffeine exposure has been linked to higher heart rates in neonates during both quiet and active sleep (Schuetze & Zeskind, 1998).

A particularly well-studied example of the sensitivity of the fetus to everyday drugs concerns the teratogenicity of ethanol (common alcohol). Jones and his colleagues published two papers in 1973 on children with similar patterns of malformation, growth deficiency, central nervous system dysfunction, and mental retardation: Noting that all the children had alcoholic mothers, this birth defect was termed *fetal alcohol syndrome* (FAS; Jones & Smith, 1973; Jones, Smith, Ulleland, & Streissguth, 1973). These publications stimulated an explosion of research on the effects of alcohol ingestion during pregnancy. FAS is now considered to be the leading cause of mental retardation with a known etiology (Abel, 1998; Connor, Sampson, Bookstein, Barr, & Streissguth, 2001). Like women who smoke, women who drink excessively during pregnancy also experience higher incidences of spontaneous abortions, stillbirths, and preterm deliveries. Diagnostic criteria for FAS include pre- or postnatal growth retardation (less than 10th percentile), central nervous system abnormalities such as microcephaly and seizures, low muscle tone and motor impairments, mental retardation, attention deficits; hyperactivity, and craniofacial abnormalities such as a narrow forehead, small nose and midface, and a low nasal bridge (Roebuck, Mattson, & Riley, 1999; Astley & Claren, 1996). Figure 4.8 shows photographs of a human child and two mouse fetuses, comparing structural abnormalities.

Importantly, Abel (1998) noted that the insidious effects of prenatally ingested alcohol are most clearly associated with alcohol abuse (e.g., having the

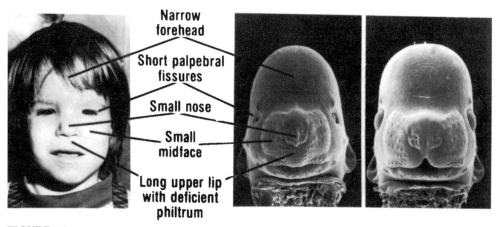

FIGURE 4.8

A child with fetal alcohol syndrome and 14-day-old mouse fetuses from ethanol-treated (*left*) and control (*right*) mothers. (Courtesy K. K. Sulik.)

equivalent of five or more drinks at a time, at least twice a week), but not necessarily with moderate or "social" drinking, although the effects of the latter are controversial. Abel (1998) proposed the term "fetal alcohol abuse syndrome," rather than fetal alcohol syndrome, to communicate to physicians that the detrimental physical, intellectual, and behavioral effects of fetal alcohol syndrome occur reliably only when alcohol is chronically abused. Polygenis and colleagues (1998) underscored this point in a meta-analysis of studies examining the effects of prenatal alcohol exposure on the infant. The results of their analyses showed no relation between moderate alcohol consumption during the first trimester of pregnancy and fetal malformations.

One must not assume, however, that moderate or "social" alcohol consumption during pregnancy has no ill effects on infants. In perhaps the most comprehensive study of prenatal alcohol's effects on some 500 children, Streissguth and her colleagues reported that consumption of an average of two drinks a day or more was related to a seven-point decrement in IQ among 7-year-old children (Streissguth, Barr, & Sampson, 1990). This decrement amounts to about one half a standard deviation, which many would view as clinically significant. In addition, Streissguth, Bookstein, Sampson, and Barr (1995) found that moderate prenatal drinking predicted consistent deficits in vigilance and attention in children from 4 to 14 years of age. In a later study, Connor, Streissguth, Sampson, Bookstein, and Barr (1999) compared 11 adults with FAS or fetal alcohol effects (FAE, which involves significant prenatal exposure to alcohol but without exhibiting the full-blown severity of FAS symptoms) with 9 adult controls with no history of prenatal exposure to alcohol on a variety of auditory and visual attention tasks. Compared to controls, the FAS/FAE group showed significant disruptions in their ability to attend to both visually and auditorially presented stimuli. Clearly, then, researchers and clinicians must take into consideration the potentially debilitating effects of prenatal exposure to alcohol on individual attentional systems.

Prenatal alcohol exposure may also have insidious long-term effects. In an extensive review of the literature on prenatal alcohol exposure, Kelly, Day, and Streissguth (2000) not only reported elevated rates of intellectual deficits in individuals experiencing prenatal alcohol exposure but also reported higher rates of criminal and sexualized behavior, depression, suicide, and parental neglect of children among adults experiencing significant exposure to alcohol before birth. Clearly, there is no one-to-one correspondence between prenatal alcohol exposure and these later difficulties. From a transactional perspective, however, it is likely that such exposure predisposes individuals toward early intellectual, attentional, and social behavior deficits that, if coupled repeatedly with unresponsive or harsh parenting, could in turn lead to more seriously maladaptive life trajectories.

Illicit drugs may also have debilitating and potentially devastating consequences for the unborn, at least in the short term. Scientific documentation of adverse perinatal effects in infants born to cocaine-abusing mothers is now widespread, raising significant concern for the well-being of these infants (Blackwell, Kirkhart, Schmitt, & Kaiser, 1998; Higgins & Katz, 1998; Lester, LaGasse, & Brunner, 1997), particularly as estimates of the prevalence of cocaine abuse among pregnant woman range from 10% to 18% in North American urban areas (Schama, Howell, & Byrd, 1998; Wheeler, 1993). Although the problem may be greatest among poor, inner-city mothers, cocaine use during pregnancy occurs in all sociodemographic groups. Cocaine is thought to inhibit the uptake and metabolism of neurotransmitters such as dopamine, norepinephrine, and serotonin, thereby increasing their levels in the brain (Gonzales & Campbell, 1994). It appears to transfer easily from mother to fetus (Krishna, Levitz, & Dancis, 1993). Epidemiological studies reveal linkages between prenatal cocaine abuse and increased rates of spontaneous abortions, stillbirths, and abruptio placentae (premature separation of the placenta), and reduced gestation lengths by an average of 15 days compared to drug-free controls. In neonates, prenatal cocaine exposure has also been linked to low birth weight, reduced head circumference and body length, high levels of irritability and tremulousness, poor state organization, and increased risk for Sudden Infant Death Syndrome (SIDS; Shama et al., 1998). Fewer researchers have examined longer-term effects, but there is evidence that children prenatally exposed to cocaine are at risk for modest intellectual and language deficits (Angelilli et al., 1994; Azuma & Chasnoff, 1993; Lester, LaGasse, & Seifer, 1998; Nulman et al., 1994; Singer et al., 1994).

Long-term effects are not always detectable, however, as Batshaw and Conlon (1997) concluded. Furthermore, it is difficult to isolate the unique effects of prenatal cocaine exposure on infant development because prenatal cocaine abuse is likely to co-occur with other factors that place infants at developmental risk, including mothers' concomitant abuse of other drugs, continued abuse of the drug after the infant's birth, poverty, parental psychopathology, and parental neglect (Cornelius, Day, Richardson, & Taylor, 1999; Hawley, 1994; Mayes & Truman, 2002). Thus, it is frequently difficult to determine whether developmental delays in infants of drug-abusing mothers are in response to drug use, poverty, parents' mental illness, and/or problems in parenting (Mayes & Bornstein, 1996, 1997a).

Mayes, Bornstein, and their colleagues conducted a systematic series of developmental studies on infants exposed to cocaine or not in utero. Experimenters were always blind to the drug exposure status of the infants. In one study, newborns were evaluated to examine the effects of maternal cocaine use on neurological integrity using the Neonatal Behavior Assessment Scale (NBAS). Cocaine-exposed infants showed significantly depressed performance on the habituation cluster of the NBAS but not on other clusters (Mayes, Granger, Frank, Schottenfeld, & Bornstein, 1993). This finding was followed up. To determine the effect of prenatal cocaine exposure on 3-month infant information-processing, the investigators used an infant-control habituation and novelty responsiveness procedure and tested infants in a developmental assessment using the Bayley Scales of Infant Development. Compared to the non-drug-exposed group, infants exposed prenatally to cocaine were significantly more likely to fail to start the habituation procedure and, for those who did, significantly more likely to react with irritability early in the procedure. The majority of infants in both groups reached the habituation criterion, however, and among those who did there were no significant differences between cocaine and non-cocaine-exposed infants in habituation or in recovery to a novel stimulus. Infants who were cocaine-exposed showed comparatively depressed performance on the motor (PDI) but not the mental (MDI) scales of the Bayley. Differences in reactivity to novelty but not in information-processing between cocaine-exposed and non-cocaine-exposed infants suggest that the effects of prenatal cocaine exposure may be on arousal and attention regulation rather than early cognitive processes (Mayes, Bornstein, Chawarska, & Granger, 1995). Further to this point, the researchers assessed language, play, emotional availability, and acceptance in cocaine-exposed and non-cocaine-exposed children and their mothers at 18 months. Cocaine-exposed youngsters showed no systematic differences in these measures from their demographically similar non-cocaine-exposed peers (Bornstein, Mayes, & Park, 1998). Consequently, the next study investigated relations between cocaine exposure and infants' regulation of arousal in response to novelty. Arousal was operationalized in terms of infant behavioral state, affective expressiveness, and attention to the stimulus. There were no differences between the two groups in baseline behavioral state or affective expression before the presentation of novel stimuli. Compared to the non-cocaine-exposed group, however, infants exposed prenatally to cocaine and other drugs were more likely to exhibit a crying state and to display negative affect on novel stimulus presentations (Mayes, Bornstein, Chawarska, Haynes, & Granger, 1996).

Finally, face-to-face interactions of polydrug-with-cocaine-using mothers and their infants at 3 and 6 months were compared to non-cocaine-but-other-drug-using mothers and mothers who used no drugs during their pregnancy. At 3 and 6 months, polydrug-with-cocaine-using mothers were less attentive to interactions, and polydrug-with-cocaine-using mothers and their infants engaged in fewer dyadic interactions than either non-cocaine or non-drug-using mothers. Compared to 3 months, polydrug-with-cocaine-using mothers at 6 months were less attentive to interactions and more frequently interrupted interactions by looking away, redirecting the infant, or withdrawing, whereas non-cocaine-using and non-drug-using mothers showed no change or an improvement in attentiveness to interactions and a decrease in interruptions. No differences emerged in the interactive behaviors of the infants of polydrug-with-cocaine-using, non-cocaine-using, or non-drug-using mothers. Cocaine use appears to represent a significant risk for diminished parental attentiveness and responsiveness to infants and for diminished interactiveness in infants (Mayes, Feldman, Granger, Haynes, Bornstein, & Schottenfeld, 1997).

However, discontinuing drug use may lead to improvements in infant development. Scherling (1994), for example, found that 40% of the children whose mothers used cocaine pre- and postnatally had IQ scores of 85 or lower (one or more standard deviations below the standardized mean of 100). By contrast, only 15% of children scored at this level when mothers stopped using cocaine postnatally. It would be important to document if mothers who discontinue drug use postnatally show improvements in parenting in comparison to mothers who remain on drugs, and whether such improvements in turn are predictive of improved infant development.

Babies born to heroin addicts are themselves addicted at birth, and such babies begin withdrawal from their addiction within 1 to 3 days after birth. Withdrawal symptoms can be severe and include tremors, irritability, vomiting, diarrhea, perspiration, and sleep disturbances (Wheeler, 1993). Heroin-addicted mothers are frequently weaned onto methadone, a drug that is taken orally and whose effects are less severe. Unfortunately, infants become addicted to methadone as well and go through a similar period of early postnatal withdrawal (Van Baar, Soepatmi, Gunning, & Akkerhuis, 1994). Prenatal heroin or methadone exposure has been linked to low birth weight, and in one study 45% of infants with heroin-abusing mothers were born too small in comparison to 15% of infants of control, non-drug abusing mothers (Glanz & Woods, 1993). Infants prenatally exposed to heroin are also at serious risk for HIV infection because their mothers frequently share needles with other addicts. Like prenatal cocaine exposure, long-range effects of heroin exposure on infant development are not clear-cut, although it may be associated with lower IQ, attentional and behavioral problems, and insecure–disorganized attachment (Batshaw & Conlon, 1997; Rodning, Beckwith, & Howard, 1990).

Like research on prenatal cocaine exposure, studies of the effects of heroin exposure are plagued by methodological shortcomings. Determining the effects of exposure to heroin is complicated by the tendency of drug users to abuse other drugs, have unhealthy lifestyles, and obtain poor prenatal care. In the postnatal period, furthermore, the drug culture has pervasive confounding negative effects on the child's family and community, exposing the child to such well-recognized environmental hazards as poverty, violence, abandonment, homelessness, inadequate health care, and inadequate parenting. Because addiction prevents many mothers from caring for their children adequately, infants born to addicts frequently experience multiple short-term foster placements, separations, and/or repeated moves (Mayes & Truman, 2002).

Tragically, seemingly harmless drugs may have simple to catastrophic consequences for babies even when parents and physicians are acting in the best interests of the mother and fetus and the drugs have no observable effects on the mothers. Simple aspirin may cause blood clotting and bleeding in the fetus (Briggs, Freeman, & Sumner, 1994), for example. Furthermore, in the late 1950s and 1960s, European physicians sometimes prescribed the sedative thalidomide for pregnant women suffering from morning sickness. Those women who took thalidomide during the period when fetal limbs were differentiating (the first trimester) subsequently gave birth to babies with limb buds rather than full limbs. Ingestion of thalidomide at other times did not have such tragic consequences (Newman, 1985). Until 1971, meanwhile, a laboratory-produced female hormone, diethylstilbestrol (DES), was sometimes prescribed for women who had difficulty bringing their pregnancies to term. The insidious nature of DES took about 30 years to make itself known. The effects included a substantially increased risk of rare cervical and vaginal cancers in grown women who were DES exposed before birth. Less frequently, DES led to the formation of cysts in the ducts where sperm are stored, low sperm counts, or abnormally shaped sperm in grown men who were so exposed in utero. Presumably, these effects are attributable to high levels of circulating estrogen at the time when fetal sex organs were differentiating (see the next section). DES daughters also have an increased risk of problem pregnancies and infertility, and even their daughters are thought to be at some risk for cancers—so exposure in the grandmother is visited on the granddaughter! Clearly, prenatal exposure to drugs has both short- and long-term consequences for developing human beings.

Environmental Toxins

The environment also poses toxic hazards for fetuses. Those that have been identified as teratogens include polychlorinated biphenyls (PCBs), DDT, mercury, and lead, and each has adverse implications for development (Farber, Yanni, & Batshaw, 1997; Needleman & Bellinger, 1994). PCBs are synthetic hydrocarbons that were used widely in industry before being banned in the United States in the 1970s. Residues of PCBs are still present in the soil, water, and air, and can be ingested by eating fish from contaminated lakes. Prenatal PCB exposure is linked to lower birth weight, smaller head circumference, shorter gestation, poorer autonomic and reflex functioning, dark pigmentation of nails and gums, and longer term deficits in memory (Jacobson & Jacobson, 1994). Radiation also has detrimental effects, as dramatically demonstrated by the strong correlation between the incidence of mental retardation and microcephaly and the proximity with which pregnant mothers lived to the Hiroshima atomic bomb explosion. The most devastating effects occurred when the fetus was less than 4 months of gestational age at the time of irradiation (Dobbing, 1968).

Teratogens are altogether insidious. The selectivity and time boundedness of their consequences combine to make them difficult to discover because they sometimes do not have easily detectable, systematic, or pervasive effects. Other factors further complicate this story; the so-called dose–effect relation is one. Usually, mechanisms of action are straightforward, such that greater amounts (in dosages or exposures) are associated with greater effects, making the effects of the toxin clear (Needleman & Bellinger, 1994). Sometimes, however, the probability of structural (anatomical) malformation in the organism follows one dose–effect curve, whereas the probability of functional (behavioral) deficit in the same organism follows an altogether different curve. In addition, structural and functional effects may not grow such that the probability of effects is directly related to dose, but instead may show a threshold growth curve (i.e., toxic effects present only after a minimum dose level is exceeded), as is the case with mercury toxicity (Weiss, 1994).

Timing

As the previous discussion illustrates, the impact of endogenous influences on infant development depends on issues of timing and duration (see Chapter 1). Frequently, the effects of exogenous (outside) experiences are time bound by endogenous forces (those arising within the organism). A *sensitive period* is defined as a time during which the organism is especially vulnerable to exogenous influences that alter or modify its structures or functions, often, though not always, in irreversible fashion (Bailey & Bruer, 2001). Sensitive periods are programmed organism–environment interactions that occur between the time a structure or function emerges and the time it reaches its mature state; typically, they encompass the epoch during which the system is undergoing most rapid growth (Bornstein, 1989). The development of each organ, limb, or sensory system is most rapid during a distinct period, and each is most vulnerable to insult or damage during this period. For example, the eyes develop most rapidly in the second month of pregnancy, and so the visual system is especially vulnerable during this period. All of the major organ systems differentiate early in gestation, and therefore as organogenesis slows toward the end of gestation, the likelihood of gross structural malformation as a result of exogenous factors declines. With respect to many teratogens, older fetuses are at much less risk than younger ones (although oxygen deprivation, for example, may be more important to the older fetus). Even if they are present for only a short time, toxins may alter the normal structure or function, or prevent it from emerging at all, whereas those structures or functions that differentiate earlier or later will remain largely unaffected. Consequently, the effects of a toxin depend as much or more on timing than on the nature of the toxin itself: Two different toxins may have very similar effects at the same phase of prenatal life, yet neither may affect development at other stages.

Prenatal experiences may also have immediate effects, as indicated by research on the effects of prenatal exposure to cocaine and heroin on neonatal functioning, and they may show long-term "sleeper" effects such as IQ deficits and behavior problems, as we discussed earlier. Finally, if exposure to teratogens continues beyond the prenatal period, risk to the child may not abate: Parents who smoke place their older infants at risk for bronchitis, pneumonia, and asthma. Exposure to lead at different times in early childhood (before or after the child's second birthday) has different consequences for the child's cognitive functioning. Lead seems to affect visuomotor and visuospatial abilities most strongly if it is ingested in the second and third years of life (Bellinger & Needleman, 1994). Findings such as these make it extremely difficult to pinpoint specific effects of prenatal exposure to teratogens.

Sexual Differentiation

To illustrate the sequences of prenatal development and to relate processes of biological and psychological development to one another, we examine sexual differentiation. Hormones may significantly affect gender-differentiated behaviors and social roles in children and adults. They determine whether the child has male or female genitals, and this affects the way parents and adults treat the child. The sex-differentiated treatment of boys and girls in turn influences the acquisition of gender identity and the development of behavioral sex differences (see Chapter 11). Although these influences may be indirect, prenatal factors clearly contribute significantly to this important aspect of personality development.

The process of sex determination begins at conception. The ovum always contains one X chromosome, because the XX pair characteristic of female cells can only split into two X-bearing gametes, whereas the XY pair characteristic of male cells splits into one X-bearing and one Y-bearing gamete. If an X-bearing sperm fertilizes the ovum it will link with the mother's X to yield a female XX constellation (as in Figure 4.2). If the Y-bearing sperm unites with the X-bearing ovum it yields a male XY pair. A single gene located on the Y chromosome appears to deliver the trigger that activates male development. For some unknown reason, more sperm that carry the X chromosome appear in the average ejaculation, but Y-bearing sperm are more likely to succeed at fertilization (Bean, 1990).

Whether or not the blastocyst has XX or XY sex chromosomes has very little direct impact on the course of early development. In the first $1^1/_2$ months after conception all embryos (regardless of sex) have a similar *primordial gonadal streak*. If the embryo has XX chromosomes, this streak develops into ovaries, whereas if there are XY chromosomes, testes will develop. This development represents the first step in the process of gender differentiation. Thereafter, as far as we know, the sex chromosomes have no direct influence on morphological, physiological, or behavioral development.

Nevertheless, several further stages occur in the development of anatomical sex differences. During the second stage, the recently differentiated gonads assume the formative role. Approximately $1\frac{1}{2}$ to 2 months after conception the testes begin to secrete the hormone testosterone. Testosterone stimulates the development of the *Wolffian duct system*. Another hormone secreted by the testes at this time, *Mullerian Inhibiting Substance* (MIS), discourages the *Mullerian duct system* (the precursor of the internal female reproductive organs) from developing. Both the Wolffian and the Mullerian ducts are present during the first "genderless" month after conception. The presence or absence of MIS and testosterone determines which of the systems will develop and which will shrivel away. In the "natural" course—that is, without testosterone—the Mullerian duct system would develop, female organs would differentiate, and the Wolffian ducts would atrophy.

The external genitalia are formed in the next stage. The presence of testosterone determines that testicles and a penis will develop. In the absence of testosterone, the undifferentiated genitalia will develop into a vulva and clitoris (see Figure 4.9).

In the fourth stage, finally, the testosterone secreted by the male testes suppresses the natural rhythmicity of function in the hypothalamus and the pituitary—the two "master glands" in the hormonal system. If testosterone is not secreted during the second and third trimesters of pregnancy, the pituitary establishes a cyclic pattern of hormone secretion, which is characteristic of females. (The suppression of cyclicity in males is further reinforced by the surge of testosterone that occurs at the onset of puberty.)

It is important to note that each stage of gender development is quite independent of the others. As in the case of toxic substances, therefore, any interference with the normal course of development will have a very specific effect on the fetus, and the nature of the effect will differ depending on its timing. Developments can be prevented from taking place but cannot be reversed. These facts were dramatically and tragically illustrated during the early 1950s, when hormonal treatments were devised to prevent women at risk of miscarrying from doing so. Unexpectedly, some ingested hormones were converted into testosterone, which had a masculinizing effect on female fetuses. When (as was usually the case) the testosterone reached the female fetuses after the third month of conception, the babies were born with normal ovaries (because these had already developed before the hormonal treatment), but they had partially developed Mullerian systems as well as partially developed Wolffian systems, and their external genitalia were similar to those of normal boys.

We can view each of the stages of anatomical sex differentiation as a gate: Whatever developments have already taken place are immune to disruption by later deviations in the developmental process. At each gate, male or female development is equally likely to occur regardless of the path followed up until that point. (When, as a result of a rare genetic defect, the fetal tissues cannot absorb the hormones released by the new testes, for example, the 2-month-old fetus will develop a female Mullerian duct system exactly as if it had ovaries rather than testes.) The key to each gate is not directly related to the previous

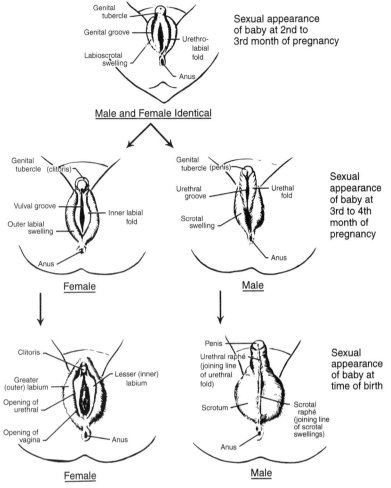

FIGURE 4.9
There are several discrete stages in the development of anatomical sex, each sharply distinguished from the adjacent ones by a series of critical events.

phase—the presence or absence of testosterone and tissues sensitive to it are critical. Furthermore, once a gate is passed it cannot be reopened.

What implications does this developmental course have for our understanding of psychological sex differences? We could speculate that the postnatal determinants of sexual differentiation are analogous to prenatal influences. Perhaps the social experiences that shape the sex-typed behaviors of boys and girls act on an organism that can readily learn to behave in either a masculine or feminine manner. The birth process may close the gates on the anatomical and physiological changes that take place in the intrauterine period, but the path to masculine- and feminine-type behavior may remain open, to be shaped by parental treatment in the first years of life. Alternatively, it may be the case that prenatal sexual differentiation "organizes" the brain in either a masculine or feminine "direction," predisposing the child to be more receptive to and perhaps seek out socialization experiences that accord with his or her prenatal sexual differentiation.

Indeed, the hormones that anatomically masculinize or feminize the fetus may produce slight but distinct behavioral sex differences as well as anatomical

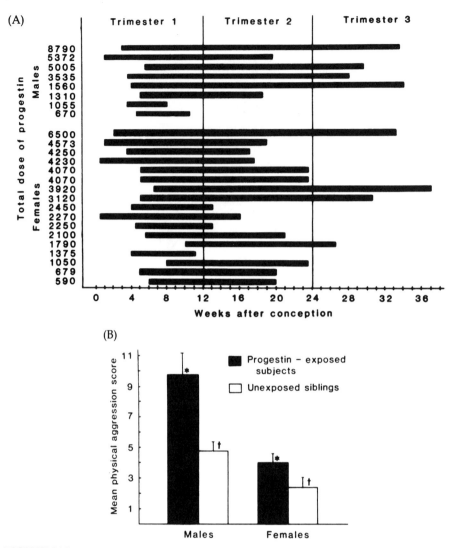

FIGURE 4.10

The effects of maternal progestin ingestion during pregnancy on children's later aggression. (A) Duration, timing, and total dose (in milligrams) of exposure to synthetic progestins in male and female human offspring. (B) Mean physical aggression scores for eight male and seventeen female offspring exposed to synthetic progestins and their unexposed matched siblings. The asterisk marks a significant difference between progestin-exposed and unexposed subjects ($P < .01$); the dagger marks a significant difference between unexposed males and unexposed females. (After Reinisch, 1981. © 1981 by the American Association for the Advancement of Science. Reprinted by permission.)

sex differences (Lustig, 1998). Reinisch (1981), for example, studied the direct influence of prenatal hormones on gender-typical behaviors. Aggression was assessed in girls and boys, about 11½ years of age, whose mothers had taken progestin (a male sex hormone sometimes prescribed to prevent miscarriage) during their pregnancies, as well as in siblings whose prenatal development involved no hormonal treatment. Figure 4.10A shows the duration, timing, and total amount of exposure to synthetic progestin in the treated sample, and Figure 4.10B shows physical aggression scores (based on children's self-reports of how they would act in conflict situations) for exposed children and their unexposed siblings. As expected, boys were more physically aggressive than girls. In addition, prenatally progestin-exposed boys *and* girls were more aggressive than matched siblings unexposed to progestin.

In another study, Hines and Kaufman (1994) examined the play styles and gender of preferred playmates in 3- to 8-year-old children with congenital adrenal hyperplasia (CAH), a genetic recessive disorder in which there is an increase in the production of androgens in the fetus. CAH females are typically born with masculinized genitalia (an enlarged clitoris and some degree of labial fusion), whereas CAH males have normal genitalia. Hines and Kaufman observed the normal sex-typed patterns of rough-and-tumble play among unaffected children (i.e., higher levels of rough-and-tumble play among non-CAH boys than among non-CAH girls). Although there was no difference between CAH and non-CAH girls in rough-and-tumble play, CAH girls were more likely to prefer males as play partners than were non-CAH girls. These studies suggest that prenatal sex hormones can affect gender-specific behaviors just as they can affect physical development.

In most cases, of course, the process of gender differentiation is continuous; chromosomal sex, internal and external reproductive organs, and sex-differentiated socialization are all consistent: The child is XY, has a male reproductive system, is reared as a boy, and develops masculine-type behavior. Biologically determined behavioral predispositions are therefore supplemented or reinforced by social experience so that all potential influences work in concert toward a common goal.

All of this means that the sex hormones have important direct and indirect effects on the development of sex differences (Ellis & Ebertz, 1998). In all likelihood, males and females are biologically predisposed to behave in certain (somewhat different) ways, but these differences are solidified when social experiences render them more distinctive and more dramatic (see Chapter 11). As we have shown in this section, it is very common for socializing factors and biological factors to collaborate, making it impossible and meaningless to say how important each is alone.

Birth and the Neonate

Birth

After approximately 274 days of gestation (at least for first-time, European American middle-income mothers with uncomplicated, spontaneous labor deliveries; Mittendorf, Williams, Berkeley, & Cotter, 1990), some unknown factor causes the mother's pituitary gland to release a hormone (oxytocin) that in turn instigates muscular contraction and expulsion of the fetus from the uterus. The uterus is actually a muscle that expands to accommodate the growing baby. *Labor* involves involuntary uterine contractions, beginning at the top of the muscle, that literally force the baby out. The duration of labor is influenced by a variety of factors, but contractions last 16 to 17 hours on the average for firstborns. Even the birth process appears to reflect cultural context, however. Shostak (1981) wrote a biography of a !Kung woman living in the Kalahari desert of Africa in the middle of the twentieth century. At the time of delivery she observed her mother simply walking a short way out of the village, sitting down against a tree, and giving birth to her brother.

Various dangers must be negotiated during the birth process. The narrowness of the birth canal leaves most newborns looking red and battered, with misshapen heads, but these effects are temporary. More significant are dangers often associated with oxygen deprivation and anesthetic use during delivery. The fetus can experience a lack of oxygen (anoxia) for many reasons:

- The umbilical cord (through which the mother supplies the baby with oxygen) is pinched during a contraction.

- The baby's orientation in the birth canal is unusual.

- The cord has wrapped around the baby.

- The baby is holding on to and squeezing the cord.

Whatever the cause of a deficiency, a baby who is deprived of oxygen for a short amount of time is in little danger; however, deprivation for just a few minutes or more is thought to risk some brain damage because brain cells require continuous oxygenation if they are to survive and function. *Anoxia* has two major effects on the brain. First, unlike other living cells, brain cells are not replaced when they die. Damage to or loss of brain cells ascribable to anoxia is permanent. Second, anoxia leads to a buildup of pressure in the blood system and, because the brain is especially vulnerable, intracranial bleeding. Fortunately, the probability of anoxia is limited because birth is a time of great stress and the infant's metabolic rate and temperature fall during delivery, reducing the need for oxygen. Moreover, minor and even moderate degrees of anoxia typically do not have long-term effects because the brain may develop alternative pathways to overcome early localized handicaps. Severe anoxia, however, places the infant at risk for brain damage and associated adverse consequences, including seizures, cerebral palsy, and impaired cognitive performance. Gray skin color is an immediate indication of anoxia, and this is recorded in the Apgar assessment of the newborn (later discussed).

The pain of childbirth has prompted some women to make use of anesthesia at some point during the process of labor and delivery. Anesthesia use at this time has been controversial, with some researchers reporting that infants whose mothers used anesthetics fare worse on a range of infant tests, and are less active and alert during interactions with mothers, than are infants whose mothers did not use anesthesia (Brackbill, 1979; Hollenbeck, Gewirtz, Sebris, & Scanlon, 1984). This is a complicated and sensitive issue, because fetal risk and maternal pain need to be considered simultaneously in decisions regarding whether to administer or withhold anesthesia during labor and delivery. It is important to note that the differences between infants of anesthetized and nonanesthetized mothers are not large, and are most evident only during the first few days postpartum (Maurer & Maurer, 1988; Rosenblith, 1992). Happily, problems associated with obstetric medication are becoming less frequent because of the popularity of natural childbirth (for example, the Lamaze method). In addition, newer local anesthetic methods such as the epidural block (Fields & Wall, 1993) appear to be effective in reducing labor pain without adverse effects on the infant (Albaladejo, Bouaziz, & Benhamou, 1998).

Babies are normally born in a vertex, or head-first, "presentation." There is a small variety of alternative presentations, the most extreme of which are breech (feet or buttocks first) or transverse (hammock position). Babies in these orientations are often delivered by cesarean sections, which now account for 20% to 25% of all births in the United States. On average, the newborn measures 20 inches (51 cm) and weighs 6 to 9 pounds (2,700 to 4,100 grams). At conception, the zygote is the size of two microscopic germ cells; by the end of the first post-natal year the child has tripled in birth weight and added 10 inches in height. The rapid rate of growth and differentiation achieved in this short period will never recur at any other point in the life cycle.

An argument can be made that birth represents a transition in a process of continuing development. The organism before and after birth does not usually deviate from the normal, genetically maturing schedule; central nervous system function and motor behavior are not discretely altered by the birth process, and at a more molecular level, physiological characteristics such as the infant's unique blood chemistry emerge slowly over the entire course of gestation. Like the fetus, the newborn is dependent on others. For example, newborn infants are unable even to maintain their own body temperature, lacking both the insulating material (subcutaneous fat) and the functional neural capacity to control body temperature. Newborns depend on caregivers to keep the temperature of their environments relatively constant so that their own limited capacities to modulate body temperature are not taxed. Undoubtedly, however, birth is also an event. With incredible suddenness, circulation and respiration are for the first time up to the child, and the newborn, unlike the fetus, is subject to hitherto unknown imbalance, deprivation, discomfort, and stimulus variety.

Preterm Birth

The typical or term infant is delivered about 40 weeks after the mother's last men-strual period. However, among the 4 million new births each year in the United States, approximately 11% are born too early and 7% are born too small (Centers for Disease Control and Prevention, 1999, May; Ventura, Martin, Curtin, & Matthews, 1995). An infant is considered preterm if born before 37 weeks gesta-tional age, and of low birth weight if born under 2,500 grams (about 5.5 lbs.). Not surprisingly, gestational age and birth weight are highly correlated.

Premature birth is a major cause of developmental delay (Friedman & Sigman, 1992; Hack, Klein, & Taylor, 1995), and rates of premature birth are unlikely to decrease. In fact, the premature birth rate in the United States in-creased 17% between 1981 and 1995 (Ventura et al., 1995), a direct result of ongoing technological advances in neonatal care that promote the viability of very small infants, that is, their ability to survive outside the womb. Serious health problems and developmental delays are more pronounced among very preterm (less than 32 weeks gestational age) and very low birth weight (less than 1,500 grams at birth) babies, who account for between 14% and 15% of all preterm, low-birth-weight births in the United States. Preterm, low birth-weight babies have average hospital stays of 45 to 50 days, and between one third and one half experience one or more rehospitalizations during the first 3 years of life (McCormick, 1992).

Babies may be born preterm for a number of reasons (Friedman & Sigman, 1992). First, abnormalities in the mother's reproductive system may prevent her from carrying the pregnancy to term. Multiple births (e.g., twins) also place excessive demands on the mother, and so many multiple births are preterm. In addition, the mother's (or fetus's) health may be such that the birth needs to be induced early to alleviate excessive stress. Second, the mother's reproductive system may be immature or may not have had sufficient time to recover from a previous pregnancy; young teen mothers are at greater risk of delivering preterm babies (Cooper, Leland, & Alexander, 1995). Third, as discussed earlier, conditions that adversely affect general health—including poverty, malnutrition, inadequate medical care, and unhealthy lifestyles—are associated with preterm delivery.

Babies who are marginally preterm often face little danger. They may be hospitalized briefly for observation or to gain weight and are then discharged. Weight gain is an issue for all preterm infants because they lack even the modest layers of fat that help insulate the baby from excess cold. A variety of medical complications can arise, however, when the degree of prematurity is more marked. For example, *respiratory distress syndrome* (RDS) is associated with infants born less than 32 weeks of gestational age (Verma, 1995). These babies often lack surfactin—a soapy substance that coats the lungs and facilitates the exchange of oxygen from the air. To assist them in breathing, preterm babies are placed in incubators in which the concentration of oxygen is much higher than in the normal environment. The actual concentration has to be titrated carefully to avoid producing *retinopathy of prematurity*, a disorder produced by excess oxygen that involves damage to the retinas, causing permanent blindness. Very young preterm babies can also develop a condition known as *bronchopulmonary dysplasia*, or chronic lung disease, identified by a thickening and inflammation of the walls of the lung and a reduced airway, resulting in a significant decrease in the amount of oxygen the infant can inhale (Vanhatalo, Ekblad, Kero, & Erkkola, 1994). Very preterm, very low birth-weight babies are also at significant risk for brain complications, such as intraventricular hemorrhage (bleeding into the ventricles) and periventricular leukomalacia (necrosis of the brain tissue that encircles the ventricles), both of which are associated with significant developmental delay (Bernbaum & Batshaw, 1997). For a number of reasons, therefore, the immature preterm infant may need close supervision in a hospital for the first weeks or months of life.

Bernbaum and Batshaw (1997) noted that the significant medical and technological developments in neonatal intensive care have led to significant increases in the survival rates of preterm, low birth-weight infants. Today, over 90% of infants with birth weights under 2,500 grams, two thirds of infants born between 750 and 1,000 grams, and one third of infants born between 500 and 750 grams survive. These rates contrast dramatically with the 1960 survival rate for all preterms, which was less than 50%. However, with increased survival rates come increased concern about the long-term prognosis and quality of life of these infants, especially those born before 32 weeks gestational age. Very preterm, very low birth-weight infants are significantly more likely than are term infants to have lower IQs and developmental and learning disabilities (Hack et al., 1995; McCormick & Workman-Daniels, 1996). In the United States, prematurity and low birth weight are linked to socioeconomic disadvantage (Paneth, 1995), and thus many preterm, low birth-weight infants are at medical and environmental risk. It is important that, in the absence of clear organic bases for abnormal development (e.g., blindness and brain damage), the degree to which preterm babies develop well or poorly appears in large part to be a function of the caregiving environment the baby encounters after discharge. Preterm babies who grow up in enriching, supportive homes do better, whereas those in more deprived environments develop more poorly (Bradley et al., 1994; Goldberg, & DiVitto, 2002; Sameroff, 1996).

TABLE 4.1 CRITERIA AND SCORING OF THE APGAR TEST

Score	A *Appearance (color)*	P *Pulse (heart rate)*	G *Grimace (reflex irritability)*	A *Activity (muscle tone)*	R *Respiration (respiratory effort)*
0	Blue, pale	Absent	No response	Limp	Absent
1	Body pink, extremities blue	Slow (below 100)	Grimace	Some flexion of extremities	Slow, irregular
2	Completely pink	Rapid (over 100)	Cry	Active motion	Good, strong cry

Infant Examinations

At about 1 minute and 5 minutes after birth, newborns in most American hospitals take their first tests, administered to determine the need for intervention to establish normal functioning. The *Apgar*, named after its originator Virginia Apgar (1953), rates babies as 0, 1, or 2 on each of five dimensions, easy to remember because of the anagram: Appearance, Pulse, Grimace, Activity, and Respiration. The criteria for each score are listed in Table 4.1, and Figure 4.11 shows two distributions of Apgar scores: the percentage of infants in a sample of nearly 28,000 babies achieving each possible score and the rate of neonatal mortality at 1 month in this same sample. As can be seen from these graphs, 75% of newborn babies scored 7 or better on the Apgar, and those who score 2 or lower were at significant risk (Apgar & James, 1962; Self & Horowitz, 1979).

The Apgar is only one of several tests designed for very young babies. It is probably the best known because it is administered right in the delivery room, but it is obviously only a gross screening instrument. Other tests have been developed to evaluate more thoroughly and systematically the status of newborns. The *Dubowitz Test* (Dubowitz & Dubowitz, 1981) is used to estimate the infant's gestational age. It scores babies on a variety of neurological items (including posture and reflexes) and external characteristics (including skin quality and gross morphology). The *Neonatal Behavioral Assessment Scale* (NBAS; Brazelton & Nugent, 1995), evaluates the baby's neurological intactness on 18 reflex items and the baby's interactional repertoire on 27 items that relate to information processing, motoric capacities, ability to control state, and response to stress.

Some important general issues surround newborn and infant testing. How infant state affects performance is one: Newborns have distinct drowsy and alert states that can affect infant performance substantially (Chapter 5). Which test or test session represents the baby best? Under what circumstances should we score the baby? Do we want to assess average or optimal performance? In what order should items be administered? Is it better to assess spontaneous or elicited behavior? The newborn is also a highly labile organism, as discussed in Chapter 3, and consequently the reliability of most newborn assessments is abysmal. Screening tests are nonetheless valuable for identifying babies who are in need of special attention, care, help, or practice. Different goals motivate developers of tests for older infants (as opposed to newborns), and in Chapter 7 we describe the most frequently administered of these tests, the Bayley and the Užgiris–Hunt tests (see Chapter 7).

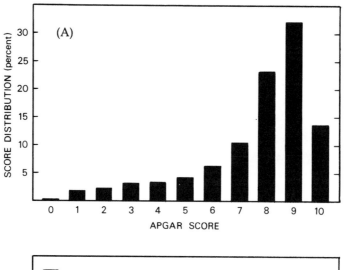

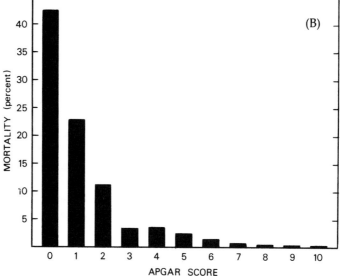

FIGURE 4.11

These data tell us about the range and validity of Apgar scores in a large population. (A) The percentage of children in a sample of nearly 28,000 who received each Apgar score. As can be seen, most newborns scored between 7 and 10 on the Apgar scale. (B) The mortality rate in the same sample at 1 month of age. The data show that infants who scored 0, 1, or 2 on the Apgar were at increased risk during early infancy. (After Apgar & James, 1962.)

Reflexes

Although human neonates certainly appear helpless, they are natively capable of a small number of integrated and organized—if limited—behaviors. Many of these *reflexes* are biologically meaningful in that they suggest survival value or adaptive significance. Reflexes are simple, unlearned stimulus–response sequences common to all members of a species, and reflexes are traditionally divided into three groups.

The *approach reflexes*, concerned with intake, include breathing and a subcomplex encompassing rooting, sucking, and swallowing (Sheppard & Mysak, 1984).

Rooting (shown in Figure 4.12A) occurs in response to stimulation around the mouth; it involves tracking, searching, and head redirection toward the source of stimulation, and it typically concludes with sucking. Clearly, rooting is of major significance to newborns because it allows infants to locate and ingest food.

A second major class of reflexes is concerned with *avoidance*. This group includes coughing, sneezing, and blinking, as well as muscle withdrawal (Figure 4.12B). A general characteristic of these reflexes is their all-or-nothing quality; if elicited, they occur in full-blown form.

A third class of reflexes, categorized under the nondescript term *other*, seems to have only vestigial meaning. In other words, phenomena like the palmer grasp, Babinski toe fanning, and Moro response may have been important at an earlier point in human history but continue now without obvious meaning. For example, the Moro reflex (Figure 4.12C) is the tendency to swing the arms wide and bring them together again in the midline (as if around the body of a care-giver). This reflex is elicited by a loud sound or when the baby suddenly falls or loses support. Similarly, the palmer grasp (Figure 4.12D) tightens when what-ever the baby is holding is suddenly raised; this grasp allows babies to support their own weight—briefly. These reflexes are still present in many nonhuman primate newborns (Figure 4.12D), helping such creatures maintain proximity to their mothers by clinging to body hair.

The regularity of reflex function in human infants provides pediatricians and neurologists with a means of assessing normal development; reflexes are involved in every major neonatal examination and screening test. Figure 4.13 shows the emergence and disappearance of a variety of reflexes before and after birth. Evidently, most reflexes develop before birth and are only present for 4 to 8 months postnatally. Unlike those reflexes, like rooting, which have obvious survival value, reflexes that have only vestigal value are believed to have their origins in the deepest and most primitive parts of the central nervous system. So long as these neurological structures dominate function, the reflexes endure. As higher cortical processes come into play, however, they appear to inhibit subcor-tical structures and thus prevent the expression of reflexes. Because the disap-pearance of some reflexes may reflect the emergence of higher cortical function, their decline is usually taken as an index of normal neurological development (see Thelen, 1984). Another developmental implication of reflex function is para-doxical: Newborns may be capable of certain activities, like those associated with swimming, which are impossible for slightly older infants.

Physical Growth and Motor Development

Perhaps because physical growth is so easy to observe and to quantify, it was a very early subject of study among individuals interested in human development. Figure 4.14 shows Count Phillippe de Montbeillard's observations of his own son's physical development; these data were gathered in the mid-eighteenth century, but they are still relatively accurate. For example, de Montbeillard's insightful decision to plot height gain over age, and not simply height, shows just how great growth is during infancy relative to all other times (including puberty).

Some principles of physical growth are sometimes considered as topics of lesser psychological import because the data are merely "descriptive." However, the story of physical growth is significant because the data provide important normative guidelines for human development; the physical characteristics of

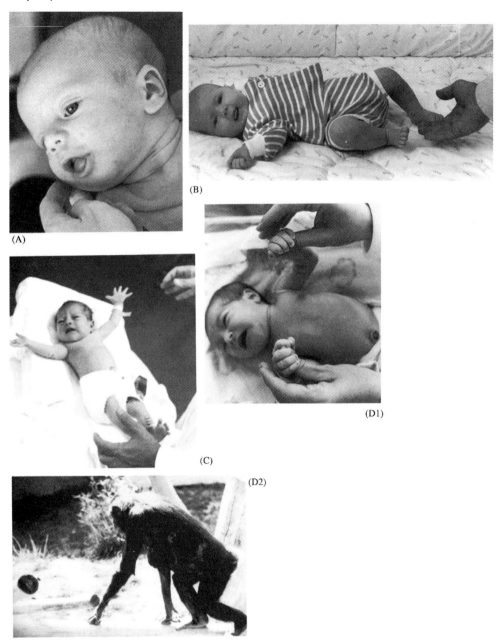

FIGURE 4.12

(*A*) The rooting reflex: A gentle touch on the cheek from breast or finger will orient the baby, mouth open and lips pursed, ready to suck. (*B*) An avoidance reflex. (*C*) The Moro reflex: When they are dropped suddenly, babies throw their arms upward and then together. (Courtesy of T. B. Brazelton.) (*D*) The palmer grasp: When an object is placed in the baby's palm the hand reacts by gripping (*D1*), sometimes so powerfully in the first hours that the baby can temporarily support his or her entire weight. Nonhuman babies, here a pygmy chimpanzee (*D2*), hold on to their mothers by grasping and clinging to ventral hair. (Courtesy of H. Papoušek.)

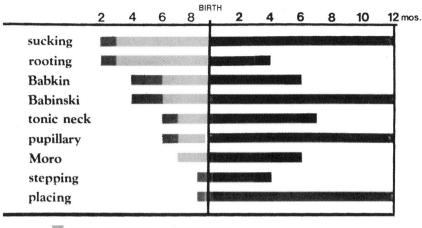

FIGURE 4.13

The variable appearance and disappearance of prenatal and postnatal reflexes. Some reflexes, like sucking and rooting, appear very early in prenatal development, whereas others, like stepping and placing, appear much later. Some reflexes, like rooting and stepping, disappear early in postnatal development, whereas others, like sucking and placing, persist well past the first year of life.

the child have implications for the child's development in many other psychological domains; and, studies of physical growth give evidence of important general principles of development. We now consider some of these principles, particularly as they bear on infancy studies.

A first general principle of physical growth is *directionality*. Whether the subject of study is anatomical growth, complexity of function, or voluntary control, development seems to follow several characteristic directions. The first is that development proceeds *cephalocaudally*, that is, from "head to tail." The visual system reaches anatomical maturity earlier than do the legs, sight reaches maturity earlier than does locomotion, and humans have voluntary visual control much earlier in life than they begin to walk. Body proportions change in this way too, as shown earlier in Figure 4.4. Second, development proceeds *proximodistally*, that is from the center of the body outward. Third, development typically proceeds in a *mass-to-specific* fashion, that is, from large muscle groups to fine ones. Fourth, development frequently involves a *hierarchical integration*; that is, simple skills develop separately and then become elaborated and more complex through mutual integration.

A second general principle of psychological development that derives from studies of physical growth is the *independence of systems*. Figure 4.15 plots the rates of growth for three major systems, illustrating that components of the human being are differentially developed at or soon after birth and grow along very different courses through the first year or two of life. By age 2 years, for example, the nervous system has achieved more than one half of its adult status, whereas physical characteristics of the body have developed to less than one third of their eventual goal, and, of course, secondary sexual characteristics have hardly developed at all.

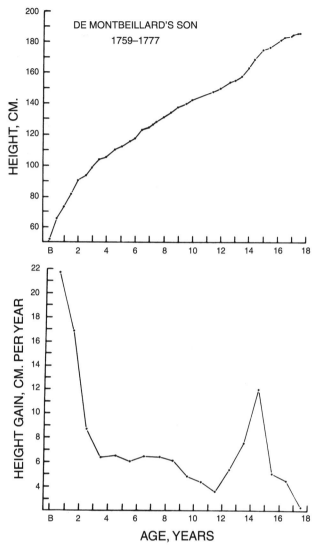

FIGURE 4.14
The growth of Count Philippe de Montbeillard's son from birth to the age of 18 years. The upper graph shows the height reached at each age; the lower graph shows the annual increments in height. (After Tanner, 1978. © 1978 by Open Books Publishing Ltd. Reprinted by permission.)

A third general principle of physical growth and development is *canalization*. The evolutionary biologist Waddington (1962) observed that life often involves the narrowing or restricting of alternatives so that one is selected in preference to others. In this view, genetic processes can correct some deflections so that phenotypic targets can be achieved despite nonoptimal environmental conditions. We can observe this phenomenon in the domain of physical development, although, again, it may apply in other realms too. The correlation between height at 2 years and at 20 years is very high. In this realm there is good predictability and, psychologically speaking, extraordinary stability. One case study illustrates the robustness of this phenomenon (Prader, Tarrer, & von Harnack, 1963). During the first year the child in question was growing normally, but just before his first

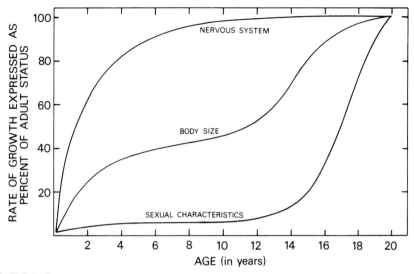

FIGURE 4.15

This figure shows that different bodily systems grow toward mature status at different rates. In infancy, the nervous system is highly developed, body size is less developed, and secondary sexual characteristics are least developed of all.

birthday the child was ill for approximately one year. During this time the child fell behind his predicted growth pattern. Following recovery, however, the child returned to his trajectory so that by his fourth birthday he was again well within the range of earlier projections. This "catch-up" when an impediment to growth is removed illustrates the principle of canalization.

Whether equivalent kinds of recovery occur in other psychological domains is an underresearched question. However, Wilson (1978) studied the canalization of intelligence in relation to preterm birth and low birth weight. Specifically, he observed identical twins who had unequal birth weights, one normal and one considerably below normal. Small babies are usually at risk for poor cognitive outcome, as we discussed earlier, but Wilson found that during development the common genotype overcame the perinatal inequality and aligned the twins: By 6 years of age their IQs were extremely highly related. Thus, catch-up from early deficit seems also to occur in the cognitive sphere.

A fourth general principle concerns the interplay between *norms* and *individual differences*. Norms are handy descriptions rather than explanations; they represent likely outcomes rather than actual or even ideal outcomes. Many physical, biological, and psychological characteristics are typically distributed in a statistically normal fashion. Consider physical height. Very few adults are either 4 or 7 feet tall; many more are 5 and 6 feet tall, and most are in between. The average may represent the distribution of some structure or function, but the range and form of the distribution are critically informative about the structure or function as well. For example, the age at which infants first walk or talk has enormous psychological import, but the true range is extraordinary, especially when considered as a proportion of the child's age. Some children first walk at 10 months, others at 18 months; some children say their first word at 9 months, others at 29 months. A given child's performance may be meaningful only for the extreme cases, however. Finally, adults all generally walk and talk sufficiently well, suggesting that the exact onset of walking or talking may be less meaningful in the long run than anxious parents and relatives often think.

Developmental variation arises in many different ways. Consider three examples: Different individuals may follow different developmental rates but eventually reach the same mature level of structure or function; different individuals may follow the same rate of development but cease growing at different levels of structure or function; and different individuals may follow different rates and reach different final developmental levels. These diverse trajectories may have many causes, some much easier to influence than others.

At birth as well as through the course of the first years, infants in affluent Western countries tend to be healthier, heavier, and longer than infants in less affluent countries. These differences presumably reflect the effects of prenatal and postnatal nutrition and care, maternal health and education, and genetic variation. By the end of the first year of postnatal life the average American toddler weighs about 20 pounds (9 kg) and is about 30 inches long (76 cm). Furthermore, within affluent countries such as the United States, children born into low socioeconomic statuses grow more slowly than those from high socioeconomic statuses, and they do not reach equivalent levels of height and weight (Schroeder, Martorell, Rivera, Ruel, & Habicht, 1995; Tanner, 1990). Clearly, adequate nutrition is critical for normal physical development.

Motor Development

Motor development is as dramatic as physical growth. Table 4.2 shows Bayley's (1993) normative findings of monthly motor accomplishments in infants between birth and 30 months. The infant's ability to coordinate physical movement develops impressively in the first $2\frac{1}{2}$ years. Movements seem uncontrolled for the first few months, but coordination develops rapidly thereafter. From the newborn, unable to roll over from the position in which originally placed, emerges the toddler who is increasingly deft (so much so, in fact, that parents quickly learn that they must constantly monitor their 2-year-olds). Certainly, this schedule of development depends on the growth of limbs and muscles sufficiently strong and organized to act in a coordinated fashion, but we can only presume a simultaneous development of neural control over muscle movement.

The sequence and coordination of motor development depend on both physical maturation and experience. Two related neurological systems direct motor activity (including reflexes): The *pyramidal system* controls precise, rapid, and skilled movements of the extremities (such as walking), and the *extrapyramidal system* controls posture and coordination. As these systems develop the infant becomes able to move about and manipulate objects. The neuromuscular systems begin developing early in the second trimester of pregnancy, and of course the child's own movement, even as a fetus, may feed back to enhance development. Several principles of such brain–behavior interrelations are described in the next chapter.

Despite these regularities of psychomotor development, it is not the case that infants automatically accomplish more mature and complicated motor feats as they mature physically. Experiences also influence the course of development, even in spheres of life thought to be largely biological. For example, Adolph

TABLE 4.2 REPRESENTATIVE ITEMS FROM THE BAYLEY SCALES
OF INFANT DEVELOPMENT

Mental Development Index	Psychomotor Development Index
Approximate Age When Observed (Months)	
1 Habituates to rattle	Thrusts arms in play
2 Follow ring in an arc	Holds head erect and steady for 15 seconds
3 Inspects own hands	Sits with support
4 Picks up cube	Sits alone momentarily
5 Looks for fallen spoon	Uses whole hand to grasp small pellet
6 Cooperates in games	Attempts to raise self to sit
7 Puts cube in cup	Rotates trunk while sitting alone
8 Turns pages of book	Walks with help
9 Pats toy in imitation	Stands alone
10 Puts six beads in box	Throws ball
11 Closes round container	Walks up stairs with help
12 Places one peg in board repeatedly	Walks backward
14 Points to two pictures	Stands on left foot with help
16 Says eight different words	Uses pads of fingertips to grasp pencil
18 Points to five pictures	Uses hand to hold paper in place
20 Uses a three-word sentence	Jumps from bottom step/stair
22 Displays verbal comprehension	Stands alone on right foot
24 Builds tower of eight cubes	Stands alone on left foot
26 Imitates vertical and horizontal strokes on paper	Walks on tiptoe for four steps
28 Discriminates pictures	Laces three beads
30 Understands concept of one	Imitates hand movements

(After Bayley, 1993.)

(1997) found that learning to locomote in infancy involves a complex reciprocal relation among maturation, perception, and experience. Although there were the expected achievements in locomotion with age (i.e., from crawling to walking), infants' ability to negotiate a challenging motor task, such as descending a sloped surface, was not automatic. Infants appear to take into account properties of the surfaces, such as the degree of slant, and explore different methods of locomotion before settling on a specific locomotive mode (e.g., crawling backward) to descend. Furthermore, once infants began walking they had to learn all over again how to descend the same slopes. Competent execution of motor systems is thus based on a dynamic interplay of biological, perceptual, and experiential influences.

As we mentioned in Chapter 1, systems theory maintains that growth in one sphere of life will have an impact on others; so psychomotor development affects multiple aspects of psychological growth (Thelen, 2000, 2001; Thelen & Spencer, 1998). Consider the development of the capacity to grasp with both hands an object offered at the midline. At the very least, this skill requires the coordination not only of fine motor movements within one hand, but of the two arms, two hands, and two eyes. The development of control over motor behaviors also makes possible the expression of intentional social- and object-related activities. Therefore, simple developments that seem primarily motoric have major implications for aspects of cognitive and social growth.

Research we previewed in Chapter 1 by Bertenthal and Campos (1990) illustrates the surprisingly formative role that motor development can play in perceptual and emotional development. It has long been believed that human infants are innately afraid of heights. This belief stems from research with animals of various species tested on the visual cliff—a table designed to create the illusion of a possible fall (see Figure 6.1). However, research with human infants suggests that babies may not innately fear heights. Although infants give evidence that they discriminate between the deep and shallow sides of the cliff at 2 months of age, it seems that they do not become afraid of height until they are able to crawl on their own, regardless of the age at which they begin to do so. Locomotion may trigger the onset of fearfulness because crawling allows the infant to calibrate distances more accurately than before; whereas the prelocomotor infant may be able to tell that one object is closer than another, the infant may not be able to tell how much closer one is than another. If this is so, the human infant may be able to see depth but may not be able to gauge depth accurately until he or she begins to move. There are other possible explanations for this finding. Crawling may merely allow infants to experience more falls and hence lead them to consider heights dangerous. Or, parents may react to near falls with intense emotion, helping the infant learn to fear heights, the way some infants learn to fear animals. Thus, there is ample evidence that motor development affects other psychological functions, clearly demonstrating the interrelatedness of developmental processes that were discussed in Chapter 1.

Finally, the baby's psychomotor development has an impressive impact on parent–infant interaction. When a baby first reaches deliberately, rolls over, stands upright, or walks, it is the occasion for joy and for telephone calls to grandparents. These achievements also signal all sorts of cognitive and social changes at home we have alluded to earlier. Change, as well as rate of change, are the impressive factors. So is the average child's physical energy. A popular—if apocryphal—anecdote that circulates among parents holds that, at the height of his physical prowess, the Olympic athlete Jim Thorpe was asked to do everything that a toddler did, exactly the way the toddler did it. As the story goes, Thorpe gave up exhausted after a few hours, while the toddler continued blithely for the rest of the day.

Summary

Physical and motor growth in infancy are impressive because they are such evident developments and because change is extremely rapid at this point in the life cycle. Developments in these spheres also have important implications for psychological development.

In this chapter we discussed genetic contributions to early growth and how they are assayed. Students of prenatal development distinguish three stages of growth (the periods of the zygote, embryo, and fetus) and recognize distinct sensitive periods during which prenatal experiences are especially influential. Perinatal tests like the Apgar, Dubowitz, and Brazelton are used to assess the status of the newborn and the degree to which newborns are prepared for extrauterine life. All emphasize important reflexes and their neurological indications. Milestones of motor development have always been of interest to parents, but contemporary scientists have tended to ignore them. However, the accomplishments of motor development have important implications for perceptual, cognitive, emotional, and social development; moreover, the principles of physical and motor development, such as directionality, independence of systems, canalization, and individual differences, provide models and metaphors for infant development in other spheres.

5

Nervous System Development in Infancy

❖

- What is the significance of states of arousal in infancy, and how does their organization change with age?
- Why does heart rate vary, and how can close study of this variation inform our understanding of infancy?
- How and why do neurons, dendrites, axa, synapses, and neural networks develop pre- and postnatally?
- What can we learn about development and individual infants by monitoring electrical activity in the brain?
- Define heart rate, vagal tone, EEG, and ERP and illustrate what each can tell us.
- Are neural cells pluripotent or specialized in function?
- How is the brain susceptible to experience?
- Describe the structural and functional development of the sensory systems.

Cycle, State, Cell, and Brain

Anatomical, physiological, and psychological growth are all dramatic in infancy, but because of its infinite complexities and astonishing ability to regulate and integrate information, nervous system development is especially noteworthy. Consider, for example, that the adult human brain contains approximately 100 billion neurons. Because new neurons generated after birth are relatively few, an average of 250,000 new cells must be generated every minute prenatally, although of course the rate is not constant across the prenatal period. In the space of approximately 9 months, a single fertilized egg evolves into a complex, self-regulating, and differentiated nervous system, and in an additional 9 to 12 months develops into a sentient child capable of intelligent feelings, thoughts, and actions.

In large measure, the diverse and remarkable accomplishments of infancy reflect impressive developments in the nervous system. However, it is difficult to establish causal relations between brain and behavior for several reasons. First, brain–behavior relations are usually bidirectional, such that genetically predetermined brain development may permit new behaviors that in turn generate new interactions with the environment that then influence brain development. Consequently, neurological growth inevitably reflects the dynamic interplay of genetic influences and selected (including self-generated) experiences. Second, much of our knowledge in this field derives from studies of nonhuman organisms, and we need to be cautious about generalizing to human beings. Third, behavior typically has multiple causes. Nevertheless, it would be surprising if development were not reflected by parallel changes in the "software" (functions) and "hardware" (structure) of the brain.

The nervous system, comprising all the neural tissues in the human body, can be considered from either a structural or a functional perspective. From the structural point of view, the nervous system may be divided into central and peripheral components: The major central components are the brain and spinal cord; peripheral components include the nerve fibers that connect the receptors and effectors to the brain. From the functional point of view, the nervous system may be divided into somatic and autonomic components: The somatic division comprises voluntary, conscious functions, and the autonomic division is concerned with visceral, automatic, and nonvoluntary processes. In this chapter we review major developments in the autonomic and somatic nervous systems from structural and functional points of view. When considering autonomic nervous system (ANS) development in the first section of the chapter, we focus particularly on states of arousal and heart rate as key psychophysiological indicators of function. When discussing central nervous system (CNS) development in the second section, we focus on different levels of neural and brain development and on aspects of early sensory development. As in Chapter 4, our goal is not to be comprehensive but to introduce select and meaningful physiological events that underpin or accompany important psychological events.

Autonomic Nervous System Development

The fetus and the newborn are physiological organisms; much of their functioning, as we have already learned, is survival oriented but not yet under conscious or voluntary control. Moreover, we have alluded to continuities as well as discontinuities between the pre- and postnatal periods. In considering ANS function in the infant, we first consider the cycles and states that overtly characterize infants, and next discuss the development of heart rate and its applications in understanding infancy. The first topic underscores the growth of self-regulation; the second highlights an important "window to the infant mind."

Cycles and States

On first observation, newborn activity appears to be spontaneous, extremely disorganized, and sporadic. When watching a new baby, even for a short time, one sees nearly constant movement of mouth, eyes, hands, and feet without apparent purpose; watching over a longer period allows one to observe apparently random and unpredictable shifts from sleep to alertness. Newborns are not quite so incoherently changeable, however: Closer and consistent inspection shows that fetuses and infants are more or less regular in many ways and that many different systems cycle in detectable patterns or rhythms. Many rhythms seem to be natural or endogenous, perhaps based on molecular "pacemaker cells." In short, apparent irregularity is only apparent, and underlying regularity characterizes much of infant behavior. How?

Involuntary infant activities—that is, infants' naturally occurring or spontaneous behaviors—are organized at fast, medium, and slow rhythms that span several orders of magnitude. Activities that occur regularly at high frequencies, perhaps once or more per second, cycle fast. Heartbeats, breathing, and sucking exemplify such fast biological rhythms that maintain life, and kicking and rocking illustrate fast behavioral stereotypes that have been linked not only to neuromuscular maturation, as was formerly believed, but also to dynamic patterns of interactions between CNS inputs, properties of the muscles and joints, gravity, and the infant's developmental status (Thelen, 1993). General body movements cycle at intermediate periodicities on the order of a minute or two; they may be seen before birth and continue to cycle at the same rate postnatally. In a short-term longitudinal study, Groome, Swiber, et al. (1999) demonstrated stable individual differences in the rates of general body movements between the late fetal period (38 weeks gestational age) and 4 weeks after birth. Thus, individual differences in activity levels of very young infants are evident even before birth. States of waking, quiet sleep (no rapid eye movements), and active sleep (coincident with rapid eye movements) are low-frequency phenomena that have cycles on the order of one or more hours in length (Papoušek, 1996). Thus, by observing infant activity over extended periods it is possible to detect underlying regular rhythms in seemingly random activity. What we see in the newborn at any one time is the simultaneous and independent cycling of several complex rhythms. No wonder outward appearance gives the impression of chaotic randomness!

The coordination and integration of different periodicities is thought by some researchers to constitute a major achievement of neurological organization (e.g., Prechtl, 1974). These rhythmic patterns may also have important implications for language development and social interaction (Chapters 9 and 11) because rhythmic pauses in babies' sucking and stages of the sleep–wake cycle help adults know when to initiate play and caregiving (Kaye, 1982). Thus many sophisticated infant activities could have their roots in prenatal and early postnatal cyclic behaviors.

State of arousal is a significant infant characteristic because newborns shift frequently among states of sleep, drowsiness, alertness, distress, and activity (Brazelton & Nugent, 1995; Halpern, MacLean, & Baumeister, 1995). Building on classic work in the 1950s and 1960s, Thoman (1990) defined ten behavioral states of arousal (see Table 5.1) that could be distinguished consistently by trained observers and that reflect reliable or stable dimensions of individuality. The distribution of time among states differed depending on whether the infants were alone or with their mothers: Babies were usually with their mothers when awake, and they were asleep when alone. The percentages of time spent in the different states are presented in the last column of Table 5.1. The degree of stability over time differed among infants in the study, and these differences later proved to have great importance: The four infants whose behavior (defined by the amount of time they spent in each state) was least stable over time all showed greater levels of medical or behavioral dysfunction, indicating that the quality of early central nervous system functioning is predictive of the quality of later behavioral organization (Thoman, 1990).

It may take months to establish a predictable schedule of states. Although Thoman (1990; Thoman & Whitney, 1990) found reasonable stability in infant

TABLE 5.1 PRIMARY BEHAVIORAL STATES

State	Characteristics	Percent of Time in This State When Alone
Awake		
Alert	Eyes open, bright, and attentively scanning	6.7
Nonalert waking	Eyes open but dull and unfocused Motor activity often high; isolated fussing is possible	2.8
Fuss	Continuous or intermittent low-intensity fussing	1.8
Cry	Intense vocalizations, singly or in succession	1.7
Transition States Between Sleep and Waking		
Drowse	Eyes either open or opening and closing slowly; usually little motor activity	4.4
Daze	Eyes glassy and immobile; usually little motor activity. This state usually occurs between episodes of Drowse and Alert.	1.0
Sleep–wake transition	Usually generalized motor activity; eyes may be closed or open and close rapidly. Isolated fusses may occur. This state usually occurs when the baby is awakening.	1.3
Sleep States		
Active sleep	Eyes closed, uneven respiration, and low muscle tone despite sporadic movement. Rapid eye movements (REMs) occur intermittently, as do smiles, frowns, grimaces, sighs, grunts, cries, mouthing, and sucking.	50.3
Quiet sleep	Eyes closed, respiration slow, regular, and deep. Tonic motor tone but limited motor activity, especially in preterm infants.	28.1
Transition Sleep State		
Active–quiet transition sleep	Typically occurs between periods of active and quiet sleep; eyes closed and little motor activity. Respiration pattern is intermediate between that of quiet and active sleep.	1.9

Adapted from the descriptions and data provided by Thoman and Whitney, 1990.

states over a 1-month period, it appears that some states, such as fussing and crying, show greater individual stability from 6 weeks to 9 months of age than do other states, such as waking (St. James-Roberts & Plęwis, 1996), and the degree to which infant states are regulated has important implications for infant care as well as parental well-being. The establishment of "stable and distinct states" may be a primary goal of preterm or compromised newborns, whereas among newborns who have already achieved this it may facilitate their ability to attend to and process environmental stimuli. State is thus significant for many reasons. First, state determines how infants present themselves. Whether and how newborn infants respond to tactile, visual, and auditory stimuli often depends on their state: In quiet alertness, for example, an infant may attend to a voice that has no effect on the baby in a period of distress. Second, infants' states influence adults' behaviors: Adults may rock and soothe distressed babies instead of trying to show them toys. Infants who are temperamentally fretful in this way elicit different patterns of care than do infants who cry only infrequently (see Chapters 10 and 11) and thus affect their own development. Third, state regularity serves as a marker of nervous system integrity. Poor state regulation is common among infants born preterm, infants who have suffered significant perinatal complications (such as intraventricular hemorrhage or asphyxia), and infants with congenital brain malformations. Poor state regulation in early infancy is also predictive of lower performance on tests of intellectual ability at the end of the first year of life (Halpern et al., 1995). Furthermore, Whitney and Thoman (1993) found abnormal sleep state patterns in premature infants, measured during the first 5 weeks after birth, to predict later neurodevelopmental dysfunction, deficits in intellectual performance, and medical problems (e.g., deafness and cerebral palsy).

Regularity of states in very young babies thus provides a window on the maturity and integrity of the nervous system. However, it does not solely reflect endogenous tendencies. The way a baby is cared for can be influential, too. In a study of very low-birth-weight infants admitted to hospital neonatal intensive care nurseries, for example, Ingersoll and Thoman (1999) found that the amount of time infants spent in quiet sleep in their isolettes was associated with the amount of caregiving (from parent or nurse) they received. Furthermore, increases in quiet sleep and decreases in active sleep and wakefulness from 33 to 35 weeks postconceptional age were associated with increases over the same period in caregiving. The organization of sleep states and sleep disturbances may also be responsive to broad cultural differences in caregiving practices. Kawasaki, Nugent, Miyashita, Miyahara, and Brazelton (1994) reported that, relative to infants in Western, industrialized countries, Japanese infants generally have better state regulation and fewer sleeping problems. This difference, they proposed, was a joint function of Japanese infants' predisposition to habituate well to aversive stimuli (e.g., noise) during sleep and the custom in Japanese culture for infants to sleep within arm's length of their parents. Such sleeping arrangements allow mothers to reach for and pull their infants close for feeding or comforting, whereas Western infants typically sleep in separate rooms from their parents. According to Kawasaki et al., therefore, cultural differences in sleep problems reflect an interaction between organismic and environmental factors.

States of quiet alertness are initially both rare and brief, but this changes noticeably over the first months of life. However infrequent and short they may be, periods of quiet alertness are extremely important because they allow infants to extract information from and adjust to the social and physical environment.

During these moments, the infant can examine and so become familiar with the features of a parent's face, or else study the mobile hanging over the crib, gradually learning how to produce interesting movements (Lamb, 1982c). Much of what infants learn about objects, people, and their own abilities appears to be acquired during periods of quiet alertness and attentiveness.

Figure 5.1 summarizes normative data on the weekly development of the sleep–wake cycle in one female infant over the first 6 months of life. (Data on waking are provided; sleep data are the reciprocal.) This girl was born at 5:16 a.m., and her sleep–wake cycle was sampled one day each week beginning at 5:16 a.m. Notice that the cumulative amount of time she was awake each day unsteadily increased over the first few months. In the first month she was awake 30% to 40% of the day, and in the sixth month 40% to 50% of the day (Figure 5.1A). (When she is an adult she will be awake 60% to 70% of the day.) Furthermore, the number of times per day that this infant awoke over the same period diminished from eight to four, and paralleled the number of feeds (discussed later): In the beginning hunger roused waking, and waking was almost uniformly followed by feeding (Figure 5.1B; in adulthood, this value diminishes to 1.) This means, of course, that the average amount of time the baby was awake in any one waking episode also increased, however unsteadily, from just over 1 hour to almost 3 hours (Figure 5.1C). (In adulthood, this value approaches 16 hours.)

Perhaps the development of the sleep–wake cycle is best captured by illustrating how time awake versus time asleep changes over the first 6 months of life. Figure 5.2 plots this infant's longest daily episodes awake and asleep. (Note that these data are shortened because each day's sample began and ended at a fixed time of day.) Two features of development are especially noteworthy. First, in these initial months this infant's asleep times are always longer than her awake times; indeed, the two curves never overlap. (In adulthood, this state of affairs will reverse.) Second, this infant's longest awake period increases only very gradually, from about 2 hours to about $3\frac{1}{2}$ hours over the first 6 months, but her sleeping bouts change dramatically over the first 2 months, from about $3\frac{1}{2}$ hours to as many as 9 hours. Time asleep thereafter remains constant, but the child's consecutive periods awake will eventually jump considerably. Figure 5.2 does not show it, but this change reflects the infant's entrainment to the day–night cycle: Beginning around 2 months of age, her longest sleep episode consistently occurred at night.

Figure 5.3 illustrates how sleep–wake patterns change over the course of the life cycle. As can be seen, the major change in the pattern of sleeping and waking occurs during the first year and is related to feeding. Figure 5.4A shows that over the first 6 months of life the number of meals this female infant took varied from day to day, but overall diminished from about 8 to about 5. (For most adults, this number eventually declines to 3.) More interesting is how her feeding times changed with age, as shown in Figure 5.4B. In this baby's first week she devoted virtually all the time she was "awake" to feeding, but over the first 2 months feeding dropped dramatically to 30% to 40% of awake time, permitting the baby to devote 60% to 70% of her awake time to social interaction and exploration of her environment. Meals during this period lasted about half an hour. After 2 months of age the proportion of awake time spent feeding fell further, to 10% to 15%, and meals became even more methodical, lasting only one fourth of an hour.

In adults, sleep and wakefulness are accompanied by recordable psychophysiological indices, such as rapid eye movements and specific patterns

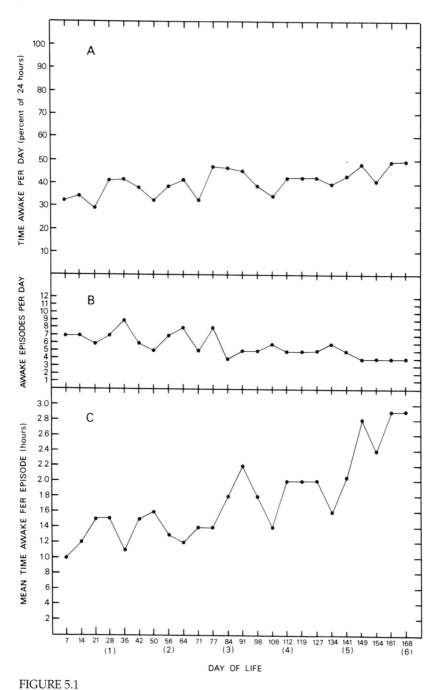

FIGURE 5.1

The sleep–wake cycle of a female infant matures week by week over the first 6 months of life. (*A*) Cumulative time awake per day increases from about one third of the day to one half. (*B*) The number of episodes awake reduces by one half. (*C*) The average duration of awake episodes triples.

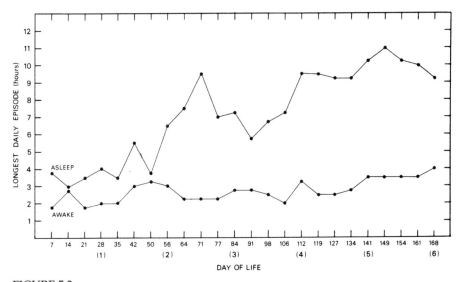

FIGURE 5.2

The longest daily episode being awake and being asleep in one infant week by week over the first 6 months of life. The longest awake episode only increases very gradually, whereas the longest asleep bout increases dramatically. This female infant entrained to the day–night cycle at about 2 months, and thereafter the longest asleep bout uniformly occurs at night.

of brain or electroencephalographic (EEG) activity. The same is true of infants, and most infant states can be reliably identified with EEG criteria by approximately 3 months of age (Papoušek & Papoušek, 1996). As we have suggested, the organization of the sleep–wake cycle reflects neurological maturation and the developing ability of babies to regulate their own states. The organization of sleep cycles is also affected by other factors, such as stressful perinatal experiences, parental caregiving, and cultural beliefs, as illustrated by Super and Harkness (1997). Among the Kipsigis in East Africa, infants sleep with their mothers and are permitted to nurse on demand. During the day they are strapped to their

FIGURE 5.3

The black areas represent sleep in this schematic representation of the basic rest–activity cycle superimposed on the sleep–wake cycle. (After Kleitman, 1963.)

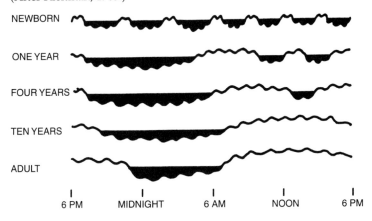

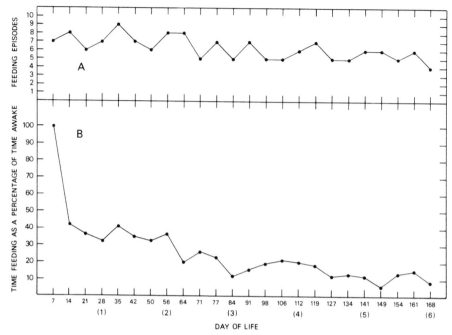

FIGURE 5.4

Feeding episodes and durations week by week during the first 6 months of life in one female infant. (*A*) The number of meals per day decreases by one half. (*B*) The duration of meals as a proportion of the time awake decreases from 50% to about 10%.

mothers' backs, accompanying them on their daily rounds of farming, household chores, and social activities. They often nap while their mothers go about their work, and so they do not begin to sleep through the night until many months later than American children. The fact that state organization can be affected by experiential factors does not really tell us why normative developmental changes take place, however.

The early growth of self-regulation, as documented by changes in the sleep–wake cycle, provides an indirect way for researchers to map the physiological maturation of the brain. The emergence of stable EEG patterns associated with different sleep states is frequently taken to indicate a major shift in the maturation of the brain. We do not know how extensive a shift in functional capacity occurs, but it is reasonable to assume that the ability to process information may increase substantially when infant states stabilize. Thus, studying the patterning of sleep states may yield information about the developmental level of underlying neural structures and so help to identify periods that have wider implications for improved psychological functioning.

Heart Rate

As we mentioned in Chapter 4, the human heart begins to beat early in the period of the embryo. At first, heart rate is rather invariable, suggesting that strong endogenous or autonomous "pacemakers" are at work; by about 24 weeks, however, heart rate switches from autonomic to neural control (Dreyfus-Brisac,

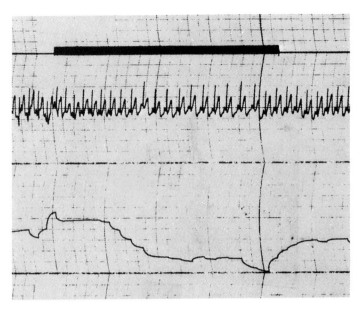

FIGURE 5.5
A heart rate deceleration (*lower curve*) occurs when the infant is shown a novel sight or hears a novel sound. The upper bar indicates the duration of the stimulus, the middle indicates heartbeats, and the lower curve the heart rate.

1968). After birth, heart rate is extremely sensitive to psychological state and has been used to help interpret what the infant may be thinking, feeling, or doing (Bornstein, 1999). It is also an important index of individual differences among infants.

In 1966, Graham and Clifton published a review articulating relations between the orienting response (described in Chapter 7) and heart rate change. They proposed that cardiac responses to brief stimuli of low intensity should be deceleratory, indicating receptiveness to incoming stimulation, whereas cardiac responses to sustained stimuli of high intensity should be acceleratory, indicating attempts to shut out stimulation. In infants, heart rate deceleration accompanying attention can be of remarkable magnitude—as many as 25 beats per minute (see Figure 5.5). So reliable is the relation between attention and heart rate deceleration that researchers have used the cardiac response since the 1960s to help determine whether an infant is actively attending to a stimulus or simply staring blankly into space in the direction of the stimulus (Bornstein & Suess, 2000b; Richards, 1997; Richards & Holley, 1999).

Changes in heart rate variability index both sustained visual attention and reactivity to psychologically meaningful stimulation (Bornstein & Suess, 2000b; Doussard-Roosevelt & Porges, 1999; Groome, Loizou, Holland, Smith, & Hoff, 1999; Stevenson-Hinde & Marshall, 1999). One aspect of heart rate variability is referred to as *respiratory sinus arrythmia* (RSA) and is used as an index of *vagal tone* (Figure 5.6); RSA reflects heart rate changes mediated by the vagus nerve, which means that they are controlled not by the sympathetic nervous system but by the parasympathetic branch of the autonomic nervous system (Porges, 1995). High vagal tone is associated with the ability to attend selectively to relevant stimuli in one's environment and to maintain attention during a task (Porges, 1995, 1997). One might expect high vagal tone to predict better functioning

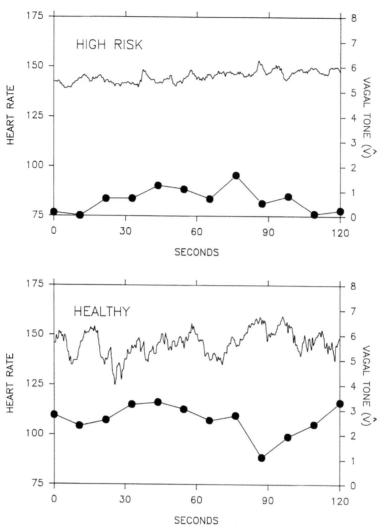

FIGURE 5.6

The figure illustrates 2 minutes of heart rate and vagal tone of two sleeping infants: One is a high-risk preterm infant monitored at approximately term; the other is a healthy term baby monitored within 36 hours of delivery. The Y axis on the left represents heart rate in beats per minute, and the Y axis on the right represents the vagal tone index. Note that heart rate is not constant for either infant. Although the heart rate levels are similar for the two infants, the healthy infant has much greater variability relative to the high-risk infant. Close observation of the two patterns identifies a striking difference in the rapid changes in heart rate that occur every 1 to 2 seconds. These oscillations are associated with respiration and reflect vagal tone.

over the long term. In very low birth-weight infants, high mean vagal tone measured as early as the neonatal period is associated with superior mental processing, social competence, and fewer behavior problems at 3 years of age (Doussard-Roosevelt, Porges, & McClenny, 1996; Doussard-Roosevelt, Porges, Scanlon, Alemi, & Scanlon, 1997). High-baseline vagal tone in normal infants under 1 year of age is associated with the ability to attend to environmental stimuli (Richards, 1994), reduced reactivity to an experimental procedure (Huffman et al., 1998), and the ability to maintain hemostasis (Groome, Loizou, et al., 1999).

In a prospective longitudinal study, vagal tone and heart period were measured twice, at 2 months and at 5 years, in both children and their mothers to evaluate and compare the development of the vagal system and its regulatory capacity at rest and during environmental task (Bornstein & Suess, 2000a, 2000b). Child baseline vagal tone and heart period were discontinuous; mother baseline vagal tone was discontinuous, but heart period was continuous. Group mean baseline-to-task change in vagal tone and heart period were continuous in both children and mothers. Children reached adult levels of baseline vagal tone by 5 years, and children and their mothers did not differ in baseline-to-task change in vagal tone or heart period. Baseline vagal tone tended to be stable, but baseline heart period and baseline-to-task change in vagal tone and heart period were unstable in children; both were stable in mothers. Baseline-to-task change in vagal tone showed consistent child-mother concordance. A second study investigated the role of cardiac vagal tone in information processing (habituation) in infants. Physiological self-regulation was operationalized as the change in vagal tone from a baseline period of measurement to habituation. Decreases in vagal tone consistently related to habituation efficiency, operationalized as accumulated looking time (ALT), in all infants twice at 2 months and twice at 5 months. Within-age and between-age suppression of vagal tone predicted ALT, but ALT did not predict suppression of vagal tone. Physiological self-regulation provided by the vagal system appears to play a role in information processing in infancy as indexed by habituation.

The regulatory functions of the vagal system are also elucidated by examining vagal tone in baseline (resting) conditions and in response to social/attentional stressors. Doussard-Roosevelt and Porges (1999) proposed that high resting vagal tone is associated with attentional skills and the ability to maintain homeostatic integrity. However, the suppression of vagal tone (the vagal "brake" response) is associated with the ability to respond successfully to social–environmental challenges and, over the long term, social interactional skills (Porges, Doussard-Roosevelt, Portales, & Greenspan, 1996). The ability of 7- to 9-month-old infants to regulate vagal tone in response to a social-attention task (such as being given an infant intelligence test by an unfamiliar examiner) predicted fewer behavior problems at 3 years of age in comparison to infants who were unable to deploy the vagal "brake." The vagal brake response is also associated with infants' soothability (Huffman et al., 1998), which has a direct impact on parental feelings of efficacy (Teti & Gelfand, 1997). Ahnert, Porges, Lamb, and Riekert (2001) found that effective emotional regulation, as indexed by vagal tone, was influenced by the quality of developing attachment relationships. As we report in Chapter 10, there is growing consensus that temperament reflects a genetic and constitutional basis of personality, and individual differences in heart rate level and vagal tone may be important manifestations of this. Ahnert et al.'s findings, however, remind us once again that constitutionally based individual differences are still susceptible to change in response to experiences.

In summary, the autonomic nervous system begins to develop regulatory functions early in prenatal life and involves regular cycles and states of arousal from birth. Both cycles and states have considerable impact on other psychological and behavioral characteristics of the developing infant and on parents. Among the best-studied aspects of autonomic nervous system functioning is heart rate, which has been used to measure sensitivity and development in many spheres of infant life, from sensation and perception to emotional reactivity and social sensibility.

Central Nervous System Development

The central nervous system is largely concerned with information processing and mediating the organism's activity. To adjust to the complex changes from interuterine to extrauterine life, the central nervous system develops in many ways at many levels simultaneously. These include the cellular level at one end of the spectrum to the overall structure of the brain at another. Not only do many structural changes take place prenatally and in infancy, but rapid and complex functional changes of many kinds, including those concerned with electrical activity of individual cells as well as the brain as a whole, occur during this period as well. In this section we discuss the measurement and evaluation of the main features of central nervous system development before and just after birth. In addition, we review principles by which experiences help to shape the growth and development of brain function.

The Cellular Level

Figure 5.7 shows a single *neuron*, whose gross morphology, including *dendrites, cell body, nucleus*, and *axon*, is clearly recognizable. Dendrites conduct information to the cell body, whereas axons transmit information away from the cell body. Information is conducted by an electrochemical exchange called the *axon potential*, along the axon fiber; this fiber can be infinitesimally short or extremely long (up to 3 or 4 feet). At the cell terminals the signal is communicated neurochemically by *neurotransmitters* to the dendrites of a connecting cell across *synapses*, which are points of interneural transmission between axons and dendrites of adjoining cells. The most common neurotransmitters are norepinephrine and acetylcholine, but more than 50 different neurotransmitters have been identified. Undeveloped cells are nude; developed cells are usually (though not always) wrapped in a sheath of *myelin*—a fatty tissue that surrounds the cell axon and greatly facilitates conduction velocity, rendering cell information transmission more efficient (Benes, 1994) and so, presumably, making it possible to effect rapid movements voluntarily.

We have already commented on the astounding proliferation of cells in the human brain. Moreover, the brain is a highly structured architectural wonder. As it develops, it follows identifiable principles. For example, cells segregate into specialized areas loosely related to function. In humans, genetic preprogramming ensures an abundance of the cells needed to perceive, think, feel, and act. In the following passages we highlight some of the central developments. Several facts about intracellular structure and function are of special interest to students of infancy. These include:

1. The birth and maturation of individual cells and of the action potential;

2. The development of interconnections among cells, including dendritic branching, synaptogenesis, neurochemical transmission, and organizational networking;

3. The specialization of cellular function, including interconnectivity, synaptic elimination, and cell death.

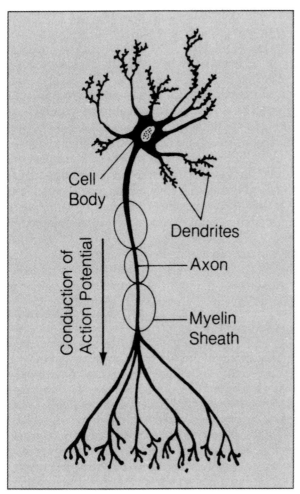

FIGURE 5.7
A single neuron showing the cell body and nucleus,
dendritic fibers, and the axon fiber, surrounded by a
myelin sheath.

Development of the central nervous system is a highly complex process whose intricacies are not fully understood. (Turn to Johnson (1997a, 1997b, 1999), Ospreen, Risser, and Edgell (1995), Goldman-Rakic, Bourgeois, and Rakic (1997), and Nowakowski (1987) for a discussion of the topic in much greater detail.) The central nervous system originates as a cell layer on the outer surface of the embryo and is already visible 1 month after conception. Neurons continue to appear throughout the period of the embryo and well into that of the fetus. After cells are born they grow, migrate, and associate with one another to form relatively stable interconnected patterns. A fascinating aspect of development in this realm is that migration routes seem to be preordained; nerve cells are even supported and guided along their routes by other (glial) cells. The layers of the brain are generated from the inside out so that cells constantly migrate. Migrating cells appear to "know" their addresses, although it is not understood exactly how: Cells may migrate to particular points or partners, or they may be drawn to these points or partners by so-called neurotrophic chemicals secreted by those partners. Whatever the process, it is fast and efficient: By the end of the sixth month of gestation, neurogenesis and migration within the cortex are complete. Furthermore, almost all cortical neurons in the human brain are generated prenatally or during very early postnatal life.

After their generation and migration, individual cells grow dendritic and axonal connections and myelinate. Dendrites and axons continue to grow, and dendrites continue to branch through adulthood. The process of myelination loosely correlates with the development of cellular function and provides a general index of maturation, although functional activity occurs in the absence of myelination. With myelination, the velocity of intracellular neurotransmission more than triples, from a rate of less than 20 feet per second to more than 60 feet per second. The visual, auditory, and somesthetic cortex myelinates before birth, whereas higher brain centers that integrate information are not completely myelinated until puberty.

Chronic alcohol intake during the prenatal period (Chapter 4) appears to inhibit the formation of axons and dendrites and the production of the neurotrophins involved in cell migration (Batshaw & Conlon, 1997). Lead damages tissue by destroying nerve cells and myelin (Ospreen et al., 1995). This helps to explain why prenatal alcohol ingestion has such profound effects on postnatal development.

Perhaps the two most important developments at the intercellular level involve biochemical neurotransmission and the restructuring of neural organization. During early maturation, increasing dendritic complexity is reflected in the growth of spines or trees connected to neighboring cells, a process called arborization. Conel (1939–1959) illustrated this facet of brain growth in humans (see Figure 5.8). In the first 2 years of life, interneural circuitry proceeds to the point where there are up to 10,000 connections per cell. Likewise, the number of synaptic vesicles regularly increases in early life, indicating an enhanced capacity for information transmission. Immature synapses can already be seen under the microscope by 4 months gestational age, and mature forms are present by 8 months. During the phases of early development, synapses are overproduced in many parts of the cerebral cortex, with no part appearing to develop faster or slower than any other. Progressive changes in the biochemistry of synaptic transmission influence behavioral development in combination with structural associations, because functionally related systems come to share the same neurotransmitters.

"Undevelopment" in the central nervous system also takes place pre- and postnatally. In vertebrates, neurons are initially overproduced and then diminish in number even before birth. Moreover, cells often lose structural features in the course of nervous system growth. As an example, Zecevic, Bourgeois, and Rakic (1989) studied the overproduction and elimination of retinal axons in the fetal rhesus monkey. About halfway into the period of the embryo, the fetal monkey has nearly 3 million retinal axons—a number that is more than twice the number present in adult monkeys. More than 1 million "extra" optic axons are generated and then eliminated before birth; soon after birth, another half million or so are eliminated. Figure 5.9 shows comparable data from humans of different ages regarding the elimination of cells in a different area of the brain.

Many explanations for this process of cellular overproduction and subsequent elimination have been offered. Typically, the number of axons associated with each cell, rather than the number of synapses, decline while each axon adds

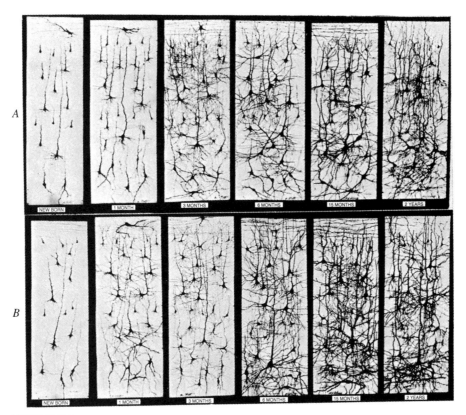

FIGURE 5.8

A schematic illustration demonstrating how dendritic arborization and the myelination of neurons increase during the first 2 years of life. (Courtesy of J. L. Conel.)

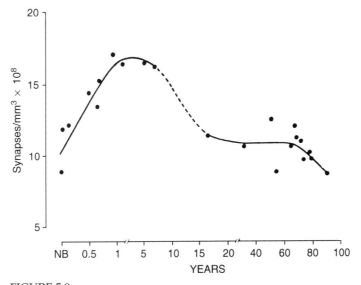

FIGURE 5.9

Synapse counts in layer 3 of the middle frontal gyrus of the human brain as a function of age. Note the rapid increase in synapses through the first year of life and the decrease by puberty and in old age. (After Huttenlocher, 1979. © 1979 by *Brain Research*. Reprinted by permission.)

new endings but connects to fewer and fewer target cells. Perhaps not all neurons connect successfully to the appropriate targets. It is possible that neurons have an intrinsic tendency to reduce the number of their connections or support only a limited number of synapses. Perhaps target cells produce a trophic agent that contributes to the formation and maintenance of only some synaptic endings; axons would thus compete, some more successfully than others. Or, perhaps, activity itself helps to establish and maintain neural circuits, with different activities determining which synapses are retained and which eliminated (Provine, 1988; Tucker, 1992). This cannot be the whole answer, however, because cells in the primary visual cortex develop even in the absence of visual stimulation or its retinal counterparts (Kuljis & Rakic, 1990). Finally, simple morphological and space considerations may force the elimination of some connections. Whatever the processes responsible for cellular elimination, a surprisingly large number of neural connections are eliminated very early in life. Cell death following neurogenesis appears to be necessary to normal development and functioning. Indeed, the failure of cell death has been associated with mental retardation and other developmental disorders (Thatcher, 1994).

In fact, early neural development involves various kinds of undevelopment, including reduction in the number of synapses among cells. Thus, the "chaotic" immature pattern of multiple intercellular connections is replaced by an "efficient" and streamlined information transmission system. Bergström (1969) formally modeled the structural development of neuronal interactions in a clear, though highly simplified, geometry. She suggested, as shown in Figure 5.10, that interneural transmission is originally *reticular*, or net-like in structure, with more or less random connections among communicating neurons. A discrete stimulus that excites this system is likely to result in a diffuse "tonic" (that is, global) response. In the more developed state, interconnections are more orderly and, in Bergström's terms, parallel rather than reticular, tract-like rather than net-like. A discrete stimulus now produces a "phasic" response that is exact in time and parallel in space with the stimulus. By way of illustration, consider how younger and older babies might respond to a loud clap. Early in life, such auditory stimulation elicits a gross response, like a whole bodily shudder. Sometime later the same clap leads to a discrete turn of the head. Thus, central nervous system development at the intercellular level is characterized by differentiation and the growth of specificity. More generally, a narrowing and progressive confinement of options and connections takes place, apparently promoting appropriate responsivity as well as reducing plasticity.

These startling developments at the intercellular level do not mean that maturation alone accounts for cellular cross talk and interconnectivity. About 50 years ago, Hebb (1949) proposed a motor–neurological theory of perceptual development, reasoning that a few rudimentary perceptual abilities—like the capacity to distinguish figure from ground—might be inborn. Beyond highly limited innate capacities like these, however, Hebb theorized that the bulk of perceptual development ought to be based on motor behavior and experience. When we see a form, we scan it and thereby develop an internal representation of it that is related to the movements of our eyes as well as to the activity of cortical neurons repeatedly excited by the form. The pathways in the brain activated by scanning the form eventually aggregate into units Hebb called "cell assemblies," or "phase sequences," which help construct familiar perceptions. Experience thus promotes the organization of cell assemblies, and metabolic changes (presumably via neurotransmitters) facilitate connections among these

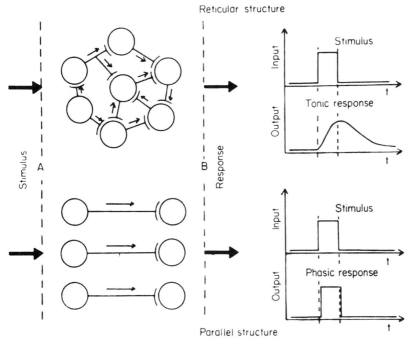

FIGURE 5.10

A schematic diagram illustrating the developmental organization of basic
interneural circuitry. Interrelations among neurons early in development are
net-like (reticular) in structure, involving more or less random connections,
and at this stage a discrete stimulus results in a tonic response. Later in
development, interneural organization is tract-like (parallel) so that a discrete
stimulus gives rise to a specific phasic response. (After Bergström, 1969.
© 1969 by Academic Press. Reprinted by permission.)

cells to promote "perceptual" pathways. With repeated experience, Hebb contended, particular stimuli persistently excite specific pathways along which
synaptic resistance is reduced and cellular cross talk is promoted. Indeed, as
the sense organs develop, the CNS relies more on sensory experience and less
on spontaneously generated neural activity for normal brain development and
functioning (Katz & Schatz, 1996).

Brain Structure

The human brain grows at a phenomenal rate as developing neurons aggregate
into cell masses that soon give the brain its characteristic structure. As can be
seen in Figure 5.11, the cortex of a human fetus in the second trimester already
reveals "convolutions" and "invaginations" indicative of its eventual adult form.
These structural characteristics are thought to develop because inner and outer
cortical layers grow at different rates.

The two hemispheres and the brain stem contain three major substruc-
tures that develop in an orderly and comprehensive fashion (Hellige, 1993;
Johnson, 1997a). Subcortical structures that control state (like the hypothalamus) and the arousal system of the reticular formation emerge first. Indeed,
nuclei of the reticular formation are among the earliest to differentiate in the

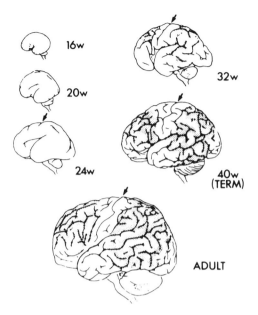

FIGURE 5.11
The developing human brain is viewed from the side in this sequence of drawings, all of which are reproduced at the same scale. The characteristic convolutions and invaginations of the brain's surface do not begin to appear until about the middle of gestation. (After Trevarthen, 1974. © 1974 by Academic Press. Reprinted by permission.)

brain. Components of the limbic system and basal ganglia, which govern emotion, "instinct," and posture, develop next. Then, finally, the cortex and cortical association areas concerned with awareness, attention, memory, and the integration of information emerge. They are also among the last to myelinate and are influenced most by experience with the outside world. Of course, the developmental phases for these three major components of the nervous system overlap, and development in each "zone" continues well past infancy.

The corpus callosum is a fiber bundle that connects the two hemispheres of the brain. We know that it is among the last CNS structures to begin to myelinate, and this fact may have startling consequences for the neurology of the newborn infant. Research with adults who have had their hemispheres surgically disconnected suggests that the two hemispheres of the brain share unequally in the distribution of mental duties, with language processed predominantly in the left hemisphere and spatial information in the right hemisphere in right-handed people (Hellige, 1993). Some time ago, Gazzaniga (1970, pp. 129 *ff*) theorized on neuromaturational grounds that "the normal neonate is born, for all practical purposes, with a split-brain.... [I]nterhemispheric communication is slight at birth, and increases with age, with good communication seen . . . starting around the ages of 2–3." If true, this state of affairs would largely prevent young babies from integrating functions on the two sides of the body or in the two halves of perceptual space. This does not mean that hemispheric dominance is not evident earlier; Hepper, Shahidullah, and White (1990) reported that fetuses as young as 15 weeks gestational age show a strong tendency to suck their right thumbs, suggesting prenatal left-brain dominance.

Electrical Activity in the Brain

Although we are unable to observe or to measure directly the activity of single cells in human beings, it is possible to assess structural and functional growth indirectly by measuring gross electrical activity in the brain. EEG recordings,

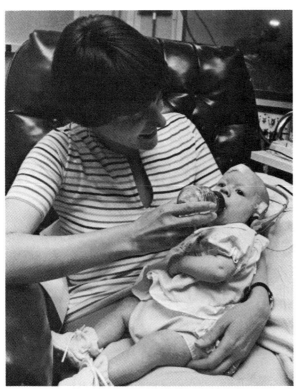

FIGURE 5.12
An infant is held by her mother while evoked brain
potentials in response to acoustic stimulation are
recorded. Leads attached painlessly to the scalp record
the endogenous electrical activity of thousands of brain
neurons. The brain waves are amplified, summed across
many presentations of the stimulus by a computer, and
an event-related brain potential is then observed.
(Courtesy of D. Shucard and D. Thomas.)

for example, reflect spontaneous electrical activity over masses of individual
cells under the scalp (Luck & Girelli, 1998). Figure 5.12 shows a baby's EEG
being assessed, and Figure 5.13 displays records of scalp EEG activity on five
occasions during the first 2 years of life. In broad outline, neonates have low-
voltage, largely undifferentiated, irregular brain activity. Over the course of the
first year the dominant rhythm in the EEG increases from about three to five
cycles per second during the first quarter of the first year of life, to seven to
nine cycles per second by the end of the first year (Bell & Fox, 1994), and by the
time they are 2 years of age, toddlers have high-amplitude and regular burst–
pause patterns of EEG activity (Thatcher, 1994). Changes in the EEG signal are
believed to reflect the excitability and organization of large neuronal masses and
so should provide clues regarding the online function of different areas of the
brain (Thatcher, 1994).

Increases in activity over the frontal areas of the cortex parallel changes in
behavior (e.g., finding hidden objects; see Chapter 7) that demand cognitive and
memory skills believed to be mediated by the frontal cortex (Bell, 1998; Bell &
Fox, 1994; Krasnegor, Lyon, & Goldman-Rakic, 1997). Figure 5.14 illustrates such

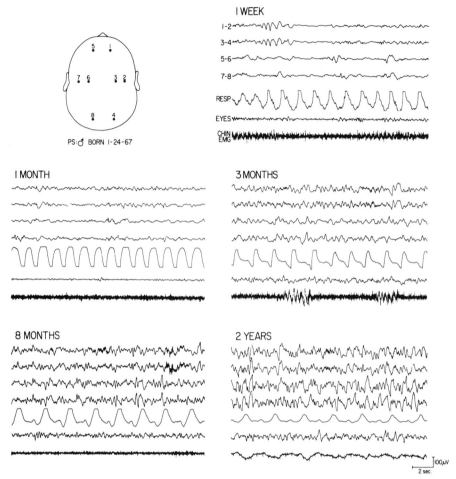

FIGURE 5.13

Records of electroencephalographic (EEG) activity, respiration, eye movements, and electromyographic (EMG) activity taken on five occasions during the first 2 years in one child's life. The first four sets of waves in each panel correspond to leads from electrodes located over different surface positions on the scalp. In broad outline, neonates show low-voltage, largely undifferentiated and irregular EEG patterns, but by the time they are 2 years of age toddlers show high amplitude and regular burst patterns in their EEGs. (After Sterman & Hoppenbrouwers, 1971. © 1971 by Academic Press. Reprinted by permission.)

brain–behavior relations and how studies of other species can sometimes be used to explore such associations. Monkey infant development outpaces human infant development. In retrieving an object from a box, for example, human infants aged 7 to 9 months will attempt to reach for the object only on the side through which they can see it even when that route is blocked (middle panel in Figure 5.14), but by 12 months human infants retrieve objects even when they have to reach around from the open side. The development in infant monkeys is faster: at 2 months they show the "awkward reach" (top panel in Figure 5.14), but by 4 months infant monkeys perform perfectly. The prefrontal cortex is intimately involved with success on this task: As shown in the lowest panel of Figure 5.14, a "prefrontal" monkey (one with that structure lesioned) behaves like a younger infant. Goldman-Rakic et al. (1997) hypothesized that a proliferation of synapses in the prefrontal cortex potentiates the ability to represent the location of the object mentally.

Another informative aspect of the EEG signal is the degree of hemispheric asymmetry, which has been identified by Henriques and Davidson (1990) and Bell and Fox (1994) as an indicator of certain temperamental styles in both infants and adults. The frontal region of the brain is involved in the expression and regulation of emotion. More specifically, activation of the right frontal cortex is typically observed during the experience or expression of negative affect (including anger and distress), whereas activation of the left frontal cortex is associated with the expression or experience of positive affect. Individual differences in frontal lobe hemispheric activation is evident in infants as young as 4 months of age. Calkins, Fox, and Marshall (1996) further showed that stable right frontal EEG activation was associated with high levels of negative affect in the first year as well as with fearfulness and behavioral inhibition in the second year. Individual differences in the magnitude of these patterns, both at baseline and in response to specific stimuli, indicate affective bias and the ability to regulate emotion and adapt to stress. Infants with a pattern of greater right-sided activation (as indicated on their EEGs) seem more likely to respond with distress or anxiety to mild stress or novelty, and this response may be a state-independent marker of the tendency to respond readily to stressful events—an early physiological index of a pattern of behavioral inhibition (Dawson, 1994b; Bell & Fox, 1994; Harman & Fox, 1997).

Individual differences in frontal lobe hemispheric activation may also relate to the affective valence of the infant's caregiving environment. Dawson, Klinger, et al. (1992) examined frontal lobe activation responses in 11- to 17-month-olds, some of whom were in the care of depressed mothers. Infants participated in a laboratory observation designed to elicit positive (a peekaboo game) and negative emotions (separation from mother). During peekaboo, the activity of the left frontal lobe was greater than in the right in infants of nondepressed mothers. This asymmetry was associated with the experience of positive affect and was not evident in infants who had depressed mothers. Furthermore, when separated from their mothers, infants with nondepressed mothers predictably responded with greater activity in the right than in the left frontal hemisphere, perhaps reflecting sadness at their mothers' departure. Paradoxically, infants with depressed mothers responded to maternal separation with increased activation of the *left* frontal lobe. These differential asymmetries were not associated with differences in the behavioral responses of infants with depressed and nondepressed mothers—there were none. Such studies illustrate the potential importance of maternal affect in organizing the central nervous system and in moderating psychophysiological responses to happy and sad events.

Event-related potentials (ERPs) average electrical activity relative to some discrete stimulus and so describe a specific pattern of brain activity evoked by a specific stimulus. It is possible to distinguish ERPs from ongoing EEG activity to help elucidate the developing functions of underlying brain structures (Chapter 3). ERPs are characterized by their waveform, latency, and amplitude (Luck & Girelli, 1998). Studies of the ontogeny of the ERP show that the waveform begins simply, with a longer delay before onset in infancy than in adulthood, and that the amplitude of the function changes across the life cycle in a fairly complex way. Short-latency ERPs are valuable when practitioners need to assess the capacities of infants too young to respond in other ways;

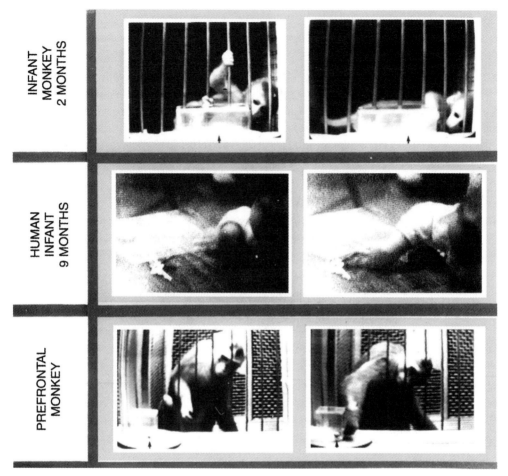

FIGURE 5.14

The awkward reach in a 2-month-old monkey, a 9-month-old human infant, and an adult monkey with a bilateral lesion of the dorsal lateral prefrontal cortex. *Frame 1*: Subject leans and looks at bait through opening of box. *Frame 2*: Subject reaches in awkwardly with far hand. *Frame 3*: Opening is on the other side of the box. Performance is the same. Subject leans and looks into the opening. *Frame 4*: Subject reaches in awkwardly with far hand. (Courtesy of A. Diamond.)

long-latency ERPs are often used to study more complex cortical functioning (Duffy, 1994).

Event-related potentials can be recorded in infants from birth (Molfese & Molfese, 1994). As shown in the top panel of Figure 5.15, the ERP for a visual stimulus at first assumes a simple form but is already quite complex by the time of birth, although it differs from the adult form, which is shown for comparison. ERP waveforms continue to vary up to 3 years of age. As shown in the bottom panel of Figure 5.15, the time between stimulus onset and the appearance of the major component of the ERP (the positive crest at P_2) shows a reasonably orderly decrease with age until it reaches adult values. The amplitude of the ERP (not shown) follows a more complex developmental course: It diminishes with age up to the normal time of birth, then increases to 3 years, then decreases again so that, in essence, adults and newborns have similar amplitudes. It is important to note that these generalizations describe normal infants shown

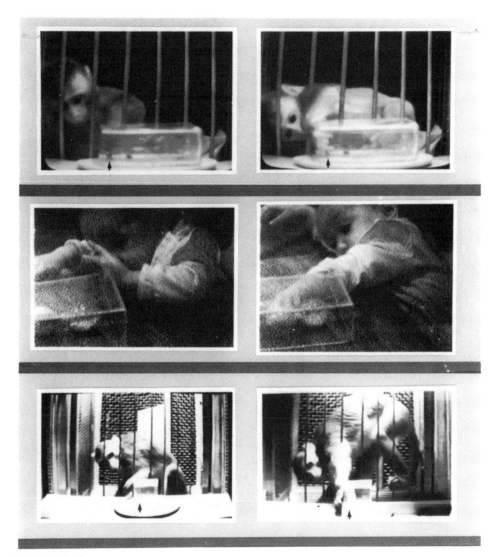

FIGURE 5.14
(*continued*)

specific stimuli; variations among infants, stimuli, and sensory systems alter them somewhat (Berg & Berg, 1987; Molfese & Molfese, 1994). In addition, Karrer, Bloom, Chaney, and Davis (1998) found significant differences between infants with Down syndrome and typical infants in several features of event-related potentials in the frontal and parietal lobes elicited by visual stimuli. Karrer et al. (1998) also showed that ERP activity can be used to document atypical intellectual development in infancy.

ERPs provide valuable information about the normal maturation of the brain, and ERPs are also very useful for determining whether and when sensory pathways function. Consider, for example, the difficulty we would encounter in trying to determine whether an infant who does not respond behaviorally to a sound (by blinking or startling) has a functioning auditory system. By recording the infant's ERPs, we can determine at least whether the infant's brain responds to sound, although of course we would not know whether the sound

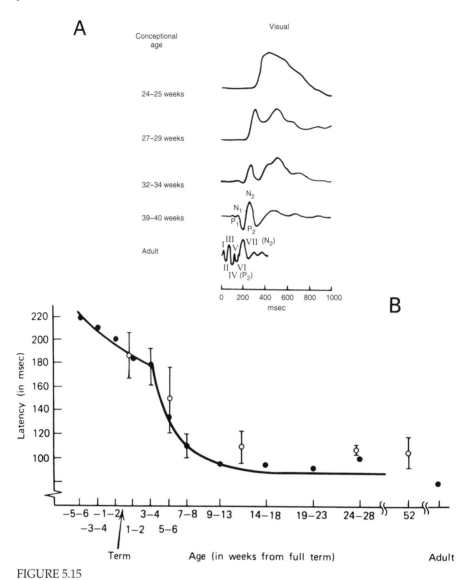

FIGURE 5.15

(*A*) Cortical responses evoked by visual stimuli in preterm infants, term newborns, and adults. (Derivations are bipolar: Oz–Pz for the visual response. Surface negativity is plotted upwards.) (*B*) Latency of the major positive component of the visual-evoked response as a function of age in weeks from term. (The solid and open symbols represent data from two different experiments. The vertical lines passing through the open symbols signify ± 1 *SD* for the group.) (After Berg & Berg, 1979. © 1979 by John Wiley. Reprinted with permission.)

was perceived (Chapter 3). ERPs have been used to document the efficiency with which infants process information, the existence of recognition memory, frontal lobe mediation of inhibitory control, and specialized brain areas associated with the development and processing of language (Diamond, Werker, & Lalonde, 1997; Mills, Coffey-Corina, & Neville, 1994; van der Molen & Molenaar, 1994). In addition, individual differences in specific features of auditory event-related potentials recorded at birth are predictive of intellectual and language abilities at 3 years of age (Molfese & Molfese, 1994).

Single-Cell Brain Activity

Typically, individual cells in the central nervous system have highly specialized functions. Consider, for example, how units in the visual system respond to light and pattern information. In 1959, Nobel laureates Hubel and Wiesel undertook a series of studies designed to ascertain how individual cells in the cat visual system respond to light. Hubel had developed a physiological technique, called microelectrode recording, with which he could measure the activity of individual cells. He and Wiesel began their research with the straightforward assumption that turning on or turning off a light in front of the cat's eyes ought to affect the activity of single cells (often called units). Instead, they found that cells in the cat's brain were not excited by the mere presence or absence of light; rather, they were excited by highly specific stimulus characteristics, such as a visual contour oriented in the vertical direction. Cells with such specialized sensitivities were present even in newborn animals that had no visual experience. Hubel and Wiesel's work provided neurophysiological evidence that the brain is prewired in ways that might aid the analysis of complex visual perceptions.

In many nonhuman species, *cell detectors* of the Hubel–Wiesel type respond to specific environmental features like angles, movement, color, and even the disparity that results from the somewhat different view of the world that each eye has. As neural systems develop, many cells seem to "know" their special functions. Cells in the visual system for the most part migrate to and interconnect with other cells in the visual system so as to respond to, analyze, and communicate visual information. Indeed, specialized neurons in the visual system connect to other neurons devoted to much the same specialization such that cells sensitive to stimulus orientation connect with other orientation-sensitive cells. In addition, the architecture of the visual system tends to be highly ordered, with, for example, vertical columns of cells in the brain devoted to the same orientation specialization, and horizontal rows of cells in the brain devoted to successive and gradual changes in preferred orientation. Incredible as it may seem, "fate maps" present during the earliest embryological differentiation of the nervous system foretell the eventual distribution of mature cells. How neurons "know" their sensitivities, where to migrate, when to stop, or with what other neurons to congregate are critical questions for which there are not yet complete answers. Some researchers believe that neuronal migration is facilitated by glial cell fibers, which serve as guides for migrating neurons (Rakic, 1987). Others have proposed that specific nerve cells seek out other specific nerve cells through a type of chemical attraction (the chemoaffinity theory; Johnson, 1999; Ospreen et al., 1995). What is clear and astonishing is the preprogramming of around 100 billion cells in the brain.

Brain Plasticity

The preceding description of cellular and structural development in the brain might lead readers to believe that, perhaps because the brain is so crucial to survival, CNS development in prenatal and early postnatal life is preprogrammed and specialized. As it turns out, however, neural development is far from fixed. For example, experimental work with animals such as ferrets and monkeys indicates that disrupting the amount of neural input from the thalamus to a specific cortical area may reduce the size of that area. In addition, if a section of cortex is moved to a different part of the brain, the transplanted part adapts structurally and functionally to its new location (e.g., if moved to the visual cortex, cells from the auditory cortex become responsive to visual stimuli; Johnson, 1997b). In this final section on CNS development, we discuss three perspectives on the effects of experience.

Greenough, Black, and Wallace (1987) showed that experience-expectant and experience-dependent processes were significantly affected by experience in ways that appear to illustrate the differences between species-typical and individual-differences factors. *Experience-expectant* processes are common to all members of the species and evolved as a neural preparation for incorporating general information from the environment efficiently and satisfactorily. The overproduction and trimming of synaptic connections between nerve cells illustrate experience-expectant information storage. By contrast, *experience-dependent* information storage processes reflect learning and brain change unique to the individual. According to Greenough and his colleagues, the neural basis of experience-dependent processes appears to involve the active formation of new synaptic connections that are a product of experience with idiosyncratic events and thereby contribute to individuality.

Both sensory or external experience and self-produced experience can modify brain structure and influence brain function. Sensory experience, via enrichment or deprivation, affects the fine and gross structure of the nervous system as well as the functional properties of cortical neurons. Such effects are evidenced by changes in the size of individual neurons and of massed brain structures as well as by the number and structure of individual synapses, enhanced neural connectivity, and strengthened neural circuitry. Rats raised in complex environments (i.e., supplied with toys and opportunities for play and exploration) develop visual cortices that are heavier and thicker than those of litter mates raised in barren, standard laboratory cages; they also show improved performance on problem-solving tasks (Greenough et al., 1987).

Less is known about the effects of *self-produced experiences*, although it has been suggested that similar influences obtain. For example, Scheibel and his associates (1985) found that lateral differences in dendritic structure increase with age, suggesting that portions of the right cortex develop more rapidly than the left, presumably because infants constantly exercise large-scale undifferentiated motor acts controlled by the right hemisphere. Later, the left hemisphere cortex becomes anatomically more complex as left hemisphere activities like language emerge. Self-produced behaviors alter perceptions in similar ways. Held and Hein (1963) showed that kittens that were allowed to explore their visual environment later mastered visual tasks in more sophisticated ways than did their yoked-control litter mates that experienced the same environment but that were motorically restrained (Chapter 7).

In light of the different sources of information and different sources of experience, it becomes clear that brain structure and function are plastic. Indeed, two kinds of plasticity are common in the nervous system: modifiability and compensation. *Modifiability* means that, although cells are predestined for specific functions, those functions may be attuned. Presumptive visual system cells, for example, can function competently in new roles with new partners when transplanted to other organ systems. To be successful, however, transplantation must occur early; after a certain sensitive period, transplanted cells will die.

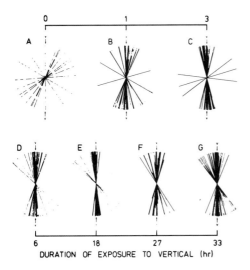

0   1   3

A   B   C

D   E   F   G

6   18   27   33

DURATION OF EXPOSURE TO VERTICAL (hr)

FIGURE 5.16
The orientation sensitivity of cells in the cat cortex as a function of experience with the vertical orientation. (*A*) With no exposure to vertical (zero hours), cells may be found in the cortex that are sensitive to all orientations. (*B*) When exposed to vertical stripes for as little as 1 hour during a sensitive period, cortical neurons begin to demonstrate a bias: Most become sensitive to vertical stimuli. (*C–G*) Three to 33 hours of exposure further sharpen cortical sensitivities to vertical stimuli, but not by much. (After Blakemore & Mitchell, 1973. © 1973 by *Nature*. Reprinted by permission.)

The modifiability of cellular sensitivity by experience is illustrated in Figure 5.16, which shows how individual cells in the cat visual cortex respond to stimuli in different orientations at 28 days of age. Figure 5.16A demonstrates that, in the absence of specific orientation experiences, the "naive" cortex contains cells sensitive to all orientations (Wiesel & Hubel, 1974). By contrast, the cat in Figure 5.16B was exposed to vertical stripes for 1 hour at a sensitive period early in its life; as can be seen, 1 hour of exposure was sufficient to bias the sensitivity of cells in its cortex. More units were devoted to vertical and near vertical orientations, whereas fewer units were devoted to other orientations. Figures 5.16C–G show that 3 to 33 hours of selective exposure did not sharpen cortical sensitivity to vertical stripes much more than 1 hour of exposure did, illustrating a threshold rather than linear dose–effect relation (see Chapter 3).

Studies like these demonstrate, first, newborn specificity at the cellular level (e.g., to orientation); second, initial equipotentiality of sensitivity (i.e., sensitivity to all orientations); third, cellular susceptibility and plasticity to experience; and, fourth, restriction of this susceptibility to early infancy. In general terms, we are apparently born with a brain ready to respond to critical features of our environment, but our brain can adapt to the environment in which we find ourselves. The window of modifiability is opened early in life so that we can prepare ourselves quickly and efficiently for the particular environment in which we will presumably develop.

Compensation is the second kind of neuronal plasticity. Compensation involves the ability of some cells to substitute for others, permitting recovery of function after neuronal loss or damage. Innumerable studies in the neurosciences show that, up to a certain point in development, local cellular defects may be compensated for by neighboring cells; after some sensitive period, however, the defect will be permanent (Chugani, 1994; Ospreen et al., 1995). The same general compensatory mechanisms seem to operate on much larger scales too. Dating back to the 1930s, a basic principle of brain plasticity has been that, when the brain is damaged early in development, subsequent functioning is less impaired than when injury is sustained late in development (Kennard, 1938). The "Kennard doctrine," however, has proved to be somewhat less robust than once believed, and by the mid-1970s it was challenged openly. Goldman (1974), for example, found that the developmental prognoses for monkeys who suffered early cortical damage were not necessarily more favorable than those of monkeys who were damaged at later ages. The effects of early damage appeared to depend on what was assessed and when it was assessed. Furthermore, children suffering lesions to the language areas of the left hemisphere in the first 2 years of life manifest major cognitive deficits, and other work indicates that the effects of early brain trauma can be severe and long lasting (Kolb, 1989). The Kennard doctrine still appears to have some validity, however, although it is not universally accurate.

Many neurologically minded psychologists have theorized about such phenomena. Lashley (1938) suggested that brain systems are largely redundant because capacities are multiply represented; therefore, young still-developing nervous systems may more easily compensate for parts that have been damaged. Perhaps different parts of the nervous system are specialized but sufficiently flexible to take over the role of damaged areas, albeit at some cost to their own special capacities. It is also possible that young neurons and young brains are less specialized with regard to function and so are able to compensate more flexibly (see Chugani, 1994; Johnson, 1997b; Kolb, 1989).

The plasticity of nervous tissue is illustrated by restoration of function following CNS damage or aging (Kolb, 1989). It has long been recognized that tissue in the peripheral nervous system regenerates, but the postnatal CNS was believed to be structurally static, such that recovery of function following damage or insult in childhood or maturity could only be mediated by the development of alternative pathways. However, the resilience and adaptability of the infant brain have impressed researchers, and the success of embryonic brain tissue grafts in nonhuman species shows that new cells or new cell processes can develop to repair damaged parts of the CNS or replace cells that have died (Johnson, 1999). We do not understand how or why such fetal nerve transplants work: Connections may develop between transplant and host brain, or fetal brain grafts may release growth hormones that promote functional recovery.

In summary, central nervous system development in infancy has been studied at the cellular level and in terms of overall brain structure, at the level of single-cell electrical activity, as well as at the level of gross activation. At each level, important questions arise concerning the interplay between strict maturational progress and the diverse array of experiences that affect the development of single cells and the brain as a whole.

Development of the Sensory Systems

The sensory systems function in utero and do not lie dormant until they are suddenly "switched on" at birth. Determining approximately when they begin to function normally is important for several reasons. First, knowing about development of the sensory systems enlarges our understanding of the general relation between structure and function. Second, it is theoretically and practically important to learn how early brain development may be influenced by sensory stimulation. Preterm babies are often born as much as $2\frac{1}{2}$ to $3\frac{1}{2}$ months before their expected due date and are therefore exposed to environmental stimulation from which they would normally be shielded. When sensory systems are not functional at this stage, preterm infants are "protected." When specific sensory systems do function, however, preterm babies may be adversely affected by the stimulating environment of the neonatal intensive care unit (NICU; Als, 1992).

As we reported in Chapter 3, Darwin observed more than 150 years ago that his son could hear, see, and probably smell soon after birth (Box 3.1), but only in the past decade have we learned very much about the structural and functional development of sensory systems before and around the time of birth. Three research tactics have been particularly informative: animal models, studies of preterm babies, and antenatal assessments in normal babies.

Two generalizations about the antenatal development of the sensory systems are well established. First, maturation within systems tends to occur peripherally before it occurs centrally. Thus, for example, the eye differentiates structurally and reaches functional maturity before the visual cortex does (Johnson, 1997a), although the retina is not fully developed at birth and development of the fovea (the part of retina where vision is most acute during the day) continues for up to 4 years of age (Banks & Shannon, 1993). Second, across systems different senses achieve structural and functional maturity at different times (Neville, 1995). Figure 5.17 shows the ontogenetic sequence of structure and function for four sensory systems—touch, position, hearing, and vision. Turkewitz and Kenny (1982) argued that this staggered developmental schedule has several biopsychological advantages, notably the fact that developmental focus on one system at a time permits the organism to "concentrate on" reaching high levels of functional maturity in each. As Gottlieb (1992) pointed out, the order in which sensory systems develop in the individual, that is ontogenetically, loosely follows the evolutionary or phylogenetic history of these systems.

Babies are reasonably well prepared to perceive the world almost as soon as extrauterine life begins: Indeed, newborns in the first hours appear to be

FIGURE 5.17
The order in which the sensory systems begin to function is similar in many species: cutaneous, vestibular, auditory, visual. (After Gottlieb, 1971b. © 1971 by Academic Press. Reprinted by permission.)

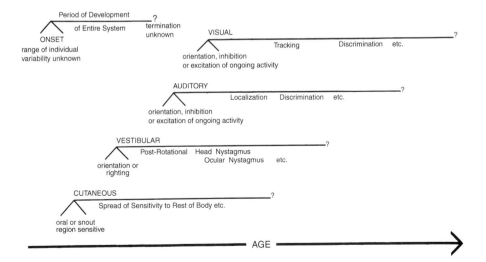

ONTOGENETIC SEQUENCE OF DEVELOPMENT OF FOUR SENSORY SYSTEMS

in a state of heightened sensory awareness, perhaps because of the prolonged rigors of the birth experience. By the second trimester of gestation, the eye and visual system, the ear and auditory system, the nose and olfactory system, the tongue and gustatory system, and the somatosensory system are essentially mature structurally, although their levels of functional competence lag (Menacker & Batshaw, 1997; Mennella & Beauchamp, 1997; Steinberg & Knightly, 1997).

How early can the conceptus–fetus–neonate sense or perceive? How good are those sensations and perceptions? These two developmental questions translate into psycho-physical ones having to do with, first, the strength of a physical stimulus that is necessary to elicit a sensation of some sort and, second, the degree to which a physical stimulus must be changed to yield a new perception. These two "threshold" questions define the basics of the study of sensation. In general, a systematic sensory psychophysics of infancy is still lacking, but we possess some rudimentary information about basic sensory sensitivities.

The "Lower" Senses

The somesthetic system regulates thermal, tactile, and positional information. Nervous tissue grows out centrally to reach the skin by the middle of the first trimester, and myelination of relevant tracts in the spinal cord has begun by the second trimester of gestation. Touch reflexes and vestibular circuitry develop precociously, and neuromotor organization in the brain stem and spinal cord produce fetal face and hand movements that suggest preadaptation for manual and oral grasp (Trevarthen, 1974). In an early study, Spelt (1948) investigated tactile sensitivity in utero with fetuses ranging from 7 to 9 months of gestational age. He used a loud clapper to elicit fetal movement, pairing clapping with vibrotactile stimulation. Spelt reported that, after as few as 15 paired stimulations, fetuses moved regularly when the tactile stimulus was presented alone. Although the fetus is known to move about spontaneously in the second trimester (Figure 4.7) and later to orient (presumably using gravity), very little is understood about prenatal development of the complex somatosensory system. Infants appear to be highly responsive to tactile stimulation, and attachment theorists have long emphasized the salience of touch for the establishment and maintenance of emotional intimacy and infant–parent attachment (Bowlby, 1969; Harlow, 1958). Systematically administered tactile stimulation appears to foster weight gain and growth in high-risk neonates such as preterms (Dieter & Emory, 1997; Goldberg & DiVitto, 2002).

The status of olfactory and gustatory function before birth is understood mostly by way of studies with animals and with preterm and term human infants. Such studies show that taste buds form and are innervated by taste nerves by about the twelfth week of gestation (Mennella & Beauchamp, 1996) and that the ability to taste develops before birth. Harris (1997) and Simbrunger (1985) found that preterm and term infants preferred a glucose solution over plain water, and a sweet solution over a salty solution, suggesting that the preference for sweet solutions may be innate. Several researchers have shown that distressed preterm and term infants can be soothed merely by giving them a glucose solution to drink, emphasizing the very high reward value that sweet tastes hold for infants (Blass, 1998; Smith & Blass, 1996; Zeifman, Delaney, & Blass, 1996).

Furthermore, neonates react with aversion when given bitter (quinine) or sour (citric acid) solutions.

Like somesthesis, gustation and olfaction are sensory systems that may reach structural maturity and functional competence early in ontogenesis. For these systems, however, birth is a significant event. The postnatal environment is not weightless; locomotion must now be self-produced; taste stimuli are homogeneous prenatally (the fetus is immersed in amniotic fluid) and heterogeneous postnatally; and odor stimuli become gaseous rather than liquid. As we shall learn in Chapter 6, somesthesis, taste, and smell, the "lower" senses have received less attention than have the "higher" senses, vision and audition, but these sensory systems play key roles in the first year, including all-important decisions about what is nourishing and what is not. The olfactory system is highly developed at birth, and preferences for pleasant (e.g., bananas or chocolate) over unpleasant odors (e.g., rotten eggs) appears to mirror adult preferences (Steiner, 1979). Indeed, the sense of smell is so good that newborn babies who breast-feed are able to identify their mothers by smell (Porter, Makin, Davis, & Christensen, 1992). The gustatory and olfactory sensory systems thus have a primitive history, advanced developmental status, and extraordinary sensitivity.

Vision

The early ontogenesis of vision has been studied most thoroughly, and two information-transmission pathways in the visual system have been identified (see Figure 5.18). Projections along the *primary visual system* originate in the retina, pass through a central thalamic relay called the lateral geniculate nucleus, and end in the occipital cortex or in other neocortical systems. The *second visual system* projects initially to the superior colliculus and then to the thalamus. The eye and the retina develop rapidly in the first and second trimesters of gestation, respectively, although the development of fine retinal structures such as the fovea is not complete until after birth (Banks & Shannon, 1993). Similarly, the optic nerve, lateral geniculate nuclei, and the layers of the cortex continue to develop with respect to cell size, myelination, and interneural connectivity well into postnatal life (Johnson, 1999; Ospreen, Risser, & Edgell, 1995). The subcortical colliculus–thalamic route is thought to approach functional maturity somewhat earlier, however.

The two visual systems have different functions: The second and phylogenetically older visual system is especially concerned with control of eye movements and information about stimulus orientation and location in space, whereas the primary visual system is concerned with information about stimulus detail and complexity.

Although the quality of visual attention seems to increase drastically after 8 months conceptional age, younger preterm infants respond to visual stimuli well before their term date. Preterms frequently express visual preferences that differ from those of conceptionally matched term babies; they also habituate less efficiently when they suffer CNS-related complications associated with prematurity, such as intraventricular hemorrhage (Ross, Tesman, Auld, & Nass, 1992), suggesting that visual functioning among preterm and term infants may differ (Bonin, Pomerleau, & Malcuit, 1998). In addition, the latency of the visually evoked cortical potential correlates with conceptional age (Thomas & Crow,

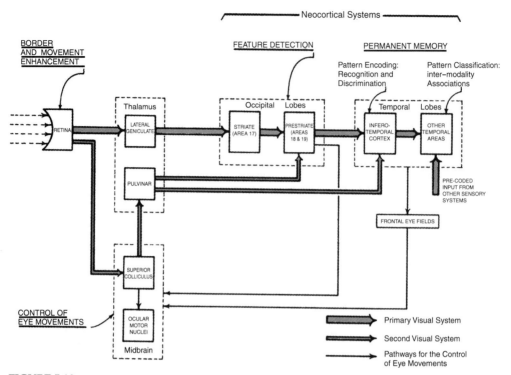

FIGURE 5.18

A simplified representation of information processing in the human visual system. (After Bronson, 1974. © 1974 by the Society for Research and Child Development. Reprinted by permission.)

1994), as illustrated in Figure 5.15B. This maturational change in responding may in turn relate to the development of attention and to the speed of visual information processing (Bornstein, Slater, Brown, Roberts, & Barrett, 1997).

It has long been observed that newborns' gross motility (Darwin, 1877; Box 3.1; Smith, 1936), pupillary reflexes (Sherman, Sherman, & Flory, 1936), and visual preferences (Hershenson, 1964) all change in response to variations in ambient illumination, indicating that newborns discriminate brightness. Indeed, they do so surprisingly well. Peeples and Teller (1975) measured brightness discrimination in 2-month-old infants using a pattern-preference technique. Infants were exposed to two homogeneous white fields, and their attention was drawn toward one when it contained a white bar that differed from the background white by as little as 5% contrast. (Adults can discriminate a 1% difference in contrast.) Pataansuu and von Hofsten (1991) demonstrated with an habituation technique that 5-month-olds discriminate between sharp and gradual changes in the brightness of a visual stimulus. Infants clearly approximate adult levels of basic visual capacity very early.

When considering the different developmental trajectories of vision and the "lower" senses, it is important to keep in mind that somesthesis, olfaction, and gustation can be stimulated and exercised before birth, whereas naturalistic, complex, patterned, and colorful visual stimulation can only be experienced after birth. To the extent that experience influences and provokes development, visual development is at a clear ecological disadvantage.

Audition

As much as seeing, newborn hearing has captured the imagination of developmentalists. The ear develops very early in gestation, and by the end of the first month after conception the cochlea is anatomically distinct. At birth, the peripheral sensory system is essentially mature (Ospreen et al., 1995; Steinberg & Knightly, 1997), as is the auditory nerve. Mature function is still inhibited, however, until amniotic fluid has drained from the middle ear.

The development of auditory sensitivity before term has been explored in several ways, but studies of electrophysiological (ERP), heart rate, and motor responses have been most common. Research with preterms indicates that the fetus responds to sounds beginning around the twelfth week of gestation, and the ability to detect sounds improves with age, stabilizing by 30 to 32 weeks of gestational age (Busnel, Granier-Deferre, & Lecanuet, 1992). The mother's abdominal wall and uterus diminish the intensity of surrounding sounds some 10 to 20 decibels but change other characteristics of the sounds very little (Bremner, 1994). Newborn infants can discriminate sounds of different intensities and frequencies, and after about 5 months of age infants can reliably identify the location of a sound (Mercer, 1998). Newborns also appear to respond selectively to sound frequencies that occur within the range of the human voice (Aslin, Jusczyk, & Pisoni, 1998).

Infants may innately prefer to attend to maternal singing that is directed toward them. In a study of 2-day-old hearing infants of deaf parents, Masataka (1999) recorded mothers singing an infant play song to their infants, and then to their adult friends. Recordings of the songs were made in Japanese and in English. Infants were then tested to determine whether they looked longer at a visual stimulus (a black-and-white checkerboard) when the infant-directed song was played than when the adult-directed song was played. Infants were clearly more attracted to singing that was infant directed, and this preference was independent of the language in which the songs were sung, indicating that infants prefer speech with melodic or prosodic variation. Furthermore, because all infants in this study had deaf parents who did not speak or sing, it was likely that this preference is innate rather than a function of prenatal or postnatal experience.

In summary, all of the senses develop during the prenatal period. One of the principal ways in which fetuses are prepared for their extrauterine future life is by substantial prenatal investment in the development of the central and peripheral sensory systems. Kessen and his colleagues (1970) once characterized human babies as "sensory surfaces." The sensory systems permit infants to register, to integrate, and to interpret many dimensions of their new world. In Chapter 6, we show how infants make use of sensory information when perceiving the world.

Summary

Major neurological developments occurring pre- and postnatally correspond to or underpin many of the observable developmental trends that interest developmental scientists. Infants initially lack the capacity to modulate their own states of arousal and thus seem to move erratically from one state to another. Nevertheless, painstaking examination over extended periods of time shows consistent (if gross) cyclic organization of infant state. In addition, neurological development appears to underlie the emergence of organized sleep patterns resembling those common in maturity. Reliable individual differences in heart rate levels and variability soon emerge, and predictable changes in heart rate in response to various types of stimulation provide a powerful tool for assessing infants' states of development and general responsivity.

In the central nervous system, intracellular and intercellular structure and function change over the first years of life as brain cells are born, develop, and connect with one another so as to permit the increasingly efficient and complex transmission of information. Alongside remarkable programmed specializations, malleability and compensation attest to the great extent of neural plasticity in infancy. The sensory capacities to taste, smell, touch, see, and hear all progress in the fetal period so that the infant is born in a state of high sensory preparedness.

6

Perceptual Development in Infancy

❖

- Can you illustrate how and why early perceptual development served as a battle-ground between nativists and empiricists?
- How do infants perceive depth?
- Why does attention play such a crucial role in the study of perceptual development in infancy?
- When and how do infants perceive forms, orientation, and movement?
- Do infants perceive color? Why was it so difficult to answer this question?
- How well do infants hear? In what ways does their sensitivity to speech sounds appear specialized?
- How and when do infants integrate information to develop cross-modal perceptions?

Beginning to Sense and Understand the World

Perception constitutes the necessary first step in experiencing and interpret-ing the world, and for this reason philosophers, psychologists, physiolo-gists, and physicists alike have been attracted to the study of perception. Our everyday experiences raise many intriguing perceptual questions. How do our perceptions come to achieve stability amidst constant fluctuations in the environment? How do perceptions come to be invested with meaning? How are the individual features of things we perceive synthesized into organized wholes? How does the perceptual quality of "bitter" differ from that of "red"? How do we see a three-dimensional world when visual processing begins with a two-dimensional image in the eye?

The study of perception was initiated by philosophers who were interested in epistemology and the nature–nurture debate about the origins of knowledge. As we read in Chapter 1, extreme views were put forward by *empiricists* on the one hand, who asserted that all knowledge comes through the senses and grows by way of experience, and by *nativists* on the other, who reasoned that human beings enter the world with rudimentary knowledge and abilities that help to order and organize what they experience. The philosophers mainly engaged in theoretical speculation and argument; it was not until physics and psychology joined forces near the dawn of the twentieth century that experimentation was introduced into the study of perception. But philosophy did focus attention on infancy, because the development of perception at or near the beginning of life is necessarily the proper period in which to study the origins and early growth of knowledge.

In addition to this philosophical purpose, studies of perception in infancy address other questions. They provide information about the quality, limits, and capacities of the sensory systems described in Chapter 5. Determining how the senses function in infancy in turn permits us to glimpse the infant's world and tells us what aspects of the environment might meaningfully influence early development. Finally, understanding perception in infancy provides a baseline against which maturation and the effects of experience can be assessed.

We start our consideration of perceptual development in infancy with a discussion of philosophical foundations and motivations for studying perceptual development empirically, and to illustrate this approach we provide an in-depth example of a classic historical controversy. We next consider the central role of attention as a means of understanding early perceptual development. Then, we turn to the heart of the matter and summarize what is known about the status of perception in infancy. Following the growth of research in this field, we emphasize the "higher" senses—sight and hearing—but also discuss some of what we know about the "lower" senses—taste, smell, and touch. In the final sections of the chapter we discuss two significant issues in infant perception: how perceptions arising from different sensory modalities interrelate and coordinate, and how experiences influence the development of perception.

Philosophical Questions and Developmental Research

Perceptual development has served as a kind of battleground between nativists and empiricists, and to illustrate this we examine one exemplary skirmish in detail. It concerns the ways infants might come to perceive depth in space. We selected this example for several reasons. First, depth perception is crucial to determining the spatial layout of the environment, recognizing objects, and guiding motor action. Second, the study of depth perception addresses an interesting psychophysical question, namely how we perceive the three dimensionality of the environment when the retina of the eye first codes information along only two dimensions. Third, debate on this question exemplifies the typical historical course: It began with hotly contested philosophical disputes that spanned the seventeenth to nineteenth centuries before prompting experimentation in the twentieth century. Throughout this time, philosophers and scientists consistently looked to infancy to help decide how depth perception develops.

A Nativist–Empiricist Debate

How do human beings come to perceive depth in visual space? Writing in the treatise *La Dioptrique* in 1638, the French philosopher René Descartes offered an answer to this question that assumed the mind's intuitive grasp of mathematical relations. Descartes believed that knowledge is inborn and that human beings are guided by "natural" laws. Our two eyes form the base of a triangle whose apex lies at the target under our gaze. When we look at a target that is far away, our lines of vision are more nearly parallel and the base angles of the triangle approach 90 degrees. When we look at a target that is nearby, the base angles of the triangle are acute. The closer the target, the more acute the angles. Descartes (1638/1824, pp. 59–66) concluded that distance is given by "an act of thinking which, being simple imagination, does not entail reasoning." Descartes was correct in observing that our eyes converge more for near than for far points of interest, and that degree of convergence is directly related to target distance. *But are we born with trigonometric tables in our heads?*

A different explanation for depth perception was later put forward by the Irish empiricist George Berkeley (1685–1753) in his *Essay Towards a New Theory of Vision* of 1709. Berkeley (1709/1901) argued that human beings do not intuit distance by "natural geometry." Rather, Berkeley theorized that infants learn object size through feedback from their tactile and motor experience. In essence, Berkeley claimed that infants associate the large apparent size of objects with bringing their two eyes close together in conjunction with the small amount they have to move their arms when reaching for nearby objects. Likewise, infants associate the small apparent size of objects with the parallel position of the two eyes and the large arm movements that need to be made when reaching for faraway objects. Berkeley hypothesized that reaching in association with convergence of the eyes and the appearance of objects leads to visual understanding of depth and distance. Touch teaches vision.

Nativists countered Berkeley's experiential argument with logic. In the *Critique of Pure Reason*, Immanuel Kant (1781/1924) asserted that the human mind does not rely on experience for meaning but innately organizes sensations into meaningful perceptions. Kant's theoretical argument was buttressed with two observations: First, depth perception emerges too early in life to be based on extensive experience and learning, and, second, adults with limited experience can perceive depth. The nativist belief that some capacity to perceive depth must be inborn also impelled some of the first experimenters in the field to seek specific biological substrates that might underlie the ability to perceive depth. Initially, such mechanisms were simply postulated by physiologists like Ewald Hering, but in more modern times sensory physiologists recording from single cells in the cortex have found hard evidence for them.

Immediately after Kant, the debate continued with a defense of empiricism. In his classic *Handbook of Physiological Optics*, Hermann Helmholtz (1866) argued that the nativists' "intuition theory is an unnecessary hypothesis." Helmholtz (1866/1925, Vol. 3) asserted that it is uneconomical to assume mechanisms of innate perception, especially when "It is not clear how the assumption of these original *'space sensations'* can help the explanation of our visual perceptions, when the adherents of this theory ultimately have to assume . . . that these sensations must be overruled by the better understanding which we get by experience."

Research Resolutions

At this juncture in history, experimental study began to supplant philosophical speculation; in fact, experimental psychology, which started only in the twentieth century, was at first specifically organized to address just such issues. Three lines of research exemplify how questions about the origins of depth perception have been addressed experimentally. All three are valuable because no one alone provides definitive information, but the three together converge to sketch how depth perception develops. The starting point for the first line of research was the following observation:

> Human infants at the creeping and toddling stage are notoriously prone to falls from more or less high places. They must be kept from going over the brink by side panels on their cribs, gates on their stairways, and vigilance of adults. As their muscular coordination matures, they begin to avoid such accidents on their own. Common sense might suggest that the child learns to recognize falling-off places by experience—that is, by falling and hurting himself. But is experience really the teacher? Or is the ability to perceive and avoid a brink part of the child's original endowment? (Gibson & Walk, 1960, p. 64)

In the early 1960s, Gibson and Walk (1960) began experiments to investigate depth perception in infants using a "visual cliff" (Figure 6.1). One side of the cliff shows the baby an illusory drop but the other side does not. Gibson and Walk found that only a very small minority of infants they tested between 6 and 14 months of age crawled across the "deep" side when their mothers called them.

FIGURE 6.1
The visual cliff. There is a glass on both sides, but on one side there is a deep space between the glass and the checkered floor; on the other side the checks are right under the glass. (Courtesy of R. Walk.)

From these results, they concluded that depth perception must be present in infants as young as 6 months of age. By 6 months, however, children may already have had plenty of experience perceiving depth. Bertenthal and Campos (1990) studied precrawling babies by monitoring heart rate when the babies were exposed to shallow and deep sides of the visual cliff. They found that babies as young as 2 months of age showed a decrease in heart rate when exposed to the deep side, indicating increased attention or interest. Thus, babies may perceive depth long before they locomote but show little fear of the drop at that age. The wariness of drops shown by older infants may result from the anxiety parents show when infants approach a drop, rather than from actual experience with falls. Infants "socially reference" their parents and use their parents' emotional cues to interpret ambiguous events (see Chapter 10).

Visual cliff experiments represent one way investigators have sought to explore the infant's capacity to perceive depth. In actuality, three types of stimulus information specify depth, and we thus organize this discussion of early depth perception around binocular, static, and kinetic cues. As Descartes and Kant argued, we have at least two bases for perceiving depth because we are *binocular* (have two eyes). Because our two eyes receive slightly different images of the visual world, the convergence angle of the two and the disparity between the two images they yield provide some information about depth perception. Binocular convergence provides information only about close-up distances, but it may provide functional information about depth as early as 2 months of age (Hainline, Riddell, Grose-Fifer, & Abramov, 1992; Kellman & Banks, 1998).

Purely *static monocular information* helps us to "see" depth as well. When normal viewing conditions are degraded, a single eye looking at a nonmoving single point of observation still cues depth. Monocular cues to depth are especially well known; artists as far back as da Vinci, Michaelangelo, and others of the Renaissance described many such ways of convincing viewers to perceive depth in a painting. One such pictorial cue is *relative size*: If two objects are known to be similar in size, having one appear smaller than the other in a two-dimensional space makes the smaller appear further away. Another is *linear perspective*: Two lines known to be parallel in real life (e.g., railroad tracks) are seen as moving away from the onlooker if they are drawn to converge in an upwardly vertical or oblique direction. *Texture gradients*, another monocular depth cue, signal depth when the elements of the textured surface gradually reduce in size across two-dimensional space (most clearly perceived when the gradient moves in a generally upward direction). Other monocular cues include *interposition* (when contours of one object partially occlude another object, the first object is perceived to be closer than the second) and *shading* (contours of an object oriented away from a light source will appear darker than will contours oriented toward the light, providing the illusion of depth). Granrud, Yonas, and their colleagues (Granrud, 1993; Yonas, Arterberry, & Granrud, 1987) conducted systematic studies organized to explore infants' responsiveness to a variety of pictorial depth cues in isolation and found that infants become sensitive to these cues at around 7 months of age.

The world and the infant perceiving it are constantly in flux, and movement information from this continuously changing structure provides additional cues to depth. There are several so-called *kinetic* cues to depth. When an object comes directly toward us on a "hit path," its image on the retina expands and we normally move to avoid the impending collision. Yonas (1981, Pettersen, Yonas, & Fisch, 1980) also conducted a series of experiments to study object "looming." Babies viewed a translucent screen onto which a silhouette of a three-dimensional objects was cast. This technique avoids actually threatening babies with a solid object and cuing them with the air changes that an actual approaching object might cause. Yonas found that babies as young as 1 month consistently blinked at approaching objects. Consider another kinetic cue, *motion parallax*: When you move through the environment, closer surfaces are perceived to occlude more distant ones: Sitting in the car, the telephone pole "moves" in front of the more distant tree. Differences in such motion gradients provide information about the relative depth of objects. Indeed, changing texture gradients as individuals or objects move through space are also used to signal depth through the *accretion or deletion of texture* (Craton & Yonas, 1990). Texture elements that become smaller with movement are perceived to be moving away in space, whereas texture elements that become larger when they move are perceived as moving closer. Even 5-month-olds use kinetic information of this kind to perceive the layout of surfaces (Kellman & Banks, 1998).

In sum, depth perception experiments have demonstrated that infants are sensitive to binocular and kinetic information by 3 to 5 months of age but may not be sensitive to static information until about 7 months of age. It is important to point out, however, that infants younger than 3 months of age probably perceive depth. Limits to our understanding of infant perception of depth are placed on us by our methods of study. There may never be a final triumph for nativism or for empiricism. It can be argued that, no matter how early in life depth perception can be demonstrated, the ability still rests on some experience, and that no matter how late depth perception emerges, it can never be proved that only experience has mattered. Nevertheless, the nativism–empiricism debate remains pervasive in the developmental study of depth perception, as well as color, speech, and (as we shall see) many other content topics in infant perceptual development.

Attention: How Perceptual Questions Are Asked of Infants and How Their Answers Are Interpreted

Much perceptual research in infancy depends critically on the attention babies pay. As we just saw in our brief review of depth perception, our understanding of infant capacity and developmental status rests on whether infants orient, look, and so forth. Attention determines which information enters the brain, and attention is the gateway to perception (Lang, Simons, & Balaban, 1997). Attention underlies awareness, experience, and interpretation of the world. Attention is therefore a significant mechanism by which infants acquire knowledge about the world. So much of the infant's maturation is hidden that whatever is observable takes on heightened significance. To what and to whom infants attend therefore serve as prominent markers of perceptual and intellectual functioning. Attention in infancy also has social consequences. Gaze is the basic unit of social exchange; establishing eye-to-eye contact with a newborn is not only rewarding to the caregiver but also sets in motion the routines and rhythms of social interaction and play. For these important reasons we now examine perceptual attention and then discuss perceptual capacity.

Attention signals information gathering from the surrounding environment, and attention therefore plays a critical role in early perception. By the mid-trimester of prenatal life, as we learned in Chapter 5, the eye and visual system, the ear and auditory system, as well as other anatomical and sensory systems have so developed that they are essentially complete structurally and very nearly mature functionally. At birth, infants can see, hear, taste, and experience touch, and so can begin to acquire information about the world through all of the senses. But the young infant (like the adult) is bombarded by sensory stimuli. An important general aspect of infant functioning is that, even from the neonatal period, babies both actively seek out and attend to certain sources of information in their environment. Patterns of attention demonstrate that infants select and, importantly, filter features of the environment and are not simply passive registrants of experience. Selectivity and activity work to the advantage of the young baby. Which stimulus features attract and hold the infant's attention? How does attention change in development? Attention is not at all simple or straightforward. Attention is composed of multiple subprocesses; attention is part reflex, part native preference, and part learned; and attention has diverse characteristics like intensity and duration.

The basic perceptual questions investigators ask infants concern the stimuli they can detect, the stimulus differences they can discriminate, and the stimuli they prefer. Methods using attention have developed to assess these capacities. For example, when habituated to one stimulus and then tested with different stimuli that are either similar to or dissimilar from the original, infants respond in a variety of ways. Four attention patterns provide information about infant detection and discrimination. The four patterns are shown graphically in Figure 6.2.

First, stimulus change following habituation may provoke attentiveness in proportion to the degree of difference between the test stimulus and the habituation stimulus (Figure 6.2A). Thus, the greater the discrepancy between a new stimulus and the habituation stimulus, the greater the discriminative response to the new stimulus. Studies of infant perception in various modalities have found that some discriminations follow just this pattern (Aslin, Jusczyk, & Pisoni, 1998; Atkinson & Hood, 1997; Bushnell, 1998; Rose & Tamis-Lemonda, 1999; Simion, Valenza, & Umilta, 1998; Slater & Johnson, 1998).

Second, change to a similar stimulus may fail to provoke a psychological discrimination (Figure 6.2B). This could reflect an actual failure to discriminate or a perceptual proclivity to group habituation and similar test stimuli together, as in categorical perception—treating two shades of blue as the same. (We discuss issues of categorization in more depth in Chapter 8.) To resolve these competing interpretations, however, it is necessary to demonstrate that under some circumstances infants can discriminate between the habituation target and the similar stimulus. To show that infants are responding at all, it is necessary to include a highly dissimilar stimulus which infants will certainly discriminate.

The third general pattern of performance might be called all-or-nothing discrimination. Here, any discriminable change in stimulation elicits roughly equivalent degrees of attention from the infant regardless of the degree of difference between the change stimulus and the habituation stimulus (Figure 6.2C). This result has been most powerfully demonstrated where stimulus change (regardless of its physical magnitude) crosses boundaries among psychological categories. Infants discriminate among different phonemes in this way (Jusczyk, 1994), as they do different hues (Kellman & Banks, 1998).

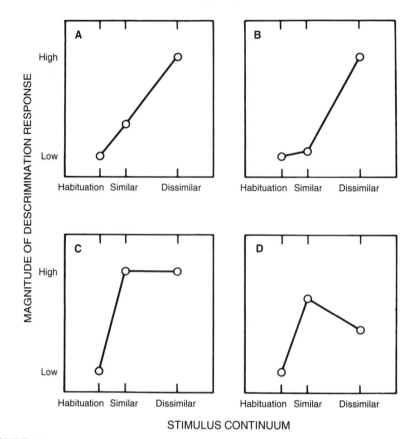

FIGURE 6.2

Four patterns of discriminative response to novel stimuli differing in psychological similarity from a habituation stimulus. (*A*) Response magnitude is a monotonic (and perhaps linear) function of the degree of difference among test and habituation stimuli. (*B*) Response magnitude is related to the degree of difference among test and habituation stimuli; habituation generalizes to similar stimuli but not to dissimilar ones. (*C*) Response magnitude reflects any difference among test and habituation stimuli; all discriminable stimuli elicit equivalent amounts of dishabituation. (*D*) Response magnitude is a nonmonotonic function of the discrepancy of test stimuli from the habituation stimulus; similar stimuli elicit more dishabituation than do dissimilar stimuli. (Position of similar and dissimilar stimuli in this figure have been scaled arbitrarily; the dissimilar stimulus is displaced three times the distance from the habituation stimulus as the similar stimulus. This is a general relation meant to be independent of any particular stimulus dimension.) (After Bornstein, 1981a © 1981 by Ablex Publishing Corporation. Reprinted by permission.)

A fourth pattern involves responses that are a nonmonotonic function of the degree of dissimilarity between the test and habituation stimuli (Figure 6.2D). Here, attending to test stimuli after habituation is an inverted-U function of the degree of discrepancy between familiar and novel stimuli. Psychologists have theorized that a moderate difference between the test stimulus and the habituation stimulus excites further exploration, whereas a test stimulus that is too novel does not sufficiently motivate the infant to explore (e.g., McCall, Kennedy, & Appelbaum, 1977; McCall & McGhee, 1977).

Certain forms of stimulation also appear to recruit infant attention, and infants have long been observed to possess and express many natural preferences favoring faces to nonfacial configurations of the same elements, three-dimensional to two-dimensional stimuli, pattern organization (symmetry) to disorganization (asymmetry), and dynamic to static configurations (Arterberry & Bornstein, 2001; Blass, 1999; Bornstein & Krinsky, 1985; Bremner, 1994; Simion, Valenza, & Umilta, 1998; Slater, 1997). They are also attracted by sweet tastes, pleasant odors, and speech-like sounds (Bertoncini, 1993; Kuhl, 1993; Mennella & Beauchamp, 1997). Visual and auditory preferences appear to be determined by stimulus characteristics, such as complexity or novelty or frequency and (relatedly) by the degree to which stimuli excite neural activity in the brain (Bornstein, 1978b).

In sum, attention serves as a principal door to perceptual functioning in infancy, as well as being among the most conspicuous indexes of infant affect and state of arousal. For these developmental and experimental reasons, attention is critical to substantive studies of infant perception.

Visual Perception

Perception is private, and there is no way for one person to know what another person's perceptions are like without making inferences from their reports or from their behaviors. Infants are mute and motorically underdeveloped, and as a result our knowledge of infants' perceptions must be inferred from behaviors such as those that index attention. However, those behaviors may vary in trustworthiness and credibility, and thus developmentalists have engineered many ways around the formidable barriers to communication that infants present. The convergence of results across techniques, laboratories, and time is critical to establishing the validity of those results (see Chapter 3). In the next sections of this chapter we discuss studies that have fleshed out our understanding of the infant's visual, auditory, chemical, and tactile worlds. Certainly our knowledge of these worlds is incomplete, but one must be impressed with how far the study of infant perception has progressed toward revealing just what perception in infancy may be like.

Two contrasting approaches to the assessment and analysis of perceptual systems exist. In this chapter, we follow the traditional "bottom-up" perspective in discussing the components of perceptual functions. The *bottom-up perspective* has two advantages. First, it closely follows the established scientific method of analysis: understanding individual aspects of a problem towards solving the problem as a whole. Second, it has a certain basis in reality, because the visual system, for example, analyzes the visual array in the world, decomposes it, and creates separate cortical representations of separate dimensions of experience. The alternative approach is, if you will, *top down*. Because objects in the environment may be specified by their sight, touch, or sound, our perception of them is invariably multimodal and is coordinated across modalities, and so it is possible to discuss perception of higher order or integrated aspects first and then move down to consider lower order sensory systems. For adults, perception is complex and normally difficult to fathom. As infants do not yet carry all of the perceptual baggage that adults do, we suspect that the most basic and general perceptual mechanisms are likely to be most salient to guide their actions and govern their acquisition of information about the world around them. For this reason, evaluating the components of perception in infants may provide insight into the basics of perception and the principles of its early development.

We begin by considering perception in the visual modality. In general, the visual world is specified by dimensions of pattern, orientation, location, movement, and color, so to gain a glimpse into the infant's visual world we review sensitivity to each of these dimensions.

Pattern, Shape, and Form

When and how well do infants first see forms? When do they see forms as a unit— as more than individual elements? In the 1960s, Kessen, Haith, and Salapatek attempted to assess sight in human newborns (Haith, 1980, 1991; Kessen, Haith, & Salapatek, 1970). They photographed the reflection of a stimulus on the front of a baby's eye, assuming that "fixating" a stimulus implied "perceiving." Some of the original findings from this research effort are still among the most provocative and still demonstrate basic principles of visual perception in the earliest part of infancy. First, the newborn actively seeks visual stimulation and input, scanning the environment in a controlled and alert fashion in order to find things to inspect . . . even in the dark. Second, newborns seem to focus most of their attention on the boundaries of figures, where the greatest amount of information is contained. So, looking strategies adopted by newborns (for whatever reason) guarantee that they will learn something about figures or objects, given the limitations under which their sensory channels operate.

Subsequent research using this technique has demonstrated that "scan patterns" develop (Haith, 1991; see Figure 6.3). In general, very young infants (under 5 weeks old) scan patterns in a limited fashion, whereas older babies

FIGURE 6.3
Typical findings obtained in studies of infant scanning. Neither 1- nor 2-month-old infants scan the entire figure. At 1 month, any contour attracts the infant's attention; at 2 months scanning is focused on the edges and angles of the figures. (Courtesy of P. Salapatek.)

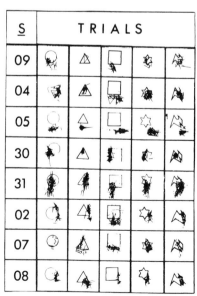

One Month Olds   Two Month Olds

scan patterns more widely and efficiently (Slater & Johnson, 1998). Studies of organized scanning indicate that newborns and young infants see something when they look at patterns, but scanning does not tell us how well infants see or what they see. After all, the fact that an infant scans an angle of a triangle does not mean that the infant resolves the contour perfectly or perceives the triangle (or even an angle of it) as adults do. Many kinds of studies have been developed to address these questions about higher order perceptions of form and pattern (e.g., de Schonen, Dervelle, Mancini, & Pascalis, 1996; Slater, 1997).

Fantz originated a preference technique to examine how well infants see, that is, visual acuity in infants. Fantz, Ordy, and Udelf (1962) capitalized on the observation that infants prefer to look at heterogeneous rather than homogeneous patterns, posting pairs of patterns for babies to look at; one member of the pair was always gray and the other a set of black-and-white stripes that varied systematically in width. (The two stimuli were also always matched in overall brightness.) The stripe width that failed to evoke a preference was viewed as giving the boundary of the baby's ability to tell stripes from solid grey. Figure 6.4 shows an infant being tested for visual acuity, and Figure 6.5 provides a concrete idea of just how well newborn babies actually see. By this measure, infants show a remarkable development in acuity between 2 weeks and 5 months. In the 40 years since Fantz's original study, techniques for measuring infant visual acuity have grown in sophistication, but the results they have yielded agree well with the initial findings (Held, 1993; Kellman & Banks, 1998; Slater, 1995; Slater & Johnson, 1998). Thus, whereas visual acuity is relatively poor in newborns, it improves rapidly and, by about 6 months of age, is almost the same as that of normal adults (Slater & Butterworth, 1997).

Infants can resolve and discriminate on the basis of visual detail, but when do infants actually perceive forms as forms? This question is interesting practically and theoretically because some theorists (Gestaltists like Koffka, 1935, for example) proposed that the perception of whole forms is innate, whereas others

FIGURE 6.4
An infant's visual acuity being tested. (Courtesy of J. Atkinson and O. Braddock.)

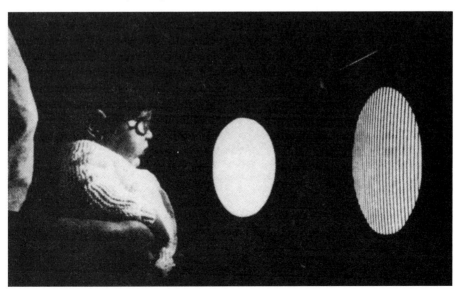

FIGURE 6.5
The face as it might appear to a newborn and to us. (Courtesy of A. Slater.)

(constructivists like Hebb, 1949, and Piaget, 1952) proposed that perception of whole forms is built up from perceptions of individual elements—lines and angles and surfaces. The question has proven remarkably difficult to answer because almost any discrimination between two forms (a triangle from a circle) can be explained as a discrimination on some simpler, featural basis (such as discriminating an angle from an arc or discriminating differing amounts of contour) without implicating "whole form" perception. Indeed, forms typically integrate multiple features (for example, color and shape), and proper perception occurs when these individual features are synthesized into a single, unified "compound" stimulus (e.g., a red triangle).

Slater, Mattock, Brown, Burnham, and Young (1991a, 1991b) demonstrated that even newborn infants have the capacity to perceive stimulus compounds. In their experiment, newborns were habituated to a pair of stimulus compounds (e.g., a green diagonal stripe that combines greenness with diagonality and a red vertical stripe that combines redness with verticality). In subsequent novelty preference test trials, infants were presented with a pair of compound stimuli: one that they had already seen (e.g., the green diagonal stripe), and one whose combined features they had not seen before (e.g., a red diagonal stripe or a green vertical stripe). All infants looked significantly longer at the unfamiliar stimulus compound than at the familiar stimulus compound. This difference in looking time could only be explained by the infants' prior memory of the compound stimuli to which they had been familiarized, because the novel stimulus compound presented during the test trials was composed of individual features (redness, greenness, verticality, and diagonality) that the infants had already seen during the habituation phase of the experiment.

Other studies indicate that very young infants can perceive whole forms through subjective contours, that is, seeing form not on the page but "in the mind's eye." Subjective contours are perceived only when component elements—in Figure 6.6, the larger pie segments—are precisely aligned. Infants can only see the square in Figure 6.6A if they fuse the component parts of the figure into a whole. Ghim's (1990) work with these stimuli demonstrated that infants as young as 3 to 4 months perceive whole forms through subjective contours. In one study, infants were habituated to Figure 6.6A (the subjective contour group) or to either Figure 6.6B, 6.6C, or 6.6D (the nonsubjective contour

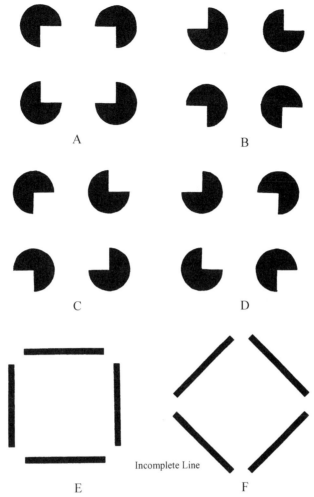

FIGURE 6.6
Four stimulus patterns used in Ghim's (1990) experiments. Pattern A produces subjective contours forming a square. Patterns B, C, and D do not produce subjective contours of a whole figure. Pattern E is an incomplete square pattern, and Pattern F is an incomplete diamond pattern. (Taken from H.-R. Ghim, 1990.)

group). Infants habituated to the subjective contour figure (Figure 6.6A) looked longer at the nonsubjective contour stimuli (Figures 6.6B, 6.6C, and 6.6D) than to the subjective contour stimulus (Figure 6.6A) during novelty preference test trials, indicating that they discriminated the subjective contour stimulus from the nonsubjective contour stimuli. By contrast, infants habituated to one of the nonsubjective contour stimuli were unable to discriminate among any of the nonsubjective contour stimuli. In a separate experiment, infants habituated to the subjective contour figure (Figure 6.6A) preferentially looked in posthabituation test trials at Figure 6.6F (the incomplete diamond form) rather than at Figure 6.6E (the incomplete square form). This indicated that the diamond pattern (Figure 6.6F) was perceived as more novel by infants habituated to the subjective contour square pattern (Figure 6.6A) than was the square pattern (Figure 6.6E). Thus, whole form perception via subjective contours, suggesting perception of complete forms, appears as early as 3 months of age.

As a special visual pattern, the face has engendered a perceptual literature of its own. Infants appear to be highly attracted to faces, although it has long been unclear whether this attraction is founded on an innate, species-specific predisposition to attend to faces (Johnson & Morton, 1993) or based on the fact that faces contain features that infants find intrinsically interesting (i.e., faces are three dimensional, move, produce sounds, and have areas of high contrast; Slater, 1993).

Early work with two-dimensional stimuli (e.g., photographs of faces) suggested that the basis for infants' attraction to faces was the presence of contrasts in facial configurations. Melhuish (1982), for example, found that 1-month-old infants did not look any longer at photographs of their mothers than at photographs of strangers, although infants preferred to look at faces with high contrast. These findings, involving two-dimensional, nonmoving stimuli, such as drawings or photographs, were replicated in a number of different laboratories (Bushnell, 1982; Kleiner, 1987). When two-dimensional stimuli in a normal face pattern, a scrambled face pattern, and a blank stimulus moved slowly in an arc-like path (see Figure 6.7), however, newborns looked at and tracked the normal face pattern significantly more than the scrambled face pattern (which was equated with the normal face pattern with respect to complexity and contrast), and in turn showed a preference for the scrambled face pattern over the blank stimulus (Johnson, Dziurawiec, Ellis, & Morton, 1991). Viewed in the context of other studies demonstrating that newborns can imitate facial expressions (happiness, sadness, surprise; Field, Woodson, Greenberg, & Cohen, 1982) and tongue protrusions (Kugiumutzakis, 1993; Meltzoff & Moore, 1977), these results suggest that newborn infants indeed possess some innate knowledge of faces and a specialized mechanism for processing facial configurations (Mondloch et al., 1999; Simion et al., 1998; Slater & Butterworth, 1997). This does not mean that infants' knowledge of faces is complete at birth. The ability to discriminate their mothers' face from others, distinguish among different facial expressions and understand the information conveyed by each, and discriminate between male versus female and young versus old faces are products of everyday experiences with faces (Bornstein & Arterberry, 2000; Bushnell, 1998; Johnson & Gilmore, 1996).

Orientation

Objects in the world are also specified by their coordination in space, including their orientation, location, and movement. Sensitivity to these spatial characteristics is critical to perception.

Physical space extends outward from the central "ego" equally in all directions, yet perceived orientation is not uniform: For adults, vertical appears to be more salient than horizontal, and horizontal is more salient than oblique

FIGURE 6.7

Experimental facial stimuli used in studies with infants. (A) The photograph of a normal face in the prototypical vertical symmetry. (B) The same face with internal features rearranged, but still symmetrical. (C) Internal facial features rearranged asymmetrically. (D) Internal facial features symmetrical, but off center. (E) The normal face turned on the horizontal. (F) The normal face, but with internal features turned on the horizontal. Such stimuli are used to assess infant sensitivity to the internal versus overall configuration of facial features and to the face as a whole.

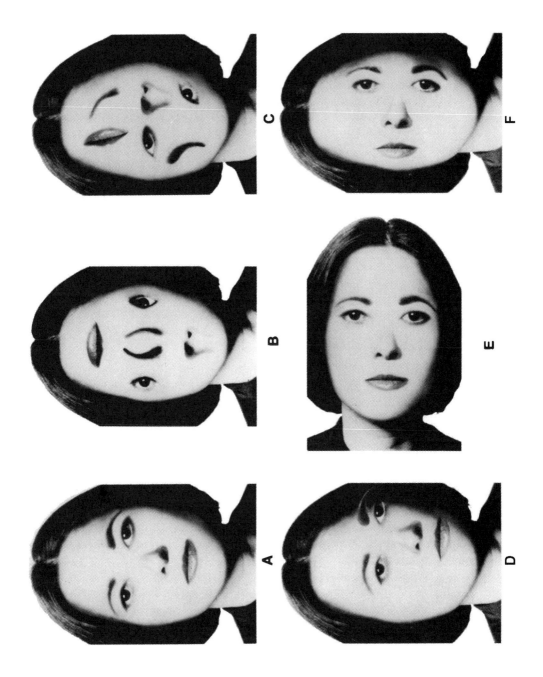

(Bornstein, 1982; Essock, 1980). For example, we accept the statement that "5 degrees is almost vertical" as somehow truer than the statement that "Vertical is almost 5 degrees" because vertical is a primary reference point. Studies of detection, discrimination, preference, and processing in infancy indicate that this same orientation salience hierarchy exists in early life—for artificial geometric forms as well as for meaningful patterns like the human face, for static as well as dynamic forms. Babies know and like the vertical: Shown pictures of a face right side up on the vertical axis (Figure 6.7A), as well as upside down or either way along the horizontal axis (Figure 6.7E), 2- to 4-month-olds clearly prefer the normal vertical orientation, showing this by smiling as well as by looking (Hayes & Watson, 1981b).

Held (1989) found that $1\frac{1}{2}$- to 12-month-old babies detect patterns aligned vertically or horizontally more readily than they detect the same patterns aligned obliquely, and that visual acuity for vertical and horizontal patterns increases more rapidly over the first year of life than does acuity for oblique patterns. Bornstein, Ferdinandsen, and Gross (1981) have likewise shown both preference and perceptual advantages for vertical and horizontal stimulus orientations: In one study with a simple grating pattern, 4-month-olds preferred vertical to horizontal, and in another with more complex symmetrical patterns 12-month-olds preferred vertical to horizontal or oblique. A moving vertical or horizontal pattern also evoked significantly greater heart rate deceleration (orienting) from 4-month-olds than did the same pattern oriented on the diagonal (Ivinskis & Findlay, 1980). Finally, babies still in the first half year of life habituated more quickly when a stimulus was oriented vertically rather than horizontally, regardless of whether the stimulus was static (Bornstein, 1981b) or dynamic (Gibson, Owsley, & Johnston, 1978).

In sum, babies between birth and about 1 year of age tend to orient to and look longest at verticals, whether the stimuli are simple or complex, static or dynamic, and so forth, and whether the response modality is psychophysiological or behavioral. This perceptual bias is undoubtedly helpful to babies because, if every orientation were equal, figuring space out might pose an even more formidable problem than it already does. How this bias arises, however, is not yet well understood. It could be that the visual system is biased; neonates only 1 to 4 days of age appear to prefer vertical to horizontal edges, and this effect might arise because infants visually scan predominantly along the horizontal (Haith, 1991). It could also be that the vertical preference is based on experience and develops quickly and naturally depending on the infant's immediate and dense exposure to a vertically oriented parent in a vertically oriented world. Everyday face-to-face communication tends to be upright and vertical. Of course, these explanations are not mutually exclusive, and any or all could conspire to influence visual perception.

Infants also discriminate orientation surprisingly well (Slater & Johnson, 1998), and babies have long been known to distinguish vertical from horizontal (Bornstein, Gross, & Wolf, 1978; Fisher, Ferdinandsen, & Bornstein 1981). Newborns tested using variants of the habituation design show orientation discrimination (Bremner, 1994), and 4-month-olds discriminate vertical from 45 degrees off vertical (Bornstein et al., 1978) as well as 10-degree disparities between different orientations of the same stimulus (Bornstein, Krinsky, & Benasich, 1986). At the same time, there is evidence that 4-month-old infants possess rudimentary shape constancy or the ability to perceive a constant form despite changes in its orientation. Bornstein et al. (1986) found that, when 4-month-olds were habituated to the same stimulus in several different orientations, the infants did not show preferential looking to the stimulus in a new orientation, but did dishabituate to an entirely new form. Slater and Johnson (1998) have proposed that both shape and size constancy (the ability to extract a constant stimulus size regardless of the viewing distance) are properties of infant perception that exist from birth.

Location

We know that young babies perceive depth in space from studies of the kind reviewed in the introductory section of this chapter. They can also find location in space; scanning studies suggest that babies seek out information in the local environment. More conclusive information about infants' sensitivity to location in space, however, comes from studies of reaching. In a longitudinal study concerned with motions, goal-directed behaviors, and types of reaches to objects located at different distances and moving at different velocities, von Hofsten (1984) found that infants as young as $4\frac{1}{2}$ months reached and contacted objects even if the objects were moving, and that their reaching was accomplished in a way that indicated good predictive targeting of location. Further development from this high level of function appeared to involve increased economy and flexibility of reaching.

The understanding of spatial location is also derived from studies of how infants find their way in large-scale spaces. Successful navigation of space develops in three steps (Spelke & Hermer, 1996). First, knowledge of spatial layout is predominantly egocentric, meaning that the infant's knowledge of location is limited by a single perspective. For example, very young infants exposed to mobiles suspended above their heads attempt to locate these mobiles by looking up even when the infants are not actually in their cribs or high chairs. Second, infants learn that objects remain in the same place when the infants move about a room. Last, infants learn that spatial relations between objects are enduring and invariant, regardless of the infants' movement or position in the room. Thus, infants' perception of spatial layout moves from a person-centered or *egocentric* perspective to an environment-centered *allocentric* perspective. Allocentric representation of space is fairly well developed by the end of the second year (Bremner & Knowles, 1994).

The facilitation of allocentric spatial perception by the onset of locomotion exemplifies the interdependence of perceptual and motor development. The study of perceptual–motor linkages has emerged as a field unto itself (Bertenthal & Clifton, 1998; Bremner, 1998). Researchers believe that a more mature, objective understanding of space depends in part on the ability to locomote (Bremner, 1997). For example, infants who crawl are more likely to avoid the deep side of the visual cliff than are those who have not yet begun to crawl (Campos, Bertenthal, & Kermoian, 1992). Infants who could locomote reacted with heart rate increases in response to the illusory drop-off, indicating increased arousal and wariness, whereas infants who were not yet crawling showed decreases in heart rate, indicating heightened interest in the drop-off. Importantly, heart rate increases also occurred in response to the visual cliff in prelocomotor infants given 30 to 40 hours of experience locomoting in walkers. Thus, these differences appeared to be specific to the experience of locomotion rather than to the infants' chronological age. Furthermore, Adolph (1997) observed that locomoting infants use perceptual information to adapt their movement accordingly. If the surface on which infants were moving appeared safe, locomotion proceeded without modification; if the surface appeared to be unsafe in any way, infants would pause, look, and sway side to side to seek out additional visual and mechanical information about the surface and their ability to maintain their balance when traversing it. Alternative forms of locomotion were used (e.g., backward rather than forward crawling), or infants refused to move at all if surfaces were deemed too risky. Adolph's work illustrates the mutually reciprocal influences of perception and locomotion during the first year of life.

Perception of Movement

Movement is an inherent feature of the world around us, and of ourselves. Movement detection is present from early infancy (Aslin & Shea, 1990; Dannemiller & Freedland, 1991), and the visual system may be preadapted to perceive movement because doing so carries distinct advantages. Things that move bring protection, nutrition, danger, and opportunities for exploration and play. Furthermore, motion provides information that is essential for developing stable perceptions of objects and spatial layouts (Kellman, 1993).

The infant's perception of motion is actually quite sophisticated. Ruff (1982a, 1985) tested the abilities of infants in the first half year to recognize and discriminate among different motions of rigid objects. For example, she first habituated babies to a series of objects, each of which moved the same way (say, from side to side), and she then tested the same infants with a novel object moving in the now familiar side to side motion and with a novel object moving in a novel way (say, from side to side and rotating). Both $3\frac{1}{2}$- and 5-month-olds discriminated the two directions of motion, and 5-months-olds also discriminated rotation from oscillation around the vertical as well as left versus right rotation. Ruff used different objects to ensure that the babies did not rely on specific shape cues to achieve these discriminations of movement.

Not only are infants sensitive to different kinds of movement, they appear to use movement cues effectively to extract additional information about position and shape. Haith (1991) and Haith and McCarty (1990) found that $3\frac{1}{2}$-month-olds could learn rules governing events in a simple spatiotemporal series (e.g., the left–right alternation of stimulus exposures) and then act on expectations formed from those events by anticipating stimulus position. Because infants may perceive object form from the experience they have with the movement of the object, it might seem that abstracting the basic form of an object while it is continuously changing would be more difficult than abstracting the form while the object is stationary. Yet perception of objects occurs naturally when they are moving, and observers appear to pick up information about objects from such perceptions. For example, Kellman and Spelke (1983) habituated 16-week-old infants to a moving stimulus such as that depicted in the top half of Figure 6.8. All elements of the stimulus (the rectangle, the rod projecting from the top of the rectangle, and the rod projecting from the bottom of the rectangle) were presented to the infants in common motion (i.e., all elements moved together, at the same rate of speed, in the same direction, at the same time). Infants were tested for dishabituation using the two test stimuli in the bottom half of Figure 6.8. Infants dishabituated to the broken rod display (bottom right of Figure 6.8) but not to the complete display (bottom left of Figure 6.8), indicating that the infants mentally connected the two rods in the habituation display.

HABITUATION DISPLAY

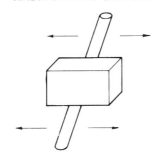

TEST DISPLAYS

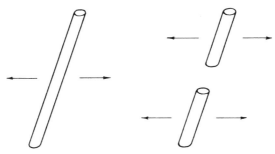

FIGURE 6.8

Habituation and test displays used to investigate infants' understanding of partly occluded objects. (Courtesy of A. Slater.)

You may wonder why common movement of the habituation stimulus was required for the infants in Kellman and Spelke's (1983) experiment to perceive the two rods as parts of a large, single object. Most adults who view the habituation stimulus as a stationary display readily perceive it as a single rod that is partially occluded by a rectangle, because mature perceivers make use of *edge-sensitive processes* to perceive object unity; this follows the Gestalt principle of *good continuation* (unconnected edges will be perceived as connected if the edges are relatable in some way; Kellman, Yin, & Shipley, 1995; see Figure 6.9). Edge-sensitive processes do not appear prior to 6 months of age, however, and very young infants must rely on *edge-insensitive processes*, which are provided by common motion, to perceive the unity of partially occluded objects (Johnson & Aslin, 1995; Kellman & Banks, 1998).

Motion also helps reveal "figural coherence." This is the perceptual grouping of elements having an invariant set of spatial relations, and it may be extracted from relative motions that are coordinated among the elements. A compelling example of figural coherence is the so-called point-light walker display, which specifies motions typical of human beings (see Figure 6.10). When adults observe such a dynamic light display they can identify the motion and the object in less than 200 milliseconds, whereas static displays of the same information are essentially uninterpretable (Slater, 1997). Infants, too, are sensitive to biomechanical motions of this kind. Similar sensitivity to structural invariance in dynamic displays, but not in static ones, is evident in infants as young as 5 months of age, and sensitivity to the three-dimensional structure of the human form is present at 9 months. Infants apparently do not perceive these displays as unrelated "swarms" of randomly moving dots, nor do they focus on the motion paths of individual

Relatable Edges

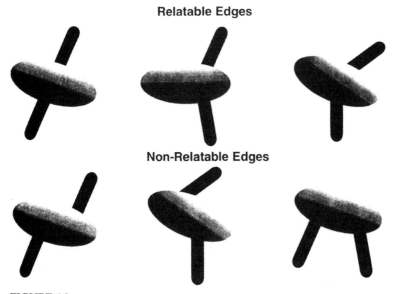

Non-Relatable Edges

FIGURE 6.9
Drawings displaying "relatable" (*top three*) and "nonrelatable" edges (*bottom three*). (From P. J. Kellman, 1996.)

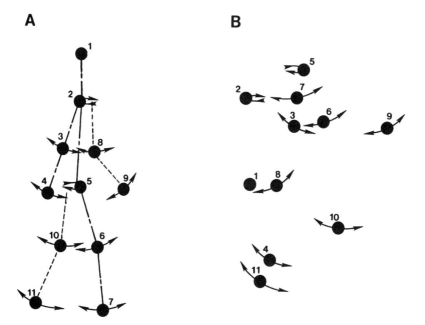

FIGURE 6.10
(*A*) An array of 11 point lights attached to the head and joints of a walking person: The head and right side of the body are numbered 1 through 7, and the numbers 8 through 11 mark those of the body's left side. The motion vectors drawn through each point light represent the perceived relative motions within the figure. (*B*) An anomalous walker identical to *A* except that the relative locations of the point lights have been scrambled as shown. (Correspondingly numbered point lights have the same absolute motions.) (© 1984 by Academic Press. Reprinted by permission.)

lights. Rather, infants are sensitive to the overall coherence of the figure based on biomechanical motion (Arterberry & Bornstein, 2001; Bertenthal, 1993).

In sum, infants in the first year of life see elements of patterns as well as pattern wholes, they show developing sensitivity to several dimensions of spatial information, including depth, orientation, location, and movement, and they even use movement to understand object form. We now turn to consider infants' perception of another visual dimension, color.

Color

Patterns and objects in the environment not only vary in terms of spatial dimensions that help specify, identify, and distinguish them, but they are also perceived as having color. Indeed, color is an intellectually impressive and aesthetically attractive kind of information. Infants see colors and seem to do so well.

Darwin speculated on the development of color vision in his son Doddy and his other children as far back as the 1870s, but real progress toward understanding the development of color vision only began a century later. Studying color vision is highly technical, and formidable problems challenge those who attempt to do so. For example, hue and brightness, the two major components of color, vary together for both adults and infants, so that whenever the color of a stimulus changes both its hue and brightness usually change as well. Therefore, in order to compare two stimuli on the basis of what we usually think of as color (hue) alone, we must first equalize or otherwise account for the brightness of both. With adults, this is relatively easy because they can be asked to match colored stimuli for brightness. In babies, however, the precise relation between brightness and color was for a long time elusive, and babies certainly cannot be asked to match brightnesses. There are also clear functional differences between infant and adult vision (e.g., Sireteanu, 1996). In short, if we show babies two circles (one red and one green) and they distinguish between the two, they may be doing so on the basis of brightness differences or on the basis of hue differences. We would not know which. As a consequence, an understanding of infant color vision needs to begin with studies of brightness perception and, on the basis of proper brightness controls, proceed to test the infant's discrimination, preference, and organization of color.

By approximately 3 months of age, babies are nearly as efficient as adults when the task is to compare brightness differences between stimuli (Kellman & Banks, 1998). It has been somewhat more challenging, however, to demonstrate that infants less than 8 weeks old can discriminate differences in hue alone, although experiments comparing chromatic or spectral sensitivity using electrophysiological and behavioral techniques agree that, across a broad range of conditions and across most of the spectrum, the infant's sensitivity to color differences is reasonably similar to that of the adult (Teller & Bornstein, 1986). Research shows, too, that red/green and yellow/blue sensitivity are similar in adults and in infants in the 1- to 3-month age range (Banks & Shannon, 1993).

When researchers wish to assess infant hue discrimination per se, it is possible to adopt several different strategies to unconfound brightnesses. For example, it is possible to match brightness using an adult standard in specific regions where infants and adults are known to match, or to vary brightness systematically or unsystematically so that brightness is not an influential factor in hue discrimination. Peeples and Teller (1975) capitalized on the baby's preference for heterogeneity, showing 2- and 3-month-olds two screens, one white and the second white with either a white or a red form projected onto it. They then systematically varied the brightness of the form around the adult match to the brightness of the background screen. When the white form was darker or brighter than the screen it created a pattern that babies favored (relative to the homogeneous white comparison); at the brightness match point, however, the babies did not prefer either screen. Just a shade difference between the form and the screen engaged the babies to look. Thus, these investigators concluded that babies' brightness sensitivity is acute. Babies *always* preferred the red form–white screen combination, however, independent of whether the red form was dimmer, equal to, or brighter than the white screen, demonstrating that even when the red bar matched the white screen in brightness, a hue difference was still evident to them. This was one of the first studies to surmount the brightness problem and to show (at least some) color vision in infants.

Adams, Courage, and Mercer (1994) used a similar procedure to demonstrate that neonates could discriminate red from grey, but not blue, green, or yellow from grey. Thus, neonates can detect some color, although their color vision is limited by the absence and immaturity of cone receptors in the retina and of postreceptor pathways for processing color information. Color vision develops very rapidly, however, and Adams, Courage, and Mercer (1991) demonstrated that infants could successfully discriminate blue, green, yellow, and red by 3 months of age.

Adults do not merely see colors; they perceive the color spectrum as organized qualitatively into categories of hue. Although we certainly recognize blends in between, we distinguish blue, green, yellow, and red as qualitatively distinct. The infant's color space is similarly organized. It could be that the way in which the visual system functions lends vision such organization, or it could be that infants learn to organize the visual world, say, when they acquire language. Bornstein, Kessen, and Weiskopf (1976a, 1976b) studied this issue using a habituation–dishabituation strategy with 4-month-olds. They found that babies who were habituated to a light of one color readily noticed when a light of a different color was shown on a test trial following habituation even when the two lights were matched in brightness. These investigators then proceeded to determine whether babies perceived color categorically, that is, whether babies regard two different blues, for example, as more similar than blue and green. We normally see blue when the wavelength of the light is around 450 nanometers (nm), green when the wavelength is around 530 nm, yellow around 580 nm, and red around 630 nm. Moreover, we tend to regard lights with wavelengths of 450 nm or 480 nm as blue even though we may see them as different blues. Similarly, we would call lights of 510 nm and 540 nm green. Capitalizing on this fact, Bornstein and his coworkers habituated babies to 480 nm, a blue near the boundary between blue and green. On test trials following habituation, the babies were shown lights of 450 nm, 480 nm, and 510 nm all matched for brightness. Thus one test stimulus was the familiar one, and two differed from the familiar stimulus by an identical amount (30 nm); however, one new test light fell into the blue range (like the familiar stimulus), whereas the other was green. Babies shown the new blue stimulus treated it and the familiar blue as the same, whereas they treated the green stimulus differently. As shown in Figure 6.11, the overall pattern of results showed that infants categorize the visible spectrum into relatively discrete hues of blue, green, yellow,

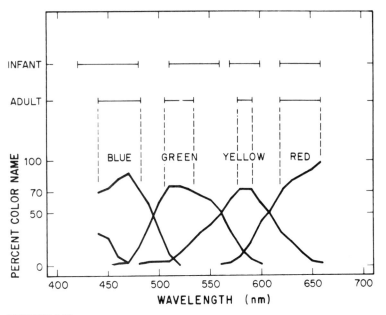

FIGURE 6.11

This figure shows how closely infants' categorical perceptions of color resemble those of adults. The lower panel indicates the likelihood that light of a given wavelength is labeled using one of the basic color names (after Boynton & Gordon, 1965). The upper panel summarizes the results of hue category studies of 4-month-old infants by Bornstein, Kessen, and Weiskopf (1976a). (From Teller & Bornstein, 1988. © 1988 by Academic Press.)

and red, and in ways similar to that of adults even though infants, like adults, can still discriminate among colors within a given category (Bornstein, 1981a).

Color controls attention, pleases, and informs. Perceiving color and doing so categorically combines with seeing pattern, locating in space, and tracking movement to aid babies in organizing and making sense of what they see. The objects babies see in the world also appear to have integrity for them.

Object Perception

To this point, we have discussed infants' perceptions of the components of objects in the world, including pattern, orientation, location, movement, and color. Do infants see objects as having integrity? In the previous section on movement perception we showed that very young infants use information conveyed by the common motion of elements in a stimulus array to perceive partially occluded objects as unitary. Proper object perception requires the ability to detect edges (*edge detection*), differentiate between edges of objects and edges of other phenomena (*edge classification*), understand which edges constitute object boundaries (*boundary assignment*), and perceive objects as single units despite the fact that, as an object or the perceiver moves through space, parts of the object disappear from view as other objects move in front of it (*unit formation*; Kellman, 1996; Kellman & Banks, 1998). The study of object perception is also incomplete without three additional considerations: (1) perceiving forms in three dimensions, (2) perceiving an object as unchanging in size despite changes in retinal projective size as the object moves away from and toward the perceiver (size constancy), and (3) perceiving substance (i.e., perceiving an object as rigid, flexible, and so forth).

Clearly, infants are preadapted to perceive objects, although mature object perception is not yet available to very young infants and appears to be a complex function of the interplay of nervous system maturation, motor development, and learning (Bertenthal & Clifton, 1998; Kellman & Banks, 1998; Slater & Johnson, 1998; Spelke, Gutheil, & Van de Walle, 1995). Edge detection, for example, appears to exist at birth, with newborns making use of differences in luminance, color, and depth to perceive edges. The ability is not fully formed at this time, however, and awaits further developments of the visual system (Kellman, 1996). Size constancy also is demonstrated by neonates and thus appears to be innate (Granrud, 1987; Slater, Mattock, & Brown, 1990), suggesting that newborns are preadapted to relate an object's projected retinal size to viewing distance. The ability to use edge-insensitive processes, which depend on information provided by common motion, to determine object unity appears very soon after birth and may be unlearned (Kellman & Spelke, 1983). Infants may be preadapted to perceive the world in certain ways, but object perception continues to develop throughout the first year of life, but more complex, mature perceptual processes (e.g., using relatable edges to perceive object unity—the edge-sensitive process) do not emerge until after 6 months of age (Spelke, Breinlinger, Jacobson, & Phillips, 1993).

Auditory Perception

Much less is known about audition than about vision in early life, even though audition is of major importance to the infant (Aslin, Jusczyk, & Pisoni, 1998; Bremner, 1994). It is an everyday observation that newborns can hear sounds: Make a sudden loud noise and a neonate will startle, as Darwin observed young Doddy to do (Box 3.1). We also know that fetuses hear in utero, as discussed in Chapter 5, and that the auditory system is very mature but not yet fully developed at the time of birth.

Sound is specified principally by two variables, frequency and amplitude. Frequency is the rate at which sound waves vibrate, and this encodes pitch, or how high or low a sound is, whereas amplitude is the intensity of sound waves, indicating how loud a sound is. Human beings hear sounds in the frequency range of approximately 20 to 20,000 Hertz (Hz). Human speech is a complex interplay of different sound frequencies at different intensities distributed over time. In recent years, developmentalists have focused principally on four basic issues; the first three concern the infant's abilities to detect sounds of different frequencies, to discriminate among frequencies, and to localize sounds in space. Curiously, however, research into these basic abilities has not captured the interest of investigators in the field of infant audition nearly so much as the fourth, namely the way babies respond to the more complex sounds that specify speech.

Basic Auditory Processes

How loud does a sound have to be for the infant to hear it? For adults, the amount of energy defining the *auditory threshold* varies with the frequency of the sound: Both low and high frequencies (above or below 1,000 Hz) require more energy than middle frequencies. Using behavioral and psychophysiolog-ical techniques (see Chapter 3), several investigators have sought to determine how the infant's threshold for intensity perception varies across the frequency spectrum. Infants appear to hear low pitch sounds less well than and high pitch sounds better than adults do, and there are nearly continuous developmental improvements in hearing at low and high frequencies during the first 2 years of life (Aslin et al., 1998).

Infants clearly discriminate among sounds of different frequencies, qual-ities, and patterns. Using head-turn techniques, Olsho and her colleagues (Olsho, Schoon, Sakai, Turpin, & Sperduto, 1982a, 1982b) first found that 5- to 8-month-olds discriminate tones differing by only about 2% in frequency in the 1,000 to 3,000 Hz range (where adult frequency discrimination is about 1%). Newborns appear to prefer music over noise, as evidenced by their propensity to alter their sucking patterns in order to hear music rather than noise (Butterfield & Siperstein, 1972). Furthermore, infants can discriminate differences in melody at 6 months of age (Trehub & Trainor, 1993) and appear to show a preference for music with common chords over music with uncommon chords. Infants may thus come into the world with biologically based predispositions to perceive certain musical patterns (Kagan & Zentner, 1996).

To determine whether an adult could locate the source of a sound, a researcher could simply ask the person to indicate the source somehow (asking may not even be necessary because people show a strong tendency to look directly toward the origin of interesting noises). It is considerably more difficult to determine whether babies can locate sounds, however. The very young are handicapped by the fact that their motor control is poor. As a result, newborns cannot orient precisely or swiftly toward the apparent origin of a sound they hear. Indeed, young babies should not be expected to be as good as adults locating sounds in space on structural grounds: They have smaller heads. The location of a sound in space depends on the fact that a sound coming, say, from the left reaches the left ear earlier than it does the right ear, even if only by a fraction of a second (Figure 6.12). Because the infant's ears are closer together than are those of the adult, this critical time difference is diminished and could impair the infant's capacity to localize a sound, especially when the sound does not come from an extreme lateral position (Clifton, Gwiazda, Bauer, Clarkson, & Held, 1988). In view of this handicap, it is especially remarkable how well (and quickly) babies find the sources of sounds in their environment. Infants in the first few days of life can turn their heads toward the general location of a sound (Brazelton & Nugent, 1995) and can reach in the direction of a sound

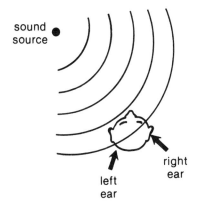

FIGURE 6.12
An illustration of how the direction from which a sound originates is specified by the slight time difference in arrival of the sound at each of the ears. (From Eimas, 1975. © 1975 by Academic Press.)

in the dark by 4 months of age (Clifton, Rochat, Robin, & Berthier, 1994). By 6 months of age, localization responses in infants are comparable to those of adults (Clifton, Perris, & Bullinger, 1991; Hillier, Hewitt, & Morrongiello, 1992).

In sum, infants are equipped with quite good hearing. The infant's auditory abilities highlighted here, along with other studies showing that infants may be especially sensitive to sounds in the spectral ranges of human speech (see next section), illustrate the biological preparedness of the infant's auditory system. Like the visual system, infants apply these basic abilities almost immediately to the highly complex tasks of perceiving, deciphering, and making sense of their world.

Speech Perception

In general, human speech is centered at relatively low frequencies, and numerous investigators have suggested that certain characteristics of human speech may be special for babies. On the most basic level, speech is characterized by great rates of acoustic change and by complex structures, both of which are preferred by infants (Aslin et al., 1998; Bertoncini, 1998).

Very young human infants seem to attend selectively to and imitate human over nonhuman sounds (Glenn, Cunningham, & Joyce, 1983), and parents also appear to accommodate infant sensitivity and capacity by speaking to babies using characteristics to which babies appear to be especially attuned (see Chapter 9). Indeed, it is difficult *not* to change one's speech so in addressing babies (Trevarthen, 1979). *Child-directed speech* differs from and simplifies normal adult-directed speech in grammar, word usage, and sound. Most germane to this discussion, it includes higher pitch, exaggerated intonation, sing-song rhythm, abbreviated utterances, and repetition (Papoušek, Papoušek, & Bornstein, 1985). Child-directed speech is also nearly universal (Aslin et al., 1998). Furthermore, very young infants prefer to listen to child-directed speech over adult-directed speech and are made happier by it (Fernald & Simon, 1984; Werker & McLeod, 1989), even when the language being spoken is different from their native tongue (Pegg, Werker, & McLeod, 1992; Werker, Pegg, & McLeod, 1994). The exaggerated pitch, intonation, and repetiveness of child-directed speech may have several functions, including attracting and keeping infants' attention (Kaplan, Goldstein, Huckeby, Owren, & Cooper, 1995), communicating information to the infant about emotion and intention (Fernald, 1992), and facilitating recognition of the mother's voice (DeCasper, LeCanuet, Busnel, Granier-Deferre, & Maugeais, 1994; Spence & Freeman, 1996). DeCasper et al. (1994), for example, found that the heart rates of fetuses in the thirty-seventh week of gestation slowed (indicating heightened attention) to an audiotaped nursery rhyme that mothers had repeatedly read aloud each day between the thirty-third and thirty-seventh week of gestation. By contrast, the infants' heart rates did not change in response to an audiotaped "control" rhyme that the mothers had not read aloud. Infants' selective attention to and preference for maternal speech patterns may result from infants' considerable experience with the *prosodic* (pitch, rhythm, and intonation) features of mothers' speech *in utero* (Lecanuet & Granier-Deferre, 1993).

Infants have the ability to perceive components of speech. Eimas, Siqueland, Jusczyk, and Vigorito (1971) reported that babies could distinguish between speech and nonspeech sounds and also that babies could distinguish among different speech sounds in an adult-like categorical manner. We discuss research on this topic at some length because it tests several basic issues in the classic nature–nurture debate.

From all of the possible speech sounds that can be produced (*phonetics*), each language uses only a subset (*phonemics*), and one dimension along which meaningful phonemes may be distinguished is their *voicing*. Variations in voicing are heard when a speaker produces different frequencies of sound waves at slightly different times. In voicing, a sound like /b/ (pronounced "ba") is produced by vibrating the vocal cords and producing higher frequencies at or before the time the lips are opened and low-frequency energy is released—/b/ is a voiced phoneme. By contrast, for sounds like /p/ (pronounced "pa"), the vocal cords do not begin to vibrate at higher frequencies until some time after the lips release lower frequencies. Thus, the high frequency components of a sound may precede the low frequency components, the two components may begin simultaneously, or the high-frequency ones may come after the low-frequency. The relative *onset times* of low and high frequencies therefore critically cue phonemic perception. It is a well-established fact that adults perceive differences in voicing more or less categorically: Although we can distinguish fine differences in the onset times of low- and high-frequency sounds, we tend to classify different examples of voiced (/b/) or voiceless (/p/) sounds as similar, but easily discriminate between voiced and voiceless sounds. In English, we distinguish voiced and voiceless sounds—/b/–/p/, /d/–/t/, and /g/–/k/. Thus, different people say /b/ and /p/ in different ways, yet we seldom misidentify these speech sounds. As we explained when describing Bornstein's research on the perception of colors, *categorical perception* involves the propensity to treat as similar a range of otherwise discriminable stimuli and to respond differently to another (even physically adjacent) range.

Many people have assumed that phenomena so ubiquitous, consistent, circumscribed, and significant as the categorical perception of speech sounds might have a biological foundation. To test this assumption, Eimas and his coworkers (1971) asked whether preverbal infants perceive voicing categorically. Using a habituation procedure in which infants' sucking turned on a sound, these investigators presented infants with a voiced phoneme (/b/) until infants habituated to it. Afterward they divided the infants into three groups: One group heard the related voiceless phoneme (/p/), a second group heard a physically different voiced phoneme from the same category (/b'/), and a third group continued to hear the habituation stimulus (/b/). The two new test stimuli (/p/ and /b'/) were equally different from the habituation stimulus (/b/) in terms of the relative onset times of low- and high-frequency components, but the two presumably differed unequally in psychological terms (because adults categorize the two /b/ sounds together and distinguish them from /p/). In fact, 1- and 4-month-olds behaved as though they perceived speech sounds categorically: Babies distinguished between /b/ and /p/, but not between the two /b/s. In other words, babies categorized sounds as either voiced or voiceless long before they themselves used language or even had extensive experience hearing language. This experiment showed that infants not only discriminated speech contrasts involving voicing, but did so categorically. The results also suggested that categorical perception of some sounds could be innate.

Eimas's experiment did not rule out a role for experience, however. In Chapter 1, we discussed several roles of experience, including facilitation, attunement, and induction. The babies who participated in the Eimas experiment were born into monolingual English-speaking families in which the voiced–voiceless distinction is common, as in *"baby"* versus *"papa."* It could be that categorical perception is partially developed at birth (as DeCasper's research shows, fetuses can hear and have experience with speech in the womb) and that its further development is facilitated or attuned over the first months of life through postnatal experience. Indeed, there is evidence to this effect. Jusczyk (1995) reported that 6-month-old infants could distinguish a great variety of phonetic contrasts, even those that did not characterize the language to which the infants were exposed. However, with continuous exposure to one language environment, the ability to distinguish phonetic contrasts outside the native language decreases, especially when the non-native contrasts do not readily conform to those found in the infant's own language (Werker, 1995). This reduced sensitivity to non-native contrasts does not appear to be permanent, however, because adults can be trained to discriminate non-native contrasts (Pisoni, Lively, & Logan, 1994). Polka and Werker (1994) found that infants show a similar pattern of early sensitivity to vowel contrasts followed by a decline in sensitivity to non-native contrasts over time. However, sensitivity to vowel contrasts occurred earlier (4 to 6 months) than that for consonants (6 months; Best, 1995), and the decline in sensitivity to vowel contrasts occurred earlier as well. Aslin et al. (1998) speculated that this earlier sensitivity to vowels occurs because vowels appear in speech with greater frequency and duration than do consonants, and thus attain greater salience to the infant earlier in development.

Categorical speech perception in infants has been documented by numerous researchers (Bertoncini, 1998; Goodman & Nusbaum, 1994; Plunkett & Schafer, 1999) who have demonstrated that infants as young as 7 months of age develop a rudimentary ability to perceive word segments (such as *cup* and *dog*) within spoken sentences (Jusczyk & Aslin, 1995). Certain perceptual discriminations seem to be universal and developed at birth; they are maintained by linguistic experiences but may be (partially) lost if absent from the language heard by the child. Other discriminations are possible at birth but can be altered by experience. Still other capacities can be induced in infants and children by exposing them to certain speech sounds. Categorical perception of speech is clearly one of the ways in which infants are prepared to learn language, a topic to which we return in Chapter 9.

Chemical and Tactile Perception

Compared with our knowledge of how infants see and hear, we possess a more rudimentary understanding of the early structure, function, and development of the senses of taste, smell, and touch. As a result, we review what is known about these three senses in one brief section.

Taste and Smell

Newborn babies, even those who have tasted nothing but amniotic fluid and smelled nothing but the delivery room, appear to discriminate among sensory qualities that signify different tastes and smells, and they even prefer certain tastes and smells to others. Compelling psychophysical evidence indicates that four basic qualities together exhaust taste experience: sweet, salt, sour, and bitter

(Brand, 1997). Tastes are, as we know, very powerful stimuli in learning: A single experience of nausea associated with a particular taste is enough to lead one to avoid that taste forever. Replicating long-forgotten findings reported in the last century by Preyer (1881/1888–1889), Steiner and his colleagues (1977, 1979; Blass, Ganchrow, & Steiner, 1984; Ganchrow, Steiner, & Daher, 1983) found that neonates display characteristic facial expressions when sweet, sour, and bitter substances are placed on their tongues (see Figure 3.5). A sweet stimulus evoked an expression of satisfaction, often accompanied by a slight smile and by sucking movements. A sour stimulus evoked lip pursing, often accompanied or followed by wrinkling the nose and blinking the eyes. A bitter fluid evoked an expression of dislike and disgust or rejection, and it was often followed by spitting or even by the preparatory movements of vomiting. These taste discriminations are organized at a primitive level of the brain, because Steiner observed them even in babies who had no cortex. The magnitude of the newborn's reaction to sweet and bitter stimuli varies with the intensity of the stimulus.

Newborns thus seem to discriminate among common tastes and even rate them. Allied research on sucking, swallowing, and breathing confirms more directly that infants prefer, and hence discriminate, among tastes. Newborns, even those born preterm, show a preference for sweet solutions (sucrose, fructose, glucose, or lactose) over neutral water; furthermore, newborns strongly dislike sour substances such as citric acid and bitter substances such as urea, but appear indifferent to salty solutions (Mennella & Beauchamp 1997). Infants begin to manifest a preference for salty solutions between 3 and 6 months of age (Beauchamp, Cowart, Mennella, & Marsh, 1994).

The preference for sweet substances and the ability to distinguish among different taste stimuli may thus be innate (Rosenstein & Oster, 1997). In fact, many species seem to prefer sweet solutions over tasteless ones, and both sweet and neutral stimuli over bitter ones (Smith & Vogt, 1997). Of course, the innate preference for sweet substances is probably reinforced by postnatal dietary practices. In the classic "cafeteria" study with babies, Davis (1928, 1934, 1939) allowed three infants to choose what they wanted to eat beginning at about 8 months, when they were still exclusively breast-fed. Infants began by trying everything that was available; later they chose what they liked (though different babies showed different preferences). Although they went on binges and food strikes from time to time, on the whole babies chose for themselves a variety and amount of food adequate for good nutrition. One baby who had rickets reportedly drank cod liver oil until he was well.

Although Davis's work seemed to suggest that infants instinctively seek out "well-balanced" diets, that was a controlled and artificial experiment. Most models of feeding emphasize the role of learning in the development of flavor preferences, taste aversions, and dietary control (e.g., Capaldi, 1996; Mennella & Beauchamp, 1997; Schafe & Bernstein, 1996). In a comprehensive review of factors influencing eating patterns, Birch and Fisher (1996) concluded that healthy eating habits develop by allowing infants and young children control of whether they eat and how much they eat, and by providing infants repeated, consistent opportunities to eat a healthy diet in positive, noncoercive contexts.

The sense of smell is less important to humans than to many other species, and this sensory modality has elicited less attention from infancy researchers than have vision, audition, and even taste. In early studies that paralleled his work on taste, Steiner (1977, 1979) observed neonates' facial expressions and reactions to odors placed on cotton swabs held beneath the nose. Steiner found that newborns responded in qualitatively different ways to different food odors. Butter and banana odors elicited positive expressions; vanilla, either positive or indifferent expressions; a fishy odor, some rejection; and the odor of rotten eggs, unanimous rejection. Indeed, soon after birth, infants discriminate among a wide variety of odors and can use their sense of smell in a host of association-learning tasks (Wilson & Sullivan, 1994).

Darwin speculated that his infant son Doddy recognized his mother by her scent (Box 3.1), and Porter (Cernoch & Porter, 1985; Porter, Bologh, & Makin, 1988) systematically compared olfactory recognition of mother, father, and stranger by breast-fed and bottle-fed infants only 12 to 18 days after birth. Babies were photographed while exposed to pairs of gauze pads worn by an adult in the underarm area on the previous night, and their duration of orienting was recorded. Only breast-feeding infants oriented preferentially and only to their own mothers' scents, thereby giving evidence that they discriminate their mothers in this way. Infants did not recognize their fathers preferentially, and bottle-fed infants did not recognize their mothers, suggesting that breast-feeding infants are exposed to and can learn unique olfactory signatures. Mothers also recognize the scent of their babies after only 1 or 2 days (Mennella & Beauchamp, 1996). Olfactory exchange in mother–infant dyads thus appears to be mutual. Porter and Winberg (1999) further noted that the chemical composition of breast fluids is similar to the chemical composition of amniotic fluid, and infants may be preattuned at birth to respond selectively to their mothers' unique olfactory cues. The ability to recognize mothers very early in life by olfactory information alone might be expected to play an important role in the early mother–infant relationship (Porter & Winberg, 1999).

In sum, newborns taste and smell, and they seem to be discriminating. However, precious little is known about the early development of these two chemical senses and about how they differentiate and develop as a result of postnatal experience and further maturation of the nervous system. Such preferences play an important role in adult daily life; it is unfortunate that so little is known about how they first form or grow.

Touch

We know from everyday experience that soothing pats can quiet a fussy infant, whereas the DPT shot almost invariably causes distress. Newborns clearly feel, but aside from a series of reports of infants' sensitivity to warmth and cold, research has not progressed very far in understanding how accurately infants localize a touch on some part of their body or how acutely infants distinguish tactile stimulation.

From information reviewed in Chapter 5 on the development of the nervous system, we can deduce that newborns respond to tactile stimulation and that infants are sensitive to touch from the moment of birth. Recall from Darwin's journal (Chapter 3) that Doddy, as a newborn, jerked his foot away when Darwin touched the baby's sole with a bit of paper (Box 3.1). The rate of response that reflects the rate of information transmission along a cell increases dramatically in infancy (Chapter 5): A newborn who has blood drawn from the heel cries and moves, but the latency to do so after the needle puncture seems seconds long, whereas at the end of just a few months a baby's reaction to an injection is immediate and demonstrative.

The tactile modality helps infants acquire knowledge about the world. As we know from combining the principles of proximodistal and cephalocaudal development (Chapter 4), the head region develops earliest, and newborns take in information early on with their eyes and ears. Very young babies will look at an object without reaching for it; they will often not bring into their line of sight an object placed in their hands. By the middle of the first year, however, babies reach for everything in sight. Gesell (1945) recognized the importance of object manipulation in infancy, but it was really Piaget (e.g., 1936/1953, 1937/1954) who brought the significance of manipulation to center stage when he proposed that such seemingly simple sensorimotor behaviors constitute the foundations of knowledge. We discuss Piaget's theory in greater depth in Chapter 7; here we simply note that Piaget grasped the fundamental significance of object manipulations when developing an understanding of how the world functions. Piaget observed that over the first 18 months of life babies repeat actions, first related to their bodies, then on simple objects, and eventually between objects. Psychologically, infants transit from simple manipulation and exploring object properties before 9 months to relational and functional activities with objects afterward (Chapter 9), and object manipulation has become an important subject of study in its own right.

Ruff (1989, 1990) filmed 6-, 9-, and 12-month-olds manipulating different kinds of objects and later scored both general behaviors (looking) as well as specific ones (alternating between looking and mouthing), noting that mouthing decreased over the second half of the first year, whereas fingering and more precise forms of manipulation both increased (accompanying the further development of fine motor coordination). Ruff also found that infants vary their exploratory activities to match the object being explored. When Ruff changed a stimulus once the infant had the chance to explore the stimulus in some detail, she found that the infant changed patterns of tactual exploration so as to maximize information acquisition about the new stimulus. For example, infants respond to a change in shape by rotating the object more, and to a change in texture by fingering the object more, and in both cases they throw, push, and drop new objects less often than familiar ones. Information processing in infancy is closely tied to tactile exploration. Tellinghuisen and Oakes (1997) found that 7- and 10-month-old infants were less distractible when they were engaged in object exploration than when they were not. Furthermore, infants explored complex objects longer than simple objects, suggesting that sustained attention to objects during tactile exploration of them reflected active information processing (Oakes & Tellinghuisen, 1994). Lansink and Richard (1997) produced findings in support of this interpretation. Six-, 9-, and 12-month-old infants were least distractible when they were in the midst of active toy manipulation and when their heart rates were decelerating (indicating focused attention) than when they were only casually attentive to the toy and when no heart rate deceleration occurred.

The sense of touch has not only been studied in the context of research on the development of object knowledge. Studies of infant–parent interaction identify gentle, tender touch as critical for the establishment of intimate parent–child relationships and secure infant–parent attachments (Barnard & Brazelton, 1990; Bowlby, 1969/1982; Harlow, 1958). Further, tactile/kinesthetic stimulation administered systematically to young infants appears to have beneficial effects on infant development (Dieter & Emory, 1997). One such program, Field's (1995) 10-day protocol of tactile/kinesthetic stimulation of infants' head, neck, shoulders, back, waist, thighs, feet, and arms, reportedly produced a 47% increase in weight gain in preterm infants relative to untreated control infants. In addition, massaged infants were more active and alert, had higher Brazelton NBAS scores, and spent 6 days less in the hospital than did comparison infants. Similar effects have been obtained with cocaine-exposed infants, infants with HIV infection, and infants of depressed mothers (Field, 1995, 2000). It is important that tactile/kinesthetic stimulation of high-risk infants such as those born prematurely should be given only after the infants are medically stable, which usually occurs sometime after 32 weeks postconceptional age (Dieter & Emory, 1997; Eckerman, Oehler, Hannan, & Molitor, 1995; Fearon, Harrison, Muir, & Kisilevsky, 1996).

Conceptually simple as touch may seem, its significance should not be underestimated. Touch works in concert with vision to inform infants about key properties of the physical world. Manipulation allows tactual exploration and enhances visual investigation. Touch also appears to be critical to the formation of infant–parent relationships and to facilitate weight gain and alertness in high-risk infants. Although the chemical and tactile senses have not been well researched in infancy, the information we do have about infant taste, smell, and touch is quite provocative. Infants demonstrate that they possess relatively advanced capacities in these domains of perception and that they use them in coming to understand the world into which they are born. Indeed, as we now note, information about the environment arriving at different sensory sources is coordinated quite early in life.

Multimodal and Cross-Modal Perception

Most research on infant perception has focused on two related goals: *status*, whether or not particular perceptual capacities are present, and *origins and processes*, the emergence, stability, and change in those individual capacities over time. This was the logical and necessary point to begin basic research on infant perceptual capacity, and the last 30 years witnessed considerable progress in reaching these goals. However, sensations are not unitary in infants (or in adults); rather, the senses interact and fuse perceptions into wholes. When we are at the ocean, for example, we see the waves, hear the surf pound, smell the salt air, and so forth. These sensory impressions go together naturally to evoke an integrated experience. In short, the world of real events is *multimodal* in that coordinated information arrives at different sensory modalities simultaneously. Furthermore, information available in only one modality can cross or transfer to another; when we feel a ball, we also "see" that it is round. Information obtained by looking, listening, and touching is often coordinated, and from very early in life.

A compelling difference of opinion exists among students of perceptual development concerning infants' multimodal and cross-modal sensitivities. This dispute centers on whether sensations are initially integrated and differentiate in development or whether they are initially differentiated and integrate in development. Integrationists propose that the newborn's senses are unified at birth, in that infants detect invariant relations across modalities and that perceptual development consists of the progressive differentiation of sources and features of environmental stimulation (Gibson, 1979). Bower (1977, pp. 68–69) wrote, "A very young baby may not know whether he is hearing something or seeing something. . . . Very rapidly, [however,] babies develop the ability to register not only the place, but also the modality of an input." In this view, a baby's perceptions are not tied to a particular modality, but rather information is perceived as *amodal*, that is, as belonging to no modality in particular. A contrasting school of thought argues that the processes involved in multimodal integration are highly complicated, that very young babies are unable to integrate information entering the brain through different sensory modalities, and that the ability to coordinate input across the senses develops over the first year(s) of life through experience (Bryant, 1974).

Research supports the integrationist view, in that newborns and very young infants have been observed to respond in a similar fashion to, or treat as equivalent, events that impinge on multiple sensory modalities, and to recognize visually what they initially perceived using a different sensory modality (Lewkowicz & Lickliter, 1994; Rochat, 1997). Newborns will orient and look toward the location of a sound, and very young infants will "match" different sound amplitudes with lights of differing brightness levels with an accuracy that rivals that of adults (Thelen & Smith, 1994). Infants in the first 6 months of life display sensitivity to a range of amodal dimensions, from the temporal synchrony of object trajectory and impact, to voice and face coordination (Bahrick, 1995; Meltzoff, 1993). For example, infants as young as 29 days of age successfully identify by sight an object they had previously explored by mouth alone (i.e., a pacifier with small nubs versus a pacifier with a smooth surface—see Figure 6.13). Infants were either given the nubbed pacifier or the smooth pacifier to suck on for 90 seconds and then were presented the two pacifiers, side by side, to look at. The infants preferred to look at the pacifier that they had initially sucked on (Meltzoff, 1993).

Infants are also sensitive to the coherence of approach/recession with loudness/softness. Approach is specified by an object appearing larger and sounding louder, recession by its appearing smaller and sounding softer. Schiff, Benasich, and Bornstein (1989) found that 5-month-olds habituate more efficiently to coherent approach or coherent recession (when the sound and image specify the same direction of motion of a person) and less efficiently to incoherent events (when the sound specifies approach but the image recedes, for example).

The study of cross-modal perception has led to insights about infants' developing sense of self. Rochat (1997) proposed that the earliest self-knowledge

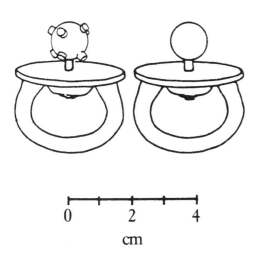

FIGURE 6.13
Two pacifiers, one with a smooth surface and one with a nubbed surface, used to examine cross-modal perception. Infants are given one of these two pacifiers to suck on without being able to see it. When presented with both pacifiers side by side, infants are more likely to look at the pacifier that they had initially sucked on. (From A. N. Meltzoff, 1993.)

FIGURE 6.14
Rochat and Morgan's (1995) apparatus for studying cross-modal perception in infants.
(From P. Rochat & R. Morgan, 1995.)

is based on the perceived intercoordination of information from perceptual systems (e.g., visual, tactile, and auditory) and motor actions such as sucking, rooting, and orienting. Rochat (1997) found the 3- to 4-week-old infants' rooting response was stronger when their cheeks were touched by the researcher's finger or a pacifier than by the infants' own hand. These findings indicate that infants can differentiate "single" touches, from a source external to their bodies, from "double" or self-touches, in which touch is felt both on the cheek and on the finger that is touching the cheek.

Rochat and Morgan (1995) provided other evidence of infants' intermodal perceptual abilities in an experiment with 3- to 5-month-olds. The infant was propped in front of a television monitor with two cameras focused on the infant's legs. Infants were propped in such a way that they were only able to see their legs on the television screen (see Figure 6.14). One of the two cameras was positioned 1 meter in front of the infant and produced a frontal view of the infant's legs (the observer's view). The other camera was placed 1 meter above the infant's head and provided a view of the infant's legs that the infant would have had if she or he was able to look down at them (the ego view). The images from the two cameras were simultaneously shown to the infants on a split screen. To attract the infants' attention to the TV screen, long, black-and-white striped socks were placed on the infants' legs, and a small microphone was positioned on the surface on which the infants' feet rested. The microphone was connected to a speaker atop the TV. Thus, infants were attracted to the TV images by the striped socks and the sounds made by their feet when they moved them around.

The infants in this experiment were shown three separate split-screen presentations of their legs (see Figure 6.15). The first (Figure 6.15A) presented the ego and observer's view of the legs. Both movement directionality and orientation differed between the two views. The second (Figure 6.15B) presented the ego view and a reversed ego view (a mirror image) of the legs. Here, movement directionality, but not orientation, differentiated the two views. The third

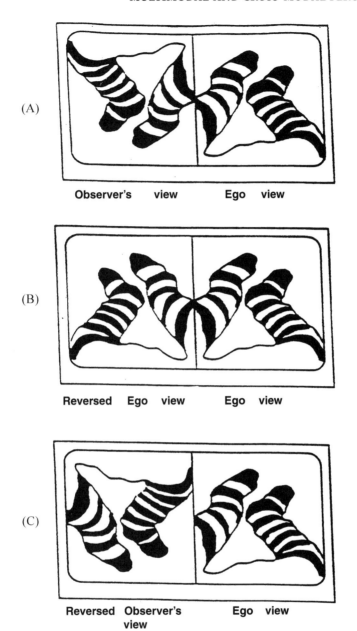

FIGURE 6.15

Different TV displays presented to infants by Rochat and Morgan (1995) to study cross-modal perception. In Figure 6.15A, the two views differed in terms of both movement directionality and orientation. In Figure 6.15B, the views differed in terms of movement directionality but not orientation. In Figure 6.15C, the two views differed in terms of orientation but not movement directionality. (From P. Rochat & R. Morgan, 1995.)

(Figure 6.15C) presented a reversed observer's view and the ego view, which varied orientation, but not movement directionality, between the two views. Infants looked significantly longer at the observer's view in Figure 6.15A and at the reversed ego view in Figure 6.15B, but did not show any preferential looking at either view in Figure 6.15C. The observer's view in Figure 6.15A and the reversed ego view in Figure 6.15B were consistent in that they differed from the adjacent view in terms of movement directionality. By contrast, when only orientation but not movement directionality differentiated the two views (Figure 6.15C), no preferential looking to either view was observed. These results indicated that infants were able to discern the difference between views of their leg movements that were congruent with their actual movements from views that were incongruent with their actual movements. The infants looked longer at TV images of their legs when the direction they felt their legs moving did not coincide with the direction of leg movement on the TV screen. This study provided further evidence for intermodal perception in infants as young as 3 months of age, in that the infants could coordinate proprioceptive (body movement and positioning) information with visual perceptual information.

Studies such as these clearly demonstrate that young infants are sensitive to multimodal information even though different senses are stimulated in distinctly different ways. It is clear that the basic sensory systems are functioning at birth, and infants then or soon after perceive highly complex and sophisticated information. Moreover, infants perceive some information arriving via the different senses in a coordinated way. Infants even make information about stimuli acquired in one modality available to other modalities. Integration of sensory information in infancy depends, of course, on the developmental status of the infant, on the task, on the stimuli used, and so forth. These kinds of research initiatives in turn raise even more formidable questions about the interaction of sensory and perceptual systems near the beginning of life, the influence of the development of one perceptual system on the development of others, and the diverse possible roles of experience on perceptual system development.

Experience and Early Perceptual Development

What are the roles of experience in early perceptual development? Which experiences matter, in what spheres of perceiving, and how early? As we have seen, perceptual abilities are already remarkably well organized at birth. However, theorists and researchers have long argued that perceptual experience is critical for normal psychological growth and development. One early classic experiment with institutionalized human newborns showed that simply introducing a visually interesting stabile into the infant's otherwise bland environment at 1 month nearly doubled visually directed reaching and visual attentiveness (White, Castle, & Held, 1964). In a second similar study, 1-month-olds who had a stabile hung over their cribs later developed a visual defensive response to its sudden approach in half the time required by a matched-age group of babies without comparable experience (Greenberg, Užgiris, & Hunt, 1968).

Some infants are born with dense central cataracts, permitting only diffuse light to be seen. In a study examining the development of visual acuity in such infants, Maurer, Lewis, Brent, and Levin (1999) found that visual acuity shortly after these cataracts were surgically removed (surgery took place anywhere between 1 week and 9 months of age) was quite impaired and no better than that of a typical newborn. However, visual acuity improved dramatically over the next month, with some improvement seen as early as 1 hour after treatment (and, thus, 1 hour after the onset of visual input). Postnatal development of visual acuity appears to depend on the presence of patterned visual stimulation.

For obvious reasons, most research on the effects of experimental manipulations of the visual system have involved animals rather than human beings.

However, Hochberg and Brooks (1962) described an infant boy who was reared in a pictureless environment until 19 months of age. When at that age the boy first saw pictures (two-dimensional arrays of three-dimensional things he knew), the child correctly named pictured objects, suggesting that name learning readily transferred from solid objects to photographs and line drawings of those objects. To study analogous effects in humans, investigators have more often had to capitalize on "natural experiments" of one sort or another (Chapter 3). Institutionalization and illness (examples of which were reviewed above) provide two such kinds of opportunistic manipulations.

Culture provides another. As we noted, prelinguistic infants distinguish certain perceptual categories associated with speech, whereas adults sometimes distinguish the same categories but sometimes distinguish different, often fewer, ones. It must be the case, therefore, that a lack of perceptual experience with certain speech distinctions fails to maintain categories, just as experiences with other speech distinctions may induce or attune the development of new discriminations (Aslin et al., 1998; Best, McRoberts, et al., 1995).

Related studies of infants and adults attest to the generality of these developmental principles of perceptual experience in nonspeech auditory domains as well as in visual perception. Studying the infant origins of musical sensitivities, Lynch, Eilers, Oller, and Urbano (1990) found that 6-month-olds from Western cultures perceive melodies based on native Western major, native Western minor, and non-native (Javanese pelog) musical scales equivalently, but that adults perceive native better than non-native scales. In a later study of infants from 6 to 12 months of age, Lynch, Short, and Chua (1996) found that the ability to detect melodic alterations in musical passages was a function of the infants' experience with music, suggesting that, as with speech perception, the processing of music is shaped by the culturally prescribed musical environments in which infants are reared. Together, nonspeech and speech studies indicate a pattern of full potential in infant perception, and they point to a major role of cultural experience in shaping perceptual development. In the domain of vision, studies of eye movement development have revealed examples of the effects of experience on perception. One kind of infant eye movement (saccades, or movements from one visual fixation point to another) are essentially mature at birth, and experience afterward maintains or attunes them; by contrast, experience seems to induce another kind of eye movement (smooth pursuit), and experience facilitates visual acuity (Slater & Johnson, 1998; Vital-Durand, Ayzac, & Pinzaru, 1996).

Bornstein initiated a series of studies designed to investigate systematic associations between specific experiences and infant perceptual development. In one experiment, Kuchuk, Vibbert, and Bornstein (1986) assessed how specific types of interactions with 3-month-olds influenced infants' perceptions. In the laboratory, infants were tested for their sensitivity to smiling faces in a series of smiles that graduated in intensity; babies showed individual variation. Concurrent observations of mother–infant interactions at home revealed that the mothers who more frequently encouraged their infants' attention to themselves when the mothers were smiling had infants who showed the most sensitivity to smiling. In a separate longitudinal study of 2- to 5-month-old infants, Bornstein and Tamis-LeMonda (1990) examined relations between mothers' calling attention to themselves versus properties, objects, or events in the environment and their infants' visual and tactual exploratory competencies. They observed several specific experience-related associations. Infants whose mothers encouraged attention to themselves had babies who attended more to them and less to the environment, whereas infants whose mothers encouraged attention to the environment had babies who explored objects more and their mothers less. Furthermore, these effects were greater among infants whose mothers engaged in actual physical, as opposed to verbal, prompting.

There can be little doubt that experiences, as well as the lack of experiences, play important roles in the maintenance, attunement, and induction of infant perceptions. It is practically axiomatic in taste development, for example, that the greater the variety of tastes the infant experiences, the more open to new tastes the child will be (Kuo, 1967). Basic perceptions are somewhat malleable to experience, and only further research will identify both the limits of that plasticity and the experiences that influence them most. At minimum, this approach to research tells us about the native perceptions of infants, the universal potential for perception, and the diverse roles of experience on shaping perceptual development in infancy.

Summary

Those who study early perceptual capacity have overcome the major impediments infants present—their silence and motoric intractability—by establishing communication with infants in a variety of ingenious psychophysiological and behavioral ways. In doing so, modern investigators have systematically and forever eradicated the notion that infants are perceptually naive. Research in infant perception addresses many questions concerning the status and natural functions of the senses near the beginning of life, the possible roles of experience, and philosophical issues about the origins of knowledge.

In this chapter we discussed functional development in five perceptual systems: vision, audition, taste, smell, and touch. All five senses are capable of function before birth, and the perceptual capacities even of the newborn baby are quite impressive. Infants are basically prepared to perceive and acquire information from the world that newly surrounds them. From the very beginning of life, furthermore, babies actively seek out that information and show distinct preferences for certain kinds of information. Soon after birth, for example, newborns prefer contours and edges, where visual information is rich; they appear to possess an innate, rudimentary knowledge of faces; and they prefer saturated colors, the sounds of language, sweet tastes, and pleasant odors.

Afterward the infant's perceptual world becomes increasingly organized. Visual acuity and the ability to detect and discriminate speech develop rapidly toward mature levels. Between the third and fifth months after birth, babies show that they can voluntarily focus on near or far objects, that they possess the rudiments of shape and size constancies, that they perceive Gestalts and recognize objects in two or three dimensions, and that they see color and discriminate complex differences among sounds. In infancy, visual–auditory and visual–tactual information is integrated into multimodal perceptual wholes. Babies distinguish and attend to properties of objects as well as to relations among properties; these abilities combine to subserve the child's cognitive understanding of the object world. Infants seem preadapted to perceive in ways that facilitate the organization of incoming information, which in turn furthers the development of their perceptual systems.

7

Mental Life in Infancy

———— ❖ ————

- What are the distinguishing characteristics of Piaget's theory of cognitive development in infancy?
- What overarching features characterize the stage of infant sensorimotor development?
- How and why have developmentalists criticized and challenged Piaget's theory?
- How do the information-processing and early learning perspectives differ from Piaget's?
- Distinguish among the three major types of learning.
- How do the processes of habituation and novelty responsiveness illustrate information processing?
- How informative and predictively valid are individual differences in habituation?
- How well do other infant tests predict later intelligence?
- How do parents shape infant intelligence?

Cognition, Learning, and Intelligence

Although it might not always be apparent, there is no question that even very young infants have an active mental life. They are constantly learning and developing new ideas, and they do so in many different ways. Moreover, what infants learn and the capacities they demonstrate in doing so affect many aspects of their later development. The questions that currently motivate thinking and research about infant mental life are these: What is infant cognition? How well can we measure it? What do infants learn about the world around them? How do they learn? How do learning and cognition develop in infancy? How do infants differ from one another in their mental abilities? How can we foster mental development in infancy and later? How do infant mental abilities relate to later cognition, emotion, and social development?

These questions have long puzzled developmentalists, and the answers advanced today constitute the major topics we cover in this chapter and the next. Specifically, in this chapter we address basic aspects of theorizing and studying mental life in infancy. The topics include Piaget's views of cognitive development and some of the important contributions of post-Piagetian researchers, learning in infancy, the information-processing approach to infant intelligence, and the ways in which the infant's interaction with

205

objects and people influence mental development. In Chapter 8, we follow this introduction to the fundamentals of infant mental life with discussions of categorization and concept formation, memory, and symbolic or pretend play.

Mental life in infancy comprises what is known, what is learned, and how infants act on the two. There are two main schools of thought about infant cognition, and they relate back to some of the ideas we introduced in Chapter 1, namely the contrasting emphases on individual differences as opposed to normative developmental functions and the debate among nativists, empiricists, interactionists, and transactionalists. Piaget was a major proponent of one school of thought; he focused on normative *developmental functions* and *qualitative descriptions* of infant mental life—what all human babies "know and do"—hypothesizing that development is discontinuous as a result of universal stages of mental growth. Proponents of the contrasting school, which includes the learning and information-processing perspectives, have emphasized the continuous, *quantitative* nature of growth in infant intelligence as well as individual differences in what, how, and why babies acquire knowledge. Remember that these different emphases—on the continuity or discontinuity of the developmental function as opposed to the stability or instability of individual differences—are independent of one another: How individuals rank in a group at different times is independent of change in the group overall, and whether or not the group function changes is independent of individual stability in terms of rank-order performance. In this chapter, we describe these general approaches to assessing mental life in infancy. At the outset, however, it is important to emphasize that these schools of thought about the infant's mental life do not compete with one another but represent coexisting and mutually informative perspectives, and we suspect that students of infant cognition will eventually achieve a synthesis of the two.

Before proceeding, consider for a moment what kind of mental life you yourself might engineer for the human infant. Certainly, you would not want to fix the infant's intelligence in advance of any actual experience; it would be shortsighted and counterproductive to eliminate the possible effects of experience because intelligence naturally includes the ability to adapt successfully to the environment. By the same token, however, you would probably not want to leave mental development wholly to experience because individual experiences can vary so much. In fact, both of these "design criteria" appear to have been met in the evolution of the development of infant cognition.

There is another point to consider: What is cognition for an infant? If we consider simple face validity we can easily agree that when infants do something, like search for and find a hidden object, the activity "looks" intelligent. We could also assess validity in terms of predictive validity, concluding that some measure of an infant assesses cognitive functioning because it predicts the child's later intelligence. For example, if efficiency in infant perception predicted intelligence test performance in elementary school, and intelligence test performance systematically related to school achievement and job performance, we would tend to believe that that aspect of infant perception was measuring something about intelligence in infancy.

Keeping the questions of design criteria and validity in mind, we now describe different ways of thinking about mental life in infancy. We begin with Piaget and the qualitative perspective on cognitive development.

The Piagetian View of Cognitive Development in Infancy

Between 1925 and 1932, the Swiss biologist and philosopher Jean Piaget watched closely as his own three children grew from infancy, taking note of the enormous intellectual progress each made during the first two years of life before they acquired language. Soon afterward, Piaget (1936/1952) published the *Origins of Intelligence in Children*, a compilation of his observations and informal experiments that led to a revolutionary theory of cognitive development in infancy.

To understand Piaget's theory, we must appreciate that Piaget saw himself as a philosopher as much as a scientist. He was initially motivated in his work by a desire to resolve the old epistemological debate about the origins of knowledge. Piaget was fascinated by the way in which the human mind seems naturally to organize knowledge into categories of, for example, space, time, causality, and substance. However, Piaget did not believe the nativist idea that these universal categories were innate; at the same time, he also disagreed with the empiricist view that all knowledge was derived from experience. (We discussed these contrasting views in both Chapters 1 and 6.) Suffice it to say that Piaget created a new and radically different solution to the philosophical problem of the origins of knowledge. Piaget suggested that each infant constructs an understanding of the world—including space, time, causality, and substance—on the basis of his or her own activity and interactions in the world.

In this part of Chapter 7, we examine several key features of Piaget's theory. They include the elements and dynamics of his theory of knowledge (the scheme, the schema, and adaptation), his view that action is the basis of knowledge, and his stage notion of development. There are, as we shall see, many unresolved aspects to Piaget's views of cognitive development in infancy.

Piaget's Theory of Knowledge

In contrast to both the nativist and empiricist views, Piaget began with the proposal that knowledge is not derived from sensations or perceptions, nor is knowledge gained from information provided by others. Rather, Piaget argued that individuals construct knowledge initially out of their own motor activity. Piaget did not deny that sensations and perceptions are important, of course, though he emphasized their role in correcting and modifying motor activity. A revolutionary implication of this assumption concerns the nature of mental representation (see also Chapter 8). If sensations and perceptions are not the sources of knowledge, then thoughts, images, and ideas in the mind—*mental representations*—cannot be the residues of sensation, as both nativists and empiricists believed. Piaget held, rather, that such mental materials involve the internalization of motor activity. His theory holds that the process of internalization is very slow for two reasons: First, motor activity initially does not closely match external reality but must come to match that reality over time. Second, motor activity might be internalized as thought or image or idea only if it is well rehearsed. Thus, in contrast to both nativism and empiricism, Piagetian theory postulates the absence of any evidence for representation until the (astonishingly late) age of approximately 18 months.

The Scheme

For the empiricists, the basic elements of knowledge were sensations; for the nativists, the basic elements were innate ideas as well as sensations. For Piaget, the basic element of infant knowledge is the *scheme*. This is a hard concept to define concisely, although the meaning is to some extent captured in the notion that schemes are central nervous system structures that produce motor activities capable of processing information in the environment. Stated simply, schemes are ways of acting on the world. In newborns, schemes are more or less automatic motor activities, although not all reflexes (sneezes and coughs) are schemes; but many can be used to acquire or process information in the environment (sucking, grasping, looking, hearing, and tasting are examples). Notice that Piaget considered looking and hearing to be actions—not simply the passive registration of sensory information. According to Piaget, knowledge develops as an elaboration of simple reflex schemes present in the newborn.

Piaget's notion of the scheme rests on the claim that knowledge begins with actions rather than with sensations. Piaget argued, however, that there must be a central mechanism for filtering out sensory inputs (i.e., we do not attend to *every* stimulus that falls on our sense organs) and for assigning meaning to sensations. He suggested that schemes allow the infant to assign meaning to stimulation. Behavioral schemes (physical activities) dominate infancy, but eventually mental schemes, that is, cognitive activities, come into play. Piaget distinguished between schemes and *schemas*, the signifiers or symbols that constitute mental life after the advent of representational abilities. In Piaget's system, the child acquires schemas at the end of infancy. Piaget took note of the fact that infant cognition is not static. Indeed, infants create, respond to, and adjust to an ever changing world; that is, infant mental development is *self-modifying*. To explain processes underlying development, he invoked the concept of adaptation.

Adaptation

Adaptation is the fundamental process whereby schemes are altered through experience. Adaptation itself involves two complementary processes, *assimilation* and *accommodation*. When information can be processed according to an existing scheme, the information is said to be assimilated, and meaning is given to the sensation. For example, a newborn infant who mouths a finger and starts sucking is said to have assimilated the finger to the sucking scheme. For the moment, the finger has a single meaning or function—it is suckable. The individual sensations—taste, pressure, vision, and so forth—that are simultaneously experienced have no meaning in themselves unless or until the infant turns his or her schemes to them. According to Piaget, assimilation is a conservative process because the infant does not change an existing way of acting on the world.

At times, however, an existing scheme cannot successfully assimilate the information in a stimulus. For example, the infant may try to mouth a fist rather than a finger, and of course will not succeed if attempts to do so are the same as attempts to mouth the finger. Two things can happen. One is that the infant can fail to assimilate and simply move on to another activity. Alternatively, the infant can change the scheme in such a way that it permits new information to be processed; for example, the mouth might be widened or changed in shape. The modification of an existing scheme to make it applicable to a new situation is termed accommodation. Notice that in Piaget's view the environment does not simply act on a passive, receptive child. Rather, the child actively changes in order to understand the environment.

Although we have described assimilation and accommodation as separate processes, the two always co-occur so that the infant's schemes can match reality and reality can be understood. Normally, the balance between assimilation and accommodation is shifting, giving temporary preeminence to one or the other process. Thus, for Piaget, assimilation predominates during play—in pretend play, for instance, reality can be interpreted in any way one wishes. Accommodation predominates during imitation—in mimicry, the actions of the child match reality as closely as possible.

Cognitive development through accommodation occurs slowly; the child does not suddenly modify all schemes to accord with physical reality. The concordance between existing schemes and the novel demands of the environment must be sufficiently good that the child knows which schemes to modify. When there is concordance between reality and the child's schemes, a state of *mental equilibrium* is said to exist. Piaget supposed that physical and mental activity are geared to maximizing the equilibration process, because it represents a crucial aspect of adaptation brought into play to resolve contradictions between the child's comprehension of the world at any given stage and the larger reality in which the child lives. Piaget was primarily interested in the processes whereby mental equilibrium at higher and higher levels can be attained.

Action as the Basis of Knowledge

Piaget contended that knowledge begins with action, that acquiring knowledge depends on doing rather than observing passively (although we know that observational learning does often occur). Thus, Piaget was a *constructivist* in that he believed that individuals actively contribute to and construct their own development. Piaget's influence is evident in the frequent stress in our book on the active role infants play in shaping their own development.

Recall Held and Hein (1963) demonstrated the critical importance of self-produced activity for the development of understanding. They created an apparatus called the kitten carousel (see Figure 7.1). This device allowed two animals to obtain essentially the same amount of exposure to an environment in two entirely different ways. One kitten was allowed to move about on its own; a second kitten was moved by the first. Thus, the second kitten's visual experience, although equivalent in extent to that of the first, was obtained passively rather than actively. The kittens were reared in the dark until they could locomote adequately, and afterward they were allowed 3 hours of visual and motor experience a day in the carousel. The results of tests given when the kittens reached maturity were compelling: The cats who had been allowed to move about on their own avoided the deep side of a visual cliff, stretched out their limbs appropriately in preparation for contact with a solid surface, and blinked at approaching objects. By contrast, even after extensive transportation in the carousel, the passively moved cats failed to show such spatially sensitive behavior. Similarly, as we all know, way finding the second time is often easier for the person who drove the car than for a passenger.

Action is clearly a strong basis of perceptual knowledge. Indeed, for infants actions it sometimes seems even more important than perceptual information. Bremner and Bryant (1985) exposed this phenomenon in a task popularized by

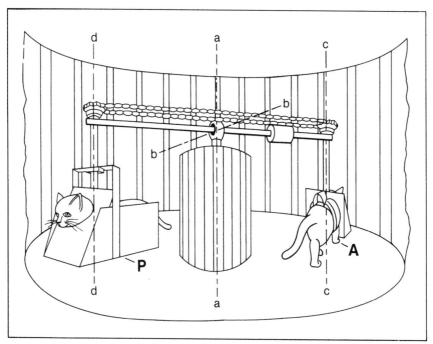

FIGURE 7.1

Kitten A roams actively under its own power, moving a second kitten passively. Both thereby received the same amount of visual stimulation. Later both are tested on various tasks, like the visual cliff. The active kittens avoid the deep side of the cliff, but the passively moved kittens do not. (After Held & Hein, 1963. © 1963 by the American Psychological Association. Reprinted by permission.)

Piaget—hiding an object and then observing whether the infant can find it. They studied the "A not B" error. This error occurs when an object is hidden repeatedly in one place (A), and the infant regularly succeeds in finding it. Then, in full view of the infant, the object is hidden in a different location (B). Bremner and Bryant hid the object in wells placed to the right or left of 9-month-old infants. The infants were allowed to uncover the hidden object five times from the same well, something these infants were able to do quite easily. Then the object was hidden in the other well. Although the infants watched the object being hidden, they did not search in the well where it was hidden, but in the well where they had found it on the five previous trials. These infants ignored perceptual information about the hiding location in favor of information about the success of their previous actions. Other studies also attest to foundations of cognition in early infant action (e.g., Haith & Benson, 1998; Willatts, 1997).

Stage Theory: The Decline of Egocentrism

Perhaps the best known feature of Piaget's theory is his doctrine of *stages*, for Piaget hypothesized that mental development unfolds in an invariant sequence of cognitive developmental periods. As a whole, infancy encompasses a *sensorimotor period*; it is followed, in the Piagetian system, by preoperational, concrete operational, and formal operational periods of childhood, early adolescence, and late adolescence, respectively. Within the sensorimotor period in infancy, Piaget detailed an additional stage-wise sequence of development. Here we illustrate that sequence with respect to the infant's move away from relatively "autistic" to relatively "realistic" ways of thinking. We call this development the *decline of egocentrism.*

Stages

Before discussing this decline, however, it is useful to review Piaget's conceptualization of stages. In the Piagetian system, observed behaviors are believed to reflect an underlying structure, and behaviors related to that stage are thought to emerge in synchrony with one another, thereby giving evidence of the stage as a whole (see Chapter 1). Thus, coherence is thought to characterize the child's interactions at any one time, making for a particular view of the world that changes across time. Importantly, the child's current stage is believed to define the way the child views the world and processes information in it. Moreover, Piaget's theory of cognitive growth posited invariant and hierarchical stage-wise progressions from infant sensorimotor behavior though formal logic in adulthood (Langer & Killen, 1998; Lutz & Sternberg, 1999).

When formulating his theory of infant cognitive development, Piaget laid stress on a central aspect—the progress of the infant away from *egocentrism.* Egocentrism for Piaget does not mean selfishness, self-centeredness, or egotism. Rather, it refers to children's understanding of the world in terms of their own motor activity, and their inability to understand it from any other perspective. Piaget described six stages in the decline of egocentrism during infancy. These stages follow a progression, and they are age-related, although their link to age is only approximate. Piaget's stages also provide evidence of the gradual realization that objects in the outside world are related to one another, at first when they are physically present and subsequently when they are representations in the mind. The notion of declining egocentrism (sometimes called *decentration*) and the associated stage theory are at the heart of Piaget's view of mental life in infancy, and so we describe these postulated stages in some detail.

Stage 1: Birth to 1 Month

At this stage of *reflex schemes*, infants accommodate to environmental stimuli very little, and thus mental development is minimal and very slow. Piaget believed that the infant in Stage 1 cannot recognize that stimuli belong to solid objects in the outside world because the different schemes appear uncoordinated (i.e., independent of one another). Consequently, because the information processed by one scheme cannot be shifted into or processed by another scheme, the infant does not know that a sound and a sight relate to the same object: They are processed independently (see the discussion of multimodal and intermodal perception in Chapter 6). Furthermore, because reflex schemes are hardly accommodated to reality, the child is most egocentric at this stage. According to Piaget, stimulation from the outside world only serves as a staging for schemes, giving the schemes something on which to operate. The infant extracts little or no information about the outside world from this stimulation.

Stage 2: 1 to 4 Months

During the second stage, the infant makes major progress toward coordinating schemes, but these intercoordinations apparently provide little information about the outside world. For example, 3-month-olds can readily coordinate their hands and mouths and may repetitively grasp and let things go, but they still appear to be repeating actions for their own sake rather than because they are learning about the outside world. Piaget used the term *primary circular reactions* to describe the infant's tendency to repeat chance discoveries involving the co-ordination of two actions. He called them "circular reactions" because they are repetitions of chance discoveries, and designated them "primary" because they are the earliest of a series of circular reactions to emerge in infancy. Another such coordination occurs when infants turn toward the source of sounds. According to Piaget, there was no evidence that infants expect to see something (but see Chapter 6); rather, infants turn in order to activate looking and hearing schemes simultaneously.

Stage 3: 4 to 7 Months

For the first time egocentrism declines noticeably, and infants now appear to be aware of the relation between their own behavior and the environment. For example, when infants accidentally produce environmental events they may re-peat them, suggesting that they want to review their effects on the environment. Because infants produce actions repeatedly (as they did in Stage 2), Piaget still spoke of circular reactions, although he called these new ones *secondary circular reactions*. Now infants begin to notice and focus on events in the outside world. Nevertheless, egocentrism is still prominent: Understanding of the world is based on action rather than on an appreciation of relations among objects. Thus, for example, if a child has discovered that kicking the side of the crib causes a mobile to move, the child may continue to kick even when the leg is too far away to reach the side of the crib. Despite the sensory evidence to the contrary, the baby repeats the previously successful action.

Stage 4: 7 to 10 Months

By Stage 4, egocentrism has declined markedly, and the infant has finally con-structed some relations among environmental stimuli. Infants now appear to understand that one object can be in front of another. Consequently, the child is only now able to remove a cover from a hidden object; this is something that should have been possible (in terms of motor abilities) far earlier *if* the child understood relations between the hidden object and the cover. Egocentrism has still not disappeared, however, and infants still commit the "A not B" error. For Piaget, this fault constituted strong evidence that perceptual information is not sufficient to account for cognitive understanding and behavior. Rather, what infants remember is their success with prior actions.

Stage 5: 10 to 18 Months

In this stage, many schemes are accommodated to the outside world, and many unexpected relations among objects are discovered. This progress is facilitated by the emergence of *tertiary circular reactions*, in which the child causes something to happen accidentally (as in secondary circular reactions) but then systematically and deliberately varies the manner in which the event is brought about. For example, a child may attempt to see whether milk leaks out of a bottle at different rates depending on the angle of the bottle and the force with which it is squeezed. Tertiary circular reactions help children to understand that they can cause action as a means of producing novel ends. This achievement anticipates the infant's capacity to engage in insightful problem solving (without trial and error) at a time when novel means must be employed to achieve novel ends.

Vestiges of egocentrism remain even at this stage, however, according to Piaget. A major limitation on the infant is the inability to conceive of *invisible displacements*. If in one continuous movement an object is hidden under and reemerges from screen A, then screen B, and finally is left behind screen C, Stage 5 infants can find the object only if they actually see the object being removed from and hidden under each screen. If the adult's hand conceals the object being hidden, infants seem to have no idea where the object is or how to go about searching for it. In short, infants still have an incomplete understanding of the possible relations between objects and screens; thus, they do not appreciate the permanence of objects and so cannot represent their invisible movements. Furthermore, although infants no longer make the "A not B" error when searching for hidden objects, their solution for new problems involves a slow trial-and-error process. This result again gives evidence that infants utilize their knowledge of previous actions rather than just sensory information.

Piaget (1953) provided a dramatic illustration of egocentrism in the Stage 5 child. He described placing his 15-month-old daughter Jacqueline in a playpen with a cardboard rooster just outside it. The rooster had to be tilted away from the child in order to be pulled between the bars of the playpen, and Jacqueline should have been able to see that the slats of the playpen would get in the way if she tried to pull the rooster in sideways. She tried to do this anyway. Moreover, although the rooster kept banging against the bars, Jacqueline did not try to adjust the orientation of the rooster. Only when the rooster fell from her hands and accidentally adopted the right orientation did she succeed in bringing the toy into the pen. However, even this accidental success did not affect her behavior when her father once again placed the rooster outside her playpen. Only after Jacqueline started to drop the rooster deliberately, systematically varying its position, was she able to solve the problem readily.

Note the importance of chance discoveries, the inattention to sensory evidence, and the deliberate variation of means only after chance success in this example. In discussing this stage of development, Piaget seemed to support an empiricist theory of problem solving but emphasized action rather than perception. He seemed to shift theoretical stance, however, when he discussed problem solving in Stage 6.

Stage 6: 18 to 24 Months

The hallmark of Stage 6 is the infant's emergent capacity for mental representation. In the case of the object concept, children can now imagine the whereabouts of an invisible object for the first time. They can also imagine invisible trajectories, so that when a ball rolls under a sofa, for example, the child will move around the sofa and anticipate the reemergence of the ball rather than attempting to follow the trajectory directly. This shows successful representation of space. Infants are now able to imitate people even in their absence (deferred imitation), which is crucial if, for example, they are ever to utter words that they have not heard for some time. Now, symbolic play becomes possible, and children also become capable of insightful problem solving. As evidence of this newfound ability, Piaget (1953) described the behavior of his other daughter, Lucienne, when she faced a problem similar to Jacqueline's. Lucienne at first pulled the toy in sideways; however, as soon as she met resistance from the slats she reoriented the toy so that she could pull it in easily. In demonstrating this sudden, successful solution of a novel problem, Lucienne met all of the criteria for what Piaget called *representation* (the ability to anticipate the solution to a problem without overt trial and error).

Stage 6, then, culminates the infant's movement away from sensorimotor egocentrism. The child's practical knowledge of the world is now so realistic that solutions to problems can be effected even prior to any direct experience with them. According to Piaget, however, attaining mental representation and insightful problem solving is made possible by many slow, struggling anticipatory accommodations. Thus, intrinsic tendencies of the organism, experience, and the emergence of new cognitive capacities play intertwined roles in the development of sensorimotor intelligence. The stage-wise decline of egocentrism with development typifies Piaget's approach to the study of cognition.

Décalage

According to Piaget, all aspects of cognitive development undergo such progressions. In Table 7.1, we list the sequences of development in four of the most important cognitive domains described by Piaget. Normally, a stage theory would suppose that all of the component features of a stage come "online" together. This is not always the case, however. *Décalage* refers to an unevenness in development across cognitive domains. Piaget (1952, 1954) described several décalages in his books on infancy. An especially striking example is the décalage shown by his children, who attained Stage 6 of imitation some weeks before they attained the same stage in object permanence, spatial understanding, or causality. This décalage is somewhat predictable if, as Piaget holds, imitation underlies the ability to represent absent objects. Piaget did not explain what he thought produces décalage. He wrote about each cognitive domain separately—there is a chapter on object permanence, one on space, and a book on imitation—and he only rarely discussed the synchrony or asynchrony of development in disparate domains. However, using the term *stage* to refer to each newly attained sensorimotor level implies that changes in cognitive capacity are fairly widespread and consistent.

Challenges to Piaget's Theory

Piaget's theory of cognitive development is unrivaled in elegance and scope, and there is empirical corroboration for many of his proposed developmental achievements and for the sequences in which they occur. The theory has clearly served as the foundation for the study of infant cognition. The topics Piaget identified, including infants' conceptions of objects, number, time, space, and causality, have served as subjects for research in infant cognition for the past four decades, and perhaps no other theory has undergone such intense scrutiny (Haith & Benson, 1998). The inevitable result of such scrutiny, however, is the emergence of a large body of work that takes issue with Piaget's formulations and basic assumptions.

One of Piaget's basic tenets is that cognition is rooted in action, without which infants would be unable to derive meaning from sensory and perceptual events (which, in Piaget's view, are disconnected and uncoordinated in early infancy). However, in grounding all knowledge in motor activity, Piaget mistakenly ignored the vital contributions of perceptual and sensory activity to representation and knowledge. Décarie (1969), for example, found that limbless children (whose mothers had ingested the sedative thalidomide during the first trimester of pregnancy—see Chapter 4) develop a normal cognitive life despite the absence of normal sensorimotor experience through infancy. Indeed, Piagetian theory does not give sufficient credit to the remarkable sensory and organizational capacities of newborns and young infants (see Chapters 5 and 6).

A second theoretical issue in Piagetian studies is whether the attainment of one stage in a given domain guarantees that the infant is in the same stage of development in another domain: Is mental development synchronous or sequential? Décalage is neither rare nor necessarily of small magnitude, and so it is necessary to examine this aspect of Piaget's theory critically. For instance, the Užgiris–Hunt (1975) Ordinal Scales of Psychological Development attempt to categorize the infant's overall performance into one of Piaget's six sensorimotor stages. However, Užgiris and Hunt (1975) found so many décalages while constructing the Ordinal Scales they were forced to conclude that progress in each area of cognitive development may be independent of progress in the others. For this reason, they opted to publish six scales of sensorimotor intelligence rather than a single scale, and they reported only modest correlations in individual performance across these scales (see below).

Fischer (1980, 1996; Fischer & Silvern, 1985) argued that the problem of décalage is so serious that it has major implications for understanding transitions from one stage of mental development to the next, for relating the development of sensorimotor intelligence to other psychological processes (such as language and emotion), and especially for understanding the strengths and limitations of the stage concept in theories of cognitive development. In order to understand décalage, Fischer stressed the importance of the environment in skill acquisition and facilitation. Like Piaget, he believes that infants have to intercoordinate a number of skills in order to shift from one stage to the next higher one and that there are cognitive skills in common across intellectual domains. Unlike Piaget, he argues that some skills are specific to each domain. If one assumes that the skills peculiar to each cognitive stage are poorly correlated with one another, then décalage should be the rule rather than the exception in cognitive development. The low correlation among measures of specific skills is ensured by environmental factors and specific experiences. An environment that facilitates the rehearsal of one cognitive skill, but not another, produces a décalage favoring the better rehearsed skill. On the other hand, because there are core cognitive structures common to all domains, there are constraints on how far the environment can "push" cognitive development in any single domain. Finally, Fischer argues that to understand cognitive development, one must first analyze the cognitive requirements for success on a given task; we should expect simultaneous attainment of stage level across different domains only when the same cognitive skills are called for (a rare event). It thus seems inappropriate to talk about cohesive "stages" of cognitive development in infancy, or even later. Stage implies synchrony of development, and synchrony may occur less frequently than the term stage connotes.

Perhaps the greatest empirical challenges to Piaget's theory of sensorimotor development, however, come from findings indicating that the capacity for mental representation of the physical world, and the emergence of object permanence, appear much earlier in development than Piaget supposed. Two

TABLE 7.1 SEQUENCE OF SOME IMPORTANT SENSORIMOTOR DEVELOPMENTS IN PIAGETIAN THEORY

Stage	Means–End Behavior	Object Permanence	Space	Imitation
1.	Reflex schemes	No special behavior toward absent objects	Practical *groups*. *Separate spaces* for each scheme (buccal space, visual space, tactile space, etc.)	"Reflexive contagion"—stimulus in environment elicits a response in the baby, which happens to match the stimulus that elicited the infant's reaction (e.g., contagion of crying in newborn nursery).
2.	Intercoordination of schemes Primary circular reactions Absence of means–end behavior	No special behavior toward absent objects	Intercoordination of schemes and of separate *spaces*. Baby can look at what he/she hears, hear what she/he says, ending what he/she grasps.	"Pseudoimitation"—only certain types of actions are "imitated": those that continue a movement of accommodation even after the stimulus is no longer perceived. Can imitate an action the infant can produce readily and that is directly available to the senses (e.g., cooing). Imitation here "paced" by the parent or model (the parent directly *elicits* the modeled action—e.g., smiling).
3.	Primitive, chance discovered, means–end relationships Secondary circular reactions	Beginning of search for objects when object is only hidden, or when object is systematically followed until it disappears.	Objects in space understood only in relationship to the infant's body and actions, but are not related to one another.	Systematic imitation of models but only with movements the infant has made and noticed self doing. Cannot imitate new, unfamiliar actions or stimuli.

4.	Deliberate means–end relationships. Means, however, must be familiar.	Objects searched for successfully after being seen hidden but only in place where previously found.	Relationships of objects to one another begin to be understood. Far-space comprehension. Size and shape constancy improve.	Imitation of actions whose performance is not visible to baby. However, the actions must already be within the infant's existing behavior repertoire. Begins new sounds and sights.
5.	Use of new means (discovered by chance) to obtain new ends. Tertiary circular reactions. Deliberate variation of means to an end.	Object searched for after being visibly displaced from one hiding place to another, but not when invisibly displaced.	Understanding of relationship of objects to one another is completed, except for absence of inclusion of self as one of the objects in space, and absence of mental representation of objects in space.	Systematic imitation of new models. Infants can imitate actions even though they cannot see themselves make the action.
6.	Insightful problem solving. New means discovered to attain a new end, even in absence of chance discovery. Internalized trial and error.	Correct, systematic search for object after multiple *invisible* displacements.	Infant relates self to other objects in space. Representation and imagination of relative position of objects.	Deferred imitation.

lines of research contribute to this conclusion. The first is represented by the work of Baillargeon (1994, 1995, 1998; Baillargeon, Kotovsky, & Needham, 1995) and Spelke (1994; Spelke & Hermer, 1996), who demonstrated that infants' capacity for perceiving and representing the physical world is much better developed than Piaget ever thought. The second is represented by the work of Meltzoff and Moore (1997, 1998, 1999), who demonstrated that infants can imitate selected facial expressions of others within minutes after birth, indicating that a rudimentary capacity to represent the external world may be present at birth. We discuss each of these lines of research in turn.

Baillargeon and Spelke employed habituation (see Chapter 3) and violation-of-expectation procedures to show that infants appear to possess knowledge about the permanence of objects much sooner than Piaget would have predicted. Spelke, Breinlinger, Macomber, and Jacobson (1992), for example, used these procedures in an experiment with $2\frac{1}{2}$-month-old infants. Figure 7.2 presents the props used in this experiment, which consisted of a platform, two thin boxes (one taller than the other), a ball, and a screen. Infants were first presented with a view of the entire platform with the ball on its extreme left and the smaller of the two boxes sitting on its edge on the extreme right. Infants were then habituated to the event depicted in Figure 7.2A, in which the screen was lowered in front of the right half of the platform, completely occluding the right half of the platform and the small box. Next, the ball was rolled from left to right across the platform and disappeared behind the screen, after which the screen was elevated to show the ball against the box.

Following habituation to this sequence, infants were shown two events, a "possible" event and an "impossible" event (which violated expectations). For each of these events, the infants were placed in front of the platform, on the right

FIGURE 7.2
Depiction of materials and event sequences used by Spelke, Breinlinger, Macomber, and Jacobson (1992). (From Baillargeon, 1998.)

Habituation Event

(A)

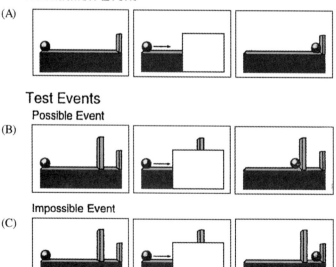

Test Events
Possible Event

(B)

Impossible Event

(C)

edge of which the smaller box had been placed, with the taller box placed on the platform a few inches from the smaller box. The screen was again lowered in front of the right half of the platform, completely occluding the right half of the platform and the smaller box, but only partially occluding the taller box. The ball was then rolled from left to right across the platform until it disappeared behind the screen, and then the screen was raised. In the possible event (Figure 7.2B), the ball rested against the taller box, which is what would be expected. In the impossible event (Figure 7.2C), the ball rested against the smaller box. Duration of infant looking was significantly longer to the impossible event than to the possible event. Such findings suggest that infants at 2½ months followed the ball's trajectory even after it disappeared behind the screen, understood that it was impossible for the ball to roll through the solid taller box, and expected the ball to be stopped by the taller box. When it did not (Figure 7.2C), infants showed surprise and looked longer.

According to Spelke et al. (1992; Spelke & Hermer, 1996), these findings suggest appreciation of object permanence in infants as young as 2 months of age. By this age, infants appear to understand that objects move *cohesively* (i.e., object parts remain connected as they move) and *continuously* through space (recall Kellman and Spelke's, 1983, study involving the occluded rod and the rectangle, discussed in Chapter 6).

Building on this work in a series of experiments on infants' developing knowledge of everyday environmental events, Baillargeon (1994, 1995, 1998; Baillargeon et al., 1995) proposed that infants are innately endowed with specific learning mechanisms that enable rapid acquisition of knowledge about *event categories* (e.g., events in which an object collides with another object, becomes occluded by another object, or supports another object) and *object categories* (e.g., animate objects, inanimate objects that move, and inanimate objects that do not move). Infants first learn about the event or object concept as a generalized whole, and with experience gradually accumulate knowledge about variables that are relevant to the concept. For example, at 2½ months of age, infants' understanding of collision is relatively simple. They expect any moving object to displace any stationary object on impact and show surprise when this does not occur. By about 6 months of age, infants can understand that a large moving object will, on impact, displace a stationary object further than will a small moving object. By 8 months, infants begin to take the stationary object's shape into account in determining whether it will be displaced by a moving object. Similar knowledge progressions are evident in infants' understanding of occlusion and support events (Baillargeon, 1998). Thus, Baillargeon and Spelke argue that the ability to mentally represent events and objects is either innate or achieved by 2 to 3 months of age, which is at least 15 months before Piaget predicted that this ability would emerge.

Meltzoff and Moore's (1998, 1999) work on infants' imitation of facial expressions within the first month of life also leads to the conclusion that a capacity for representation is present from birth. However, they hold that representational capacity continues to develop after birth, and that object permanence is not complete until about 9 months of age, resulting from innumerable interactions between the infant and the physical and social worlds. This view is embodied in what Meltzoff has termed *representational–development theory*.

In brief, representational–development theory posits that infants have the capacity for representation, allowing them to acquire and retain information about the world through observation and perception long before they act on

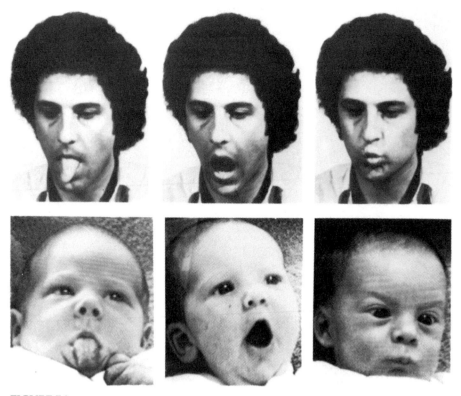

FIGURE 7.3

These photographs show 2- to 3-week-old infants imitating. (From Meltzoff & Moore, 1977. © 1977 by the American Association for the Advancement of Science. Reprinted by permission.)

objects. The ability to imitate various facial expressions has been demonstrated in infants less than 1 month old (see Figure 7.3) and even within a few moments after birth (see Chapter 6). These observations indicate that, from birth, infants form mental representations of events from observation alone and can reproduce these events immediately. Note that these data contrast with Piaget's contention that infants do not imitate until the fourth substage of sensorimotor development (10–12 months of age) and do not develop representational abilities until the sixth substage (18–24 months). Perhaps even more compelling are observations that infants can engage in deferred imitation of a model's novel actions on an object as early as 6 months of age (almost a full year before Piaget said it occurred) and of a model's facial expressions within the first 2 months of life. For example, Meltzoff (1988a) had 6- to 9-month-old infants observe an adult model lean forward and press a panel with his forehead (a highly unusual, novel behavior). One week later, the infants who had viewed this behavior, and a control group of infants who had not, returned to the laboratory and were presented with the panel. No control infants exhibited the forehead-to-panel response, whereas 66% of the infants who had previously witnessed this behavior did. Furthermore, Meltzoff and Moore (1999) demonstrated that 6-week-old infants who witnessed an adult model's facial gestures could reproduce these expressions 24 hours later when they saw the same adult displaying a neutral face.

Other work documents that very young infants have the ability to represent external actions that persist across time and contexts (Meltzoff & Moore,

1997). Meltzoff and Moore (1999) termed this capacity *representational persistence* and argued that it was not equivalent to the representational capacity of infants in the second year of life. Rather, representational persistence is viewed as the beginning state of infant cognition, which continues to develop with maturation and the infant's ongoing experience with the world and does not imply awareness of object permanence, which requires the understanding that objects exist continuously in the world. Indeed, Meltzoff and Moore (1999) argue that the experimental work of Spelke and Baillargeon provides evidence that young infants recognize an object's identity, which serves as a prerequisite for, but is not the same as, object permanence.

Evidence that one can distinguish infants who understand object permanence (and, therefore, object identity as well) from infants who understand object identity but not object permanence was provided by Moore, Borton, and Darby (1978) in a visual tracking experiment. In this experiment, 5- and 9-month-old infants watched a ball pass in continuous movement from left to right behind two nontransparent split screens (see Figure 7.4C). The ball passed behind the

FIGURE 7.4

Visual tracking tasks used by Moore, Borton, and Darby (1978) to identify and differentiate infants who understand object permanence (and therefore, object identity) from infants who understand object identity only. In Figure 7.4A, a ball moves from left to right behind a screen, and a square emerges from the other end of the screen. Figure 7.4B depicts a ball disappearing behind the screen and emerging from the other end of the screen sooner than expected, based on the ball's initial rate of speed. Figure 7.4C shows a ball disappearing behind the first screen, not passing between the two screens, and an identical ball emerging from behind the second screen. Infants who understand object identity are surprised by the events in Figures 7.4A and 7.4B, in which features of the moving objects are altered as the objects pass from left to right, but not by the event depicted in 7.4C, which does not vary the appearance of the ball. By contrast, infants who understand object permanence show surprise to all three events, indicating that they not only detect featural changes in the moving objects, but they are also aware that the ball that emerged from the second screen in Figure 7.4C could not have been the same as the one that disappeared behind the first screen. (From Meltzoff & Moore, 1999, Lawrence Erlbaum Associates.)

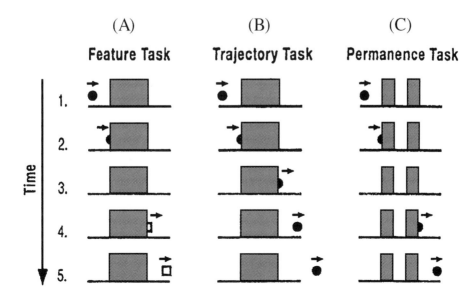

first screen and then emerged from behind the second screen without passing through the open gap between the two screens. The ball that emerged from the second screen looked exactly like the ball that disappeared behind the first screen. Moore et al. (1978) hypothesized that infants with an understanding of object permanence would perceive this state of affairs as a violation of expectations. If only one ball was involved it should in its passage have been occluded by the first screen, become visible between the two screens, be occluded again by the second screen, and become visible again when it reemerged from behind the second screen. Infants with object permanence would regard the ball that emerged from the second screen as a new ball and scan the edges of the first screen for the original, thus showing that they perceived the first ball as continuing to exist even though it disappeared. By contrast, infants who understand object identity but not yet object permanence should not perceive this event as a violation of expectations, because the ball that emerged from the second screen was identical to the ball that disappeared behind the first screen. Moore and his colleagues also expected that infants who understood object identity, whether or not they had also achieved object permanence, would be sensitive to changes in the features and trajectory of an object as it moved from left to right behind a nontransparent screen. In the feature task (Figure 7.4A), a ball moved behind a screen and a box emerged from the other side of the screen along the same trajectory. In the trajectory task (Figure 7.4B), a ball moved behind a screen and emerged from the other side sooner than expected, based on its initial speed.

As predicted, both 5- and 9-month-old infants were sensitive to identity violations. They looked away from the object that emerged from the right side of the screen, which differed from the original in terms of features (Figure 7.4A) or trajectory (Figure 7.4B) and scanned the edges of the screen in apparent search for the original. However, only the 9-month-old infants showed such behavior in the permanence task (Figure 7.4C). The 5-month-olds did search for the original ball, presumably because they perceived the ball that emerged from the second screen to be the same ball that disappeared behind the first screen. These findings collectively showed that object permanence emerges sometime between 5 and 9 months of age and that what appeared as evidence for object permanence in younger infants (e.g., Spelke et al., 1995) was actually evidence for object identity.

Thus, although Meltzoff, Spelke, and Baillargeon agree that representational capacity exists from birth, Meltzoff and Moore (1998, 1999) argue that the ability to represent events and objects across time and space, which they term representational persistence, does not imply the understanding that objects exist in the world as permanent entities. Rather, early representational persistence predisposes infants to maintain the identity of objects, which serves as a developmental precursor to object permanence.

This work and that of others (e.g., Maratos, 1998; Thelen, Schooner, Scherer, & Smith, 2001) indicates that Piaget seriously underestimated infants' perceptual and cognitive capacities. Indeed, Haith and Benson (1998) cite many studies that illustrate that infants' competencies in understanding temporally ordered events, means–ends relations, space, causality, and number become evident much earlier in development than Piaget would have predicted. In their view, this has led to the emergence of a variety of "mini theories" that purport to explain the developmental course of specific infant competencies in specific domains of development, using very specific methodologies. Perhaps this was inevitable in light of the oft-made criticism that Piaget's theory was too general and too all-encompassing to explain the whole of infant cognition. On the other hand, Haith and Benson (1998) argue that such specialization and overfocus on specific infant abilities has led post-Piagetian researchers to be more concerned with demonstrating the precocity of newborns at the expense of understanding how a particular ability develops. They wrote:

> The main task is to lay out the course of accomplishment and what controls this course. The focus on issues about innateness and obtaining the earliest evidence for a skill distracts us from this difficult task and . . . leads to dichotomous characterizations of cognitive growth. We are disappointed that there is a dearth of studies that include multiple age groups and a relative lack of interest in describing the course of development. More studies are needed that ask how concepts develop, with less concern about whether evidence [for an infant ability] is positive at a particular age. (p. 245)

Although it has become clear that infants are more organized and sophisticated than Piaget thought, his contributions laid the foundation for the study of infant cognition today. Furthermore, even with the impressive developments of post-Piagetian researchers, there remains a clear need to understand the roles of neurophysiological growth and memory in cognitive development, and mechanisms of acquisition and change. We now turn to other approaches to the study of infant mental life that address these issues.

Early Learning and Information Processing

In the preceding part of this chapter, we discussed Piaget and post-Piagetian perspectives on normative cognitive development and the idea of qualitative periods and transformations that all infants traverse. Our goal was to describe *how* infants may come to understand the world on the basis of their biological inheritance and common experiences they have interacting with the world. In this part of the chapter we introduce a more quantitative approach to the study of intelligence in infancy. Here we focus on learning and information-processing perspectives, those that interpret cognitive development in terms of the acquisition of associations and the use of processing mechanisms to bring information from the environment into the cognitive system. When we refer to these processes we mean the formation and encoding of information; in Chapter 8 we discuss what happens to that information afterward, that is, in memory and use. Like Piaget, these theories propose some species-general rules, for it was once widely held that the "laws of learning" were universal and applied to all individuals and to all species. Unlike Piaget, these viewpoints concentrate on the measurement and long-term implications of individual differences in cognitive functioning early in life.

Even newborns learn to make associations and subsequently can make use of what they have learned. Learning and information processing are believed to underlie the infant's slow but steady acquisition of knowledge about the world: After all, learning reflects underlying brain plasticity and change. In Chapter 3 we introduced the basic concepts and procedures behind learning paradigms (e.g., operant conditioning) and behind two components of information processing (habituation and novelty responsiveness) while showing how each is applied as a methodological technique in infancy studies. In this section we discuss learning and information processing again, this time as components of infant mental life. Toward that end, we review research on their early emergence, individual variation and reliability, and patterns of developmental change.

Classical and Operant Learning and Imitation

Three Types of Learning

Recall that *classical conditioning* capitalizes on the existence of stimulus–response relations built into the organism, as when a loud sound elicits an eye blink. The loud sound is called the *unconditioned stimulus* (UCS), and the response it gives rise to is called the *unconditioned response* (UCR). In classical conditioning, a *conditioned stimulus* (CS), one that is initially neutral and does not elicit the response, is paired with a UCS. After repeated pairings of the CS with the UCS, the CS begins to take on properties of the UCS and elicits a *conditioned response* (CR) like the UCR. That is, learning by association takes place.

Several infant reflexive behaviors lend themselves readily to classical conditioning. Ivkovich, Collins, Eckerman, Krasnegor, and Stanton (1999), for example, conditioned eye blink responses in 4- and 5-month-old infants to a tone (the CS) that was paired with an air puff (the UCS) directed at the infants' right eye. Classical conditioning appears to be a very basic and fundamental learning process (Smotherman & Robinson, 1996; Wilson & Sullivan, 1994) that can be demonstrated even in newborns. For example, Blass, Ganchrow, and Steiner (1984) showed how 1- to 2-day-old newborns could be classically conditioned. Newborns were gently stroked on the head for 10 seconds immediately before delivery of a sucrose solution into their mouths. Compared with infants in control groups, neonates who had this training showed more head-orienting and sucking responses during the stroking session. When the stroking was no longer followed by sucrose, the babies showed extinction (the decline in response strength that occurs when the UCS is no longer guaranteed). Blass also reported that infants in the experimental group cried during extinction. They suggest that this negative affect reflected the violation of a learned relation between touch, which is a naturally occurring biological stimulus, and sucrose, a potent nutrient reinforcer. Of course the babies protested!

Operant conditioning, or the selection of operant behavior by its consequences, involves associations between one's own action and the consequence of that action. Actions that are reinforced are more likely to be repeated in the future, whereas actions that are punished are less likely to be repeated. The major difference between operant conditioning and classical conditioning is that in classical conditioning a previously neutral signal comes to elicit a response through association, whereas in operant conditioning the probability of a naturally occurring response is increased by reinforcement and decreased by punishment.

Different operant conditioning paradigms tap different voluntarily controlled motor activities, such as sucking, head turning, or kicking (Rovee-Collier, 1996a; Weisberg & Rovee-Collier, 1998). Like classical conditioning, operant conditioning is a fundamental process that is demonstrable from birth. DeCasper and Fifer (1980) provided an example of operant conditioning in 3-day-old babies using the sound of mother's voice as a contingent reinforcer of infant sucking. The experimenters first measured the infants' baseline operant rate of sucking, and they then determined the average interval between the babies' spontaneous sucking bursts. Next, the infants were divided into two groups: Those in one group were presented with the sound of their mother's voice whenever the interval between their sucking bursts was greater than their baseline average; those in the other group heard their mother's voice when their interburst interval was less than their baseline average. Both groups heard the voice of another infant's mother whenever the interburst interval was the opposite of that scheduled to produce their own mother's voice, that is, when the interval was less than the average for the first group and more than the average for the second group. Most infants in the study changed from their baseline interburst sucking intervals so as to produce their own mother's voices. Similarly, Floccia and Christophe (1997) demonstrated that neonatal sucking rates increased when sucking on a pacifier was followed immediately by human speech sounds (/ba/ and /fu/). Sucking rates did not increase, however, when the speech sound variations were delivered noncontingently. These two studies indicate that social stimuli, such as the mother's voice and human speech sounds, can serve as potent reinforcers of infant behavior even in the neonatal period.

Operant researchers need to distinguish events that are rewarding from events that are reinforcing. Events that reward an organism are frequently but incorrectly construed as reinforcers. A reward *may* function as a reinforcer (i.e., it may increase the frequency of occurrence of a particular response; Catania, 1998), but researchers must take pains to identify those events that actually function as reinforcers of specific responses in infancy and be sensitive to changes in the reinforcing capacities of different stimuli as the infant develops and matures. This same point applies to aversive events, which are often assumed to be punishers.

For operant learning to succeed, it is also crucial that infants be able to perceive the contingency between their action and its consequence (Watson, 1966a, 1972). With very young infants, whose attention spans and memory capacities are more limited than those of older infants, simple, isolated events that occur immediately in response to the target behavior are more likely to be perceived as contingent than are more complex and/or delayed events.

Imitation is a third and particularly efficient way to learn. During infancy, imitation provides a mechanism for acquiring information of all sorts—just by watching or listening. How early infants imitate and what they can imitate are significant research issues, as we showed when discussing the ability to imitate facial movements such as tongue protrusions, mouth openings, and lip pursing (see Figure 7.3). However, some controversy has attended the reliability and interpretation of early infant imitation. Developmental studies of infant imitation have shown that imitations of tongue protrusions and mouth openings decrease over the first 3 months of life, whereas imitations of vocalizations, finger movements, and other simple motor actions increase in frequency over the first year (Abravanel & Sigafoos, 1984; Décarie & Ricard, 1996; Jacobson, 1979, Pawlby, 1977). Why would imitation of facial gestures decline over time if they indeed reflect a capacity for imitation that is present and develops from birth? Maratos (1998) proposed that infants' early imitation of facial gestures is possible because infants are born with a preconception of the human face (a point we discussed in Chapter 6), an innate capacity for perceiving the equivalence between the facial movements of others and movements of their own face and the ability to represent the human face at a purely sensory level. Maratos (1998) proposed that early infant imitation represents an effort to communicate on a purely emotional level, and that the decline in facial imitation takes place because other, more complex and more effective means of communication (e.g., smiling and vocal and gestural imitation) emerge with time. Maratos thus views early facial imitation as additional evidence of a preadapted capacity to recognize and communicate with other members of the human species (see Chapter 6).

Limiting Conditions on Learning

Even when necessary cognitive capacities are present and the learning task is well designed, many factors influence the course of learning in infants. Three such limiting conditions are prominent. One major factor is behavioral state (see Chapter 5). At least the first steps in learning require that the infant be alert long enough to perceive a signal and to respond to it appropriately. If state is not accounted for when learning, the baby's opportunities to learn may be curtailed unfairly. Long ago, Papoušek and Bernstein (1969) demonstrated that conditionability in infants depends on state. They found that learning took place most readily during periods of quiet alertness; little acquisition appeared to take place when infants were drowsy or asleep.

It was once assumed that any stimulus–response association could be learned. We now know that this is not the case. Even with older infants, among whom conditioning is easier, it is by no means axiomatic, for example, that classical conditioning can be established with *any* stimulus, that *any* behavior can be strengthened through operant reinforcement, or that *any* act can be imitated. So, second, there are natural constraints on learning, and this means that tests of the infant's ability to learn have to be designed with extreme care; negative findings may indicate that a particular association cannot be learned, not that learning itself is impossible. The researcher has to determine whether the infant is physically capable of the response demanded and whether the stimulus can be perceived. Ethologists (Hinde & Stevenson-Hinde, 1973) and learning theorists (Seligman, 1970) have argued that certain associations are *prepared*, in that they are biologically more appropriate than others, and so are learned more readily. Blass and his coworkers (1984) claimed that their success in classically conditioning newborns in the first days of life directly reflected their choice of an associative link between a natural mode of parent–infant communication (facial touch) and a nutrient reinforcer (sugar). Certain stimuli and responses appear to "go together" naturally, and it is easier to learn to associate such naturally co-occurring contingencies.

According to Weisberg and Rovee-Collier (1998; Rovee-Collier, 1996a, 1996b), all infants are capable of conditioning. When researchers have failed to demonstrate conditionability, it is because the *economics of the response* demanded of the infant require too great an expenditure of effort to be worthwhile. When the response is less demanding, infants readily emit it and so appear to be conditionable. Thus, third, the associations that newborn infants are most likely to learn involve responses that do not require too great an expenditure of energy, whether classical, operant, or imitative in nature. In short, if the energy cost of responding exceeds the value of the reward, infants cannot afford to perform the response and so will seem not to learn the association.

Before leaving this discussion, it is essential to point out that a special focus on learning, and optimal arrangements for it in laboratory study, can overestimate the infant's learning capacities, at least relative to everyday life. In other words, the fact that infants *can* learn does not guarantee that they make use of all these learning devices at all times in their daily life. This is a good example of the competence–performance distinction we raised in Chapter 3.

Information Processing: Habituation and Novelty Responsiveness

Conditioning techniques provide reasonably clear data about learning because babies respond actively, voluntarily, and definitively, clearly "communicating" about their functional abilities. However, conditioning often takes time and is relatively difficult to implement. We can also learn something about babies' cognition simply by observing them as they regard the world and process information about it. Information processing tells us about the activities infants use in representing and manipulating information mentally; it is not a comprehensive theory of cognition or of development, but rather an approach to studying mental processes (Bornstein, Brown, & Slater, 1996; Bornstein, Slater, Brown, Roberts, & Barrett, 1997).

An infant will typically orient and attend to a novel stimulus, but if that stimulus remains available to view, the infant's attention to it will usually diminish. *Habituation* is the decline in responding to a stimulus that is available continuously or is presented repeatedly. If the infant is tested with both familiar and novel stimuli after such familiarization, the infant will tend to look at the familiar stimulus less than at the new stimulus. The greater attention to the new stimulus is called *novelty responsiveness*.

Habituation and novelty responsiveness must reflect (at least) two component processes: the construction of some sort of central mental representation of the stimulus material, and the continuing comparison between the stimulus being presented and that mental representation. The infant's declining interest in the now familiar stimulus presumably indicates that the infant has learned something about the stimulus, and the infant's novelty response to the new stimulus presumably indicates that the infant can discriminate between the new and the familiar stimulus. If external stimulus and representation match—giving evidence that the baby has come to "know" the stimulus—there is little reason to continue to look once the baby has habituated to the original stimulus; however, mismatches appear to maintain the infant's attention so that a novel stimulus, introduced after habituation to the (now) familiar stimulus, typically reexcites attention. Habituation therefore gives a strong face valid indication that it has something to do with information processing (Bornstein, 1985; Rose & Tamis-LeMonda, 1999).

Three additional points help to confirm an information-processing interpretation of habituation. First, older infants habituate more efficiently than younger infants (as we discuss in the next section). Second, infants of the same age require more time to encode information from a complex stimulus than from a simple one. Caron and Caron (1969) demonstrated this effect clearly. They showed three groups of 3½-month-olds four different multicolored geometric designs serially on four trials followed by five repeated presentations of either 2×2, 12×12, or 24×24 checkerboards. As shown in Figure 7.5, all three groups maintained a high level of looking on the initial four trials, during which stimulation varied; all three groups looked less on the repetition trials, furthermore, but the groups declined differentially, and habituation clearly reflected stimulus complexity. Following habituation, infants showed a novelty response to the new stimulus introduced in three additional trials. Third, habituation appears to be a "central" process: Slater, Morison, and Rose (1983a) showed that newborn babies who habituated to a stimulus while viewing it through only one eye later

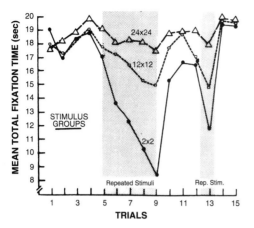

FIGURE 7.5

Mean total fixation during varied (1–4, 10–12, 14–15) and repeated (5–9, 13) 20–second trials for three stimulus groups. (After Caron & Caron, 1969. © 1969 by the Psychonomic Society. Reprinted by permission.)

recovered attention when shown a novel stimulus through the other eye. This *interocular transfer* indicates that information about the stimulus is processed centrally. Recovery in crossmodal transfer (Chapter 6) suggests that central processing and mental representations are involved in habituation as well (Bornstein & Tamis-LeMonda, 1994).

Even newborns habituate. Slater and his colleagues showed clear and consistent evidence of visual habituation in babies at term (Slater, 1995; Slater, Brown, Mattock, & Bornstein, 1996). Many other researchers have demonstrated habituation of heart rate, high-amplitude sucking, and visual responding in the first month of life (Wyly, 1997).

Habituation of attention is not restricted to laboratory investigation, but is probably typical of the infant's everyday interactions with people and objects in the world. Bornstein and Ludemann (1989) documented habituation of attention and novelty responsiveness in naturally occurring, home-based interactions of infants with faces and with objects. The two processes of habituation and novelty responsiveness also appear to be loosely related. Colombo, Mitchell, O'Brien, and Horowitz (1987) found that shorter looking was consistently associated with higher magnitude novelty responsiveness in 4- to 9-month-old infants. In addition, Bornstein and Tamis-LeMonda (1991) found that 2-month-olds' novelty preferences predicted their habituation at 5 months. The two processes differ, nonetheless, and involve complementary capabilities. Novelty responsiveness evaluates the infant's reaction to an aspect of the environment that is new or changed; habituation assesses the infant's reaction to an aspect of the environment that is unchanging.

Like classical and operant conditioning, habituation and novelty responsiveness have their requisite experimental controls. To the extent that these processes are believed to reflect change in the central nervous system, it is necessary to rule out the possibility that habituation or familiarization can be accounted for by other, more peripheral factors. These include (1) fatigue of sensory receptors resulting from repeated stimulation and (2) fatigue in the response system or in state. Two *pseudohabituation* control procedures are therefore common in infancy studies (see Bertenthal, Haith, & Campos, 1983; Bornstein, 1985). One involves presenting a novel stimulus in the same sensory modality and thereby activating the same receptors as the habituation stimulus. Response recovery to the novel, but not the familiar, stimulus rules out pseudohabituation. The second control procedure involves presenting a pretest stimulus (before habituation) and the same stimulus as a posttest (after habituation). Comparable responding to the two implies that the intervening decrement in responding does not reflect fatigue or a simple change in infant state. When controls for pseudohabituation are lacking, it is often not possible to arrive at firm conclusions about the infant's learning or about central nervous system function with respect to the stimulation.

Learning and information processing give good evidence of mental functioning in infancy. The next logical questions are: Do some infants learn or process stimulus information more quickly, efficiently, or completely than others? Is infant performance reliable over the short term? How do learning and information processing change and develop over the course of infancy? Do learning, habituation, or novelty responsiveness inform us about concurrent cognitive differences among infants? Do they tell us anything about future childhood cognitive capacities? It turns out that habituation has been studied most with respect to these questions, novelty responsiveness less, and classical and operant conditioning and imitation least, if at all.

Individual Variation and Reliability

Considerable research has been conducted to date on two important measurement concerns with respect to information processing, namely, distinguishing individual variation among babies and determining whether individual differences constitute reliable, that is replicable, characteristics of babies. As we see later in this chapter, individual variation among babies may say quite a lot about their future mental life.

There is ample evidence, as we have learned, that infants habituate and show novelty reactions even in the first days of life, just as they may be conditioned. Importantly, infants differ considerably among themselves in habituating and reacting to novelty; that is, they show *individual variation* (Ashmead & Davis, 1996; Bornstein et al., 1996; Colombo, Frick, & Gorman, 1997; Fagan & Haiken-Vasen, 1997; Orlian & Rose, 1997; Rose & Feldman, 1997; Sigman, Cohen, & Beckwith, 1997; Zelazo & Stack, 1997). Other things being equal, infants vary among themselves with respect to the amount of looking or rate of decrement in habituating. For example, some 5-month-olds who are shown a single human face wearing a single expression habituate in seconds, whereas others may take minutes. Likewise, babies who are shown a given stimulus for a fixed amount of time vary in their response to a new stimulus following familiarization: Some show a novelty response (giving more than 50% of their total looking to the novel stimulus), some perform at chance levels, and some give a familiarity preference.

Qualitatively speaking, infants appear to show (at least) three consistent "styles" in habituating. McCall and Kagan (1970) identified "rapid habituators," "slow habituators," and "idiosyncratic habituators" among 5-month-old babies who saw a group of three realistic stimuli. (They also found a group of babies who looked too briefly to be classified reliably.) Bornstein and Benasich (1986) identified parallel "linear/exponential decrease," "increase–decrease," and "fluctuating" patterns of habituation among 5-month-olds shown a single face or a single geometric pattern. Figure 7.6 shows an example of each kind of baby. The baby in the top panel looks a lot at the stimulus at first and then rapidly stops looking; this baby exemplifies a rapid habituator who shows a linear or exponential decrease in looking. The baby in the middle panel looks only a little at first, but then appears to get interested in the stimulus before finally habituating; this baby

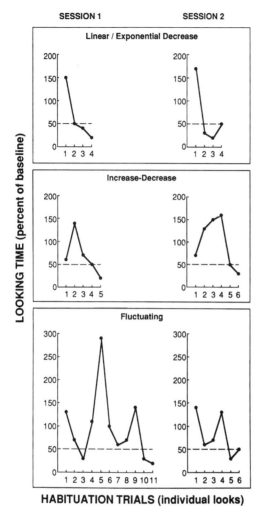

SESSION 1   SESSION 2

Linear / Exponential Decrease

Increase-Decrease

Fluctuating

LOOKING TIME (percent of baseline)

HABITUATION TRIALS (individual looks)

FIGURE 7.6

Results of two infant-control habituation sessions for three infants who were shown a single female face wearing an affectively neutral expression. Individual looks are plotted as a percentage of the mean of the first two looks, called the baseline and set equal to 100%. These infants illustrate three main patterns of habituation and the short-term reliability of habituation patterns. The infant at the top showed a linear or exponential decrease from baseline to a 50% habituation criterion in two sessions; the infant in the middle first looked more, then rapidly habituated to criterion both times. The infant at the bottom showed a fluctuating looking-time function in each session before reaching the habituation criterion. (In these plots, data points are rounded to the nearest 10%.) Exponential decrease habituators require significantly less accumulated looking and fewer exposures to the stimulus than increase–decrease or fluctuating habituators. (After Bornstein & Benasich, 1986. © 1986 by the Society for Research in Child Development. Reprinted by permission.)

illustrates an habituator whose looking increases before decreasing. The looking preferences of the baby in the bottom panel seem to fluctuate before looking stabilizes at habituation. Linear/exponential decrease babies constituted about 60% of a sample of 5-month-olds shown a single stimulus; increase–decrease babies about 10% of the sample; and fluctuating babies about 30% of the sample. Importantly, linear/exponential babies required approximately half as much exposure to a stimulus to habituate as increase–decrease or fluctuating babies.

Whether measured quantitatively or qualitatively, these individual differences in habituation also appear to show moderate short-term stability. That is, given the same testing conditions, a baby is likely to habituate in approximately the same way on different occasions spaced reasonably close together in time (Bornstein et al., 1997). Reliability of habituation has been assessed in several studies. Some researchers have measured infants as young as 2 months, others infants 1 year of age and older; some have measured infants twice on the same day, others with 3 months or 1 year between testings. Some have used the same stimuli, others slightly different stimuli on the two tests (e.g., Bornstein et al.,

1996; Colombo, 1993; Hood & Murray, 1996; Slater, Brown, et al., 1996). Habituation patterns are also reliable from session to session (see Figure 7.6).

Despite differences in procedures across studies as well as other sources of unreliability—infant age, infant state, and the nature of the stimuli can be expected to affect infant performance—infants tend to show considerable variation in how they habituate and recover, and they also tend to process information in these ways in a reasonably consistent fashion on different occasions spaced close together in time. Variation and reliability are important because they say that, at least to some degree, infants differ in response sensitivity and those differences are in the infant rather than in the procedure, the stimulus, or the situation. These facts in turn allow us to have confidence when these measures are used in other ways (see below).

Developmental Changes in Learning and Information Processing

Newborns (and even fetuses) learn, but this does not mean that developmental changes in learning do not occur during and after infancy. The nervous system matures rapidly during the first postnatal months, permitting longer periods of alertness and better organization of infantile state (see Chapter 5). By 3 months of age, infants are readily conditioned in a variety of paradigms. By 6 months, almost all the physiological immaturities that might restrict attention, perception, and information processing in the early period of postnatal life have disappeared, further facilitating learning. In addition, the child's curiosity ensures repeated opportunities to learn.

Indeed, as they age, infants change impressively in their learning (Weisberg & Rovee-Collier, 1998), although longitudinal studies of infant conditioning are rare. For example, Hoffman, Cohen, and DeVito (1985) compared the performance of 8-month-old infants directly with that of adults in classically conditioning an eye blink, normally elicited by a tap to the glabella (the flat region of skin between the eyebrows). A tone was the CS. Infants acquired the conditioned association more slowly than adults, and the latency of their conditioned responses was slower (even though the latency of the unconditioned response was faster in infants).

Habituation also improves with age. One of the first papers on infant habituation ever published (Fantz, 1964) documented this increasing efficiency, and, as we saw in Chapter 3 (Figure 3.1), the cumulative amount of time needed to habituate to a stimulus decreases dramatically over the first year. Bornstein, Pêcheux, and Lécuyer (1988) traced the development of both habituation and novelty responsiveness longitudinally. They habituated and tested a small group of infants with different stimuli each week between their third and seventh months. Figure 7.7 shows a steady and regular developmental change in the amount of time one infant required to inspect a novel stimulus in order to habituate over her first half year of life. Indeed, at 2 to 3 months of age she required nearly $6\frac{1}{2}$ times as much exposure to the stimulus as she required at 6 to 7 months of age. This result cannot be accounted for by repeated habituation experiences; Bornstein and his coworkers also showed that a control group, only tested at 5 months, habituated in the same way as babies tested repeatedly to that point.

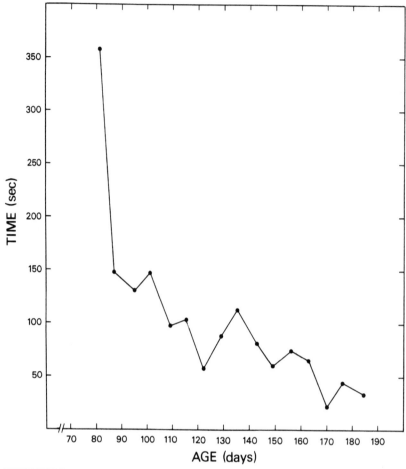

FIGURE 7.7

Total accumulated looking time to reach a constant habituation criterion in one infant studied weekly between her second and seventh months. The time required to habituate is long in early infancy and declines steadily and rapidly toward middle infancy. (After Bornstein, Pêcheux, & Lécuyer, 1988.)

Several mechanisms may plausibly account for individual differences in infant habituation rates and for developmental improvements in these rates. Speed of information processing is one such mechanism. Rapid processing is presumably what accounts for mental agility and "quickness," whereas slow processing has been associated with deficits in IQ (Bornstein, Slater, et al., 1997; Rose & Tamis-LeMonda, 1999). Several researchers have linked infants' performance on visual attention tasks with infants' latency to respond to specific stimulus events (Jacobson et al., 1992; Tamis-LeMonda & McClure, 1994), suggesting that speed of processing indeed underlies individual differences in performance on visual attention tasks. Another such mechanism is short-term memory. Variations in the ability to remember stimuli presented over time may account for variations in habituation and novelty preference tasks. Rose and Feldman (1995, 1997) found that infants' performance on a visual recognition memory task at 7 months predicted their performance on a variety of cognitive tasks at 11 years of age. It is perhaps intuitive that short-term memory capacity would be implicated, given that habituation cannot take place without a working memory of the stimulus event. A third mechanism is the infant's ability to deploy attention efficiently, focusing on relevant stimulus features and inhibiting attention to irrelevant stimuli (McCall, 1994; McCall & Mash, 1995). In older children, performance in a variety of cognitive tasks is associated with the ability to inhibit attention to distracting stimuli (Dempster & Brainerd, 1995). Finally, Cohen (1998) has proposed that processing efficiency increases with age because infants become able to encode progressively larger units of information.

In learning, and especially in information processing, researchers have developed techniques that allow them some access to the mind of the child. Very young babies learn and imitate, habituate attention to familiar stimuli, and recover attention to novel stimulation. Individual differences in the latter processes are reasonably reliable, and these processes become more efficient over the course of infancy. We now consider the implications of these mental processes in infancy for cognitive functioning in childhood.

Infant Mental Life and the Question of Validity

To this point we have reviewed two schools of thought about infant cognition, learning, and intelligence. The school associated with Piaget describes qualitative stages of development in early thinking and stresses universal processes of mental life in infancy. A second school, which is associated with learning and information-processing theories, describes the development of thinking abilities in quantitative terms and emphasizes variation among individuals. With these views in mind, we now return to the validity questions posed at the outset of the chapter. How do we know what infants "know"? Does what infants know tell us about their later development? We think that we know something about the infant's performance on tasks and in situations that seem to require thinking or intelligence. Before addressing these questions, however, it will be instructive to review briefly the history of attempts to assess infant intelligence.

Traditional Tests of Infant Intelligence

Assessments of intelligence only date from the beginning of the twentieth century. Around 1900, the forward-thinking Ministry of Public Education in Paris authorized Alfred Binet, an experimental psychologist, to develop a mental test with the purpose of identifying children in the public schools who might need remedial education. Binet's test initiated major developments in the field of mental assessment (Bornstein, 1994).

To be sure, by Binet's time other researchers in Europe and in the United States had also begun to develop tests of mental ability. Among the leaders of this movement was James McKeen Cattell, who had studied with Wilhelm Wundt in Germany, where experimental psychology was founded. Cattell (1890) thought that the individual variation he observed in adults' physical and perceptual functions (for example, in reaction time) reflected individual variation in their mental functioning. However, Binet went beyond this sensory perspective to consider "higher" mental processes, by which he meant attention, comprehension, and memory (Binet & Henri, 1895, 1896). Specifically, he wrote: "To judge well, to comprehend well, to reason well, these are the essentials of intelligence"

(Binet & Simon, 1905, p. 196). The first editions of the Binet scale set the tone for most succeeding efforts, both with children and eventually with infants. Binet's inclusion of "cognitive" items, as well as items of clearly different levels of difficulty, was readily adopted by others. Age norms were developed as the testing movement spread quickly, although the focus remained on adults and school-age children. Cyril Burt (1921) translated the Binet test for the English, as Lewis Terman (1916) at Stanford did for Americans.

Soon after the tradition of intelligence testing took root and flourished, two compelling questions related to the earliest manifestations and development of intelligence naturally arose. Can we measure "intelligence" in infancy? What does "intelligence" in infancy tell us about "intelligence" later in life? At the end of the nineteenth century, infants and young children were being credited with intelligence (Figure 7.8), and between the turn of that century and the present the assessment of intelligence in infancy and the prediction of adult cognition from infancy have become abiding topics of research, provoking considerable theoretical controversy and attracting wide popular attention.

Recall from our discussion of the first baby biographies (Chapter 3) that in the last quarter of the nineteenth century—following Darwin and just preceding Binet—many astute observers of children documented the basics of infant

FIGURE 7.8

The Young Architect, from *The Nursery* (1875). This infant has invented his own game using dominoes as building blocks. (Courtesy of the Winterthur Museum, Winterthur, Delaware.)

development. Infant diaries thus provided a wealth of ideas for items that could be adopted for use in "intelligence" tests for babies. Moreover, the evidence developed from baby biographies had two important implications. First, baby biographies showed that infants of different ages were competent at different tasks; that is, items in infant tests could be graded for difficulty like the items in children's tests were. Second, baby biographies gave evidence of wide individual variation among infants of the same age; that is, infants vary among themselves like children and adults do.

Many early investigators developed standardized tasks for infants that were graded in difficulty by age, and for years their sequences, scales, and schedules of infant behavior proved valuable in defining normative development. Although the 1920s witnessed several attempts of this sort, the best-known and most widely adopted tests were not developed until somewhat later. Of these, the most successful has been the Bayley Scales of Infant Development, although the Užgiris-Hunt Ordinal Scales of Psychological Development also merit discussion.

Beginning in the 1920s, Nancy Bayley endeavored to measure mental and motor growth from infancy. As part of the Berkeley Growth Study, Bayley (1933a) published the California First Year Mental Scale. She based this scale on the performance of middle-income children observed monthly from birth through $1^1/_2$ years of age. In the 1960s, Bayley (1969) published a major revision and restandardization of this effort, called the Bayley Scales of Infant Development (BSID), and this assessment was again revised and restandardized in the 1990s to become the BSID-II (Bayley, 1993). The BSID are divided into a Mental Development Index (the MDI consists of 178 items) and a Psychomotor Development Index (the PDI consists of 111 items). The BSID assess motor, sensation, perception, cognition, memory, language, and social behavior in infants over the first $2^1/_2$ years of life (see Table 4.2).

When Piaget was eventually translated into English in the 1950s, his work began to affect research in many areas. Up to that time, a psychometric tradition following Binet had dominated testing and assessment of infants (Bayley's test represents a traditional psychometric approach to assessment). In this approach, the philosophy of child testing is essentially scaled down to infants. Faithful to a learning-style orientation, this tradition sees developmental progress as incremental, adding bits to one's knowledge base over time, and it relates achievements to one another based on their emergence at common chronological ages. Piaget's approach, as we learned earlier in this chapter, has at its base a progressive, cumulative nature as well—albeit with a different integrative slant.

The best-known infant test to have developed from the Piagetian approach is the Užgiris–Hunt (1975) Ordinal Scales of Psychological Development. Užgiris and Hunt devised a series of tasks radically different from the psychometric testing approach. For example, their Ordinal Scales assume *hierarchical relations* among infant achievements at different levels, in that they consider later occurring, higher order accomplishments to encompass and subsume earlier occurring lower order ones. Furthermore, their scales are not tied to chronological age, but the succession of tasks within any sequence is believed to follow an intrinsically logical order. The Ordinal Scales consist of six sets of distinct sequences appropriate for infants ranging from 1 or 2 to about 24 months of age. Briefly, one scale is concerned with the infant's increasing knowledge of the existence of objects outside the immediate context, based on the infant's visual pursuit and object permanence. The second assesses means–end relations, such as the use of implements to obtain objects out of reach. The third concentrates on imitation of vocalization and gesture. The fourth uses anticipatory behaviors for identifying the infant's comprehension of antecedent–consequent relations, called operational causality. The fifth follows the infant's ability to track and locate objects and therefore to appreciate space. The sixth evaluates the changing role of toys as extensions of the infant, as objects of curiosity, and eventually as functional units.

Bayley and Užgiris and Hunt were by no means alone in their efforts to develop infant tests (Stack & Poulin-Dubois, 1998). During the first part of this century, many others, both in the United States (e.g., Cattell, 1940/1960; Escalona & Corman, 1969; Gesell, 1945, 1954; Shirley, 1933) and abroad (e.g., Buhler & Hetzer in Austria, 1935; Griffiths in England, 1954), worked toward the development of assessment instruments for infants. We have selected the Bayley and Užgiris–Hunt tests for special consideration here in part because of their historical primacy, in part because of the traditions they represent, and in part because they have been used most frequently in research on infant mental development.

Traditional Infant Tests and Their Predictive Validity

When researchers want to assess the validity of an IQ measure, say among college students, they can ask how well IQ scores correlate with student performance on an everyday index of intelligence, like achievement in school. (The answer is moderately well.) In other words, with adults and even older children, the degree to which a test measures what it was designed to measure can be assessed by actually comparing test scores with independent measures of achievement. In infants, however, there is no definitive or obvious concurrent external index of cognitive performance with which to compare test performance in order to assess validity. This has been tried, as we shall see, but the validity of infant tests has more typically been assessed by comparing infants' performance early in life with their performance years later as children or even adults. Logically, researchers argue, if individuals who perform well on infant tests do well on standardized IQ tests as children, then the infant tests must be telling us something about "intelligence" in infancy. This is the general approach to assessing the predictive validity of infant measures.

Bayley (1949) conducted a classic longitudinal study in this regard, and her results exemplify both the findings and far-reaching conclusions that characterize much of the early tradition in infant testing. Bayley followed 27 children from 3 months to 18 years of age, correlating their BSID scores in infancy and early childhood with their intelligence test scores in young adulthood. Figure 7.9 shows her results. As can be seen, she found essentially no correlation between infants' and children's test performance in the first 3 to 4 years of life and their intelligence test performance at 18 years. Only after children reached about 5 years of age did the association between child scores and eventual adult scores emerge, subsequently attaining a very high level between 11 and 18 years. The predictive validity of the Užgiris–Hunt Ordinal Scales is not better, except after 18 to 20 months, when a variety of scales appears to predict IQ to 24 and 31 months (Užgiris, 1989).

Such findings have been replicated many times. Developmental tests, such as the BSID, administered to infants in the first year of life are not good predictors of later IQ (Harris & Langkamp, 1994; Palti & Adler, 1994; Wyly, 1997).

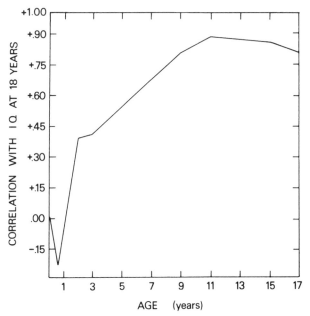

FIGURE 7.9

The correlation of test performance at different ages with IQ at 18 years of age. The correlation between test performance in the first 3 or 4 years of life and IQ test performance in maturity is low; the correlation after 5 to 6 years is substantially higher. (After Bayley, 1949.)

Such tests administered to infants older than 12 months show somewhat better predictive power than do tests administered in the first year (DiLalla et al., 1990; Molfese & Acheson, 1997), and predictive relations may be stronger for high-risk and retarded infants than for normal babies (Aiken, 1996; Siegel, 1989). With only a few exceptions, however, scores achieved in the first year of life on traditional developmental tests usually fail to provide meaningful information about intelligence in later childhood (Bornstein et al., 1997).

The intent of this analysis is not to condemn traditional infant tests like the BSID; after all, they are quite useful in evaluating developmental problems in infants (Sandall, 1997). Still, many theorists argue that there is no general intelligence factor (g) in mental life; otherwise, smarter infants would be smarter children. Some argue that if g exists, it is not fixed or stable at least across the early part of the lifespan. Finally, some argue that mental growth follows a stage-like progression wherein intelligence in infancy is very different from mature intelligence, and therefore individual variation in infancy represents not stable differences, but temporary variations in stage progression (see Bornstein et al., 1997; Colombo, 1993; McCall & Carriger, 1993). These interpretations of mental development in childhood differ greatly, but all are based on data showing the inability of traditional infant tests to predict later intelligence.

The repeated finding that there is little or no stability in mental development from infancy to later childhood may be a function of limitations inherent in traditional standardized tests, however. The test–retest reliability of traditional infant tests is frequently poor (Colombo, 1993; Fagen & Ohr, 1990; Užgiris, 1989): Infant performance at one time typically does not accurately predict infant performance just a short time later. Poor stability in test performance in infancy may occur for many reasons. Infancy is a period of rapid "fits and starts" in development, and thus the same infant may behave differently from one test session to the next. Alternatively, infants may simply be too underdeveloped, undermotivated, and underregulated, so that unreliability of performance is inherent to this phase of life. The problem of reliability is especially serious when one considers its relation to validity, that is how well a test measures what it is supposed to measure. Reliability places a kind of measurement "ceiling" on validity, because one measure cannot be expected to relate to some other measure (of the same or of a related phenomenon) better than it relates to itself. Thus, if the reliability of a measure is poor, its validity will usually be poor also.

In addition, the kinds of items put to young infants in such traditional infant tests as the Bayley and Užgiris–Hunt largely tap sensory capacities, motor achievements, and affective responses like orienting, reaching, and smiling (see Table 4.2). For an older child, very different items are used in evaluating intelligence—normally skills related to language, reasoning, and memory. Thus, the constructs compared bear little or no conceptual relation to one another. In essence, children are asked such different "questions" across developmental periods that there is little reason to expect stability between performance on traditional infant tests and performance on subsequent intelligence tests.

For these reasons, it is understandable that the predictive validity of the Bayley, the Užgiris-Hunt, and other traditional infant tests are all relatively poor for normal populations of infants. This means that the low age-to-age correlations between performance on the standard array of infant tests and later intelligence tests may be valid, but it would be invalid to conclude because of them that there is no stability in mental development from infancy.

Rather, to assess stability in mental development from infancy, measures that evaluate more purely "cognitive" functioning and performance must be employed. New longitudinal assessments of cognitive predictability beginning in infancy should tap information-processing skills in ways that are psychometrically sound, that are relatively free of motor requirements and affective components, and that conceptually parallel (to the degree possible) cognitive functions in childhood. In the next section, we review the results of validity research on various types of information-processing measures in infancy, notably habituation and novelty responsiveness. As we have already seen, these measures show individual variation and possess reasonable reliability; as we shall see, performance on them predicts cognitive competencies in childhood, not perfectly, but better than do scores on traditional infant tests.

The Information-Processing Orientation to the Assessment of Cognitive Competencies in Infancy

Attention has long been considered to be a basic component of mental life (Binet & Henri, 1895, 1896; see Chapter 6), and attention is viewed as a key facet of intelligence (Rose & Tamis-LeMonda, 1999). Generally speaking, infants who process information more efficiently are thought to acquire knowledge more quickly. Thus, as we discussed earlier in this chapter, quicker decays and lower total looking times in habituation are generally considered indexes of more efficient information processing. We certainly understand the everyday meaning of "quick" and "slow" when used to connote a person's intelligence (Marr &

Sternberg, 1987). Learning rate and reactivity are traditional parts of our definition of intelligence (Bloom, 1976; Durkin, 1966; Glaser & Rosner, 1975), and there is an established relation between reaction time on the one hand and intelligence test performance on the other (Vernon, 1987); inspecting and reacting quickly do not always signify mental speed, however. This relation is thought to be partly inherited and to build on a "neural efficiency" model of information processing.

Similarly, more looking at new stimuli and less looking at familiar stimuli also appear to index efficient information processing (Bornstein, 1998; Rose & Tamis-LeMonda, 1999). Research in novelty responsiveness is usually intramodal: the infant sees one stimulus and is later tested with both familiar and novel visual stimuli. However, there is evidence that infant novelty responsiveness across modalities—being familiarized with a stimulus tactually and then distinguishing a novel stimulus from the familiar one visually—predicts later cognitive competence as well (Rose, Feldman, Futterweit, & Jankowski, 1998).

Habituation and novelty responsiveness appear to denote meaningful individual differences in cognition. Procedures having to do with both (whether intramodal or crossmodal) were originally developed to assess facets of infant perception and cognition (like discrimination and memory), and infants are believed to mentally represent the stimuli presented during these procedures (Chapter 8). An understanding that decrement and recovery of attention involve information processing accounts for the widespread acceptance of these measures as techniques of study in infancy. We now consider specifically how well these measures serve as indexes of cognitive competencies in infancy and in later childhood.

It is difficult to know what would constitute a proper independent measure of infant "cognition" but there are some possible candidates. Infants (and young children) who habituate efficiently tend to explore their environment more competently and to play in more sophisticated ways (Tamis-LeMonda & Bornstein, 1989, 1993). Furthermore, infants who are expected to differ in intelligence later in life show commensurate individual differences in decrement as well as in recovery of attention. Perinatal risk and developmental disabilities such as Down syndrome adversely affect both decrement and recovery (Jacobson, Jacobson, Sokol, Martier, & Ager, 1993; Miranda & Fantz, 1974; Rose, 1994; Rose & Feldman, 1996; Zelazo & Stack, 1997).

Beyond these concurrent considerations, a key question for any new infant evaluation is whether it predicts scores on intelligence tests administered later in life. Measures of both decrement and recovery of attention in infancy have moderate validity in this regard. A large body of literature documents that young infants who show efficient visual information processing perform better on traditional assessments of cognitive competence in childhood and adolescence (Bornstein et al., 1997; Colombo, 1993; Dougherty & Haith, 1997; Fagan & Vasen, 1997; McCall & Carriger, 1993; McCall & Mash, 1995; Rose & Feldman, 1995; Rose et al., 1998; Sigman, Cohen, & Beckwith, 1997). Importantly, this stability is found in different laboratories, with different populations of both normal and at-risk infants, for different measures in infancy and across different modalities, including visual and auditory. Although it is far from perfect, the prediction between information-processing measures in infancy and cognitive performance in childhood is also notably higher than that between traditional infant tests and childhood IQ tests.

Some pertinent points must be raised concerning this predictive relation, however. First, this finding may be robust because decrement and recovery of attention are related to central cognitive capacities in infants and prediction is not limited to one modality or to one population. Second, as we note below, habituation in infancy predicts cognitive status in childhood independent of family influences that one might expect to affect performance (including maternal behaviors), thereby suggesting an unmediated (direct) tie between habituation performance in infants and their cognitive skills as children. In short, stability appears to be *in* the individual. Third, habituation could covary with some other factor(s), and it may be those that are responsible for the predictive association between habituation performance in infancy and later intelligence. For example, an infant presumably needs to be developed perceptually, to possess a vigilant or persistent cognitive style, and to have an attentive temperament to succeed first at habituation and later in an intelligence test. Alternatively, it could be that babies who process information efficiently also expose themselves to more appropriate amounts, kinds, or patterns of environmental stimulation (Bornstein, 1985c).

Taken together, however, these results substantiate a new view of mental development, one that supports the notion that there is some stability in individual cognitive performance from infancy. Measures of attention in the first year of life show moderate predictive validity for selected measures of cognitive competence perhaps through adolescence. Bayley herself seems to have anticipated these findings: In reflecting on her original longitudinal results, Bayley (1949, p. 167) speculated that "it may be that . . . we have not yet found the right tests, [and] search will reveal some infant behaviors which are characteristic of underlying intellectual functions, whose nature is such that they can be used for purposes of predicting the quality of intelligence at later ages."

Although these data on stability in mental development are telling, they certainly do not mean that intelligence is innate or fixed in early life. They do, however, overturn the view that cognition in infancy is not meaningfully associated with later development. In the final section of this chapter we take up the important consideration of how the social and physical environments in which the infants grow, and whatever capacities infants bring to these settings, jointly contribute to intellectual development.

Mental Development in Its Social Context

How does the mind bring itself into close coordination with physical and social reality? In the strong form of the maturationist argument, mental life in infancy is given genetically and unfolds biologically, being wholly within the child. There is undeniably some validity to this position. Modern behavior geneticists argue that individual differences among infants reflect inheritance in substantial degree, and there are reliable familial similarities with respect to IQ (Bouchard, Lykken, McGue, Segal, & Tellegen, 1990; Pipp-Siegel, Robinson, Bridges, & Bartholomew, 1997). Under a variety of testing conditions and comparisons, maternal IQ correlates strongly with child IQ (e.g., Loehlin, Horn, & Willerman, 1997), and a review of the "world's literature" points to the fact that the more closely individuals are related, the more similarly they perform on IQ tests (Chipuer, Rovine, & Plomin, 1990). The performance and developmental pattern of infants on traditional tests (like the Bayley) have been linked to hereditary endowment as well. As predicted by a genetic model (Chapter 3), Wilson (1983, 1984) found that identical twins are more alike in their scores on the Bayley

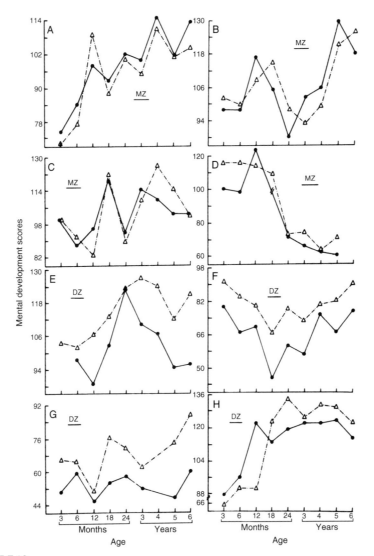

FIGURE 7.10

Illustrative mental development curves for monozygotic (MZ) and dizygotic (DZ) twins. *A–D*: These four pairs of monozygotic twins show regularly increasing, nonmonotonic, and regularly decreasing mental development test scores between 3 months and 6 years of age; their functions follow similar curves. *E–H*: These four pairs of dizygotic twins show how mental development curves within the same age range can vary in form, show consistent absolute differences, differ in trajectory over time, or differ in onset of growth spurt. (After Wilson, 1978. © 1978 by the American Association for the Advancement of Sciences. Reprinted with permission.)

and later tests than are fraternal twins or mere siblings. Wilson studied children from 3 months to 6 years of age, and Figure 7.10 shows some of his results. Monozygotic (MZ) twins (A–D in Figure 7.10) are similar across ages, even paralleling each other with respect to spurts and lags in development. Dizygotic (DZ) twins (E–H in Figure 7.10) are less similar over time.

Certainly genetics contribute to mental development, but all other prominent theories put experience in the world either as the principal source of individual cognitive growth or as a major contributing component (Dixon & Lerner,

FIGURE 7.11

Pierre Auguste Renoire (1841–1919), *Gabrielle et Jean*
(1895–1896). (Courtesy of Jean Walter and Paul Guillaume,
Musée de L'Orangerie, Paris.)

1999; Lutz & Sternberg, 1999; see Figure 7.11). In this final section of the chapter
we make explicit some specific views on how infant learning is assisted and
guided by others—the social context of mental development in infancy.

Parental Interaction and Teaching

Many theories of development hold that the environment exerts a strong influence (Chapter 2). Behaviorism propounded this view as a "main effect"
(Chapter 1), and many social scientists have argued that aggregate-level variables, like social status or cultural practice, constitute the chief influences on
mental development in children (e.g., Bornstein, 1991; Bornstein & Bradley,
2002). As we wrote in Chapter 2, such "global" factors exert tremendous control
over many aspects of early development. For example, in an extensive review,
Huston (1999) summarized the adverse effects of low socioeconomic status on
intellectual development in children.

Individual modes of caregiving presumably mediate between global influences on the one hand and individual variation in mental functioning and cognitive growth on the other, however. McLoyd (1998), for example, cited punitive,
harsh parental discipline as an important mediator of relations between poverty

and intellectual deficits and socioemotional difficulties in childhood. Extensive studies comparing mental growth in children from adoptive versus nonadoptive families (as those from the Colorado and Texas Adoption Projects—see Loehlin et al., 1997; Plomin, 1999) confirm the view that aspects of the mother–infant relationship also predict later developmental status in the child, free from genetic confounds. This position warrants intense empirical focus on everyday activities in the family. As a consequence, we turn to a closer scrutiny of behaviors thought to affect cognitive development from infancy. Echoing our orientation laid out in Chapter 1, one of our principal reference points in making sense of this literature is the *specificity principle* (Bornstein, 2002), namely, that specific experiences at specific times in early life may affect specific aspects of the child's growth in specific ways. Whereas the overall level of parental stimulation was once believed to affect the child's overall level of development (see Maccoby & Martin, 1983), evidence increasingly suggests that specific environmental events and parental activities relate concurrently and predictively to specific aspects of child performance and that parent and infant alike influence mental development (Bornstein, 1989b; Bornstein & Tamis-LeMonda, 1997; Feldman, Greenbaum, & Yirmiya, 1999; Tzuriel, 1999; Wachs, 1999).

Perhaps the most influential early proponent of a transactional perspective was Lev Vygotsky (1978), who emphasized the crucial importance of interaction with others for cognitive development. He contended that the more advanced or expert partner (e.g., the mother) raises the level of performance of the less advanced or expert partner (the infant) through social interaction (Rogoff, Mistry, Göncu, & Mosier, 1993). The difference between children's spontaneous performance at a task without guidance, and that observed with guidance, represents a central cognitive concept in Vygotskian theory known as the *zone of proximal development* (ZPD); (Lloyd & Fernyhough, 1999). Vygotsky's (1978, p. 86) idea of the ZPD centers on "problem solving under adult guidance," even in infancy.

Before children are old enough to enter formal social-learning situations like school, or even informal ones like play groups, the vast majority of their experiences stem directly from interactions they have within the family. Adult caregiving figures are responsible for determining most, if not all, of the infants' early experiences. What then are prominent caregiving strategies that relate to cognitive functioning in infancy? Parents take principal responsibility for structuring teaching exchanges with infants: They engage infants in early games as well as in turn-taking exchanges in play (Bornstein, 2002). Bruner (1983) identified the informal teaching roles adults adopt in interactions with infants under the rubric of *scaffolds*. As carpenters would in constructing a building, parents sometimes use these temporary aids to help the child advance. Later the scaffold may be replaced or taken away entirely. Some scaffolding strategies may be more effective than others, depending on the nature and age of the child, and parents can be expected to vary in the scaffolds they favor. Joint attention appears to be a one that potentiates cognitively successful interactions: Joint attention in infancy has been linked to infants' Bayley scores and communicative competence (Carpenter, Nagell, & Tomasello, 1998; Hirose & Barnard, 1997; Saxon, 1997). Parental responsiveness appears to be another (Bornstein, 2002). The environmental provisions (e.g., toys and books) that parents make for their infants constitute a third (Bradley, 2002). In terms of individual variation, some parents demonstrate more, others guide more (Landry, Garner, Swank, & Baldwin, 1996). European American mothers tend to encourage infant exploration more than Kenyan Gusii mothers (LaVine, 1997). Finally, sensitive parents tailor their scaffolding behaviors to match their infants' developmental progress (Rochat, Querido, & Striano, 1999), for example, by providing more "mediated learning experiences" as infants age (Tzuriel, 1999).

In a series of studies designed to evaluate different kinds of caregiving effects on infant development, Bornstein and his colleagues found that mothers show individual differences in these activities, that parenting has short-term reliability, and that these activities relate regularly to different forms of early mental growth, such as visual and tactual exploration in 2- and 5-month-olds, perceptual–cognitive competence in 3-month-olds, language and play in 13-month-olds, and intellectual ability in preschoolers (Bornstein & Tamis-LeMonda, 1990, 1997; Bornstein, Tamis-LeMonda, & Haynes, 1999; Tamis-LeMonda & Bornstein, 1990, 1994; Vibbert & Bornstein, 1989).

The Joint Contribution of Parent and Infant to Infant Mental Development

Rogoff and her colleagues have formally studied maternal teaching in infancy from the perspective of Vygotsky's ZPD, and they have discussed adult-assisted learning in children, pointing out that learning and socialization are actually interactive processes that require joint problem solving (Chavajay & Rogoff, 1999; Rogoff, 1996, 1997; Rogoff, Ellis, & Gardner, 1999; Rogoff, Matusov, & White, 1996). They looked at variations in role relations of infants and toddlers and their families in cultural communities as far flung as Turkey, Guatemala, India, and the United States, and documented how toddlers experience multiple settings, multiple caregivers, and widely contrasting outcomes in growing up. In all of these interactions, however, children participate actively in culturally organized activities, and in this way gain an understanding of the world they live in. As *apprentices* in daily living skills, infants and toddlers must learn to think, argue, act, and interact with all of the central characters in their culture in order to grow up and adapt successfully.

Thus, infant and caregiver jointly contribute to developing cognitive competence. Bornstein (1985c) provided evidence to this effect in a study that measured infant habituation at 4 months, productive language at 1 year, and intelligence test performance at 4 years as well as their mothers' home-based didactic interactions when the infants were 4 months and 1 year of age. Habituation and maternal stimulation in infancy each independently predicted language production and intelligence test performance in childhood. Tamis-LeMonda and Bornstein (1989) showed that habituation and maternal stimulation at 5 months predicted language comprehension and play sophistication at 13 months. In addition, Bornstein and Tamis-LeMonda (1997) found that infant habituation rates at 5 months and mothers' contingent responsivity to infant vocalizations and explorations were correlated such that more rapid infant habituation was associated with higher levels of maternal responsiveness. This could mean that mothers are predisposed to be more responsive to infants with better information-processing (and thus, better cognitive) skills, or that contingent social input from caregivers actually fosters information-processing abilities, in which case it might be possible to facilitate infant development by training mothers to be more sensitive. Of course, the link could also be bidirectional, reflecting a transactional process that predicts intellectual competence over the long term.

What motivates infants' parents to behave in the ways they do? In Chapter 11, we discuss parental belief systems and the factors that determine how parents interact with their infants. Whatever the reasons, parents bring more to interactions with their infants than simple learning; they promote their infants' mental development through the structures they create and the meanings they place on those structures. By the same token, infants bring an active mental life to their everyday interactions with adults; they also carry more away from their interactions than simply the contents of individual lessons.

Summary

The assessment of cognitive capacity early in life, analyses of the endogenous and exogenous factors that shape its origins and expression, and study of its predictive validity are abiding and compelling topics. In this chapter we described the fundamental premises and objectives of two major schools of thought about mental life in infancy. In his theory of sensorimotor intelligence, Piaget differs from empiricist and nativist theorists by emphasizing the importance of constructivism and motor activity in the development of knowledge. Post-Piagetian researchers have since elaborated on, and in some cases refuted, some of Piaget's basic tenets regarding sensorimotor development. Learning- and information-processing theorists have advanced an alternative view of infant mental life, noting that even newborns can be operantly and classically conditioned, imitate, and habituate and show novelty responsiveness. These competing schools work toward different scientific goals. The quantitative attempts to define antecedents of cognition and learning and focuses on individual differences—the ABCs of how children learn, acquire, and process information about the environment. By contrast, Piaget defined a qualitative series of invariant and universal stages in development. Both traditions teach us some "truths" about cognitive status and development from infancy, and so at some level (or, so many theorists believe) they may complement one another.

In recent years, two revolutions have taken place in the study of infant cognitive development. Whereas earlier infant assessments did not predict later cognitive stature in the child, contemporary studies using new techniques have unearthed significant levels of cognitive stability from infancy. And, whereas investigators suspected that early experiences ought to influence intellectual growth but could not find predictive relations, researchers have more recently developed specific measures that are predictively telling. The social environment also promotes cognitive development. Together these diverse points of view meet the design criteria for mental development and show that both endogenous and exogenous forces help to bring the individual's mind in line with the external physical and social reality.

8

Representation in Infancy

———— ❖ ————

- What is representation?
- Do babies categorize their perceptions? How do we know?
- How does categorization change developmentally?
- How does memory develop?
- Which behavioral and electrophysiological techniques have been used to study memory development? How?
- What factors affect how well infants remember?
- How is play related to memory and categorization?
- How does play change developmentally?
- How do interactions with adults shape play?
- How does play prepare infants to learn language?

Categories and Concepts, Memory, and Pretense

Armed with increasingly sophisticated ways of asking empirical questions of infants and obtaining answers from them, researchers have acquired a good understanding of infant capabilities. We have seen the fruits of those labors, and the resultant change in our basic understanding of infant perceptual sensitivities and cognitive competencies in the chapters preceding this one. Now developmentalists have traveled considerably beyond asking whether or not the senses function in infancy, beyond a rudimentary understanding of the perceptual world of the infant, and even beyond the question of whether infants think, to look at more sophisticated infant capacities. One of the most significant of these is *mental representation*, first discussed in Chapter 7 and further explored here.

As we indicated in Chapter 7, Piaget proposed that the first 2 years of life culminate in the development of representational thinking—the ability to think about people and objects that are not present. The Russian developmental psychologist Vygotsky also focused on this transition. He theorized that a critical change in infancy consisted of "interiorization," making the external world accessible to the internal. Thus, with development, infants more and more represent the external world in their internal thoughts. Vygotsky (1967) hypothesized that thinking in growing children consists of internalizing speech. Although the capacity for representation appears to exist from birth (see

Chapter 7), many developmentalists consider the study of how representational capacities develop to be crucial to understanding mental growth in early life. In their classic study *Symbol Formation*, Werner and Kaplan (1963) argued that the child develops principally in terms of symbolic and representational capacities, and does so in a variety of dramatically interrelated ways: thus, out of infancy there are telling changes in memory, problem solving, imitation, verbal competence, and play.

For Piaget (1962), Werner and Kaplan (1963), and Vygotsky (1967), representational ability is integrally related to the issue of object independence. In essence, these theorists argued that the child does not display truly symbolic understanding until there is clear movement beyond prerepresentational thinking (dependence on immediate perceptual and contextual support) to representational thinking (mental manipulation in the absence of feedback from objects). This development is sometimes called *decontextualization*. (We shall meet this concept again in Chapter 9, "Origins of Language in Infancy," when we note that real naming may only occur when the child can refer accurately to something even when it is not present.)

Using different investigative techniques, researchers have further differentiated the concept of representation and pushed the period of demonstrated representation to considerably younger ages. In the Piagetian view (Chapter 7), for example, there is little or no integration of incoming sensory information at birth, and the construction of an integrated world from "disconnected sights, sounds, and touches" is only accomplished over a considerable amount of time, ending in sensorimotor schemas of a solid, three-dimensional world. Babies thus derive a knowledge of objects from manual activity. Indeed, Piaget even characterized children's first words as imitative schemas not yet invested with representation. The perceptual world is coherent and differentiated much earlier in life than Piaget supposed, however. For example, work on cross-modal transfer indicates that information arriving at the senses is interrelated across modalities, and there is therefore considerably greater coherence to infants' perceptual experience than was once thought (see Chapter 6).

When Piaget studied acquisition of the object concept in his own children, he relied on their manual search for a hidden object. In an elementary sense, this mode of testing underestimates the child's competence, because children may still know something about the properties of a hidden object yet be constrained by their manual abilities, their understanding of how to search manually, or even their motivation to search. This point is persuasively demonstrated by the experimental work discussed in Chapter 7 that showed the capacity for mental representation is present at birth or very shortly thereafter, many months before infants develop manual search skills. Understanding of object permanence might emerge by 9 months of age, perhaps because even young infants need these capacities to master the flood of interactions with the physical world.

It is important to note, however, that representation hardly begins or ends with the child's attainment of the object concept, and that the term representation refers to a broad range of mental phenomena (e.g., memory, action, and the use of signs and symbols; Klahr, 1999; Mascolo & Fischer, 1999). Furthermore, perhaps the essence of cognitive growth in infancy and beyond lies in the manner in which different representational capacities and skills emerge and develop over time. DeLoache and Smith (1999), for example, documented a rather more sophisticated change in the young child's ability to understand symbolic relations. In their work, a miniature toy was hidden in a scale model of an actual room while a young child watched. Then the child was brought into the actual room and was asked to find the toy. Three-year-olds knew precisely where to search for the hidden toy, but children only 6 months younger (2½ years old) did not. As DeLoache and Smith noted, the failure of 2½-year-olds to find the toy was not because of faulty memory of the hiding event—most 2½-year-olds could readily find the miniature toy in the scale model. Instead, it appeared that these younger children were unable to use the hiding event to symbolize the hidden location of the real toy in the actual room.

It is important, therefore, to keep in mind that the study of early representation not only tells us about the nature of the young child's mind, but also tells us about the child's ability to use his or her mind. In DeLoache's task, the child must understand that the model represents the room. A moment's reflection reveals that the appreciation of books and television requires similar abilities. When and to what degree do children believe that what they see and hear actually represent reality?

In this chapter, we address three topics that, in one way or another, demand mental representation. More specifically, we describe and review categorization and conceptual understanding in babies, the development of memory in infancy, and the growth of pretend play at the end of infancy. Each of these capacities reflects the infant's increasing cognitive sophistication and flexibility. We address questions such as: What is the nature of representation? How does it develop? How do infants access it? How do they use it? Each of these topics has elicited a surge of empirical and theoretical activity in recent years. Infancy is the period of life without language—or with only rudimentary language—yet each one of these abilities articulates with or is presumptive of language. Many theorists have argued that, as linguistic comprehension begins before the first year, even young infants must possess a representational system that enables language learning. On this account, we also refer from time to time in this chapter to emerging relations between categories and concepts, memory, and play on the one hand with the dawning of language capacities in infants on the other. The origins of language takes center stage in Chapter 9.

Categories and Concepts

Early on, conceptual abilities were only inferred when infants demonstrated object permanence as described by Piaget, with the ability to retrieve a hidden object taken as evidence for the existence of an object concept. From this perspective, retrieval of the object implied that the infant had knowledge about the object beyond immediate perceptual feedback—a mental representation. There are, however, very different ways to think about conceptual abilities: exactly when infants start forming concepts about the world and what specifically defines a concept in infancy have been topics of much debate. We begin this section with a discussion of categorization and its study in infancy. We then address some perspectives on category formation and ask whether and when categories in infancy can be considered conceptual.

Categorization

Adults frequently treat discriminably different properties, objects, or events as effectively similar; that is, they categorize. Categorization involves the grouping of separate items into a set according to some type of precept or rule (Bornstein, 1984; Gelman & Diesendruck, 1999a, 1999b; Hayne, 1996; Mandler & McDonough, 1998; Quinn & Eimas, 1996). Members of a category may be classified together because they share a common attribute, element, or relation, or they may be classified via extension or intention. The *extension* of a set is constituted of the members, and the *intention* of a set comprises characteristics that define set membership. For example, a set may be defined as "vehicles with four wheels," from which one can deduce membership, or examples may be provided from which the set definition may be induced. Sets have breadths (the variety of stimuli which are included), prototypes (best examples), and boundaries (regions or instances of marginal inclusion). The demonstration of categorization requires that, in one context, properties, objects, or events are discriminable and that, in another, the same set of discriminable stimuli is grouped together.

Categorization reflects mental activity in three distinct spheres (Bornstein, 1984). First, categorization structures and clarifies perception. The environment into which infants are born and in which they develop provides an infinite variety of stimulation and is physically unstable, and infants themselves experience the world out of a constant biological flux. Both these major sources of variation must be reduced if perception is to proceed with any degree of organization, order, or coherence. Second, categorization facilitates the storage and retrieval of information. It supplies a principle of organization by which more information can be banked efficiently in memory: The infant doesn't have to remember every one of mother's facial expressions to recognize her face. Third, even elementary kinds of categorization anticipate modes of advanced information processing. In this process, the knowledge of some attribute or property often implies knowledge of other attributes or properties; thus, categorization also entails a rudimentary kind of logical inference.

Methods of Studying Categorization in Infancy

For older children and adults, who can sort and discriminate objects by verbal labeling, evidence of categorization in infancy relies on detailed observations of object manipulation in *sequential touching* and *familiarization/novelty preference* tasks (Hayne, 1996). For very young infants with limited manipulation skills, *habituation* and *operant conditioning* paradigms have been used (Merriman, Rovee-Collier, & Wilk, 1997). As part of a sequence of experiments, Rakison and Butterworth (1998a) used a sequential touching, object manipulation task to demonstrate categorization in the second year of life. The infants were shown four small (4 to 6 cm) three-dimensional models belonging to two categories: animals (cow, dog, goose, and walrus) and vehicles (train, bus, motorbike, and all-terrain vehicle). All eight stimuli were presented on a table in front of the infant, in random order, and the experimenter encouraged the infant to play with them. In this paradigm, categorization was inferred if the infant sequentially manipulated the objects within a category more frequently (i.e., at greater than chance levels) than objects across categories. That was indeed the case. Infants moved sequentially from one animal to another, and from one vehicle to another, significantly more frequently than they switched from animal to vehicle or from vehicle to animal. Rakison and Butterworth thus demonstrated that infants could discriminate animals from vehicles and categorize within each set in the second year of life.

In the familiarization/novelty preference paradigm, infants are first familiarized with several exemplars from the same category and are then presented with a novel exemplar from the same category and a novel exemplar from a different category. Categorization is inferred if infants pay more attention to the novel, out-of-category stimulus than to the novel, in-category stimulus. Oakes, Coppage, and Dingel (1997) employed the familiarization/novelty preference paradigm to demonstrate categorization skills in 10- and 13-month-olds. Infants were seated in a high chair and were given a series of small toys, one at a time, for 30 seconds. The toys belonged either to a land animals category (tiger, horse, dog, and zebra) or a sea animals category (killer whale, harp seal, humpback whale, and dolphin). Each toy in the land or sea animal category was presented three times for a total of twelve 30-second trials (the familiarization phase), and infants were allowed to manipulate the toys as they wished. Three subsequent trials constituted the test phase. Following the twelfth familiarization trial, infants were given a novel land animal (e.g., a rhinoceros), a novel sea animal (e.g., a manatee), and a novel toy that did not belong to either category (e.g., a truck). Both the 10-month-old and 13-month-old infants attended less across the familiarization trials, evidencing habituation. In the test phase, 10-month-olds dishabituated only to the truck but not to the novel, out-of-category animal stimuli, whereas the 13-month-olds dishabituated to both the novel, out-of-category animal stimulus and the truck. Thus, 10-month-old infants appeared capable of distinguishing animals from trucks but not land from sea animals—they appeared to form one broad, global category of "animals" that included both land and sea creatures—whereas the 13-month-olds appeared to distinguish between two categories, one of land animals, and the other of sea animals. These findings may reflect a generalized developmental sequence in categorization skills, from global to more basic categories with increasing age, a point that we revisit later in this section.

More traditional habituation/novelty preference paradigms have been employed to study categorization abilities in younger infants (under 6 months of age), whose object manipulation skills are more limited than those of older infants (Arterberry & Bornstein, 2001; Hayne, 1996). In a typical case, the infant is habituated to one or a small number of category exemplars (e.g., animals). Then a novel stimulus is presented that does not belong to the category (e.g., a vehicle). If the infant attends longer to the vehicle than to the last animal presented in the habituation series, it suggests that the infant distinguishes animals from vehicles and thus that the infant has formed a category of animals. Habituation paradigms have been used widely to document the ability to categorize geometric forms (e.g., triangles and squares), dot and line patterns, animals (cats, dogs, birds, and horses), phonemes, colors, gender of human voices, furniture, and spatial relations (e.g., above and below; Haith & Benson, 1998; Hayne, 1996; Jusczyk, 1995; Quinn, 1999; Quinn & Eimas, 1996).

The fact that infant behavior can be shaped by its consequences (see Chapter 7) has led to the development of another method for studying categorization in young infants. This method, termed the *mobile conjugate reinforcement paradigm*, makes use of 2- to 6-month-old infants' ability to learn, while lying face up in a crib, to make an overhead mobile move by kicking their feet (Rovee-Collier & Shyi, 1992). A ribbon connects the infant's ankle to the overhead mobile, and young infants readily learn that the harder they kick, the greater the amount of movement they produce in the mobile (hence the term *conjugate reinforcement*, reinforcement whose intensity is proportional to the intensity and vigor of the

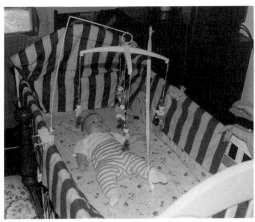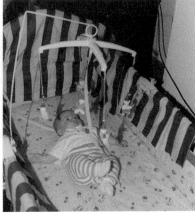

FIGURE 8.1
The mobile conjugate reinforcement paradigm. *Left panel*: an infant during a nonreinforcement phase with the ankle ribbon attached to the empty mobile stand. *Right panel*: the same infant during a reinforcement phase with the ankle ribbon attached to the stand from which the mobile hangs. (From H. Hayne, 1996.)

response). This paradigm is illustrated in Figure 8.1. It typically involves a brief (3-minute) baseline measure of infant foot kicks without the ribbon connecting the infant's foot to the mobile. This is followed by a 9-minute reinforcement period, during which the infant's foot is connected to the mobile, thus enabling the infant to move the mobile by kicking her or his foot. A 3-minute posttraining nonreinforcement phase then follows, during which the infant's foot is disconnected from the mobile and rate of foot-kicking is measured to test the infant's immediate retention of the event.

The mobile conjugate reinforcement paradigm is used to examine infant categorization in two ways: In the *simple forgetting procedure*, the infant is trained on a variety of different mobile exemplars on different days. Training is then followed by a delay of a day or more, followed in turn by a 3-minute posttraining, nonreinforcement retention phase, during which the infant is presented with a novel mobile that is not moving and not connected to the infant's foot. If the infant's rate of foot-kicking is similar to the rate observed during actual training (when the foot and mobile were connected), it suggests that the infant views the novel mobile as belonging to the same category as the exemplars used during training. If the infant's foot-kicking rate does not differ from the baseline rate, categorization is not assumed.

Figure 8.2A shows one of several mobile training exemplars used by Greco, Hayne, and Rovee-Collier (1990) when they tested categorization in 3-month-olds who participated in a study of simple forgetting. All training exemplars were mobiles from which were suspended five same-size, colored blocks, all of which displayed either the letter A or the number 2. On three consecutive days the infants received training with mobiles that had the same alphanumeric character (either A or 2) but that varied the color of that character across days (e.g., Day 1: Blue A; Day 2: Red A; Day 3: Green A). After a 24-hour delay the infants were tested with one of the four novel mobiles depicted in Figures 8B to 8E. Infants' foot-kicking rates were highest in response to the nursery mobile (Figure 8.2B), next highest in response to the stars mobile (Figure 8.2C), and at

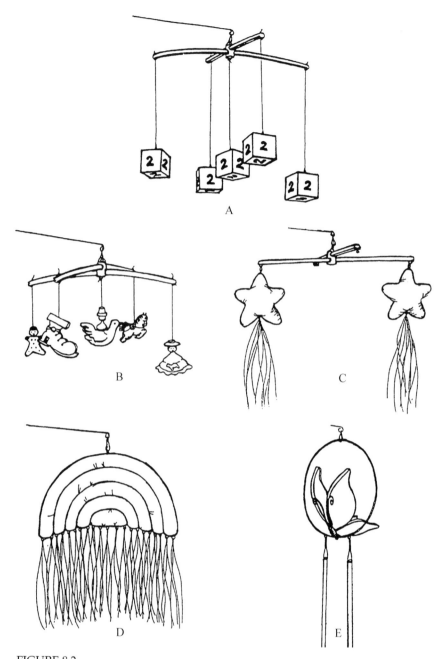

FIGURE 8.2

Mobile training and test mobiles used by Greco, Hayne, and Rovee-Collier (1990).
Figure 8.2A depicts one of the Blocks training mobiles. Figures 8.2B–8.2E depict
the Nursery (8.2B), Stars (8.2C), Rainbow (8.2D), and Butterfly (8.2E) test mobiles.
(Drawings by Paula Penno. From H. Hayne, 1996.)

levels not different from pretraining baseline in response to the rainbow and
butterfly mobiles (Figures 8.2D and 8.2E). Thus, 3-month-old infants placed the
nursery and stars mobiles within the same category as the training mobiles, but
did not do so with the rainbow or butterfly mobile. This categorization appeared
to be based on perceptual similarities between the test mobiles and the training

mobiles, and this interpretation was supported by similarity ratings provided by adults. Prior to this experiment, adults had rated the nursery mobile highest in physical similarity to the training mobiles, followed by the stars mobile, and then by the rainbow and butterfly mobiles (Greco et al., 1990).

A variant of the simple forgetting procedure that tests for categorization using the mobile reinforcement paradigm is the *reactivation procedure*, in which the infant is given a "reminder" session designed to reactivate the infant's memory of the training event prior to the retention test. The reminder session involves a 3-minute, noncontingent exposure to a mobile that was used in the training phase. In this session, movement of the mobile is produced by the experimenter at a rate similar to that produced by the infant during training, but the infant's foot and the mobile are not connected, so the infant cannot control the mobile's movement during the reminder. Evidence for categorization, involving a novel mobile, is assessed hours or days later using the procedure described earlier (Hayne, 1996).

Issues in the Study of Categorization

Interest in infant categorization exploded in the past two decades. Perhaps inevitably, this has led to a number of controversies about the nature and development of categorization in infancy.

Global-to-Basic or Basic-to-Global Categories?

How does categorization proceed as infants develop? Do infants first categorize at a global, superordinate level (e.g., forming the global category of "animals with four legs"), before they form finer-grained categories (e.g., dogs vs. cats)? Or do infants categorize at a more narrow, basic level first (e.g., differentiating dogs and cats based on the presence or absence of whiskers) before placing dogs and cats into a superordinate category (e.g., animals with four legs)?

Traditionally, a basic-to-global progression was assumed (Rosch, Mervis, Gray, Johnson, & Boyes-Braem, 1976; Mervis & Rosch, 1981), but later studies cast doubt on this view. Younger and Fearing (1999, 2000), for example, conducted a series of experiments with 4-, 7-, and 10-month-old infants using the habituation/novelty preference paradigm. Infants in the first experiment received ten familiarization trials in which they were presented randomly with five pairs of cats and five pairs of horses. Three test comparisons followed. The first two test comparisons involved a novel (never before seen) cat and dog, or a novel horse and a different dog. The third test comparison involved a novel cat or horse and a car. If the infants had formed basic-level categories they would be expected to look longer at the dog than at the novel cat or horse in the first two test comparisons. If the infants had formed a global category of "animals" (cats, dogs, and horses), they would be expected to look longer at the car in the third test comparison than at the novel cat or horse, and to show no preferential looking in the novel cat–dog and novel horse–dog test comparisons. In fact, younger (4- and 7-month-old) infants showed preferential looking to the car in the third test comparison, but no preferential looking in the first two test comparisons, suggesting that they had formed a global category (animals) that they distinguished from a nonanimal exemplar (the car). By contrast, 10-month-old infants looked reliably longer at the dogs than at the novel cat or horse in the first two test comparisons, suggesting that, by 10 months of age, infants could form more differentiated categories (i.e., cats and horses in one category, dogs in another, or cats, horses, and dogs all in separate categories). This apparent global-to-basic developmental progression was also evident in two subsequent experiments that involved familiarization with exemplars that contrasted strongly (e.g., cat and car exemplars, followed by test comparisons involving a novel cat with a dog and a novel car with a truck) and exemplars that contrasted moderately (e.g., cat and bird exemplars, followed by test comparisons involving a novel cat with a dog and a novel bird with a bat; Younger & Fearing, 2000). Data from other laboratories also provided support for the global-to-basic shift in infant categorization skills over time (Mandler, 1998, 2000; Mandler & McDonough, 1998; Quinn & Johnson, 2000).

The tendencies to form global or basic categories depend greatly on the nature of the experimental stimuli used and the manner in which the stimuli are presented, however. Younger and Fearing (2000) noted, for example, that 7-month-olds could form basic level categories when the categories used were more distinctive. Similarly, Oakes et al. (1997) found that the kinds of categories infants formed depended on the degree to which the exemplars provided to infants during familiarization trials were perceptually distinct. Taking the contrary argument a step further, Rakison (2000; Rakison & Butterworth, 1998a, 1998b) argued that the global-to-basic progression in infant categorization is illusory, citing a host of findings suggesting that infants categorize on the basis of whatever attributes a set of exemplars have in common. Thus, although a global-to-basic trend in the development of categorization in infancy has some support, this perspective has been challenged on empirical grounds and its confirmation awaits additional research.

Is Infant Categorization Perceptual or Conceptual?

This question has stimulated heated controversy, but there is no straightforward, easy answer to it, perhaps because researchers do not agree how "concepts" should be defined (Quinn & Eimas, 1996). Some argue that a concept is a theory one uses to help make sense of the world (Gelman & Diesendruck, 1999a, 1999b), whereas Mandler (1998) proposed that concepts are ideas about kinds of things that go beyond simple perceptual associations among different elements in a category. For example, horses, dogs, and cats are different kinds of animals, and an animal is a different kind of thing than is a car. To have a concept of animals, from this perspective, the infant must understand, even at a rudimentary level, that animals have a set of common features that supersede perceptual similarities (i.e., that they can move, make sounds, interact with each other, have babies, and so forth). Rudimentary concepts such as these, Mandler (1998, 2000) argued, begin developing very early in life and become more and more elaborated, sophisticated, and differentiated with maturation and experience. Indeed, she cited evidence for the global-to-basic trend in the development of infant categorization as an indication that infants first form rather holistic, undifferentiated concepts about the world (e.g., animals, vehicles) before fine-tuning those broad concepts into smaller, more fine-grained conceptual categories (e.g., dogs and cats).

Others, however, believe that it is more parsimonious to explain very early categorization on the basis of perceptual similarities among stimuli (Mareschal & French, 2000; Quinn, Johnson, Mareschal, Rakison, & Younger, 2000; Rakison, 2000). Quinn et al. (2000) noted that the apparent global-to-basic progression in categorical development occurs because global categories are more easily distinguished perceptually than are basic categories. For example, it is easier to distinguish animals from furniture perceptually than it is to distinguish dogs from cats, which would account for infants' ability to make global distinctions earlier in development than basic distinctions.

When Does a Category Become Conceptual?

If infant categorization is initially perceptual in nature, then the question arises as to when a given category actually attains the status of a concept (Bornstein, 1984). Mandler (2000) proposed that concepts begin in early infancy, as infants learn the kinds of things that comprise their world by virtue of their interrelated characteristics, features, and functions, and that separate developmental mechanisms govern categorization at perceptual and conceptual levels. Indeed, Mandler (1997) proposed a mechanism, *perceptual analysis*, to account for the development of conceptual categories. Perceptual analysis, Mandler argued, is an active cognitive process that involves recoding perceptual information into higher order, more abstract characteristics. This process may begin as early as 3 to 4 months of age, at which point infants have already begun forming perceptually based categories. Quinn and Eimas (1996), by contrast, argued that there was no need to postulate a separate mechanism for concept formation, and that conceptual categories emerge over time as new information about the features, roles, and interrelations among members of a given perceptual set is acquired with the development of language and memory. Quinn and Eimas (1996) view the transition from perceptual to conceptual categorization as gradual, not sudden, despite outward appearance to the contrary.

Although these controversies present real challenges to researchers, it is clear that the study of infant categorization has contributed greatly to our understanding of early cognitive development, particularly regarding the manner in which infants are preadapted to make sense of the world around them. Categorization represents a many-to-one reduction process that functions adaptively in many different spheres of infant thinking. Indeed, it would be difficult to overstate the significance of categorization for cognition and its development. Categorization is pervasive and essential for perceiving, thinking, remembering, and communicating. Haith and Benson (1998, p. 229) illustrate this point succinctly:

> Imagine an infant who must learn anew its parents' face for each perspective rotation, each expression, and each change of hair style. Or, consider the task of an infant who must acquire a new knowledge base for each separate cat that it encounters—that each meows, drinks, eats, and so on. And, one can appreciate the utility of categorization. By incorporating individual percepts of the mom's face into a mom–face category and individual cats into a cat category, infants gain enormous leverage in accumulating knowledge. Each piece of information one acquires with an individual exemplar can generalize to the whole set, permitting appropriate expectations and behavior in encounters with completely new instances.

Memory

It is obviously important that infants attend to stimuli and events in their environment, but it is also crucial that they be able to store, retrieve, and use that information later. Memory representations underlie the infant's awareness, experience, knowledge, and interpretation of the world. Developmentalists are interested in all dimensions of infant memory, in what infants can remember, and the nature of their memory representations, in the ways in which infants remember, and in how good infant memory is. In this section of the chapter, we describe the tools researchers have exploited to study infant memory, and with these tools, what has been learned about the common parameters of early memory development, including age, study time, duration of memory, and interference.

Memory plays a key role in the general model of mental functioning. This model is traditionally believed to involve (at least) three stages:

1. The sensory register temporarily stores attended-to information.

2. Short-term memory has limited and momentary capacity for information.

3. Long-term memory represents a limitless, permanent storehouse of knowledge, but one that depends on "control" processes that are generally unavailable to infants or even very young children. (Failure to remember is more likely to result from an inability to retrieve information from long-term store rather than actual loss of information; as a consequence, memory strategies play a key role in long-term memory.)

Learning and memory are interrelated but not identical phenomena. The types of learning paradigms discussed in Chapters 3 and 7 demand more than simply remembering whether a stimulus was encountered before. In conditioned head turning, for example, the infant must recognize a sound and remember to turn to one side when that sound is heard. It is quite conceivable, however, that the infant will remember the sound and perhaps even remembers the response contingency, yet choose not to perform. Alternately, the baby may be incapable of a response yet recognize the learning situation very well. Therefore, the study of memory development is important in its own right.

Many aspects of memory change during childhood and adolescence (Cowan, 1997; Hartshorn et al., 1998; Herbert & Hayne, 2000; Nelson, 1997a, 1997b), and so adults' memory systems and memories differ from those of infants in many ways. Putative neuropsychological sites of memory (e.g., the hippocampus, thalamus, rhinal cortex, basal forebrain, and orbital prefrontal cortex) are still forming during the first year (Nelson, 1997a), whereas all of the requisite physiological wiring is (presumably) present in adults. Adults process information much more rapidly than infants. Adults have had many more experiences, and hence many more memories to associate with new to-be-remembered material, thereby facilitating mnemonic processes, although these past experiences often interfere with memory retrieval and accuracy as well.

Interest in the dynamics of memory development in infancy has developed alongside the rise to prominence of the information-processing approach in research on adult cognition (Chapter 7). With infants, information-processing theorists seek, first, to identify component skills involved in remembering certain types of information and, then, by assessing development of each of these component skills, to determine whether their immaturity slows the attainment of more competent memory skills (Rose & Tamis-LeMonda, 1999). This approach promises to tell us much about the nature of representation in memory and about the ways in which memory and representation develop.

Cognitive scientists who study memory typically distinguish between two major pairs of processes. One pair involves encoding and retrieval. *Encoding* specifies the transformation of incoming information into memory; *retrieval* specifies the search-and-find process(es) used to get information out of memory. The second pair of processes further differentiates retrieval into recognition and recall. To retrieve via *recognition* requires only that we remember having experienced previously whatever is to be remembered, and contextual cues are provided to help with recognition. To retrieve via *recall* requires that we be able to remember a prior experience without being afforded any cues. Cognitive scientists also distinguish between two different kinds of memory. *Declarative*, or *explicit memory*, is defined as memory for names, events, places, and so forth (Bauer, in press). Subsumed within declarative memory are the more well-known *episodic memory* (memory of events that have been experienced) and *semantic memory* (memory of facts about the world), a dichotomy that Tulving (1985) introduced. Four basic features characterize declarative memory: (1) It is conscious (i.e., memories are accessed by conscious effort); (2) it is fast (i.e., memories can be formed in an instant); (3) it is fallible (i.e., memories can fade or cannot be retrieved); and (4) it is flexible (i.e., memories tend not to be context dependent; Bauer, in press; Zola-Morgan & Squire, 1993). By contrast, *nondeclarative (or procedural) memory* refers to habits and skills that are shaped by experience (e.g., riding a bike). These memories (1) are largely unconscious; (2) slow to develop; (3) relatively infallible (i.e., not prone to forgetting); and (4) inflexible (i.e., dependent on context; Bauer, 1997, in press; Parkin, 1997). The vast majority of experiments on infant memory involve declarative memories, although we note here that nondeclarative memories may be particularly important for understanding the development of social relationships (e.g., Crittenden, Lang, Claussen, & Partridge, 2000). We will have more to say about this in Chapter 11.

Interestingly, it was believed for years that infants could not remember much of anything, because adults typically have great difficulty remembering events that took place before 3 to 4 years of age (Bauer, 1996; Rovee-Collier & Gerhardstein, 1997). Indeed, Freud (1916–1917/1966) coined the term *infantile amnesia* to describe this phenomenon, which he attributed to repression of memories of traumatic events, or of the inability to form coherent memories of events (Bauer, in press; Weigle & Bauer, 2000). Piaget (1954) supported this view, arguing that recall may not be possible during the first year because it demands the capacity to encode symbolically, which he thought only emerged during the transition from sensorimotor to preoperational intelligence at about 2 years of age.

We now know that this view is premature and inaccurate. Infants are not only quite capable of recognizing previously experienced events (over which there was less controversy), but also of recalling events. We begin with a discussion of methods employed to study infant memory, and then move to a discussion of factors that influence memory formation, and of developmental changes in infant memory over time.

Techniques Used to Study Infant Memory

Students of memory capacity in infancy have used five different techniques. Two are *habituation* and *novelty-responsiveness procedures* that we know from Chapters 3 and 7, which specifically tap recognition memory. Look back to Figure 3.8 on page 79. When an infant looks at a repeated study stimulus less on its fifth showing than on its first, the loss of interest—barring artifact—strongly suggests that the baby is coming to recognize the stimulus. Presumably, the baby is comparing each new stimulus presentation with a memory, or mental representation of the study stimulus based on previous exposures. Figure 3.8 shows this decrement clearly. A recovery in attention to a novel or test stimulus following familiarization necessarily indicates differential treatment of study from test stimuli based on prior study experience. Figure 3.8 shows such recovery.

Once habituation is complete, the study stimulus and a new or test stimulus are presented. If the baby looks more at the test than at the study stimulus, researchers infer that the baby has recognized the study stimulus and so in some rudimentary and unspecified way has remembered something about the study stimulus. That is, a low level of looking at the study stimulus on retest is usually interpreted as recognition, or memory of the study stimulus, whereas recovery of looking at the study stimulus is interpreted as forgetting. Strictly speaking, however, if the baby regards the test and the study stimuli equally, researchers cannot assume that the baby failed to remember. Instead, the infant may simply find the familiar stimulus as interesting as the novel stimulus. Because "interestingness" is determined by many factors (other than novelty), the absence of recovery is always difficult to interpret (Bornstein, 1985).

Habituation and novelty responsiveness are taken to involve development of both mental representation and memory, and students of infancy have transformed the two paradigms into versatile and powerful tools with which to investigate the ontogeny of memory (e.g., De Saint Victor, Smith, & Loboschefski, 1997). Using habituation, for example, it is possible to track the rate at which a stimulus is encoded; presumably, faster habituation is an index of quicker encoding. It is also possible to monitor the course of mental construction because one can "probe" during habituation for discrimination to assess the ongoing development or consolidation of memory structures. By habituating or familiarizing infants and testing them immediately afterward with the same stimulus, it is also possible to study short-term recognition memory, just as it is possible to impose a delay between habituation and a later test in order to assess long-term recognition memory. Similarly, a "savings method" that compares the rate of habituation to a stimulus at one time with habituation to the same stimulus but at a later time can be used to assess short- or long-term retention of a stimulus depending on the length of time between the two tests.

A third approach designed to tap into infant recognition memory involves a variety of operant conditioning techniques, discussed earlier in this chapter in our coverage of infant categorization. Rovee-Collier and her colleagues employed techniques like the mobile conjugate reinforcement paradigm to study memory capacity in infancy (Adler, Inslicht, Rovee-Collier, & Gerhardstein, 1998; Hartshorn & Rovee-Collier, 1997; Rovee-Collier & Boller, 1995; Rovee-Collier & Gerhardstein, 1997). Refer to Figure 8.1. In this technique, a baseline reading is taken of how often an infant kicks. A ribbon is then tied from the baby's ankle to a mobile hanging over the crib. Quickly, the baby learns that foot kicking moves the mobile. When attached to the mobile in this way, the baby kicks at two to three times the baseline rate. When an infant who has previously learned the association between kicking and mobile-moving relearns that response more rapidly than a similar-age child who has not previously learned the response, then the difference, or "savings," indexes memory. This paradigm is particularly useful with very young infants who have not yet developed fine-motor control and manual search skills.

Another operant conditioning paradigm, the *train paradigm*, has been used to study memory in infants older than 6 months of age (Hartshorn & Rovee-Collier,

FIGURE 8.3
The train operant conditioning memory task, used with 6- through 18-months-olds.
Each lever press moves the train around the track for 2 seconds. (From C. Rovee-Collier
& P. Gerhardstein, 1997.)

1997). In this procedure, the infant learns to press a lever to move a miniature
electric train around a track (see Figure 8.3). Like the mobile conjugate reinforcement paradigm, infants learn the association between their response (the lever
press) and its consequence (e.g., movement of the train car). The infants are then
tested after a delay of 2 or more weeks with the same apparatus. Retention of the
event is assumed if the infant presses the lever at a rate that equals or exceeds
the rate observed at the end of training (Rovee-Collier & Gerhardstein, 1997).

Other research techniques are designed specifically to assess infant recall.
For example, in the *search technique*, the experimenter hides an object of interest
to the infant and then observes whether the infant seeks it and, if so, whether
the search is appropriate and successful (Bjorklund & Douglas, 1997; Reznick,
Fueser, & Bosquet, 1998). Reznick et al. (1998), for example, hid a toy in one of
three wells in front of 7-month-old and 9-month-old infants, and then allowed
the infants to search for the toy after a short delay. The 7-month-olds spent equal
proportions of time searching in all three wells, whereas the 9-month-olds were
able to find the toy more often than would be expected by chance. Even if the
9-month-olds erred on their first try they tended to succeed on their second try
despite delays of 10 to 20 seconds between hiding the toy and infant search.

Ahmed and Ruffman (2000) similarly observed a capacity for remembering
simple event sequences in 8- to 12-month-old infants tested in a Piagetian "A not
B" search task, and in a "not-search" task that involved a violation of expectations. The infants made the typical "A not B" errors at this age (i.e., they searched
at place A for an object after watching the experimenter first hide the object at
place A, then retrieve it from place A and rehide it at place B; see Chapter 7).
The infants nevertheless demonstrated some memory for the correct location of
the object in the not-search task. In this task, infants watched the experimenter

hide the toy at place A, and then watched the experimenter retrieve the object from place A and rehide it at place B. The experimenter then produced the object from place A (an impossible event) or at place B (a possible event). The infants looked significantly longer at the impossible, unexpected event than at the possible, expected event, demonstrating some memory of the object's correct location. These results, considered with those of Reznick et al. (1998), suggest that the ability to recall simple event sequences emerges between 7 and 9 months of age.

Finally, *deferred imitation*, or imitation of a modeled sequence of events after a nontrivial time delay, gives evidence of infant recall. Piaget argued that infants could not defer imitation until the sixth stage of sensorimotor development, beginning at roughly 18 months of age (see Chapter 7). Since Piaget's time, however, many researchers have demonstrated deferred imitation in the first year, even in infants as young as 6 months of age. For example, Barr, Dowden, and Hayne (1996) modeled a three-step event sequence of (1) removing a mitten from a puppet's hand, (2) shaking the mitten (which rang a bell inside the mitten), and (3) putting the mitten back on the puppet's hand. After a 24-hour delay, infants were given the puppet and mitten. About 75% of infants imitated at least one of the three events in the sequence, but only 25% appeared able to imitate at least two of the steps in the order demonstrated. Six-month-olds, thus, had memory for content of individual events but not yet for the temporal order of the events. Consistent with memory research using search paradigms (e.g., Reznick et al., 1998), however, deferred imitation of modeled event sequences is apparent by 9 months of age, even after a 5-week delay (Carver & Bauer, 1999), suggesting that critically important memory functions, particularly the long-term recall of ordered events, become consolidated in infants between 6 and 9 months of age (Bauer, in press).

The five techniques we have outlined to this point all rely on behavioral responses in infants. One *psycho-physiological* technique, *event-related potentials* (ERPs; see Chapter 5), may be especially useful in documenting not only when learning in infancy takes place, but also which neural substrates might mediate it (Nelson, 1997a, 1997b). Carver, Bauer, and Nelson (2000) used ERPs to demonstrate the recall of ordered events in infants. Infants who demonstrated, with deferred imitation, recall of an ordered event sequence showed a different ERP response from specific brain regions than did infants who did not recall the ordered sequence.

Five behavioral and one electrophysiological technique have been used to study memory in infancy. Each has advantages and limitations with regard to the ages and types of memory to which it can be applied. No one technique alone is sufficient to study the dimensions and limitations of infant memory, but the several techniques complement one another and in a short time have yielded a surprisingly detailed picture of the dimensions of memory in infancy.

Influences on Infant Memory

Infant age is a major parameter affecting memory, and several important questions flow from this observation: How early in life do infants begin to remember? Does age affect memory processing? Does age influence forgetting? Perhaps the fact that so few of us remember anything about our infancy provokes this intense interest, although reports of habituation and novelty responsiveness in newborns strongly imply memory at birth (see Chapter 7). Indeed, memory may even go back to the prenatal period: One classic prenatal conditioning study

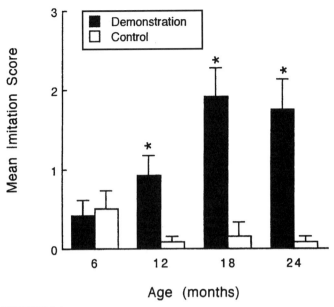

FIGURE 8.4

Mean imitation scores of 6-, 12-, 18-, and 24-month-old infants tested after a 24-hour delay in the puppet–mitten task as a function of experimental group (Demonstration, Control). An asterisk indicates that the mean imitation score of the demonstration group (solid bars) was significantly above the mean imitation score of their age-matched control group (open bars). Units on the Y axis are the mean number of events, out of three that were modeled, that were correctly imitated. (From R. Barr & H. Hayne, 2000.)

reported that a fetus retained a learned association for 18 days (Spelt, 1948). We also learned in Chapters 3 and 7 that infants habituate more, more quickly, and more efficiently as they grow older.

Infant age also affects the ability to remember. As might be expected, infants can recall more information, across longer periods of time, as they get older. Using a deferred imitation task involving a three-event sequence (pulling a mitten off a puppet's hand, shaking the mitten, and then putting the mitten back on the puppet's hand), Barr and Hayne (2000) found that recall of these events after a 24-hour delay was highest among 18- and 24-month-olds, lowest among 6-month-olds (who did not perform any better than infants who never observed the modeled sequence), and intermediate among 12-month-olds (see Figure 8.4). Figure 8.5 illustrates the relation between infant age and retention duration, or the maximum number of weeks between training and retention testing in either the mobile conjugate reinforcement or train electric paradigms across which forgetting did not occur. It is clear that older infants recalled across longer time intervals than did younger infants, and that, for the age groups tested, this relation was linear. Bauer, Wenner, Dropik, and Wewerka (2000) also demonstrated, with a deferred imitation task involving three- and four-step sequences, that 20-month-old infants recalled more information across delays of 1, 3, 6, 9, and 12 months than did 16-month-olds, who in turn recalled more than did 13-month-olds. Thus, as infants develop, they recall more information, more accurately, across longer and longer periods of time.

Study time also affects infant memory. Familiarization-test experiments suggest that babies do not require extremely long exposures to to-be-remembered information to develop a mental representation on the basis of which they can

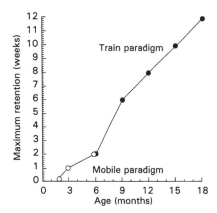

FIGURE 8.5

Maximum retention duration, using the mobile conjugate reinforcement and train operant conditioning paradigms, plotted against infant age. The mobile paradigm was used with infants 6 months of age or younger. The train paradigm was used with infants between 6 and 18 months. (From Hartshorn, K., Rovee-Collier, C., Gerhardstein, P., Bhatt, R. S., Wondoloski, T. L., Klein, P. J., Gilch, J., Wurtzel, N., & Campos-de-Carvalho, M. (1998). The ontogeny of long-term memory over the first year-and-a-half of life. *Developmental Psychobiology, 32,* 69–89.)

recognize the study stimulus, or, at least, prefer a novel stimulus by comparison. As we reviewed earlier, a characteristic feature of declarative memory is that it is fast (i.e., it can be formed quickly). At the same time, practice, or repeated experience with an event facilitates memory. Barr and Hayne (2000), for example, enlisted two groups of 18-month-old infants in the puppet–mitten task described earlier. One group of infants, the practice group, was given three opportunities to imitate the sequence of actions performed by the experimenter. The other group, the no-practice group, was shown the action sequence six times by the experimenter but was given no opportunity to perform the actions. Six weeks later, half of the infants in both groups were given a "memory reactivation," or reminder, session, which involved a brief exposure to the same puppet and experimenter but without the experimenter modeling the action sequence. All infants then received the retention test. Retention of the action sequence was significantly better among infants in the practice group, which was given the reminder, indicating that prior practice with the event facilitated memory of it.

In another study, Bauer, Hertsgaard, and Wewerka (1995) reported facilitative effects of repeated exposure to an event on later recall. Thirteen- and 15-month-old infants who were shown a novel event sequence three times reproduced it significantly better than did those who saw the sequence only once. Recall is also facilitated when the modeled action sequences are reenacted between the time of initial exposure to them (training) and retention testing. Hudson and Sheffield (1998) trained 18-month-olds on eight novel tasks in a playroom and then brought the infants back to the laboratory to reenact the same tasks 15 minutes, 2 weeks, or 8 weeks after training. Retention testing occurred 6 to 8 weeks after reenactment. Reenacting the tasks improved infants' recall of the tasks relative to control infants who did not observe the reenactments. Interestingly, reenacting only half of the tasks facilitated retention just as well as reenacting all of them. Furthermore, reenactment improved recall even better after longer delays than after shorter delays, suggesting that a memory "refresher" is especially useful the closer one gets to forgetting the event. Thus, like memory in older children and adults, infant memory can be facilitated by repeated exposure and/or practice (Rovee-Collier & Gerhardstein, 1997).

Finally, infant memory—especially long-term memory—appears to be sensitive to *interference effects* (Rovee-Collier & Boller, 1995), further suggesting that the same basic processes that contribute to forgetting in adults are at work in infancy as well. Unlike adult memory, however, infant memory appears to be more closely bound by the context in which the memory is acquired, and context plays a role in memory retrieval. Rovee-Collier's work underscores this point (Butler & Rovee-Collier, 1989; Rovee-Collier, Griesler, & Early, 1985). Three-month-olds learned an association between foot kicking and mobile moving in one situation, and were then tested either in the same or a different situation. Retention was not affected after 1 day, but a change of context disrupted memory after delays of 3 and 7 days. Memory becomes less and less bound by contextual cues, however, over the course of the first year.

In summary, habituation, novelty responsiveness, conditioning, search, and imitation convincingly demonstrate that infants have a sophisticated capacity to remember, and researchers have progressed beyond asking simple questions about whether or not infants *can* remember. Clearly, even newborns can. Investigators now ask how infants remember, that is, what skills or strategies infants use, and what the dimensions of memory in infancy are. Encoding skills and short-term memory improve rapidly over the first year, whereas retrieval skills and long-term memory improve later and gradually. Even in the first weeks of life, babies give good evidence of recognition (as, for example, for their mothers' face, voice, and scent), and their memories may last. As infants age they demonstrate an ability to hold events in memory for longer time spans, and they require fewer cues and shorter periods of familiarization to recall past events. Babies appear to have specific memories, however, and they can retrieve seemingly forgotten information if they are given a reminder. This may be especially true for patterned, repeated events, such as those that occur in the context of parent–child interactions, which infants can recall with greater and greater accuracy from the second half of the first year of life onward. Although the capacity for ordered recall at this point in development is quite rudimentary, it develops rapidly, and with it the potential for memories to guide and influence subsequent reactions to and behavior with objects and people.

Play

It may seem odd at first to combine discussions of play and mental representation. Isn't play social and affective? Of course, it is. But imagine for a moment what play looks like in its earliest state. Play is certainly fun and interactive, but play also involves studying a doll alone, manipulating a busy-box, building with a set of blocks, or entertaining no one else at a make-believe tea party. Play frequently imitates life, and it is quite common to observe toddlers reenacting in play specific events that they observe or participate in routinely (e.g., "driving" a toy car). Such instances in the second year of life indicate that infants represent events mentally and can reproduce them in play. The increase during the second year of life in symbolic or pretend play, as well as in language, reflects underlying developmental progressions in the capacity for representation (Bornstein & O'Reilly, 1993).

Play reflects and influences the infant's level of competence in linguistic, socioemotional, and physical–motor domains of development (Beeghly, 1993; Bergman & Lefcourt, 1994; Creasey, Jarvis, & Berk, 1998; Pellegrini & Smith, 1998; Tamis-LeMonda & Bornstein, 1996). Eisert and Lamorey (1996) found that the quality of play related to adaptive and fine-motor skills among 12-month-olds. Lyytinen, Laakso, Poikkeus, and Rita (1999) found that the quality of symbolic play at 14 months predicted intellectual and linguistic development at

24 months, and Kelly-Vance, Needelman, Troia, and Ryalls (1999) also found a strong linkage between a play-based assessment and the Bayley Scales of Infant Development among 2-year-olds. And the quality of toddlers' exploratory and social play with peers has been linked to the security of infant–mother attachment (Belsky, Garduque, & Hrncir, 1984). Thus, infant play holds special significance to professionals with a wide range of interests.

In this section of the chapter, we first describe the early development of play, which, in bold outline, begins as inspection and manipulation and moves gradually to higher order pretense. Then we examine the study of play and the ways in which play becomes embedded in interaction. Afterward, we link symbolic play with other developing mental abilities near the end of infancy. Play brings the child into contact with diverse physical and social features of the environment and in many ways is a critical kind of self-initiated learning.

The Development of Play

Piaget (1954, 1962) was among the first theorists to study play seriously. Because Piaget was primarily concerned with the philosophical problems of epistemology (Chapter 1), most of his research on infant cognitive development focused on children's beliefs about space, objects, and causation, in other words, children's understanding of physical laws governing actions and objects. However, Piagetian theory also provoked examination of a variety of related mental processes, and Piaget himself saw infant play activity as a means for integrating strategies. He studied play (among other things) for the light it promised to throw on cognitive development in infancy generally. Play is exploration, and how exploration proceeds reveals much about mental growth. For Piaget, activities with a single object were the most primitive. The very youngest infant manipulates a single object at a single time, relying on sensorimotor behaviors alone (pushing, pulling, and so forth). Older infants move on to a more advanced level, manipulating the parts of objects or juxtaposing two objects to look at object relations (putting a spoon into a cup), so that the use children make of objects in play appears to reflect developmental changes in intelligence. Many researchers have studied play in order to learn what it tells us about children's cognitive development, what knowledge children possess, how they acquire new knowledge, and how various factors affect the acquisition and exercise of that knowledge base.

Piaget examined his own children's play closely and articulated four major principles about play:

1. Play follows an ordinal developmental sequence.

2. Action is the basis of knowledge, as exemplified in the slow decentration (i.e., decreasing egocentrism) of child play.

3. Representational ("pretend") play has a late onset and slow development.

4. Pretend play shifts from play that involves only the self (e.g., pretending to sleep), through pretense involving self–object relations (e.g., pretending to drink from a cup), to pretense involving objects exclusively (e.g., having a doll pretend to eat).

Piaget's heirs have confirmed many of these observations, but they have also found need for considerable refinement. Play assessments have been operationalized and further elaborated by many different investigators (e.g., Bornstein & O'Reilly, 1993; Bornstein & Tamis-LeMonda, 1995; McCune, 1995; Tamis-LeMonda & Bornstein, 1996; Tamis-LeMonda, Užgiris, & Bornstein, 2002). Assessments vary depending on the use of naturalistic, unstructured free play or modeling and prompting of play with a prespecified set of toys that range in complexity and developmental level in order to "pull" for different levels of play. Some play assessments are also integrated into intervention efforts with special-needs children (e.g., Linder, 1990). These assessments, based on careful, systematic observations of infants' interactions with toys, reveal that the earliest forms of play involve the repetition of actions. Objects in the environment do not play an important role in the child's play during the first 2 or 3 months of life. Three-month-olds, for instance, may coo repeatedly or kick their legs while lying awake in their cribs, or they may arch their backs and drop their bodies onto the mattress over and over again. These actions are recognizable as Piaget's *primary circular reactions*—activities apparently repeated for their own sake (Chapter 7). Even after infants have developed manipulative skills they appear to be primarily interested in the actions they can perform rather than in the objects being manipulated. Thus, very young babies may look at a toy in their field of vision (see Figure 8.6), but rarely scan systematically or study the objects they are playing with; instead they put them into their mouths immediately (see Figure 8.7). Even when two objects appear related to one another—a cup and a spoon—the older infant often focuses on actions—banging the spoon in the cup—rather than on the objects. Remove the spoon, and the action is likely to continue.

At around 9 months of age, a major change in the complexity and quality of infant play seems to occur. Infants begin to engage in what is called *functional*, *relational*, and *functional–relational* play. In relational play, the infant brings together two unrelated objects (e.g., a spoon and a block) with no indication of

FIGURE 8.6
A baby in the earliest stage of play can only look at the toy.

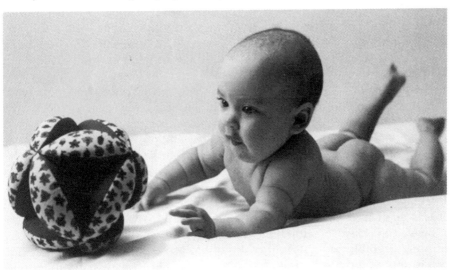

FIGURE 8.7
An infant in a later stage of play mouths the toy.

pretense (see Figure 8.8). Functional play involves playing with an object in the way the object was intended to be played with (e.g., rolling a toy car on its wheels across the floor). Functional–relational play brings together two objects in a meaningful and appropriate way. For example, the child may take a spoon and stir it inside a cup or place blocks inside a container of some sort (see Figure 8.9).

For the next several months, infants show little that resembles clear-cut pretense or symbolic play. According to Piaget, pretense requires bringing to mind a physically absent object, and hence involves representational skills that (he wrote) are not attained until the second year of life. Consistent with this notion, pretend play does not regularly occur until the second year of life, although some infants show this capacity as early as 13 months of age.

Symbolic play can be clearly identified in the second year by the emergence of object substitution. When the young child builds a tower out of blocks, the tower seems to mean more to the child than the characteristics of the blocks per se. There may therefore be two kinds of representation reflected in object substitutions (Leslie, 1988a, 1988b). First, *primary representations* reflect representations of the objects based on their current perception; blocks have substance, shape, and color, and so different blocks may be used for different purposes. There are also *metarepresentations* of the objects comprising representations of objects apart from their normal meaning; assembled, a set of blocks is now a tower. The object substitutions of younger toddlers tend to be restricted by physical resemblance—different colors of blocks—whereas older toddlers are not as dependent on physical characteristics, so blocks may stand for people

FIGURE 8.8
An infant in a still later stage of play may
bring two objects into juxtaposition.

(Pederson, Rook-Green, & Elder, 1981; Ungerer, Zelazo, Kearsley, & O'Leary, 1981). Thus, Ungerer and her colleagues (1981) observed that in the second year toddlers use objects to represent other objects to which they may bear no physical resemblance.

Even when the child is operating at the level of pretense, play initially centers on the child's own body and actions (Belsky & Most, 1981; Fenson & Ramsay, 1980). For instance, children might pretend that they are going to sleep, or they may pretend to drink from a cup or talk on a telephone (see Figure 8.10). It is not until later that the child decenters pretense by beginning to involve objects other than the self. Children may then first pretend to sleep themselves by lying down on a pillow and only later make a doll lie down and sleep. And, even after this decentration has taken place, significant developmental changes lie ahead. McCune-Nicolich (1981c) observed how play becomes more complex with age through the incorporation of combinations and sequences of pretend actions. Older children also make more elaborate plans for future play, as when they play "kitchen" and appear to prepare a whole meal (see Figure 8.11).

We can broadly summarize the development of play. In the first year, play is predominantly characterized by sensorimotor manipulation; infant play appears designed to extract information about objects, what objects do, what perceivable qualities they have, and what immediate effects they can produce. This form of play is commonly referred to as *exploratory*, or *nonsymbolic*, because children's play activities are tied to the tangible properties of objects rather than being representative. In the second year, children's play actions take on more of a nonliteral quality: The goal of play now appears to be *symbolic*, or *representational*. Play is increasingly generative, as children enact activities performed by self,

FIGURE 8.9
A toddler at play can use two objects together
functionally.

others, and objects in simple pretense scenarios, pretending to drink from empty
teacups, to talk on toy telephones, and the like (Bornstein & O'Reilly, 1993;
McCune, 1995; Tamis-LeMonda & Bornstein, 1996).

These two broad developmental stages of play, exploratory and symbolic,
have each been further analyzed into sublevels of sophistication. In nonsymbolic play, actions are at first directed toward a single object: The child squeezes
a foam ball. Then actions incorporate combinations of two or more objects, initially treated inappropriately and later appropriately: The child first juxtaposes
a nesting block with a busy-box and later inserts the block in its appropriately
shaped hole. In symbolic play, pretense schemes are applied to the self before
they are applied to others: The child pretends to drink from a cup before feeding
a doll. Single-scheme pretense appears before multischeme pretense: The child
pretends to drink from a cup and later pretends to pour and drink. Finally, pretense with literal objects precedes pretense with substitution objects: The child
first represents a telephone with a telephone and later uses a stick to represent
a telephone handset.

Table 8.1 shows a single comprehensive scheme of play for infants (Tamis-
LeMonda & Bornstein, 1996). Eight basic play levels are defined, and the table
shows predominant play acts for each level that toddlers of 13 and 20 months
might exhibit, along with an index of the relative frequency of those examples.
The eight play levels are: (1) Unitary functional activity, (2) Inappropriate combinatorial activity, (3) Appropriate combinatorial activity, (4) Transitional play,

FIGURE 8.10
A toddler in a still later stage of play can pretend to
use a telephone.

(5) Self-directed pretense, (6) Other-directed pretense, (7) Sequential pretense, and (8) Substitution pretense. Note that Levels 1 to 4 constitute exploratory play and that Levels 5 to 8 constitute symbolic play. Tamis-LeMonda and Bornstein (1991) assessed the development of these eight play levels in toddlers: They found that more sophisticated forms of play became increasingly common with age among American as well as Japanese infants.

We have introduced the distinction between exploratory (nonsymbolic) and (symbolic) representational play as a guide to the general developmental changes that take place in infancy, but there are also individual differences in the rate at which children achieve representation, and there may be individual differences in children's levels of achievement. The scheme we describe represents the idealized developmental progression: Most children traverse this progression, but children of a given age vary greatly among themselves with respect to, say, their symbolic play. For example, Tamis-LeMonda and Bornstein (1990) found that 15% of 13-month-old toddlers' total play was symbolic, but data on individual toddlers indicated that some never exhibited symbolic play, whereas as much as 51% of the play by others was symbolic. At 20 months, 31% of toddlers' total play was symbolic, but data on individual toddlers indicated that for some as little as 2% was symbolic, whereas for others 83% was symbolic. Furthermore, 13-month symbolic-play levels predicted 20-month symbolic-play levels—toddlers who showed more representational play at 13 months also showed more representational play at

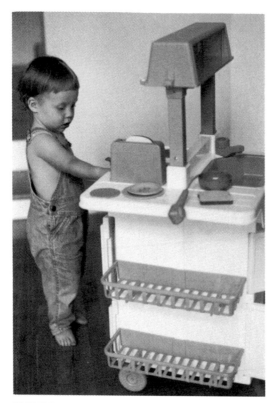

FIGURE 8.11
A toddler in higher stages of play can engage in
sequences of pretense play.

20 months—but this stability was dependent on the supportive roles played
by the mothers.

In overview, much as Piaget proposed, infants transit from undifferentiated
exploratory play not specific to the object manipulated, through functional–
relational play tailored to specific objects, to pretend play with objects or freedom from them altogether. The fact that play is so well studied does not mean
that even fundamental definitions are settled, however, for the discrimination
between play and other activities is difficult (see Rubin, Fein, & Vandenberg,
1983). Nonetheless, McCall (McCall, Eichorn, & Hogarty, 1977; Weisler &
McCall, 1976) has summarized the developmental trajectory as follows:

1.   The object is what I do.

2.   What is this object and what can it do?

3.   What can I do with the object?

Play Development and Social Interaction

"Play is something contented children do when adults are not bothering them
to do other things; and play is something adults tell demanding children to do
to get them out of the way" (Fein, 1991, p. 144). As this statement exemplifies,

TABLE 8.1 TODDLER PLAY LEVELS

Play Level	Definition	Predominant Examples	
		13 Months	*20 Months*
1. Unitary functional activity	Production of an effect that is unique to a single object	Throw or squeeze foam ball (25%)[a]	Dial telephone (21%)
2. Inappropriate combinatorial activity	Inappropriate juxtaposition of two or more objects	Put ball in vehicle[b]	Put ball in vehicle[b]
3. Appropriate combinatorial activity	Appropriate juxtaposition of two or more objects	Put lid on teapot (44%)	Nest blocks (27%)
4. Transitional play	Approximate of pretense but without confirmatory evidence	Put telephone receiver to ear (without vocalization, 44%)	Put telephone receiver to ear (without vocalization, 57%)
5. Self-directed pretense	Clear pretense activity directed toward self	Eat from spoon or cup (39%)	Eat from spoon or cup (36%)
6. Other-directed pretense	Clear pretense activity directed toward other	Kiss or hug doll (41%)	Pretend vehicle makes sound (48%)
7. Sequential pretense	Link of two or more pretense actions	Dial telephone and speak into receiver (45%)	Dial telephone and speak into receiver (30%)
8. Substitution pretense	Pretend activity involving one or more object substitutions	Pretend block is telephone and talk into it[b]	Pretend block is telephone and talk into it[b]

[a] Percentages in parentheses reflect the frequency of the associated example over the total frequency of play acts at that level.
[b] Because any inappropriate combination for Level 2 or any object substitution for Level 8 exemplifies that play level, none dominated.

many early researchers looked at play as a solitary child activity (Fein & Apfel, 1979; Fenson & Ramsay, 1980), whereas Vygotsky (1978) proposed that social interaction fostered symbolic functioning in the individual. The achievement of symbolic play is now seen as a reflection of individual growth in the context of interpersonal interaction and sociocultural context. Indeed, Vygotsky fostered a major conceptual shift in the study of play, regarding it not as a solitary activity reflecting underlying cognitive schema that the child already possessed, but as a formative activity shaped in large measure by the child's interactions with the parent (Smolucha & Smolucha, 1998).

It is quite normal to think of play in the context of social interaction. Play emerges in the child, but adults influence its development by provisioning the play environment, engaging children actively, and responding to their overtures. How does interaction affect play? How does play affect social interaction?

Bornstein, Tamis-LeMonda, and their colleagues have addressed these questions in a series of studies examining infant play in the context of mother–infant interaction. Bornstein, Haynes, O'Reilly, and Painter (1996) found that the social play of 20-month-olds with their mothers was more sophisticated, complex, and varied than the infants' solitary play. Importantly, what the mothers did with their infants during social play with objects appeared to affect the quality of the infants' later object play. Mothers of 20-month-olds who initiated symbolic play at high frequencies had toddlers who also engaged in symbolic play frequently, whether initiated by mother or the child. Similarly, Tamis-LeMonda and Bornstein (1991) and Bornstein, Haynes, Pascual, Painter, and Galperín (1999) reported significant concurrent associations between mothers' and infants' nonsymbolic free play, and between their symbolic free play, when infants were 20 months of age. Mothers and infants thus appear to be attuned to each other during play, with the play level of one partner geared closely to the play level of the other. In addition, individual differences in symbolic play between mothers and infants appear to be stable, at least over the short term (Bornstein, Haynes, Legler, O'Reilly, & Painter, 1997). In two longitudinal studies, Tamis-LeMonda, Bornstein, Baumwell, and Damast (1996) further illustrated that, when attempting to understand how parent–infant interaction shapes infant development over time, it is critical to assess predictive relations within very specific domains of functioning. Thus, maternal responsivity to infant vocalizations predicted later language development, whereas mothers' responsivity to infant play predicted the quality of later play.

Importantly, Tamis-LeMonda, Damast, and Bornstein (1994) found that what mothers know about play and how it develops may predict the degree to which mothers can facilitate the sophistication of their infants' play. Mothers of 21-month-olds were shown an elaboration of the play scale depicted in Table 8.1 and were asked to rank order the items from least to most sophisticated. Generally speaking, mothers recognized that simple exploratory play (e.g., mouthing and simple, nonfunctional manipulation) was less sophisticated than functional play, and that functional play was less sophisticated than symbolic, pretend play. On the other hand, there was much variability in the mothers' ratings; some mothers had more accurate knowledge of play sophistication than others. These accuracy differences, in turn, predicted the degree to which the mothers successfully "scaffolded" their toddlers' play. That is, mothers who had an accurate knowledge of play tended to prompt their children to play at a more sophisticated level than did mothers with less accurate knowledge. Thus, the more parents know about play and how it develops, the more they may actually foster their infants' play during daily interactions.

Evidence for social–interactional determinants of play quality in infancy also comes from many quarters. For example, mothers' ability to time and attune their emotional displays appropriately to their infants' emotional states during face-to-face exchanges in the first year of life predict toddlers' symbolic play at 24 months of age (Feldman & Greenbaum, 1997), suggesting that successful emotional signaling and responsivity in the first year may lay the foundation for later symbolic development. In a longitudinal study of mother–infant play interaction, Stilson and Harding (1997) found that, when mothers responded to their 18-month-olds' object play in an "options-promoting" manner (i.e., encouraging, affirming, and/or expanding on the child's activities), the children engaged in significantly higher levels of symbolic play at 40 months of age than did children whose mothers responded in an "options-limiting" manner (i.e., disapproving of or obstructing the child's play). Clearly, both holistic characteristics of parenting (quality of emotional attunement) as well as parents' specific behaviors during play with their infants affect play competence in infancy and beyond.

Culture, Social Context, and Play

Research on developmental milestones and individual variation in emerging play, as well as research on parental mediators and correlates of individual variation in play, have been based almost exclusively on investigations in Western families. Such a monocultural emphasis restricts our understanding of early development because those characteristics of growth—in this instance play in infancy—that are universal cannot be distinguished from those that are culturally specific (Rogoff, 1993; Rogoff, Mistry, Gönçu, & Mosier, 1993; Roopnarine, Lasker, Sacks, & Stores, 1998). In some cultures, for example, play is viewed as predominantly a child's activity (e.g., Mayan and tribal Indian cultures), whereas other cultures assign an important role to the parent as a play partner (e.g., middle-income U.S. culture). Differences between cultures also exist in views about the value of play. Some cultures, for example, believe that play provides important development-promoting experiences. Others see play functioning primarily to amuse (Tamis-LeMonda & Bornstein, 1996). Presumably, cultural beliefs about play may affect the nature and frequency of infants' play with parents, siblings, and peers.

Bornstein, Tamis-LeMonda, and colleagues also engaged in a series of cross-cultural studies of mother–infant play in the United States, Argentina, and Japan (Bornstein, Azuma, Tamis-LeMonda, & Ogino, 1990; Bornstein, Haynes, Pascual, et al., 1999; Tamis-LeMonda, Bornstein, Cyphers, Toda, & Ogino, 1992). Japan represents a provocative base for comparison with America in this respect because these two countries maintain reasonably similar levels of modernity and living standards, and both are child centered, but at the same time the two differ dramatically in terms of history, culture, beliefs, and childrearing goals, as well as in the activities mothers in each country emphasize in interactions with young infants and children. In general, American mothers are believed to promote autonomy and organize social interactions so as to foster physical and verbal assertiveness in children, as well as interest in the external environment, whereas Japanese mothers organize social interactions so as to consolidate and strengthen mutual dependence within the dyad (LeVine, 1997; Rothbaum et al., 2000).

Generally speaking, Japanese infants and mothers tend to engage in more symbolic play than their American counterparts, and American mothers tend to engage in more exploratory play. Moreover, the differential emphasis by Japanese mothers on symbolic play is specifically reflected in increased levels of demonstrating and solicitation of other-directed pretense. Thus, in line with the common cultural characterization, Japanese mothers organize infant-directed pretense play in ways that encourage incorporation of a partner into play. Japanese mothers encourage interactive (other-directed) pretense ("Feed the dolly"), whereas American mothers encourage self-exploration at functional and combinatorial play levels ("Push the bus"). Childrearing practices in Japan emphasize closeness and interdependency between dyad members, whereas Americans encourage interest in the environment and interpersonal independence supplemented by information-oriented verbal interactions. For Americans, play and the toys used during play are more frequently the topic or object of communication; by contrast, the play setting and associated toys appear to mediate dyadic communication and interaction among the Japanese. This functional contrast is reflected prominently in the differential use of specific levels of play by mothers in these two societies.

It quite difficult to study play in a social context, but this setting also gives play credibility and ecological validity in child development. As a result, researchers have struggled harder to study play and its development in everyday contexts. One such endeavor concerns the role of *scripts*. Much of our thinking about the very young child's astuteness in symbolic play—the tea party or the racetrack—may be disabused by a closer consideration of the child's everyday routines and the incremental developments in representation that spring from them. That is, the child's earliest mental representations of events in everyday life reflect something about common routines acquired through repeated direct experience with the world (Fivush, 1997). These representations are ordered in complexity, and higher order representations depend for their elaboration on representations of simple initial ones (Halford, 1999). Thus, the child's early experiences, their richness and consistency, inform the content and functioning of the child's later representations.

An *event* is an interaction that is often utilitarian in nature; it has a goal. Such interactions consist of temporal and causal behavioral sequences that typically have a beginning, middle, and end. The entire sequence may also be labeled. For the infant, he or she cries, and the mother responds verbally or prepares a bottle or breast and feeds. For the toddler, the routine of "going shopping" begins with making a list, going out, selecting items at the supermarket, and ends with putting them away or even making dinner. On this account, parents are highly influential in the development of basic event representations for the child. The mother may organize the child's environment and time so that daily events are consistent and predictable; she may regulate the child's behavior when engaging in them; she may verbally label them before, during, and after; and she may show how simple events map onto other larger daily activities and goals. Having both the nondeclarative, procedural knowledge (how to carry out an event) as well as the declarative, explicit knowledge (the actual label for the event) should facilitate the child's retrieval of actions embodied in the event representation.

Representation Reconsidered

Play clearly changes dramatically during infancy, developing from exploration and functional manipulation toward more sophisticated acts of differentiated pretense. At the same time, infants exhibit equally rapid increases in related spheres of development. For example, toddlers begin to say and to understand sound sequences that function as true naming as they shift away from the context-restricted use of words and phrases to more flexible use across contexts (see Chapter 9). Over the same period, moreover, sustained attention becomes longer, more controlled, and more focused, as toddlers make rapid strides in coordinating attention and in disregarding extraneous environmental intrusions on the focus of their attention (see Chapter 6).

Several investigators have examined competencies across these seemingly diverse domains of development—play, language, and attention—within the same populations of children. Some have studied language and play (e.g., Bornstein, Tamis-LeMonda, & Haynes, 1999; Stevens, Blake, Vitale, & MacDonald, 1998) under the assumption that language and play are different manifestations of a common representational substrate. Other investigators have studied links between play and attention (Morgan, MacTurk, & Hrncir, 1995). In general, they find that advances in play and language go together, as do advances in play and attention.

Wolf and Gardner (1981) provided an example of play–language relations. They followed a small group of young children longitudinally and observed the emergence of two styles. One group of children, called *patterners*, focused their play on the object world, particularly physical characteristics and spatial arrangements of objects and toys in two- and three-dimensional arrays. The early vocabulary of patterners was characterized by names for objects, animals, and locations. The other group of children, called *dramatists*, was more involved with social play. They preferred to reproduce aspects of interaction in their symbolic play, and they elected to use materials (telephones and puppets) in interpersonal activities. Dramatists had more early words that were expressions of feeling and names, and later words that stood for emotions, moods, and the like. In the field of language development, as we will see in Chapter 9, developmental psycholinguists have formally distinguished between *referential* and *expressive toddlers*, namely, those who have many words for things as opposed to those who use language in the service of social interaction.

Tamis-LeMonda and Bornstein (1990) designed a study to assess infants' language, play competence, and attention span in order to examine interrelations among these three important areas of competence in the same children. It could be that individual differences in children are consistent in language, play, and attention, and therefore relations among these domains are global. In this case, a single representational process might underlie individual variation among children in these seemingly divergent areas. Or, it could be that associations among these three domains are more differentiated and that only certain pairs of abilities go together. This would suggest that different underlying representational processes are at work in early mental development. Data on language, play, and attention in 13-month-olds were all collected during a single home visit. An indication of the toddlers' language comprehension was obtained from a maternal language inventory, and children's play competence and attention span were coded from a videotape of the play session. Maternal stimulation was also coded from the same videotape. Infant play competence and language comprehension go together, as do play competence and attention span. Children who are good at one proved good at the other. However, language comprehension did not relate to attention span. Children who were good at one were not necessarily good at the other. These associations obtained even when the contribution of maternal stimulation was eliminated from consideration.

The pattern of associations obtained supports an emerging consensus that language and play skills reflect one kind of underlying capacity for representation that itself emerges during late infancy. Researchers have long emphasized the common representational nature of flexible language and pretense play. In both, people, experiences, and actions can be symbolically depicted. The observed coemergence of pretense play and flexible language at the start of the second year, along with the observed association between the rankings of individual infants on play and language proficiency, lend empirical support to the notion that a single cognitive component might underlie these two domains. Notably, this representational competence is stable in infants between 13 and 20 months (Tamis-LeMonda & Bornstein, 1991). Children's play competence is associated with their language comprehension, and it is independently associated with their attention span. To this point, we have followed the association between play and language. But what of the association between play and attention span? The observed pattern of associations points to the inherent multidimensional nature of play. In the second year of life, play might be partitioned into (at least) two independent components—a "play-language" factor and a "play-attention" factor—that reflect different underlying mental capacities in the toddler. Although these two factors share the same index of children's play sophistication, they are independent of one another, and a high level of ability in one domain does not automatically imply a high ability level in another.

Of course, child's play does not solely reflect mental representation. Many researchers have suggested that play depends on motivational as well as other factors (Dichter-Blancher, Busch-Rossnagel, & Knauf-Jensen, 1997; Harmon & Morgan, 1999; MacTurk & Morgan, 1995). Thus, *mastery motivation* might help us understand the side of play competence that relates strictly to attention. In fact, the motivation to master the environment often results in longer periods of object exploration (i.e., attention) and therefore increased competence in ongoing play (Barrett & Morgan, 1995).

As we noted in Chapter 7, Piaget (1952) believed that a moderate degree of discrepancy between an external stimulus and the child's representation provokes a state of disequilibrated arousal that the child needs to reduce through physical or mental activity. Children derive pleasure from such activity, but the achievement of equilibrium or mastery also results in satisfaction, joy, or efficacy. These positive affective reactions presumably reinforce mastery efforts and promote future mastery activity. Some theorists suggest that infants might even be intrinsically motivated to engage in simple behaviors such as looking at and grasping objects (White, 1959), and they have studied individual differences and the degree to which this motive may be identified in infant behavior (MacTurk, Morgan, & Jennings, 1995). Other theorists assume that individual differences in mastery motivation may be explained by parents' behavior toward their children in the early years. From this perspective, perhaps, adult reactions to young children's efforts at mastery may have important implications for children's persistence at becoming competent. For example, intrusive, controlling parenting may deflate infants' motivation for mastery, whereas parenting that sensitively scaffolds and supports infant play is likely to promote it (Busch-Rossnagel, Knauf-Jensen, & DesRosiers, 1995; Kelley & Brownell, 2000).

Wachs (1987; Wachs & Combs, 1995) distinguished at least three forms of mastery motivation in infancy:

1. *Object mastery* is concerned with physical tasks.

2. *Social mastery* is concerned with maintaining and influencing social interactions.

3. *Social-object mastery* is concerned with using objects in adult–infant interactions.

In Wachs' view, object and social mastery are independent constructs. Different aspects of the environment predicted different forms of mastery motivation: Wachs obtained positive correlations between the physical structure of the 1-year-old child's environment and laboratory assessments of object mastery. Parental interference during play with objects was associated with reduced object mastery, whereas parental object naming, showing, and demonstrating were positively associated with social-object mastery.

The kind of representation discussed in this chapter is circumscribed to infant play and hardly approximates the full-blown, dramatic pretense so often observed in children after infancy. In older toddlers and young children, play extends into emotional and more intricate social concerns. For example, psychoanalysts like Erikson (1977) proposed that pretense is appealing to young children because it permits them to deal with otherwise deeply emotional concerns involving fear, abandonment, and violation. This kind of pretense allows emotionally charged material to be approached and processed with a certain amount of control. Full-blown dramatic pretense spills over into clinical and therapy issues well-known in other spheres of psychology (Woolgar, 1999). Pretense is the forum in which children may create and rework symbolic representations that are charged with deep emotional meanings.

In summary, we have described infants' solitary play with objects and infant play in the context of social interaction with parents and as a reflection of broader cultural themes and values. Solitary play with objects in infancy is believed to be a window on cognitive level, with play proceeding in the first year of life from simple manipulation and mouthing to functional activities that exploit objects' unique properties. In the second year of life, infants increasingly engage in symbolic, pretend forms of play that, along with the growth of language at this time, reflects the further development, refinement, and elaboration of representational capacities. Play clearly has social, emotional, attentional, and mastery components and does not develop in isolation; indeed, it is fostered during social interactions with parents when parents are attuned to their infant's emotional cues and developmental level.

Summary

In this chapter, we reviewed what is known about three prominent forms of mental representation in infancy. Infancy itself represents a period in which central mental abilities, such as categorization and concept formation, memory, and pretend play emerge and develop. Representation stands for the information that is stored in the head. How that information is stored, the nature of that information, its availability, and its use are the central concerns of this chapter. Our understanding of cognition in all its forms depends on our understanding of the nature of mental representations. Studies of representational abilities inform us about the developing capacity to acquire, share, and use information about the environment. To understand the foundations and mechanisms that underpin mental growth in childhood we must understand representation in its several forms, including categorization and concept formation, memory, and play. Each reflects important (and perhaps related) mental processes, although each is also quite complex and multifactorial. In this chapter we treated the topics of categorization and concept formation, memory, and play separately, and discussed them largely independent of cognition and language. However, these are artificial distinctions because all these processes are integrally interrelated. Clearly, the infant has a rich mental life, and our study of the mental life of the infant is still at a frontier.

The transition from sensorimotor behavior to linguistic intelligence is awe-inspiring. This process is well ordered and universal, and the achievement impressive, building as it does on representation in the forms of categorization and concept formation, memory, and play.

9

Origins of Language
in Infancy

———— ❖ ————

- What are the three levels or domains of infant language development?
- Distinguish between production and comprehension of language.
- What does the study of norms in infant language development tell us?
- What does the study of quantitative and qualitative individual differences in infant language development tell us?
- Give examples of how physical, perceptual, cognitive, and social development aid infant language acquisition.
- Briefly discuss the three major ways we gain knowledge about infants' acquisition of language.
- What is "infant-directed speech" and name some of its main characteristics.
- What are similarities and differences between hearing and deaf infants' language learning?
- What is "reference," and how do babies master it?
- What is the significance of the context-restricted to context-flexible shift in semantic development?
- Give evidence of nativist and empiricist accounts of infant word learning.
- Give evidence of nativist and empiricist accounts of infants learning grammar.

The Building Blocks of Communication

Our generic terms *infant* and *baby* both have their origins in language-related concepts. The word *infant* derives from the Latin *in + fans*, translated literally as "nonspeaker," and the word baby shares a Middle English root with *babble*. In the estimation of many, children only leave infancy when they begin to communicate verbally with those around them. As we shall see in this chapter, however, "conversations" with babies begin well before words come into consideration.

Language lies at the nexus of impressive accomplishments in the perceptual, cognitive, and social spheres of development. Human language is also a very complicated matter to study, for it simultaneously involves several overlapping levels of analysis. Sounds that are to be linguistically meaningful must be produced and perceived, according to the *phonology* (sound structure) of the

279

language. The *semantics*, or *meaning*, of words and phrases must be learned, as well as the *syntax* or *grammar* of the language, which defines the ways in which words and phrases are structured and arranged in order to ensure meaningful communication. Consider a toddler's task in understanding mother's meaning when she says simply, "Yourteddyislyingonthecouchsweetie." The child must segregate the sound stream into individual word forms, understand what each word means, and analyze the grammatical structure linking the word forms. To complicate matters further, these three types of decoding must take place simultaneously as the speech is heard. Nevertheless, however complex, abstract, and formidable language is, the cognitively immature child rapidly becomes facile in both understanding and speaking.

Some theoreticians have argued that language learning proceeds strictly on the basis of the child's experiences: St. Augustine (398/1961) wrote that children learn language by imitating their elders, and B.F. Skinner (1957) argued that children learn language just as they do any system of behavioral contingencies— through reinforcement. In contrast, other theorists have asserted that language acquisition could only develop on innate biological grounds (Bickerton, 1990; Chomsky, 1965; Jakobson, 1968; Lenneberg, 1967). However, language is surely too rich, unique, and complex a system for the infant simply to "learn" passively, just as it is too rich, unique, and complex a system for the newborn simply to "know." One observer of the historical give-and-take between these nurture and nature views of the origins of language dubbed this "the debate between the impossible and the miraculous."

In this chapter we describe how children develop from nonverbal individualists into interactive conversationalists, willing and able to articulate their cares, needs, desires, and dreams to others. We start with a brief consideration of norms and individual variation of verbal development, along with some important principles related to the mechanics of studying early language. We then turn to discuss how infants' experiences complement their capacities by channeling the development of communication toward increasingly effective interactions and integration into the social world. Next, we take up production and comprehension in the three levels of language. In this central part of the chapter we show how anatomical and sensory capacities of the infant relate to producing and perceiving the sound aspects of language; we examine theory and data on how children begin to acquire semantic forms and how they match function in early language growth; and, we discuss the rudiments of grammatical expression and understanding. As we shall see, infants are surprisingly prepared in each of these realms, possessing both the motivation and the competencies to ensure that they quickly become full linguistic participants. The acquisition of language reflects a complex interaction between the child's developing competencies and the larger context of adult–infant social communication.

Language Norms and Methods of Study

Figure 9.1 depicts in a simplified format some milestones of language development in infancy. In the first month of life, infants coo and babble; by their twenty-fourth month, toddlers generate grammatically correct sentences. In the first month, infants respond to the human voice; by their twenty-fourth month, toddlers comprehend the meaning of prepositions. The very existence of this chart reflects the strong normative tradition in the field of "developmental

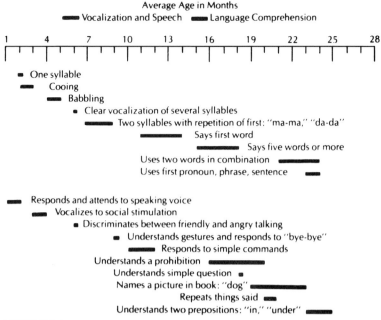

FIGURE 9.1

Approximate age norms for the development of expression and comprehension in infants over the first 2½ years of life. At the top are examples of the time periods when different kinds of vocalization and speech first appear. At the bottom are analogous milestones for language comprehension.

psycholinguistics," the popularity of description, and the fundamental distinction between production and comprehension in language study. However, it also masks a central everyday consideration of individual differences.

Comprehension and Production

When examining child language, it is first necessary to distinguish between comprehension and production. If you play with a 1-year-old, you might notice that the child can follow your instructions well but cannot tell you anything about the simple game he or she is playing so artfully. Comprehension nearly always precedes production developmentally (see Darwin, 1877, Box 3.1). For example, Benedict (1979) listed the first 50 words comprehended and produced by infants. Infants first understood words at 9 months but didn't say any until 12 months, on average, and comprehension reached a 50-word milestone at around 13 months, whereas production reached this point at 18 months. As we shall see, though, the story is not so simple. These averages do not reflect the tremendous variability among children, and neither comprehension nor production are all-or-nothing affairs. In the latter half of the second year, many children exhibit rapid increases in both productive and receptive language. The source and nature of this "vocabulary burst" have been the focus of debate. One observation relevant to understanding the vocabulary burst is that productive and receptive vocabularies increase together. Children who comprehend more words are also likely to produce more words (Bates, Bretherton, & Snyder, 1988; Bretherton & Bates,

1984; Snyder, Bates, & Bretherton, 1981; Vibbert & Bornstein, 1989), and this is true in the United States as well as in Japan (Tamis-LeMonda, Bornstein, Cyphers, Toda, & Ogino, 1990). Although the statistical association between productive and receptive vocabularies is not always strong, this link indicates that acceleration in word learning rates is not simply a consequence of improvement in articulation; rather, some aspect of word understanding is implicated. Perhaps vocabularies take off as soon as children realize that things have names. On occasion this epiphany is witnessed by parents, as their little son or daughter suddenly seems to "get it" and begins labeling objects and learning words with abandon (Kamhi, 1986).

However, the expansion in vocabulary does not always have this sudden character. For most children, the rate of word learning does indeed increase a great deal in the second year, but this increase does not necessarily begin with a sudden leap; children seem to gradually get better and better at word learning (Bates & Carnevale, 1993). This is likely to be due to a wide range of cognitive changes, including improvements in interpreting continuous speech (Fernald, Pinto, Swingley, Weinberg, & McRoberts, 1998; Plunkett, 1993), development of categorization skills (Gopnik & Meltzoff, 1987a), and greater appreciation of the pragmatics of language use (Ninio, 1995). On this view, children's conscious notion of what language is for, including the naming insight, is just one of the many cognitive developments that result in better and faster word learning.

Individual Variation

Children of the same age vary dramatically among themselves on nearly every index of language development, and individual differences in children's language, as well as their sources of variation, occupy a central position in the study of language acquisition (Bates & Carnevale, 1993; Goldfield & Snow, 1989; Thal & Bates, 1990). Perhaps the classic illustration of individual differences in early language production was provided by Brown (1973), who traced speech development in three children—Adam, Eve, and Sarah; he indexed their verbal growth in terms of changing mean length of utterance (discussed later). Figure 9.2 shows that all three children achieved common goals and that growth rates were nearly equivalent among them. However, Eve began considerably earlier than did Adam or Sarah, and Eve appears to make the same progress from 19 to 27 months that Adam and Sarah make from 26 to 42 months. For example, Eve used an average of three utterances at about 2 years of age, whereas Adam and Sarah did not do so until approximately 3 years of age—one third of their lifetimes later.

Snyder and her colleagues (1981) studied the range of one-word vocabularies among 13-month-olds: Comprehension ranged from 11 to 97 words, and production from 0 to 45 words. Tamis-LeMonda and Bornstein (1990, 1991) also studied comprehension and production of words longitudinally between 13 and 20 months, looking in particular at those words infants could use or understand without immediate environmental cues (so-called context flexible vocabularies). At 13 months, some toddlers comprehended 10 words, others 75; some produced 0 words, others 27. At 20 months, individual toddlers ranged from 8 to 434 words in their productive vocabularies. This study also looked at a variety of other verbal abilities at 20 months. The average length in morphemes (meaningful units of speech, such as *jump* and *ing* in *jumping*) of children's longest utterances was 2.6; however, some children only expressed single-morpheme utterances, whereas

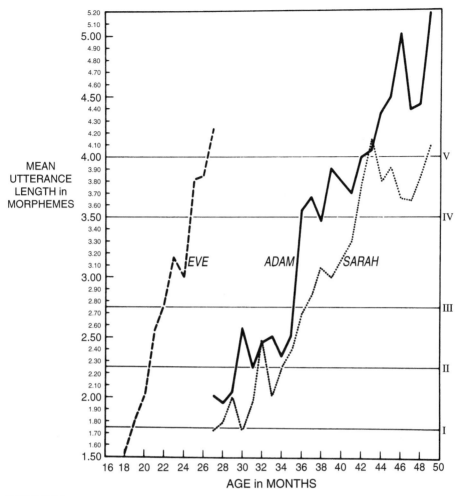

FIGURE 9.2

Mean utterance length by age in three children. (After Brown, 1973. © 1971 by Harvard University Press. Reprinted with permission.)

others linked over 5 morphemes. Children also varied in their use of different pragmatic categories—topics such as actor, action, possession, recipient, rejection/objection, and playful routine, with some children using only 3 and others using as many as 15. Over the second year, there is also a fair amount of consistency within individual children: 13-month productive vocabulary size predicts 20-month productive vocabulary size, grammar, and pragmatic diversity, and 13-month language comprehension predicts 20-month pragmatic diversity. That is, those children who had high scores on these measures also had high scores at 20 months, and those with lower scores continued to have lower scores when they were older.

This work exemplifies a quantitative approach to studying individual differences in infants' language acquisition. Other investigators have endeavored to capture the qualitative variation in very young children's speech. Following Halliday (1975), Nelson (1981) hypothesized a continuum of verbal styles of production in the second year of life. At one end are *referential* ("analytic" or "code-oriented") children, whose early vocabularies are marked by a high proportion of object labels and whose speech is organized around providing information. (Perhaps they are the "patterners" we discussed in Chapter 8.) At the other end of the continuum are *expressive* ("Gestalt" or "message-oriented") children, whose early vocabularies comprise relatively more pronouns and action words, and whose speech is marked by social formulae and routines intended to communicate feelings and desires. (They may be the "dramatists.") Goldfield (1985/1986) provided a descriptive account of two children who represent lexical extremes in the study of early word learning. She videotaped the children at play with their mothers at home at 12, 15, and 18 months of age. Johanna was a prototypical referential child. Of Johanna's first 50 words, 49 were names for things. In play, approximately half of her attempts to engage her mother involved her giving or showing a toy, and reciprocally Johanna's mother consistently labeled toys for her. Talk about toys was the most frequent category of maternal speech, and naming was a frequent strategy. Caitlin was a prototypical expressive child. Nearly two thirds of Caitlin's first 50 words consisted of social expressions, many of them in phrases. She included a toy in less than one fifth of her bids to her mother, preferring instead to engage in routines of social play. These two styles of communicating appear to function differently for children: For referential youngsters the purposes of language are to label, describe, and exchange information, whereas for expressive youngsters language is to denote or confirm activity.

Clearly, Caitlin and Johanna are extremes; most children exhibit a more balanced picture of referential and expressive speech, and differences between them are therefore "a matter of degree" (Bretherton, McNew, Snyder, & Bates, 1983). In fact, a given child may sometimes look referential and at other times look expressive, depending on demands of the situation—book reading may call for a more referential style, whereas social games call for an expressive style (Peters, 1997). It is also not entirely clear at present just how this continuum is related to other dimensions of variation in children's linguistic styles.

Lieven, Pine, and Barnes (1992) have suggested that the referential/ expressive distinction might best be characterized in terms of whether children tend to use single words or unanalyzed "frozen" phrases (like "That's mine"). They argue that the single-word children (who have also been described as analytical) will go on to produce multiword utterances by combining the words they know into new combinations, whereas the frozen-phrase children will begin producing multiword speech by varying the phrases they know, for example, by moving from "That's mine" to "That's yours."

Individual variation in language ability probably has several sources. Some developmental psycholinguists have argued that different children may have different cognitive organizations that underpin individual differences, such as the referential–expressive distinction (Nelson, 1973b). For example, children may differ in their hypotheses about what language is for—to categorize objects or to talk about one's self. However, it seems likely that different "hypotheses" of this kind have their roots in how parents and infants interact, rather than innate biases that differ among children. As we will see later in the chapter, variation in several aspects of communication between parents and children has been associated with the size and composition of children's vocabularies.

The maturational status and physical integrity of the infant appear to play a part in language development. Over the first 5 years of life, high-risk preterm children yield a consistent (if slight) lag in the achievement of most stages of language development relative to those born at term (Largo, Molinari,

Comendale-Pinto, Weber, & Duc, 1986). Expectedly, preterm children with cerebral palsy are even more delayed. Birth weight and gestational age are negatively associated with language development across the first 5 years of life. Siegel (1982a, 1982b) showed that, for preterm infants, severity of illness in the perinatal period was among the most robust predictors of language comprehension and expression at age 3 years.

A Note on Methods of Language Study

To understand how language learning proceeds, it would seem very easy—and ultimately valid—simply to observe, record, and analyze what children themselves appear to understand and naturally say as they grow up. Indeed, until relatively recently virtually all studies in developmental psycholinguistics used naturalistic observational methods. In adopting the observational strategy, of course, the researcher has to decide how long and how frequently to listen to the child in order to be satisfied that the child's language skills have been sampled adequately.

In addition, pictures of a child's verbal abilities may differ depending on the social and physical contexts of observation. Every parent has lamented his or her young child's not saying something with a stranger, or even a grandparent, that the same child says often when with the parent alone. Thus, whether the child is recorded when alone, with a friend or strange adult, or interacting with parents can make a difference in estimating the child's language activity. Furthermore, free play with parents will elicit one set of linguistic skills from children, whereas structured interaction (say, while eating or learning) can be expected to elicit quite a different set. The physical setting therefore constitutes another potentially influential, but often neglected, factor in language assessment (Belsky, 1980; Bornstein, Haynes, Painter, & Genevro, 2000; Bornstein, Tamis-LeMonda, & Haynes, 1999; Stevenson, Leavitt, Roach, Chapman, & Miller, 1986). One study compared naturalistic samples of three features of language in 2-year-olds—total utterances, word roots, and MLU—in the home in three contrasting situations: the child observed playing by her/himself with mother near by, the child and mother observed in direct play interaction, and the child and mother unobserved at a time the mother judged would provide a sample of the child's "optimal" language (Bornstein, Painter, & Park, 2002). Children produced more utterances and word roots and expressed themselves in longer MLU when in interaction than when playing alone, but children's utterances, word roots, and MLU were greatest in the optimal language production situation.

Elicited production techniques have been widely used to complement transcripts of children's spontaneous speech. The general idea is to set up a situation that increases the likelihood of children using a given word or sentence construction, either by directly asking children to say something or by providing toys or other aids that tend to elicit the desired kinds of comments. This is a useful technique because the constructions tested might be rare or absent in diary data, but nevertheless a part of children's productive ability. Also, the tested constructions can use words invented by the experimenter to be certain that the child's response is not simply an imitation of something he or she heard before. For example, Tomasello and Brooks (1998) taught 24-month-olds invented verbs in transitive (with a direct object) sentences, such as "The ball is dacking the car," and in intransitive sentences (no direct object, such as "The ball is dacking").

Children were later asked, "What is the ball doing", to see if they would use the verb transitively in new sentences ("Dacking the house"). Children who had been taught the verb in intransitive sentences almost never used it transitively, suggesting that 2-year-olds are conservative in using verbs in novel syntactic constructions.

Another strategy used to assess beginning language competence in babies employs parents as reporters, and much of the classic information about language development has been obtained from parental diaries (e.g., Bloom, 1976; Dromi, 1987; Leopold, 1949; Weir, 1962). As sources of information, diaries can be quite detailed, informative, and thought provoking, although they may also be biased and describe unrepresentative children (Miller, 1981; see our discussion of baby biographies in Chapter 3). Instead of having parents report their own spontaneous and sometimes idiosyncratic impressions, interviews can be conducted (Tamis-LeMonda & Bornstein, 2002). An interviewer might ask parents if the child understands and produces specific words. A modern comprehensive variant of this method is the structured parental report. Language checklists offer advantages over traditional diary methods in the same way that recognition facilitates memory over recall. Two widely used instruments are *The Clinical Linguistic and Auditory Milestone Scale* (CLAMS; Capute et al., 1986; Capute, Shapiro, Wachtel, Gunther, & Palmer, 1986) and the *MacArthur Communicative Development Inventories* (MCDI; Fenson, Dale, Reznick, Hartung, & Burgess, 1990; see Maital, Dromi, Sagi, & Bornstein, 2000).

How well do measures of child language derived from these three sources, including observations of the child's speech with mother, experimenter assessments, and maternal reports, agree? Bornstein and Haynes (1998) studied a total of 184 20-month-olds and their mothers to address this question. In fact, strong relations among child language measures derived from observations of the child's speech with mother, experimenter assessments, and maternal reports emerged. Those children who use more words and longer utterances in everyday speech with their mothers were those whom experimenters assessed as comprehending and being able to produce more vocabulary, and they were also the children whose mothers independently reported and rated that they know and speak in more sophisticated ways.

The fact that children generally understand more than they can say means that much language development occurs "underground": Children's discoveries about language are not automatically reflected in what they say to us. This has important methodological consequences even in the study of children's speech: If a child says, "bap," for *bottle*, is it because she does not know how *bottle* sounds, or because she cannot perfectly produce the word she perceives? In recent years investigators have used a number of methods to help uncover some of infants' "underground" developments and have substantially refined traditional techniques based on analysis of children's speech.

Some of these are referred to as *preference methods*. Preference methods in speech research ultimately derive from Fantz, who (as you will recall from Chapter 6) was interested in visual development. In his studies, the fact that infants preferred to look at one panel (a set of thin stripes) rather than another (a plain gray field) indicated that infants could see the difference between them; infants' acuity was good enough to spot the lines. Of course, you can't tell what an infant is listening to by checking where his ears are pointing; to study infants' attention to sounds, a trick is required. This trick is to make presentation of sounds contingent on infants' looking behavior: while infants look in a particular direction, they hear something; when they look away, the sounds stop. Thus, infants can control how long they listen to a stimulus, just as Fantz's infants controlled how long they looked at the visual displays. In the first studies using this *headturn preference method*, infants' preference itself was of interest. For example, Fernald (1985) found that 4-month-olds preferred to listen to "infant-directed" speech, over "adult-directed" speech, possibly because infants responded to it emotionally (see the next section). In many subsequent studies, researchers were less interested in preferences per se than in the fact that infants would demonstrate (via listening times) that they had distinguished different sets of speech sounds. Jusczyk and Aslin (1995) played 8-month-olds lists of words (dog...dog...dog...cup...cup...cup...) and then tested their preference for little stories that contained these words or that contained *feet* and *bike* instead. Children preferred the stories with the familiar words. (Other children heard "feet...feet...bike..." and preferred the "feet–bike" stories.) The important result was that young children could recognize words in continuous speech; the fact that they happened to prefer the familiar-word passages rather than the unfamiliar-word passages was only of incidental interest.

One of the disadvantages of some of these experimental methods, including the auditory preference procedures used with infants, is that relatively little information is learned about each child—typically just one number, the difference between his or her listening times to one type of speech and another type of speech. As a result, these methods are not well suited to the study of individual differences. In most studies, groups of infants are evaluated, and conclusions can be drawn over these groups (for example, 6-month-olds may behave one way, 8-month-olds another). Thus, although auditory preference tasks have been uniquely informative about the earliest stages of language learning, they have not been able to tell us much about differences between children at a given age.

A second preference method whose use is becoming increasingly widespread is (somewhat confusingly) referred to as *preferential looking*. This task is used to evaluate children's *understanding* of words and other linguistic structures. The idea is simple: Children see two pictures or movies side by side (such as a ball and a car). Then an experimenter (or a recording) says something about one of the pictures (such as "Where's the ball?"). A number of studies have shown that even 12-month-olds will look more at the named picture than the distracter picture (Hollich et al., 2000). This technique is useful for studying the process of word learning: first a word is taught for a novel object, and then recognition of this word is tested using preferential looking. It is also possible to determine how quickly infants can recognize words, by carefully measuring how much time elapses between the beginning of the spoken word and the beginning of the infant's eye movement from the distracter picture to the named picture (Fernald et al., 1989).

Another methodological advance in studying early language has been to make high-quality recordings of infants' speech and then analyze these recordings. Some careful studies have shown that children's early production of speech is more sophisticated than it sounds. For example, when children first start saying words, they may fail to make certain distinctions clear; a child might seem to pronounce the *p* and *b* at the beginnings of words in exactly the same way. This suggests that children fail to notice the distinction when they hear *p* and *b* words. However, analyses of recordings of children's attempts at *p* and *b* sounds (and related contrasts such as *t* vs. *d* and *k* vs. *g*) have revealed a developmental period in which some children do make the sounds differently, but not differently enough for adults to hear the distinction clearly (e.g., Macken & Barton, 1980). The theoretical message of this study is that children's learning of these distinctions cannot be due to adult reinforcement because adults can hardly hear children's initial improvements. The methodological message is that our naked ears may underestimate what children know. This echoes a theme that has arisen again and again in the study of language development: The roots of complex behaviors may be discovered long before those behaviors are clear and overt, and many capacities that seem to bloom overnight have in fact been gestating for months.

In summary, a wide range of methods is available for the study of infant language development. The choice of methods depends on the questions to be answered and (to some extent) the ages of the infants to be tested. In the study of infants under about 12 months, experimental designs are available for characterizing trends in learning over groups of children. A wider variety of options is available for research on children's speech: intensive analyses of children's spontaneous speech, elicited production tasks, and parental interviews have been used. The most reliable information comes from the use of several measurement techniques together, to get around the limitations of individual techniques. One general conclusion that may be drawn is that, although there are "milestones" of language development that nearly all children pass, there are vast individual differences among children in when these milestones are reached and, to some extent, what path children follow in reaching them.

Synchrony in Speech

Infants obviously come very far very fast in acquiring the complex and symbolic system that is language. In the task of learning the different constituents of language, the child is neither ill equipped nor alone, however. In this section, we examine some of the sophisticated elements of language that infants and their caregivers bring to the acquisition process. Here we focus on infant-directed speech, turn taking, gesture, and dynamic sensitivity to illustrate this parent–infant synchrony. By synchrony, we mean true interaction, continual adjustment, and mutual accommodation. In the description that follows, we decompose the dyad and alternate between baby and mother for descriptive purposes only; baby and mother always communicate with one another.

Infant-Directed Speech

As we learned in Chapter 6, infants possess innate perceptual propensities and capacities, however primitive, that aid language learning. Moreover, even in the womb they hear and process more than mere bits of sound and pieces of language. Relatedly, parents repackage the language aimed at infants to match presumed or evaluated infant capacities. This synchrony is thought to facilitate language acquisition.

Specifically, mothers, fathers, caregivers, and even older children adopt a special dialect when addressing infants, called variously baby talk, motherese, parentese, or more neutrally *infant-directed speech*. The special characteristics of infant-directed speech include: prosodic features (higher pitch, greater range of frequencies, more varied and exaggerated intonation); simplicity features (shorter utterances, slower tempo, longer pauses between phrases, fewer embedded clauses, fewer auxiliaries); redundancy features (more repetition over shorter amounts of time, more immediate repetition); lexical features (special forms like "mama"); and content features (restriction of topics to the child's world). Infant-directed speech may be intuitive and nonconscious (Bernstein Ratner & Luberoff, 1984; Fernald & Simon, 1984; Fernald et al., 1989; Garnica, 1977; Hoff-Ginsberg & Shatz, 1982; Papoušek & Papoušek, 1991; Papoušek, Papoušek, & Haekel, 1987; Stern, Spiker, Barnett, & McCain, 1983), and cross-cultural developmental study attests that infant-directed speech is (essentially) universal (Jacobson et al., 1983; Papoušek & Papoušek, 1981, 1991; Papoušek, Papoušek, & Bornstein, 1985; Snow, 1977a), although not without exception (Bernstein Ratner & Pye, 1984). Interestingly, when communicating with their infants, deaf mothers modify their sign language very much the way hearing mothers use infant-directed speech (Erting, Thumann-Prezioso, & Benedict, 2000). Dunn and Kendrick (1982c) observed that even 2- to 3-year-olds engage in such systematic language adjustments—they increase attentional utterances and repetitions and shorten utterances in general—when speaking to their year-old siblings as opposed to their mothers.

One of the most frequently investigated features of infant-directed speech is the alteration in pitch, and we can use it as an illustration. Ervin-Tripp (1973) noted that mothers address younger babies with higher pitch. Jacobson and his colleagues (1983) found that nonparents, males and females, who had little prior experience with infants modified their speech as much as parents, and both groups modified their speech when an infant or small child was actually present or even when asked to imagine speaking to an infant or small child (Jacobson, Boersma, Fields, & Olson, 1983). Fernald and her colleagues (1989) analyzed the fundamental frequency as well as utterance duration and pause duration of mothers' and fathers' naturalistic speech to preverbal infants in French, Italian, German, Japanese, British English, and American English. Figure 9.3 shows cross-language consistency in patterns of prosodic modification used by parents: Mothers and fathers alike used higher mean, minimum, and maximum fundamental frequency and a greater variability in fundamental frequency (and they also used shorter utterances and longer pauses) in infant-directed speech than in adult-directed speech. Such data provide valuable information about features of the early linguistic environment that are culturally widespread as well as those that are specific to particular language communities. Although these results were consistent, select variations were notable. For example, the adjustment in mothers' speech is more pronounced than in fathers' speech. Similarly, the adjustment in American English is more pronounced than in the speech of other cultures (Fernald et al., 1989).

Why do people use baby talk? It has been proposed that the characteristic prosodic patterns of infant-directed speech might elicit attention, modulate arousal and communicate affect, and facilitate language comprehension (Cooper & Aslin, 1989; Fernald et al., 1989). With regard to eliciting attention, infants respond more to their own mothers' voice when she is speaking motherese (Glenn & Cunningham, 1983); infants also prefer to listen to infant-directed speech than to adult-directed speech even when spoken by strangers (Fernald, 1985; Fernald & Kuhl, 1987).

Second, the prosody of infant-directed speech might regulate infant arousal level and communicate affect to the infant. Charles Darwin (1877, Box 3.1)

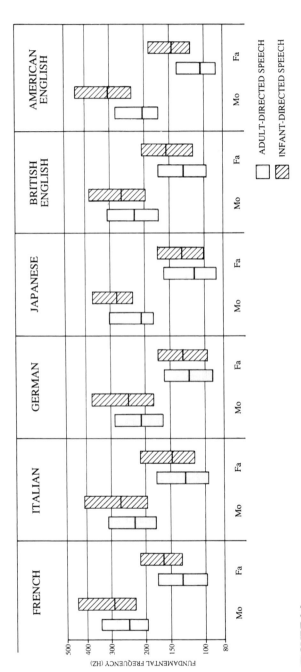

FIGURE 9.3

Cross-language comparison of fundamental frequency (F_0) characteristics of mothers' (Mo) and fathers' (Fa) speech to adults and to infants. (For each bar, the bottom line represents the mean F_0-minimum, the top line represents the mean F_0-maximum, and the intersecting line indicates the mean-F_0 per utterance. The extent of the bar corresponds to F_0-range. Open box, adult-directed speech; hatch box, infant-directed speech.) Note that mothers increase their peak fundamental frequency relatively more than fathers when speaking to their infants, and American English speakers tend to use more exaggerated prosody when interacting with an infant than do the speakers of most other languages.

reported that Doddy "understood intonation and gestures" before he was 1 year old. The infant's understanding of such features—and, perhaps, meaning—in human speech before language is understood turns on analyzing the coincidence of specific kinds of prosodic contours in infant-directed speech, the specific interactional contexts in which they occur, and their effects on a baby. For example, Papoušek and Papoušek (1991) examined culture-universal and culture-specific linkages in the coordination of intonation in parental speech to prelinguistic infants and the communicative intent of adults in specific parenting contexts. The Papoušeks' work leads to the conclusion that certain intonation contours in mothers' speech to baby recur with greater than chance regularity in particular interactions, and that these regularities characterize a wide variety of languages, such as American English, German, and Mandarin Chinese. As Figure 9.4 shows, mothers use rising pitch contours to engage infant attention and elicit a response from an infant, falling contours to soothe a distressed infant, and bell-shaped contours to maintain infant attention (Papoušek & Papoušek, 1991; Papoušek et al., 1985; see also Fernald, 1985, 1989; Marcos, 1987; Stern, Spiker, & MacKain, 1982). The prosodic patterns of infant-directed speech may provide the infant with reliable cues about the communicative intent of the speaker. Here, again, there may be something to Darwin's early observation of Doddy's first understanding the meaningfulness of speech through prosody and intonation rather than through words.

Finally, the prosodic modifications of infant-directed speech appear to facilitate speech processing and language comprehension on the part of the infant. Exaggerated prosody is thought to help infants follow and segment the speech stream as well as provide some acoustic cues to the syntactic structure of linguistic messages (Hirsh-Pasek et al., 1987; Peters, 1983). For example, infants discriminate speech sounds embedded in multisyllabic sequences better in infant-directed speech than in adult-directed speech (Karzon, 1985). On the direct question of whether and how infant-directed speech affects children's language development, opinions vary (see Hoff-Ginsberg & Shatz, 1982; Schwartz & Camarata, 1985), and one should not take away from this characterization of infant-directed speech a strong form of the "motherese hypothesis," namely that special properties of infant-directed speech play a causal role in learning syntax (Gleitman, Newport, & Gleitman, 1984; Wexler & Culicover, 1980). Indeed, Gleitman and her colleagues (1984) suggest that in principle the language-learning child would actually be put at a long-term disadvantage by the simplifying aspects of infant-directed speech, because that speech does not match the language corpus the child actually has to learn. Of course, the counterargument is that most learning proceeds by beginning with simple structures and then moving on to more complex ones (Furrow & Nelson, 1986).

Out of the wide variety of adjustments that characterize infant-directed speech, we selected prosodic change. There are many others, as we listed.

Moreover, fathers appear to be sensitive to infant language status but to play complementary roles to mothers with regard to the quality and quantity of speech directed to infants (Rondal, 1980). By and large, paternal speech displays the same simplification processes found in maternal speech. However, mothers tend to focus more on social and emotional expression, whereas fathers tend to focus on directives, questions, and providing information (Leaper, Anderson, & Sanders, 1998).

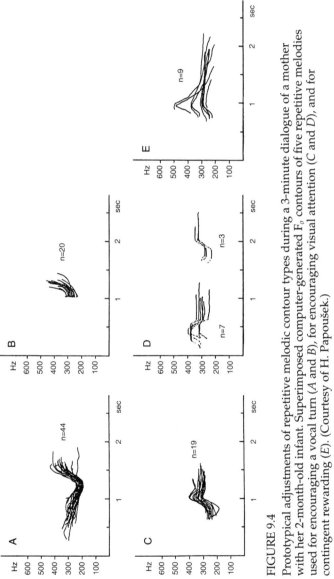

FIGURE 9.4

Prototypical adjustments of repetitive melodic contour types during a 3-minute dialogue of a mother with her 2-month-old infant. Superimposed computer-generated F_0 contours of five repetitive melodies used for encouraging a vocal turn (A and B), for encouraging visual attention (C and D), and for contingent rewarding (E). (Courtesy of H. Papoušek.)

Turn Taking

Observations of infant-directed speech lead to a deeper conversational realm of mother–infant synchrony that merits close attention as a base of language learning. It is *turn taking*. Adults conversing with one another tend to match certain temporal factors in their speech, and turn taking is fundamental to the structure of adult dialogue. It is impolite to interrupt; rather, we wait our turn to speak.

Turn taking in mother–infant exchange is common, with roots apparently deep in their initial interactions. Kaye (1982) uncovered a nonverbal "dialogue" between mothers feeding their newborns: When the infant pauses sucking, the mother "jiggles," and when the mother ceases to jiggle, the infant responds by sucking again. From an extremely early age infants produce different sounds, and their caregivers respond differently to different infant vocalizations depending on their interpretation. Keller and Schölmerich (1987) studied the relation between infants' first vocalizations and parental reactions over the initial 4 months of life. They classified infant vocalizations as positive, effortful, negative, and physiological; they coded maternal behaviors as tactile, vestibular, and verbal/vocal; and they assessed interactional states between the two. Even 2-week-olds produced different types of vocalizations, and in this 4-month period rates of infant vocalization were related to interactional state: Infants tended to produce more positive vocalizations during eye contact with parents, and parents tended to respond to their infants' positive vocalizations with verbal/vocal reactions, whereas parents predominantly responded to physiological, negative, and effort vocalizations with tactile and vestibular behaviors.

Jasnow and Feldstein (1986) have closely analyzed the temporal mechanics of speech between mothers and their 9-month-old infants. They found that dyads engaged in alternating vocalizations to a much greater degree than simultaneous vocalizations. Stevenson, Ver Hoeve, Roach, and Leavitt (1986) confirmed that patterns of mother–infant vocal exchange are structurally similar to patterns typical of adult conversation: They observed that mothers' and babies' initiating vocalizations were followed by suppression of vocalization, thereby permitting the partner to join the conversation.

In turn, Bloom and her associates (Bloom, 1979; Bloom, Russell, & Wassenburg, 1987) studied the effects of turn taking in mother–infant conversation, first on infant vocalization, and next on the quality of subsequent mother vocalization. In their first experiment, one group of 3-month-olds experienced conversational turn taking and another random responsiveness on the part of an adult. Infant vocalizations were then counted and categorized as either speech-like or nonspeech-like. When the adult maintained the prototypic conversational give-and-take pattern, infants produced a relatively higher ratio of speech-like to nonspeech-like sounds. In their second experiment, adult responsiveness consisted of conversational turn taking or random responsiveness using nonverbal vocalizations, smiling, and touching the infant's abdomen. Again, turn taking facilitated a speak–listen pattern of vocalizing by the infant, but this time, in the absence of a verbal component of the adult's response, turn taking did not facilitate the infants' production of speech-like sounds. The two experiments together show that infants participating in normal "conversation" vocalize more like they are "really talking," and that what adults "say" to 3-month-olds influences what those infants are likely to "reply" in return.

This is not to say that covocalization does not occur in mother–infant vocal episodes (Elias, Hayes, & Broerse, 1986). Although two early studies reported that covocalization exceeds alternating vocalization between mothers and infants, these studies involved very young infants, and covocalization decreases steadily from 3 months to 18 months, possibly because mothers try harder to figure out what infants are saying as infants become more competent communicators (Elias & Broerse, 1996).

Mothers promote turn taking: They typically vocalize rapidly after an infant vocalization, and they often prolong pauses after their own vocalizations to increase the likelihood that infant vocalizations will become part of a "conversational chain" (Hayes, 1984). Furthermore, mothers follow a brief interval of silence with informative speech, whereas noninformative speech tends to occur during mother–infant covocalization (Elias, Hayes, & Broerse, 1988).

In short, mothers act in verbal exchanges with their preverbal infants like sophisticated conversationalists. Perhaps mothers behave in this way because it is their normal way of interacting. Alternatively, turn taking may be a socializing aspect of maternal conversation with infants. Perhaps, too, alternating is a fundamental recognition on the part of mothers that conversations must take place in turns because the human nervous system cannot simultaneously produce and understand speech.

Gesture

Mothers and infants provide one another with a range of nonverbal supports to communication and language learning. *Gesture* is one such mutually shared prop. By the time their infants are 9 months of age, parents already engage in much *ostensive definition*—labeling something and also nonverbally indicating direction of regard, such as pointing (Baldwin & Markman, 1989). Nine months is the earliest age at which infants are prone to look in the direction indicated by adult pointing rather than looking at the pointing finger itself (Butterworth & Grover, 1990; Leung & Rhinegold, 1981).

Shatz (1982) identified seven discrete types of hand gestures used by mothers, and she found that distinct hand gestures co-occurred reliably with naturally occurring topics of conversation. For example, a mother might point and at the same time ask the question "What is that?" or "Is that a ball?" On the basis of a subsequent comparative analysis of mother–infant play, where one group of mothers was free to use their hands and another group was instructed not to, Schnur and Shatz (1984) concluded that mothers' gestures serve principally to maintain infant attention, thereby exerting an indirect influence over language acquisition. In Schnur and Shatz, children's overall attentiveness declined in the ungestured group.

Infants are more likely to attend to objects previously pointed to and labeled than to objects that received no labels. Baldwin and Markman (1989) showed infants from two age groups (10–14 months and 17–20 months) pairs of unfamiliar toys in two situations: a pointing alone condition and a labeling and pointing condition. When pointing occurred, infants looked equally long at the target when it was labeled as when it was not. During a later play session, however, infants looked longer at target toys that had been labeled than at those that had not. Language labeling increases infants' attention to objects beyond the time that the labeling itself actually occurs, and language maintains infant attention to objects over and above pointing.

When mothers engage their infants verbally in the second year, they are usually doing something at the same time; that is, language occurs in an "action context and not as an isolated output" (Schaffer, Hepburn, & Collis, 1983, p. 337). This observation further highlights the importance of *joint attention* (Bornstein, 1985c). Mothers tend to speak when the child's visual and/or motor involvement with particular objects make her speech most meaningful and comprehensible. The addition of nonverbal cues to verbal directives toward infants 15 and 24 months of age significantly increases the chances of obtaining the child's compliance to attention-focusing controls (Schaffer & Crook, 1980).

For their part, children are not only active in comprehending and speaking when they acquire language, but in making use of nonverbal supports such as gesturing. Long before the end of their first year, infants communicate differentially about objects by pointing, giving, referring, and showing. Perhaps the prototypical gesture for language-learning children in this age range is pointing. In *Symbol Formation*, Werner and Kaplan (1963) hypothesized that pointing marks a transitional milestone in symbolic development (see Chapters 7 and 8). They considered pointing transitional because it refers to properties, objects, and events in the immediate physical surround, but only so and not to things not present. Pointing is also social because pointing permits the infant to initiate a topic of conversation.

The median age of onset of pointing is about $12\frac{1}{2}$ months (Lempers, 1979; Leung & Rhinegold, 1981); expectedly, language-delayed (autistic) children show relatively low levels of pointing (Mundy, Sigman, Unger, & Sherman, 1986). Masur (1982, 1983) studied individual differences in infant pointing and their consequences. The range of individual differences in onset varies sixfold (9–19 months), and mothers label in response to children's pointing more than to their reaching for objects. Moreover, mothers' labeling responses to infants' pointing significantly predicts children's later object-naming vocabularies. Indeed, the use of "referential" gestures in many ways anticipates language development in the child. Carpenter, Mastergeorge, and Coggins (1983) observed babies 8 to 15 months of age monthly in free-play interactions with their mothers and found that babies at 8 months gestured and vocalized in communication, but by 15 months gestures had been replaced in communicative intent by single-word utterances.

Dynamic Sensitivity

One of the principal tasks of the first $2\frac{1}{2}$ years of life is for the infant to develop into a "conversant." Adult and infant alike are geared to this common goal. Parental speech adjustments to infants are not just attention getting and attention holding, regulating, and contextually apt, they also appear to be *dynamically sensitive* to infants' changing capacities. Parents modify all systems of their speech relative to their infant's development. Generally, prosodic modifications diminish markedly after infancy, and semantic and syntactic modifications change constantly to match toddlers' newly developing linguistic competencies, in this way creating and maintaining appropriate vocal environments for infants (Papoušek et al., 1985).

Parents are sensitive both to infant age and to infant capacity. Bellinger (1980) collected transcripts of codable utterances from mother and child pairs in four age groupings from 1 year to 5 years, and analyzed them to yield information about various aspects of mothers' speech. On the basis of the organization of a given mother's language, Bellinger found that he could predict the exact age of the child.

In fact, however, mothers' speech tends usually to follow child performance more closely than child age. (In much of the speech literature, however, child age and language level are confounded; see Wells, 1979.) For example, McLaughlin, White, McDevitt, and Raskin (1983) found that the mean length of mothers' utterances matches the mean length of their $1\frac{1}{2}$- to $3\frac{1}{2}$-year-olds' utterances. Certainly, age and level of language development both exert influences over the characteristics of maternal speech, as other child characteristics must do as well. Temperament—activity level, task persistence, and affect discussed in Chapter 10—may be one (Smolak, 1987). However, maternal language appears to reflect an understanding of child competence level—the language the child is likely to understand.

Infants' universal propensities and their idiosyncratic tendencies are matched by the many ways adults help them to "crack the linguistic code." The language system starts at a certain basal level of accomplishment and progresses reasonably consistently to greater levels of sophistication; its growth in turn signals the social environment to alter input in accord with its changing level. A corollary of this view is that a single kind of input may affect development differently at different times, perhaps because the changing system interprets and utilizes even constant input differently at different times. Thus, early in life the intonations of infant-directed maternal speech may maintain attention or modulate arousal, whereas at later points it may communicate affect, help to identify the mother, or facilitate speech perception.

In this section we have previewed the intricate coordination of infant and parent roles in first language learning. In succeeding sections we analyze language acquisition in the child by treating major subcomponents of language separately, and further analyze the roles of interpersonal interactions in language acquisition. Toward the conclusion, when we take up issues of the child's learning grammar, we again confront the truism that conversation and communication in language are inherently social and interactive phenomena whose foundations are laid very early in life.

Making and Understanding Speech

The auditory signal that specifies speech involves a complex interplay of frequencies and intensities of sound waves arrayed over time. A speech spectrograph, like the one shown in Figure 9.5, makes visible such a pattern; specifically, it depicts the sound waves produced by the vocal folds and articulated in the oral cavity when we say, "development in infancy." The dark bands reflect sounds above threshold intensity at different frequencies, and the light areas reflect silence.

On hearing, the infant's tasks are to decode the complex vibratory pattern that sound projects onto the auditory apparatus and to reconstruct it into a

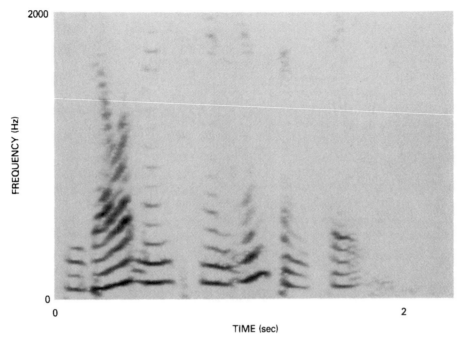

FIGURE 9.5

A speech spectrograph for the utterance "development in infancy." The dark areas show patterns of energy focused at different frequencies, called formants. Also indicated are different specific sound patterns, such as voicing.

psychologically meaningful pattern. On speaking, the infant must determine what will go into the array and then articulate it. How do babies accomplish these tasks? In this section of the chapter we focus on these primitive aspects of speech perception and production. This focus is appropriate because this text is about babies. In the two sections following, we raise and discuss what we know about the infant's rudimentary understanding and use of first word forms and grammar.

Sound Perception

We learned in Chapters 5 and 6 that the auditory system is quite well developed before birth. Even newborns are equipped to hear, orient to, and distinguish sounds, and babies seem especially primed to perceive and appreciate sound in the dynamic form and range of human speech. They are acutely sensitive to its salient components and significant complexities. Consider, however, the seemingly impossible task of segmenting the speech stream—knowing where one word ends and the next begins—before knowing any words or even what a word is. Moreover, infants have to do this for different speakers speaking in different contexts. The following sets of experiments illustrate some infant competencies that have evolved to address three problems, namely segmenting sounds, matching sounds and sights, and recognizing speech.

Infants perceive categories in speech, described in Chapter 6. Using sucking-habituation and head-turn paradigms, speech researchers have shown that even

FIGURE 9.6
Peter Bruegel (1525/1530–1569), *The Tower of Babel* (1563). (Courtesy of Museum Boymans/van Beuningen, Rotterdam.)

babies under 6 months of age categorize some speech sounds much as adults do. For years theorists had argued that because sounds vary so much from one language to another—as Peter Bruegel reminds us vividly in his 1563 painting *The Tower of Babel* (see Figure 9.6)—meaningful distinctions among sounds must be shaped by experience, implying that early in development speech would be perceived as a random mishmash of sounds. Cross-language research confirms that, although many sounds are possible (*phonetics*), languages use only relatively small numbers of distinct sounds in their speech (*phonemics*). Some Polynesian languages use as few as 15 phonemes, for example, whereas some European and Asian languages use as many as 75. English uses 45. But as we have seen (see Chapter 6), some phonemes are distinguished essentially universally, and these are the ones that tend to be represented in the early perceptual capacities of young babies. Contrary to early beliefs, therefore, it appears that the sounds of speech are not experienced as wholly random or confusing, but rather, even near the beginning of life, many sounds are naturally partitioned into smaller (and presumably more manageable) categories. Other animals (like chinchillas and monkeys) parse speech sounds too (Bornstein, 1985; Harnad, 1987), and so categorical perception of speech does not necessarily imply a "language"-specific mechanism. Moreover, speech sounds are certainly not invested with meaning in infancy, even if they are quickly discriminated by babies as psychological units. Apparently, the auditory system is structured so as to group together select complex sounds and does so without the requirement of extensive linguistic experience. However, as we learned from Werker's research (Chapter 6) experience is necessary for maintaining perceptual discrimination of speech. The categories that infants are able to discriminate innately are adjusted over time to fit the phonological requirements of the language babies hear. Some distinctions will disappear (as in the Hindi contrast among the

English-learning infants studied by Werker). In other cases the prototypical sound within a category will have to shift somewhat to match the local dialect, although the developmental course of this process is not well understood.

Infants also appear to be able to identify particular speakers quite early. As described in Chapter 5, DeCasper and Fifer (1980) tape-recorded mothers reading Dr. Seuss's *To Think That I Saw It on Mulberry Street*, and then made the infant's own mother's voice, or the voice of another mother, available to newborns for sucking on a pacifier. The babies were all less than 3 days of age at testing and could only have been exposed postnatally to their own mothers' voices for 12 hours. These newborns not only discriminated their mothers' voices from those of female strangers, they also "worked" (that is, sucked more) to produce their own mothers' voices in preference to the voice of the other female. These results suggest that prenatal or only very brief postnatal experience influences babies' auditory perceptions and performance. The question of which one was resolved in a follow-up study. Spence and DeCasper (1984) found that newborns prefer stories their mothers had read to them in utero over stories that were new. That is, prenatal auditory experience determined postnatal preference.

During their first year, infants learn a tremendous amount about how their language sounds. As we saw in Chapter 6, infants become increasingly attuned to the phonological categories used in the ambient language. In addition, infants learn a great deal about what words in their language are like. One example of this is *phonotactic learning*. Phonotactics refers to constraints on the combination of speech sounds in words. In English, the sounds "n" and "k" can occur together in a syllable, but only at the end (*sink*) and only in that order (*sikn*, *nkis*, and *knis* are not possible words of English). Although there are similarities in these rules across languages, there are also clear differences; for example, in Dutch, *kn* is a possible word onset—the Dutch word for *knee* (*knie*) is pronounced exactly like the English, except that the Dutch pronounce the initial *k*. Studies by Jusczyk, Friederici, Wessels, Svenkerud, and Jusczyk (1993) using the auditory preference procedure showed that infants have begun to learn these regularities by 9 months. In one of these studies, American and Dutch babies heard lists of words that were "legal" in Dutch but not English (such as *knoest*) or legal in English but not Dutch (such as *stewed*, whose final *d* is not permitted in Dutch). Infants preferred to listen to lists consistent with their own language's phonotactics.

What might this phonological knowledge be good for? One problem that infants must solve in order to understand language is to discover which elements of the continuous speech signal are words. This is called the *segmentation problem*. Acoustic analyses of speech show that when we talk we tend to run words together without pausing between words or otherwise indicating word boundaries. This is true even when we talk to infants. Consider "Yourteddyislyingonthecouchsweetie." The number of ways to divide this sentence into possible words is very large, presenting a problem for word finding. But if you know that *rt* cannot start a word, this gives you a head start because you can rule out "You rteddy...." Of course, phonotactics is not a complete solution—there isn't anything un-English about a possible word like *teddyis*—but they could help. Another potentially helpful regularity of English is that stressed syllables tend to be the first syllable in a word. Knowing this, it makes more sense to guess that *teddy* and *lying* are words than that *yourte* or *thecouch* are words. Indeed, infants in English-language environments seem to divide speech sequences in just this way. Jusczyk, Houston, and Newsome (1999) used the auditory preference procedure to evaluate infants' segmentation of words with stressed first syllables (like *hamlet*) or second syllables (like *device*). Seven-month-olds first heard either two "hamlet"-type words repeated several times, or two "device"-type words. Then infants heard short stories containing the familiarized words or not. Only infants tested with initial-stress words showed a preference for the stories containing the familiarized words; other infants showed no preference, suggesting that they had been unable to detect the final-stress words in the stories. This failure actually comes as good news because it would seem that infants are unlikely to guess that *thecouch* (a final-stress sequence) is a word.

An additional cue to word identity is a statistical one. Consider the three syllables that make up "your teddy." Infants hear many phrases starting with *your*: "your nose," "your shoe," "your diaper", and so on. This variety actually helps identify *your* as a word—after hearing your *x*, your *y*, and your *z*, "your teddy" is not likely to be segmented as *yourte dy*. By contrast, the *te* of *teddy* is relatively likely to be followed by *dy*, suggesting that *teddy* is a word. A number of studies have shown that infants use this kind of statistical patterning to group syllables together. Goodsitt, Morgan, and Kuhl (1993) taught 7-month-olds to make a response whenever they heard the syllable *ti*. Then the experimenters hid the *ti* in a two-syllable context like *koga*, producing *kogati*. Some infants were tested on *invariant contexts* (always *koga*); others were tested on *variant contexts* (sometimes *koga*, sometimes *gako*). Infants were much better at finding the *ti* when the context was invariant. Because *ko* and *ga* always appeared together and in the same order, infants stuck them together, making the *ti* easier to find. It is the "sticking together" that is of interest: If infants spontaneously group together syllables that have this kind of statistical consistency, it could help them find words. More dramatic evidence of this phenomenon was provided by Aslin, Saffran, and Newport (1998). First infants heard a series of invented words, strung together in a continuous sequence (a bit like hearing "bermudacolossusmandiblecolossusbermuda...", but with made-up words like *daropi* and without any syllables stressed). Then infants heard lists containing isolated versions of the words (*bermuda...bermuda...*) or bits of words (*dacolos...dacolos...*). Eight-month-olds reliably preferred the bits of words. The fact that infants could distinguish the two kinds of lists demonstrates that they had been able to detect the statistical structure of the syllables: *da* always followed *mu*, which always followed *ber*. Analyses of speech to infants suggest that this clustering according to statistical structure could help in the discovery of English words (Swingley, 1999).

Researchers using computational modeling have shown that speech to infants contains various statistical regularities that could in principle be used by infants to guide their solution of the segmentation problem. For example, phonotactics could be learned by paying attention to the sounds that begin and end utterances. Because utterances have to start with the beginning of a word and must finish with the end of the word, infants might get a preliminary fix on how words are allowed to begin and end by paying attention to whole utterances. Christiansen, Allen, and Seidenberg (1998) demonstrated the feasibility of this approach by training a "connectionist" computer model to go through a transcribed corpus of infant-directed speech sound by sound, guessing at each step what the next sound would be and whether it was about to reach the end of an utterance (and modifying its guessing strategy according to whether it had guessed correctly). Eventually the system began guessing "end of utterance" not only for utterance ends but for word ends too, because it had generalized phonotactic regularities from utterances to words. In another computational analysis, Brent and Cartwright (1996) showed that many words could be learned by hearing words in short utterances and then using these words to help detect other words. For example, if you know *shoe* is a word, you can guess that *my* is a word when you hear "my shoe." Both of these computational models show that a lot of information about word segmentation is contained in the phonological sequences infants hear.

These several lines of research illustrate the ingenuity and energy of researchers and human infants alike in figuring out speech. They tell us that, either natively or on the basis of very little experience, babies partition the speech stream, coordinate correspondences between eye and ear, and recognize the source of speech. These capabilities and others yet to be discovered, no matter how advanced in and of themselves, certainly do not make infants fully sophisticated listeners. However, each gives infants some advantage, ensuring that they begin the task of deciphering language from a less than naive starting point.

Sound Production

Most investigators agree that all infants traverse three initial stages in early verbal development: a prelinguistic, a one-word, and a multiword stage, with important transitions in between. In this section we are concerned with two early manifestations of infant prelinguistic vocalizations—cry and babbling. In the next section, we discuss more of what is known about formal semantic development.

Cry

The infant's cry is a very revealing kind of vocalization (Lester & Boukydis, 1985). On the basis of cry characteristics, it is possible to differentiate among a variety of developmental problems—in utero cocaine exposure, nutritional deficiency, respiratory disorder, sudden infant death syndrome, prematurity, and trisomy-21, among them (e.g., Colton, Steinschneider, Black, & Gleason, 1985; Lester & Boukydis, 1991; Thoden, Jarvenpaa, & Michelsson, 1985). Furthermore, different infant physiological states (e.g., hunger and sleepiness) are associated with different spectrographic patterns of crying (Wasz-Hockert, Michelsson, & Lind, 1985).

Few adults can deny or disregard a baby's cry; it compels us to respond (Bowlby, 1969), and the nearly universal response is to be nurturant in some way (Bornstein, Tal, Tamis-LeMonda, 1991). However, infants' cries and our responses to them are often highly differentiated, and to this extent cries represent extremely effective communicative signals (e.g., Lester & Boukydis, 1991). For example, adults reliably distinguish a pain cry and a hunger cry (see Darwin's, 1877, comments in Box 3.1) and presumably respond to the two in different ways. Figure 9.7 illustrates a mother's autonomic sensitivity to her infant's hunger cry. The white spots in this surface heat thermograph show that mammary blood and milk flow are automatically stimulated by such cries.

How and on what bases do adults identify infants' cries? Sagi (1981) investigated sensitivity to cries in mothers and nonmothers who were themselves either experienced or inexperienced in childcare. He asked every participant in his study to identify hunger, pain, and pleasure cries of newborn to 7-month-old infants. Regardless of the number of children they themselves had, mothers

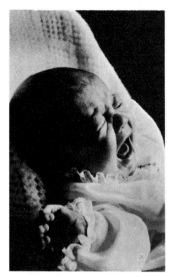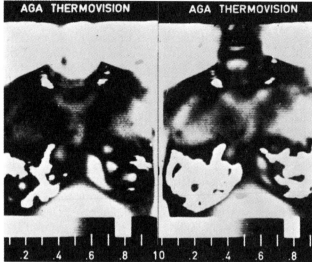

FIGURE 9.7
How an infant's cry influences the mother. White spots in the heat thermograph to the right indicate mammary blood and milk flow before and during an infant's cry. (Courtesy of S. McCarroll and J. Lind.)

identified infant cries more accurately than did nonmothers. Apparently being a parent rather than experience with infants per se aids in interpreting the infant's cry.

The perception and interpretation of cries are important, because cries and their distinguishing features play a significant role in many aspects of normal and atypical child development (Brazelton, 1985; Murray, 1979, 1985). Thoman, Acebo, and Becker (1983), for example, found that by 1 month infants' crying contributes to establishing interactional stability in mother–infant dyads. Preterm babies usually have shriller and more penetrating cries, and adults perceive them as more aversive than the cries of healthy term babies (Frodi, Lamb, & Wille, 1981; Frodi & Thompson, 1985; Murray, 1985; Zeskind & Lester, 1978). Lounsbury and Bates (1982) found that babies who were rated as having "difficult" temperaments by their parents (Chapter 10) have cries whose fundamental frequency is 50 Hz higher than that of babies not considered difficult.

Babbling

Although babies' cries inform parents about their state, babbling is the first significant nondistress communication. Babbling typically accompanies excitation and motor activity in the first half of the first year of life, and alternates with attentive listening in the second half. Babbling represents a deceptively simple development, and several aspects of babbling have led psycholinguists to conclude that there is more to infants' babbling than at first meets the ear. Perhaps babbling assumes heightened significance because it comprises infants' first "structured" vocalizations, because it sounds like fun, and because it fills the eerie void between the silence or crying so common to early infancy on the one hand and advent of the first intelligible words of toddlerhood on the other.

Relations between the development of early babbling and first speech are obscure. Some have argued that the two are distinct and separate periods of vocal production, the earlier random and ephemeral, and the later structured and fixed (Jakobson, 1968). However, it is now known that, while there are various developmental stages in babbling, there is not a firm discontinuity between babble and early talk, as had been proposed by Jakobson. Babble and first words rest on the same innately programmed articulatory mechanisms; they share the same fundamental speech sounds; and babbling production continues to coexist with first words for 4 or 5 months (Boysson-Bardies & Vihman, 1991; Locke, 1983; McCune & Vihman, 1987; Oller, 2000; Vihman & Miller, 1988). In babbling, there are frequent repetitions of the same syllable sound or syllable, and this practice makes perfect in the sounds, syllables, and sequences of syllables that will comprise full-blown speech. Oller (2000) defined "canonical" syllables as the first units of child speech to exhibit the timing characteristics of adult consonant and vowel production. These typically appear at about 6 to 8 months in normal-hearing infants, whatever the ambient language. Children usually also draw their early lexicon from the phonetic repertoire established in the course of babbling (Stoel-Gammon & Cooper, 1984; Vihman, Macken, Miller, Simmons, & Miller, 1985). However, productive vocabulary depends on increasing control of vocalization as well as the development of conceptual schemata. Elbers and Ton (1985) examined the babbling monologues of a Dutch child in the one and one half months following acquisition of the first word. They found that the child's word production related to concurrent babbling in a mutually facilitative way: Babbling predisposed talking toward words with a certain phonological form, and talking reciprocally influenced the nature of babbling.

A classic study by Bayley and her associates promised great significance to such early vocalizing: They found that girls who vocalized more on a cluster of BSID items from 5 through 12 months scored higher on verbal IQ tests between 6 and 26 years (Cameron, Livson, & Bayley, 1967). Although this early work has not been systematically followed up, from time to time it has received provocative confirmations. For example, Roe and her colleagues (Roe, McClure, & Roe, 1983) reported that infants' "differential vocal response" to stimulation by mother versus a female stranger predicts later verbal-cognitive and academic functioning and discriminates groups of infants who are later expected to show differential levels of verbal intelligence. McCune and Vihman (1987) found a positive association between the diversity and frequency of infant consonant production and their general lexical advance. DiLalla and her colleagues (1990) found that the total number of different syllables uttered by 7- to 9-month-olds predicted Bayley scores at 1 and 2 years and Stanford Binet scores at 3 years (DiLalla et al., 1990). Indeed, Thompson and Plomin (1988) reported that the number of different syllable sounds 7- to 9-month-olds make predicts their parents' average IQ.

The production of speech has been called the most complex of human action patterns, and origins of regularity in early speech production constitute one of several convergences of nature and nurture in language development. For this reason we examine some significant features in detail. Sound production in newborns is constrained by the anatomy of the oral cavity and by respiratory patterns (Laver, 1980; Lester & Boukydis, 1991). The vocal tracts of adults and infants differ, and these differences have profound effects on articulation, imitation, and learning speech (Kent & Murray, 1982). Although anatomical constraints do not force all children to babble in the same way, these constraints do appear to promote a particular developmental scheme for speech sound production.

The linguistic theorist Jakobson (1968, 1971) proposed the romantic view that infants produce all of the sounds of world's languages but that, when they

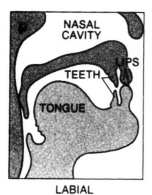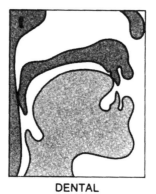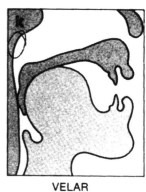

FIGURE 9.8

How sounds are articulated in the vocal tract. Labials such as /p/ are articulated at the front of the mouth by the two lips, dentals like /t/ by the tongue at the roof of the mouth, and velars like /k/ at the back of the mouth. (After Miller, 1981. © 1981 by W. H. Freeman and Co. Reprinted with permission.)

first began to speak, children limit their articulations to a highly restricted set of contrasts and that infants' initial sound productions follow a universal pattern. He was partly right. Infants do produce a range of sounds even in their first months, but these sounds are not truly phonemes and can be quite difficult to assign to standard phoneme categories; furthermore, there is not much variety in these early sounds (Oller, 2000). The difficulty of interpreting the sounds of early babble is not surprising given the immaturity of infants' control over the oral articulators. However, it is true that infants' first vocalizations are not dependent on the language infants hear and thus are universal (Locke, 1983). Figure 9.8 shows the oral cavity and vocal tract configuration involved in articulating labials (/p/ and /b/), dentals (/t/ and /d/), and velars (/k/ and /g/). Vowel sounds (/o/, /e/, and /a/) are articulated at roughly parallel points. Jakobson argued that articulation follows a general developmental progression among consonants from labials and dentals to velars and among vowels from back vowels like /u/ to front vowels like /i/. This means that infants' earliest complex combinations ought to be front (labial) or perhaps dental (or nasal) consonants with back (velar) vowels: that is, /p/ or /b/ or /d/ or /m/ with /a/. Note that this descriptive account does not imply that infants separately program the articulation of consonants and vowels even when they have reached the canonical babbling stage. MacNeilage and Davis (1990, 2000) pointed out that infants commonly produce syllables sounding like /ba/ and /di/ but are relatively less likely to produce /bi/, probably because making a /b/ results in a tongue position well suited to following with /a/ but not /i/. This suggests that infants have control over syllables rather than individual phonemes even if we tend to think of babble in terms of phonemes.

Such constraints on prespeech capacities appear to foretell the composition of first words (e.g., Locke, 1983; MacNeilage & Davis, 2000; Vihman, Macken, Miller, Simmons, & Miller, 1985). Early babbling production is rooted in anatomical biases and ease of motor control common to all children (Kent, 1984; Locke, 1983). Vihman (1991) studied infants and toddlers in four language communities—Japanese, French, Swedish, and English. A very small number of syllables accounted for half of those produced in all the groups, and the two highest-use syllables, /da/ and /ba/, were used by all language groups.

It did not long escape notice that the highest probability syllabic combinations in infant speech, based on Jakobson's theory, tend to be those that connote important meanings very early in life. Cross-cultural linguistic research showed that the most likely first sound combinations should be /pa/, /ba/, /da/, and /ma/, and further, that /pa/-like, /da/-like, and /ma/-like sounds are used as parental kin terms in an unusually large proportion of language communities. Of the four logically possible combinations, the front consonant with back vowel pairs were used in 57% of 1,072 languages studied, where only 25% would be expected by chance (Murdock, 1959). Recall, too, that Doddy's first articulate sound, according to his father, was /da/. The implication seems to be that parents (or languages) have directly adopted as generic labels for themselves their own infants' earliest, anatomically determined vocal productions.

Finally, there is evidence that babbling is the product of an amodal brain-based language capacity under maturational control. Petitto and Marentette (1991) observed manual babbling in deaf infants 10 to 16 months of age exposed to sign languages from birth, and on the basis of a comparison with babbling in hearing infants concluded that experience with speech per se is not critical to the onset or nature of babbling, but rather that the similarities in manual and vocal babbling indicate that babbling is an abstract and generalized language capacity of human beings related to expressive capacity. In fact, Petitto and her colleagues subsequently demonstrated differences in the manual gestures of hearing infants exposed to sign language, and hearing infants exposed to speech. The infants exposed to sign language made an additional range of slow-moving gestures, positioned directly in front of their bodies, apparently mimicking the gestures of their signing parents. This gestural "babble" shows that the hand and arm movements seen in the first study were a consequence of exposure to sign language and not somehow a consequence of deafness itself (Petitto, Holowka, Sergio, & Ostry, 2001).

If the earliest manifestations of vocal babbling emerge naturally and are anatomically constrained, different kinds of linguistic experience should not differentially influence it, nor should the ontogeny of babbling depend on any particular experience. Spanish-, Japanese-, and English-learning babies show no great differences in their basic sound production repertoires, suggesting that grossly different linguistic experiences do not shape the elements of first vocal babbling very much (Locke, 1983; Nakazima, 1975; Oller & Eilers, 1982). However, some early experience clearly does matter.

Every child uses two sources of perceptual information when beginning to speak: feedback from his or her own speech and the speech of others. This is at base a constructivist point of view. Studies show that deaf infants' babbles fall behind those of hearing infants (Gilbert, 1982; Oller, 2000). For example, Oller and Eilers (1988) recorded babbling in deaf and hearing infants longitudinally. Normal-hearing babies entered the canonical babbling stage between 6 and 10 months of age, whereas the range for deaf babies was 11 to 25 months. Hearing-impaired infants also produce fewer consonant types, show a decrease in types over time, and use a lower proportion of multisyllabic utterances, whereas normal-hearing babies show a larger number of consonant types, increase in such types over time, and increase in proportion of multisyllabic utterances (Stoel-Gammon & Otomo, 1986). Deaf infants almost never learn to speak normally (although, of course, their language production in a signed language may be perfectly fluent). It would appear from these studies, therefore, that auditory input is necessary for the normal and timely development of the range of adult-like syllables.

In addition, some components of early babbling are positively influenced by local auditory input. Clearly, infants born into different language communities rapidly grow up to speak different languages. Boysson-Bardies, Sagart, and Durand (1984) first recorded pure samples of babbling among 6-, 8-, and 10-month-old French, Arabic, and Chinese babies from Paris, Tunis or Algiers, and Hong Kong, respectively, noting that the French, Arabic, and Cantonese languages differ from one another in voice quality, stress, and proportion of consonantal versus vocalic sounds. They then asked French monolingual adult judges—both experienced phoneticians and lay people—to identify which babbling samples came from French babies. The phoneticians could correctly identify the country of origin in 6-month-olds; both the trained and lay groups correctly identified the patrimony of 8- and 10-month-olds. Analysis of the speech samples revealed that intonation in pitch and intensity contours strongly cued adults' perceptions, whereas particular sounds that are meaningful to the specific language did not. Because the language the infant hears is the only conceivable cause of such an effect, it is highly likely that infants as young as 6 months of age have already been influenced by the language they hear. Thus, the environment swiftly and surely channels early speech development toward the adult target language, and so very young infants must be extraordinarily sensitive to particular auditory experiences.

Ethological studies illustrate a complementary point in nonhuman animals. Birds provide a parallel, if not a model, of the basic relations between biology and experience in vocal development. Marler and his associates (Marler, 1987; Marler & Peters, 1989) observed the development of bird song in white-crowned sparrows from two communities, one on the south of San Francisco Bay at Sunset Beach and the other on the north of San Francisco Bay in Marin County. Marler spectrographically analyzed bird songs in the two communities and noticed that the birds' basic song patterns resembled one another but that overtone patterns distinguished the two dialects. Marler then placed the eggs of Oakland sparrows in the nests of Marin County birds, and vice versa. Hatchlings in both communities grew up to sing the songs common to their respective vocal environments rather than their "native" songs. Birds reared in a laboratory setting (and under conditions of auditory isolation) began to experiment with song and eventually "crystallized" a song that was atypical and highly schematic, but one that still showed many of the basic features of the normal sparrow pattern. From these studies it can be concluded that white-crowned sparrows are "programmed" to sing but that the particular dialect they sing is determined by the linguistic community in which they are reared. Similarly, human beings in all speech communities are apparently born with capacity and motivation for speech, but different language communities shape this tendency into different mature patterns.

How is first language production shaped? In a classic learning study, Rheingold, Gewirtz, and Ross (1959) demonstrated that vocalizations in babies as young as 3 months of age can be operantly conditioned by providing contingent social reinforcement. Another major avenue to infant language learning must be imitation (Valentine, 1930), including innate imitation of sound making, elicitation of imitation of action, and reflexive imitation. Piaget (1962) suggested that vocal imitation might develop through "contagion," as an empathic response to the other interactant's behavior. Human beings are among the only animals who acquire their cultural vocal repertoire by listening and imitation.

Infants even in the first 6 months of life imitate prosodic aspects of speech, as, for example, pitch (Lieberman, 1984; Papoušek & Papoušek, 1981; Piaget, 1962) and speech sounds (Kuhl & Meltzoff, 1988).

Many studies therefore confirm the subtle and not so subtle effects that the environment exerts over the development of infant vocalization. In several different cultures, middle-income mothers have been observed to speak to their infants more frequently and with more varied sounds than do lower-income mothers, although mothers in the two groups may behave similarly with respect to physical contact and nurturance (Hoff, 2002; Ninio, 1980). In turn, middle-income babies produce more sounds in the first months of life than do babies of lower-income parents (Papoušek et al., 1985). American mothers vocally play with their infants more than Central American Guatemalan Indian, European Dutch, African Zambian, and Japanese mothers do, and, presumably in consequence, American infants vocalize at greater rates (Goldberg, 1977; Kagan & Klein, 1973; Rebelsky, 1967; Tamis-LeMonda et al., 1991). Expectedly, therefore, social deprivation influences infant vocalization. Figure 9.9 shows that infants who were reared in orphanages during the first 6 months of life (earlier in the twentieth century) produced fewer different types of vowels and consonants and vocalized vowels and consonants less frequently than did infants reared in normal intact families (Brodbeck & Irwin, 1946). Of course, in natural experimental comparisons such as this one, we must be certain that the groups of infants were equivalent initially so that any eventual

FIGURE 9.9

Children reared in intact families consistently vocalize more different types of vowels and consonants and with greater frequency in the first half year of life than do infants reared in orphanages. (Left column vowels, right column consonants; age level 1 = birth to 2 months; 2 = 2 to 4 months; 3 = 4 to 6 months). (After Brodbeck & Irwin, 1946.)

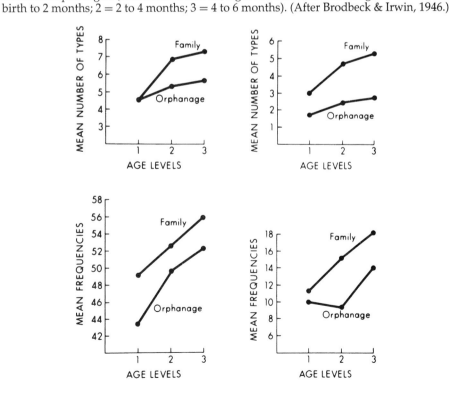

differences between them can be attributed unambiguously to the class, culture, or social deprivation "manipulation" of the experiment, and not to preexisting differences between the groups. Unfortunately, such baseline data are often lacking. Thus, any one of these results may be suspect. However, the pattern of findings across all conditions concerning the environment's role in infant vocalization is consistent and telling.

In summary, infants' very earliest sensitivities to sound and their earliest vocal expressions give evidence of strong biological influences. Very soon, however, both perception and production of sound become subject to the linguistic environments provided by parent, home, and culture. We now turn to consider a second system of language development, semantics, and the ways by which infants' initial verbalizations transform into meaning in speech.

Semantics

Infants cry, babble, and even gesture to communicate effectively before they acquire and use words. But these methods of communication have severe limitations: It may be impossible for an infant to use gesture to share a memory with his or her mother, and all parents can attest to the ambiguity of cries and babble. The next step is for infants to start learning the arbitrary connections between sounds and meanings that are characteristic of human language but unique to each language. This learning problem is the focus of this section.

Reference and First Words

A major obstacle confronting the language-learning child is the problem of *reference*, or the link between sounds and their meaning. Recall once again the "Yourteddyislyingonthecouchsweetie" problem and consider that to understand this simple statement, even after parsing the signal into separate units correctly, the child (*Sweetie*) must determine which unit refers to him- or herself, which to objects (*teddy, couch*) in the environment, which to an action (*is lying*), and so forth. After all, connections between word sounds and word meanings are essentially arbitrary, rendering the decoding task nontrivial. Much psychological, linguistic, and philosophical energy has been spent on this issue, but just how semantic development transpires still remains something of a mystery. In this section we discuss some major questions about semantic development. How is reference defined, when does it begin, and what are its origins? Later in this chapter we take up the equally formidable question of how the infant figures out the rule system interrelating words.

Let's begin with an appreciation of even the most basic aspect of the problem, namely, defining what a child's first word is. Even this, as it turns out, is somewhat problematic because what is meant by *word* is itself open to considerable dispute. Different developmental psycholinguists peg the onset of so-called *nominal insight*, or referential naming (Dore, 1978; Kamhi, 1986; McShane, 1980) to various times straddling the child's first birthday. Some argue that children who clearly comprehend words and phrases and produce conventional sounds ought to be credited with nominal insight. These abilities are typically evident from parents' observations at about 9 or 10 months, although work using preferential looking techniques has suggested that even 6-month-olds know that *mommy* (or the word used in the family) goes with the mother and *daddy* with the father (Tincoff & Jusczyk, 1999). By 9 months, many children use single sounds in regular or stereotyped ways: *mama* as request, *dat* to show, *bam* for things falling. Thus, although the child may not have pronunciations and word meanings that are aligned with those of English, he or she has taken an important step by using particular sounds to mean things, even if this usage is only apparent within a specific and limited context. For example, a child might use *bam* to refer to falling, but only falling from a high chair, or *car* to refer only to cars when seen from inside the house (Bloom, 1973). Other psycholinguists contend that such context-constrained sounds do not evince true nominal insight because they are not applied to classes of people, properties, objects, or events. These theorists argue more conservatively that the achievement of reference is only attained when children use sounds that clearly "name" people, properties, objects, or events. By the time they are 12 or 13 months of age, children use *mama* to mean mother in a variety of settings and situations, for example, and not exclusively when their mother is in a particular place or performing a specific activity. A third group of psycholinguists is more conservative still, crediting children with nominal insight only when, around 16 to 18 months, children use single words to convey sentential meaning. The most conservative attribution of word knowledge involves the child's understanding or using labels even when the referent is not present. Meeting this standard requires understanding and producing words to refer to things that are not available in the scene—for example, asking when the family dog will be back from the kennel.

In both comprehension and production, this development gives evidence of a true shift from *context-restricted* to *flexible* use, signifying a distinct, mature level of understanding of what names mean. Flexible language is consistently shown to be a reliable measure of language ability and to be a valid predictor of current and later linguistic and cognitive competencies (Bates, Bretherton, & Snyder, 1988; Bornstein & Tamis-LeMonda, 1989; Bretherton & Bates, 1984; Tamis-LeMonda & Bornstein, 1989, 1990).

To what do children's first words refer? One might expect that children's first words would be those that they hear most often and that the syntactic classes (noun, verb, etc.) of first words would be proportional to the number of words children hear in each class. But this is not true—or at least the story is not this simple. The two most frequent English words in speech to infants are *you* and *the*, which are rarely if ever in the top 50 first-produced words. So word frequency is not the sole key to early vocabularies (although all other factors being equal, frequency matters; American children learn *cat* before *cap*). What about the syntactic class of early words? Here there has been a great deal of debate, with some researchers saying that nouns predominate in early vocabularies and others saying they do not. Part of the problem in answering this question is that it is not clear what young children mean when they use a word. If a child says, "Bye-bye," the child might be referring to waving (a verb), the waving gesture (a noun), a social routine (whose syntactic class is hard to identify in any case), or any of several other possibilities. Setting this issue aside, most studies of English have found that a large number of early words are nouns, at least if the words are identified in terms of their adult class.

A number of explanations for this finding have been proposed. They are not exclusive: One or all of them may be true to some degree. The standard view is that the key factor is the ability of children to learn the concept to which a word refers. Nouns often refer to concrete objects, and verbs often refer to relations between things. Because notions like "dog" are easier to grasp than notions like "give," children learn more nouns (Gentner, 1982). A related view is that nouns are learned more readily because it is easier for children to figure out which aspects of a scene grown-ups are talking about when they use nouns than when they use verbs—that is, it's not the concepts themselves that are hard to grasp, it's identifying which concept an adult is using a word for (Gleitman & Gleitman, 1992). Finally, as Sandhofer, Smith, and Luo (2000) have argued, the noun "advantage" may arise because many nouns tend to be used the same way, being words referring to things—once you learn a few nouns, learning more object nouns is easy because they refer to similar kinds of categories (e.g., baby, book, or dog). Verbs, on the other hand, are more heterogenous, referring to movement (*go*), desires (*want*, *like*), manipulation of objects (*put*, *get*), and other things (*play*, *find*). These accounts do not explain the fact that infants learn nouns that do not refer to objects (*night*, *birthday*), however.

Input factors play a role as well. Studies of languages other than English show that sometimes children do not produce more nouns than verbs. For example, children learning Korean (Choi & Gopnik, 1995) and Mandarin Chinese (Tardif, 1996) have been heard to say more verbs than nouns. Two plausible explanations for this phenomenon have been offered. First, in both Korean and Mandarin verbs are much more likely to appear at the ends of utterances than in English, where the last word in a maternal sentence tends to be a noun. Perceptual studies have shown that it is easier for children to recognize familiar words at the ends of sentences (Fernald, McRoberts, & Swingley, 2001), suggesting that this structural feature of languages influences rates of word learning as well. Second, Korean and Mandarin mothers tend to talk about actions more than do English mothers, who tend to focus on labeling things. Goldfield (1993) showed that American mothers who used more nouns tended to have infants with a higher proportion of nouns in their vocabularies; if this correlation is present within English-learning infants it would be surprising if it were absent across languages. These differences in the speech heard by infants may neutralize the conceptual advantages enjoyed by nouns.

The Problem of Word Learning

Word learning is an example of *induction*, or using a limited set of examples to draw conclusions that permit inferences about new cases. Suppose a child sees a cup referred to as *cup*. For the child to recognize that the same word refers to other cups too requires an inductive inference: going beyond the taught example to other examples. As we will see, this is not as simple as it sounds. Research has addressed several facets of this process. First there is what we might call the *immediate reference problem*: What does the speaker mean when he or she says, "cup," right now? Sometimes the speaker will be pointing to an object when labeling it, but even in these seemingly clear cases there are many logical possibilities for what the word might refer to (Quine, 1960). It might mean "cup," but could mean "handle," "hot liquid," "drinking," "not appropriate for babies your age," or any of an infinite number of conceivable meanings. How do infants get it right? The second facet of word learning may be called the *extension problem*: once the infant has guessed which particular entity was referred to, he or she should then be willing to extend this word to other entities belonging to the same category—unless the word is a proper name. But what makes a cup a "cup"? Its shape? Color? Function? We cannot simply say, "things that are similar to the original cup," because this begs the question; without a definition of similarity we're right back where we started.

One straightforward hypothesis is that infants are not biased in any way: on hearing a word, they store in memory every percept in their senses: what they are seeing, feeling, tasting, and so on. Over multiple exposures to the word, only a few percepts will be present every time the word is heard, and over time the meaning of the word will be isolated. Some context-restricted uses of words seem to arise from this kind of process; if an infant only uses *car* for a specific situation, or only while sitting in a particular location, it suggests that the meaning of the word is not distinct from a wide range of sensory associations. However, this account cannot be the general solution to how infants learn word meanings. First, words are sometimes used when their referents are absent. If a parent says "I'm gonna go get your cup," on this account the learner should rule out the hypothesis that *cup* refers to a drinking vessel (because it's not there) and start considering things like the floor (which has been there every time). Second, chance co-occurrences would result in implausible word meanings. Suppose a parent happens to use *cup* several times when the cup is full but not when it's empty, and in the morning but not the evening. In this case the meaning of cup would be something like "full drinking container in the morning," but children do not seem to come up with these odd definitions. Third, and most importantly, children have been shown to learn words too quickly for a purely associative account in which meanings must be narrowed down over multiple exposures in different contexts. This "fast mapping" has been shown in many studies: Adults name an object a few times, and children seem to pick up the name of that object quickly (Heibeck & Markman, 1987).

Thus, psycholinguists agree that infants must be constrained in their guesses about word meaning. Three of these constraints were proposed by Markman (1989), one of which is the *whole object assumption*. Under this argument, it is assumed that when an adult points to an object and labels it, the child first perceives the novel label as referring to the whole object and not to its parts, substance, or other properties, although it could very well refer to these other things (e.g., Markman & Hutchinson, 1984). A second example is that children appear to be biased in interpreting nouns they hear as *category labels* (Markman & Hutchinson, 1984; Mervis, 1987; Waxman & Gelman, 1986), a bias that Markman termed the *taxonomic constraint*. On this assumption, children are said to interpret new words as referring not only to the object that they first see labeled with a word, but other objects that are the same kind of thing; that is, children try to solve the extension problem (rather than assuming all words are proper names, like Paris or Cicero), and their first guesses will be based on what the object is rather than what the object might be associated to. A third much-studied constraint is the *mutual exclusivity*, a claim that children assume that any given object should have only one name. This constraint is related to alternative constraints such as *contrast* (the assumption that there are no true synonyms; Clark, 1987, 1988) and the *novel–noun–nameless–category* (the assumption that children are biased to link a noun and an object category if both are new to the child; Golinkoff, Mervis, & Hirsh-Pasek, 1994). For the most part, the operation of these biases in word learning has been demonstrated in experiments in which children are shown two objects and then hear a novel word apparently intended to refer to one of the objects. For example, Markman and Wachtel (1988) presented 3-year-olds with a familiar object (like a cup) and an unfamiliar object (a pair of tongs) and asked, "Show me the dak." Children nearly always picked out the unfamiliar object, suggesting that they had rejected the notion that the novel word could be applied to an object already having a name (the cup).

A number of authors have suggested that the *constraints perspective* on word learning misses important facts about the process. No one denies the robustness and replicability of the effects shown in the numerous studies testing constraints; rather, the relevance of these constraints to the "bigger picture" of word learning has been questioned. Deák (2000), for example, argued that word learning constraints *describe* children's behavior but do not explain it. Others have suggested that we need more general theories of word learning that are not limited to object labels; after all, as we have seen, many of children's first words are not names for things.

Children are able to "pick up" word meanings outside of the stereotypical "point and label" situation (*ostensive naming*). The Western habit of picture book reading and pointing out categories ("That's a truck. See the truck.") is not a good model for learning many verbs, for example. Tomasello and Cale Kruger (1992) studied a group of mothers interacting with their 1-year-old children. Mothers' uses of verbs were divided into those referring to actions that were about to happen ("impending" actions), actions that were going on during the sentence ("ongoing" actions), and actions occurring after the sentence ("completed" actions). By far the largest number of verb uses were for impending actions: either requests that the child do something or comments about what the child or mother was about to do. Among the 19-month-olds, children whose mothers tended to use impending-action verbs to refer to whatever the child was focused on tended to have more verbs in their vocabularies, suggesting that verb learning is actually easier when the verbs describe what is about to happen rather than what is happening now. Indeed, in a follow-up experiment teaching novel verbs under these three conditions, Tomasello and Cale Kruger found that 24-month-olds were more likely to say words taught under "impending" conditions than "ongoing" or "completed." Perhaps, then, ostensive definitions are not the best way for young children to learn verbs.

Children are also sensitive to *communicative intent* in their thinking about what a word refers to; children recognize that language is about people's ideas and intentions. In a number of studies, Baldwin and her colleagues have shown that simple co-occurrence of a word and infants' attention to an object are not sufficient for word learning if social aspects of the situation do not support a linkage between word and object. For example, in one study children who were focused on exploring a novel toy heard an adult say, "A toma! It's a toma." For some children, the speaker was in view and was clearly talking to the child; for other children, the speaker was hidden behind a rice-paper screen and had previously been seen talking on the telephone. Children in the former condition learned that the object was a "toma"; by contrast, children in the latter condition did not learn the word (Baldwin, Markham, Bill, Desjardins, & Irwin, 1996). This result is striking because on a simple associative view of word learning, one would imagine that hearing a new word and attending to a new toy would be sufficient for word learning, but this is not the case.

These experiments show children's flexibility in determining what thing in the world (be it an object or an action) is referred to by a novel word. But this still leaves the question of extension: Which additional cases also qualify for the label? Markman's taxonomic constraint says that children will try to find another thing of the same kind, but what defines a kind? Work on this issue has shown that there is no simple answer to this question. In a typical study, children are taught a novel label for a novel object ("This is a mido"). Then they are presented with two additional objects: one shares one property of the original; the other shares another. Children are asked, "Can you find another mido?" Their choice indicates which property they thought criterial for identifying the category. In one well-known study using this method, Gentner (1978) taught 2- to 5-year-olds two new words for distinctive objects: one with a face whose expression could be changed by pushing a button (a "jiggy") and another that produced jelly beans at the press of a lever (a "zimbo"). When children were shown a third object that had a face like the first but yielded candy like the second, they were more likely to call it a jiggy, suggesting that they considered appearance or shape more important than function.

This study was followed by a considerable number of experiments trying to sort out the basis of children's extensions of word meanings. One study showed that the basis of children's word extension can vary with the kind of thing being named. Soja, Carey, and Spelke (1991) showed 25-month-olds an unfamiliar object (such as a copper plumbing T-junction) or an unfamiliar substance arranged in a particular shape (such as a crescent-shaped heap of sawdust). The object or substance was named: "This is my stad." Next, children were shown another object or substance configuration with the same shape as the original (for example, a plastic T-junction or a crescent-shaped heap of tiny chunks of leather) and also a few pieces of the original named thing (a few bits of copper or three round heaps of sawdust). Which would children pick out as the "stad"— the choice with the same shape but different substance, or the choice with the same substance but not the same shape? The results were clear: When taught the word for an object, like the T-junction, children generalized on the basis of shape, calling the plastic T a "stad." But when taught the word for the substance, like the sawdust, children generalized on the basis of substance, calling the additional rounded heaps of sawdust "stad." This experiment demonstrated that shape does not always determine word meaning for children; they modulate their interpretation based on what kind of thing the word stands for.

Additional experiments varying these kinds of situations in a number of ways have pointed to the complexity of the problem; there does not seem to be any single rule that determines how young children extend words, and the topic is the focus of a great deal of debate even in studies of older children.

Individual Differences in Vocabulary Learning

Various attempts have been made to account for the widespread differences in children's early vocabularies. Suggesting that early reference relates to maturation and growth, the Emperor Constantine wrote that infants could not speak well or form words because their teeth had not yet erupted, which would suggest that vocabulary size should be correlated with teething, a prediction for which we know of no supporting evidence. Most subsequent accounts have focused on differences in children's experience, primarily in the speech children hear from their parents. Hart and Risley (1995) found that parents differ in how much they talk to their infants, with parents lower in socioeconomic status talking substantially less than more affluent parents. But there is also a great deal of variation that is independent of socioeconomic status. Bornstein and Ruddy (1984) studied mothers whose socioeconomic status (SES) and education levels were relatively similar and found that these mothers varied widely in the frequency with which they talked to their babies. Some mothers talked to their 4-month-olds in as little as 3% and some in as much as 97% of a typical home observation period, and, notably, these individual differences were stable across the infants' first year of life. Thus, the range of basic language that washes over babies is virtually as large as it can be, even in mothers who are otherwise relatively similar. These differences matter. For example, Nelson (1973b) reported a strong concurrent relation between mothers' and their 2-year-olds' use of nouns. Findings such as these suggest that mothers whose speech emphasizes objects have children whose language likewise emphasizes objects.

Of course, interpretation of direction of influence is always uncertain in correlational studies (Bates, Bretherton, Beeghly-Smith, & McNew, 1982; Pine, Lieven, & Rowland, 1997). It could be that maternal speech influences child speech or that children who use nouns earlier promote the use of nouns by their mothers. Studies utilizing experimental designs (Belsky, Goode, & Most, 1980; Lucariello, 1987), statistical techniques (Bornstein, 1985; Olson, Bayles, & Bates, 1986; Tamis-LeMonda & Bornstein, 1989), and strategies for demonstrating specific links between individual inputs and particular language acquisitions (Goldfield, 1987) have increasingly bolstered the assumption that specific parental activities or aspects of the environment have significant roles to play in the growth of specific infant verbal skills. Mothers vary substantially in the quality and quantity of language they provide their children. When both language amount and verbal responsiveness are considered, however, verbal responsiveness is found to contribute uniquely to children's emerging language (Bornstein, Tamis-LeMonda, & Haynes, 1999; Tamis-LeMonda, Bornstein, & Baumwell, 2001). For example, children with verbally responsive mothers achieve the vocabulary spurt and combine words into simple sentences sooner in development than do children with less verbally responsive mothers (Tamis-LeMonda & Bornstein, 2002). Indeed, most contemporary theoretical formulations about how specific parent–child interactions contribute to language development (Bruner, 1983; Werner & Kaplan, 1963; Vygotsky, 1978) challenge investigators to consider specific relations between types of interactions and the acquisition of verbal skills at different points in time (see, for example, Bornstein, 1989; Wachs & Gruen, 1982; Wohlwill, 1973).

Many investigators concerned with early language have therefore turned to examine detailed aspects of parental speech (physical and prosodic parameters, references, questions, verb forms, and elaboration on child utterance) in relation to specific kinds of linguistic gains in children (Barnes, Gutfreund, Satterly, & Wells, 1983; Goldfield, 1987; Hoff-Ginsberg, 1985; Hoff-Ginsberg & Shatz, 1982). Messer (1981) measured the relative amplitude of labels and nonlabels in the speech of mothers while they showed toys to their 1-year-old infants. He found that labels had nearly a .50 probability of being the loudest word in the sentence. From this observation, Messer supposed that the relative loudness of labels could cue infants to map new words onto referent objects. Others have pointed to links between prosody of maternal speech and the object focus. For example, Fernald and Mazzie (1991) found that mothers' speech to infants consistently positions words at points of perceptual prominence in the speech stream—notably on exaggerated fundamental frequency peaks in utterance-final position—whereas in speech to adults the use of a prosodic emphasis is more variable. (We learned about the importance of such intonation contours in infant-directed speech earlier.) Many authors have supposed that infants discover linguistically relevant units in continuous speech by taking advantage of prosodic cues which may be regularly correlated with words, phrases, and clauses. This is the so-called *prosodic bootstrapping hypothesis* (Morgan & Demuth, 1996). Of course, maternal language also serves as a model for infant language.

Mothers often verbally refer to objects, activities, or events in the environment by describing, labelling, or asking about the unique qualities of the referent ("That's a spoon" and "What color is the spoon?"). This form of referential language is reputedly associated with vocabulary expansion during early language development (Furrow, Nelson, & Benedict, 1979; Newport, Gleitman, & Gleitman, 1977). Gogate and her colleagues showed that, when mothers teach infants a name for a novel toy, mothers have a strong tendency to move the toy in synchrony with their verbal label, which may help infants make the association (Gogate, Bahrick, & Watson, 2000).

Other investigators have focused on the role of social orientation (quality of attachment, parent responsiveness, involvement, sensitivity, and control style) in predicting early language competence (Bornstein & Tamis-LeMonda, 1989; Grolnick, Frodi, & Bridges, 1984; Matas, Arend, & Sroufe, 1978; Slade, 1987a, 1987b; Sorce & Emde, 1981). Still others have stressed the influence of the general intellectual climate (providing enriching toys, reading books, encouraging attention to surroundings) to growth in the language sphere (Belsky et al., 1980; Bornstein, 1985; Bradley, Caldwell, & Elardo, 1979; Carew, 1980; Olson et al., 1986; Tamis-LeMonda & Bornstein, 1989; Wachs & Gruen, 1982). Bee and her associates (1982) looked prospectively at the outcome of such experiences in predicting receptive and expressive language. They found that perinatal physical status and infant performance on a Bayley-type examination were poor predictors, but that mother–infant interaction (maternal attentiveness and mood during feeding) and environmental quality in infancy were strong predictors of 3-year-old child language comprehension. Similarly, Olson, Bates, and Bayles (1984) found that mothers' affectionately touching, rocking, holding, and smiling at 6-month-olds significantly predicted a composite measure of cognitive–linguistic competence in the same children at 2 years.

Bornstein and his associates analyzed influences of interactive maternal activities on the growth of early productive and receptive vocabulary and later verbal intelligence in a series of concurrent and prospective studies. In one, Vibbert and Bornstein (1989) found a positive association between the extent to which mothers verbally or physically encouraged their 1-year-olds to attend to new properties, objects, or events in the environment and how many words toddlers understood. Tamis-LeMonda and Bornstein (1990) also found that mothers' didactic encouragement relates to their 1-year-olds' language comprehension. In a predictive study, Bornstein (1985) recorded the frequency with which mothers encouraged their infants' attention to the environment in physical and verbal ways. When the babies reached 1 year of age, mother–infant interaction was observed and expressive vocabulary size in toddlers was assessed. Finally, at 4 years, the children completed a standardized intelligence test. Mothers who spoke more and prompted their infants more at 4 months had 1-year-olds with larger productive vocabularies and 4-year-olds who scored higher on the IQ test, suggesting that maternal stimulation facilitates the growth of infant language skills. In a follow-up short-term longitudinal study, mothers' encouragement of attention and infants' habituation at 5 months were found to predict toddlers' language comprehension and language production at 13 months (Tamis-LeMonda & Bornstein, 1989). A related study showed that maternal verbal *responsiveness*, or likelihood of the mother talking about what the child says or does, is strongly associated with vocabulary development: Children of highly responsive mothers reach the milestone of saying 50 different words earlier than children of less responsive mothers (Tamis-LeMonda et al., 1998).

In Chapter 2, we learned that research on the developmental effects of daycare is complicated because of questions surrounding the definition of quality of daycare, age of entry, and other factors. Nevertheless, because of the prominence of nonparental care of infants today it is of interest to look at the effects of daycare versus home care on children's early language development. One study of several hundred infants found that, generally speaking, children who spend some time in daycare centers do not differ much in their language achievements from children who are cared for exclusively in the home (NICHD Early Child Care Research Network, 2000). All other factors being equal, childcare in centers appears to have a small advantage over home-based daycare or exclusive maternal care, perhaps because children in daycare centers are exposed to a wider variety of language-based interactions. It is important to note, though, that the quality of the daycare arrangement is as important as what sort of care it is. Language development is facilitated by environments in which caregivers talk to children, and not all daycare centers provide this stimulation equally. Thus, the measured quality of the childcare situation has a modest but consistent effect on children's language performance.

Other aspects of the child's physical environment appear to influence communicative development. Wachs and Chan (1986) demonstrated this association. During four visits to the homes of 1-year-olds, they assessed different aspects of the environment in conjunction with different dimensions of infants' communicative performance. Their data show, for example, that parents who provide their child with new toys and changes in room decorations are also likely to name those objects for the child, but the physical parameters of the environment exert an influence on child language acquisition in and of themselves and not simply as a function of parental naming.

Clearly, neither nativist nor empiricist accounts alone tell us the whole story about early semantic development. Together, each has something to say about major influences on language acquisition. Consider what modern behavior genetic findings tell us about hereditary versus environmental influences on the growth of communicative competencies of infants. The Colorado Adoption Project (Hardy-Brown, 1983; Hardy-Brown & Plomin, 1985; Hardy-Brown, Plomin, & DeFries, 1981; Plomin & DeFries, 1985) reported rates of communicative development (language items from the BSID) in groups of 12-month-olds either born or adopted into intact families. Significant associations between adoptees and their biological parents, and between adoptees and their adoptive parents indicate, respectively, genetic influences on individual differences in infant communicative performance versus experiential influences. There is ample evidence for both in language development: Adoptive mothers' activities, like imitation of infant vocalization and contingent vocal responsiveness to infant vocalization, predict infant language competencies as do shared genetics (Rose et al., 1980; Scarr & Weinberg, 1983).

Of course, infants are by no means passive in the acquisition of semantics. A significant class of so-called infant effects arises when the infant influences his or her own development indirectly by influencing the behaviors of parents or other caregivers. Some evidence for such effects in language learning comes from a study of mother–toddler interaction as related to child semantic development reviewed earlier. When Vibbert and Bornstein (1989) evaluated maternal didactic and social interactions in relation to toddler language, the influence of maternal didactic activities was shown to relate to maternal social activities and to the role of the child in the interaction. In the case of the infant's comprehension of nouns, for example, where mothers initiated and maintained object-centered interactions more than their toddlers, toddlers showed virtually continuous gains in language to the degree that their mothers also engaged in social activities. On the other hand, where toddlers initiated and maintained object-centered interactions more than their mothers, maternal social input was unassociated with language acquisition. These complex relations show that infants are not simply vessels to be filled with language to a greater or lesser extent depending on characteristics of parents; infants actively participate in their own language learning (Bloom, Margulis, Tinker, & Fujita, 1996).

As we see in the foregoing discussion, determining exact relations between interactions on the one hand and semantic acquisition on the other has proven both conceptually and empirically challenging. Simple one-to-one correspondences between demographic variables (e.g., parent IQ, educational status, SES, employment status), interaction styles, and infant language skills appear not to exist. Even within homogeneous socioeconomic samples, it is a truism that mothers show wide variation in their proclivities toward verbal interaction and that infants vary considerably in early verbal skills. Research demonstrating specific links between parent verbal and nonverbal stimulation with objects and child semantic development suggests that parental efforts to channel child attention to extradyadic foci may make the representational function of language (i.e., words stand for things) more salient. Perhaps in this way, language becomes associated with things outside of the strongly interpersonal mother–infant relationship, and labels acquire concrete reference points for new-talking toddlers. Both "object-focus" and "encouragement of attention" aspects of didactics appear to play key parts in language acquisition.

Once the child attains one-word speech, word learning appears to proceed rapidly. If lexical size estimates are at all accurate, the average 3-year-old possesses a vocabulary of 3,000 words. Therefore, between approximately 12 and 36 months, the child is acquiring four new words per day on average. In so doing, children demonstrate not only perceptual attentiveness, but exploratory venturesomeness and mental absorptiveness. Babies and their experiences vary enormously, and in recent years studies of individual differences in early language learning have adopted both quantitative and qualitative approaches to understanding those differences.

Syntax

Syntax means grammar, the rules for combining words into meaningful and interpretable communications. Syntactic competence in children is a wonder to behold; particularly remarkable is children's ability to detect syntactic rules and regularities. These vary enormously across languages. In English, for example, subjects usually precede verbs, which in turn usually precede objects. Thus, when you hear "Larry thumped the ape," you know the monkey got hit by Larry. As English speakers, we are so accustomed to this word order regularity that it seems natural and perhaps even logical (Figure 9.10). But a great many languages don't work this way; for example, in Welsh the verb usually comes

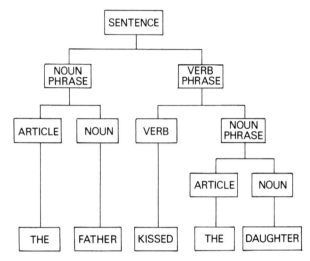

FIGURE 9.10
The basic structure of an English sentence, "The father kissed the daughter," and its grammatical decomposition.

first. In Turkish and Japanese, although many sentences place the verb last, subjects and objects do not have a fixed order. To tell who is who, these languages attach a suffix to objects, and word order is used instead for focus (emphasizing what is new and important in the conversation). Given that these rules vary across languages, they must be learned. Some structures are trickier than others; for example, the English passive is learned late, and even French adults need to look up some irregular French verb inflections, but generally speaking the rate at which children learn, and the fact that children make far fewer errors than one might imagine based on their learning of nonlinguistic regularities, suggest that children come to the task of language learning prepared to view language in certain circumscribed ways.

One example of this is provided by children learning Turkish. As Slobin (1982) and his colleagues found, by about 24 months these children make very few errors in inflecting verbs, which may not sound so impressive until you learn that Turkish verbs can be inflected for voice (e.g., active/passive), negation (isn't/is), tense (e.g., present/past), person (e.g. me/you), and number (singular/plural), among other things. Verbs do not always need all of these inflections, but children's ability to get it right is astonishing. For example, Aksu-Koç and Slobin (1985) report a 25-month-old appropriately (and grammatically) saying sentences like "getir-me-di-n," which may be glossed as "bring-negative-past-you," or "you didn't bring." Consider the particle *di*, which here denotes the past tense. To learn this morpheme, the child must have extracted it from words, analyzed the situations in which it was used, and drawn the conclusion that it tended to be used when referring to past events. As Maratsos (1998) points out, this analysis of situations is an enormous computational problem; across languages, words may be inflected not only for tense (which happens to be relevant for Turkish *di*), but also gender, shape, animacy (living/nonliving), social status, aspect (whether an action is ongoing or completed), number, and several other properties. And as we will see, parents cannot be counted on to explicitly point out what inflections are for: no mother is telling her 19-month-old, "Listen carefully: in our language, *d* at the end of a verb means something that already happened, except in some verbs like *hide*." Children sort these things out for themselves, and they are good at it.

Most researchers agree that there must be innate constraints on the hypotheses that children entertain when trying to learn how words and combinations of words align with meanings. But what are these constraints? Here we find one of the great debates in psychology and language.

One early view, offered by Bloomfield (1933), was that children learn grammatical rules by imitation and reinforcement. A similar view was later offered by Skinner in *Verbal Behavior* (1957). On this account, grammar can be characterized as an associative chain of words linked by transitions of greater or lesser probabilities. According to the behaviorist view, children learn *transitional probabilities* among words. Acquiring a grammar is therefore simply a matter of learning that "The dog ate" is English (*dog* can follow *the*, and *ate* can follow *dog*), but that "dog the ate" is not. Word-specific facts like these are learned by imitation and reinforcement, as we know infants can: On this view, adults produce grammatical statements for children to model, and they also systematically reward children's grammatically correct statements.

In what must still be the best-known book review in psychology or linguistics, Chomsky (1958) argued that Skinner's account of syntax development was fatally oversimplified. Some of Chomsky's main criticisms were these: Grammar involves more than elementary transitional probabilities among units of language that otherwise have no intrinsic order. The grammatically correct use and meaning of an initial word in a sentence just as often depends on the end of the sentence (that is, on an overall sentence plan) as it does on the next word, as is implied in a transitional probability approach. For example, the sentence "Colorless green ideas sleep furiously" is perfectly grammatical, although the actual transitional probabilities in the word string are absurdly low. Thus, transitional probabilities from one word to the next do not provide a reasonable account of grammar, and therefore cannot serve as the guiding principle of language learning. Second, Skinner's notion of reinforcement required parents to selectively reward children for producing grammatical utterances. Yet research has shown that parents do not do this reliably enough to account for language acquisition. In fact, parents are much more likely to correct young children's factual errors than their grammar. If a child says, "Me eat banana," parents are more prone to saying, "No, that was an apple" than "No, say 'I ate a banana' " (Brown & Hanlon, 1970; Morgan & Travis, 1989). Thus, parents do not directly teach children grammar the way schoolteachers do; children *induce* grammar from daily conversational interactions. Two other facts militate against a schoolteacher–pupil view of language acquisition: first, even expert linguists disagree about how to characterize grammatical rules—certainly this knowledge is not available to every parent. Second, children seem extremely resistant to explicit correction of grammar; a child saying "Me eat banana" will not generally switch to "I ate a banana" on being corrected.

Chomsky's attack went beyond mere criticism. He argued constructively that accounting for grammar requires sets of rules that operate over phrases rather than words. These phrases each have a chief element, or "head," that is drawn from a limited set of formal categories such as "noun" and "verb" (thus, a noun phrase has a noun as its head, a verb phrase has a verb, and so on). Grammatical rules determine how these categories may be arranged into *syntactic structures*. For example, possible noun phrases include "Ernie," "the socks," "twelve hungry ducks," or "the burritos left over from lunch"; these noun phrases could all fit in the part of a sentence calling for a noun phrase. Thus, "Ernie arrived," "The socks arrived," and so on are all grammatical sentences (although they might not make much sense). You could also say, "Did you know that Ernie / the socks / twelve ducks . . . arrived?" One of Chomsky's crucial contributions was to introduce into psychology the idea that any adequate description of language has to refer to structures like these and not just words. This idea is called *structure dependence*: Grammatical rules are defined not only over words, but also over syntactic phrases such as noun phrase. Structure dependence explains why the "colorless green ideas" sentence is grammatical even though it is improbable: "colorless green ideas" is a noun phrase and is allowed the full syntactic rights of noun phrases. Structure dependence is a critical constraint on the possible rules of grammar. Languages do not have rules like "To form a question, trade the first and fourth words" or "Form the past tense by adding /wa/ to the second word."

One of the boldest of Chomsky's claims was that structure dependence, and a number of other aspects of syntax, are innate, built into every infant in what he called Universal Grammar (UG). UG is said to account for the fact that, while children's language environments differ enormously, children's syntactic outcomes are strikingly homogeneous; whereas variation in the vocabularies of English-learning children can be traced to environmental factors such as amount of parent speech, variation in grammar seems hardly to exist among children learning a given language. Chomsky likened language learning to the growth of an organ like the liver: As long as certain very basic preconditions are met, both develop in all children. The claim is not that language itself is innate; that would imply that an English child reared in a Cantonese family would learn English instead of Cantonese. Rather, the claim is that children are innately biased to interpret language in certain ways. Some of these biases, such as structure dependence, are widely agreed on; other innate knowledge, such as specific constraints on what a pronoun can refer to, or the existence of innate categories like "noun" and "verb," are the focus of intense debate.

A current version of Chomsky's theory is referred to as the Principles and Parameters approach, which holds that in some basic respects (such as structure dependence) all languages share a set of basic principles; and that languages' grammars vary in only a restricted number of ways, called parameters. As children gain experience with language, they discover the values of the parameters. For example, in some languages it is grammatical to leave off the subject of a sentence, whereas in other languages this is ungrammatical. Thus, in Spanish, one may say, "Yo canto" (*I sing*) or just "Canto" (which also means "I sing," but the *I* is implied by the *o* ending of the verb). But in French, like English, one must say, "Je chante," to mean "I sing"; leaving off the *je* changes the meaning of the sentence. Whether or not it is grammatical to omit the subject of a sentence in these constructions is argued to be a parameter that all languages have; children must learn whether their language is a "subject-drop-okay" language or a "subject-drop-not-okay" language. An interesting feature of the Principles and Parameters approach is that some parameter values are held to be innate default settings. A candidate default was the "subject-drop-okay" value. Because children often omit subjects of sentences, the theory went, perhaps all children at first behave as if they were learning a language like Spanish or Italian. Children who really are learning these languages stick with the default parameter setting, whereas children who are not, such as English learners, must switch. Recent research has shown that in fact English learners do not drop subjects under the same circumstances as Italian learners (or Italian adults), complicating this simple account (Rizzi, 2000). However, attempts to find ways in which language learners behave similarly across languages and across development remain important endeavors in the study of syntax acquisition.

A crucial feature of UG is that the innately specified knowledge is particular to language; Universal Grammar applies to no other domain. The notion that languages either require subjects of sentences or do not, for example, is not a kind of innate knowledge that could be shared with other cognitive processes like visual perception or memory. For those who do not share the Chomskyan perspective, the innate specification of linguistic structure is a key sticking point (Elman et al., 1996). For these researchers there may be innate biases that concern children's ways of interpreting the world, including the interpretation of speech. But these biases are not particular to language. For example, proponents of the standard Chomskyan approach argue that there are innate rules that tell children that, in sentences like "Julien brought him a ladder," it is impossible for *Julien* and *him* to refer to the same person (by contrast with "When he came, Julien brought a ladder," which allows *he* and *Julien* to be the same). Some psychologists consider this level of detail in innate specification unlikely (Elman et al., 1996).

If language is like an organ, as Chomsky proposed, is it an organ that can be identified as a biological structure in the brain? At present it is not possible to give a complete answer to this question, but it is certain that there is no special knot of brain tissue that can be said to wholly contain the language faculty. Neuroscientific studies of adult linguistic performance show that certain structures in the brain are involved in particular aspects of language processing; for example, injury to Broca's area (in the left frontal lobe) tends to cause problems in producing fluent speech and in comprehending syntactic structure, whereas injury to Wernicke's area (in the left temporal lobe) tends to cause poor comprehension generally and fluent but relatively meaningless speech. See Figure 9.11. The discovery of brain areas specialized for language (although not a unitary language module) is consistent with a nativist theory. But it is also consistent with more general theories proposing that certain areas of the brain are good at processing stimuli of various sorts, and therefore are nearly always recruited for language. And there is nothing in brain specialization that proves the innateness of syntactic parameters.

Nevertheless, this question has motivated some interesting research on the neuropsychology of language processing in infancy. Because of methodological problems in doing neuroscience with infants, much of this research has been limited to whether infants, like most adults, show a tendency to process language in the left hemisphere of the brain. Molfese and Molfese (1994) provided electrophysiological evidence regarding hemispheric specialization for speech in newborn infants. They presented syllables, words, and mechanical sounds to infants and discovered consistent stimulus-dependent asymmetries in auditory evoked responses. As expected, the evoked response to speech stimuli was larger over the left temporal region than over the right, and the evoked response to mechanical sounds was larger over the right temporal region than over the left. They also found that the disparity of hemispheric response in infancy predicts children's level of language skill assessed on the McCarthy scale at 3 years (see Figure 9.12). Similarly, Best, Hoffman, and Glanville (1982), recording heart function, found a left-hemisphere advantage for discriminating speech sounds and a right-hemisphere advantage for timbre in 3- and 4-month-olds. MacKain

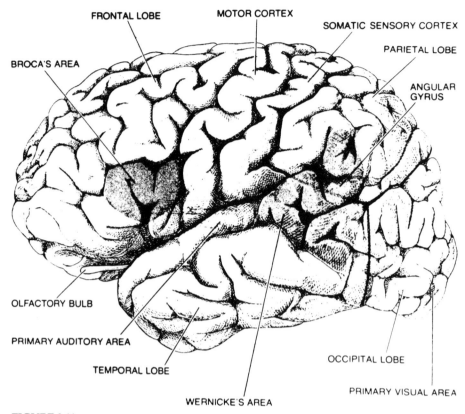

FIGURE 9.11

A view of the left side of the human brain indicating the major features and
highlighting two areas of speech, Broca's area and Wernike's area, concerned
respectively with producing and comprehending language.

and her associates (1983) found that infants of 5 months behaviorally match
synchronized optic-acoustic displays of speech in the right visual field, suggesting a left-hemisphere cerebral advantage. These sorts of effects may be better
described as a left-hemisphere speech analysis specialization than a language
specialization more generally (Locke, 1997). Studies by Mills, Coffey-Corina,
and Neville (1993, 1997) using electrophysiological measures found differential
responses to words that were reported as known or unknown to the 1-year-olds
they tested. In infants from 13 to 17 months of age, differences in responses to
known and unknown words were the same in the left and right hemispheres;
at 20 months, responses to known and unknown words differed only in the left
hemisphere. These results suggest functional specialization sometime in the second year. Developmental speech research of this sort is quite difficult to conduct,
and care must be taken not to overinterpret even such provocative results. However, available evidence suggests that anatomical and functional hemispheric
asymmetries may already exist at or soon after birth.

A second controversial source of neurological information on language acquisition comes from comparisons of individuals who have sustained cerebral
damage at different times in their lives. When the left hemisphere in a very
young child is damaged, the child typically develops normally with regard to
language, presumably because the two hemispheres of the brain are "plastic" in

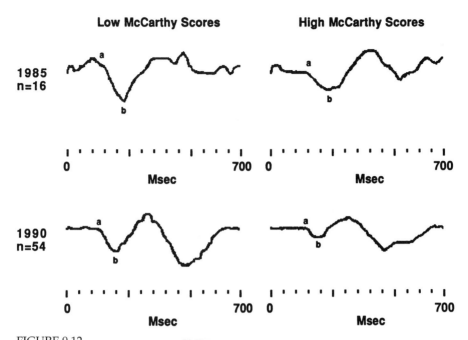

FIGURE 9.12

Auditory evoked responses (AERs) from two studies (in 1985 and 1990) from groups of newborn infants. AERs collected within a day of birth predict children's language scores as measured at 3 years of age. AER amplitude is larger as measured from point a to point b for lower scoring children in both samples and smaller for higher performing groups.

the very young; that is, they may be sharpened by experience, and one hemisphere assumes the functions of the other in the wake of the injury. (This depends, of course, on the site, nature, and severity of the injury.) When injuries are sustained after the onset of language, however, recovery is slower, if there is recovery at all. An adult whose left hemisphere is traumatized, as for example by stroke, may suffer permanent aphasia, the inability to use language (Almli & Finger, 1987). José Ribera's *The Club-Footed Boy* (1642) was one of the first formal representations of this syndrome. Notice in Figure 9.13 that the child Ribera painted is unilaterally affected: His right arm and right leg show evidence of hemiplegia, which means that the child was injured in the left hemisphere that controls the right half of the body. We know that the child is mute as well because he carries with him the written message: "Da Mihi Elemosinam Propter Amorem Dei" (For the love of God give me alms).

The question of whether children possess a "natural language" has been asked with surprising frequency in history—and by a surprising group of individuals, from pharoahs to phoneticians. James I of England (1566–1625), for example, posed the question and thought of how to address it. Long interested in the Bible—his is the King James version—James sought to identify the original language of Adam and Eve, and to do so he conceived of a unique experiment. He proposed to place two infants on an otherwise uninhabited island in the care of a deaf-mute nurse. James reasoned that, if the two spontaneously developed speech, theirs would be the natural language of humankind. Although probably within his power, King James never (to our knowledge) conducted his study. To determine natural language, and whether or not linguistic structures develop

FIGURE 9.13

José Ribera (1589–1656), *The Club-Footed Boy* (1642). The child evidences hemiplegia on the right side, indicating left-hemisphere damage, and the sign he carries suggests that he is mute.

spontaneously and reflect worldly experience, would constitute a telling experiment, but a wholly unethical one (Chapter 3).

Experiments of opportunity that approximate King James's conditions tend to confirm that children develop functional "language categories" in the absence of formal linguistic experience. Goldin-Meadow and Mylander (1983, 1984), for example, studied language development in deaf infants who are of normal

TABLE 9.1 THE EARLY EXPRESSION OF COMMON MEANING RELATIONS

Relations	English	Russian	German	Samoan
Agent-action	teddy fall	mama prua (Mama walk)	Puppe kommt (doll comes)	pa'u pepe (fall doll)
Action-object	hit ball	day chasy (give watch)	tur aufmachen (door open)	tapale' oe (hit you)
Entity-location	there car	Tosya tam (Tosya there)	buch da (book there)	Keith lea (Keith there)
Possessor-possession	mama dress	pup moya (navel my)	mein ball (my ball)	lol a'u (candy my)
Entity-attribute	big truck	papa bol'shoy (papa big)	milch heiss (milk hot)	fa'ali'i pepe (headstrong baby)
Rejection-action	no wash	vody net (water no)	nicht blasen (not blow)	le 'ai (not eat)

intelligence but whose parents (for various reasons) have prohibited their learning manual sign language. As a consequence, these children have essentially no experience with any formal language, although their other life experiences are normal. Goldin-Meadow categorized these children's communicative gestures into units (analogous to words) and connected multisign units (analogous to phrases). By the middle of the second year, the children give good evidence that they developed signs to refer to objects, people, and actions, and they combine signs into phrases to express relations among words in ordered ways. Their communication system is not only structured, it incorporates many properties found in child languages. Clearly, in the absence of formal training and imitation, children develop comprehensible syntactic rules: They sign actors before actions, and acts before objects acted on. Further analysis of mothers' interactions with their children showed that the children (rather than their mothers) originate such sign systems. These researchers concluded that "even under difficult circumstances" human children reveal a natural inclination to develop a grammatically structured communication system. Furthermore, the timing of children's invention of communication systems is roughly the same as that of hearing children learning spoken languages—their first "words" appear at around 12 months, and their first combinations of words appear several months later.

These results suggest that children are somehow driven to produce language, or at least communication systems with some kind of structure. Intriguing evidence in support of this notion has emerged from studies of deaf children in Nicaragua, where until relatively recently no sign language existed. Deaf children from around the country converged on a special school in Managua, where teachers (unsuccessfully) tried to teach them to lip-read Spanish. Children began using a gesture system to communicate with each other, and over time this system acquired complex features that are found in true sign languages (Senghas & Coppola, 2001). Later-arriving children learned the language from children already at the school, and these children improved on the language in ways that made it more similar in complexity and grammar to mature languages.

The Sources of Language in Language Learning

The Chomskyan argument and data that support it give conviction to a radical and counterintuitive biological view of the origins of grammar in language. It is still uncertain, however, that the regular development of grammar necessarily reflects a purely biological language faculty. The logic of the Chomskyan argument is that no known learning mechanism could acquire language consistently and with such a limited range of errors without being constrained in some language-specific way. However, there is also no known genetic mechanism that could account for the transmission of language-specific rules. The nativist position amounts to a claim that no general-purpose learning mechanism will ever be sufficient to account for children's facility in language learning. The empiricist position, by contrast, is that the science of learning mechanisms is not sufficiently advanced to permit this conclusion. Indeed, computer scientists have made significant advances in understanding what sorts of learning from sparse or idiosyncratic data are possible. There are no computer programs that can learn language the way a child does, or even at all, but some researchers argue that it's too early to say for sure that grammar is actually unlearnable from the kinds of speech infants hear, coupled with constraints that are more general than those envisioned by the Chomskyan account (e.g., Elman et al., 1996). This is very much an open issue at present.

It is important to keep in mind that although we have seen that there seems to be a kind of "drive" in children to produce language in a certain way (as in the case of the Nicaraguan signers), children are not alone in language acquisition, and to some degree variability among parents in their language use has measurable consequences for the rate at which aspects of children's syntactic development proceeds. For example, mothers who more frequently provoke their young children to speak have children with higher mean length of utterances (MLUs) (Peterson & Sherrod, 1982). Similarly, the noun-to-pronoun use and abbreviated utterance length of mothers are positively correlated with language development (Furrow et al., 1979). Children's tendency to use fixed multiword phrases (apparently without recognizing the words within them) is affected by maternal speech: Mothers who vary sentence structure in such a way that word boundaries are illustrated (e.g., by repeating the word *baby* in different sentence frames: That's a baby; show me the baby, the baby likes you) have children who are less likely to use unanalyzed phrases (Pine et al., 1997). We have also seen that word learning is strongly affected by characteristics of maternal speech. However, relatively speaking, the learning of syntax appears to be much less affected by variation in the input than the learning of words. Whether this is due to an innate syntactic module remains to be determined.

Summary

Infancy literally translates to mean "incapable of speech," yet infancy is paradoxically the point of departure for understanding language development and the time of some of the greatest achievements in language learning. Because the adult end point of language acquisition is so complex and variable, many have argued that specific sounds, semantics, and syntax, indeed the act of communicating, must all be learned. On the same grounds, however, others have argued that the intricate and multifaceted edifice of language could not but be constructed on inborn propensities and abilities. These diametric positions occupy the heart of the debate between "the impossible and the miraculous."

In this chapter on the origins of language learning in infancy, we have only scratched the surface of some of the topography, yet still unearthed treasure remains in a very rich field. Many more questions than we have answered await the next generation of developmental psycholinguists. In the space of about 2 years, infants master language without explicit instruction. By that time, babies comprehend others and express themselves using the complex symbol system we know as language. Children everywhere seem to get on the same road to achieve basic linguistic proficiency and travel at more or less the same rate down that road, largely (although not wholly) independent of their general intelligence, the language community in which they are reared, and the amount of tuition they receive. On the other hand, all manifestations of the language system are constructed or transformed by specific experiences: Toddlers learn only the particular language (and even the idiosyncratic dialect) to which they are exposed, and individual experiences seem regularly to be associated with individual differences in language competencies. Happily, parents readily adjust the language they direct to their infants in ways that appear to ease their infants' task. Thus, language acquisition must be both rigid and flexible; it must assure desired outcomes even in the face of environmental instability while at the same time encouraging flexibility in response to environmental diversity.

Language lies at the intersection of perceptual, cognitive, and social competencies. Language learning is critical to successful communication, but the challenge of language also forms a "problem space" in its own right, to be met and mastered for its own sake. The child brings perceptual prerequisites and sophisticated cognitive concepts to language learning as well as extensive experience with meaning, intent, and the dialogue nature of protolinguistic social interactions. In addition, language growth is fostered in a medium of fine-tuned accommodation that coexists between caregiver and child: In speaking to their young, parents adopt a special dialect, called infant-directed speech, that modifies normal adult-directed conversation to meet the preferences and limited information-processing capabilities of their infant partners. For their part, even young babies signal adults in many special ways, from smile and cry to gesture and look, that serve the purposes of communicating. Despite the barriers to normal everyday interchanges that nature has erected between caregivers and newborns, both actively strive and succeed impressively in conversing.

10

Emotions and
Temperament in Infancy

❖

- What distinguishes among emotions, emotional communication, emotional expression, and emotional experiences in infants?
- What functions do emotions serve in infancy?
- How can emotional expressions be studied in infancy and how do they change developmentally?
- What role does imitation play in infant emotional development?
- How sensitive are babies to emotional signals?
- What are the strengths and weaknesses of the learning, psychoanalytic, cognitive, and ethological theories of emotional development?
- What is temperament in infancy? What determines temperament?
- What are the principal dimensions of infant temperament?
- How does temperament affect infant development?
- What are the strengths and weaknesses of different ways of measuring infant temperament?

Individual Sensitivity and Style

Emotional development and temperamental individuality have been topics of compelling interest to students of infancy because they help shape the child's encounters with the social and object world. Emotional reactions organize how a baby responds to events, and parents devote careful attention to these reactions in their efforts to manage, pacify, accentuate, or redirect them. Over the course of the first 2 years of life, changes in a child's emotional reactions demarcate important transitions in development that are meaningful to caregivers, whether they concern the first elicited smiles, the earliest indications of stranger wariness, or the emergence of nascent expressions of embarrassment. These emotional reactions are significant also because they are viewed by parents as indicators of an emerging individuality—as cues to what the child's behavioral style is like now and will be like in future years. Along with variations in activity level and other dimensions, individual differences in predominant mood, soothability, and emotional intensity define dimensions of temperamental individuality by which infants become behaviorally organized early in life, and by which parents increasingly characterize their children. Indeed, Rothbart and Bates (1998) defined temperament partly in terms of individual differences in emotional reactivity, which they view as constitutionally based (i.e., genetically or biologically based), showing stability over time, and having an impact on the child's interaction with social partners. Thus, studies of emotions and temperament are not only linked because they involve similar aspects of behavioral individuality, but because they significantly guide the child's immediate reactions and enduring predispositions in encounters with the surrounding world.

In this chapter we discuss important features of early emotional and temperamental development. We begin with emotional development and consider how emotions have been defined and measured in infancy. Then we turn to more substantive questions concerning the development of emotional responses and the infant's developing sensitivity to the emotional cues of others. We conclude this section with a consideration of the various theories that have sought to explain these developmental changes. Next, we discuss temperament, about which definitional and measurement issues are also important. With respect to temperament, however, we also consider the questions of how temperamental differences affect infants' behavioral functioning, and the factors that can account for stability of temperament over time. As we shall see the study of emotional development and temperamental individuality remind us again of how significantly the infant affects the surrounding world through salient emotional expressions and an enduring behavioral style that includes emotional features.

Toward a Definition of Emotions

The study of emotional development is challenging because it poses fundamental questions for the measurement and interpretation of infant behavior. Do a baby's facial expressions reliably reflect underlying emotional experience? Does the infant's capacity to differentiate facial expressions of emotion in others reflect an understanding of these emotions? How should emotion be defined? In this section, we begin to consider these questions, starting with the definition of *emotions*.

If you stop to consider how you would define an emotion, you may find this task to be more challenging than it first appears. Indeed, philosophers have disagreed about the nature of emotions. Plato and Socrates believed that emotions got in the way of good judgment and thus should be kept under control and serve reason (rather than the other way around). Twentieth-century formulations about emotion have attempted to integrate views from neurologists and behavioral scientists into a broad conceptual definition (Solomon, 2000). You might approach the task of defining emotions by describing the range of emotions of which people are capable and the different components of an emotional experience, such as the accompanying patterns of physiological arousal, characteristic facial and vocal expressions, conditions that elicit specific emotions, and the like. *Structuralist* approaches define emotion in terms of constituent processes and identify the range of emotions that developing individuals can experience at different ages. The range of emotions depends on underlying cognitive, experiential, and physiological processes. The structuralist approach has dominated the study of emotional development for decades, just as it has dominated the psychological study of emotions more generally. Most of the theories of emotional development that we consider later in this chapter embrace structuralist definitions of emotion, including psychoanalytic, learning, and cognitive theories.

Lewis's (2000a) theory of emotions is an example of a structuralist view that identifies five defining characteristics of emotions. First, there are *emotion elicitors*, internal and external events that trigger biological changes that are the basis for emotion. Second, there are *emotion receptors* in the brain that facilitate the person's capacity to register and encode emotion-relevant events. Third, there are *emotion states* that involve changes in somatic and psychophysiological activity when emotional receptors are activated. Fourth, there are *emotional expressions*, including facial, gestural, and other behaviors. Finally, there is *emotional experience*, which is the interpretation and evaluation by individuals of their perceived emotional state and expression. Like most researchers, Lewis believes that emotional development depends, in part, on underlying changes in cognition, physiological arousal, and experience (especially social experience).

Structural theorists also devote considerable effort to identifying the basic or *primary emotions* of which people are capable from early in life. Not surprisingly, there is often vigorous debate concerning the criteria that define a primary emotion as well as the taxonomy of primary emotions offered by various theorists (Plutchik, 1980). Izard (Izard & Malatesta, 1987), for example, identified eleven primary emotions: interest, joy, surprise, sadness, anger, disgust, contempt, fear, shame, guilt, and shyness. Other theorists reject emotions like interest as primary, while adding others, such as affection (Campos, Barrett, Lamb, Goldsmith, & Stenberg, 1983). There remains, therefore, disagreement concerning the specific variety of primary emotions. In general, most structural theorists believe that a capacity for a primary emotion must be so deeply rooted within the human biological heritage that it is either innate or very early developing. Thus, primary emotions are distinct from *secondary emotions*, which depend on more advanced developmental capacities. Lewis (2000a) believes, for example, that the emergence of secondary emotions of embarrassment, pride, guilt, shame, and envy during the second and third years of life depends on a developing capacity for self-referent thought that makes these emotional experiences impossible for younger infants.

In general, structuralist views have contributed to the study of emotional development by describing some of the constituent processes involved in emotional experience, even in young infants. By identifying cognitive influences underlying emotional reactions, for example, structural theorists have helped us understand how events are evaluated and interpreted in different ways by infants of various ages, and how these appraisals affect emotionality. Similarly, by devoting intensive study to the facial expressions that usually accompany emotional experiences, researchers have developed useful methodologies for studying emotion in very young infants. However, some critics of structuralist views have argued that in so doing structuralists sometimes portray emotion as nothing more than a by-product of the perceptual or cognitive processes that underlie emotional development, and this makes the study of emotions rather uninteresting. In a sense, if emotion is portrayed as the outcome of other developmental achievements, then researchers tend to neglect how emotional development may, in turn, influence perception, cognition, and sociability. Thus, emphasizing the constituent processes yields useful insights, but may at times mislead students of emotional development to underestimate the reciprocal influence of emotion on other aspects of development.

Another way you might choose to define emotion, however, would be to consider what emotion does in your everyday experience. Emotions provide potent and informative internal cues, for example, that may cause you to reevaluate your current circumstances and make new plans. Emotions also provide significant cues to others concerning your current state that may alter that state as others "read" your visible emotional cues and respond differently. These perspectives are consistent with a *functionalist* view of emotions, which emphasizes the purposes and roles of emotion in the ongoing transactions between individuals and their environments (Campos, 1994; Campos et al., 1983; Frijda, 2000). Functionalist definitions of emotion derive, in part, from ethological theories that emphasize the adaptive purposes of emotion in human evolution. (We will consider ethological theories later in this chapter.)

Exemplary of a functionalist approach is the definition of emotions provided by Campos, Campos, and Barrett (1989, p. 395): Emotions are "processes of establishing, maintaining, or disrupting the relations between the person and the internal or external environment, when such relations are significant to the individual." Events can obtain personal significance in various ways. First, and most important, events may be directly relevant to an individual's goals or objectives, and emotional reactions derive from whether or not these goals are achieved. Second, some events (such as sudden, loud noises or noxious odors) are inherent elicitors of emotion because of how they trigger innate emotive processes. And third, events may induce affective resonance—in which an individual takes on the emotional experience of another—that can lead to emotional arousal. As we shall see, infants can experience emotions in all of these ways.

Within a functionalist view, emotions can be further defined in terms of what they do (Campos, 1994). For example, emotions can regulate other internal psychological processes: They influence perception, cognition, and motivation. Doing so may cause people to reevaluate their current conditions and adjust their actions accordingly. Emotions and emotion terms influence how people appraise and interpret events and how they organize their experiences conceptually. Emotions also can regulate interpersonal behavior, because individuals respond socially to the emotions they "read" in others, and people regulate the expression of their own emotions to achieve social goals. Observing someone approaching who is visibly angry (with clenched fists, a flushed face, and an angry facial expression) arouses different emotions and reactions than observing someone who looks joyful or fearful. Finally, emotions are also directly related to an individual's action tendencies by organizing and motivating reactions to environmental events that may be biologically and/or psychologically adaptive. Compare, for example, the goals, appreciation, action tendencies, and adaptive functions of the emotions of joy, anger, sadness, and fear presented in Table 10.1. Joy is expressed when an organism concludes that a significant objective or goal has been attained, and this emotional experience energizes the organism, reinforces the activity, encourages others to maintain the pleasurable interaction, and stimulates the organism to attempt new challenges. Anger, by contrast, derives from the perception of obstacles to goal attainment, and anger motivates efforts to restore progress toward achieving the goal, change the behavior of others, and/or strive for revenge or retaliation.

TABLE 10.1 GENERALIZED SCHEMA FOR PREDICTING ELICITATION
OF SOME BASIC EMOTIONS

Emotion	Goal	Appreciation	Action Tendency	Adaptive Function
Joy	Any significant objective	Goal is perceived or predicted to be attained	Approach Energizing	Reinforcement of successful strategy
				Facilitation of rehearsal of new challenges
				Social message to initiate or continue interaction
Anger	Any significant objective	Perception of or anticipation of an obstacle to attainment of goal; perception of obstacle as not easily removable	Elimination (not just removal) of properties of an object that make it an obstacle	Restoration of progress toward a goal
				Effecting a change in behavior of a social other
				In later development: revenge, retaliation
Sadness	Securing or maintaining an engagement with either an animate or inanimate object	Perception of the goal as unattainable	Disengagement	Conservation of energy
				Eventual redirection of resources to other pursuits perceived to be more attainable
				Encourages nurturance from others
Fear	Maintenance of integrity of the self, including self-survival and, later, self-esteem	Perception that the goal is not likely to be attained, unless protective action is taken	Flight, withdrawal	Survival
				Avoidance of pain
				Maintenance of self-esteem
				Alert others to avoid the situation or help

Adapted from Campos et al. (1983). Reprinted by permission of John Wiley and Sons and the authors.

It is clear that functionalist views of emotion avoid many of the pitfalls of structuralist views. In regarding emotion as a central organizing feature of human experience, for example, functionalist theorists recognize that emotions are influenced by perception and cognition but are never the mere by-product of these internal processes. This heightens interest in emotional development as a catalyst for other developmental processes that is enhanced by a theoretical emphasis on the purposes and functions of emotion, rather than its structural constituents. Functionalist theorists argue that by focusing on the roles of emotion in human behavior we come closer to understanding their adaptive and maladaptive influences. Functionalist perspectives are criticized, however, for a lack of clarity about precisely how emotions are related to other aspects of human motivation. By defining emotions as being related to the "significant" interests of the individual and by relating emotional arousal to broadly defined adaptive functions, functionalist definitions of emotion seem unduly expansive (encompassing, it would seem, most of human motivation, including drives related to hunger, thirst, and sexuality) and thus are imprecise. Functionalist views also tend to identify the purposes of emotion better than they explain why these functions emerge when they do.

In some respects, the differences between classical structuralist and newer functionalist views of emotion may be viewed as differences in emphasis rather than of substance: The two often explain identical emotional processes in complementary ways (compare, for example, Izard & Ackerman, 2000, with Barrett & Campos, 1987). However, these approaches also differ with respect to the substantive questions that underlie the study of emotion in general and of emotional development in particular. Can young infants experience a broad variety of discrete emotions, or do different emotions emerge out of a less differentiated ability to express distress and pleasure at birth? How are emotional experience and emotional expression—especially facial and vocal expression—linked early in life, and does their association change with development? What roles do developmental changes in perception and cognition assume in emotional development? How are emotions socialized in infancy, and how does a capacity to regulate or manage emotional arousal emerge during this period? There are no clear answers to any of these questions, which explains researchers' continuing strong interest in early emotional development and the importance of definitions (structuralist or functionalist) that guide alternative approaches to these issues. Some provisional answers are beginning to emerge from research on the development of emotional expressions in infancy, however.

Methodological Issues in the Study of Emotions in Infancy

Understanding emotional development in prelinguistic infants presents formidable challenges to researchers because infants cannot introspect and report on their subjective experiences in the ways that adults can. As a consequence, the study of emotional sensitivity is inextricably linked to the development of emotional expressions in infancy: It is difficult to study one without studying the other, even though expressions may not always reliably index underlying experience. For this reason, we first examine methodological issues in the study of emotional development in the first 2 years of life.

Darwin (1872/1975) anticipated the current reliance of researchers on facial expressions of emotion with his observation that certain expressions are remarkably consistent across age and culture. In Figure 10.1, we reproduce Darwin's pictures of emotional distress in children, illustrating his belief in the universality of emotional expressions (see, too, his comments on Doddy's emotions in Box 3.1).

Because the face is full of muscle activity and can convey a broad range of expressions with subtle variations, and because we commonly use the face as our primary means of evaluating another's emotional experience, researchers have devoted considerable effort to devising measurement systems to appraise facial expressions of emotion in infants. These researchers have devised highly detailed, anatomically based measurement systems for coding specific muscle movements in the face. Ekman's Facial Action Coding System (FACS; Ekman & Friesen, 1976, 1978) illustrates this measurement approach for adults, with a

FIGURE 10.1
Expressions of distress in infants suffering slight pain, moderate
hunger, or discomfort. (From Darwin, 1872/1975.)

broad range of specific and complex facial muscular activity discretely coded
in a detailed and time-consuming procedure. Oster modified this system for
infants (called Baby FACS), taking into account the unique facial configurations of young babies (Oster, Hegley, & Nagel, 1992). Similarly, Izard (1979;
Izard & Dougherty, 1982) developed a detailed system, called the Maximally

Discriminative Facial Movements Code (MAX), that is designed for use with infants and allows users to identify 27 distinct components or patterns that may be organized to specify particular emotions. A simplified version of MAX (called AFFEX) is also available, and examples of MAX coding criteria are found in Table 10.2.

If we are confident that facial expressions reliably reflect underlying emotional arousal in infants, the primary benefit of this level of detail is that it enables the researcher to specify precisely and unambiguously when a particular emotion is being experienced, as well as delineating specific transitions or fluctuations between emotions and the temporal course of emotional arousal and decline. This is especially useful when researchers are studying the baby's emotional reactions to social events—such as the approach of an unfamiliar adult—in which short-term changes in the infant's facial expressions may reveal significant changes in the infant's appraisal of the stranger. Because these detailed, anatomically based systems typically require the coding of videotaped records at very slow speeds (a fraction of the rate at which they occur in real time), they provide a level of detail and sophistication that more general systems cannot provide. For example, Messinger, Fogel, and Dickson (2001) described four types of smiles: smiling alone involving neither cheek raising nor mouth opening (simple smiling), cheek-raise smiling without mouth opening (Duchenne smiling), open mouth smiling without cheek raising (play smiling), and open-mouth cheek-raise smiling (duplay smiling). They went on to describe how these different types of smiles actually signal different emotions in infants 1 to 6 months of age.

But how well do facial expressions index underlying emotional experience in infants? Because we rely on facial expressions in our everyday estimates of others' emotional experiences, these measures carry considerable "face validity," as evident in the infant facial expressions depicted in Figure 10.2, each of which can be coded in detail using MAX, AFFEX, or Baby FACS. In this figure, it is rather clear which baby is expressing fear, joy, anger, and other discrete emotions. However, students of early emotional development have also questioned how reliably facial expressions observed in young infants reflect a baby's underlying emotional experience. For example, Camras, Lambrecht, and Michel (1996) found that an open mouth, raised eyebrows facial expression (identified by facial coding schemes as "surprise"—see Figure 10.2) may not always denote surprise in infants. They found that raised eyebrows and open mouths were typical of 5- to 7-month-old infants engaged in routine object exploration: Raised eyebrows frequently occurred after the infants began mouthing the toy. In an earlier study, adult judges frequently identified different infant facial expressions (i.e., anger, sadness, and pain/discomfort) than did users of the MAX coding system (Camras, Sullivan, & George, 1993). These observations have led some theorists to argue that the linkages between facial expressions of emotion and underlying emotional experiences are not innate (as theorists like Izard & Malatesta, 1987, believe), but instead develop over time through social experience, nervous system maturation, and a growing emotional repertoire (Saarni, 2000).

As an alternative or as a convergent measure, researchers have turned to vocal or gestural expressions. Johnstone, Van Reekum and Scherer (2001; Scherer, 1999) showed in research with adults using synthesized and filtered speech that there are a number of reliable vocal indicators of emotional state in adults. Happiness, for example, is expressed by high vocal pitch, pitch variability,

TABLE 10.2 FACIAL EXPRESSION CRITERIA AND ILLUSTRATION

Selection of Maximally Discriminative Facial Movements (MAX) Codes

Brows (B), Forehead (F), Nasal root (N)	Eyes/Nose/Cheeks	Mouth/Lips
20. B: Raised in arched or normal shape. F: long transverse furrows or thickening; N: narrowed.	30. Enlarged, roundish appearance of eye region owing to tissue between upper lid and brow being stretched (upper eye furrow may be visible); upper eyelids not raised.	50. Opened, roundish or oval.
21. B: One brow raised higher than other (other one may be slightly lowered).	31. Eye fissure widened, upper lid raised (white shows more than normal).	51. Opened, relaxed.
22. B: Raised; drawn together, straight or normal shape. F: short transverse furrows or thickening in mid-region; N: narrowed.	33. Narrowed or squinted (by action of eye sphincters or brow depressors).	52. Corners pulled back and slightly up (open or closed).
23. B: Inner corners raised; shape under inner corner. F: bulge or furrows in center above brow corners; N: narrowed.	36. Gaze downward, askance.	53. Opened, tense, corners retracted straight back.
24. B: Drawn together, but neither raised nor lowered. F: Vertical furrows in center above brow corners; N: narrowed.	37. Eye fissure scrouged, tightly closed.	54. Angular, squarish (open).
25. B: Lowered and drawn together F: vertical furrows or bulge between brows; N: broadened, bulged.	38. Cheeks raised.	56. Corners drawn downward–outward (open or closed); chin may push up center or lower lip.
	39. Gaze cast downward, head tilted back.	59A (= 51/66). Opened, relaxed; tongue forward (beyond gum line), may be moving.
	42. Nasal bridge furrowed (or shows lumpy ridge running diagonally upward from nasolabial fold). (42 need not be coded separately; it can be used as an additional cue in coding 54 and 59B.)	61. Upper lip raised on one side
		63. Lower lip lowered (may be slightly forward).
		64. Lower lip (or both lips) rolled inward (not illustrated and not observed in video records of infants).
		65. Lips pursed.
		66. Tongue forward (beyond gum line), may be moving.

From Campos et al. (1983). Reprinted by permission of John Wiley and Sons and the authors.

fast tempo, and high intensity, whereas sadness is specified by low pitch, low intensity, slow tempo, and diminished pitch variability. But we know very little about how different emotions are expressed vocally by infants and whether different emotions have distinct vocalic correlates. Thus, for example, researchers studying the infant cry have debated whether infants possess distinct cries for hunger, pain, anger, and other states, or whether caregivers infer these states in babies on the basis of time and context (e.g., when the baby was last fed) rather than on the basis of the cry itself. Adults do, however, rate certain cries as more distressed and aversive than others: Babies who cry with a high pitch, with great intensity, and for a long duration tend to elicit faster responses than do infants who cry briefly or minimally, because adults accurately interpret the cry as more distressed (Barr, Hopkins, & Green, 2000). However, much more research is needed before cry features can be reliably associated with distinct emotions in infants' particularly as the cry itself changes during infancy because of developmental changes in the fundamental frequency, the structure of the vocal apparatus, nervous system organization, cognition, and social experience (Barr et al., 2000; Lester & Boukydis, 1991). Consequently, cries may mean somewhat different things in newborns than in 1-year-olds.

We know even less about the gestures, movements, and other behaviors that may indicate emotional arousal in infants. Darwin observed that Doddy regularly used gestures "to explain his wishes" (Box 3.1), but Papoušek and Papoušek (1978) are among the few researchers to study gestural means of identifying infants' behavioral and emotional states. Figure 10.3 shows stimuli they used in a study of parents' and nonparents' identification of infants' behavior and emotional states, and reveals that infants signal their states gesturally with considerable clarity. Moreover, infants become very still when they are interested in an event, turn away from stimuli that evoke fear, show a slumped posture when sad, look intently (often with a double take) at stimuli that surprise them, and try to repeat or duplicate experiences they find joyful. Although such behaviors are certainly not associated with different emotions in a one-to-one fashion, they provide useful convergent measures when used in tandem with facial and/or vocal measures to tell us about infants' emotions.

Clearly, in sum, reliance on any single index of emotional arousal in infants—whether facial, vocal, or gestural—risks erroneous conclusions, and thus the use of multiple convergent measures of emotion is probably the best course in studies of early emotional development. Unfortunately, because of the labor-intensive demands required for obtaining such measures, few research studies incorporate such multimethod strategies.

Development of Emotional Expressions

Because emotional reactions are associated with biologically and psychologically adaptive action tendencies (as functionalist approaches note), it should not be surprising that emotional expressions can be observed during the newborn period, often in response to survival-related experiences. We have already discussed (see Chapter 6) neonates' emotional reactions to the taste of sour, sweet, and bitter substances. Neonates clearly responded to a sweet taste with what adults interpret as positive facial expressions, and to other tastes with various negative expressions of disgust or "distaste" as if to eliminate the noxious

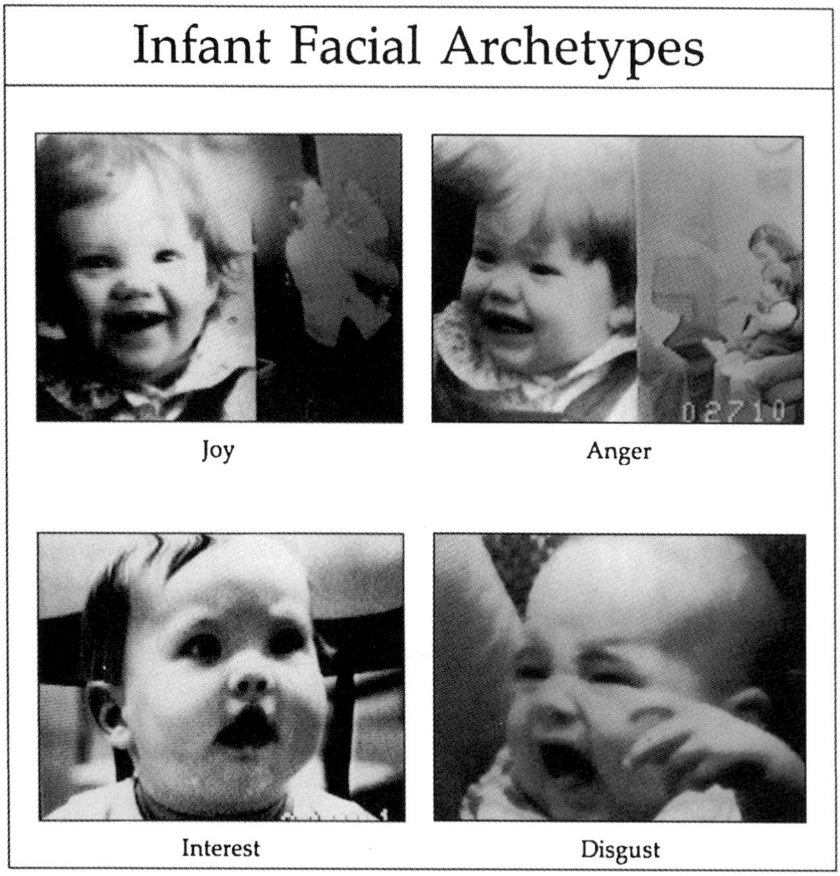

Infant Facial Archetypes

Joy

Anger

Interest

Disgust

FIGURE 10.2

Infant facial archetypes. Joy: Mouth forms smile, cheeks lifted, twinkle in eyes. Anger: Brows drawn together and downward, eyes fixed, mouth squarish. Interest: Brows raised or knit, mouth may be softly rounded, lips pursed. Disgust: Nose wrinkled, upper lip raised, tongue pushed outward. Surprise: Brows raised, eyes widened, mouth rounded in oval shape. Distress/Pain: Eyes tightly closed, mouth, as in anger, squared and angular. Sadness: Brows' inner corners raised, mouth corners drawn out and down. Fear: Brows level, drawn in and up, eyelids lifted, mouth corner retracted straight back. (Courtesy of C. Izard, L. Izard, 1995.)

substance. Although newborns are capable of a more limited range of discrete emotional expressions than older infants, some basic emotions appear to be within the neonate's expressive repertoire.

Distress is, of course, also one of these primary emotions. Lewis (2000a) viewed distress as one of three early appearing primary emotions, available to infants from the very first moment of life. Distress further differentiates as a function of maturation and experience into sadness, disgust, fear, and anger by 6 months of age. Lemerise and Dodge (2000) found that anger expressions in infancy have been observed as early as 3 to 4 months of age, and that as infants age, anger, rather than generalized distress, becomes increasingly typical in response to events that are unpleasant or restricting. In their studies of the emotional responses of young infants to painful inoculations, Izard and his colleagues (Izard, Hembree, Dougherty, & Spizzirri, 1983; Izard, Hembree, & Huebner, 1987) reported that distress was preeminent in the expressions of infants at 2 months

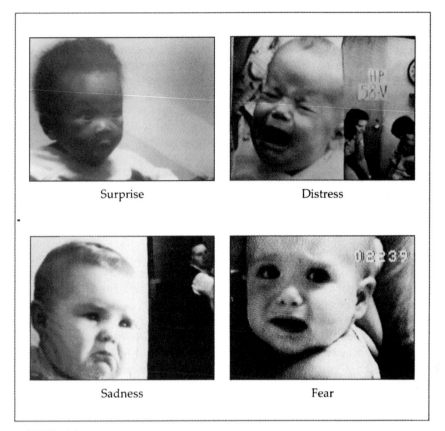

Surprise	Distress
Sadness	Fear

FIGURE 10.2
(*Continued*)

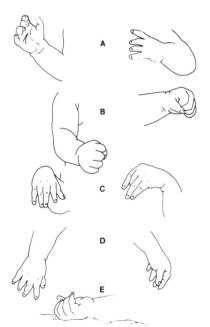

FIGURE 10.3

Observable cues indicating behavioral and emotional states of infants as seen in the position of hands: (*A*) Alert waking state; (*B*) Closed fists in uncomfortable or distressing situations; (*C*) Passive waking state; (*D*) Transition to sleep; (*E*) Sleep. (Courtesy of H. Papoušek.)

of age, but by 19 months anger expressions predominated. They reasoned from these findings that very young infants are capable only of an immediate emergency reaction to physical pain that distress expressions indicate, but that with increasing age they can inhibit this emergency reaction enough to mobilize angry feelings, which motivate more sophisticated actions to alleviate the painful stimulus. When one is angry, in other words, one is motivated to change the eliciting circumstances, whereas this does not as commonly occur with physical distress (see Table 10.1), and this may reflect the older infant's cognitive maturation (e.g., the growth of means–ends understanding) as well as the growth of neurophysiological inhibitory processes.

In this connection, Buss and Goldsmith (1998) examined 6-, 12-, and 18-month-old infants' emotional and behavioral reactions in two episodes designed to elicit anger (i.e., placing a desired toy behind a barrier and stopping infant play by restraining the infant's arms) and two episodes designed to elicit fear (i.e., having a remote-controlled spider and a remote-controlled dog whose behavior was noisy unpredictably approach the infant). As expected, the anger- and fear-eliciting episodes produced AFFEX-defined expressions of anger and fear in the infants (Izard, Dougherty, & Hembree, 1983). Intensity of fear expressions was associated with less approach toward and more withdrawal from the fear stimuli and more looks toward mother. Intensity of anger was associated with greater resistance against the arm restraint and more attempts by the infant to distract her- or himself from the stimulus by focusing on another object. Interestingly, infants' resistance against the arm restraint and their distraction attempts during the anger episodes predicted lower levels of subsequent anger expressions, suggesting that such behaviors served to regulate underlying feelings of anger. No such predictive relations were found between the reactions to the fear-eliciting stimuli and subsequent expressions of fear, however, suggesting that emotion regulation functions differently for different affective systems (Buss & Goldsmith, 1998).

Sadness is another early emerging emotional expression and has been observed in infants as young as $2\frac{1}{2}$ months of age (Izard et al., 1995). Tronick, Cohn, and their collaborators (Cohn & Tronick, 1983a, 1983b; Tronick, Cohn, & Shea, 1986) have observed that, when mothers play with their 3-month-old infants and then suddenly become impassive and unresponsive, their babies show signs of withdrawal, "wariness," and sadness in their facial and postural expressions. Expressions of sadness have also been reported in infants of depressed mothers (Field, 1987; Field et al., 1988). Fear is also apparent early. Yonas (1981) reported that the withdrawal component of fear appears when 3-month-olds confront looming stimuli, although facial expressions have not been measured in this situation. After the half-year point, infants also begin to show fearful reactions to visual cliffs, approaching strangers, and other sudden or unusual events.

A capacity for expressing positive emotions also emerges in early infancy (Lewis, 2000a). The earliest elicited smiles begin to appear toward the end of the first month of life and can be evoked through social interaction, such as the sound of a high-pitched human voice or the appearance of a nodding face (Emde & Harmon, 1972; Wolff, 1966). Clear expressions of joy can be observed by $2\frac{1}{2}$ months, when infants are engaged in social play with their mothers (Izard et al., 1995), and by 3 to 4 months of age infants begin laughing in response to stimulation (especially social stimulation) that is more arousing and intense (Field, 1982; Sroufe & Wunsch, 1972; Sroufe & Waters, 1976). Joy is also apparent in response to nonsocial eliciting conditions: Lewis, Alessandri, and

Sullivan (1990) found increased expressions of joy and interest when infants as young as 2 months of age were learning a contingent game, and expressions of anger when the learned expectancies from this game were later violated.

Taken together, infants from birth and shortly thereafter are capable of expressing a range of different emotions, including distress, disgust (or "distaste"), anger, sadness, fear, surprise, and joy in a range of laboratory and naturalistic situations. The fact that such a large proportion of primary emotions is present so early in life and that they appear in survival-related situations (such as tasting noxious substances, experiencing a painful inoculation, or confronting a looming stimulus) gives credence to functionalist views that emotional arousal motivates and directs biologically adaptive action tendencies, even very early in infancy. It also supports the structuralist perspective that early emotional expressions may be organized around these kinds of discrete emotional experiences.

Instead of using highly detailed direct observations to determine whether or not emotions are present in young infants, an alternative research strategy is to ask untrained observers, such as mothers, nurses, or students, to identify the emotions displayed in photographs of infants. Whether the emotions are depicted in still photographs or in videotaped segments, these untrained identifications tend to be accurate (see Hiltunen, Moilanen, Szajnberg, & Gardner, 1999), although perhaps more so for expressions of joy, interest, surprise, and distress and less so for expressions of fear, anger, sadness, and disgust (Oster, Hegley, & Nagel, 1992). Researchers have also asked infant caregivers to describe the range of emotions they perceive in their babies. Emde and his colleagues reported that, by the time their infants reached 1 month of age, 99% of mothers believe that their babies express interest, 95% joy, 84% anger, 75% surprise, 58% fear, and 34% sadness (Johnson et al., 1982). In response to specific questions, the mothers described vocal and facial expressions, along with gestures and arm movements, as the bases for their judgments (Johnson et al., 1982; Klinnert, Sorce, Emde, Stenberg, & Gaensbauer, 1984). It is not clear, of course, whether these judgments reflect the infants' expressive capacities alone or whether mothers' subjective inferences and use of contextual cues assumed a predominant role. However, because mothers commonly respond differently to different perceived emotional messages, they have frequent opportunities to refine their inferences depending on how their babies respond to them (Sorce & Emde, 1982). Thus, there may be good reasons for confidence in maternal judgments such as these.

As infants grow older, they become capable of a broadened range of emotional expressions, and they become responsive to a growing variety of eliciting conditions. Changes in neurophysiological organization contribute to the inhibition of primitive distress reactions and the enlistment of more complex emotional responses to events such as anger. Other neurophysiological changes later in the first year may also provide infants with a capacity for emotional inhibition and self-regulation, especially of negative emotions (Fox & Calkins, 2000). Cognitive changes also contribute to emotional growth by enabling infants to evaluate situations more complexly. Toward the end of the first year, for example, an infant's reactions to a stranger entail not only an evaluation of the adult's unfamiliarity, but also of the context (e.g., mother's presence or absence), the setting (e.g., a comfortable and familiar environment or an unfamiliar laboratory), the stranger's appearance (e.g., male or female, child or adult) and behavior (e.g., approaching fast or slow, looming overhead or looking at eye level), as well as many other considerations (Thompson & Limber, 1990). These findings have been an important corrective to theoretical views of emotional development (discussed below) that link stranger anxiety directly to maturational processes or the simple perception of unfamiliarity and indicate that the growth of information-processing skills and reasoning processes (such as the capacity to anticipate events or to link means and ends) contributes to changes in complex appraisal processes underlying these and other emotional reactions later in the first year. In other words, as infants become more sophisticated thinkers, their emotional responses also become more sophisticated. Moreover, growing language skills provide opportunities for alternative forms of emotional expression—through words rather than cries or clenched fists—and alter emotionality as well (Cole, Michel, & Teti, 1994).

Social experience also assumes a significant role in shaping emotional expression (Denham, 1998; Eisenberg, Fabes, & Losoya, 1997; Saarni, 2000). Malatesta and Haviland (1982, 1985), for example, studied infants and their mothers during periods of face-to-face play and reported that mothers changed their facial expressions an average of seven to nine times a minute. Roughly 25% of the time, however, the mothers responded promptly to their infants' expressions. Typically, this involved imitating or responding positively to infants' positive expressions, especially those of younger infants, and ignoring their negative expressions. This kind of contingent emotional responding could reinforce the expression of positive emotions and mute the expression of negative emotions. Bornstein and his colleagues have also noticed this kind of mother–infant reciprocity of positive emotionality: They found a strong association between smiling by mothers and their 3-month-olds (Kuchuk, Vibbert, & Bornstein, 1986).

Malatesta (1985; Malatesta, Grigoryev, Lamb, Albin, & Culver, 1986) subsequently reported that, as their infants grew older (to 7½ months), mothers became increasingly responsive to expressions of interest and decreasingly responsive to expressions of pain. Not surprisingly, infants also changed in their expressive patterns over this period by increasing their positive expressions and decreasing their negative expressions, partly in response to maternal behavior. In these and other studies (Malatesta, Culver, Tesman, & Shepard, 1989; Malatesta & Haviland, 1982), mothers and infants showed considerable consistency in their expressive behavior over time and also substantial similarity in their expressions, suggesting that mothers may socialize their infants' expressive styles from the early months of life. Of course, it is also possible that these familial similarities in expressiveness reflect a temperamental dimension of genetic origin, and we shall consider this question later in this chapter. On the other hand, Harkness and Super (1985; see also Super & Harkness, 1982) described several ways in which adults from different cultures socialize the emotional displays of their infants by responding in accordance with culture-specific interpretations of the infants' expressions and emotions.

Kaye (1982) considered the ways that parents socialize emotion in infants through three kinds of imitation: *Minimizing imitation* occurs when the parent imitates a negative expression briefly before switching to a positive expression, *modulating imitation* occurs when the parent maintains the expression but tempers its intensity, and *maximizing imitation* occurs when the parent exaggerates the infant's expression. In addition, Malatesta and others have noted that mothers respond differently to the emotional expressions of sons and daughters, perhaps in accordance with sex-typed display rules for the expression of emotion in our culture.

In more extreme circumstances, a parent's behavior can foster affective disturbances in young offspring through similar socialization processes (Field, 2000). In one investigation, Field and her colleagues (1988) noted that the infants of depressed mothers not only showed depressed social behavior (withdrawn, immobile, and nonresponsive) when interacting with their mothers but also when interacting with a stranger who knew nothing about the baby. They suggested several ways that infants were likely to have acquired and generalized such a socioemotional style: through the effects of reduced opportunities for social stimulation and the development of social skills at home, through generalized imitation of maternal behaviors, through genetic similarity, and/or through the psychological effects of the mother's depression on the baby (e.g., the baby's learned helplessness, coping activities, and so forth). Higher levels of negative affect among infants of depressed mothers is well documented (Gelfand & Teti, 1990; Teti & Gelfand, 1997), and it is important for researchers to disentangle these diverse and overlapping influences because of the importance of doing so for the design of social intervention and remediation.

Emotional development can be socialized in another way also: through the baby's emotionally resonant or empathic response to the parent's emotional state. Darwin wrote that Doddy may have expressed sympathy when his nurse pretended to cry although the boy was only 6 months old (Box 3.1). Researchers still know relatively little about how a capacity for empathy develops in infancy, but there is evidence that preempathic capacities emerge very early in a form of emotional "contagion" in which the baby spontaneously resonates with another's salient emotional expressions (Saarni, Mumme, & Campos, 1998). This response later becomes more genuinely empathic in quality with the emergence of self-other differentiation and growth in the understanding of others' emotional expressions (Thompson, 1998). Additional studies suggest that young infants respond resonantly to caregivers' emotional expressions. In informal observations (Buhler, 1930, 1933) and in experimental studies (Haviland & Lelwica, 1987; Termine & Izard, 1988), infants have been observed to assume an emotional expression similar to that of an adult, showing negative emotion when adults were posing anger or fear and displaying joy when adults were posing happiness or interest.

Finally, another catalyst to emotional growth later in infancy is the development of self-awareness that permits, for the first time, a variety of self-conscious "secondary" emotions such as embarrassment, shame, and later guilt and pride (Lewis, Sullivan, Stanger, & Weiss, 1989; Lewis, 2000b). Lewis and his colleagues observed 15- to 24-month-old infants during an assessment of self-recognition and subsequently in a series of situations designed to elicit self-conscious emotions like embarrassment. He found that those infants who showed self-recognition also looked embarrassed when, for example, they were effusively praised by an adult: They smiled and looked away, covered their faces with their hands, and showed related behaviors. Infants who did not show self-recognition did not exhibit these reactions to adult praise. The emergence of self-awareness also fosters interpersonal understanding, of course, including a better understanding of the emotions of others (Dunn, 2000a), which we consider in the next section.

In summary, current findings convincingly attest that newborns and young infants show a variety of emotional expressions that are predictably related to specific eliciting conditions. These findings support both structuralist and functionalist portrayals of emotional development. With subsequent growth across a variety of developmental domains, the infant's emotional repertoire continues to broaden, infants become responsive to a greater range of eliciting conditions, the capacity to cope with or regulate emotional experience is enhanced, and more complex emotions and emotional interrelations emerge. But the story of emotional development includes not only these internal changes, but also changes in the socializing influences of adult partners as infants respond to the emotional expressions of others.

Development of Sensitivity to Emotional Signals

Emotional development involves reading as well as sending emotional signals, and many researchers have studied the capacity to read the facial expressions of emotion in others. It is important to note, however, that discriminating different facial expressions is not the same as understanding their meaning, and thus "reading" requires important interpretive as well as perceptual capacities.

As we saw in Chapter 6, visual acuity in early infancy is limited, making it hard for newborns to distinguish among different facial features and expressive patterns. At around $1\frac{1}{2}$ to 2 months of age, however, infants begin to discriminate among different facial expressions of emotion (Barrera & Maurer, 1981a, 1981b; Bornstein & Arterberry, 2000; Oster, 1981; Schwartz, Izard, & Ansul, 1985), and they can even distinguish variations in the intensity of some emotional expressions (Kuchuk, Vibbert, & Bornstein, 1986). However, this does not mean that the emotional meaning of the expression is understood by the child. Infants of this age may respond differently to different facial configurations (e.g., eyebrow position or mouth open or closed) without assigning specific emotional meanings to them. However, because of their newly acquired sensitivity to internal facial features, infants begin at this time to respond discriminatively by protesting or fussing when their mothers adopt unresponsive "still-faces" (Cohn & Tronick, 1983a, 1983b). Earlier in the first year, they do not appear to expect adults to respond socially, and infants may develop early expectations concerning their caregiver's emotional and social propensities.

When infants reach 4 to 9 months of age, emotional expressions are not only distinguished but also become emotionally meaningful, and as a result infants become more emotionally responsive to the expressions they observe. As earlier noted, a number of researchers have shown that infants of this age can "resonate" to the emotional expressions of adults (i.e., matching expressions they see) and may also acquire more enduring socioemotional dispositions when, for example, their caregivers are depressed (Teti & Gelfand, 1997). This is also the period during which infants begin to respond differently to different vocal correlates of emotional expression and to coordinate vocal and facial features of emotional expressions (Walker-Andrews, 1997). The emotional expressions of others are, in short, regarded more comprehensively and meaningfully by infants.

Starting around 8 to 9 months of age, infants begin to appreciate that others' emotional messages pertain to specific objects or events. They now understand the referent of communication, including emotional messages (Blackford & Walden, 1998; Klinnert, 1984; Saarni, 2000). Infants can now understand not only that facial expressions have emotional meaning, but that they have meaning with reference to specific objects or events. They can thus use others' emotional expressions as guides to their own reactions to events and so *social referencing*—the deliberate search for information to help clarify uncertain events—begins. As defined by Campos and Stenberg (1981), social referencing is the tendency of individuals to use others' emotional expressions to help "disambiguate uncertainty"—that is, to understand the situation and thus relieve any uncertainty about it. By 9 to 12 months of age, infants reliably seek information from adults to help them interpret many types of unfamiliar events. Infants look to fathers as well as mothers for emotional cues (Dickstein & Parke, 1988; Hirshberg & Svejda, 1990), and they even reference previously unfamiliar experimenters with whom they have become acquainted (Klinnert et al., 1986). Hornik, Risenhoover, and Gunnar (1987) found that infants not only play with unusual toys when their mothers show disgust as opposed to pleasure, but when the same toys are presented a few minutes later infants show the same responses even when their mothers are no longer posing distinct emotional expressions but are instead silent and neutral. This suggests that infants continue to apply what they have learned through referencing about ambiguous stimuli even when parents are no longer providing compelling emotional cues about the event. Mumme, Fernald, and Herrera (1996) found that infants use mothers' vocal emotional signals to interpret ambiguous events. Mothers who used a fear voice ("Oh, how frightful!") in response to the introduction of a battery-operated robot or cow elicited more negative affect, more looks toward the mother, and less toy interaction than did mothers who used a neutral voice ("How insightful.").

Taken together, research on social referencing, like research on the development of sensitivity to emotional signals, indicates that facial and vocal expressions of emotion assume great significance in a baby's experience of the world once they can be perceived clearly. This is hardly surprising: Emotional expressions are among the most important social signals relevant to a baby's well-being, and thus we should expect that babies become attuned to these signals from early in life. As infants proceed through their second year, their increased social competence and sensitivity are fostered, in part, by the enhanced sophistication of their skills at "reading" the emotions of others. Although their sensitivity to others' emotions sometimes leads to prosocial behavior (i.e., sharing toys), it is also the basis for conflict with siblings and other family members when it is manifested in teasing, testing the limits of parental demands, and arguments (Dunn, 1998, 2000b). In a sense, the development of emotional sensitivity provides the basis for enlisting this sensitivity for the full variety of social motives of which infants become capable in the second year.

Theorizing About Emotions in Infancy

Although developmental changes in emotional expressions and growth in sensitivity to others' emotional signals have somewhat independent early pathways, they converge in critical ways later in infancy. These dual facets of emotional development—changes in the production of emotional expressions and growth in the perception of emotions of others—have been the subject of considerable theoretical speculation. Indeed, no fewer than four major groups of theorists have attempted to explain the production and perception of emotions in infancy: learning theorists, psychoanalysts, cognitive theorists, and ethologists. After reviewing the research on emotional development, the strengths and weaknesses of alternative theoretical views will be more clearly apparent.

Learning Theories

One of the first theorists to explain the early course of emotional development was John B. Watson, who believed that there are three basic emotions—fear, rage, and love—elicited by a set of unconditioned stimuli that have the inherent capacity to evoke emotion. Infants do not have to learn to react fearfully to sudden noises in dark settings, for example, or to lunging large animals because these are unconditioned responses. Watson believed, however, that most emotional reactions are the result of learned associations between an unconditioned stimulus and a neutral event so that the neutral event becomes capable of eliciting the emotional response through classical conditioning (see Chapter 7). Most emotional reactions are produced through learning or conditioning, in other words, such as when infants acquire positive responses to a mother's face and voice because of their association with food, warmth, and other innate elicitors of pleasure. In one application of this view, Watson (1927) advised parents that children commonly learn to fear the dark through the association of darkness with an earlier, frightening event (such as the sudden clap of thunder during a storm). He suggested that this fear could be unlearned (or extinguished) if children go to bed in progressively darker bedrooms without being alerted by frightening events.

Operant conditioning (Brackbill, 1958; Etzel & Gewirtz, 1967; Gewirtz & Pelaez-Nogueras, 2000) and observational learning (Bandura, 1969) may also affect how much and what kinds of emotions are produced by infants. The range and quality of a baby's early facial expressions of emotion are doubtlessly influenced by patterns of reinforcing responses from caregivers and by opportunities to observe and imitate adult expressive behavior. But the learning theorists' success in explaining how emotional responses become socialized or associated with new events does not provide a complete theory of emotional development, because they cannot satisfactorily explain why emotional reactions occur in the first place. Why, for example, do babies start smiling at about 6 weeks of age? It is not a direct result of feeding, holding, or stroking (Spitz, 1965), nor does it occur by imitation, because blind babies begin to smile at the same age as sighted infants (Fraiberg, 1977). For a more satisfactory explanation, developmentalists usually turn to alternative theoretical views.

Psychoanalytic Theories

One of these alternatives is psychoanalytic theory. Many psychoanalytic theorists, like Spitz (1965), believe that emotional development is partly a result of ego development in the context of parent–infant interaction. Spitz argued that parent–infant interaction is related to emotional development in two ways. First, the caregiver assures gratification of the baby's physical needs, and this has a direct influence on emotions as well as lending the caregiver special significance in a baby's psychological life. Second, the parent must often frustrate the child—and thus elicit negative emotions—in order to facilitate the child's integration into society by instilling self-control. This parent–infant interaction produces a variety of positive emotions (through need gratification) and negative emotions (through socialization).

The emotions that result from need gratification were believed by Spitz to help organize the ego processes of perception, cognition, and memory in early infancy. They organize perception and attention by heightening the salience to the baby of those environmental stimuli that coincide with need and need reduction. When parent–infant interaction is associated with need reduction, for example, stimuli associated with the parent—especially the parent's facial features—are likely to be especially meaningful and significant to the baby. In particular, according to Spitz, the configuration of facial features involving the forehead, eyes, and nose becomes (once it can be perceptually distinguished) a *social releaser* that can elicit the baby's smile. In a sense, emotional perception derives from the same psychological processes of need gratification that underlie emotional production in infancy. Note how this interpretation of the onset of early smiling differs from the learning account. To learning theorists, the face becomes a *conditioned elicitor* of smiling through learning, whereas in psychoanalytic theory, the facial configuration is an *automatic elicitor* of smiling. The emotions related to need and need reduction also help organize memory: The baby learns that the appearance of the facial configuration signals that a reduction of needs is about to occur. Hence, Spitz used the term *sign gestalt* to refer to the facial features that elicit the social smile in young infants. It is a *gestalt* because only a specific facial configuration will successfully elicit the smile, and it is a *sign* because it is a signal of impending need reduction.

Spitz (1965) also used the older infant's developing ability to represent the parent in memory to explain the onset of stranger anxiety (which commences around 7 to 9 months of age). He argued that stranger anxiety results from a rudimentary inference process: The child compares the stranger to an internal representation of the parent. If the parent is absent, the baby anticipates that the parent will not be available to satisfy needs, and distress results. Finally, a third important transition in early emotional development occurs during the second year with, interestingly enough, the child's increasing use of the word "No!"—an indicator of enhanced self-awareness, ego development, and new arenas for emotional growth (Spitz, 1965).

Spitz's account of emotional development is not the only psychoanalytic formulation. For example, Mahler, Pine, and Bergman (1975) noted that important transitions in early emotional development occur because the child becomes, over time, psychologically differentiated from the parent and experiences considerable ambivalence about becoming autonomous. But Spitz's theory alone underscores the centrality of parent–infant interaction to the emerging range and quality of emotional responsiveness in infancy and how the "emotional climate" of the home can influence emotional development in direct and indirect ways.

Psychoanalytic theories have more difficulty explaining other aspects of emotional development, however. For example, early emotional responsiveness occurs not just to stimuli associated with the parent but also to a variety of other stimulus events. One-and-one-half to 3-month-olds smile not only at faces but also at bull's-eye patterns and bells; 6- to 9-month-olds show fear not only to strangers but also to heights, masks, jacks-in-the-box, and other such events (Campos, 1976; Emde & Harmon, 1972; Scarr & Salapatek, 1970). It is not clear how this range of stimulus events relates to the processes of ego development and parent–infant interaction by which emotional development is explained within psychoanalytic theory. Moreover, the specific ways that parent–infant interaction affects emotional development are rather unspecified by psychoanalytic theorists, and researchers have identified a number of influence processes—such as through social referencing and emotional contagion—that move beyond these theoretical formulations. Finally, as discussed in Chapter 1, psychoanalytic theory also involves a number of implicit assumptions about the nature of human development and about the critical role of early life experiences that have not proven correct.

Cognitive Theories

Recognizing the failures of both psychoanalytic and learning theories to explain emotional development, several cognitive interpretations have been offered. The most influential was initially proposed by Hebb (1946) to account for the unlearned, spontaneous expressions of fear in chimpanzees. Hebb postulated that perceptual experiences establish a set of memory traces in the form of neurological circuits that he called *phase sequences*. Whenever a new perceptual experience is sufficiently similar to previous ones to activate a phase sequence, yet not similar enough to maintain the continued smooth functioning of this neural circuit, the brain is disrupted in a way that produces the subjective experience of fear. By extrapolation from Hebb's theory, fear of strangers in infancy occurs because infants have established memory traces of familiar individuals that are activated—but disrupted—when unfamiliar persons are encountered. Similarly, masks, jacks-in-the-box, and other fear-producing events at this age can also be explained as discrepancies between perceptual experience and the memory traces or expectations they evoke. In short, when stimuli are familiar but discrepant from well-established memory traces of familiar stimuli, they produce fear in the young.

One important problem with this explanation is that infants can usually discriminate visually between mothers and strangers by 3 months of age, yet they do not show fear of strangers until 6 or 7 months of age (Berenson, 1996). Consequently, Kagan amended Hebb's theory by arguing that until 6 months of age discrepancy between perceptual experience and memory traces yields interest rather than fear (Kagan, 1974; Kagan, Kearsley, & Zelazo, 1978). After this age, however, the infant acquires the cognitive capacity to spontaneously generate hypotheses to explain the discrepancy and, according to Kagan, when an interesting discrepant event fails to be explained by the hypotheses the child generates, fear or distress ensues. Kagan's modification of Hebb's theory thus explains stranger reactions, separation distress, as well as wariness of novel stimuli such as jacks-in-the-box and masks as the result of failures to explain discrepancies between environmental events and memory traces or expectations. If the child knew what happened to the mother or could predict what the stranger would do, for example, no negative reactions would result.

In another modification of Hebb's theory, Sroufe argued that discrepancy can account for the intensity of an emotional reaction to a stimulus event, but it cannot account for the positive or negative quality of that reaction (Sroufe, 1979; Sroufe, Waters, & Matas, 1974). Whether an emotional reaction is positive or negative depends, among other things, on the context in which a stimulus event is encountered. Infant speech is more sophisticated with mothers than with strangers (Bornstein, Haynes, Painter, & Genevro, 2000), but as we earlier noted, infants respond more positively to strangers in familiar circumstances (such as at home) than in unfamiliar contexts (such as a laboratory; Sroufe et al., 1974). Friendliness toward strangers is also more apparent when strangers approach slowly and gradually rather than suddenly and abruptly, and when the mother or another trusted adult reacts positively to the stranger (Boccia & Campos, 1983). Thus the "strangeness" (or discrepancy) of the unfamiliar adult does not, in itself, determine the baby's emotional reaction; rather, the context in which the stranger is encountered influences whether the baby is scared or sociable (Thompson & Limber, 1990).

Cognitive theories have in common the advantage of linking emotional production to changes in cognitive functions—memory traces, perceptual processes, appraisals, and the like—that underscore the manner in which emotion is integrated with other developing behavioral processes. Indeed, these theories (with the exception of Sroufe's) are sometimes criticized for unduly emphasizing how emotion is a derivative of cognitive processes, without considering also how emotion may reciprocally influence cognition. A more important criticism, however, is that theoretical reliance on difficult to measure processes like "discrepancy from memory traces" and "hypotheses to explain discrepancy" makes these formulations difficult to test. In other words, whereas cognitive theories offer rather interesting post hoc explanations for the emotional reactions we observe in infants, it is difficult to specify beforehand how discrepant a stimulus event is from a baby's cognitive expectations—and thus the emotional reaction that event will elicit—because it is hard to measure degrees of discrepancy or the hypotheses a baby spontaneously generates to explain them. Consequently, cognitive theories have not generated the amount of research inquiry that their intriguing explanations for emotional development might otherwise warrant.

Ethological Theories

Other theories of emotion emphasize the biological or maturational determinants of emotional development. The importance of these determinants is reflected in two research literatures that are germane to the field of emotional development. The first consists of studies of rhesus monkeys raised in isolation who nevertheless respond with fear or aversion to pictures of other monkeys in threatening postures (Sackett, 1966). Because these monkeys were denied opportunities for social learning or conditioning of emotional behavior, this literature suggests that certain emotional reactions may have innate, biological bases (Nelson, 1987). The second literature indicates that the developmental course of many emotional responses early in life appears to adhere to a strong maturational timetable, including early social smiling, separation reactions, and other behaviors (Izard & Ackerman, 2000). This adds further credence to the view that emotional development has important biomaturational origins, independent of social determinants.

The impressiveness of these findings has increased the popularity of ethological theorizing about emotional development. Ethological theories emphasize that emotions are associated with behavioral processes that have fostered species survival and reproductive success throughout our evolutionary history. Emotions are important because they provide significant signals to social partners and are associated with autonomic behavioral reactions that facilitate adaptive responses to threat, danger, or stress (Campos, 1994). There is accumulating evidence that some of the expressive patterns associated with emotion are culturally universal and thus may be innate (Ekman, 1984), and together with evidence concerning the similarity of human and primate expressive patterns (Parker, 1998), this suggests that emotional reactions are part of biologically adaptive response patterns that probably evolved early in human phylogenesis to foster species survival.

Consider, for example, the emotion of fear. Virtually from birth, infants startle to sudden, intense events, and they later exhibit fear or wariness in response to unfamiliar people, strange objects, or unexpected stimuli of strong intensity. When these events occur, infants typically exhibit components of a classic "fear face" (see Figure 10.2), emit loud, distinctive distress vocalizations, and typically retreat and seek a trusted attachment figure. This constellation of responses has been described by some researchers as a "fear/wariness behavioral system" (Chapter 11). It is easy to see how such reactions can be viewed as adaptive (Bowlby, 1973). In the savannah settings in which humans presumably evolved, infants were likely to encounter strange objects, people, or events that might prove dangerous or threatening, and consequently the behaviors associated with the arousal of fear would contribute to the infant's withdrawal from these stimuli and protection by caregivers. Indeed, the peremptory responses of adults to the sight or sound of a fearful infant promote this protective care. Other emotions can similarly be viewed as the consequence of adaptation.

These ethological formulations provide valuable perspectives on emotional development because they address important questions concerning the evolutionary meaning of emotional expressions and the significance of the child's understanding of others' emotional expressions. Ultimately, and uniquely, ethological theories provide a valuable context for explaining why the emotional signals of infants have such a compelling effect on adult caregivers, and conversely why the expressions of others elicit such interest and (at times) resonant responses from young infants. As noted earlier, ethological views have provided an important foundation for the functionalist perspective to emotion and its portrayal of the adaptive functions of basic emotions (see Table 10.1). Despite these strengths, however, ethological formulations do a much better job of describing the evolutionary meaning of emotional reactions than of explaining the developmental processes by which these emotional reactions unfold. Beyond positing rather simple maturational explanations, ethological theorists tend not to address these essential developmental inquiries very successfully.

Conclusion

If the current status of developmental formulations of infant emotions seems rather disappointing, it is because each is striving to explain an extraordinarily complex developmental process. Indeed, the existing shortcomings of each theory are balanced by the contributions each makes to explaining emotional development—either in terms of learning influences, the "emotional climate" of parent–infant interaction, cognitive development, or the biological heritage of the human species—and our earlier review of research in this area indicates that each theory helps to explain a small but important aspect of emotional development in infancy. The same is true of the contributions of classic structuralist views of emotion—those that emphasize the organization of emotional response systems—and newer functionalist portrayals that underscore the adaptive purposes of emotional arousal. In the end, the development of a more comprehensive and integrated theory of early emotional development requires a more comprehensive, integrated theory of infancy than has yet been offered.

Temperamental Individuality

Emotional expressions are one important way that infants influence those around them. Temperamental individuality is another. Parents and other caregivers devote considerable energy to identifying, adapting to, and channeling the temperamental features of their offspring, just as they try to interpret, respond to, and manage their infants' emotional states (Figure 10.4). In this respect, emotion and temperament have similar implications for adults. Moreover, temperamental features often have an emotional quality—such as variations in predominant mood, difficulty, proneness to fear or to smiling and laughter—although they also embrace variations in activity level, predictability, sociability, and other aspects of individuality. Thus emotionality and temperament share some common features.

In other respects, however, these socioemotional processes are quite different. Whereas a baby's emotional states are often fleeting, we commonly think of temperamental attributes as more enduring characteristics of the child. Infants may show momentary periods of fussiness owing to changes in routine or unfamiliar people nearby, but when fussiness is part of the baby's more persistent

FIGURE 10.4
Temperament has long been recognized as a hallmark of infancy. In early iconographies, the bodily "humours" were represented as infants. This illustration represents the sweet placidity of infancy.

style we usually view it as an attribute of the child (rather than of immediate circumstances) and thus temperamental in quality. This example illustrates another way that the study of emotional development and temperamental individuality differ. Short-term fluctuations in a child's emotional state are rarely regarded as prognostic of long-term consequences for the child, but temperamental attributes attain significance in the minds of parents and other caregivers for what they foreshadow about the child's later personality.

Indeed, the study of temperament has become important because temperament is viewed as an early foundation for personality. Whereas personality includes temperament but also the effects of social experience, self-referent belief systems, knowledge structures, values and goals, and other complex processes, many of these processes have not yet developed or become consolidated in infancy. Socializing influences are only beginning, and thus the hereditary and/or constitutional bases for temperamental individuality are likely to be most apparent. To the extent that we can see the person-to-be in the baby, we see the personality-to-be in temperament.

As we shall see, considerable effort has been devoted to characterizing the various dimensions along which infants differ temperamentally and determining whether these dimensions aggregate into broader temperamental profiles. Many researchers have explored the stability of these temperamental features over time, as well as the factors that can account for consistency and change over time. The study of temperament is interesting for an additional reason: It raises fascinating questions about how the baby's enduring individuality influences growth. By studying the effects of temperament on social interaction, cognition, behavioral problems, and other domains, researchers are acquiring an understanding of the complex roles played by temperament.

Here is an illustration. Earlier we noted that the infant's growing emotional understanding influences sibling interaction as children learn how to tease, sympathize, dominate, and enlist other social strategies that rely on an acute "reading" of the sibling's emotional reactions. How does temperament affect sibling interaction? This question was posed by Munn and Dunn (1989), who observed episodes of sibling conflict on two occasions, when the younger sibling was 2 and 3 years old, and also collected maternal reports of the temperamental attributes of each child each time. Little insight into the nature of sibling conflict was achieved when they examined the contribution of each child's temperament in isolation, so they created a measure of the difference between siblings' scores on each dimension of temperament. The difference measures were strongly related to sibling conflict on each occasion, especially when siblings differed on measures of negative mood and emotional intensity. These findings suggest that, regardless of the particular temperamental profile of each child, it is the extent of the dissonance between the two children's temperaments that contributes to their conflict. In a sense, some siblings do not get along because their behavioral styles collide with each other.

Consistent with this view, researchers have long believed that whether a child's long-term adjustment is favorable or unfavorable depends on an interaction between the child's temperament and the demands of the environment—more specifically, on the "goodness of fit" or match between them (Chess & Thomas, 1996; Lerner & Lerner, 1994; Seifer, 2000). A child with a low activity level, positive mood, and poor adaptability "fits" well in a home or school setting that makes few demands and provides many opportunities for self-direction. But such an environment is a poorer fit for a child with a high activity level, high distractibility, and poorer mood. A child's successful adjustment thus depends on an interaction between his or her temperamental attributes and the demands of the setting. In this light, it is clear that a temperamentally difficult child will not inevitably experience later problems if, say, parents understand and are tolerant of the child's behavioral style and can provide activities in which the child's characteristics can be channeled and valued. Conversely, even a temperamentally easy child will experience problems if parents impose excessive demands or ignore reasonable needs. As a consequence, the sensitivity and adaptability of parents to their child's temperamental profile is an important predictor of long-term adjustment (Teti & Candelaria, 2002).

From a behavior genetics perspective, other temperamental theorists argue for even more complex models of how temperament influences development (Plomin et al., 1993). Scarr (1993), for example, suggested that children evoke certain responses from others based on their temperamental attributes and that these responses, in turn, affect development. A highly sociable infant tends to elicit interest and play from adults, and this social stimulation has many benefits for the child. Moreover, as children grow older their temperamental features may lead them to prefer certain environments over others, especially those settings that best suit their behavioral style. A highly active child may choose to become involved in sports, whereas a low-activity child may select settings fostering sedentary activities, like reading or conversation. Admittedly, this kind of "niche picking" is harder for an infant to accomplish, but similar preferences may be expressed in the baby's selective interest in certain activities over others (e.g., highly active play with father versus more low-key activities with mother), and these preferences will still be developmentally stimulating in different ways.

Alternatively, Wachs (in press) argues that individuals do not necessarily shape environments, they simply experience them differently depending on their temperamental attributes. An unexpected encounter with a friendly but unfamiliar adult will be experienced much differently, for example, by a child who is temperamentally sociable and positive in mood than by a child who is low in adaptability and high in fear. In a study motivated by this "organismic specificity hypothesis," Gandour (1989) observed 15-month-old toddlers at home and measured children's exploratory activity as well as the mothers' efforts to guide and stimulate; temperamental measures of the children were also obtained. Gandour found that toddlers with low activity levels whose mothers provided lots of stimulation explored more than low-activity toddlers with understimulating mothers, as one might expect. High-activity toddlers, however, explored most when they had mothers who were *not* highly stimulating, perhaps because they had less need for stimulation and were more easily overwhelmed when caregivers gave them lots of guidance and stimulation. In a sense, the effects of parental care—and of other environmental influences—depends in part on the baby's temperamental profile.

Taken together, the study of the effects of temperament on development provides researchers with a much richer picture of how a child's individual characteristics interact with environmental demands to shape and guide developmental outcomes. Contrary to simpler (main effects) views that "good" temperamental features lead to optimal developmental outcomes and "bad" features predict later behavioral problems, it appears that the consequences of a particular temperamental profile for a child depend in part on the demands of the environments in which the child is living, the sensitivity and adaptability of social partners within those settings, and how temperament itself guides the child's choice of activities and interpretation of experiences. The result is more complex transactional predictions of later outcomes, in which temperament is an important but certainly not an exclusive determinant.

Conceptualizing Infant Temperament

Although theorists portray the dimensions and origins of temperament in many different ways, we can regard temperament as the biologically based source of individual differences in behavioral functioning that tend to be stable over time. Temperament emerges early in life and expresses itself behaviorally in various ways, but temperament itself is the underlying construct inferred from these observable behaviors. In other words, a temperamentally sociable child is likely to manifest that high sociability (if it remains consistent) in different ways at different ages: in smiles and reaches as an infant, in approaching and exploring other people as a toddler, in animated conversation as a preschooler, and in the development of a range of more complex social skills as a grade-schooler. Temperament may be manifested differently in age-appropriate ways, but it reflects a consistent core of underlying individuality. This view has implications for measurement: A child's underlying temperamental characteristics may endure over time even though the behavioral manifestations of temperament change. Distinguishing between underlying temperamental features and the behaviors associated with them at a given time is a tricky conceptual and methodological challenge.

Temperamental features are biologically based, but their biological basis does not necessarily mean that these features are genetically fixed or that experience has little impact on temperament. Researchers now agree that an adequate portrayal of temperament must acknowledge the reciprocal influences that exist between temperament and the environment, and that temperament is affected by this transactional process (Rothbart & Bates, 1998).

Despite differences between alternative theoretical portrayals of the underlying dimensions of temperament, researchers tend to agree on the kinds of individual variability that are likely to be temperamental in quality. In particular, two characteristics of individual behavior have been of special interest. One is the *temporal* features of behavior, including how fast the behaviors begin after stimulation (latency), how rapidly they escalate (rise time), how long they last (duration), and how slowly they go away (decay or recovery). Another is the *intensive* features of behavior, including how strongly behaviors express themselves (amplitude) and how sensitive they are to stimulation (threshold). In general, although interest in these characteristics has led to varying portrayals of temperamental dimensions, three attributes tend to emerge across most conceptualizations of temperament: variations in activity level, sociability, and emotionality.

Scientific interest in infant temperament has a fairly long history. Gesell and Ames (1937) first conducted rudimentary research on infant temperament in the 1930s, but it was not until Thomas, Chess, and their colleagues founded the New York Longitudinal Study (NYLS) in the 1950s that interest in infant temperament reawakened and research on this topic began in earnest. This interest has magnified during the past decade, during which new conceptualizations of temperament have emerged, several programmatic research efforts have been inaugurated, and studies of temperament and its impact have mushroomed.

TABLE 10.3 DIMENSIONS OF TEMPERAMENT PORTRAYED
BY MAJOR THEORISTS

Thomas and Chess	Buss and Plomin	Rothbart and Derryberry
1. Activity level	1. Activity level	1. Activity level
2. Approach–withdrawal	2. Emotionality	2. Fear
3. Adaptability	3. Sociability	3. Distress to limitations (frustration)
4. Quality of mood		
5. Attention span and persistence		4. Smiling and laughter
6. Distractability		5. Soothability
7. Rhythmicity (regularity)		6. Duration of orienting
8. Intensity of reaction		
9. Threshold of responsiveness		

The New York Longitudinal Study

Thomas and Chess began their longitudinal studies when infants were 2 or 3 months of age, at which time mothers were interviewed extensively about their infants. From these interviews, babies were rated on several dimensions, listed in Table 10.3 (Chess & Thomas, 1984, 1986; Thomas & Chess, 1977, 1980; Thomas, Chess, & Birch, 1970; Thomas, Chess, Birch, Hertzig, & Korn, 1963). In devising these dimensions—including activity level, rhythmicity, attention span, quality of mood, and several others—Thomas and Chess sought to delineate the stylistic features of the infant's emerging individuality, or consistencies in how activities are performed (rather than what is done or why they are performed). In distinguishing temperament from motivations, abilities, or personality, Thomas and Chess viewed temperament as early emerging, constitutionally based behavioral tendencies that influence the impact of the environment on the child. These nine dimensions were selected because they could be evaluated in all children, and they appeared to be important dimensions of individuality that should affect development.

From nine dimensions, Thomas and Chess created a four-way typology of broader temperamental profiles. "Easy" babies were positive in mood, regular in body functions, and adaptable; these babies approached new situations positively and reacted with low or moderate intensity. Approximately 40% of the babies in the NYLS were deemed easy. "Difficult" babies, by contrast, were negative in mood, irregular, and slow to adapt; they withdrew from new situations and reacted with high intensity. Difficult children accounted for about 10% of the NYLS sample. "Slow-to-warm-up" babies were negative in mood and slow to adapt; they withdrew from new situations, reacted with low to moderate intensity, and were low in activity. They constituted about 15% of the sample. The remaining babies (about 35%) constituted "average" babies and did not fit into the other profiles.

Thomas and Chess followed these children at regular intervals from infancy to young adulthood in their effort to understand the temperamental origins of later behavioral disorders, and thus created one of the most ambitious longitudinal studies that continues to this day. The results of this investigation suggest that early temperamental individuality can have long-term consequences, but by no means determines later development. Some behavioral features, of course, have a strong influence on later development: Lerner, Hertzog, Hooker, Hassibi, and Thomas (1988) found, in a re-analysis of the NYLS data, that high levels of childhood aggression predict adjustment problems in adolescence. But early temperamental individuality need not always foreshadow long-term outcomes in part because temperament and the environment jointly determine the "goodness of fit." It is difficult to predict long-term outcomes for a child based on temperament alone because the "fit" with the environment might be good or bad, and might change with development.

Another reason temperament does not always foreshadow long-term outcomes, according to Thomas and Chess, is that temperament itself might change as the result of environmental challenges and personality development. Whereas environmental experiences reinforce certain temperamental attributes, they may modify or help to change others. Furthermore, as the result of emerging personality capacities, children may acquire strategies for controlling certain temperamental attributes (like activity level) that are poorly suited for certain settings (like school). As a consequence, developmental outcomes are influenced not only by the "fit" between temperament and environments, but also by how temperamental attributes themselves evolve through the transactions between settings and the child's emerging personality. For these reasons, we might be most concerned about individuals who maintain a difficult temperament throughout much of their lives, and this is, indeed, warranted. Tubman and Lerner (1992), in a further analysis of the NYLS data, found that individuals who had high ratings for difficult temperament throughout adolescence and early adulthood exhibited the lowest levels of adjustment.

Like many pioneering studies, the NYLS has been criticized on various grounds. Some researchers questioned the reliance on parent interviews and the extent to which the interviewers were familiar with the families they studied and thus possibly biased their evaluations. In this regard, researchers have more recently benefitted from the work of Carey (1970), who developed the Infant Temperament Questionnaire (ITQ), which was later revised by Carey and McDevitt into the RITQ (1978a, 1978b), which in turn was revised into the Early Infancy Temperament Questionnaire (EITQ; Medoff-Cooper, Carey, & McDevitt, 1993) for use with infants about 4 months old and younger. The ITQ, RITQ, and EITQ are standardized parent-report questionnaires in which infants are rated along each of the nine temperament dimensions. Some critics question whether the nine dimensions of temperament best characterize behavioral individuality, however, and they have proposed different, and fewer, dimensions.

Buss and Plomin

Whereas Thomas and Chess began their temperamental studies from a clinical tradition, Buss and Plomin (1984) approached the study of temperament from a behavioral genetics perspective. To these researchers, temperament is a set of inherited personality traits that appear early in life. Buss and Plomin's conceptualization of temperament differs from Thomas and Chess's in at least four ways. First, they do not seek to distinguish temperament from personality but instead regard temperament as an early core of personality As a result, temperament includes motivation and other characteristics that Thomas and Chess excluded from their definition. Second, they view temperament as having exclusively genetic rather than constitutional origins; this is important because hereditary influences on behavioral style are presumed to be more stable than are constitutional factors (such as consequences of prenatal experience). Third, Buss and Plomin underscore that temperamental attributes remain highly stable throughout life, consistent with their genetic origins, and thus have enduring effects on personality development. Fourth, Buss and Plomin differ in their description of temperamental dimensions (see Table 10.3). Rather than nine, they identify only three (activity level, sociability, and negative emotionality), which are also the same dimensions that Thomas and Chess, and other researchers use to identify "difficult" temperaments (Bates & Wachs, 1994). These three dimensions were identified by Buss and Plomin because they appear very early in life, are strongly inherited, and are sufficiently distinct to be characterized as independent. (In an earlier version of their theory, Buss and Plomin, 1975, had identified a fourth temperamental dimension—impulsivity—that was later excluded because research did not provide convincing evidence of its heritability.)

Although Buss and Plomin underscore the genetic and stable attributes of temperament, they do not ignore the importance of environmental influences. A child's adjustment is influenced, they note, by the match between temperamental attributes and environmental demands (similar to the "goodness of fit" concept), and individuals may choose environmental settings that match their inherited behavioral characteristics (Buss & Plomin, 1984). Buss and Plomin believe, however, that the environment has a limited effect on temperament and that temperamental attributes may influence setting events as much as the reverse, especially when individuals have strong temperamental features. Sociable people tend to make their environments more interactive, while active people tend naturally to quicken the tempo of a setting. Moreover, they note that individuals can modify the nature of their environments even when setting demands are fixed. For example, a child with a high activity level who is restricted to his or her room may nevertheless manage to expend a high amount of energy in that setting, perhaps to the dismay of the parents.

Rothbart and Derryberry

Rothbart's (Rothbart & Derryberry, 1981; see also Rothbart & Ahadi, 1994; Putnam, Sanson, & Rothbart, 2002; Rothbart, Posner, & Hershey, 1995) view of temperamental individuality integrates developmental perspectives with work from the cognitive sciences, psychobiology, adult personality, and Pavlovian research in the Soviet tradition. Rothbart defines temperament in terms of relatively stable, primarily biologically based individual differences in reactivity and self-regulation. "Reactivity" refers to the excitability or arousability of the individual's response systems and is measured in terms of the response parameters (time and intensity) we defined earlier. Self-regulation refers to the processes that modulate reactivity through approach or avoidance, inhibition, or attentional processes. Rothbart argues that individual differences in these tendencies have genetic and/or constitutional origins, and are based in specifiable neurophysiological, endocrinological, and/or behavioral processes (see Rothbart & Bates, 1998).

Rothbart and her colleagues focused on six temperamental dimensions that reflect these broader reactive and self-regulatory processes: activity level, soothability, fear, distress to limitations (frustration), smiling and laughter, and duration of orienting. As can be seen in Table 10.3, these dimensions overlap in some ways with those of Thomas and Chess and Buss and Plomin, but there are some independent features as well. For example, Rothbart includes individual differences in frustration and fear that resemble Buss and Plomin's emotionality dimension, but she also includes positive emotionality, and her fear dimension is somewhat similar to Thomas and Chess's dimensions of approach–withdrawal and adaptability. Like many other theorists, Rothbart views personality as a much broader construct than temperament, with temperament perhaps as the biological foundation.

Rothbart's conceptualization of temperament also emphasizes development. Temperament is modified over time not only because of the various environmental influences discussed above, but also because the constituent biological response systems grow and mature. With neurocortical maturation, for example, infants gradually develop self-control over activity and emotion in ways that affect the self-regulatory features of temperamental individuality (Thompson, 1990b). The growth of emotional responsiveness discussed earlier also has implications for emotion-based temperamental dimensions like distress to limitations, smiling and laughter, and fear. Partly for these reasons, Rothbart concludes that, although temperamental dimensions are more likely to be stable over time than are other aspects of behavioral individuality, stability is more likely within rather than between periods of rapid developmental change. In their conceptualization, in other words, the stability of temperament is a highly contingent rather than an absolute feature, depending not only on environmental demands but also on intrinsic maturational processes.

Conclusion

Other temperament researchers have offered different but more limited portrayals of temperament. Bates (1986a, 1986b, 2001; Bates, Freeland, & Lounsbury, 1979), for example, focused on a "fussy-difficult" dimension, which appears to be associated with patterns of parent–infant interaction and with a child's long-term behavioral problems. Difficult temperament is one of the dimensions assessed by his Infant Characteristics Questionnaire (ICQ), along with "unadaptability," "dullness," and "unpredictability." Bornstein (Bornstein, Gaughran, & Homel, 1986; Bornstein et al., 1991) developed a combined home observation and matching parent-report procedure to assess infants' spontaneous activity as well as their responsiveness in both free-play and structured situations. Their dimensions are intended to capture basic tendencies to approach and react to the immediate social and material environment, and their method entails evaluation of observational reports from mothers and unrelated observers, as well as global maternal ratings.

It is clear from this discussion (and from inspection of Table 10.3) that theorists differ significantly in their conceptualization of temperament and in the dimensions of temperament that they identify, and it is unclear whether this diversity of approaches is desirable or not. On the one hand, research efforts are proceeding in different directions as research groups embrace conceptualizations of temperament that lead them to ask different questions of different behavioral processes, often concerning individuals at markedly different periods of development. This undermines the integration of findings from different research groups. On the other hand, temperamental research is still in its infancy, and the proliferation of viewpoints is not only a common but a desirable feature of new inquiry. Indeed, given the willingness of most theorists to revise their theories (see Rothbart & Bates, 1998) and the current generation of new research findings that may contribute to such revisions, there is good reason to be optimistic that diverse theories catalyze useful new studies that converge on common issues. If, in the end, the value of these theories is measured by their usefulness in explaining what research tells us about temperamental individuality, theorists may be approaching a common set of definitional features. In the meantime, it is useful to consider what we have learned about the effects of temperament on later development.

Origins and Consequences of Temperamental Individuality

Psychobiological Correlates

Given the reliance of most theorists on underlying differences in biological processes (e.g., heredity and constitutional factors), research on these processes and their links to temperament are important. Two sets of studies—one concerning autonomic nervous system correlates of dispositionally inhibited and reactive children, and the other concerning the heritability of temperamental differences in twins—contribute to understanding these psychobiological correlates.

In a longitudinal study conducted by Kagan and his colleagues, 4-month-old infants were classified as either high (showing high levels of motor activity and distress in response to a battery of auditory, olfactory, and visual stimuli) or low (showing low-level reactions to the same stimuli) in reactivity and were then examined at 14 and 21 months (Kagan & Arcus, 1994), $4\frac{1}{2}$ years (Kagan, Snidman, & Arcus, 1998), and 7 years of age (Kagan, Snidman, Zentner, & Peterson, 1999). Temperamental reactivity was fairly stable over time. Children classified as highly reactive in infancy were significantly more likely to react fearfully to novel stimuli at 14 and 21 months than were children classified as unreactive. By $4\frac{1}{2}$ years, highly reactive children showed less spontaneity and sociability with adults than unreactive children did, but highly reactive children at this age were not as likely to appear fearful in response to novelty than they were at younger ages. By 7 years, highly reactive children were more likely to manifest symptoms of anxiety than were unreactive children. Highly reactive children were also more likely to have a higher diastolic blood pressure and more narrow faces than were unreactive children. Kagan and his colleagues speculated that dispositionally inhibited children have a lower threshold of reactivity in limbic structures (like the hypothalamus and amygdala) that mediate fear and defense, whereas uninhibited children have higher reactivity thresholds. Because of these differences in sympathetic arousal, inhibited children show more fearful, wary, and shy behavior, whereas uninhibited children are generally more outgoing and emotionally more labile (Kagan, Reznick, & Snidman, 1999). Fox and his colleagues (Fox, Henderson, Rubin, Calkins, & Schmidt, 2001) reported similar stability in temperamental reactivity and proneness to distress from 4 months to 4 years of age.

These studies indicate that indexes of autonomic reactivity are related in a predictable manner to stable behavioral measures of reactivity and inhibition/self-regulation (which are Rothbart's, 1981, dual aspects of temperamental individuality). The links between these findings and issues of temperament are underscored by reports that these behavioral and physiological indexes are heritable (Healy, Fox, & Porges, 1988). According to Kagan (1997), stability of individual differences in inhibition is enhanced in these samples because children who are dispositionally inhibited or uninhibited tend to fall toward the extremes of the normal distribution of behavior (representing no more than 10% of the population) and thus represent distinct temperamental types. He also noted, however, that these characteristics are not immutable and sometimes change as a result of concerted efforts by parents to modify their children's attributes. In general, then, these findings suggest that significant differences in temperament related to reactivity and inhibition have correlates in autonomic nervous system functioning that tend to be stable over time. We still need to learn more about the origins of these nervous system differences and whether they antedate or follow the development of behavioral indicators of inhibition or reactivity. Their relations to other temperamental attributes also merit examination. Rothbart and Bates (1998), for example, found that individual differences in inhibition are inversely related to positive emotional expressions, suggesting a link between emotionality and inhibition in infancy.

Other insights into the psychobiological correlates of temperament come from twin studies. As discussed in Chapter 3, researchers often study infant twins to sort out the extent to which behaviors have identifiable genetic contributions. Monozygotic (MZ) twins share 100% of their genes, whereas dizygotic (DZ) twins share only 50% on average (as do siblings). If a behavior has a significant genetic component, therefore, MZ twins ought to behave more similarly than DZ twins, barring more equal treatment of MZ than DZ twins by those around them. In general, twin studies indicate that individual differences in emotionality (especially distress and fearfulness), activity level, and sociability (or shyness) are heritable (Caspi, 1998; Goldsmith & Lemery, 2000; Goldsmith, Lemery, Aksan, & Buss, 2000), precisely the dimensions of temperament identified in Buss and Plomin's (1984) genetic-based theory of temperament. Whereas correlations between MZ twins ranged from .50 to .80, correlations between DZ twins were .50 or less (see Figure 10.5).

These findings are consistent with the behavior genetics approach adopted by Buss and Plomin (1984) and other temperament researchers who believe that temperamental individuality is strongly determined by individual genotypes (see also Lemery & Goldsmith, 1999; Scarr & Kidd, 1983; Schmitz et al., 1999). In this view, people are inclined by their unique genetic endowments to act and respond to events in particular ways. Their genetic endowments also guide their selection of environmental settings and partners within those settings that are consistent with their heritable behavioral style ("niche picking"). Furthermore, these behavioral tendencies exert additional influence over the environment because they evoke reactions from others that are consistent with their genotypical characteristics.

Because we too readily tend to equate early genetic influence with immutable and unchanging consequences, it is wise to remember why behavioral geneticists do not do so (Goldsmith & Lemery, 2000; Lemery & Goldsmith, 1999; Plomin, 2000). First, heritability estimates are specific to the population that is studied, and the heritability of certain dispositional attributes changes during

FIGURE 10.5
Monozygotic twins may look alike and behave similarly, but dizygotic twins look alike and behave dissimilarly, because on average they are no more alike than any siblings.

the early years. Second, gene action may be discontinuous over time, and genetic influences may also account for developmental accelerations and lags rather than smooth underlying growth functions. Moreover, some children may be genetically inconsistent; their hereditary make-up will "program" changes over time. Third, experience can alter temperament by modifying physiological systems through which genes affect behavior (Dienstbier, 1989).

Thus, in considering the psychobiological correlates of temperamental individuality—whether revealed by studies of autonomic functioning or twin similarity—the evidence indicates that certain temperamental attributes are associated with differences in underlying biological or genetic functions, but that these attributes are not necessarily stable and unchanging. Although variability in dispositional behaviors associated with emotional reactivity (especially of negative emotion), sociability/shyness/inhibition, and activity level has strong psychobiological correlates, these systems are also plastic such that individual differences in these attributes are likely to remain more stable over time than are other behavioral characteristics, although they are not immutable and fixed.

Culture and Temperament

In contradistinction to the psychobiological underpinnings of temperament, some developmental anthropologists have examined whether cultural groups differ temperamentally in meaningful ways; to paraphrase the famous anthropologist Ruth Benedict, "Culture may be temperament writ large." Such inquiry almost inevitably invites overgeneralization and misinterpretation, and cultural differences—when they are observed—can be portrayed in ways that misrepresent the culture. Nevertheless, such differences have been observed, and their source is a subject of perennial interest (see Arbiter, Sato-Tanaka, Kolvin, & Leitch, 1999; Bornstein, 1991).

In comparing cultural groups on temperament, culture and gene pool are naturally confounded, so it is difficult to determine whether observed temperamental differences are due to differences in social customs and socialization practices, or instead to genetic differences (see Figure 10.6). This is one reason that researchers have focused on cultural differences in neonates or very young infants, observed presumably before socialization influences are significant or long-standing (Bornstein, 1989b; Chisholm, 1989). Cross-cultural studies of neonates using Brazelton's (Brazelton & Nugent, 1995) Neonatal Behavioral Assessment Scale (NBAS) have found, for example, that Chinese American and Japanese American newborns are less perturbable, better able to soothe themselves, and experience less lability in arousal than their European American counterparts (Camras, Oster, Campos, Miyaki, & Bradshaw, 1992). Kagan et al. (1994) argued that these differences were not due to cultural differences between the caregiving practices of U.S. and Asian mothers. In their study, Kagan et al. administered to 9-month-old infants from Boston, Dublin, and Beijing the same set of visual, auditory, and olfactory stimuli used in their studies of reactivity discussed earlier. The Caucasian infants, regardless of origin, were more arousable and prone to distress than were the Chinese infants. Of course, the conclusion that these differences represent constitutionally based, temperamental differences rather than cultural differences in caregiving awaits additional studies done both within and across cultural groups.

(A)

(B)

FIGURE 10.6
Children growing up in different cultures have radically different experiences that interact with genetic differences. Here are shown infants bathing (*A*) in India and (*B*) in Guatemala. (Courtesy of M. Bornstein and B. Rogoff.)

Gender Differences

Studies of gender differences in temperament also illustrate how difficult it is to disentangle the experiential and genetic bases of temperamental individuality. Few systematic studies of gender differences have been undertaken, but they have revealed no strong and consistent gender differences in temperament (e.g., Mathiesen & Tambs, 1999; Sanson, Prior, Smart, & Oberklaid, 1993), although some researchers have shown that boys appear to have a higher activity level than girls (Eaton & Enns, 1986), and at least one study has reported higher distress to novelty in 6-month-old girls than in same-age boys (Martin, Wisenbaker, Baker, & Huttunen, 1997).

How should we interpret the gender difference in temperamental activity? A nativist explanation would propose that such differences are genetically based. On the other hand, we will discover in the next chapter that parents and other caregivers treat male and female infants differently from birth in ways that are consistent with cultural stereotypes, including beliefs about the higher activity level of males.

Temperament and Thought

Among the more intriguing effects of temperament on behavioral functioning is the possibility that temperamental individuality affects the child's cognitive processing. Several dimensions of temperament have been linked to cognitive functioning in infancy. For example, persistence in infancy has been associated with mastery skills (MacTurk, Morgan, & Jennings, 1995). Wachs and Gandour (1983) noted that temperamentally "easy" 6-month-olds did better on the Užgiris–Hunt Ordinal Scales of Infant Development than did temperamentally difficult infants. Furthermore, Wachs (1987) found infant difficulty in 12-month-olds was negatively associated with levels of mastery motivation in structured laboratory tasks, whereas Pipp-Siegel, Robinson, Bridges, and Bartholomew (1997) found modest but significant inverse relations between shyness in 20- and 24-month-olds and various indexes of social cognition, including role-taking and self-recognition abilities.

What can account for these influences? On the one hand, certain temperamental attributes may facilitate the child's cognitive performance. Infants who are high in positive emotionality and persistence are likely to approach cognitive tasks more constructively than infants with more negative or distractable dispositions. On the other hand, these temperamental features may facilitate cognitive functioning more indirectly by evoking responses from others that promote cognitive development. If parents and other caregivers are likely to interact more positively and with infants who have positive, persistent, and sociable temperaments (Teti & Candelaria, 2002), these characteristics may indirectly foster cognitive performance because the social responses they promote are development enhancing. Or, consider a third possible explanation. Infants with these temperamental characteristics may receive better scores on cognitive performance measures because they respond better to strange examiners, adapt better to unfamiliar testing procedures, and/or are perceived more positively by testers (Lamb, 1981a). Indeed, the role of infant temperament in predicting development in cognitive and other developmental domains may depend on the quality of "fit" between the infant and the environment (Wachs, in press).

Difficultness

There continues to be interest in the developmental sequelae of infant difficultness and its impact on parent–infant relationships. This stems in part from Thomas Chess and Birch (1970) findings that the majority (70%) of "difficult" infants went on to develop behavior problems in later childhood (so some 30% did not), whereas only 18% of the "easy" infants did. Although continuing re-assessments of the NYLS longitudinal data have failed to confirm the strength of these early predictions (Bates, 1987), other researchers have found that temperamental difficultness figures importantly in the development of clinical and "subclinical" behavioral problems at later ages.

"Difficultness" has at its core the frequent and intense expression of negative emotion (Figure 10.7) and thus is consistent with other emotion-based theories of temperament reviewed earlier. Two central elements of temperamental difficultness, irritability and proneness to distress, tend to remain moderately stable during the first few years of life (Rothbart & Bates, 1998). However, prediction from infant difficultness to later behavior problems has been inconsistent

FIGURE 10.7
Infant "difficultness." Rembrandt von Rijn
(1616–1669). *The Naughty Child* (1635).
(Courtesy of Kupferstichkabinett, SMPK,
Berlin.)

(Teti & Candelaria, 2002). This is perhaps because the manner in which parents respond to questions about infant difficultness may have as much or more to do with the emergence of later behavior problems than infant difficultness alone. Indeed, temperamental traits such as high irritability and proneness-to-distress are associated with parental withdrawal, anger, and coercive discipline (Bates, Pettit, & Dodge, 1995; Lee & Bates, 1985; van den Boom, 1991). When parents respond to an irritable, difficult-to-soothe infant with hostility and anger, the infant is placed at even greater risk for later maladjustment than she or he is by difficult temperament alone. Bates et al. (1995), for example, found that harsh parental reactions to 4-year-olds identified in infancy as temperamentally difficult contributed to externalizing behavior in adolescence beyond the contribution of early temperamental difficulty. Similarly, Belsky, Hsieh, and Crnic (1998) found that affectively negative and intrusive mothering predicted externalizing behavior only in 3-year-olds judged at 1 year of age to be temperamentally difficult. Clearly, favorable child outcomes are not fostered by harsh parental reactions to temperamentally challenging infants.

At the same time, it is important to note that temperamental difficulty in infancy need not lead to parenting failures and child maladjustment. For example, Bates, Pettit, Dodge, and Ridge (1998) found that restrictive maternal control in the first 2 years of life (i.e., prohibitions, scolding, and restricting child behavior that was of potential harm to the child) in the general absence of physical discipline led to more positive outcomes in children who were difficult to control in infancy. Specifically, longitudinal associations between resistance to control in infancy and later "acting-out" were weaker in the presence of maternal restrictive control. According to Bates et al., consistent, firm parental control, without physical coercion, was an adaptive parental response to temperamental difficulty and may have fostered the child's ability to self-regulate and develop internalized standards of conduct. These findings are reminiscent of Thomas and Chess's (1977) premise that child developmental outcomes are best understood in terms of the goodness-of-fit between specific temperamental profiles and characteristics of the caregiving environment. They also support, broadly speaking, Wach's (in press) organismic-specificity hypothesis, which posits that the effects of any particular environment on child development will depend on the quality of fit between characteristics of the child and those of that environment.

Equally important, however, is the fact that easiness and difficulty are subjectively judged. Infant characteristics that some adults find difficult may not pose significant challenges for other caregivers. In this sense, "difficultness" resides not only in the infant but also in the caregiving context. Consequently, researchers and practitioners have been wise to apply the label "difficult" sparingly because different caregivers may find different characteristics to be challenging, and because such a label (and the treatment of children it fosters) may contribute to the problematic attributes themselves. In the end, temperamental constructs like difficultness must be understood in the context of infant–caregiver interaction.

Conclusion

Based on what researchers have learned about the nature of temperamental individuality, its diverse origins, and the complex, transactional influences that exist between temperament and various aspects of the environment, it should be clear that popular notions of temperament as early emerging, rigidly stable attributes that resist modification and have consistent long-term influences on the individual are inaccurate. Although temperamental attributes *tend* to be stable over time, the expression of temperamental individuality—and the nature of one's underlying temperamental "profile"—may change due to development and maturation, experiential influences, the contexts in which temperament is expressed, and the integration of temperamental features into an emerging personality organization. Similar complexity accompanies efforts to predict the consequences of temperament for later behavioral functioning. Researchers have learned that temperament is only one factor in the calculus of influences that predict later outcomes and that temperamental effects are best understood in the interactional contexts in which they are manifested, interpreted, modified, and accommodated.

Perhaps for these reasons, the temporal stability of temperamental features varies depending on the particular dimension of temperament studied, the period of time over which stability is assessed, the measures of temperament that are employed, the age of the infants studied, the consistency of environmental settings in which children live, and a variety of other influences (Rothbart & Bates, 1998). In short, the stability of temperament is contingent, never absolute. And this is sensible, given the complexity of behavior of which temperament is a part.

The Measurement of Infant Temperament

Our discussion of temperamental difficultness and its consequences for infant–parent interaction raise an intriguing question: Do temperamental features reside primarily within the child or in perceptions of the child by others? This question poses formidable challenges for those who measure temperament. On the one hand, caregivers are likely to provide highly insightful reports of a child's temperamental attributes based on their long-term and intimate experience with the child. However, reliance on caregiver-report measures invites problems of bias in measurement owing to the caregiver's subjective viewpoint, personality dispositions, unique experiences, and other factors that may inappropriately influence reports of the child's temperamental features. On the other hand, efforts to measure temperament more objectively through direct observations by unacquainted researchers inevitably involve limited sampling, observer effects, context effects (as in the difference between laboratory and home observations), and other potential biases. In short, alternative approaches to measurement both have strengths and weaknesses. Because these measurement issues fundamentally affect validity, the operational assessment of temperament remains a basic problem in this field of study (Rothbart & Bates, 1998).

Other challenges attend efforts to develop useful measures of temperament. If parent-report measures (usually questionnaires or interviews) are used, considerable effort must be made to select items representing the desired range of temperamental attributes in a broad variety of situations. If observational measures (whether home or laboratory) are used, they must be based on a broad sampling of infant behavior in situations that will reveal the range of temperamental attributes to be studied. Whether parent-report, home-observation or laboratory-observation measures are used, two psychometric issues figure prominently in the evaluation of how useful measures are to researchers. They are reliability and validity.

Reliability

Reliability concerns how consistently a temperament measure yields the same information about the same child. One kind of reliability estimate is *test–retest reliability*: Does the measure provide the same score on one day that it does on another day (assuming temperament remains stable, especially over short periods)? Not surprisingly, test–retest reliability is greater over short periods than over longer intervals, and ranges in most cases from moderate to high correlations between early and later assessments of temperament. For example, Rothbart (1981) reported that stability for the six dimensions of her Infant Behavior Questionnaire (IBQ) varies from good to excellent for periods as long as 6 to 9 months. Obviously, if temperamental features in infancy can be altered by developmental and experiential influences, test–retest reliability over long periods of time is affected by potential changes in temperament itself, rather than the actual reliability of the measure.

Another kind of reliability estimate is *interrater reliability*: Does the measure provide the same score when it is used by different observers? If the child's temperamental features are clear and the measure is objective, correlations between the scores assigned by different observers should be high. Unfortunately, when parents and nonrelated observers rate a child's temperament, reported convergence is only fair (Bornstein et al., 1991; Seifer, Sameroff, Barrett, & Krafchuk, 1994), as is agreement between mothers and fathers (Rothbart & Bates, 1998) or between mothers and daycare providers (Goldsmith, Rieser-Danner, & Briggs, 1991). This may be attributable, in part, to the fact that different observers note different features of the child's behavior because they have often had different experiences with the child.

A third kind of reliability estimate is *internal consistency*: Does the baby receive the same scores on items that tap the same temperamental features? Most measures include a number of items that are intended to assess the same temperamental dimension (activity level, emotionality, and so forth). If the measure is well designed, and if each item relates to the same temperamental dimension, individual scores on each of these items should agree. Unfortunately, internal consistency estimates for dimensions of many infant temperament measures are quite variable (Rothbart & Bates, 1998). In other words, many temperamental scales are not consistent and coherent.

Overall, there is considerable variability in how well current measures yield consistent information about a child.

Validity

Do these measures actually assess the dispositions we define as temperamental? This is obviously a crucial measurement issue because the conclusions researchers derive about temperament depend on the validity of the measures they employ.

There are at least two kinds of assessments that are pertinent to evaluating the validity of popular measures. The first is *discriminant validity*: Does the measure index dimensions of temperament that are independent and nonoverlapping? To the extent that temperament dimensions are genuinely independent of each other, the scores for each dimension yielded by a temperament measure should be uncorrelated with each other. Unfortunately, most researchers provide little clear information about discriminant validity, perhaps because some degree of mutual overlap (e.g., between emotionality and sociability) might be theoretically expected.

A second kind of validity index is *predictive validity*: Does the temperament measure provide scores that enable us to predict related behavior by the child in other circumstances? Does a child rated high in activity level behave actively in everyday settings? Predictive validity can entail either contemporaneous behavioral predictions or predictions of later behavior. Predictive validity is important because of concerns, discussed earlier, that parental perceptions of temperament may be biased by characteristics of the parent. Indeed, there is some evidence that maternal personality characteristics are associated with mothers' temperament ratings of their infants (Diener, Goldstein, & Mangelsdorf, 1995; Mebert, 1991). These findings suggest that parents are not necessarily accurate reporters of their child's temperamental features, although their objectivity can be enhanced through procedures by which parents provide very specific behavioral ratings based on observations of their infants over delineated periods of time, rather than providing general conclusions about their child's temperamental attributes (Bornstein et al., 1991).

Some researchers point out that researchers should study the extent to which these perceptions and their origins make important contributions to temperamental individuality (Bates, 1994; Bornstein et al., 1991; Rothbart, 1995). Importantly, however, the validity of observational measures of temperament is not necessarily any better than that of parental reports, and the field awaits a large-scale study that can assess the strengths and limitations of both approaches more definitively (Rothbart & Bates, 1998). As these psychometric issues indicate, considerably more progress in the development and refinement of temperamental measures is required before satisfactory levels of reliability and validity can be demonstrated and research findings clearly interpreted. In the end, the most useful studies of temperament will likely entail convergent multimethod approaches in which the unique and common variance associated with parent and observer ratings can be studied and compared (see Bornstein et al., 1991, for an example). This is, of course, the same conclusion derived from our earlier discussion of thorny methodological issues in the measurement of emotion and reflects the same problems associated with reliance on single methods whose relations to the constructs of interest are often only partial and indirect.

Summary

As we have noted throughout this chapter, emotional expressions and temperamental individuality share many common features. Most theorists regard variability in emotionality (especially negative emotion) as an important feature, and a baby's emotional expressions influence the caregiving environment in ways that are similar to the effects of activity level, sociability, and other dimensions of temperament. In focusing on emotional development and temperamental individuality, researchers increasingly acknowledge that infants make significant contributions to their interactions with the social world. This conclusion is not new, of course, but research shows both the sophistication of the baby's socioemotional contributions and the complexity of their influence on social relationships. As a result, earlier portrayals of the infant as a diffusely reactive emotive organism guided by underlying, unchanging dispositional attributes have been replaced by portrayals that recognize the multidimensionality of the baby's emotional life and the diverse influences on temperamental individuality. At the same time, images of the caregiving context are being modified to reflect caregiving influences that accommodate, interpret, and channel as well as shape the child's socioemotional characteristics. Because of the transactional influences underlying these portrayals of infant and context, the study of emotional development and temperamental individuality contributes to a much richer, and more provocative, understanding of infant development.

11

Social Development in Infancy

❖

- Describe the phases of infant–parent attachment.
- How and to whom do infant attachments form?
- What is the attachment behavior system, and how does it work?
- What is security of attachment, how is it determined, and how is it typically measured?
- How stable and predictively valid are individual differences in infant attachment security?
- What factors affect the quality of parental behavior?
- What are the principal domains of parent–infant interaction?
- How stable are individual differences in characteristics of parent–infant interaction?
- Do boys and girls have different social experiences?

Attachments and Interactions

To many theorists, the development of relationships with other people (mainly parents) constitutes one of the most important aspects of social development in infancy, and in this chapter we describe stages in the development of the infant's first social relationships, commonly referred to as attachments. After considering what appear to be universal developmental stages, we review speculations concerning the origins of individual differences in attachments—differences that may be consequences of very early interactions between parents or other caregivers and infants. As we then show, there are differences in the types of attachment infants form with their parents, and these differences may affect children's later cognitive, social, and personality development. The quality of infant–parent attachments is itself influenced by a variety of factors, of which the harmony of infant–parent interaction and the infant's temperament have been most widely studied.

Following a consideration of attachments, we discuss infant–parent interaction. In particular, we describe prominent domains of infant–mother interaction, individual differences in interactions, stability and continuity of those domains, and correspondences between infant and parent activities. The chapter concludes with a brief review of sex differences in social behavior and development. Of course, interactions with people other than parents and caregivers (for example, siblings and peers) also affect the child's development, as we pointed out in Chapter 2.

All the major theories of emotional development have addressed the development of attachments, and all contribute something to our understanding of this important phenomenon. However, the most popular explanation of the process of attachment formation was provided by John Bowlby (1969), a psychoanalyst who was much impressed by the capacity of ethological theorists to explain early emotional communications and the formation of social bonds in nonhuman species.

Bowlby began with the assumption that the behavioral propensities of infants and parents are most profitably considered in the context of the environment in which our species evolved. In that "environment of evolutionary adaptedness," the survival of infants would have depended on their ability to maintain proximity to protective adults in order to obtain nourishment, comfort, and security. Unlike the young of many other species, however, human infants are unable to move closer to or to follow adults for several months after birth, and they are even incapable of clinging to adults in order to stay in contact. Instead, human infants rely on signals of various sorts to entice adults to approach them. In order for these signals to be effective, adults must be predisposed to respond to them. The best example of such a prepotent signal is the infant cry, which very effectively entices adults to approach, pick up, and soothe the infant (Barr et al., 2000). As they grow older, infants develop a variety of means of achieving proximity or contact, including independent locomotion, and gradually come to focus their bids on people with whom they are most familiar, thereby forming attachments to them (Figure 11.1).

Basic Phases of Social Development

Bowlby (1969) described four phases in the development of infant–parent attachments: the newborn phase of indiscriminate social responsiveness (months 1 to 2), the phase of discriminating sociability (2 to 7 months), "maintenance of proximity to a discriminated figure by means of locomotion as well as signals" (month 7 through the second year), and finally the phase of goal-corrected partnership (year 3 on). We will concentrate on the first three phases, because the fourth does not begin until after infancy.

Phase 1: Newborn Indiscriminate Social Responsiveness (1 to 2 Months of Age)

This first phase in the attachment process is marked by the development of a repertoire of signals. From the time of birth, at least one very effective signal is at the baby's disposal—the cry. Crying motivates adults to soothe infants by picking them up and is the first-emerging example of a class of behaviors labeled *attachment behaviors* by Bowlby. The defining or common characteristic of these behaviors is that they all help to provide comfort and security

FIGURE 11.1

It was commonly believed that infants developed attachments
to the individuals responsible for their basic care and feeding.
In a classic study involving rhesus monkey infants, however,
Harlow and Zimmermann (1959) showed that infants form
attachments to cuddly terrycloth mother surrogates rather than
the wire surrogates that fed them. This study helped pave the
way for Bowlby's theory of attachment, which placed emphasis
on proximity and contact seeking rather than feeding. (Courtesy
of S. J. Suomi.)

by bringing the baby close to a protective, caregiving adult (Figure 11.2).
Another potent attachment behavior enters the baby's repertoire in the second month of life—smiling. Like crying, smiling is a signal that powerfully
affects adult behavior. However, smiles are effective because they encourage
adults to stay near the baby, whereas cries encourage adults to approach the
baby.

From birth, therefore, babies are capable of affecting the social environment
around them: Adults respond differentially to various newborn behaviors and
signals. The defining feature of this phase, however, is that babies are indiscriminate in the use of proximity-promoting signals: They appear to be satisfied whoever responds to their cries, smiles, and other similar signals. Adults,
of course, respond selectively depending on their relative investment and
responsibility.

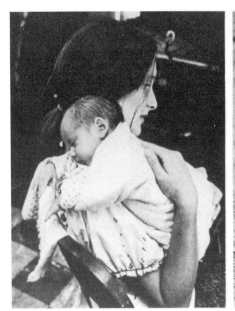

FIGURE 11.2
Physical contact between young infants and their parents dominates interactions early in life.

The newborn baby is characterized by marked, sudden, unpredictable changes in state (levels of arousal and distress) and by poor coordination of movements (Chapters 4 and 5). Behavior becomes more organized over time as internal neural control mechanisms develop (Chapter 5). During the first 2 months, caregivers have a major impact on the baby's state of arousal. When babies are distressed, adults intervene to soothe them; even when babies are drowsy they become alert when held erect at the adult's shoulder (Brazelton & Nugent, 1995). Doing so is obviously important, because infants can learn little about their environment—either social or physical—outside these periods of alertness. Relatively long periods of alertness simply do not occur spontaneously during this early phase: It is only through adult intervention that their value can be optimized. Practically, this means that when infants are alert and able to learn about the environment they are often in the arms of their caregivers. Because the caregivers who are close by can be felt, smelled, heard, and seen when infants are alert, babies may come to learn a great deal about them, and rapidly learn to associate their presence with alertness and the relief of distress (Thompson, 1998). This association may be one of the earliest, and certainly one of the most dramatic, associations that infants acquire. For example, Lamb and Malkin (1986) found that babies rapidly learned to expect their parents to respond when they cried, and so began to quit crying as soon as they heard or saw their mothers approaching, rather than when they were actually picked up.

Distress-relief sequences are not the only contexts in which young infants interact with their parents, of course. Various caregiving routines, including feeding (e.g., Bentley, Gavin, Black, & Teti, 1999) and social play (Fogel et al., 1997) provide the context for social interaction. Kaye (1982) described the interactions between mothers and their very young infants during feeding. He found a consistent tendency for mothers and infants to take turns, with the mother jiggling the nipple in the baby's mouth whenever the infant paused (Chapter 9). This turn taking, of course, alerts the infant to the basic principle of *reciprocity*. In addition, mothers (and presumably fathers as well) try to capture and maintain their infants' attention in the course of face-to-face play by moving their heads, exaggerating their facial expressions, and modulating the intonation of their voices. At 2 months, social and didactic interactions are equally emphasized by mothers, but over time didactic interactions (those in which the parent encourages the child to examine some property, object, or event in the environment) become increasingly prominent (Bornstein & Tamis-LeMonda, 1990). Correspondingly, 2-month-olds are oriented to social interactions, whereas 5-month-olds are focused more on exploration of the environment.

Frequent encounters with adults at times when infants are alert may also facilitate infants' capacities to recognize their parents, and Bowlby suggested that acquisition of the ability to recognize specific people marked the transition to the second phase of attachment development. As described in Chapter 6, however, studies show that infants are able to recognize their own mothers' voice and smell within the first 2 weeks of life, much earlier than Bowlby believed.

Phase 2: Discriminating Sociability (2 to 7 Months of Age)

Bowlby (1969) suggested that discriminating sociability began in the second or third month of life, although this capacity may in fact emerge much earlier. Presumably because significant others (such as parents) have been associated with pleasurable experiences (e.g., feeding, cuddling, rocking, and play) and with the relief of distress from early in life, familiar people become persons with whom the baby prefers to interact. Initially, these preferences manifest themselves in fairly subtle ways: Certain people will be able to soothe the baby more easily, and to elicit smiles and coos more readily, broadly, and frequently. Parents are enormously rewarded by this change in their baby's behavior: It indicates that they are special to the baby and that the child (at last) appreciates the effort they have put into caregiving. Prior to this phase, the baby appeared to enjoy interacting with anyone without apparent preference.

During this second phase of social development, babies are far more coordinated behaviorally than they were earlier. Their arousal level is far less variable, and (as described in Chapter 5) infants now spend larger proportions of their time in alert states. Distress is less frequent, and interactions with adults more often involve play. In many Western cultures, face-to-face games make their appearance in the first phase, becoming most prominent when infants are between 3 and 6 months of age (Adamson & Bakeman, 1984), following which infants become more interested in exploration than in social play (Bornstein & Tamis-LeMonda, 1990). In early face-to-face interactions, the adult assumes major responsibility for keeping the interaction going: Babies coo or smile or stick out their tongues, and adults respond with similar actions (Kaye, 1982). However, babies are not simply passive partners in face-to-face games. Two- to 3-month-olds begin to respond with boredom, distress, or withdrawal when their mothers adopt unresponsive "still-faces" instead of behaving in their typical interactive fashion (Moore, Cohn, & Campbell, 2001). They seem concerned over adults' failure to follow the rules of interaction, indicating that infants may indeed understand these rules, find synchronized and reciprocal interactions more enjoyable, and "expect" their partners to follow the rules (Chapter 9).

From repeated experiences in face-to-face play and distress-relief sequences, the baby seems to learn at least three important things: The first is the rule of *reciprocity*: In social interaction, partners take turns acting and reacting to the other's behavior. Second is *effectance*: The baby learns that her or his behavior can affect the behavior of others in a consistent and predictable fashion. The third is *trust*: The caregiver can be counted on to respond when signaled. Attaining these concepts means a major development in the process of becoming social. Once infants realize that their cries, smiles, and coos elicit predictable responses from others, they begin to develop a coherent view of the social world and concepts of themselves as individuals who significantly affect others. The degree to which babies feel confident in their predictions regarding the behavior of others— that is, the degree to which they trust or have faith in the reliability of specific people—may influence the security of their attachment relationships, a topic about which we shall have much to say in a later section. Individual differences in the amount of trust or perceived effectance each infant develops probably depend on individual differences in the responsiveness of the adults with whom the baby interacts in a variety of contexts (play, feeding, distress-relief, and so forth).

Phase 3: Attachments (7 to 24 Months of Age)

By 6 or 7 months of age, the infant bears little resemblance to the neonate. Seven-month-olds clearly understand and respect the rule of reciprocity in their inter-actions. Their confidence in others reinforced, 7-month-olds enjoy their newly acquired ability to creep around and to take responsibility for getting close to their parents at will, instead of waiting for others to come in response to their cries or coos. Between 6 and 12 months of age, infants are increasingly likely to initiate interaction using directed social behaviors, whereas mothers more frequently initiate games, terminate or redirect their infants' activities, and issue verbal requests (Green et al., 1980).

In addition to assuming an increasingly active role in their relationships, babies also begin in Phase 3 to protest (by crying) when left by attachment figures (Figure 11.3). According to Bowlby, separation protest should be viewed as a signal aimed at making attachment figures come back to the baby, and its emergence can be linked to attaining some primitive conception of person permanence (Ainsworth, 1973)—the notion that people have a permanent existence independent of the infant (see Chapter 7).

Major changes in social relationships occur between 7 to 8 months (the beginning of Phase 3) and at about 24 months (the end of this phase): Infants become increasingly sophisticated in their abilities to behave intentionally, communicate verbally, and respond appropriately in different contexts. As infants grow older, they initiate an increasing proportion of their interactions and are therefore respondents in a decreasing proportion. They can tolerate a growing distance from attachment figures, and (as noted in the Chapter 2) they become more and more adept at interacting with peers and unfamiliar adults. Figure 11.4 shows that these developmental trends are the same across a variety of primates, including langurs, baboons, gorillas, and humans.

FIGURE 11.3
A toddler cries as the parent leaves the room, and goes
to the door in an attempt to follow. Separation protest is
a hallmark of Phase 3 in the development of attachment.
(Courtesy of R. A. Thompson.)

For humans, however, this stage is marked by the emergence of discriminating attachments, which we discuss in detail following a brief discussion of Phase 4.

Phase 4: Goal-Corrected Partnerships (Year 3 Onward)

According to Bowlby (1969), the next major transition occurs at the beginning of the third year of life, when children become able to take their parents' needs into account when interacting with them. For example, they now appear to recognize for the first time (and begrudgingly) that parents must sometimes give priority to other activities, whereas the child's needs or wants must wait. Indeed, research on attachment has also focused on the study of attachment in preschoolers and school-age children (Teti, 1999). This focus includes the examination of patterns of interaction between children and their attachment figures, but in light of preschoolers' improved abilities in memory and language, the study of attachment in the preschool years has also focused on children's verbal representations of attachment relationships, in particular the child's recollections and expectations about the parent's behavior in hypothetical situations (Solomon & George, 1999; Teti, 1999, 2001).

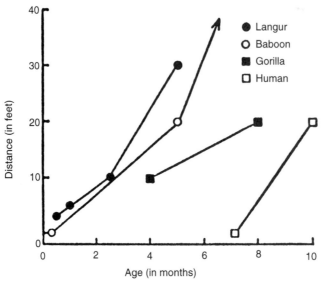

FIGURE 11.4

Distances between infants and mothers of some primate species at a variety of ages; the data points represent the maximum distances observed at each age, with the curve for the baboon reaching 90 feet at the end of 10 months. (After Rheingold and Eckerman, 1970. © 1970 by the American Association for the Advancement of Science. Reprinted by permission.)

Some Features of Attachment Bonds

The beginning of Phase 3 marks (by consensus) the time at which the first infant–adult attachments are formed. *Attachments* are specific, enduring, emotional bonds whose existence is of major importance in the process of sociopersonality development. In light of this, it is necessary to ask: What are the processes by which attachments form? To whom do infants become attached?

How Do Attachments Form?

Studying young ducklings, Konrad Lorenz (1935/1970) described what seemed to be an innate predisposition to "imprint on" an object—attempt to remain close to whatever salient moving object is present during a "sensitive period" occurring shortly after hatching (Bornstein, 1989). Attachment formation takes far longer in humans than in birds, and we doubt whether imprinting in ducklings and attachment in humans should be viewed as the result of similar mechanisms. Nevertheless, Bowlby was influenced by Lorenz's work on imprinting when proposing a comparable predisposition in humans to form attachments. According to Bowlby, the consistency of the adults' presence and availability during the sensitive period—the first 6 postnatal months—determines to whom the baby will become attached. If there is no consistent caregiver over this period (as might occur in institutions like hospitals, for example), the baby would not form attachments (Figure 11.5). Bowlby and his cotheorist, Mary Ainsworth, believed that most babies develop a hierarchy of attachment figures and that their primary caregivers—usually their mothers—become primary attachment

FIGURE 11.5
These children following their teacher remind us of the ducklings in Lorenz's
description of imprinting.

figures before any other relationships are formed. Once infants have this foundation, Ainsworth and Bowlby argued, they may (and often do) form relationships
with others, for example, fathers, daycare workers, and older siblings. Obviously,
there must be a minimal amount of time that these other individuals regularly
interact with infants if attachments are to form, but unfortunately we do not
know what this minimum level is or how it varies depending on the style or
quality of interaction.

The amount of time adults spend with infants is not the only factor determining whether infant–adult attachments will form: The quality of adult–infant
interaction also appears to be important. Bowlby and Ainsworth believed that
infants become attached to those persons who have been associated over time
with consistent, predictable, and appropriate responses to the baby's signals, as
well as to their needs (e.g., Ainsworth, Blehar, Waters, & Wall, 1978; Cummings &
Cummings, 2002; Thompson, 1998, 1999). The importance of the quality of
interaction over and above the quantity of interaction is underscored by the
evidence reviewed below, indicating that babies may become attached to both
of their parents at about the same time, contrary to Ainsworth and Bowlby's
hypothesis, even though they spend much less time with their fathers than
with their mothers. Whether or not a baby becomes attached to and protests
separation from someone seems to depend on the quality of their interaction,
not on the amount of time (over and above some minimum) the baby spends
with the person.

To Whom Do Infants Become Attached?

Before the mid-1970s, developmentalists assumed that infants formed their first
and most important relationships with their mothers. Researchers still agree
that mothers play a central role and that the stages and processes described

above apply especially well to the infant–mother attachment. This conception is too narrow, however, because it pays little attention to the ways in which the mother's other relationships might affect her relationship with the child and to the possible influences of fathers and other caregivers (Chapter 2). Developmental researchers are now keenly aware not only of the number of individuals (other than mothers) who may directly influence the child, but also of the elaborate ways in which children's behavior is affected by the multiple other social relationships in which they are involved. Because most of this chapter is implicitly concerned with the infant–mother relationship, here we focus most directly on infant–father relationships.

The Development of Father–Infant Attachments

There is substantial evidence that infants develop attachments to both their mothers and fathers (see Lamb, 1997, and 2002, for reviews). However, it was unclear how early in their lives infants form these attachments, because no data were available concerning the period between 6 and 9 months of age. Controversy also arose concerning the existence of preferences for mothers over fathers—some studies reported such preferences, whereas others failed to find them—and no data were available concerning father–infant interaction in the unstructured home environment rather than in the laboratory.

As Lamb (1997, 2002) concluded, studies of infant–mother and infant–father attachments have indicated that 7-, 8-, 12-, and 13-month-old infants show no systematic preference for either parent over the other on attachment behavior measures (their propensity to stay near, approach, touch, cry to, and ask to be held by specific adults), although these measures all show preferences for parents over a relatively unfamiliar adult visitor. Measures of separation protest and greeting behavior also show no preferences for either parent. Thus, most infants form attachments to both their parents at about the same time. When distressed, the display of attachment behaviors increases, and infants organize their behavior similarly around whichever parent is present. When both parents are present, distressed infants turn to their mothers preferentially. Interestingly, some boys show strong preferences for their fathers at home during the period that they turn to their mothers preferentially when distressed, suggesting that mothers are still deemed more reliable sources of comfort and security even when fathers become more desirable partners for playful interaction. These findings suggest that, although many infants become attached to both of their parents at the same time, they rank attachment figures in a hierarchy, with primary caregivers preferred.

Characteristics of Mother– and Father–Infant Interaction

Even in the first postnatal trimester, fathers and mothers appear to engage their infants in different types of interactions. When videotaped in face-to-face play with their one-half to 6-month-old infants, for example, fathers tend to provide staccato bursts of both physical and social stimulation, whereas mothers tend to be more rhythmic and containing (Barnard & Solchany, 2002; Parke, 2002; Teti, Bond, & Gibbs, 1988). Fathers continue to be more playful than mothers when interacting with their infants (Lamb, 1976b, 1977). Contrary to popular misconceptions, however, fathers are neither inept nor uninterested in interacting with their newborns. When observed feeding their infants, for example, both fathers and mothers respond to their infants' cues, either with social bids or by adjusting the pace of the feeding (Lamb, 1999, 2000, 2002). Although fathers are capable of behaving sensitively, however, they tend to yield responsibility for child-tending chores to their wives when not asked to demonstrate their competence for investigators (Parke, 1996). With older infants, fathers tend to engage in more physically stimulating, unpredictable, and arousing play than do mothers (Lamb, 2002; Parke & Buriel, 1998).

Pedersen, Cain, and Zaslow (1982) suggested that these patterns of interaction may differ, at least in middle-income families, when both parents are employed full-time, however. When observed with their infants, employed mothers stimulated more than homemaker mothers and were far more active than their husbands. Fathers with homemaker wives played with their infants more than did the mothers, but this pattern was reversed in families with working mothers, even though maternal responsibility for caregiving did not differ depending on the mothers' employment status. In other research involving families in which Swedish fathers assumed a major role in childcare, as well as traditional Swedish (Lamb et al., 1982a) and American (Belsky, Gilstrap, & Rovine, 1984) families, however, parental gender appeared to have a much more powerful influence than did parental role and employment status: Fathers and mothers tended to behave in characteristically distinct ways. Mothers were more likely to kiss, hug, talk to, smile at, tend, or hold their infants than fathers were, regardless of their degree of involvement in caregiving.

On average, it appears that fathers spend less time than mothers do with their infants, and this is true of families in the United States, Australia, Belgium, and Great Britain, and of families of varying ethnicity in the United States (European American, African American, and Latin American) (Parke & Buriel, 1998). Despite recent increases in the amount of time children spend with their fathers, however, most fathers continue to assume little or no responsibility for their infants' care and rearing. Fathers typically see themselves (and are seen by their partners and others) as helpers rather than parents with a primary responsibility for caregiving. All parties see breadwinning as the primary responsibility of fathers. However, most infants must have enough "quality" interaction with their fathers, despite the low quantity, because most infants become attached to their fathers (Lamb, 2002). And when fathers do take a greater role in infant care, their responsiveness and sensitivity appear to increase (Lamb, 1997, 2002).

In summary, infants generally form attachments around the middle of the first year of life to those adults with whom they have had most consistent and extended interaction. Infants generally establish significant relationships with both of their parents, even though they tend to have three or four times as much interaction with their mothers as with their fathers. The types of interactions that infants have with their parents also tend to differ. When mothers assume primary responsibility for childcare within the family (as they typically do), infant–mother interactions are characterized by childcare activities, whereas infant–father interactions are dominated by play. As a result, relationships with the two parents are distinctive from a very early age. Infants also form relationships with siblings, peers, and nonfamilial caregivers as well as their parents (as we reported in Chapter 2). These early relationships with mothers, fathers, brothers, sisters, and others all ensure that the social world of the young infant is rich and that we need to consider all the people in the child's social world when trying to understand the social context in which the infant is developing.

Behavior Systems Relevant to Infant Attachment

In this section, we want to examine more closely the characteristics of infant–parent attachments, particularly those that distinguish attachment from nonattachment relationships. To do so, we must consider some additional facets of attachment theory. Ethologically oriented attachment theorists are particularly interested in the biologically adaptive function (i.e., survival value) of infants' behavioral tendencies. As a result, Bowlby (1969) stressed the fact that attachment behaviors promote proximity between infants and adults; proximity to protective caregivers is of obvious adaptive value to dependent and helpless infants. Bowlby drew on control systems theory to derive a metaphor for the functioning of the so-called attachment behavior system, which mediates multiple distinct behaviors (for example, directed crying and approaching), employed to achieve the same goal (proximity and protection). In addition to the attachment system, theorists such as Bischof (1975; Gubler & Bischof, 1991) suggested that three other systems also mediate infant social behavior. Each system controls a set of behaviors that have a common utility in achieving an adaptive goal. In this section we describe the four behavioral systems and the interrelations that exist among them.

Four Behavior Systems

The *attachment behavior system* controls or coordinates infant activities most clearly and obviously related to attaining and maintaining proximity to or contact with attachment figures. Examples of these behaviors are gestures or signals indicating a desire to be held, crying to a person, and so forth. These attachment behaviors are infrequently directed to persons to whom infants are not attached, which means that researchers can identify attachment figures by determining to whom babies direct these behaviors. The function of the attachment behavior system is to ensure that infants retain access to persons on whom they can rely for nurturance and protection. In the eyes of the ethologically oriented theorists, such behavioral propensities would have been of adaptive significance (i.e., would have maximized the probability of infant survival) in the "environment of evolutionary adaptedness."

The second behavior system is the *fear/wariness system*. It coordinates avoidant, wary, or fearful responses to strangers (Figure 11.6). These behaviors are quite unlike those controlled by the attachment behavior system, although both systems are of adaptive value. For the same reason that it is important for infants to ensure access or proximity to protective adults, it is of survival value to avoid encounters with unknown and potentially dangerous persons and situations. As we described in Chapter 10, apprehension over the appearance of strange persons becomes marked in many infants around 7 to 8 months of age. This apprehension is a product of the fear/wariness system.

Although it may be adaptive to be wary when first encountering strange persons, it is assuredly not adaptive for human infants to refuse all contact or

FIGURE 11.6
Although he had been interacting quite happily with this stranger a moment ago, this toddler is concerned when the stranger picks him up and soon reaches out toward his mother. (Courtesy of R. A. Thompson.)

interaction with nonattachment figures. Persons other than parents have a profound impact on psychosocial development, and most interactions in later life involve people to whom children are not attached. Consequently, it is not surprising that the wariness response diminishes rapidly over time, and infants eventually enter, albeit tentatively at first, into friendly interactions with non-attachment figures. This kind of interaction typically involves distal social behaviors like smiling and vocalizing and is mediated by the third behavior system, the *affiliative system*. During an intermediate period when both affiliation and fear/wariness are activated, coy responses may be prominent.

Unlike attachment behaviors, affiliative behaviors do not promote physical contact with the person to whom they are directed, and consequently affiliative behaviors (like vocalizing) are often used in interaction with attachment figures as well as with persons to whom babies are not attached. It is not possible to investigate attachment relations by considering only behaviors such as smiling, because they may reflect either attachment or affiliation.

The existence of the affiliative behavior system speaks to the importance of infants' interactions with persons to whom they are not attached. In the course of interaction with other people, babies have the opportunity to gain social competence and learn social skills through modeling and reinforcement (Figure 11.7). Affiliating with a variety of individuals sets the occasion for infants to learn how to modulate their style of interaction in accordance with each individual's characteristic and unique interpersonal style. Social stimulation also seems to influence the rate of cognitive development (Chapter 7). In all, therefore, infants benefit from their social interactions in a variety of ways.

Infants also engage in interaction with their physical environment in order to develop competence in and mastery over it (Wachs, in press). The *exploratory*

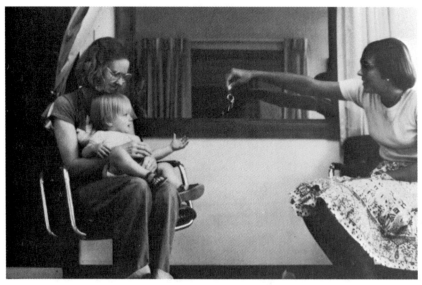

FIGURE 11.7
While gaining security from the close contact with mother, the toddler engages in
friendly interaction with a stranger. (Courtesy of R. A. Thompson.)

behavior system mediates contacts with the physical or nonsocial environment,
whereas "exploratory" social encounters are mediated by the affiliative system.
The exploration and manipulation of objects also facilitate the development
of cognitive competencies (Bornstein, 2002; Bornstein & Tamis-LeMonda, 1990;
Keller & Boigs, 1991).

Interdependencies Among the Behavior Systems

One major claim of the ethological theorists is that the four behavior systems
are complementary and interrelated rather than independent of one another.
Furthermore, the immediate goals of all the behavior systems usually cannot be
achieved simultaneously. Consequently, the degree to which one of the systems
is activated influences arousal or inhibition of the others. The specific effects
that any one system has on the arousal or inhibition of others can be predicted
by considering the adaptive functions of the four systems; these predictions are
generally supported by both anecdotal and scientific evidence about infant behavior. A few examples will suffice to demonstrate how these behavior systems
operate and interrelate.

The appearance of an unfamiliar individual should, according to the ethological model, arouse the infant's fear/wariness behavioral system. In most cases,
the infant's response involves both an attempt to avoid interaction with the
stranger (fear/wariness) and an attempt to move closer to the familiar attachment figure (attachment). Furthermore, activation of either (or both) of these
systems is incompatible with affiliation or exploration. Consequently, affiliation and exploration are typically inhibited when either the attachment or the
fear/wariness system is activated. The corollary is also true: When infants are not
distressed and are in familiar (and thus not anxiety-provoking) surroundings,
they may feel free to engage in interaction with less familiar persons (i.e., the

affiliative system is activated) and to explore the environment actively (i.e., the exploratory system is activated) without notable concern for remaining near their attachment figures (i.e., the attachment system is either not activated or is inhibited). According to Ainsworth, the presence of attachment figures provides infants with sufficient security that they are able to explore the environment extensively and adaptively. Thus attachment figures provide infants with the "secure base" from which they can engage in interaction with other persons and explore the physical environment. In the next section we discuss individual differences in attachment and the extent to which adults actually serve as secure bases for their children.

The Security of Infant–Parent Attachments

Many proponents of attachment theory are clinically oriented scholars primarily interested in the ways that early attachment relationships affect subsequent development. To explore this question, Ainsworth developed a procedure—the Strange Situation—for assessing what she called "the security of attachment" (Ainsworth et al., 1978). She also provided an elegant and persuasive account of the relationships among early infant–mother interaction, security of infant attachment, and subsequent child development. In this section we first describe the Strange Situation procedure and Ainsworth's hypotheses concerning security of attachment and then summarize major research on this topic.

The "Strange Situation"

This popular technique to study attachment can be used only when infants are old enough to have formed attachments and are mobile, yet are not so old that brief separations and encounters with strangers are no longer noteworthy. As a result, the Strange Situation is appropriate for infants ranging in age from about 10 to 24 months. The procedure has seven episodes, which are outlined in Table 11.1. The procedure is designed to expose infants to increasing amounts of stress in order to observe how they organize their attachment behaviors around their parents when distressed. Stress is stimulated by an unfamiliar environment, the entrance of an unfamiliar adult, and two brief separations from the parent.

A Typology of Attachments

As suggested earlier, infants should be able to use attachment figures as secure bases from which to explore the novel environment. Considering the four behavior systems, the stranger's entrance should lead infants to inhibit exploration and draw a little closer to their parents, at least temporarily. The parents' departure should lead infants to attempt to bring them back by crying or searching, and to reduced exploration and affiliation. Following the parents' return, infants should seek to reengage in interaction and, if distressed, may wish to be cuddled and comforted. The same responses should occur, with somewhat greater intensity, following the second separation and reunion. In fact, this is precisely how about 65% of the infants studied in the United States behave in

TABLE 11.1 THE STRANGE SITUATION[a]

Episode[b]	Persons Present	Change
1.	Parent, infant	Enter room
2.	Parent, infant, stranger	Unfamiliar adult joins the dyad
3.	Infant, stranger	Parent leaves
4.	Parent, infant	Parent returns, stranger leaves
5.	Infant	Parent leaves
6.	Infant, stranger	Stranger returns
7.	Parent, infant	Parent returns, Stranger leaves

[a] After Ainsworth and Wittig (1969).
[b] All episodes are usually 3 minutes long, but episodes 3, 5, and 6 can be curtailed if the infant becomes too distressed, and episodes 4 and 7 are sometimes extended.

the Strange Situation (Teti & Teti, 1996; Thompson, 1998). Following the practices of Ainsworth and her colleagues, these infants (designated Type B) are regarded as securely attached because their behavior conforms to theoretical predictions about how babies should behave in relation to attachment figures.

By contrast, some infants seem unable to use their parents as secure bases from which to explore. Furthermore, although they are distressed by their parents' absence, they behave ambivalently on reunion, both seeking contact and interaction and angrily rejecting it when it is offered (Figure 11.8). These infants

FIGURE 11.8
When mother returns after a brief absence, the securely attached toddler approaches her and requests to be picked up. Insecurely attached toddlers may turn away or behave angrily toward their mothers after similar separations. (Courtesy of R. A. Thompson.)

are conventionally labeled insecure–resistant or ambivalent (Type C). They typically account for about 10% to 15% of the infants in American research samples (Teti & Teti, 1996; Thompson, 1998).

A third group of infants seems little concerned by their parents' absence. Instead of greeting their parents on reunion, they actively avoid interaction and ignore their parents' bids. The infants are said to exhibit insecure–avoidant attachments (Type A); they typically constitute about 20% of the infants in American samples (Teti & Teti, 1996; Thompson, 1998). Main and her colleagues have also described a fourth group of infants whose behavior is "disoriented" and/or "disorganized" (Type D; Main & Solomon, 1991). These infants simultaneously display contradictory behavior patterns, manifest incomplete or indirected movements, and appear confused or apprehensive about approaching their parents.

Determinants of Strange Situation Behavior

Considerable debate has ensued about the origins of individual differences in infants' Strange Situation behavior. Attachment theorists have emphasized the role played by prior infant–mother interactions; critics have suggested that Strange Situation behavior reflects temperament as much as attachment security.

Parent–Child Interaction and Attachment Security

According to ethological attachment theorists, infants count on attachment figures to protect them and to be accessible when needed, and so use them as secure bases from which to explore and interact with other people. As noted above, however, infants do not trust their attachment figures equally, and these differences in security of attachment might affect how willingly infants will use their attachment figures as bases of security in situations like the Strange Situation. Almost from birth, infants learn about people from their interactions with them. Because adults differ in their style and sensitivity, differences should be evident among infants in the extent to which infants have confidence in their own effectance (ability to act on the environment successfully) and in the reliability of others (Ainsworth et al., 1978; Lamb, 1981a).

Since Ainsworth's hypotheses were proposed, many researchers have attempted to test them in independent longitudinal studies (see reviews by Thompson, 1998; Weinfield, Sroufe, Egeland, & Carlson, 1999). There appears to be general support for the notion that sensitive parenting—that is, nurturant, attentive, nonrestrictive parental care—and synchronous infant–mother interactions are associated with secure (Type B) infant behavior in the Strange Situation, and this appears to be true of U.S.-based samples as well as samples from cultures outside the United States (De Wolff & van IJzendoorn, 1997; Posada et al., 1999; Thompson, 1998). The mothers of infants who behave in either insecure–avoidant (Type A) or insecure–resistant (Type C) fashions manifest less socially desirable patterns of behavior: They may over- or understimulate, fail to make their behaviors contingent on infant behavior, appear cold or rejecting, and sometimes act ineptly. Because there is much variability in these results, it is difficult to identify precisely what aspects of parental behavior are important. Some studies identify warmth but not sensitivity, some patterning of stimulation but not warmth or amount of stimulation, and so forth. There does appear to be some consensus, however, that insecure–avoidant attachments are associated with intrusive, overstimulating, rejecting parenting, whereas insecure–resistant attachments are linked to inconsistent, unresponsive parenting (Belsky, 1999; De Wolff & van IJzendoorn, 1997). Although the antecedents of disorganized (Type D) attachments are less well established, Type D attachments are more common among abused and maltreated infants and among infants exposed to other pathological caregiving environments (Lyons-Ruth & Jacobvitz, 1999; Teti, Gelfand, Messinger, & Isabella, 1995) and may be consequences of parental behaviors that infants find frightening or disturbing (Main & Hesse, 1990; Schuengel, Bakermans-Kranenburg, van IJzendoorn, & Bloom, 1999).

The Role of Infant Temperament

Although studies exploring the linkage between early temperament and attachment security are inconclusive, most researchers now believe that infant temperament has at least an indirect effect on Strange Situation behavior because it likely affects the quality of infant–parent interaction. In addition, temperament may affect how infants are influenced by their parents: Distractible babies, for example, may be less affected by their parents' behavior than attentive babies are. Most researchers suggest that temperament does not have a direct effect on whether or not infants are classified as Type A, B, or C, although early temperamental irritability does predict insecurity in later infancy (Crockenberg, 1981; Susman-Stillman, Kalkoske, Egeland, & Waldman, 1996; van den Boom, 1994; Vaughn & Bost, 1999).

Such findings do not specify the relation between temperament and attachment security. Most researchers have relied on parent-report measures of temperament, which are potentially unreliable, telling us not only about the baby's style but also about the parent's personality (Chapter 10). Thompson and Lamb (1982) suggested that temperament may affect only the degree of distress manifest in the Strange Situation. Thus, whereas the quality of infant–parent interaction would determine whether the child will become securely or insecurely attached, constitutionally based differences in irritability would determine whether the insecurity will be manifest in a low distress (i.e., avoidant) or high distress (i.e., resistant) fashion, and whether security will be manifest by high levels of distal interaction or high levels of contact seeking. Findings consistent with this hypothesis have also been reported by other researchers (Belsky & Rovine, 1987; Frodi & Thompson, 1985; Vaughn, Lefever, Seifer, & Barglow, 1989), but researchers using more objective measures of adrenocortical reactivity or emotional reactivity have obtained less conclusive results (Calkins & Fox, 1992; Gunnar, Mangelsdorf, Larson, & Hertsgaard, 1989; Hertsgaard, Gunnar, Erikson, & Nachmias, 1995; Nachmias, Gunnar, Mangelsdorf, Parritz, & Buss, 1996; Thompson & Lamb, 1984), leaving uncertain the constitutional bases of Strange Situation behavior. It remains likely, however, that temperament and attachment security are independent dimensions, with temperament affecting irritability and emotionality but not the security of attachment per se.

Such findings add credence to Ainsworth's (1989) notions about the origins of individual differences in Strange Situation behavior. Relatedly, Rothbart and Bates (1998) follow the lead of Thomas and Chess (1977), who argued that the "goodness-of-fit" between child and parent or context is of paramount importance, as it affects the quality of their interaction. From this perspective, the nature of the child's temperament is less important than the fit between that temperament and the parents' own temperament and expectations. Because the same infant temperament may fit well with one parent and poorly with another, the role played by temperament in the establishment of attachment relationships is much harder to study and specify than it would have been had the association between temperament and attachment security been direct.

Stability of Infant Attachment

The notion that Strange Situation behavior reflects something that is not ephemeral but intrinsic to the relationship was initially supported by findings showing that there is remarkable stability over time in these patterns of infant behavior. Both Connell (1976) and Waters (1978) reported stability between 12 and 18 months of age in the way infants behaved in the Strange Situation when observed more than once with the same parent. According to Waters, 48 out of 50 infants—96%—obtained the same classification on both occasions. Later, Main and Cassidy (1988) reported a high degree of stability (84%) between 12-month assessments in the Strange Situation and 6-year assessments using a new observational procedure designed by Cassidy to study older children.

However, test–retest reliability is not always so high, and, in fact, short-term stability estimates for Strange Situation classifications show much variation (Thompson, 1998). In some cases, instability of attachment classifications are lawfully related to changes in infants' "social ecology." For example, in their study of attachment stability in an economically disadvantaged sample, Vaughn, Egeland, Sroufe, and Waters (1979) found that many infants changed from one classification to another between 12 and 18 months of age and that such changes were systematic: When the families had experienced considerable social stress during the 6-month period, Type B attachments often changed to Type A or C, although when families experienced a low degree of stress, Type A or C attachments did not necessarily become Type B. In a middle-income sample, Thompson, Lamb, and Estes (1982) found that major changes in family circumstances or caregiving arrangements (e.g., the onset of maternal employment) led to changes in infants' Strange Situation behavior, but they did not necessarily engender change from the more desirable B to the less desirable A and C types any more often than the reverse. In another study involving a middle-income sample, Belsky, Campbell, Cohn, and Moore (1996) found no stability in attachment security between 12 and 18 to 20 months of age, nor were they able to identify any reliable correlates of instability. Attachment theory would predict that changes in stability of attachments over time should be associated in some way with lawful changes in parental sensitivity (for example, a change from secure to insecure should coincide with a decrease across the same time period in parental sensitivity).

At this point, a coherent explanation of stability or instability in Strange Situation classifications remains to be provided. We propose that stability and instability of attachments in infancy may indeed be explained by continuities and discontinuities in parental behavior, although researchers still need to study representative samples of parents and infants in multiple, ecologically valid contexts over time in order to provide an adequate test of this hypothesis. It is also likely that changes in attachment security may be partially independent of parenting quality and may relate to normative family life transitions experienced by children. Teti, Sakin, Kucera, Corns, and Das Eiden (1996), for example, found that the birth of a second child predicted a significant decrease in attachment security among firstborn children and that this decrease was not linked to changes, from before to after the birth, in mothers' sensitivity with their firstborns, mothers' levels of psychiatric symptoms, or mothers' reports of marital harmony. Indeed, the decrease in firstborn attachment security may have reflected changes in the children's perceptions of their relationships with their mothers in response to the introduction of the new family members, who may have been perceived as threats (Teti, 2002). Studies of attachment stability thus should take into consideration not just continuity and change in life circumstances and in parenting but also the manner in which children cope with and perceive normative life transitions.

Predictive Validity of Attachment Classifications

Another reason why attachment classifications intrigue developmentalists is that they appear to predict aspects of the child's future behavior. Like Erikson (1950), attachment theorists believe that when babies encounter people for the first time, they tend to assume that those persons will treat them in the same way that other people have treated them in the past. Thus, babies who have developed trust in their attachment figures will tend to regard the new people they encounter as trustworthy too. As babies get to know each individual, of course, they develop a set of expectations about that specific individual.

The relation between Strange Situation behavior and styles of interaction with others has been well documented (Berlin & Cassidy, 1999; Kerns, 1996; Sroufe, 1996; Teti, in press). Babies with Type B attachments to their mothers were later more cooperatively playful when interacting with a friendly stranger than were Type A or C infants. Similarly, quality of early attachment relates to social relationships in encounters with peers both at the same and at later points in time. Strange Situation behavior may affect social relationships in contemporaneous encounters with peers. Type B infants engage in more frequent, more prosocial, and more mature forms of interaction with their siblings and peers, sharing more and showing a greater capacity to initiate and maintain interactions, for example.

Other researchers have examined the relation between Strange Situation classifications and aspects of later achievement motivation in children (Frankel & Bates, 1990; Grossmann, Grossmann, & Zimmerman, 1999; Sroufe, 1983a, 1983b). They report that secure infant–mother attachments at 12 or 18 months are associated with superior problem-solving abilities in a variety of stressful and challenging contexts in the preschool years. In particular, children who showed Type B attachments to their mothers as infants persist longer and more enthusiastically in cognitively challenging situations than do children who had Type A or Type C attachments. Type B infants also seem to be more resilient and robust when stressed or challenged and appear more socially competent and independent when they later enter preschool (Teti & Teti, 1996). Insecure attachment in infancy, and in particular the disorganized/disoriented (Type D) classification, predict elevated rates of antisocial behavior in later childhood (Lyons-Ruth, Easterbrooks, Davidson, & Bronfman, 1995; Shaw, Owens, Vondra, Keenan, & Winslow, 1997).

Evidence concerning the temporal stability of Strange Situation behavior and its relations to measures of earlier infant–child interaction and later child achievement and personality suggests that the Strange Situation measures some meaningful aspect of mother–infant attachment and has important implications for understanding and predicting development. Presumably, Strange Situation behavior with fathers affects development in analogous ways, although the child's relationships with primary attachment figures, be they mothers or fathers, is likely to be more significant than other attachment relationships.

Lamb and his colleagues (Lamb, Thompson, Gardner, & Charnov, 1985; Thompson, 1998) point out, however, that the degree of predictive validity is far from perfect. Rather, the relation between Strange Situation behavior in infancy and subsequent child behavior is found only when there is stability in caregiving arrangements and family circumstances, which (as we noted previously) seem to maintain stability in patterns of parent–child interaction subsequently reflected in similar patterns of Strange Situation behavior. This raises the interesting question we first encountered when considering the stability of cognition in infancy: Is the prediction over time attributable to individual differences in the quality of early infant–parent attachments? Or, is it attributable to the continuing quality of child–parent interactions over time? Researchers often assume the former, namely that Strange Situation behavior reflects a part of the child's personality. But, if the latter were true, it would imply that the quality of early relationships was predictively valuable not because it caused later differences directly, but because it presaged later differences in the quality of relationships that in turn support continuing differences in the child's behavior. Such a pattern of findings would place the locus of stability in continuing parent–child interactions rather than in some aspect of the child's personality. Surprisingly, this possibility has not yet been tested directly, although it has major relevance for long-standing assumptions concerning the critical importance of early experiences and is consistent with the transactional view of development.

Although Strange Situation behavior, prior infant–parent interaction, and the child's later behavior are all interrelated, correlations obtained among them are not very strong. This suggests that factors other than quality of attachment, such as temperament or familiarity with strangers and brief separations, influence Strange Situation behavior. In turn, this means that researchers need to rely on multiple converging methods to assess constructs as complex and as important as the quality of infant attachments, rather than rely on a single measure like the Strange Situation in which behavior is influenced by factors other than quality of attachment.

Cross-Cultural Research on the Attachment Typology

As Table 11.2 shows, the distribution of infants across the A, B, and C categories in many other countries appear to differ from that typically found in American samples, even though secondary analyses have shown that researchers in different countries apply the coding and classification criteria similarly (van IJzendoorn & Kroonenberg, 1990). These results could mean that parents in the cultures concerned were either much more or less sensitive than American parents, but this ethnocentric interpretation seems incorrect. Rather, the results may underscore the importance of factors other than the quality of parental behavior in explaining infant behavior in the Strange Situation (Lamb et al., 1985;

TABLE 11.2 DISTRIBUTION OF INFANTS ACROSS ATTACHMENT TYPES IN SELECTED STUDIES[a]

Country	Reference	A	B	C
United States	Ainsworth et al. (1978)	23	70	13
	Thompson et al. (1982)	7	30	6
	Belsky and Rovine (1988)	11	69	11
	Fracasso, Busch-Rossnagel, and Fisher (1993) (Latino immigrants)	15	25	10
Japan	Takahashi (1986)	0	41	19
	Durrett, Otaki, and Richards (1984)	5	24	7
Germany	Grossmann et al. (1981)	24	16	6
Israel	Sagi et al. (1985)	7	47	28
	Sagi et al. (1994)	0	20	5
The Netherlands	van IJzendoorn, Goossens, Kroonenberg, and Tavecchio (1985)	14	27	0
Sweden	Lamb et al. (1982)	11	38	2

[a] Values represent actual numbers of infants in each attachment category.

Thompson, 1998). For example, the high degrees of stress manifest by Japanese and Israeli babies in the Strange Situation may have led to increases in the proportion of infants classified as Type C. The Japanese infants may appear inordinately distressed either because they have much less experience with separations from their mothers than American infants typically have, or because their mothers are much more stressed by the procedures (Grossmann & Grossmann, 1990); in either case the situation would not be psychologically similar for Japanese and American babies. Likewise, for infants growing up on Israeli kibbutzim, encounters with total strangers are more unusual and thus elicit great distress. Again, even though the procedure was structurally the same for Japanese, Israeli, and American infants, the psychological experiences or meaning for infants from each culture may have been very different (Bornstein, 1995). In addition, Miyake, Chen, and Campos (1985) reported that Japanese infants who were classified as Type C were temperamentally more irritable than Type B infants from birth. Thus, it appears that culture-specific rearing practices or temperamental differences may help to account for at least some of the variation in Strange Situation classifications across cultures. van IJzendoorn and Kroonenberg (1988) also showed that there is a great deal of intracultural variability, making it important not to reach conclusions about cross-cultural differences on the basis of small and often unrepresentative samples from each culture.

In summary, the picture emerging from the many studies in which Strange Situation behavior was assessed is complex. Strange Situation behavior appears to reflect individual differences in patterns of infant–parent interaction, with Type B attachments potentiated in Western cultures by warm, sensitive, and supportive parental behavior. Infant temperament appears to affect the degree of distress infants manifest in contexts like the Strange Situation (Vaughn & Bost, 1999), but it does not clearly determine the degree of security that the baby will manifest. However, other factors seem to be important as well, notably, culture-specific rearing practices. To understand the formative importance of infant–parent attachment, we need to obtain multiple measures of attachment rather than rely exclusively on observations in the Strange Situation.

Parental Behavior and Interaction with Infants

Origins of Parenting Characteristics

The origins of individual differences in parenting are extremely complex, as we noted in Chapter 2, but most researchers consider six spheres of influence to be of paramount importance: (1) parents' enduring personality characteristics, (2) parents' beliefs, (3) situational influences on parents' psychological state, (4) the actual or perceived characteristics of the infants, (5) parents' attachment representations, and (6) critical events. In this section we discuss these factors as well as the principal domains of parenting interaction, including their stability, continuity, and covariation, correspondence with infant activity, and some cross-cultural variations in parental behavior.

Personality

Theorists have usually assumed that parental sensitivity reflects adults' enduring personality traits or predispositions, and that sensitive parenting is more likely to occur when parents are psychologically healthy (Belsky, 1999; Belsky & Barends, 2002; Teti et al., 1995). Characteristics such as self-centeredness and adaptability might be especially pertinent, for example. Parents' adaptability may be important in the infants' first few months, during which their infants' activities appear unpredictable and disorganized, their cues less distinct and undifferentiated, and the infants themselves generally less "readable." Self-centeredness may lead to insensitivity when adults fail to put infants' needs ahead of their own. Other important aspects of parental personality include self-efficacy in the parenting role, cheerfulness, agreeableness, and low levels of depression and anxiety (Belsky, 1999; Teti et al., 1995; Teti & Gelfand, 1997).

A central concept in understanding the determinants of parental sensitivity is the adults' perception of his or her *efficacy* as a parent (Teti & Gelfand, 1991, 1997). By definition, parents who believe that they are efficacious see themselves as competent caregivers and interpret interactions between themselves and their infants as enjoyable for the infants. Parental skill, of course, is not the only relevant factor here. A parent who feels incompetent may feel rewarded by even modest levels of success, and the infant's temperament, readability, predictability, and responsiveness also influence the effectiveness of any adult intervention. The same behavioral intervention may rapidly soothe one infant yet seem totally ineffective when another infant is involved, leading the parents of different infants to reach very different conclusions about their own competence as parents, despite superficial similarities in their behavioral styles. Through the quality and contingency of infants' responses, meanwhile, infants have a major impact on how parents perceive their own effectiveness. We return to these so-called infant effects later in this section.

Perceived efficacy is likely to affect parental sensitivity because parents who feel effective are reinforced and thus motivated to engage in further interaction, which in turn provides additional opportunities to read infants' signals, interpret them correctly, and respond appropriately. Furthermore, the more rewarding the interaction, the more motivated are parents to seek "quality" interaction again. Teti and Gelfand (1991), for example, found mothers' feelings of efficacy in the parental role to be a stronger predictor of parenting competence (i.e., sensitivity and warmth) in interactions with their infants than were mothers' levels of depressive symptoms, social and marital supports, and perceptions of their infants' temperament.

Perhaps one of the strongest predictors of parental feelings of inefficacy is depression. Many parents—mothers *and* fathers—experience bouts of depression from time to time. Some reflect enduring psychological characteristics; others may be transient, as a response to economic circumstances or even following the birth the baby. These feelings influence parental perceptions and behaviors toward baby, perhaps by making parents less responsive. Certainly, too, depressed mothers fail to experience—and convey to their infants—much happiness with life. Tronick and his colleagues observed that depressed mothers are less responsive to infant signals, and therefore more often engage in inadequately coordinated interactions (Giannino & Tronick, 1988). In turn, depressed behaviors have short- as well as long-term consequences for infants. For example, Wright, George, Burke, Gelfand, and Teti (2000) found that clinical levels of maternal depression when children were between 3 months and 3 years of age were associated with more behavior problems (i.e., aggressive and antisocial behaviors) at 5 to 8 years of age than were observed in children whose mothers were not depressed during this early period. These associations were evident even when the mothers' current depressive symptoms were accounted for.

Some influential aspects of adult personality may be enduring, but most researchers also assume a more dynamic view of personality. A parent's personality is likely to change as a result of formative experiences, such as childbirth, marriage, prolonged hostility from a spouse, divorce, or intolerable degrees of stress. In addition, beliefs and intuitions are thought to be related to parental behaviors.

Parental Belief Systems

Goodnow (2002) has discussed the developmental scripts or developmental scenarios that represent parents' informal theories of development. She assumes that most parents have implicit assumptions regarding the relations between behavior and age, so parents continually assess children's level of development in formulating how best and most productively to interact with them. Parents' scripts are constantly in flux, as the adults actively acquire new information about children through observation, feedback, experimentation, and so forth. These parental belief systems play an important role in shaping parental behavior. McGillicuddy-DeLisi (1985, p. 196), for example, pointed out that, when parents see children as active participants in their own development, parents are more likely to use teaching strategies that "stimulate the child to anticipate, reconstruct, and think in representational terms. . . ." When parents believe that they have little or no effect on their children's intelligence or temperament, they may not assume a very active role in teaching children at all. So the ways in which parents choose to interact with their children seem to be strongly related to the parents' own general belief systems.

These suppositions about beliefs beg the question: How do parents develop belief systems? Family constellation, socioeconomic status, culture, as well as factors such as spousal beliefs, childhood experiences, and the beliefs of one's own parents, have been identified as potential sources of influence (Bornstein, Cote, & Venuti, 2001; Cote & Bornstein, 2000b; Sigel, McGillicuddy-DeLisi, & Goodnow, 1992). Interest in parents' beliefs and actions with respect to their children's development is increasing (Chiang, Caplovitz, & Nunez, 2000; Gaskins, 1999; Savage & Gauvain, 1998; Tamis-LeMonda, Chen, & Bornstein, 1998; Wentzell, 1998). For example, in a study of parents and children who experienced Head Start, Galper, Wigfield, and Seefeldt (1997) found that optimistic parental beliefs about how well their children would do in school correlated positively with the children's own attitudes toward school and measures of how well children performed in math and reading.

Some components of parenting are driven by individual personality characteristics and beliefs and are in this way thoughtful and conscious. However, Papoušek and Papoušek (2002) developed a complementary notion of *intuitive parenting*. Intuitive parenting consists of behaviors enacted in a nonconscious fashion that are sensitive and developmentally suited to the ability and stage of a child, and thus enhance child adaptation. We reviewed an example of intuitive parenting when we discussed infant-directed speech in Chapter 9. Parents (as well as others) unconsciously and habitually modulate myriad aspects of their communication, presumably to match infant competencies appropriately. Parents find it difficult to modify such intuitive behaviors, even when asked. Intuitive behaviors, in the Papoušeks' view, do not require the time and effort usually required by conscious decision making, and, being more rapid and efficient, they utilize much less of the parent's attentional reserve.

Social–Situational Factors

Parents' personalities and perceptions of their roles and responsibilities clearly constitute sets of social factors that influence their behavior toward infants. Of course there are other ways that social factors can be influential. Most important among these are stress and the availability of social support (Cochran & Niego, 2002). Financial and social stress presumably demand attention from parents, and as a result reduce their attentiveness, patience, and tolerance, and adversely affect their general well-being and psychological health. It is not surprising, therefore, that child maltreatment is more common when parents are subjected to high levels of economic or social stress and are socially and emotionally isolated from potential support networks (DePanfilis & Zuravin, 1999; Kotch, Browne, DuFort, & Winsor, 1999).

A number of researchers have demonstrated that the quality of parenting is influenced by the levels of stress *and* social support available to parents, even when the stresses are modest and the quality of parenting is clearly not abusive (Gordon, 2000; Smith, Landry, & Swank, 2000). Thus, well-supported mothers are less restrictive and punitive with their infants than are relatively unsupported mothers, and the quality and frequency of contacts with significant others is associated with the quality of parent–child relationships (Burchinal, Follmer, & Bryant, 1996) as well as the parents' sense of their own effectance and competence (Teti & Gelfand, 1991). Belsky (1999) proposed that intimate support from husbands combines with mothers' broader social networks (i.e., community and friendship support) to predict parenting quality.

Infant Characteristics

Most theorists acknowledge that infants' characteristics affect parental behavior, but disagreement about the relative importance of parental and infant contributions to interaction and development is long-standing (compare Bell & Harper, 1977, with Ainsworth, 1979).

Very young infants cannot construct complex internal representations of their parents' behavior because their cognitive capacities are limited (Marvin & Britner, 1999). Consequently, they cannot alter their behavior in order to mesh their activities and emotions with those of their interactive partners. Parents, by contrast, presumably can generate internal models of infant behavior and alter their behavioral strategies in order to elicit specific responses and to mesh with their infants' activities and needs. With age and experience, babies begin to interpret the behaviors of others.

Infants have innate behavioral propensities that permit them to provide contingent feedback to their parents, and these in turn contribute to feelings of effectance in their parents. The readiness to respond to social stimulation, mutual eye contact, and soothing when held indicates to parents that their behaviors are effective and enjoyable. Furthermore, under ordinary conditions, specific infant behaviors predictably elicit from parents responses that allow infants to develop notions of effectance as well. Successful dyadic interactions thus help parents and infants alike to perceive themselves as effective and their relationships as positive.

Goldberg (1977) and Lamb and Easterbrooks (1981) list a number of infant characteristics that affect parental effectance; these include infants' responsiveness, readability, and predictability. Responsiveness refers to the extent and quality of infant reactivity to stimulation, and readability to the definitiveness of infant behavioral signals. An "easily read" infant is one who produces unambiguous cues that allow caregivers to recognize the infant's states quickly, interpret the infant's signals promptly, and thus respond contingently. Predictability refers to the degree to which the infant's behaviors can be anticipated reliably from contextual events or the infant's own preceding behaviors. The health and developmental maturity of infants also affect the parents' behavior and the quality of infant–parent interaction, as has been illustrated in the research on preterm infants and their parents (Goldberg & DiVitto, 2002).

Studies of healthy preterm infants and mothers consistently show that these infants are more passive and reactive and that their mothers are more active and directive than are term infants of comparable age and their mothers (Teti, O'Connell, & Reiner, 1996; see Figure 11.9). This does not necessarily mean that the mothers of preterm infants are more insensitive, however. Rather, the differences may arise in part because preterm infants are immature and call for more social "buffering" and directiveness from their adult partners. Thus, the differences may actually attest to the sensitivity of these mothers. Support for this view can be found in the fact that the interaction styles of preterm infants and their mothers are similar to those involving younger term infants—infants who are of the same conceptional age but have spent a briefer period of time outside the womb. Such findings indicate that the maturity level of the child influences social interactions.

Child characteristics other than maturity can influence parents as well. When newborns are unhealthy, for example, they seem to require more "work" from their adult partners to complement their own low energy level and sluggishness (Goldberg & DiVitto, 2002), and these differences become evident

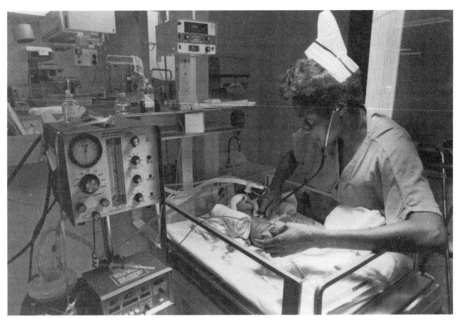

FIGURE 11.9
A small preterm baby in an incubator.

when infants are compared with conceptional agemates as well as chronological agemates. Furthermore, whereas the differences attributed to maturity level appear to diminish over time, those attributable to ill health may be more enduring. Therefore, perhaps as a result of deficiencies in both social and perceptual–cognitive arenas, very small and unhealthy preterm infants often grow up to have cognitive and educational deficits (Hack et al., 2002; Minde, 2000; Wood et al., 2000). The effects of infant health may even be exacerbated, unfortunately, by pervasive stereotypes that lead adults to treat ill and/or preterm infants differently, regardless of their actual characteristics (Stern, Karraker, Sopko, & Norman, 2000).

One problem researchers face when trying to identify the cause of poor developmental outcomes among infants is that risk factors co-occur. Preterm births are more common in poor, ill-nourished, and socially stressed families, and it is not known how great an impact these factors have, separately or together. It is known, however, that preterms growing up in advantaged circumstances are much more likely to achieve normal cognitive and intellectual status at school age than are those reared in disadvantaged situations (Bendersky & Lewis, 1994; The Infant Health and Development Program, 1990; see Chapter 1). Indeed, it was this observation that fostered the development of Sameroff's transactional theory (see Chapter 1). Presumably, more affluent parents are spared many of the stresses that distract poorer parents and are able to have higher quality interactions with their children.

Parental Attachment Representations

The manner in which parents mentally represent attachment relationships also predicts parental quality. These representations are believed to be rooted in the parent's own attachment-related experiences with her or his own parents during childhood, although attachment theorists openly acknowledge that how one represents attachment relationships can undergo considerable revision as one enters into and experiences new relationships (Hesse, 1999). Most researchers have used the Adult Attachment Interview (AAI; George et al., 1985), in which the parent discusses her or his relationships with her or his own mother and father, and the rater pays particular attention not to the content of the response per se (i.e., whether the relationship is described positively or negatively), but whether the parent can provide convincing details to back up her or his descriptions. The interview yields four adult attachment groupings: Autonomous (Group F) parents relate experiences and relationships in an open, fluid, objective, coherent manner, clearly value and appreciate attachment relationships, and view them as important influences on their lives. Dismissing (Group D) parents, by contrast, view attachment relationships as having limited influence on their lives and appear to avoid detailed discussions of early attachment experiences. Idealization of parental figures is typical, as is lack of recall for attachment-related experiences. Preoccupied (Group E) parents are mentally entangled, conflicted, and angry about past and present attachment relationships. Their extensive preoccupation with past and present parental transgressions precludes an ability to describe these events objectively and coherently. Finally, unresolved (Group U) parents give evidence of mental disorganization over abuse or loss, indicating that such events continue to have a major disorganizing influence on the quality of their thinking and discourse.

Parental AAI classifications are predictive of corresponding infant–parent attachment classifications (Hesse, 1999). That is, mothers classified with the AAI as autonomous (the analog of a secure attachment in infancy) are more likely to have securely attached infants. Mothers classified as dismissing (analogous to insecure–avoidant infant–mother attachment) are likely to have insecure–avoidant infants. Mothers classified as preoccupied (analogous to an insecure–resistant attachment in infancy) are likely to have insecure–resistant attachments. Finally, mothers classified as unresolved (conceptually akin to insecure–disorganized attachment in infancy) are likely to have insecure–disorganized infants (Hesse, 1999). In addition, autonomous mothers are more sensitive toward their infants than are nonautonomous mothers. Importantly, adults need not recall a history of nurturant parenting in order to be classified as autonomous. It is not uncommon for parents who report problematic childhoods to have forgiven their parents for perceived transgressions and to see how they might have contributed to some of the difficulties they encountered. Adult attachment representations appear to be quite specific with respect to the manner in which adults represent attachment relationships and are not related to intelligence, memory of nonattachment related events, or social desirability (Bakermans-Kranenburg & van IJzendoorn, 1993; Sagi et al., 1994).

Critical Events

There has been long-standing interest in the possibility that certain critical life experiences might affect parental behavior. One of these is early mother–neonate contact, which is believed by some to influence the process of mother–infant bonding and thus the quality of subsequent maternal behavior. A second is the mother's own experience of abuse as a child.

There is no question that childbirth is one of the most profound emotional experiences that parents have, and recent changes in obstetrical practice have been designed to maximize the opportunity for new parents to share in and to enjoy the experience. Klaus and Kennell (e.g., 1981; Kennell, Voos, & Klaus, 1979) and De Chateau (1980) argued that there exists in human mothers a "sensitive period" immediately after delivery, during which skin-to-skin contact is more likely to produce affectionate bonding to infants than at any other time. When this bonding process is interrupted, Klaus and Kennell warned, various forms of aberrant parental behavior, including child abuse and neglect, are more likely to occur, and suboptimal child development is more probable. Prior to about 1980, the obstetrical practices prevalent throughout the Western world (especially the United States) involved regular mother–infant separations immediately after birth. This meant, according to Klaus and Kennell, that many dyads were placed at risk for parenting failure.

Klaus and Kennell's critique of obstetrical practices provided the "scientific" support needed to convince a skeptical medical establishment to accept changes that should have been welcomed on humanitarian grounds alone. Although the reforms they spurred were long overdue, empirical evidence has not supported Klaus and Kennell's claims regarding the importance of early maternal contact (Eyer, 1992a, 1992b, 1994; Teti & Teti, 1996), however, and there is no evidence that birth attendance affects the behavior and attitudes of fathers either (Palkovitz, 1985).

Most researchers now agree that brief early contact with infants has little or no enduring effect on parental behavior, at least in part because early contact is only one of many factors that affect the bonding process. A similar conclusion is appropriate when considering claims concerning the effects of a history of maltreatment on parents. As Burgess and Youngblade (1988, p. 1) wrote, "Conventional wisdom suggests that abusive parents were, themselves, maltreated as children. . . . It is also assumed that the basic mechanisms of transmission are well-known. Attachment-based research has suggested that the insecure attachment an infant forms with its mother sets the infant at risk for later maltreatment. . . . Similarly, social learning research . . . has suggested that the lessons a child learns at home, whether they be through modeling or reinforcement contingencies, play a significant role as mechanisms of transmission; in effect, 'teaching' this child to use violence and probably maltreat a child later."

Abused rhesus monkeys become abusive with their own first offspring, although they can provide adequate mothering to laterborn children (Maestripieri & Carroll, 1998; Suomi & Ripp, 1983). However, it is not the case that abused children automatically become abusive parents or engage in violent behavior. In a 25-year longitudinal study, Widom (2000) found that, although individuals who had been abused in childhood were more likely to be violent and antisocial in adulthood than were nonabused individuals, the percentage of abused individuals with violent histories was only 26.4% (vs. 15.6% for controls). Whether or not early abuse predicts abusive parenting behavior is believed to be a complex function of a variety of personality and social–ecological factors, all of which make it more or less likely that individuals will engage in violence and/or abuse (Cicchetti & Toth, 2000; Thompson, 2000). Indeed, it is no longer justifiable simply to assume that abused children are likely to become abusive parents as adults; we now need to determine which abused children are likely to behave in this fashion and why. The answers presumably can be found in consideration of the parents' personality, the characteristics of their children, and the family's economic and social circumstances.

Infant–Parent Interactions

Research has shown that in many ways interactions between parents and infants model an intricate dance, not only in rhythm, but in style. Mother does one kind of step and the infant may do the same, or a different step, and it is not always clear who is in the lead. More directly, as we suggested in Chapter 7, parent and child alike may have idiosyncratic styles or patterns of interacting, and one may influence the short- and long-term development of the other. The transactional perspective on infant–parent interaction proposes that infants not only are shaped by the environment but also alter the environment as they interact with it and interpret the environment in their own ways (Bornstein, 2002). In other words, infant and environment actively shape one another through time. What are the activities infants and parents bring to their interactions with one another? What is their nature? What are their effects?

Domains of Interaction

Despite the dynamic range and intricacy of individual activities infants naturally engage in with their parents, many authorities have operationally distinguished two major domains of infant–parent interaction beyond basic nurturing, feeding, bathing, and changing. They are conceptually separable and developmentally significant. The two have been called animate versus inanimate, affective versus informational, person oriented versus environment oriented, social versus didactic, or dyadic versus extradyadic (e.g., Bornstein, 1989a, 2002; Goldfield, 1987; Penman, Cross, Milgrom-Friedman, & Meares, 1983; Schaffer, 1984; Sherrod, 1981; Stern, 1985). The *dyadic*, or social, domain describes those interactions that, for the infant, have their focus on mother and baby. For mother, dyadic activities encompass physical and verbal strategies used in engaging the infant interpersonally. Many published studies of the infant–mother relationship have naturally concentrated on dyadic interactions; within the first year of life, however, babies (and their parents) increasingly incorporate the outside world into their interactions. An *extradyadic,* or didactic, domain describes interactions that turn outward from the dyad and a focus on properties, objects, and events in the environment. Importantly, dyadic and extradyadic styles appear to be largely unrelated to one another: Infants and mothers who focus more on one another are not necessarily or automatically more or less attentive to the environment, and infants and mothers who attend more to the environment are not necessarily or automatically more or less attentive to one another. As Bornstein and his colleagues have found, this is true in American as well as in French and Japanese dyads (Bornstein & Tamis-LeMonda, 1990; Bornstein, Tamis-LeMonda, Pêcheux, & Rahn, 1991; Bornstein, Tamis-LeMonda, Tal, & Ludemann et al., 1992). In other words, infants and their mothers appear to specialize in particular kinds of activities.

Stability and Continuity in Interaction

Having defined domains of infant–mother interaction, we can examine the stability of individual variation over time as well as the continuity in group behavior over time. Recall from Chapter 1 that stability in the relative ranks of individuals over time is independent of continuity in the absolute level of group performance over time.

Between 2 and 5 months of age, infants' behavior is very unstable, although Fish (1998) found that decreases in negative emotional expressivity were associated with alertness in the newborn period and the quality of mothers' social supports. Greater stability in infant interactive tendencies has been found at later ages, however. Nicely, Tamis-LeMonda, and Grolnick (1999) reported that infant expressive behavior (intensity and tempo, positive and negative facial expressions, vocalizations, and body movements) was stable from 9 to 13 months of age, and this tended to be true even after taking into account affective maternal responses that "matched" the infants' responses (in intensity, tempo, or rhythm). In other words, the stability in infant behavior could not be accounted for by maternal support of the infants' behavior. Maternal activities (e.g., maternal speech) tend to be more stable early in the infant's life than are infant behaviors (see Table 1.1; Bornstein & Tamis-LeMonda, 1990; Holden & Miller, 1999). Klein (1988) found that Israeli mothers were also highly consistent with respect to the quality of stimulation they provided between the time their infants were 6 and 24 months of age.

Summarizing across a wide variety of samples, time intervals, and home assessments, Gottfried (1984) determined that parent-provided environmental variables are very consistent during the early years. Other investigators have also reported stability of caregiving between 1 and 9 months (Belsky, Taylor, & Rovine, 1984), 6 and 13 months (Petit & Bates, 1984), and 1 and 12 months (Levy-Shiff, Dimitrovsky, Shulman, & Har-Even, 1998). It is important to note, however, that stability of parent and infant characteristics derived from observations of parents and infants also depends on the duration of the observations and whether the dyads are observed across consistent or inconsistent contexts. Leyendecker et al. (1997), for example, found that relatively brief (1- and 2-hour long) naturalistic observations did not yield reliable measures of parent–infant behavior (perhaps because abbreviated observations are not sufficient to obtain representative samples of interaction) and that behavior differed in different contexts. Importantly, these findings were replicated in diverse cultural groups.

Stability of individual differences does not imply continuity. Many investigators have suggested that, around the middle of the first year, the nature of infant–mother interaction changes from dyad-oriented foci to environmental-oriented foci (Bornstein & Tamis-LeMonda, 1990; Kaye, 1982; Schaffer, 1984). Mothers show continuity in some activities but discontinuity in other activities. For example, Klein (1988) found that Israeli mothers provide increasing numbers of learning experiences across the first 2 years. Further, Levy-Shiff et al. (1998) found, not surprisingly, that maternal caregiving behavior (i.e., feeding and changing diapers) decreased significantly over the first year of life, whereas maternal affiliative behavior (i.e., playing and expressing affection) increased across this same period of time.

Correspondence in Infant–Mother Interaction

Traditionally, developmentalists believed that the child's overall level of development was affected by the overall level of parental engagement (see Maccoby & Martin, 1983) but more recent research indicates that specific infant activities relate concurrently and predictively to specific parental activities (Baumwell, Tamis-LeMonda, & Bornstein, 1997; Bornstein, Haynes, Pascual, Painter, & Galperin, 1999; Bornstein & Tamis-LeMonda, 1997; Bornstein,

Tamis-LeMonda, & Haynes, 1999; Tamis-LeMonda, Bornstein, Baumwell, & Damast, 1996). In achieving correspondence (consistency in the rank-order status of infant and parent activities), infants who perform a specific kind of activity more have parents who perform a corresponding activity more. Studies of infant–parent correspondence offer answers to important questions about interaction. Are infant activities linked to specific and conceptually relevant maternal activities? Are these patterns of correspondence consistent in the infant's first months? Furthermore, concurrent and predictive correspondences begin to define the mutual influences that infant and parent exert on one another.

For example, Bornstein and Tamis-LeMonda (1997) found that only maternal responsiveness to infant nondistress activities (e.g., exploration and play) predicted infant attention span and level of symbolic play at 13 months. Maternal responsivity to infant distress bore no such relations, suggesting that infant development in a specific domain can be facilitated by parental behavior that is appropriately responsive to infant functioning within that specific domain. Tamis-LeMonda et al. (1996) found that maternal responsivity to 13-month-olds' vocalizations specifically predicted child language use at 21 months, whereas maternal responsivity to 13-month-olds' play predicted child play competence at 21 months. Furthermore, mothers' verbal responses to infants at 20 months were sensitive to increases in infant vocabulary from 13 to 20 months (Bornstein et al., 1996). The specificity of mother-infant influence is evident in other cultures as well. In a study of U.S. and Argentine mothers of 20-month-olds, Bornstein, Haynes, et al. (1999) found that girls in both cultures engaged in more symbolic play than did boys, whereas boys in both cultures engaged in more exploratory play than did girls. In both cultures, mothers engaged in more symbolic play with girls and in more exploratory play with boys, which is consistent with the premise that infant functioning in a particular developmental domain is tied closely to parental input received in that domain.

In summary, parental personality, beliefs and intuitions, aspects of social and economic circumstances, infant characteristics, parents' attachment representations, and critical events all play important roles in determining parenting behavior, as do the characteristics of their infants. The complex formative interactions among these factors continue to tease researchers and challenge those who would like to intervene with parents in order to improve the quality of infants' lives.

Sex Differences in Social Development

Earlier in this chapter, as well as in Chapter 10, we discussed the roles that children's endogenous temperamental characteristics play in shaping their development. Temperament is not the only such characteristic that children bring to bear on their own social development, however: Gender is another important variable of this sort. Like temperament, the infant's gender may not only be associated with unlearned differences in behavioral style and potential; it may also influence the ways in which others perceive and relate to the child.

Evidence about innate sex differences in neonatal behavior always seems to be controversial (e.g., Ruble & Martin, 1998). There is some evidence that male infants are more active than female infants (Campbell & Eaton, 1999; Martin, Wisenbaker, Baker, & Huttunen, 1997). In addition, Martin et al. (1997) found higher levels of distress to novelty in female infants than in male infants. These sex differences are sometimes more apparent than real, however, and researchers studying them must take into consideration prevailing stereotypes about boys and girls as well as differences in the early experiential histories of babies that can affect adult perceptions. For example, attempts to verify whether or not innate sex differences exist are hampered by the tendency to perceive sex-stereotyped proclivities in babies, whether or not there is any objective basis for these perceptions (Stern et al., 2000). For example, Teichner, Ames, and Kerig (1997) found that mothers and fathers of 4-month-old infants tended to view their daughters in more negative terms as their infants' crying increased. No such negative perceptions emerged when sons cried more. In fact, higher levels of crying by boys were associated with a maternal tendency to rate their sons as more powerful, whereas higher levels of crying in daughters were associated with tendencies to rate their daughters as less powerful.

Similar biases are evident in maternal appraisals of infant crawling. Mondschein, Adolph, and Tamis-LeMonda (2000) found that mothers of 11-month-old male infants overestimated how well their babies would crawl down a sloped pathway, whereas mothers of 11-month-old female infants underestimated how well their babies would do (subsequent tests of crawling ability on the sloped path revealed no sex differences whatsoever in infant crawling). Such findings are consistent with the premise that adult perceptions of infant competencies and characteristics tend to favor boys over girls. Furthermore, these gender biases do not appear to have diminished with the passage of time. For example, Rubin, Provenzano, and Luria (1974) found that parents (especially fathers) described their sons with terms like "sturdy," "handsome," and "strong," and their daughters with terms like "dainty," "pretty," and "fragile." Condry and Condry (1976) even found that the behavior of the same infant in the same videotape was described differently depending on whether raters thought the child was a girl or boy: When the child was identified as John, "he" was perceived as inquisitive and adventurous, whereas when the child in the same film was identified as Mary, "she" was considered fearful and anxious. Thus, to study sex differences in newborns, it is necessary to avoid unwittingly reflecting the effects of observer expectations (e.g., by dressing boys and girls similarly and eliminating any gender labels).

In some respects, male and female infants are treated differently from birth. Newborn nurseries use color codes (blue for boy and pink for girl) to differentiate the sexes, and early presents to infants use similarly sex-typed color codes (Fagot & Leinbach, 1993; Fagot, Rodgers, & Leinbach, 2000). In addition, from birth onward, fathers appear to interact preferentially with sons and mothers with daughters (Lamb, 1997). In a study of mothers' and fathers' behavior with male infants while shopping at a mall, Roggman (1992) found that fathers were more likely than were mothers to accompany their infants to toy stores than to clothing stores, lending support to the premise that fathers are more likely to pursue play activities with their male infants than are mothers (Yogman, 1990). Fathers play more boisterous games with sons than with daughters, whereas mothers' interactions with both boys and girls tend to be didactic (Clarke-Stewart & Hevey, 1981; Huston, 1983). Mother–daughter interactions are characterized by greater levels of closeness and intimacy than are mother–son interactions: Lindahl and Heimann (1997) found that mothers of 9-month-old girls played in closer proximity to each other than did mothers of same-age sons. Whatever their origins, sex-typed differences in play are evident by the end of the first year and do not change much thereafter.

The sex typing of infant–parent play is perennially fascinating because girls and boys gravitate in such different directions, apparently regardless of the parents' professed beliefs. Children, and especially boys, begin to show preferences for male-typed toys (e.g., toy trucks) as early as the second year of life (O'Brien et al., 2000). Furthermore, parents choose sex-typed toys for infant girls and, especially, boys (Eisenberg, Wolchik, Hernandez, & Pasternack, 1985; Fagot, 1995). Masculine toys (trucks) are associated with relatively low levels of questioning and teaching, with low proximity between parents and children, and with more animated sounds (beeps) rather than statements that convey or elicit information from the child (Caldera, Huston, & O'Brien, 1989). Feminine toys (dolls) elicit close physical proximity and more verbal interactions in the form of comments and questions. These patterns of interaction emerge for both fathers and mothers and for both boys and girls. Gender neutral toys (puzzles) elicit more positive and informative verbal behaviors from parents than either feminine or masculine toys.

To determine the age at which toddlers begin to exhibit consistent sex-stereotype toy choices and investigate the association between parents' expectations and the children's own knowledge of gender-typed toys, O'Brien and Huston (1985a, 1985b) observed the development of sex-typed play behavior in toddlers beginning at 18 months of age. Children were observed in a daycare center for 1 hour a day 1 week per month for 14 months with a set of masculine, feminine, and neutral toys. In addition, the homes of some of the boys and girls were visited, and the toys available to them were counted and classified. Parents were also asked to predict their children's liking for the toys used at the daycare center. Both boys and girls played significantly more often with same-sex-typed toys. Older girls played more often with same-sex-typed toys and less with cross-sex-typed toys than the younger girls. Boys' preference for masculine toys was high throughout. Both boys and girls had more sex-typed than cross-sex-typed toys in their homes, and parents predicted that their children would choose to play with same-sex-typed toys. Mothers' and fathers' behaviors toward the toy play of their infant sons and daughters even earlier—at 10, 14, and 18 months—were observed in the laboratory where sex-typed toys and neutral toys were provided (Roopnarine, 1986). Sex differences were found in infant toy choice starting at 10 months for dolls; for example, girls were more likely to play with dolls and to give them to their parents. Moreover, both parents were more likely to attend to the block play of sons than of daughters.

The effects of gender expectancies—formed and met—spill over to other spheres of infant development. Children who acquire gender labels before they are nearing the end of the second year are also more sex-typed in their toy choices than late labelers (Fagot, 1995; Fagot et al., 2000). Parents' responses to the child's sex-type play at $1\frac{1}{2}$ years predicts whether the child will be early or late in acquiring the ability to label gender. Parents of children who label early give more attention (both positive and negative) when their children play with either male- or female-sex-typed toys, regardless of sex of child.

Summary

In this chapter we have reviewed evidence concerning the earliest development of social relationships, emphasizing infant–parent attachments and infant–parent interactions. We began by describing major stages in the development of attachments. Initially, infants cannot recognize specific people. Once this capacity develops, infants begin to interact preferentially with familiar people, and attachments are gradually formed with them. Infants form attachments to those adults who have been consistently and reliably accessible during the first months of their lives. Most form attachments to both their mothers and fathers at the same time, although they tend to prefer whoever is the primary caregiver.

Individual differences in the security of attachment relationships seem to depend on the quality of early interactions, which is itself determined by the infant's actual and perceived temperament and by adults' behavioral propensities. When the interaction between infant and adult is warm and well meshed, "secure" attachments are likely to develop. Mismatches between infants and parents lead to insecure attachments. Instead of using their attachment figures as bases of security from which to explore, and as sources of comfort when distressed, insecure infants either avoid their attachment figures or interact angrily with them. Strange Situation behavior is related to patterns of interaction with strange adults and peers, and thus may have pervasive effects on the child's development. Long-term predictions between type of attachment and measures of later child behavior emerge only where there appears to be stability in family circumstances, which presumably ensures continuity in the quality of parent–child relationships.

Infant behaviors with parents are divisible into domains, and, parents tend to show consistency among themselves over time in certain of these domains, but infants do not. Most infant activities increase in frequency, whereas some aspects of parenting increase and others decrease over the course of infancy. The interactive aspects of infant and parent activities have important consequences for the after-infancy development of a child.

Sex differences in infant behavior are initially quite ephemeral. Over time, however, adults help to shape infants' gender-stereotyped patterns of behavior.

12

Conclusions

What We Have Learned

From and About Infants

—————— ❖ ——————

Because *Development in Infancy* is a topically organized book, we have devoted separate chapters to each of the major substantive aspects of development in infancy. Such an organization, however, can have the unfortunate consequence of obscuring issues that cut across individual topics and the essential coherence of development across domains. In this chapter, therefore, we use the development of social cognition in infancy to illustrate these interrelations among different aspects of development. Although we present some new facts about infancy in this chapter, primarily we recall details presented earlier and integrate them into a broader, comprehensive perspective on infancy. We hope to leave readers with a clear appreciation of the unity of development: of the fact that psychophysical, cognitive, perceptual, verbal, emotional, and social development are parallel and intimately related lines of development in infancy.

The Shared Mind: Fitting the Pieces Together

To illustrate interrelations among different aspects of development, consider the growth of social cognition in infancy. *Social cognition* refers both to the ways that young infants perceive and understand social interaction and the people with whom they interact. The crucial concern of those who study social cognition in infancy is with the formation and elaboration of concepts about people. Concept formation is a well-established research focus among students of cognitive development, and by dealing simply with the formation of concepts about people it is possible to illustrate the essential arbitrariness of the distinction between social and cognitive development. Much of what we have discussed in the chapter on social development can be examined rather fruitfully from the perspective of cognitive function, especially if we also integrate what we know about the organization of state, sensory development, and perception.

Much of the research in early social cognition explored how the infant develops the capacity to identify, remember, and recognize people as intentional agents and distinct from inanimate objects in the environment. After making these distinctions, the baby embarks on the complex task of learning how to make inferences about the properties, behavioral propensities, motivations, and emotions of other people that in turn underlie the developing ability to attend to, understand, and communicate with others. At every stage, as we shall repeatedly emphasize, perceptual and cognitive immaturity limits the nature of the infant's social relationships and his or her ability to attribute meaning to social experiences. The three aspects of development to be examined in this chapter are (1) the development of concepts about people who are of emotional importance, (2) the development of an elementary self-concept (perceived effectance), and (3) the developing ability to detect and appraise affective information or cues provided by others. Because their origins appear to be very similar, the first two aspects are discussed together. These topics are somewhat more abstract than those described in the previous chapters because, although we relate their development to observable behaviors and events, we are in fact describing the development of unobservable processes that account for the continuity and coherence of observable behavior.

Recall the first three stages of social awareness described by Bowlby (1969) and introduced in Chapter 11. The first stage is that of undiscriminating sociability. It ends when the infant discriminates easily among individuals and responds more positively to some people than to others. This development marks the onset of the stage of discriminating sociability, lasting until roughly the end of the first half year of life. In turn, this stage ends with the formation of attachments: enduring, specific relationships with the people for whom the baby has been showing preferences in the preceding months. According to attachment theorists, by the third stage babies have sufficient (cognitive) awareness of object and person permanence to notice the absence of a particular person and try to call that person back. Babies have some primitive appreciation, in other words, that people continue to exist even when they cannot be seen or heard.

Although the term *socially indiscriminate* implies that the earlier period is characterized by incompetencies, the magnitude of the progress that the infant actually makes is remarkable. Newborns presumably arrive in the world without knowledge of people, with physiological systems that keep them in a state of drowsiness or sleep most of the time, and with only primitive perceptual skills. Yet within a few weeks they distinguish among people, recognize one or more special people, and even associate those people with certain pleasurable events. These developments comprise the major attainments of this first phase. How are such dramatic developments possible?

The answer lies in closer inspection of newborn capacities, as described in Chapters 5 and 6, which not only permit newborns to form concepts of specific people but actually bias newborns so that they are likely to form those concepts rapidly. Despite their limited acuity, newborn infants examine visual stimuli systematically. When they are alert, they actively search the environment, and especially faces, for visual inspection. At first, their mode of exploring is rather disorganized, and attention seems to focus only on small parts of figures—usually an external or limiting contour. Soon, however, infants inspect figures fully. Furthermore, human faces appear to have intrinsic appeal to young infants, and human faces rank among the most interesting stimuli that babies normally encounter. Because babies study human faces more intently than they study any other stimuli, the rates at which they learn about them, associate other stimuli with them, and come to recognize specific people are accelerated. There is growing evidence that auditory and visual stimulation are linked: Babies attend visually when there is simultaneous sound. Not only does this propensity help form a visual concept that permits recognition of specific faces, it also helps form audiovisual concepts. Thus, a coordination of the caregiver's face and voice may well be among the very first concepts developed in infancy.

Watson (1985) has proposed that in the course of everyday learning infants go far beyond whatever simple associations may be present at the moment. In this view, infants' experiences, especially in controlling contingent stimulation, lead them to develop a sense of *effectance* (see also Teti et al., 1996). In other words, babies come to learn the greater lesson that they are able to control their own experiences. Moreover, as they recognize that their behaviors exert an effect on the environment, babies also become increasingly motivated to learn and thus attempt to control the environment more. As a result, babies who have more experiences with controllable stimulation control stimulation in other contexts more readily. By contrast, babies whose experiences are uncontrollable and are not contingent on their own actions may not be motivated to establish control over the environment even when that is possible.

This momentous consequence of learning should not be underestimated, for it affects children's performance in many learning situations and it applies to the many everyday experiences young infants encounter. Simple learning surely accounts for much of the infant's early discovery and mastery of the environment, and it is through simple contingent associations between behavior and environmental consequences—be they physical or social—that the baby learns about the environment and the roles she or he can play in that environment. Frequent associations between crying and being picked up and soothed, or between banging and hearing a sound, may form the basic foundations on which to build a notion of personal effectance (see Chapter 11). Effectance can thus be seen as an especially important type of motivation—a motivation to try to act on and alter the environment that comes from knowing that to do so successfully is indeed within one's grasp (White, 1959).

By the time infants are 6 or 7 months old they may have developed this sense of personal effectance and are able to recognize specific individuals and associate them with pleasurable events. At around this age the primitive appreciation that people continue to exist even when they cannot be seen or heard makes possible another advance toward maturity in the baby's social relationships. At last, true, enduring, affectionate relationships are possible because of the infant's new (albeit primitive) understanding of person permanence. This transition is marked by the fact that infants begin to protest separation from their parents for the first time. Because infants are now able to recognize specific individuals they learn not simply that certain responses occur predictably, but that a particular individual (or individuals) can be counted on to respond to certain signals.

Recognition of the reliability and predictability of particular persons follows and constitutes an immensely important step in social development. Parents differ in their responsiveness to infant signals (Ainsworth, Blehar, Waters, & Wall, 1978; Bornstein & Tamis-LeMonda, 1997; DeWolff & van IJzendoorn, 1997), and so their infants develop different degrees of trust in parental predictability. When infants can count on their attachment figures to be accessible and to respond appropriately and contingently, they gain enough security to move away in order to engage in active exploration of the environment and seek affiliation with other children and adults. When they are distressed, these infants do not hesitate to seek comfort from their attachment figures. When parents have behaved less sensitively, however, infants have less certainty about their parents' behavior. These babies may cling anxiously to their parents and ignore the environment simply because they cannot count on their parents to remain accessible if they move away to explore.

Infants' concepts of the predictability of their attachment figures' behavior develop gradually as a result of their interactions during the first year. These expectations in turn help to determine how infants behave in relation to their caregivers or attachment figures. Each of the patterns of behavior one observes in the Strange Situation can be viewed as a consequence of infants' expectations about their parents' behavior—expectations developed through interaction in the preceding months (Lamb, 1981c). Infants learn to expect their caregivers to behave and respond in fairly stable and predictable ways (securely attached infants), in inconsistent and unpredictable ways (resistant or angry infants), or in predictably aversive ways (avoidant infants). Because of the cognitive constraints discussed earlier (the ability to recognize specific individuals, the ability to remember associations between one's own behaviors and their environmental consequences), it seems likely that the experiences occurring from the second month on may be particularly important in shaping these behavior patterns, although clear effects on children's interactions with their attachment figures are not evident until later in the year.

Central aspects of socioemotional development can be analyzed in very cognitive terms. Indeed, all-important aspects of development have to be seen as developments of a complete organism rather than as purely social, cognitive, psychophysiological, or perceptual developments. Another illustration of how these sources combine to determine the infant's social cognition is provided by the development of social referencing, which we mentioned in Chapter 10. *Social referencing* refers to the way infants 9 to 12 months of age and older systematically rely on emotional cues provided by significant others to help regulate their own behavior in uncertain settings, for example, by positioning themselves to keep others' faces in view.

An example makes this concept clear. Imagine an infant exploring a new room. She or he encounters an unfamiliar insect. In most infants the insect would arouse ambivalent reactions: It is a novel and intriguing sight, yet there is some evidence that insects intrinsically elicit wariness. To help resolve the ambiguity, the infant will typically look to mother or father to see how the parent is appraising the situation. If the parent appears fearful, the infant is likely to retreat from the bug. If the parent smiles and speaks in a friendly, supportive voice, the infant is likely to approach the insect to examine it more closely.

Note that perception, sensorimotor intelligence, attachment, emotion as communication, and learning are all at play in this situation. First, the infant is unable to evaluate the situation alone and so seeks clarifying information from others. Second, the infant must have the perceptual ability to detect the affective expressions of the parent. If vision or hearing is impaired or perceptual development is not sufficiently advanced for the visual or vocal information to be processed, social referencing will be seriously hampered or absent altogether. (Indeed, parents of infants with sensory deficits frequently report being much more directive and controlling in their interaction with the infants: These parents have to work harder to influence their babies' behavior; Meadow-Orlans, 2002.) Third, if emotions did not have social communicative significance, and if the infant had not developed a sense of trust in the parents, there would be no sense in appraising the parents' expressions. Fourth, to ensure that the parent's expression pertains to the stimulus in question the infant must note whether the parent is oriented toward the ambiguous stimulus. Understanding the interrelation between two environmental stimuli (the parent's eyes and the object in question) is not cognitively possible before Stage 4 of sensorimotor intelligence, and not fully established until Stage 5. Finally, the child must learn how to behave toward this stimulus in future encounters when the parent is unavailable: She or he needs to associate the bug with the emotional information the parent provides.

Social referencing may be developmentally important because it facilitates learning through indirect experience. By responding to and learning from the parent's emotional cues in uncertain but potentially harmful circumstances (e.g., electric outlets, noxious chemicals, or poisonous plants) infants learn to avoid these dangers without first experiencing the unpleasant consequences of direct experience with them.

By 12 months of age, infants clearly make use of facial information provided by their parents to regulate their own behaviors in uncertain settings. Consider, for example, the willingness of 1-year-olds to cross the visual cliff (see Figures 12.1 and 12.2). To make the visual cliff somewhat ambiguous, the apparent drop-off can be reduced from its usual depth, say, a little more than the height of an average stair step. Infants are placed on the shallow side of the cliff table and enticed toward the deep side by an interesting moving toy and the smiling faces of their mothers from across the deep side. When the infants reach the center of the cliff table, the mothers' facial expression then shifts in accordance with instructions given to them: They either pose an intense fear face or a broader smile (see Figures 12.1 and 12.2). In situations like this, the results are quite clear: When mothers smile, their infants cross the deep side to get to the mother and the toy, whereas when mothers show fear their infants avoid crossing. Infants also use the vocal intonations of trusted adults as emotional cues in uncertain situations, beginning as early as 8 months of age. By 1 year, therefore, social referencing appears to play a powerful role in the regulation of infant behavior. Social referencing truly involves a cognitive appraisal process: When the cliff table is modified so that there is no drop-off, babies tend not to seek information from their mothers, and when they do, the mothers' facial expressions do not influence the babies' tendency to cross the table. Only when the situation is somewhat ambiguous is social referencing employed.

Why does social referencing affect the behavior of 1-year-olds? Some theorists argue that infants derive important information from an adult's emotional cues that assists in the children's own appraisal of events. Others believe that parents' cues directly influence infant emotional state, which in turn affects the infant's reactions to an event. Evidence for both kinds of influence is apparent in current research, so neither explanation can be rejected (e.g., Hala, 1997; Hirshberg, 1990; Mumme & Fernald, 1996; Recchia, 1997; Stenberg & Hagekull, 1997; Walden & Knieps, 1996). Social referencing is also triggered by situational uncertainty; events that elicit distinctly positive or negative reactions from infants do not provoke referencing (Gunnar & Stone, 1984). For example, in the research by Sorce, Emde, Campos, and Klinnert (1985) illustrated in Figures 12.1 and 12.2, babies did not seek information from their mothers when the cliff table was modified so that there was no drop-off at all. Only when the situation was somewhat ambiguous was social referencing employed to obtain clarifying emotional cues from an adult. Finally, infant characteristics, including their

FIGURE 12.1

This figure demonstrates the power of the mother's
emotional expressions in regulating her infant's behavior
when the baby is in an uncertain situation. (*A*) The
12-month-old has reached the edge of a visual cliff table
and looks down at the 12-inch drop. (*B*) The infant looks
in a questioning fashion to her mother, who responds
with a continued broad smile. (*C*) This infant, like most
other 12-month-olds who reference a smiling mother,
crosses the deep side of the cliff. (Courtesy of J. Sorce,
R. Emde, & M. Klinnert.)

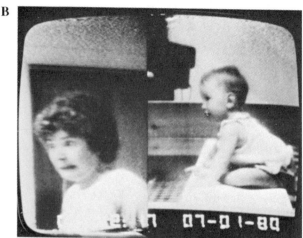

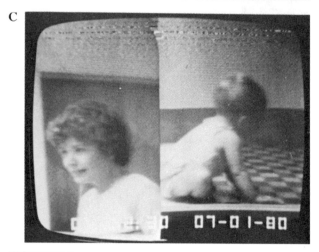

FIGURE 12.2

This figure demonstrates the effect of the mother posing a
fear face to a different 12-month-old. (*A*) The baby looks
down at the deep side. (*B*) She references the mother, who
is posing an intense fear face. (C) The infant backs away
from the center of the cliff table and subsequently begins to
cry. (Courtesy of J. Sorce, R. Emde, & M. Klinnert.)

sensory capacities (Walker-Andrews & Dickson, 1997), temperamental wariness (Blackford & Walden, 1998; Hornik & Gunnar, 1988), as well as the quality of their attachment to the mother (Ainsworth, 1992; Baldwin & Moses, 1996; Dickstein, Thompson, Estes, Malkin, & Lamb, 1984), also influence the incidence of social referencing.

Social referencing can have a powerful effect not only on reactions to inanimate stimuli—such as strange toys or a visual cliff—but on social behavior, such as reactions to strangers. As we stressed in Chapter 10, developmental scientists have long been interested in the fact that infants in the middle of the first year often react negatively to unfamiliar adults (i.e., infants manifest stranger anxiety), and theorists have proposed diverse explanations for this phenomenon (Thompson & Limber, 1990). To some, it is a biological process that is explainable by simple maturation (e.g., Freedman, 1974); to others, it is a product of cognitive development (e.g., Kagan, 1974); to others still, it derives from ego development (e.g., Spitz, 1965). But studies of social referencing provide another possibility: Strangers are somewhat uncertain and ambiguous for young infants, who turn to trusted adults for emotional information. Consistent with this interpretation, several researchers have shown that infants respond less negatively, and even positively, to strangers when the parent responds positively to them (Boccia & Campos, 1989; Denzin, 1992; Feiring, Lewis, & Starr, 1984), and even when strangers interact positively with other strangers (Feiring et al., 1984). These observations suggest that it is not the strangers' unfamiliarity *per se* that elicits fearfulness in infants of this age, but the reactions of trusted adults who are referenced by an uncertain infant. When adults are positive and sociable, infants are likely to respond with greater friendliness than fearfulness.

Summary

In this chapter, we reassert the coherence of infant development and the place of infancy in human development. Both social and cognitive developments are facilitated by the simple perceptual strategies or predispositions characteristic of young infants. Furthermore, important aspects of personality development—the development of self-concept—and important social processes—trust in the reliability of other people and social referencing—depend on the baby's cognitive understanding of the relation between her or his own behavior and specific environmental consequences. Learning associations between social behaviors and social consequences may be facilitated by the regularity and frequency of these associations. We also showed that infants may appraise the emotional expressions of their parents to reduce ambiguity in uncertain situations and thus decide how to behave. This chapter illustrates the inescapable intimate relations among physical, perceptual, cognitive, verbal, emotional, and social development in infancy.

References

Abel, E. L. (1984). *Fetal alcohol syndrome and fetal alcohol effects*. New York: Plenum.

Abramovitch, R., Corter, C., & Lando, B. (1979). Sibling interaction in the home. *Child Development, 50,* 997–1003.

Abravanel, E., & Sigafoos, A. D. (1984). Exploring the presence of imitation in early infancy. *Child Development, 55,* 381–392.

Adams, R. J., Courage, M. L., & Mercer, M. E. (1991). Deficiencies in human neonates' color vision: Photoreceptoral and neural explanations. *Behavioural Brain Research, 43,* 109–114.

Adams, R. J., Courage, M. L., & Mercer, M. E. (1994). Systematic measurement of human neonatal color vision. *Vision Research, 34,* 1691–1701.

Adamson, L. B., & Bakeman, R. (1984). Mothers' communicative acts: Changes during infancy. *Infant Behavior and Development, 7,* 467–478.

Adamson, L. B., & Bakeman, R. (1985). Affect and attention: Infants observed with mothers and peers. *Child Development, 56,* 582–593.

Adler, S. A., Inslicht, S., Rovee-Collier, C., & Gerhardstein, P. C. (1998). Perceptual asymmetry and memory retrieval in 3-month-old infants. *Infant Behavior and Development, 21,* 253–272.

Adolph, K. E. (1997). Learning in the development of infant locomotion. *Monographs of the Society for Research in Child Development, 62*(3, Serial No. 251).

Ahmed, A., & Ruffman, T. (2000). Why do infants make A not B errors in a search task, yet show memory for the location of hidden objects in a nonsearch task? In D. Muir & A. Slater (Eds.), *Infant development: The essential readings. Essential readings in development psychology* (pp. 216–235). Malden, MA: Blackwell.

Ahnert, L., & Lamb, M. E. (2001). The East German child care system: Associations with caretaking and caretaking beliefs, and children's early attachment and adjustment. *American Behavioral Scientist, 44,* 1843–1863.

Ahnert, L., Lamb, M. E., Porges, S. W., & Rickert, H. (2002, April 19). Infant emotions and cardiac reactivity during adjustment to child care I: Perspectives from infant-mother attachment. Poster presented at the International Conference on Infant Studies, Toronto, Canada.

Aiken, L. R. (1996). *Assessment of intellectual functioning* (2nd ed.). New York: Plenum.

Ainsworth, M. D. S. (1967). *Infancy in Uganda.* Baltimore: Johns Hopkins University Press.

Ainsworth, M. D. S. (1973). The development of infant–mother attachment. In B. M. Caldwell & H. N. Ricciuti (Eds.), *Review of child development research* (Vol. 3). Chicago: University of Chicago Press.

Ainsworth, M. D. S. (1979). Attachment as related to mother–infant interaction. In J. S. Rosenblatt, R. A. Hinde, C. Beer, & M. Busnel (Eds.), *Advances in the study of behavior* (Vol. 9). New York: Academic.

Ainsworth, M. D. S. (1992). A consideration of social referencing in the context of attachment theory and research. In S. Feinman (Ed.), *Social referencing and the social construction of reality* (pp. 349–367). New York: Plenum.

Ainsworth, M. D. S. (1989). Attachments beyond infancy. *American Psychologist, 44,* 709–716.

Ainsworth, M. D. S., Bell, S. M., & Stayton, D. J. (1974). Infant–mother attachment and social development: "Socialisation" as a product of reciprocal responsiveness to signals. In M. P. M. Richards (Ed.), *The integration of a child into a social world* (pp. 91–135). London: Cambridge University Press.

Ainsworth, M. D. S., Blehar, M. C., Waters, E., & Wall, S. (1978). *Patterns of attachment: A psychological study of the Strange Situation.* Hillsdale, NJ: Lawrence Erlbaum Associates.

Ainsworth, M. D. S., & Wittig, B. A. (1969). Attachment and exploratory behavior of one-year-olds in a strange situation. In B. M. Foss (Ed.), *Determinants of Infant Behaviour* (Vol. 4, pp. 111–136). London: Routledge Methuen.

Aksu-Koç, A. A., & Slobin, D. I. (1985). The acquisition of Turkish. In D. I. Slobin (Ed.), *The crosslinguistic study of language acquisition* (Vol. 1, pp. 15–68). Hillsdale, NJ: Lawrence Erlbaum Associates.

Albaladejo, P., Bouaziz, H., & Benhamou, D. (1998). Epidural analgesics: How can safety and efficacy be improved? *CNS Drugs, 10,* 91–104.

Almli, R. C., & Finger, S. (1987). Neural insult and critical period concepts. In M. H. Bornstein (Ed.), *Sensitive periods in development: Interdisciplinary perspectives* (pp. 123–143). Hillsdale, NJ: Lawrence Erlbaum Associates.

Als, H. (1992). Individualized, family-focused developmental care for the very low birthweight preterm infant in the NICU. In S. L. Friedman & M. D. Sigman (Eds.), *The psychological development of low-birthweight children. Annual Advances in Applied Developmental Psychology* (Vol. 6, pp. 341–388). Norwood, NJ: Ablex.

American Psychological Association. (1992). Ethical principles of psychologists and code of conduct. *American Psychologist, 47,* 1597–1611.

Anastasi, A. (1958). Heredity, environment, and the question, "how?" *Psychological Review, 65,* 197–208.

Angelilli, M. L., Fischer, H., Delaney-Black, V., Rubinstein, M., Ager, J. W., & Sokol, R. J. (1994). History of in utero cocaine exposure in language-delayed children. *Clinical Pediatrics, 33,* 514–516.

Apgar, V. A. (1953). Proposal for a new method of evaluation of the newborn infant. *Anesthesia and Analgesia, Current Researches, 22,* 260.

Apgar, V. A., & James, L. S. (1962). Further observations on the newborn scoring system. *American Journal of Diseases of Children, 104,* 418–428.

Arbiter, E., Sato-Tanaka, R., Kolvin, I., & Leitch, I. (1999). Differences in behaviour and temperament between Japanese and British toddlers living in London: A pilot study. *Child Psychology and Psychiatry Review, 4,* 117–125.

Arterberry, M. E., & Bornstein, M. H. (2001). Three-month-old infants' categorization of animals and vehicles based on static and dynamic attributes. *Journal of Experimental Child Psychology, 80,* 333–346.

Ashmead, D. H., & Davis, D. L. (1996). Measuring habituation in infants: An approach using regression analysis. *Child Development, 67,* 2677–2690.

Aslin, R. N. (1981a). Development of smooth pursuit in human infants. In D. F. Fisher, R. A. Monty, & E. J. Senders (Eds.), *Eye movements: Cognition and visual perception* (pp. 31–51). Hillsdale, NJ: Lawrence Erlbaum Associates.

Aslin, R. N. (1981b). Experiential influences and sensitive periods in perceptual development: A unified model. In R. N. Aslin, J. R. Alberts, & M. R. Peterson (Eds.), *Development of perception: Psychobiological perspectives: Vol. 21. The visual system.* New York: Academic.

Aslin, R. N. (1988). Anatomical constraints on oculomotor development: Implications for infant perception. In A. Yonas (Ed.), *Minnesota Symposium*

Aslin, R. N., Saffran, J. R., & Newport, E. L. (1998). Computation of conditional probability statistics by 8-month-old infants. *Psychological Science, 9,* 321–324.

Aslin, R. N., & Shea, S. L. (1990). Velocity thresholds in human infants: Implications for the perception of motion. *Developmental Psychology, 26,* 589–598.

Aslin, R. N., Jusczyk, P. W., & Pisoni, D. B. (1998). Speech and auditory processing during infancy: Constraints on and precursors to language. In W. Damon (Editor-in-Chief), D. Kuhn, & R. S. Siegler (Vol. Eds.), *Handbook of child psychology: Vol. 2. Cognition, perception, and language* (5th ed., pp. 147–198). New York: Wiley.

Astley, S. J., & Clarren, S. K. (1996). A case definition and photographic screening tool for the facial phenotype of fetal alcohol syndrome. *Journal of Pediatrics, 129,* 33–41.

Atkinson, J., & Braddick, O. (1989). Development of basic visual functions. In A. Slater & G. Bremner (Eds.), *Infant development* (pp. 7–41). Hillsdale, NJ: Lawrence Erlbaum Associates.

Atkinson, J., & Hood, B. (1997). Development of visual attention: Bridging disciplines. In J. A. Burack & J. T. Enns (Eds.), *Attention, development, and psychopathology* (pp. 31–54). New York: Guilford.

Azuma, S. D., & Chasnoff, L. J. (1993). Outcome of children prenatally exposed to cocaine and other drugs: A path analysis of three-year data. *Pediatrics, 92,* 396–402.

Bahrick, L. E. (1995). Intermodal origins of self-perception. In P. Rochat (Ed.), *The self in infancy: Theory and research. Advances in psychology* (Vol. 112, pp. 349–373). Amsterdam: North-Holland/Elsevier.

Bahrick, L. E., Hernandez-Reif, M., & Pickens, J. N. (1997). The effect of retrieval cues on visual preferences and memory in infancy: Evidence for a four-phase attention function. *Journal of Experimental Child Psychology, 67,* 1–20.

Bailey, D. B., Jr., & Bruer, J. T. (Eds.). (2001). *Critical thinking about critical periods.* Baltimore: Brookes.

Baillargeon, R. (1994). How do infants learn about the physical world? *Current Directions in Psychological Science, 3,* 133–140.

Baillargeon, R. (1995). A model of physical reasoning in infancy. In C. Rovee-Collier & L. P. Lipsitt (Eds.), *Advances in infancy research* (Vol. 9, pp. 305–371). Norwood, NJ: Ablex.

Baillargeon, R. (1998). Infants' understanding of the physical world. In M. Sabourin, F. Craik,

& M. Robert (Eds.), *Advances in psychological science*: Vol. 2. *Biological and cognitive aspects* (pp. 503–529). East Sussex, England: Psychology Press.

Baillargeon, R., Kotovsky, L., & Needham, A. (1995). The acquisition of physical knowledge in infancy. In D. Sperber, D. Premack, & A. J. Premack (Eds.), *Causal cognition: A multidisciplinary debate* (pp. 79–116). Oxford: Clarendon.

Bakermans-Kranenburg, M. J., & van IJzendoorn, M. H. (1993). A psychometric study of the Adult Attachment Interview: Reliability and discriminant validity. *Developmental Psychology, 29,* 870–880.

Baldwin, D. A., & Markmam, E. M. (1989). Establishing word–object relations: A first step. *Child Development, 60,* 381–398.

Baldwin, D. A., & Moses, L. J. (1996). The ontogeny of social information gathering. *Child Development, 67,* 1915–1939.

Baldwin, D. A., Markham, E. M., Bill, B., Desjardins, R. N., & Irwin, J. M. (1996). Infants' reliance on a social criterion for establishing word–object relations. *Child Development, 67,* 3135–3153.

Ball, R. S. (1977). The Gesell developmental schedules: Arnold Gesell (1880–1961). *Journal of Abnormal Child Psychology, 5,* 233–239.

Bandura, A. (1969). *Principles of behavior modification.* New York: Holt, Rinehart, & Winston.

Banks, M. S., & Shannon, E. (1993). Spatial and chromatic visual efficiency in human neonates. In C. E. Granrud (Ed.), *Visual perception and cognition in infancy* (pp. 1–46). Hillsdale, NJ: Lawrence Erlbaum Associates.

Barnard, K. E., & Brazelton, T. B. (Eds.). (1990). *Touch: The foundation of experience.* Madison, CT: International Universities Press.

Barnard, K. E., & Solchany, J. (2002). Mothering. In M. H. Bornstein (Ed.), *Handbook of parenting Vol. 3 Status and social conditions of parenting* (2nd ed., pp. 3–25). Mahwah, NJ: Lawrence Erlbaum Associates.

Barnes, S., Gutfreund, M., Satterly, D., & Wells, G. (1983). Characteristics of adult speech which predict children's language development. *Journal of Child Language, 10,* 65–84.

Barr, R., & Hayne, H. (2000). Age-related changes in imitation: Implications for memory development. In C. Rovee-Collier, L. P. Lipsitt, & H. Hayne (Eds.), *Progress in infancy research* (Vol. 1, pp. 21–67). Mahwah, NJ: Lawrence Erlbaum Associates.

Barr, R., Dowden, A., & Hayne, H. (1996). Developmental changes in deferred imitation by 6- to 24-month-old infants. *Infant Behavior and Development, 19,* 159–170.

Barr, R. G., Hopkins, B., & Green, J. A. (Eds.). (2000). Crying as a sign, a symptom, and a signal: Clinical, emotional, and developmental aspects of infant and toddler crying (*Clinics in Developmental Medicine*, No. 152). New York: Cambridge University Press.

Barrera, M. E., & Maurer, D. (1981a). Recognition of mother's photographed face by the three-month-old infant. *Child Development, 52,* 714–716.

Barrera, M. E., & Maurer, D. (1981b). The perception of facial expressions by the three-month-old. *Child Development, 52,* 203–206.

Barrett, K., & Campos, J. J. (1987). Perspectives on emotional development: II. A functionalist approach to emotions. In J. D. Osofsky (Ed.), *Handbook of infant development* (2nd ed., pp. 555–578). New York: Wiley.

Barrett, K. C., & Morgan, G. A. (1995). Continuities and discontinuities in mastery motivation during infancy and toddlerhood: A conceptualization and review. In R. H. MacTurk & G. A. Morgan (Eds.), *Mastery motivation: Origins, conceptualizations, and applications* (pp. 57–93). Norwood, NJ: Ablex.

Bates, E., & Carnevale, G. F. (1993). New directions in research on language development. *Development Review, 13,* 436–470.

Bates, E., Bretherton, I., & Snyder, L. (1988). *From first words to grammar.* New York: Cambridge University Press.

Bates, E., Bretherton, I., Beeghly-Smith, M., & McNew, S. (1982). Social bases of language development: A reassessment. In H. Reese & L. Lipsitt (Eds.), *Advances in child development and behavior* (Vol. 16, pp. 8–75). New York: Academic.

Bates, J. E. (1986a). The measurement of temperament. In R. Plomin & J. Dunn (Eds.), *The study of temperament: Changes, continuities, and challenges.* Hillsdale, NJ: Lawrence Erlbaum Associates.

Bates, J. E. (1986b). Temperament in infancy. In J. D. Osofsky (Ed.), *Handbook of infant development.* New York: Wiley.

Bates, J. E. (1987). Temperament in infancy. In J. D. Osofsky (Ed.), *Handbook of infant development (2nd ed.). Wiley series on personality processes* (pp. 1101–1149). Oxford, England: John Wiley & Sons.

Bates, J. E. (1994). Parents as scientific observers of their children's development. In S. L. Friedman & H. C. Haywood (Eds.), *Developmental follow-up: Concepts, domains, and methods* (pp. 197–216). New York: Academic.

Bates, J. E. (2001). Adjustment style in childhood as a product of parenting and temperament. In T. D. Wachs & G. A. Kohnstamm (Eds.), *Temperament in context* (pp. 173–200). Mahwah, NJ: Lawrence Erlbaum Associates.

Bates, J. E., & Wachs, T. D. (Eds.). (1994). *Temperament: Individual differences at the interface of biology and behavior.* Washington, DC: American Psychological Association.

Bates, J. E., Freeland, C. A., & Lounsbury, M. L. (1979). Measurement of infant difficultness. *Child Development, 50,* 794–803.

Bates, J. E., Maslin, C. A., & Frankel, K. A. (1985). Attachment security, mother–child interaction, and temperament as predictors of behavior problem ratings at age three years. In I. Bretherton & E. Waters (Eds.), *Growing points of attachment theory and research. Monographs of the Society for Research in Child Development, 50* (Serial No. 209).

Bates, J. E., Petit, G. S., & Bayles, K. (1985). *Infancy and preschool antecedents of behavior problems at 5 years.* Paper presented at the biennial meetings of the Society for Research in Child Development, Toronto, Canada.

Bates, J. E., Pettit, G. S., & Dodge, K. A. (1995). Family and child factors in stability and change in children's aggressiveness in elementary school. In J. McCord (Ed.), *Coercion and punishment in long-term perspectives* (pp. 124–138). New York: Cambridge University Press.

Bates, J. E., Pettit, G. S., Dodge, K. A., & Ridge, B. (1998). Interaction of temperamental resistance to control and restrictive parenting in the development of externalizing behavior. *Developmental Psychology, 34,* 982–995.

Batshaw, M. L. (1997). Understanding your chromosomes. In M. L. Batshaw (Ed.), *Children with disabilities* (4th ed., pp. 3–16). Baltimore: Brookes.

Batshaw, M. L., & Conlon, C. J. (1997). Substance abuse: A preventable threat to development. In M. L. Batshaw (Ed.), *Children with disabilities* (4th ed., pp. 143–162). Baltimore: Brookes.

Bauer, P. J. (1996). What do infants recall of their lives? Memory for specific events by one- to two-year-olds. *American Psychologist, 51,* 29–41.

Bauer, P. J. (1997). Development of memory in early childhood. In C. Hulme (Series Ed.) & N. Cowan (Vol. Ed.), *The development of memory in childhood. Studies in developmental psychology* (pp. 83–111). Hove, England: Psychology Press.

Bauer, P. J. (in press). New developments in the study of infant memory. In D. M. Teti (Ed.), *Handbook of research methods in developmental psychology.* Malden, MA: Blackwell.

Bauer, P. J., Hertsgaard, L. A., & Wewerka, S. S. (1995). Effects of experience and reminding on long-term recall in infancy: Remembering not to forget. *Journal of Experimental Child Psychology, 59,* 260–298.

Bauer, P. J., Wenner, J. A., Dropik, P. L., & Wewerka, S. S. (2000). Parameters of remembering and forgetting in the transition from infancy to early childhood. *Monographs of the Society for Research in Child Development, 65* (4, Serial No. 263).

Baumwell, L., Tamis-LeMonda, C. S., & Bornstein, M. H. (1997). Maternal verbal sensitivity and child language comprehension. *Infant Behavior and Development, 20,* 247–258.

Baydar, N., Greek, A., & Brooks-Gunn, J. (1997). A longitudinal study of the effects of the birth of a sibling during the first 6 years of life. *Journal of Marriage and the Family, 59,* 939–956.

Bayley, N. (1933a). *The California first year mental scale.* Berkeley, CA: University of California Press.

Bayley, N. (1933b). Mental growth during the first three years. *Genetic Psychology, 14,* 1–92.

Bayley, N. (1949). Consistency and variability in the growth of intelligence from birth to eighteen years. *Journal of Genetic Psychology, 75,* 165–196.

Bayley, N. (1969). *Bayley scales of infant development.* New York: Psychological Corporation.

Bayley, N. (1993). *Bayley scales of infant development* (2nd ed., manual). Orlando, FL: Psychological Corporation.

Bean, B. (1990). Progenitive sex ratio among functioning sperm cells. *American Journal of Human Genetics, 47,* 351–353.

Beauchamp, G. K., Cowart, B. L., Mennella, J. A., & Marsh, R. R. (1994). Infant salt taste: Developmental, methodological and contextual factors. *Developmental Psychobiology, 27,* 353–365.

Bee, H. L., Barnard, K. E., Eyres, S. J., Gray, C. A., Hammond, M. A., Spietz, A. L., Snyder, C., & Clark, B. (1982). Prediction of IQ and language skill from perinatal status, child performance, family characteristics, and mother–infant interaction. *Child Development, 53,* 1134–1156.

Beeghly, M. (1993). Parent–infant play as a window on infant competence: An organizational approach to assessment. In K. MacDonald (Ed.), *Parent–child play: Descriptions and implications* (pp. 71–112). Albany, NY: State University of New York Press.

Befu, H. (1986). Social and cultural background for child development in Japan and the United States. In H. W. Stevenson, H. Azuma, & K. Hakuta (Eds.), *Child development and education in Japan* (pp. 13–27). San Francisco: Freeman.

Beit-Halachmi, B., & Rabin, A. I. (1977). The kibbutz as a social experiment and as a child rearing laboratory. *American Psychologist, 32,* 532–541.

Bell, M. A. (1998). Frontal lobe function during infancy: Implications for the development of cognition and attention. In J. E. Richards (Ed.), *Cognitive neuroscience of attention: A developmental perspective* (pp. 287–316). Mahwah, NJ: Lawrence Erlbaum Associates.

Bell, M. A., & Fox, N. A. (1994). Brain development over the first year of life: Relations between electroencephalographic frequency and coherence and cognitive and affective behaviors. In G. Dawson & K. W. Fischer (Eds.), *Human behavior and the developing brain* (pp. 314–345). New York: Guilford.

Bell, R. Q., & Harper, L. (1977). *Child effects on adults*. Hillsdale, NJ: Lawrence Erlbaum Associates.

Bellinger, D. (1980). Consistency in the pattern of change in mother's speech: Some discriminant analyses. *Journal of Child Language, 7*, 469–487.

Bellinger, D., & Needleman, H. L. (1994). The neurotoxicity of prenatal exposure to lead: Kinetics, mechanisms, and expressions. In H. L. Needleman & D. Bellinger (Eds.), *Prenatal exposure to toxicants: Developmental consequences* (pp. 89–111). Baltimore: Johns Hopkins University Press.

Belsky, J. (1980). Mother–infant interaction at home and in the laboratory: A comparative study. *Journal of Genetic Psychology, 137*, 37–47.

Belsky, J. (1999). Interactional and contextual determinants of attachment security. In J. Cassidy & P. R. Shaver (Eds.), *Handbook of attachment: Theory, research, and clinical applications* (pp. 249–264). New York: Guilford.

Belsky, J., & Barends, N. (2002). Personality and parenting. In M. H. Bornstein (Ed.), *Handbook of parenting:* Vol. 3 *Status and social ecology of parenting* (pp. 415–438). Mahwah, NJ: Lawrence Erlbaum Associates.

Belsky, J., & Cassidy, J. (1995). Attachment: Theory and evidence. In M. L. Rutter, D. F. Hay, & S. Baron-Cohen (Eds.), *Developmental principles and clinical issues in psychology and psychiatry* (pp. 373–402). Oxford, England: Blackwell.

Belsky, J., & Most, R. K. (1981). From exploration to play: A cross-sectional study of infant free play behavior. *Developmental Psychology, 17*, 630–639.

Belsky, J., & Rovine, M. (1987). Temperament and attachment security in the Strange Situation: An empirical rapprochement. *Child Development, 58*, 787–795.

Belsky, J., Campbell, S. B., Cohn, J. F., & Moore, G. (1996). Instability of infant–parent attachment security. *Developmental Psychology, 32*, 921–924.

Belsky, J., Garduque, L., & Hrncir, E. (1984). Assessing performance, competence, and executive capacity in infant play: Relations to home environment and security of attachment. *Developmental Psychology, 20*, 406–417.

Belsky, J., Gilstrap, B., & Rovine, M. (1984). The Pennsylvania Infant and Family Development Project I: Stability and change in mother–infant and father–infant interaction in a family setting—1- to 3- to 9-months. *Child Development, 55*, 692–705.

Belsky, J., Goode, M. K., & Most, R. K. (1980). Maternal stimulation and infant exploratory competence: Cross-sectional, correlational, and experimental analyses. *Child Development, 51*, 1163–1178.

Belsky, J., Hsieh, K.-H., & Crnic, K. (1998). Mothering, fathering, and infant negativity as antecedents of boys' externalizing problems and inhibition at age 3 years: Differential susceptibility to rearing experience? *Development and Psychopathology, 10*, 301–319.

Belsky, J., Rovine, M., & Taylor, D. (1984). The Pennsylvania Infant and Family Development Project III: The origins of individual differences in infant–mother attachment: Maternal and infant contributions. *Child Development, 35*, 706–717.

Belsky, J., Taylor, D., & Rovine, M. (1984). The Pennsylvania Infant and Family Development Project, II: The development of reciprocal interaction in the mother–infant dyad. *Child Development, 55*, 706–717.

Bendersky, M., & Lewis, M. (1994). Environmental risk, biological risk, and developmental outcome. *Developmental Psychology, 30*, 484–494.

Benedict, H. (1979). Early lexical development: Comprehension and production. *Journal of Child Language, 6*, 183–200.

Benes, F. M. (1994). Development of the cortico-limbic system. In G. Dawson & K. W. Fischer (Eds.), *Human behavior and the developing brain* (pp. 176–206). New York: Guilford.

Bentley, M., Gavin, L., Black, M. M., & Teti, L. (1999). Infant feeding practices of low-income, African-American, adolescent mothers: An ecological, multigenerational perspective. *Social Science and Medicine, 49*, 1085–1100.

Berenson, C. K. (1996). Anxiety and the developing child. *American Psychiatric Press Review of Psychiatry, 15*, 383–404.

Berg, W. K., & Berg, K. M. (1987). Psychophysiological development in infancy: State, startle, and attention. In J. D. Osofsky (Ed.), *Handbook of infant development* (2nd ed., pp. 238–317). New York: Wiley.

Bergman, A., & Lefcourt, I. S. (1994). Self-other action play: A window into the representational world of the infant. In A. Slade & D. P. Wolf (Eds.), *Children at play: Clinical and developmental approaches to meaning and representation* (pp. 133–147). New York: Oxford University Press.

Bergström, R. M. (1969). Electrical parameters of the brain during ontogeny. In R. J. Robinson (Ed.), *Brain and early behavior: Development in the fetus and infant*. New York: Academic.

Berkeley, G. (1901). *An essay toward a new theory of vision*. Oxford, England: Clarendon. (Originally published 1709.)

Berkowitz, G. S., & Skovron, M. L. (1990). Delayed childbearing and the outcome of pregnancy. *New England Journal of Medicine, 322*, 659–665.

Berlin, L. J., & Cassidy, J. (1999). Relations among relationships: Contributions from attachment theory and research. In J. Cassidy & P. R. Shaver (Eds.), *Handbook of attachment: Theory, research, and clinical applications* (pp. 688–712). New York: Guilford.

Bernbaum, J. C., & Batshaw, M. L. (1997). Born too soon, born too small. In M. L. Batshaw (Ed.),

Children with disabilities (4th ed., pp. 115–139). Baltimore: Brookes.

Bernstein Ratner, N., & Luberoff, A. (1984). Cues to post-vocalic voicing in mother-child speech. *Journal of Phonetics, 12,* 285–289.

Bernstein Ratner, N., & Pye, C. (1984). Higher pitch in BT is not universal: Acoustic evidence from Quiche Mayan. *Journal of Child Language, 11,* 515–522.

Bertenthal, B. I. (1993). Infants' perception of biomechanical motions: Intrinsic image and knowledge-based constraints. In C. Granrud (Ed.), *Visual perception and cognition in infancy* (pp. 175–214). Hillsdale, NJ: Lawrence Erlbaum Associates.

Bertenthal, B. I., & Campos, J. J. (1984). A reexamination of fear and its determinants on the visual cliff. *Psychophysiology, 21,* 413–417.

Bertenthal, B. I., & Campos, J. J. (1990). A systems approach to the organizing effects of self-produced locomotion during infancy. In C. Rovee-Collier & L. P. Lipsitt (Eds.), *Advances in infancy research* (Vol. 6, pp. 1–60). Norwood, NJ: Ablex.

Bertenthal, B. I., & Clifton, R. R. (1998). Perception and action. In W. Damon (Editor-in-Chief), D. Kuhn, & R. S. Siegler (Vol. Eds.), *Handbook of child psychology:* Volume 2. *Cognition, perception, and language* (5th ed., pp. 51–102). New York: Wiley.

Bertenthal, B. I., Campos, J., & Haith, M. (1980). Development of visual organization: Perception of subjective contours. *Child Development, 51,* 1072–1080.

Bertenthal, B. I., Haith, M. M., & Campos, J. J. (1983). The partial-lag design: A method for controlling spontaneous regression in the infant-control habituation paradigm. *Infant Behavior and Development, 6,* 331–338.

Bertoncini, J. (1993). Infants' perception of speech units: Primary representation capacities. In B. de Boysson-Bardies, S. de Schonen, P. Jusczyk, P. McNeilage, & J. Morton (Eds.), *Developmental neurocognition: Speech and face processing in the first year of life* (pp. 249–257). Dordrecht, the Netherlands: Kluwer Academic.

Bertoncini, J. (1998). Initial capacities for speech processing: Infants' attention to prosodic cues for segmentation. In F. Simion & G. Butterworth (Eds.), *The development of sensory, motor, and cognitive capacities in early infancy: From perception to cognition* (pp. 161–170). London: Psychology Press.

Best, C. T., Hoffman, H., & Glanville, B. B. (1982). Development of infant ear asymmetries for speech and music. *Perception and Psychophysics, 31,* 75–85.

Best, C. T., McRoberts, G. W., LaFleur, R., Silver-Isenstadt, J. (1995). Divergent developmental patterns for infants' perceptions of two nonnative consonant contrasts. *Infant Behavior and Development, 18,* 339–350.

Bettelheim, B. (1969). *The children of the dream.* London: MacMillan.

Bickerton, D. (1990). *Language and species.* Chicago: University of Chicago Press.

Binet, A., & Henri, V. (1895). La Mémoire des phrases. *L'Année Psychologique, 1,* 24–59.

Binet, A., & Henri, V. (1896). La psychologie individuelle. *L'Année Psychologique, 2,* 411–465.

Binet, A., & Simon, T. (1905). Méthodes nouvelles pour le diagnostic du niveau intellectuel des normaux. *L'Année Psychologique, 11,* 191–244.

Birch, L. L., & Fisher, J. A. (1996). The role of experience in the development of children's eating behavior. In E. D. Capaldi (Ed.), *Why we eat what we eat* (pp. 113–141). Washington, DC: American Psychological Association.

Birns, B., & Hay, D. F. (Eds.). (1988). *The different faces of motherhood.* New York: Plenum.

Bischof, N. (1975). A systems approach toward the functional connections of attachment and fear. *Child Development, 46,* 801–817.

Bjorklund, D. F., & Douglas, R. N. (1997). The development of memory strategies. In C. Hulme (Series Ed.) & N. Cowan (Ed.), *The development of memory in childhood. Studies in developmental psychology* (pp. 201–246). Hove, England: Psychology Press.

Blackford, J. U., & Walden, T. A. (1998). Individual differences in social referencing. *Infant Behavior and Development, 21,* 89–102.

Blackwell, P., Kirkhart, I., Schmitt, D., & Kaiser, M. (1998). Cocaine/polydrug affected dyads: Implications for infant cognitive development and mother–infant interaction during the first six postnatal months. *Journal of Applied Developmental Psychology, 19,* 235–248.

Blakemore, C., & Mitchell, D. E. (1973). Environmental modification of the visual cortex and the neural basis of learning and memory. *Nature, 241,* 467–468.

Blasco, P. A. (1989). Preterm birth: To correct or not to correct. *Developmental Medicine and Child Neurology, 31,* 816–821.

Blass, E. M. (1998). Changing influences of sucrose and visual engagement in 2- to 12-week-old human infants: Implications for maternal face recognition. *Infant Behavior and Development, 20,* 423–434.

Blass, E. M. (1999). The ontogeny of human infant face recognition: Orogustatory, visual, and social influences. In P. Rochat (Ed.), *Early social cognition: Understanding others in the first months of life* (pp. 35–65). Mahwah, NJ: Lawrence Erlbaum Associates.

Blass, E. M., Ganchrow, J. R., & Steiner, J. E. (1984). Classical conditioning in newborn humans 2–48 hours of age. *Infant Behavior and Development, 7,* 223–235.

Bloch, H. (1989). On early coordinations and their future. In A. de Ribaupierre (Ed.), *Transition mechanisms in child development: The longitudinal perspective* (pp. 259–282). New York: Cambridge University Press.

Block, J. H., & Block, J. (1980). The role of ego-control and ego-resiliency in the organization of behavior. In W. A. Collins (Ed.), *Minnesota Symposium on Child Psychology* (Vol. 13, pp. 39–101). Hillsdale, NJ: Lawrence Erlbaum Associates.

Bloom, B. S. (1964). *Stability and change in human characteristics*. New York: Wiley.

Bloom, B. S. (1976). *Human characteristics and school learning*. New York: McGraw-Hill.

Bloom, K. (1979). Evaluation of infant vocal conditioning. *Journal of Experimental Child Psychology, 27*, 60–70.

Bloom, K., Russell, A., & Wassenberg, K. (1987). Turn taking affects the quality of infant vocalizations. *Journal of Child Language, 14*, 211–227.

Bloom, L. (1973). *One word at a time*. The Hague, the Netherlands: Mouton.

Bloom, L., & Capatides, J. B. (1987). Expression of affect and the emergence of language. *Child Development, 58*, 1513–1522.

Bloom, L., Margulis, C., Tinker, E., & Fujita, N. (1996). Early conversations and word learning: Contributions from child and adult. *Child Development, 67*, 3154–3175.

Bloomfield, L. (1933). *Language*. New York: Holt, Rinehart, & Winston.

Boccia, M., & Campos, J. J. (1983, April). *Maternal emotional signalling: Its effect on infants' reaction to strangers*. Paper presented at the meeting of the Society for Research in Child Development, Detroit, MI.

Boccia, M., & Campos, J. J. (1989). Maternal emotional signals, social referencing, and infants' reactions to strangers. *New Directions for Child Development*, No. 44, pp. 25–49. San Francisco: Jossey-Bass.

Bonin, M., Pomerleau, A., & Malcuit, G. (1998). A longitudinal study of visual attention and psychomotor development in preterm and full-term infants during the first six months of life. *Infant Behavior and Development, 21*, 103–118.

Bornstein, M. H. (1978a). Chromatic vision in infancy. In H. W. Reese & L. P. Lipsitt (Eds.), *Advances in child development and behavior* (Vol. 12, pp. 117–182). New York: Academic.

Bornstein, M. H. (1978b). Visual behavior of the young human infant: Relationships between chromatic and spatial perception and the activity of underlying brain mechanisms. *Journal of Experimental Child Psychology, 26*, 174–192.

Bornstein, M. H. (1981a). Psychological studies of color perception in human infants: Habituation, discrimination and categorization, recognition, and conceptualization. In L. P. Lipsitt (Ed.), *Advances in infancy research* (Vol. 1, pp. 1–40). Norwood, NJ: Ablex.

Bornstein, M. H. (1981b). Two kinds of perceptual organization near the beginning of life. In W. A. Collins (Ed.), *Minnesota Symposia on Child Psychology* (Vol. 14, pp. 39–91). Hillsdale, NJ: Lawrence Erlbaum Associates.

Bornstein, M. H. (1982). Perceptual anisotropies in infancy: Ontogenetic origins and implications of inequalities in spatial vision. In H. W. Reese & L. P. Lipsitt (Eds.), *Advances in child development and behavior* (Vol. 16, pp. 77–123). New York: Academic.

Bornstein, M. H. (1984). A descriptive taxonomy of psychological categories used by infants. In C. Sophian (Ed.), *Origins of cognitive skills* (pp. 313–338). Hillsdale, NJ: Lawrence Erlbaum Associates.

Bornstein, M. H. (1985a). Colour–name versus shape–name learning in young children. *Journal of Child Language, 12*, 387–393.

Bornstein, M. H. (1985b). Habituation of attention as a measure of visual information processing in human infants: Summary, systematization, and synthesis. In G. Gottlieb & N. A. Krasnegor (Eds.), *Measurement of audition and vision in the first year of postnatal life: A methodological overview* (pp. 253–300). Norwood, NJ: Ablex.

Bornstein, M. H. (1985c). How infant and mother jointly contribute to developing cognitive competence in the child. *Proceedings of the National Academy of Sciences* (United States), *82*, 7470–7473.

Bornstein, M. H. (1985d). Infant into adult: Unity to diversity in the development of visual categorization. In J. Mehler & R. Fox (Eds.), *Neonate cognition: Beyond the blooming, buzzing confusion* (pp. 115–138). Hillsdale, NJ: Lawrence Erlbaum Associates.

Bornstein, M. H. (1985e). On the development of color naming in young children: Data and theory. *Brain and Language, 26*, 72–93.

Bornstein, M. H. (1989a). Between caretakers and their young: Two modes of interaction and their consequences for cognitive growth. In M. H. Bornstein & J. S. Bruner (Eds.), *Interaction in human development* (pp. 147–170). Hillsdale, NJ: Lawrence Erlbaum Associates.

Bornstein, M. H. (1989b). Cross-cultural developmental comparisons: The case of Japanese—American infant and mother activities and interactions. What we know, what we need to know, and why we need to know. *Developmental Review, 9*, 171–204.

Bornstein, M. H. (Ed.). (1989c). *Maternal responsiveness: Characteristics and consequences*. San Francisco: Jossey-Bass.

Bornstein, M. H. (1989d). Sensitive periods in development: Structural characteristics and causal interpretations. *Psychological Bulletin, 105*, 179–197.

Bornstein, M. H. (1989e). Stability in early mental development: From attention and information processing in infancy to language and cognition in childhood. In M. H. Bornstein & N. A. Krasnegor (Eds.), *Stability and continuity in mental development: Behavioral and biological perspectives* (pp. 147–170). Hillsdale, NJ: Lawrence Erlbaum Associates.

Bornstein, M. H. (1991a). Approaches to parenting in culture. In M. H. Bornstein (Ed.), *Cultural approaches to parenting* (pp. 3–19). Hillsdale, NJ: Lawrence Erlbaum Associates.

Bornstein, M. H. (Ed.). (1991b). *Cultural approaches to parenting.* Hillsdale, NJ: Lawrence Erlbaum Associates.

Bornstein, M. H. (1994). Alfred Binet, the origins of mental testing, and the consequences for understanding the development of human intelligence. In P. Fraisse & J. Sequi (Eds.), *Les Origines de la Psychologie Scientfique: Centenaire de l'Anné Psycholoque* (pp. 145–161). Paris: Presses Universitaires de France.

Bornstein, M. H. (1995). Form and function: Implications for studies of culture and human development. *Culture & Psychology, 1,* 123–137.

Bornstein, M. H. (1998). Stability in mental development from early life: Methods, measures, models, meanings, and myths. In F. Simion & G. Butterworth (Eds.), *The development of sensory, motor and cognitive capacities in early infancy: From perception to cognition* (pp. 301–332). Hove, England: Psychology Press.

Bornstein, M. H. (2000). Infant into conversant: Language and nonlanguage processes in developing early communication. In N. Budwig, I. Č. Užgiris, & J. V. Wertsch (Eds.), *Communication: An arena of development. Advances in applied developmental psychology* (pp. 109–129). Stamford, CT: Ablex.

Bornstein, M. H. (2001). Arnold Lucius Gesell. *Pediatrics and Related Topics/Pädiatrie and Grenzgebiete, 40,* 395–409.

Bornstein, M. H. (2002). Parenting infants. In M. H. Bornstein (Ed.), *Handbook of parenting* (2nd ed., Vol. I, pp. 3–43). Mahwah, NJ: Lawrence Erlbaum Associates.

Bornstein, M. H., & Arterberry, M. E. (2000). *Discrimination, categorization, and apperception of smiling by 5-month-old infants.* Unpublished Manuscript, NICHD Bethesda, MD.

Bornstein, M. H., Azuma, H., Tamis-LeMonda, C. S., & Ogino, M. (1990). Mother and infant activity and interaction in Japan and in the United States: I. A comparative macroanalysis of naturalistic exchanges. *International Journal of Behavioural Development, 13,* 267–287.

Bornstein, M. H., & Benasich, A. A. (1986). Infant habituation: Assessments of individual differences and short-term reliability at five months. *Child Development, 57,* 87–99.

Bornstein, M. H., & Bradley, R. H. (Eds.). (2002). *Socioeconomic status, parenting, and child development.* Mahwah, NJ: Lawrence Erlbaum Associates.

Bornstein, M. H., Brown, E. M., & Slater, A. (1996). Patterns of stability and continuity in attention across early infancy. *Journal of Reproductive and Infant Psychology, 14,* 195–200.

Bornstein, M. H., & Cote, L. R. (2001). Mother-infant interaction and acculturation I: Behavioral comparisons in Japanese American and South American families. *International Journal of Behavioral Development, 25,* 549–563.

Bornstein, M. H., Cote, L. R., & Venuti, P. (2001). Parenting beliefs and behaviors in northern and southern groups of Italian mothers of young infants. *Journal of Family Psychology, 15,* 663–675.

Bornstein, M. H., DiPietro, J. A., Hahn, C. H., Painter, K. M., Haynes, O. M., & Costigan, K. A. (2002). Prenatal cardiac function and postnatal cognitive development: An exploratory study. *Infancy, 3.*

Bornstein, M. H., Ferdinandsen, K., & Gross, C. G. (1981). Perception of symmetry in infancy. *Developmental Psychology, 17,* 82–86.

Bornstein, M. H., Gaughran, J. M., & Homel, P. (1986). Infant temperament: Theory, tradition, critique, and new assessments. In C. E. Izard & P. B. Read (Eds.), *Measuring emotions in infants and children* (Vol. 2, pp. 172–199). New York: Cambridge University Press.

Bornstein, M. H., Gaughran, J. M., & Segui, I. (1991). Multimethod assessment of infant temperament: Mother questionnaire and mother and observer reports evaluated and compared at five months using the Infant Temperament Measure. *International Journal of Behavioral Development, 14,* 131–151.

Bornstein, M. H., Gross, C. G., & Wolf, J. Z. (1978). Perceptual similarity of mirror images in infancy. *Cognition, 6,* 89–116.

Bornstein, M. H., Hahn, C.-S., Suwalsky, J. T. D., & Haynes, O. M. (2002). Socioeconomic status, parenting, and child development: The Hollingshead Four-Factor Index of Social Status and the Socioeconomic Index of Occupations. In M. H. Bornstein & R. H. Bradley (Eds.), *Socio-economic status, parenting, and child development.* Mahwah, NJ: Lawrence Erlbaum Associates.

Bornstein, M. H., & Haynes, O. M. (1998). Vocabulary competence in early childhood: Measurement, latent construct, and predictive validity. *Child Development, 69,* 654–671.

Bornstein, M. H., Haynes, O. M., Azuma, H., Galperín, C., Maital, S., Ogino, M., Painter, K., Pascual, L., Pêcheux, M. G., Rahn, C., Toda, S., Venuti, P. A., & Wright, B. (1998). A cross-national study of self-evaluations and attributions in parenting: Argentina, Belgium, France, Israel, Italy, Japan, and the United States. *Developmental Psychology, 34,* 662–676.

Bornstein, M. H., Haynes, O. M., Legler, J. M., O'Reilly, A. W., & Painter, K. M. (1997).

Symbolic play in childhood: Interpersonal and environmental context and stability. *Infant Behavior and Development, 20,* 197–207.

Bornstein, M. H., Haynes, O. M., O'Reilly, A. W., & Painter, K. (1996). Solitary and collaborative pretense play in early childhood: Sources of individual variation in the development of representational competence. *Child Development, 67,* 2910–2929.

Bornstein, M. H., Haynes, O. M., Painter, K. M., & Genevro, J. L. (2000). Child language with mother and with stranger at home and in the laboratory: A methodological study. *Journal of Child Language, 27,* 407–420.

Bornstein, M. H., Haynes, O. M., Pascual, L., Painter, K. M., & Galperin, C. (1999). Play in two societies: Pervasiveness of process, specificity of structure. *Child Development, 70,* 317–331.

Bornstein, M. H., Kessen, W., & Weiskopf, S. (1976a). The categories of hue in infancy. *Science, 191,* 201–202.

Bornstein, M. H., Kessen, W., & Weiskopf, S. (1976b). Color vision and hue categorization in young human infants. *Journal of Experimental Psychology: Human Perception and Performance, 2,* 115–129.

Bornstein, M. H., & Krinsky, S. (1985). Perception of symmetry in infancy: The salience of vertical symmetry and the perception of pattern wholes. *Journal of Experimental Child Psychology, 39,* 1–19.

Bornstein, M. H., Krinsky, S. J., & Benasich, A. A. (1986). Fine orientation discrimination and shape constancy in young infants. *Journal of Experimental Child Psychology, 41,* 49–60.

Bornstein, M. H., & Lamb, M. E. (Eds.). (1999). *Developmental psychology: An advanced textbook* (4th ed.). Mahwah, NJ: Lawrence Erlbaum Associates.

Bornstein, M. H., & Ludemann, P. L. (1989). Habituation at home. *Infant Behavior and Development, 12,* 525–529.

Bornstein, M. H., Maital, S. L., & Tal, J. (1997). Contexts of collaboration in caregiving: Infant interactions with Israeli kibbutz mothers and caregivers. *Early Child Development and Care, 135,* 145–171.

Bornstein, M. H., & Mayes, L. (1991). Taking the measure of infant mind. In F. S. Kessel, M. H. Bornstein, & A. J. Sameroff (Eds.), *Contemporary constructions of the child.* Hillsdale, NJ: Lawrence Erlbaum Associates.

Bornstein, M. H., Mayes, L. C., & Park, J. (1998). Language, play, emotional availability, and acceptance in cocaine-exposed and non-cocaine exposed young children and their mothers. *Revue Parole, 7/8,* 235–260.

Bornstein, M. H., & O'Reilly, A. W. (Eds.). (1993). *The role of play in the development of thought.* San Francisco: Jossey-Bass.

Bornstein, M. H., Painter, K. P., & Park, J. (2002). Naturalistic language sampling in typically developing children. *Journal of Child Language.*

Bornstein, M. H., Pêcheux, M. G., & Lécuyer, R. (1988). Visual habituation in human infants: Development and rearing circumstances. *Psychological Research, 50,* 130–133.

Bornstein, M. H., & Ruddy, M. G. (1984). Infant attention and maternal stimulation: Prediction of cognitive and linguistic development in singletons and twins. In H. Bouma & D. G. Bouwhuis (Eds.), *Attention and performance X: Control Language Processes* (pp. 433–445). London: Lawrence Erlbaum Associates.

Bornstein, M. H., Slater, A., Brown, E. M., Roberts, E., & Barrett, J. (1997). Stability of mental development from infancy to later childhood: Three "waves" of research. In G. Bremner, A. Slater, & G. Butterworth (Eds.), *Infant development: Recent advances* (pp. 191–215). Hove, England: Psychology Press.

Bornstein, M. H., & Suess, P. E. (2000a). Child and mother cardiac vagal tone: Continuity, stability, and concordance across the first 5 years. *Developmental Psychology, 36,* 54–65.

Bornstein, M. H., & Suess, P. E. (2000b). Physiological self-regulation and information processing in infancy: Cardiac vagal tone and habituation. *Child Development, 71,* 273–287.

Bornstein, M. H., Tal, J., & Tamis-LeMonda, C. S. (1991). Parenting in cross-cultural perspective: The United States, France, and Japan. In M. H. Bornstein (Ed.), *Cultural approaches to parenting* (pp. 69–90). Hillsdale, NJ: Lawrence Erlbaum Associates.

Bornstein, M. H., & Tamis-LeMonda, C. S. (1989). Maternal responsiveness and cognitive development in children. In M. H. Bornstein (Ed.), *Maternal responsiveness: Characteristics and consequences* (pp. 49–61). San Francisco: Jossey-Bass.

Bornstein, M. H., & Tamis-LeMonda, C. S. (1990). Activities and interactions of mothers and their firstborn infants in the first six months of life: Covariation, stability, continuity, correspondence, and prediction. *Child Development, 61,* 1206–1217.

Bornstein, M. H., & Tamis-LeMonda, C. S. (1991). *Origins of cognitive skills in infants.* Paper presented at the International Conference on Infant Studies, Los Angeles.

Bornstein, M. H., & Tamis-LeMonda, C. S. (1994). Antecedents of information-processing skills in infants: Habituation, novelty, responsiveness, and cross-modal transfer. *Infant Behavior and Development, 17,* 371–380.

Bornstein, M. H., & Tamis-LeMonda, C. S. (1995). Parent-child symbolic play: Three theories in search of an effect. *Developmental Review, 15,* 382–400.

Bornstein, M. H., & Tamis-LeMonda, C. S. (1997a). Maternal responsiveness and infant mental abilities: Specific predictive relations. *Infant Behavior and Development, 20,* 283–296.

Bornstein, M. H., Tamis-LeMonda, C. S., & Haynes, O. M. (1999). First words in the second year: Continuity, stability, and models of concurrent and predictive correspondence in vocabulary and verbal responsiveness across age and context. *Infant Behavior and Development, 22,* 65–85.

Bornstein, M. H., Tamis-LeMonda, C. S., Pascual, L., Haynes, O. M., Painter, K., Galperín, C., & Pêcheux, M. G. (1996). Ideas about parenting in Argentina, France, and the United States. *International Journal of Behavioral Development, 19,* 347–367.

Bornstein, M. H., Tamis-LeMonda, C. S., Pêcheux, M. G., & Rahn, C. W. (1991). Mother and infant activity and interaction in France and in the United States: A comparative study. *International Journal of Behavioral Development, 14,* 21–43.

Bornstein, M. H., Tamis-LeMonda, C. S., Tal, J., Ludemann, P., Toda, S., Rahn, C. W., Pêcheux, M.-G., Azuma, H., & Vardi, D. (1992). Maternal responsiveness to infants in three societies: The United States, France, and Japan. *Child Development, 63,* 808–821.

Bornstein, M. H., Toda, S., Azuma, H., Tamis-LeMonda, C. S., & Ogino, M. (1990). Mother and infant activity and interaction in Japan and in the United States: II. A comparative microanalysis of naturalistic interactions focused on the organization of infant attention. *International Journal of Behavoural Development, 13,* 289–308.

Bouchard, T. J. (1997). IQ similarity in twins reared apart: Findings and responses to critics. In R. J. Sternberg & E. L. Grigorenko (Ed.), *Intelligence, heredity, and environment* (pp. 126–160). New York: Cambridge University Press.

Bouchard, T. J., Lykken, D. T., McGue, M., Segal, N. L., & Tellegen, A. (1990). Sources of human psychological differences: The Minnesota study of twins reared apart. *Science, 250,* 223–228.

Bower, T. G. R. (1977). *A primer of infant development.* San Francisco: Freeman.

Bowlby, J. (1951). *Maternal care and mental health.* Geneva, Switzerland: World Health Organization.

Bowlby, J. (1969). *Attachment and loss: Vol. 1. Attachment.* New York: Basic Books.

Bowlby, J. (1973). *Attachment and loss: Vol. 2. Separation.* New York: Basic Books.

Boysson-Bardies, B. de, Sagart, L., & Durand, C. (1984). Discernible differences in the babbling of infants according to target language. *Journal of Child Language, 11,* 1–15.

Boyton, R. M., & Gordon, J. (1965). Bezold-Brüke hue shift measured by color-naming technique. *Journal of the Optical Society of America, 55,* 78–86.

Brackbill, Y. (1958). Extinction of the smiling response in infants as a function of reinforcement schedule. *Child Development, 29,* 115–124.

Brackbill, Y. (1979). Obstetrical medication and infant behavior. In J. D. Osofsky (Ed.), *Handbook*

of infant development (pp. 76–125). New York: Wiley.

Bradley, R. H. (2002). Environment and parenting. In M. H. Bornstein (Ed.), *Handbook of parenting: Vol. 2. Biology and ecology of parenting* (pp. 235–261). Mahwah, NJ: Lawrence Erlbaum Associates.

Bradley, R. H., Burchinal, M. R., & Casey, P. H. (2001). Early intervention: The moderating role of the home environment. *Applied Developmental Science, 5,* 2–8.

Bradley, R. H., Caldwell, B. M., & Elardo, R. (1979). Home environment and cognitive development in the first 2 years: A crosslagged panel analysis. *Developmental Psychology, 15,* 246–250.

Bradley, R. H., Caldwell, B. M., & Rock, S. L. (1988). Home environment and school performance: A ten-year follow-up and examination of three models of environmental action. *Child Development, 59,* 852–867.

Bradley, R. H., Whiteside, L., Mundfrom, D. J., Casey, P. H., Kelleher, K. J., & Pope, S. K. (1994). Early indications of resilience and their relation to experiences in the home environments of low birthweight, premature children living in poverty. *Child Development, 65,* 346–360.

Brand, J. G. (1997). Biophysics of taste. In E. C. Carterette & M. P. Friedman (Series Eds.) & G. K. Beauchamp & L. Bartoshuk (Eds.), *Tasting and smelling. Handbook of perception and cognition* (2nd ed., pp. 1–24). San Diego: Academic.

Brandt, I., & Sticker, E. J. (1991). Bedeutung der alterskorrektur bei fryuhgeborenen. *Monatsschr Kinderheilkd, 139,* 16–21.

Brazelton, T. B. (1985). Application of cry research to clinical perspectives. In B. M. Lester & C. F. Z. Boukydis (Eds.), *Infant crying: Theoretical and research perspectives* (pp. 325–340). New York: Plenum.

Brazelton, T. B., & Nugent, J. K. (1995). *Neonatal Behavioral Assessment Scale* (3rd ed.). London: Cambridge University Press.

Bremner, J. G. (1994). *Infancy* (2nd ed.). Oxford, England, & Cambridge, MA: Blackwell.

Bremner, J. G. (1997). From perception to cognition. In G. Bremner, A. Slater, & G. Butterworth (Eds.), *Infant development: Recent advances* (pp. 55–74). Hove, England: Psychology Press.

Bremner, J. G. (1998). From perception to action: The early development of knowledge. In F. Simion & G. Butterworth (Eds.), *The development of sensory, motor, and cognitive capacities in early infancy: From perception to cognition* (pp. 239–255). London: Psychology Press.

Bremner, J. G., & Bryant, P. E. (1985). Active movement and development of spatial abilities in infancy. In H. M. Wellman (Ed.), *Children's searching: The development of search skill and spatial representation.* Hillsdale, NJ: Lawrence Erlbaum Associates.

Bremner, J. G., & Knowles, L. (1994). Processes underlying young children's spatial orientation during movement. *Journal of Experimental Child Psychology, 57,* 355–376.

Brent, M. R., & Cartwright, T. A. (1996). Distributional regularity and phonotactic constraints are useful for segmentation. *Cognition, 61,* 93–125.

Bretherton, I., & Bates, E. (1984). The development of representation from 10 to 28 months. In R. N. Emde & R. J. Harmon (Eds.), *Continuities and discontinuities in development* (pp. 229–261). New York: Plenum.

Bretherton, I., McNew, S., Snyder, L., & Bates, E. (1983). Individual differences at 20 months: Analytic and holistic strategies in language acquisition. *Journal of Child Language, 10,* 293–320.

Briggs, G. G., Freeman, R. K., & Sumner, J. Y. (Eds.). (1994). *Drugs in pregnancy and lactation.* Baltimore: Williams & Wilkins.

Broberg, A., Lamb, M. E., & Hwang, P. (1990). Inhibition: Its stability and correlates in sixteen- to forty-month-old children. *Child Development, 61,* 1153–1163.

Broberg, A., Hwang, C. P., Lamb, M. E., & Ketterlinus, R. D. (1989). Child care effects on socioemotional and intellectual competence in Swedish preschoolers. In J. S. Lande, S. Scarr, & N. Gunzenhauser (Eds.), *Caring for children: Challenge to America* (pp. 49–75). Hillsdale, NJ: Lawrence Erlbaum Associates.

Brodbeck, A. J., & Irwin, D. L. (1946). The speech behavior of infants without families. *Child Development, 17,* 145–156.

Brody, G. H., Stoneman, Z., & McCoy, J. K. (1994). Contributions of family relationships and child temperaments to longitudinal variations in sibling relationship quality and sibling relationship styles. *Journal of Family Psychology, 8,* 274–286.

Bronfenbrenner, U. (1961). The changing American child. *Journal of Social Issues, 17,* 6–18.

Bronfenbrenner, U. (1975). *The ecology of human development: A research perspective.* Paper presented to the American Psychological Asociation, Chicago.

Bronfenbrenner, U. (1999). Environments in developmental perspective: Theoretical and operational models. In S. L. Friedman & T. D. Wachs (Eds.), *Measuring environment across the life span: Emerging methods and concepts* (pp. 3–28). Washington, DC: American Psychological Association.

Bronson, G. W. (1974). The postnatal growth of visual capacity. *Child Development, 45,* 873–890.

Bronstein, P., & Cowan, C. P. (Eds.). (1988). *Fatherhood today: Men's changing role in the family.* New York: Wiley.

Brooks-Gunn, J., Klebanov, P. K., Liaw, F., & Spiker, D. (1993). Enhancing the development of low-birthweight, premature infants: Changes in cognition and behavior over the first three years. *Child Development, 64,* 736–753.

Brown, R. (1973). *A first language: The early stages.* London: George Allen.

Brown, R., & Hanlon, C. (1970). Derivational complexity and order of acquisition in child speech. In J. R. Hayes (Ed.), *Cognition and the development of language* (pp. 155–207). New York: Wiley.

Bruner, J. S. (1983). *Child's talk: Learning to use language.* New York: Norton.

Bryant, P. E. (1974). *Perception and understanding in young children: An experimental approach.* London: Methuen.

Buhler, C. (1930). *The first year of life.* New York: Day.

Buhler, C. (1933). The social behavior of children. In C. Murchison (Ed.), *Handbook of child psychology.* Worcester, MA: Clark University Press.

Buhler, C., & Hetzer, H. (1935). *Testing children's development from birth to school age.* New York: Farrar & Rinehart.

Burchinal, M. R., Follmer, A., & Bryant, D. M. (1996). The relations of maternal social support and family structure with maternal responsiveness and child outcomes among African American families. *Developmental Psychology, 32,* 1073–1083.

Burchinal, M. R., Roberts, J. E., Nabors, L. A., & Bryant, D. M. (1996). Quality of center child care and infant cognitive and language development. *Child Development, 67,* 606–620.

Burgess, R. L., & Youngblade, L. M. (1988). Social incompetence and the intergenerational transmission of abusive parental practices. In R. Gelles, G. Hotaling, D. Finkelhor, & M. Straus (Eds.), *Family abuse and its consequences: New directions in family violence research.* Beverly Hills, CA: Sage.

Burt, C. (1921). *Mental and scholastic tests.* London: King.

Busch-Rossnagel, N. A., Knauf-Jensen, D. E., & DesRosiers, F. A. (1995). Mothers and others: The role of the socializing environment in the development of mastery motivation. In R. H. MacTurk & G. A. Morgan (Eds.), *Mastery motivation: Origins, conceptualizations, and applications. Advances in applied developmental psychology* (Vol. 12, pp. 117–145). Stamford, CT: Ablex.

Bushnell, I. W. R. (1982). Discrimination of faces by young infants. *Journal of Experimental Child Psychology, 33,* 298–308.

Bushnell, I. W. R. (1998). The origins of face perception. In F. Simion & G. Butterworth (Eds.), *The development of sensory, motor, and cognitive capacities in early infancy: From perception to cognition* (pp. 69–86). London: Psychology Press.

Busnel, M. C., Granier-Deferre, C., & Lecanuet, J. P. (1992). Fetal audition: *Annals of the New York Academy of Sciences, 662,* 118–134.

Buss, A. H., & Plomin, R. (1975). *A temperament theory of personality.* New York: Wiley.

Buss, A. H., & Plomin, R. (1984). *Temperament: Early developing personality traits.* Hillsdale, NJ: Lawrence Erlbaum Associates.

Buss, K. A., & Goldsmith, H. H. (1998). Fear and anger regulation in infancy: Effects on the temporal dynamics of affective expression. *Child Development, 69,* 359–374.

Butler, J., & Rovee-Collier, C. (1989). Contextual gating of memory retrieval. *Developmental Psychobiology, 22,* 533–552.

Butterfield, E. C., & Siperstein, G. N. (1972). Influence of contingent auditory stimulation upon non-nutritional suckle. In J. F. Bosoma (Ed.), *Third Symposium on Oral Sensation and Perception: The Mouth of the Infant.* Springfield, IL: Thomas.

Butterworth, G., & Grover, L. (1990). Joint visual attention, manual pointing, and preverbal communication in human infancy. In M. Jeannerod (Ed.), *Attention and performance: Vol. 13. Motor representation and control* (pp. 605–624). Mahwah, NJ: Lawrence Erlbaum Associates.

Cairns, R. B. (1998). The making of developmental psychology. In W. Damon (Series Ed.) & R. M. Lerner (Vol. Ed.), *Handbook of child psychology: Vol. 1. Theoretical models of human development* (5th ed., pp. 25–105). New York: Wiley.

Caldera, Y. M., Huston, A. C., & O'Brien, M. (1989). Social interactions and play patterns of parents and toddlers with feminine, masculine, and neutral toys. *Child Development, 60,* 70–76.

Calkins, S. D., & Fox, N. (1992). The relations among infant temperament, security of attachment, and behavioral inhibition at twenty-four months. *Child Development, 63,* 1456–1472.

Calkins, S. D., Fox, N. A., & Marshall, T. R. (1996). Behavioral and physiological antecedents of inhibited and uninhibited behavior. *Child Development, 67,* 523–540.

Cameron, J., Livson, N., & Bayley, N. (1967). Infant vocalizations and their relationship to mature intelligence. *Science, 157,* 331–333.

Campbell, D. W., & Eaton, W. O. (1999). Sex differences in the activity level of infants. *Infant and Child Development, 8,* 1–17.

Campos, J. J. (1976). Heart rate: A sensitive tool for the study of emotional development in the infant. In L. P. Lipsitt (Ed.), *Developmental psychobiology: The significance of infancy.* Hillsdale, NJ: Lawrence Erlbaum Associates.

Campos, J. J. (1994, Spring). The new functionalism of emotion. *SRCD Newsletter,* pp. 2, 4, 7.

Campos, J., Barrett, K. C., Lamb, M. E., Goldsmith, H., & Stenberg, C. (1983). Socioemotional development. In P. H. Mussen (Gen. Ed.) & M. M. Haith & J. J. Campos (Vol. Eds.), *Handbook of child psychology: Vol. 2. Infancy and developmental psychobiology* (pp. 783–916). New York: Wiley.

Campos, J., Bertenthal, B. I., & Kermoian, R. (1992). Early experience and emotional development: The emergence of wariness of heights. *Psychological Science, 3,* 61–64.

Campos, J. J., Campos, R. G., & Barrett, K. C. (1989). Emergent themes in the study of emotional development and emotional regulation. *Developmental Psychology, 25,* 394–402.

Campos, J. J., & Stenberg, C. (1981). Perception, appraisal, and emotions: The onset of social referencing. In M. E. Lamb & L. R. Sherrod (Eds.), *Infant social cognition: Empirical and theoretical considerations* (pp. 273–314). Hillsdale, NJ: Lawrence Erlbaum Associates.

Camras, L. A., Lambrecht, L., & Michel, G. F. (1996). Infant "surprise" expressions as coordinative motor structures. *Journal of Nonverbal Behavior, 20,* 183–195.

Camras, L. A., Sullivan, J., & George, M. (1993). Do infants express discrete emotions? Adult judgments of facial, vocal, and body actions. *Journal of Nonverbal Behavior, 17,* 171–186.

Camras, L. A., Oster, H., Campos, J. J., Miyaki, K., & Bradshaw, D. (1992). Japanese and American infants' response to arm restraint. *Developmental Psychology, 28,* 578–583.

Capaldi, E. D. (1996). Conditioned food preferences. In E. D. Capaldi (Ed.), *Why we eat what we eat* (pp. 53–80). Washington, DC: American Psychological Association.

Capute, A. J., Palmer, F. B., Shapiro, B. K., Wachtel, R. C., Schmidt, S., & Ross, A. (1986). Clinical Linguistic and Auditory Milestone Scale: Prediction of cognition in infancy. *Developmental Medicine and Child Neurology, 28,* 762–771.

Capute, A. J., Shapiro, B. K., Wachtel, R. C., Gunther, V. A., & Palmer, F. B. (1986). The Clinical Linguistic and Auditory Milestone Scale (CLAMS): Identification of cognitive defects in motor-delayed children. *American Journal of Diseases of Children, 140,* 694–698.

Carew, J. V. (1980). Experience and the development of intelligence in young children at home and in day care. *Monographs for Society for Research in Child Development, 45*(67, Serial No. 187).

Carey, W. B. (1970). A simplified method for measuring infant temperament. *Journal of Pediatrics, 77,* 188–194.

Carey, W. B., & McDevitt, S. C. (1978a). Revision of the Infant Temperament Questionnaire. *Pediatrics, 61,* 735–739.

Carey, W. B., & McDevitt, S. C. (1978b). Stability and change in individual temperamental diagnoses from infancy to early childhood. *Journal of the American Academy of Child Psychiatry, 17,* 331–337.

Caron, A. J., & Caron, R. F. (1969). Degree of stimulus complexity and habituation of visual fixation in infants. *Psychonomic Science, 14,* 78–79.

Carpenter, M., Nagell, K., & Tomasello, M. (1998). Social cognition, joint attention, and communicative competence from 9 to 15 months of age. *Monographs of the Society for Research in Child Development, 63*(4, Serial No. 255), 1–143.

Carpenter, R. L., Mastergeorge, A. M., & Coggins, T. E. (1983). The acquisition of communicative intentions in infants eight to fifteen months of age. *Language and Speech, 216,* 101–116.

Carver, L. J., & Bauer, P. J. (1999). When the event is more than the sum of its parts: Nine-month-olds' long-term ordered recall. *Memory, 7,* 147–174.

Carver, L. J., Bauer, P. J., & Nelson, C. A. (2000). Associations between infant brain activity and recall memory. *Developmental Science, 3,* 234–246.

Casper, L. M. (1997, Nov.). *Who's minding our preschoolers?* (Current Population Reports, P70-62). Washington, DC: U.S. Bureau of the Census.

Caspi, A. (1998). Personality development across the life course. In W. Damon (Editor-in-Chief) & N. Eisenberg (Vol. Ed.), *Social, emotional and personality development: Vol. 3. Handbook of child psychology* (5th ed., pp. 311–388). New York: Wiley.

Catania, A. C. (1998). *Learning* (4th ed.). Saddle River, NJ: Prentice-Hall.

Cattell, J. (1890). Mental tests and measurements. *Mind, 15,* 373–381.

Cattell, P. (1940/1960). *The measure of intelligence in infants and young children.* New York: Psychological Corporation.

Centers for Disease Control and Prevention. (1989). *HIV/AIDS Surveillance.* Washington, DC: U.S. Department of Health and Human Services.

Centers for Disease Control and Prevention. (1994). *Down syndrome prevalence at birth: United States, 1983–1990.* Morbidity & Mortality Weekly Report, 43, 617–622.

Centers for Disease Control and Prevention. (1995b). *Chorionic villus sampling and amniocentesis: Recommendations for prenatal counseling.* Morbidity & Mortality Weekly Report, 44, (RR-9), 1–12. Washington, DC: U.S. Department of Health and Human Services.

Centers for Disease Control and Prevention. (1998, April). *Guidelines for the use of antiretroviral agents in pediatric HIV infection.* Morbidity & Mortality Weekly Report, 47, (RR-4), 1–31.

Centers for Disease Control and Prevention. (1999). *Status of perinatal HIV prevention: U.S. declines continue.* CDC-NCHSTP-Division of HIV/AIDS Prevention. Washington, DC: U.S. Department of Health and Human Services.

Centers for Disease Control and Prevention. (1999a). *Birthweight and gestation* (National Vital Statistics Reports, 47, No. 18). Washington, DC: U.S. Department of Health and Human Services.

Cernoch, J. M., & Porter, R. H. (1985). Recognition of maternal axillary odors by infants. *Child Development, 56,* 1593–1598.

Chavajay, P., & Rogoff, B. (1999). Cultural variation in management of attention by children and their caregivers. *Developmental Psychology, 35,* 1079–1090.

Cherney, S. S., Fulker, D. W., & Hewitt, J. K. (1997). Cognitive development from infancy to middle childhood. In R. J. Sternberg & E. L. Grigorenko (Eds.), *Intelligence, heredity, and environment* (pp. 463–482). New York: Cambridge University Press.

Chervenak, F. A., & McCullough, L. B. (1998). Ethical dimensions of ultrasound screening for fetal anomalies. *Annals of the New York Academy of Sciences, 847,* 185–190.

Chess, S., & Thomas, A. (1984). *Origins and evolution of behavior disorders from infancy to early adult life.* New York: Brunner/Mazel.

Chess, S., & Thomas, A. (1986). *Temperament in clinical practice.* New York: Guilford.

Chess, S., & Thomas, A. (1996). *Temperament: Theory and practice.* Philadelphia: Brunner/Mazel.

Chiang, T.-M., Caplovitz, K. B., & Nunez, N. N. (2000). Maternal attributions of Taiwanese and American toddlers' misdeeds and accomplishments. *Journal of Cross-Cultural Psychology, 31,* 349–368.

Chipuer, H. M., Rovine, M. J., & Plomin, R. (1990). LISREL modeling: Genetic and environmental influences on IQ revisited. *Intelligence, 14,* 11–29.

Chisholm, J. S. (1989). Biology, culture, and the development of temperament: A Navajo example. In J. K. Nugent, B. M. Lester, & T. B. Brazelton (Eds.), *The cultural context of infancy* (Vol. 1, pp. 341–364). Norwood, NJ: Ablex.

Choi, S., & Gopnik, A. (1995). Early acquisition of verbs in Korean: A cross-linguistic study. *Journal of Child Language, 22,* 497–529.

Chomsky, N. (1958). Review of the book *Verbal Behavior* by B. F. Skinner. *Language, 35,* 26–58.

Chomsky, N. (1965). *Aspects of the theory of syntax.* Cambridge, MA: MIT Press.

Christiansen, M. H., Allen, J., & Seidenberg, M. S. (1998). Learning to segment speech using multiple cues: A connectionist model. *Language & Cognitive Processes, 13,* 221–268.

Chugani, H. T. (1994). Development of regional brain glucose metabolism in relation to behavior and plasticity. In G. Dawson & K. W. Fischer (Eds.), *Human behavior and the developing brain* (pp. 153–175). New York: Guilford.

Cicchetti, D., & Toth, S. L. (2000). Developmental processes in maltreated children. In R. A. Dienstbier (Series Ed.) & D. J. Hansen (Vol. Ed.), *Motivation and child maltreatment (Nebraska Symposium on Motivation* (Vol. 46, pp. 85–160). Lincoln: University of Nebraska Press.

Clark, E. V. (1987). The principle of contrast: A constraint on language acquisition. In B. MacWhinney (Ed.), *Mechanisms of language acquisition* (pp. 1–33). Hillsdale, NJ: Lawrence Erlbaum Associates.

Clark, E. V. (1988). On the logic of contrast. *Journal of Child Language, 15*, 317–335.

Clark, E. V. (1990). On the pragmatics of contrast. *Journal of Child Language, 17*, 417–431.

Clarke, A. M., & Clarke, A. D. B. (2000). *Early experience and the life path.* Bristol, PA: Kingsley.

Clarke-Stewart, K. A., & Allhusen, V. D. (2002). Nonparental caregiving. In M. H. Bornstein (Eds.), *Handbook of parenting* (2nd ed., pp. 215–252). Mahwah, NJ: Lawrence Erlbaum Associates.

Clarke-Stewart, K. A., & Hevey, C. M. (1981). Longitudinal relations in repeated observations of mother–child interaction from 1 to $2^{1}/_{2}$ years. *Developmental Psychology, 17*, 127–145.

Clifton, R. K., Gwiazda, J., Bauer, J. A., Clarkson, M. G., & Held, R. M. (1988). Growth in head size during infancy: Implications for sound localization. *Developmental Psychology, 24*, 477–483.

Clifton, R. K., Perris, E., & Bullinger, A. (1991). Infants' perception of auditory space. *Developmental Psychology, 27*, 161–171.

Clifton, R. K., Rochat, P., Robin, D. J., & Berthier, N. E. (1994). Multimodal perception in the control of infant reaching. *Journal of Experimental Psychology: Human Perception and Performance, 20*, 876–886.

Cochran, M., & Niego, S. (2002). Parenting and social networks. In M. H. Bornstein (Ed.), *Handbook of parenting: Vol. 4. Applied parenting* (pp. 123–148). Mahwah, NJ: Lawrence Erlbaum Associates.

Cohen, L. B. (1998). An information-processing approach to infant perception and cognition. In F. Simion & G. Butterworth (Ed.), *The development of sensory, motor, and cognitive capacities in early infancy: From perception to cognition* (pp. 277–300). Hove, England: Psychology Press.

Cohn, J., & Tronick, E. (1983a). Communicative rules and the sequential structure of infant behavior during normal and depressed interaction. In E. Tronick (Ed.), *The development of human communication and the joint regulation of behavior.* Baltimore: University Park Press.

Cohn, J. E., & Tronick, E. Z. (1983b). Three-month-old infants' reaction to simulated maternal depression. *Child Development, 54*, 185–193.

Cole, M. (1999). Culture in development. In M. H. Bornstein & M. E. Lamb (Eds.), *Developmental psychology: An advanced textbook* (4th ed., pp. 73–123). Mahwah, NJ: Lawrence Erlbaum Associates.

Cole, P. M., Michel, M., & Teti, L. (1994). The development of emotional regulation and dysregulation: A clinical perspective. In N. A. Fox (Ed.), *The development of emotion regulation: Biological and behavioral considerations. Monographs of the Society for Research in Child Development, 59*(Serial No. 240), 73–100.

Collins, W. A., Maccoby, E. E., Steinberg, L., Hetherington, E. M., & Bornstein, M. (2000). Contemporary research on parenting: The case for nature and nurture. *American Psychologist, 55*, 218–232.

Colombo, J. (1993). *Infant cognition: Predicting later intellectual functioning.* Newbury Park, CA: Sage.

Colombo, J., & Mitchell, D. W. (1990). Individual differences in early visual attention: Fixation time and information processing. In J. Colombo & J. Fagen (Eds.), *Individual differences in infancy: Reliability, stability, prediction* (pp. 193–228). Hillsdale, NJ: Lawrence Erlbaum Associates.

Colombo, J., Frick, J. E., & Gorman, S. A. (1997). Sensitization during visual habituation sequences: Procedural effects and individual differences. *Journal of Experimental Child Psychology, 67*, 223–235.

Colombo, J., Mitchell, D. W., O'Brien, M., & Horowitz, F. D. (1987). The stability of visual habituation during the first year of life. *Child Development, 57*, 474–488.

Colombo, J., O'Brien, M., Mitchell, D. W., Roberts, K., & Horowitz, F. D. (1987). A lower boundary for category formation in preverbal infants. *Journal of Child Language, 14*, 383–385.

Colton, R. H., Steinschneider, A., Black, L., & Gleason, J. (1985). The newborn infant cry: Its potential implications for development and SIDS. In B. M. Lester & C. F. Z. Boukydis (Eds.), *Infant crying: Theoretical and research perspectives* (pp. 119–137). New York: Plenum.

Condry, J., & Condry, S. (1976). Sex differences: A study of the eye of the beholder. *Child Development, 47*, 812–819.

Conel, J. L. (1939–1959). *The postnatal development of the human cerebral cortex* (Vols. 1–6). Cambridge, MA: Harvard University Press.

Connell, D. B. (1976). *Individual differences in attachment: An investigation into stability, implications, and relationships to structure of early language development.* Unpublished doctoral dissertation, Syracuse University.

Connor, P. D., Sampson, P. D., Bookstein, F. L., & Streisguth, A. (2001). Direct and indirect effects of prenatal alcohol damage on executive function. *Developmental Neuropsychology, 18*, 331–333.

Connor, P. D., Streissguth, A. P., Sampson, P. D., Bookstein, F. L., & Barr, H. M. (1999). Individual differences in auditory and visual attention among fetal alcohol-affective adults. *Alcoholism: Clinical and Experimental Research, 23*, 1395–1402.

Conrad, R. (1998). Darwin's baby and baby's Darwin: Mutual recognition in observational research. *Human Development, 41*, 47–64.

Consortium for Longitudinal Studies. (1983). *As the twig is bent: Lasting effects of preschool programs.* Hillsdale, NJ: Lawrence Erlbaum Associates.

Cooper, L. G., Leland, N. L., & Alexander, G. (1995). Effects of maternal age on birth outcomes among young adolescents. *Social Biology, 42*, 22–35.

Cooper, R. P., & Aslin, R. N. (1989). The language environment of the young infant: Implications for early perceptual development. *Canadian Journal of Psychology, 43*, 247–265.

Cornelius, M. D., Day, N. L., Richardson, G. A., & Taylor, P. M. (1999). Epidemiology of substance abuse during pregnancy. In P. J. Ott & R. E. Tarter (Eds.), *Sourcebook on substance abuse: Etiology, epidemiology, assessment, and treatment* (pp. 1–13). Boston: Allyn & Bacon.

Cost, quality, and child outcome in child care centers. (1995). Economics Department, University of Colorado at Denver, Denver, CO.

Cote, L. R., & Bornstein, M. H. (2000a). Mother–infant interaction and acculturation II: Behavioural coherence and correspondence in Japanese American and South American families. *International Journal of Behavioural Development, 25*, 564–576.

Cote, L. R., & Bornstein, M. H. (2000b). Social and didactic parenting behaviors and beliefs among Japanese American and South American mothers of infants. *Infancy, 1*, 363–374.

Cote, L. R., & Bornstein, M. H. (2001). Mother–infant interaction and acculturation II: Behavioral coherence and correspondence in Japanese American and South American families. *International Journal of Behavioral Development, 25*, 564–576.

Cowan, C. P., & Cowan, P. A. (1992). *When partners become parents*. New York: Basic Books.

Cowan, N. (Ed.). (1997). *The development of memory in childhood. Studies in developmental psychology*. Hove, England: Psychology Press.

Craton, L. G., & Yonas, A. (1990). The role of motion in infants' perception of occlusion. In T. E. James (Ed.), *Advances in psychology: 69. The development of attention: Research and theory*. Amsterdam: North-Holland.

Creasey, G. L., Jarvis, P. A., & Berk, L. E. (1998). Play and social competence. In O. N. Saracho & B. Spodek (Eds.), Multiple perspectives on play and early childhood education: Inquiries and insights (pp. 116–143). Albany: State University of New York Press.

Crittenden, P. M., Lang, C., Claussen, A. H., & Partridge, M. F. (2000). Relations among mothers' dispositional representations of parenting. In P. M. Crittenden & A. H. Claussen (Eds.), *The organization of attachment relationships: Maturation, culture, and context* (pp. 214–248). Cambridge, England: Cambridge University Press.

Crockenberg, S. B. (1981). Infant irritability, mother responsiveness, and social support influences on the security of infant–mother attachment. *Child Development, 52*, 857–865.

Crockenberg, S. B. (1988). Social suport and parenting. In H. E. Fitzgerald, B. M. Lester, & M. W. Yogman (Eds.), *Theory and research in behavioral pediatrics* (Vol. 4, pp. 141–174). New York: Plenum.

Cumming, E. M., & Cummings, J. S. (2002). Parenting and attachment. In M. H. Bornstein (Ed.), *Handbook of parenting: Vol. 5. Practical parenting* (pp. 35–58). Mahwah, NJ: Lawrence Erlbaum Associates.

Dannemiller, J. L., & Freedland, R. L. (1991). Detection of relative motion by human infants. *Developmental Psychology, 27*, 67–78.

Darwin, C. R. (1859). *The origin of species*. London: Murray.

Darwin, C. R. (1875). *The expression of the emotions in man and animals*. Chicago: University of Chicago Press. (Original work published 1872.)

Darwin, C. R. (1877). A biographical sketch of an infant. *Mind, 2*, 286–294.

Davies, P. T., & Cummings, E. M. (1998). Exploring children's emotional security as a mediator of the link between marital relations and child adjustment. *Child Development, 69*, 124–139.

Davis, C. M. (1928). Self-selection of diet by newly weaned infants. *American Journal of Diseases of Children, 36*, 651–679.

Davis, C. M. (1934). Studies in the self-selection of diet by young children. *Journal of the American Dental Association, 21*, 636–640.

Davis, C. M. (1935). Choice of formulas made by three infants throughout the nursing period. *American Journal of Diseases, 50*, 385–394.

Davis, C. M. (1939). Results of the self-selection of diets by young children. *Canadian Medical Association Journal, 41*, 257–261.

Dawson, G. (1994a). Development of emotional expression and emotion regulation in infancy: Contributions of the frontal lobe. In G. Dawson & K. W. Fischer (Eds.), *Human behavior and the developing brain* (pp. 346–379). New York: Guilford.

Dawson, G. (1994b). Frontal electroencephalographic correlates of individual differences in emotion expression in infants: A brain systems perspective on emotion. *Monographs of the Society for Research in Child Development, 59*(2–3), 135–151.

Dawson, G., Ashman, S. B., & Carver, L. J. (2000). The role of early experience in shaping behavioral and brain development and its implications for social policy. *Development and Psychopathology, 12*, 695–712.

Dawson, G., Klinger, L. G., Panagiotides, H., Hill, D., & Spieker, S. (1992). Frontal lobe activity and affective behavior of infants of mothers with depressive symptoms. *Child Development, 63*, 725–737.

Deàk, G. O. (2000). Hunting the fox of word learning: Why "constraints" fail to capture it. *Departmental Review, 20*, 29–80.

Deater-Deckard, K., & Plomin, R. (1999). An adoption study of the etiology of teacher and parent reports of externalizing behavior problems in middle childhood. *Child Development, 70,* 144–154.

Décarie, T. G. (1969). A study of the mental and emotional development of the thalidomide child. In B. M. Foss (Ed.), *Determinants of infant behavior* (Vol. 4). London: Methuen.

Décarie, T. G., & Ricard, M. (1996). Revisiting Piaget revisited or the vulnerability of Piaget's infancy theory in the 1990s. In G. G. Noam & K. W. Fischer (Eds.), *Development and vulnerability in close relationships* (pp. 113–132). Mahwah, NJ: Lawrence Erlbaum Associates.

DeCasper, A. J., & Fifer, W. P. (1980). Of human bonding: Newborns prefer their mothers' voices. *Science, 208,* 1174–1176.

DeCasper, A. J., Lecanuet, J. P., Busnel, M. C., Granier-Deferre, C., & Maugeais, R. (1994). Fetal reactions to recurrent maternal speech. *Infant Behavior and Development, 17,* 159–164.

De Chateau, P. (1980). Parent–neonate interaction and its long term effects. In E. G. Simmel (Ed.), *Early experiences and early behavior.* New York: Academic.

DeLoache, J. S., & Smith, C. M. (1999). Early symbolic representation. In I. E. Sigel (Ed.), *Development of mental representation: Theories and applications* (pp. 61–86). Mahwah, NJ: Lawrence Erlbaum Associates.

Dempster, F. N., & Brainerd, C. J. (Eds.). (1995). *Interference and inhibition in cognition* (pp. 175–204). San Diego, CA: Academic.

Denham, S. A. (1998). *Emotional development in young children.* New York: Guilford.

Dennis, W. (1940). Infant reaction to restraint. *Transactions of the New York Academy of Science, 2,* 211–212.

Dennis, W. (1949). Historical beginnings of child psychology. *Psychological Bulletin, 46,* 224–235.

Dennis, W., & Dennis, M. G. (1940). The effect of cradling practices upon the onset of walking in Hopi children. *Journal of Genetic Psychology, 56,* 77–86.

Denzin, N. K. (1992). A phenomenological analysis of social referencing. In S. Feinman (Ed.), *Social referencing and the social construction of reality in infancy* (pp. 95–114). New York: Plenum.

DePanfilis, D., & Zuravin, S. J. (1999). Predicting child maltreatment recurrences during treatment. *Child Abuse and Neglect, 23,* 729–743.

De Saint Victor, C., Smith, P. H., & Loboschefski, T. (1997). Ten-month-old infants' retrieval of familiar information from short-term memory. *Infant Behavior and Development, 20,* 111–122.

Descartes, R. (1824). La dioptrique. In V. Coursin (Ed.), *Oeuvres de Descartes* (M. D. Boring, Trans.). Paris: n.p. (Original work published 1638.)

De Schonen, S., Deruelle, C., Mancini, J., & Pascalis, O. (1996). Pattern processing in infancy: Hemispheric differences and brain maturation. In F. Vital-Durand, J. Atkinson, & O. J.

Braddick (Eds.), *Infant vision* (pp. 327–344). Oxford, England: Oxford University Press.

Devlin, B., Fienberg, S. E., Resnick, D. P., & Roeder, K. (1995). Galton redux: Intelligence, race, and society: A review of the bell curve: Intelligence and class structure in American life. *American Statistician, 90,* 1483–1488.

De Wolff, M. S., & van IJzendoorn, M. H. (1997). Sensitivity and attachment: A meta-analysis of parental antecedents of infant attachment. *Child Development, 68,* 571–591.

Diamond, A. E., Werker, J. F., & Lalonde, C. (1994). Toward understanding commonalities in the development of object search, detour navigation, categorization, and speech perception. In G. Dawson & K. W. Fischer (Eds.), *Human behavior and the developing brain* (pp. 380–426). New York: Guilford.

Dichter-Blancher, T. B., Busch-Rossnagel, N. A., & Knauf-Jensen, D. E. (1997). Mastery motivation: Appropriate tasks for toddlers. *Infant Behavior and Development, 20,* 545–548.

Dickstein, S., & Parke, R. D. (1988). Social referencing in infancy: A glance at fathers and marriage. *Child Development, 59,* 506–511.

Dickstein, S., Thompson, R. A., Estes, D., Malkin, C., & Lamb, M. E. (1984). Social referencing and the security of attachment. *Infant Behavior and Development, 7,* 507–516.

Diener, M. L., Goldstein, L. H., & Mangelsdorf, S. C. (1995). The role of prenatal expectations in parents' reports of infant temperament. *Merrill-Palmer Quarterly, 41,* 172–190.

Dienstbier, R. A. (1989). Arousal and physiological toughness: Implications for mental and physical health. *Psychological Review, 96,* 84–100.

Dieter, J. N. I., & Emory, E. K. (1997). Supplemental stimulation of premature infants: A treatment model. *Journal of Pediatric Psychology, 22,* 281–295.

DiLalla, L. F., Thompson, L. A., Plomin, R., Phillips, K., Fagan, J. F., Haith, M. M., Cyphers, L. H., & Fulker, D. W. (1990). Infant predictors of preschool and adult IQ: A study of infant twins and their parents. *Developmental Psychology, 26,* 759–769.

DiPietro, J. A., & Allen, M. C. (1991). Estimation of gestational age: Implications for developmental research. *Child Development, 62,* 1184–1199.

DiPietro, J. A., Bornstein, M. H., Costigan, K. A., Pressman, E. K., Hahn, C. S., Painter, K. M., Smith, B. A., & Yi, L. J. (2002). What does fetal movement predict about behavior during the first two years of life? *Developmental Psychobiology.*

Dixon, R. A., & Lerner, R. M. (1999). History and systems in developmental psychology. In M. H. Bornstein & M. E. Lamb (Eds.), *Developmental psychology: An advanced textbook* (4th ed., pp. 3–45). Mahwah, NJ: Lawrence Erlbaum Associates.

Dobbing, J. (1968). Vulnerable periods in developing brain. In A. N. Davison & J. Dobbing (Eds.), *Applied neurochemistry*. Oxford, England: Blackwell.

Dobbing, J., & Sands, J. C. (1973). The quantitative growth and development of the human brain. *Archives of Diseases of Childhood, 48,* 757–767.

Dollard, J., & Miller, N. (1950). *Personality and psychotherapy.* New York: McGraw-Hill.

Dore, J. (1978). Variation in preschool children's conversational performances. In K. Nelson (Ed.), *Children's language* (Vol. 1). New York: Gardner.

Dougherty, T. M., & Haith, M. M. (1997). Infant expectations and reaction time as predictors of childhood speed of processing and IQ. *Developmental Psychology, 33,* 146–155.

Doussard-Roosevelt, J. A., & Porges, S. W. (1999). The role of neurobehavioral organization in stress responses: A polyvagal model. In M. Lewis & D. Ramsay (Eds.), *Soothing and stress* (pp. 57–76). Mahwah, NJ: Lawrence Erlbaum Associates.

Doussard-Roosevelt, J., Porges, S. W., & McClenny, B. D. (1996). Behavioral sleep states in very low birth weight preterm neonates: Relation to neonatal health and vagal maturation. *Journal of Pediatric Psychology, 21,* 785–802.

Doussard-Roosevelt, J. A., Porges, S. W., Scanlon, J. W., Alemi, B., & Scanlon, K. B. (1997). Vagal regulation of heart rate in the prediction of developmental outcome for very low birth weight preterm infants. *Child Development, 68,* 173–186.

Dreyfus-Brisac, C. (1968). Sleep ontogenesis in early human prematurity from 24 to 27 weeks of conceptional age. *Developmental Psychology, 1,* 162–169.

Dromi, E. (1987). *Early lexical development.* Cambridge, England: Cambridge University Press.

Dubowitz, L., & Dubowitz, V. (1981). *The neurological assessment of the preterm and fullterm newborn infant* (Clinics in Developmental Medicine, No. 79). London: Spastics International Medical Publications.

Duffy, F. H. (1994). The role of quantified electroencephalography in psychological research. In G. Dawson & K. W. Fischer (Eds.), *Human behavior and the developing brain* (pp. 93–133). New York: Guilford.

Duncan, G. J., Brooks-Gunn, J., & Klebanov, P. K. (1994). Economic deprivation and early childhood development. *Child Development, 65,* 296–318.

Duncan, S. C., Duncan, T. E., & Hops, H. (1996). Analysis of longitudinal data within accelerated longitudinal designs. *Psychological Methods, 1,* 236–248.

Dunn, J. (1988). *The beginnings of social understanding.* Cambridge: Harvard University Press.

Dunn, J. (2000a). Mind-reading, emotion understanding, and relationships. *International Journal of Behavioral Development, 24,* 142–144.

Dunn, J. (2000b). State of the art: Siblings. *Psychologist, 13,* 244–248.

Dunn, J., & Kendrick, C. (1980). The arrival of a sibling: Changes in patterns of interaction between mother and first-born child. *Journal of Child Psychology and Psychiatry, 21,* 119–132.

Dunn, J., & Kendrick, C. (1981). Interaction between young siblings: Associations with the interactions between mothers and first-born. *Developmental Psychology, 17,* 336–343.

Dunn, J., & Kendrick, C. (1982a). *Siblings: Love, envy, and understanding.* Cambridge, MA: Harvard University Press.

Dunn, J., & Kendrick, C. (1982b). Siblings and their mothers: Relationships within the family. In M. E. Lamb & B. Sutton-Smith (Eds.), *Sibling relationships: Their nature and significance across the life span* (pp. 39–60). Hillsdale, NJ: Lawrence Erlbaum Associates.

Dunn, J., & Kendrick, C. (1982c). The speech of two- and three-year-olds to infant siblings: "Baby talk" and the context of communication. *Journal of Child Language, 9,* 579–595.

Dunn, J., & Plomin, R. (1991). *Separate lives: Why siblings are so different.* New York: Basic Books.

Durkin, D. (1966). *Children who read early.* New York: Teachers College Press.

Eaton, W. O., & Enns, L. R. (1986). Sex differences in human motor activity level. *Psychological Bulletin, 100,* 19–28.

Eckerman, C. O., & Oehler, J. M. (1992). Very-low-birthweight newborns and parents as early social partners. In I. E. Sigel (Series Ed.) & S. L. Friedman & M. D. Sigman (Eds.), *The psychological development of low birthweight children* (pp. 91–123). Norwood, NJ: Ablex.

Eckerman, C. O., Oehler, J. M., Hannan, T. E., & Molitor, A. (1995). The development prior to term age of very prematurely born newborns' responsiveness in face exchanges. *Infant Behavior and Development, 18,* 283–297.

Edwards, D. D., & Edwards, J. S. (1970). Fetal movement: Development and time course. *Science, 169,* 95–97.

Eimas, P. D. (1975). Speech perception in early infancy. In L. B. Cohen & P. Salapatek (Eds.), *Infant perception: From sensation to cognition* (Vol. 2). New York: Academic.

Eimas, P. D., Siqueland, E. R., Jusczyk, P., & Vigorito, J. (1971). Speech perception in infants. *Science, 171,* 303–306.

Eisenberg, N., Fabes, R. A., & Losoya, S. (1997). Emotional responding: Regulation, social correlates, and socialization. In P. Solovey & D. J. Sluyter (Eds.), *Emotional development and emotional intelligence: Educational implications* (pp. 129–167). New York: Basic Books.

Eisenberg, N., Wolchik, S. A., Hernandez, R., & Pasternack, J. F. (1985). Parental socialization of young children's play: A short-term longitudinal study. *Child Development, 56,* 1506–1513.

Eisert, D., & Lamorey, S. (1996). Play as a window on child development: The relationship between play and other developmental domains. *Early Education and Development, 7,* 221–235.

Ekman, P. (1984). Expression and the nature of emotion. In K. R. Scherer & P. Ekman (Eds.), *Approaches to emotion* (pp. 319–343). Hillsdale, NJ: Lawrence Erlbaum Associates.

Ekman, P., & Friesen, W. (1976). Measuring facial movement. *Environmental Psychology and Verbal Behavior, 1,* 56–75.

Ekman, P., & Friesen, W. (1978). *Facial action coding system.* Palo Alto, CA: Consulting Psychologists Press.

Ekman, P., & Oster, H. (1979). Facial expressions of emotion. In M. R. Rosenzweig & L. W. Porter (Eds.), *Annual review of psychology.* Palo Alto, CA: Annual Reviews.

Elbers, L., & Ton, J. (1985). Play pen monologues: The interplay of words and babbles in the first words period. *Journal of Child Language, 12,* 551–565.

Elias, G., & Broerse, J. (1996). Development changes in the incidence and likelihood of simultaneous talk during the first two years: A question of function. *Journal of Child Language, 23,* 201–217.

Elias, G., Hayes, A., & Broerse, J. (1986). Maternal control of co-vocalization and inter-speaker silences in mother–infant vocal engagements. *Journal of Child Psychology and Psychiatry, 27,* 409–415.

Elias, G., Hayes, A., & Broerse, J. (1988). Aspects of structure and content of maternal talk with infants. *Journal of Child Psychology and Psychiatry, 29,* 523–531.

Eliot, L. (1999). *What's going on in there? How the brain and mind develop in the first five years of life.* New York: Bantam Books.

Ellis, L., & Ebertz, L. (Eds.). (1998). *Males, females, and behavior: Toward biological understanding.* Westport, CT: Praeger.

Elman, J. L., Bates, E. A., Johnson, M. H., Karmiloff-Smith, A., Parisi, D., & Plunkett, K. (1996). *Rethinking innateness: A connectionist perspective on development.* Cambridge, MA: MIT Press.

Emde, R. N., & Harmon, R. J. (1972). Endogenous and exogenous smiling systems in early infancy. *Journal of the American Academy of Child Psychiatry, 11,* 177–200.

Emde, R. N., & Hewitt, J. K. (Eds.). (2001). *Infancy to early childhood: Genetic and environmental influences on developmental change.* New York: Oxford University Press.

Entwisle, D. R., & Astone, N. M. (1994). Some practical guidelines for measuring youth's race, ethnicity and socioeconomic status. *Child Development, 65,* 1521–1540.

Erickson, M., Sroufe, L. A., & Egeland, B. (1985). The relationship between quality of attachment and behavior problems in preschool in a high-risk sample. In I. Bretherton & E. Waters (Eds.), *Growing point in attachment theory and research* (pp. 147–161). *Monographs of the Society for Research in Child Development, 50* (1–2, Serial No. 209).

Erikson, E. H. (1950). *Childhood and society.* New York: Norton.

Erikson, E. H. (1977). *Toys and reason.* New York: Norton.

Erting, C. J., Thumann-Prezioso, C., & Benedict, B. S. (2000). Bilingualism in a deaf family: Fingerspelling in early childhood. In P. E. Spencer & C. J. Erting (Eds.), *The deaf child in the family and at school: Essays in honor of Kathryn P. Meadow-Orlans* (pp. 41–54). Mahwah, NJ: Lawrence Erlbaum Associates.

Ervin-Tripp, S. (1973). *Language acquisition and communication.* Stanford, CA: Stanford University Press.

Escalona, S. K., & Corman, H. (1969). *Albert Einstein scales of sensorimotor development.* New York: Einstein College of Medicine of Yeshiva University.

Essock, E. A. (1980). The oblique effect of stimulus identification considered with respect to two classes of oblique effects. *Perception, 9,* 37–46.

Etzel, B., & Gewirtz, J. (1967). Experimental modification of caretaker-maintained high rate operant crying in a 6- and a 20-week-old infant. (*Infans tyrannotearus*): Extinction of crying with reinforcement of eye contact and smiling. *Journal of Experimental Child Psychology, 5,* 303–317.

Eyer, D. E. (1992a). The bonding hype. In M. E. Lamb & J. B. Lancaster (Eds.), *Birth management: Biosocial perspectives.* Hawthorne, NY: de Gruyter.

Eyer, D. E. (1992b). *Mother–infant bonding: A scientific fiction.* New Haven, CT: Yale University Press.

Eyer, D. E. (1994). Mother–infant bodnig: A scientific fiction. *Human Nature, 5,* 69–94.

Fagan, J. F., & Vasen, J. H. (1997). Selective attention to novelty as a measure of information processing across the lifespan. In J. A. Burack & J. T. Enns (Eds.), *Attention development and psychopathology* (pp. 55–73). New York: Guilford.

Fagen, J. W., & Ohr, P. S. (1990). Individual differences in infant conditioning and memory. In J. Colombo & J. Fagen (Eds.), *Individual differences in infancy: Reliability, stability, prediction* (pp. 155–192). Hillsdale, NJ: Lawrence Erlbaum Associates.

Fagot, B. I. (1995). Psychsocial and cognitive determinants of early gender-role development. *Annual Review of Sex Research, 6,* 1–31.

Fagot, B. I., & Leinbach, M. D. (1993). Gender-role development in young children: From discrimination to labeling. *Developmental Review, 13,* 205–224.

Fagot, B. I., Rodgers, C. S., & Leinbach, M. D. (2000). Theories of gender socialization. In T. Eckes & H. M. Trautner (Ed.), *The developmental social psychology of gender* (pp. 65–89). Mahwah, NJ: Lawrence Erlbaum Associates.

Fantz, R. L. (1964). Visual experience in infants: Decreased attention to familiar patterns relative to novel ones. *Science, 146,* 668–670.

Fantz, R. L., Ordy, J. M., & Udelf, M. S. (1962). Maturation of pattern vision in infants during the first six months. *Journal of Comparative and Physiological Psychology, 55,* 907–917.

Farber, A. F., Yanni, C. C., & Batshaw, M. L. (1997). Nutrition: Good and bad. In M. L. Batshaw (Ed.), *Children with disabilities* (4th ed., pp. 182–210). Baltimore: Brookes.

Feagans, L., & Farran, D. C. (Eds.). (1982). *The language of children reared in poverty.* New York: Academic.

Fearon, I., Harrison, L. L., Muir, D. W., & Kisilevsky, B. S. (1996, April). *Naturalistic parental touch in the NICU: Developmental changes in preterm infants' behavioural and physiological responses.* Paper presented at the International Conference on Infant Studies, Providence, RI.

Fein, G. G. (1991). Bloodsuckers, blisters, cooked babies, and other curiosities: Affective themes in pretense. In F. S. Kessel, M. H. Bornstein, & A. J. Sameroff (Eds.), *Contemporary constructions of the child* (pp. 143–157). Hillsdale, NJ: Lawrence Erlbaum Associates.

Fein, G. G., & Apfel, A. (1979). The development of play: Style, structure and situation. *Genetic Psychology Monographs, 99,* 231–250.

Feiring, C., Lewis, M., & Starr, M. D. (1984). Indirect effects and infants' reactions to strangers. *Developmental Psychology, 20,* 485–491.

Feldman, R., & Greenbaum, C. W. (1997). Affect regulation and synchrony in mother–infant play as precursors to the development of symbolic competence. *Infant Mental Health Journal, 18,* 4–23.

Feldman, R., Greenbaum, C. W., & Yirmiya, N. (1999). Mother–infant synchrony as an antecedent of the emergence of self-control. *Developmental Psychology, 35,* 223–231.

Fenichel, E., Lurie-Hurvitz, E., & Griffin, A. (1999). Seizing the moment to build momentum for quality infant/toddler child care: Highlights of the Child Bureau and Head Start Bureau's National Leadership Forum on Quality Care for Infants and Toddlers. *Zero to Three, 19,* 3–17.

Fenson, L., & Ramsay, D. (1980). Decentration and integration of the child's play in the second year. *Child Development, 51,* 171–178.

Fenson, L., Dale, P., Reznick, S., Hartung, J., & Burgess, S. (1990). *Norms for the MacArthur Communicative Development Inventories.* Poster presented at the International Conference on Infant Studies, Montreal, Canada.

Fernald, A. (1985). Four-month-old infants prefer to listen to motherese. *Infant Behavior and Development, 8,* 181–182.

Fernald, A. (1989). Intonation and communicative intent in mothers' speech to infants: Is the melody the message? *Child Development, 60,* 1497–1510.

Fernald, A. (1992). Meaningful melodies in mothers' speech to infants. In H. Papoušek, U. Jürgens, & M. Papoušek (Eds.), *Origins and development of nonverbal vocal communication: Evolutionary, comparative, and methodological aspects* (pp. 262–282). Cambridge, England: Cambridge University Press.

Fernald, A. (1998). Approval and disapproval: Infant responsiveness to vocal affect in familiar and unfamiliar languages. *Child development, 64,* 657–674.

Fernald, A., & Kuhl, P. (1987). Acoustic determinants of infant preference for motherese speech. *Infant Behavior and Development, 10,* 279–293.

Fernald, A., & Mazzie, C. (1991). Prosody and focus in speech to infants and adults. *Developmental Psychology, 27,* 209–221.

Fernald, A., Pinto, J. P., Swingley, D., Weinberg, A., & McRoberts, G. W. (1998). Rapid gains in speed of verbal processing by infants in the 2nd year. *Psychological Science, 9,* 228–231.

Fernald, A., & Simon, T. (1984). Expanded intonation contours in mothers' speech to newborns. *Developmental Psychology, 20,* 104–113.

Fernald, A., McRoberts, G., & Swingley, D. (2001). Infants' developing competence in recognizing and understanding words in fluent speech. In J. Weissenborn & B. Höhle (Eds.), *Approaches to bootstrapping in early languages acquisition* (Vol. 1, pp. 97–123). Amsterdam: Benjamins.

Fernald, A., Taeschner, T., Dunn, J., Papoušek, M., Boysson-Bardies, B., & Fukui, I. (1989). A cross-language study of prosodic modifications in mothers' and fathers' speech to preverbal infants. *Journal of Child Language, 16,* 477–501.

Field, T. (1987). Affective and interactive disturbances in infants. In J. D. Osofsky (Ed.), *Handbook of infant development* (2nd ed., pp. 972–1005). New York: Wiley.

Field, T. (1995). Infant massage therapy. In T. M. Field (Ed.), *Touch in early development* (pp. 105–114). Mahwah, NJ: Lawrence Erlbaum Associates.

Field, T. (1998). Maternal cocaine use and fetal development. In E. A. Blechman & K. D. Brownell (Eds.), *Behavioral medicine and women: A comprehensive handbook* (pp. 27–30). New York: Guilford.

Field, T. (2000). Infant massage therapy. In C. H. Zeanah (Ed.), *Handbook of infant mental health* (2nd ed., pp. 494–500). New York: Guilford.

Field, T., Healy, B., Goldstein, S., Perry, S., Bendell, D., Schanberg, S., Zimmerman, E. A., & Kuhn, C. (1988). Infants of depressed mothers show "depressed" behavior even with nondepressed adults. *Child Development, 59,* 1569–1579.

Field, T., Pickens, J., Fox, N. A., Gonzalez, J., & Nawrocki, T. (1998). Facial expression and EEG responses to happy and sad faces/voices by 3-month-old infants of depressed mothers. *British Journal of Developmental Psychology, 16,* 485–494.

Field, T. M. (1982). Individual differences in the expressivity of neonates and young infants. In R. Feldman (Ed.), *Development of nonverbal behavior in children.* New York: Springer-Verlag.

Field, T. M., Woodson, R. W., Greenberg, R., & Cohen, C. (1982). Discrimination and imitation of facial expressions by neonates. *Science, 218,* 179–181.

Fields, S. A., & Wall, E. M. (1993). Obstetric analgesia and anesthesia. *Primary Care, 20,* 705–712.

Fischer, K. W. (1980). A theory of cognitive development: The control and construction of hierarchies of skills. *Psychological Review, 87,* 477–531.

Fischer, K. W. (1996). Infants' construction of actions in context: Piaget's contribution to research on early development. *Psychological Science, 7,* 204–210.

Fischer, K. W., & Silvern, L. (1985). Stages and individual differences in cognitive development. *Annual Review Psychology, 36,* 613–648.

Fiscus, S. A., Adimora, A. A., Schoenbach, V. J., Lim, W., McKinney, R., Rupar, D., Kenny, J., Woods, C., & Wilfert, C. (1996). Perinatal HIV infection and the effect of zidovudine therapy on transmission in rural and urban counties. *Journal of the American Medical Association, 275,* 1483–1488.

Fish, M. (1998). Negative emotionality and positive/social behavior in rural Appalachian infants: Prediction from caregiver and infant characteristics. *Infant Behavior and Development, 21,* 685–698.

Fisher, C. B., Ferdinandsen, K., & Bornstein, M. H. (1981). The role of symmetry in infant form perception. *Child Development, 52,* 457–462.

Fisher, C. B., Hatashita-Wong, M., & Greene, L. I. (1999). Ethical and legal issues. In W. K. Silverman & T. H. Ollendick (Eds.), *Developmental issues in the clinical treatment of children* (pp. 470–486). Boston: Allyn & Bacon.

Fivush, R. (1997). Event memory in early childhood. In C. Hulme (Series Ed.) & N. Cowan (Ed.), *The development of memory in childhood. Studies in developmental psychology* (pp. 139–161). Hove, England: Psychology Press.

Floccia, C., & Christophe, A. (1997). High-amplitude sucking and newborns: The quest for underlying mechanisms. *Journal of Experimental Child Psychology, 64,* 175–198.

Fogel, A., Dickson, K. L., Hsu, H. C., Messinger, D., Nelson-Goens, G. C., & Nwokah, E. (1997). Communication of smiling and laughter in mother–infant play: Research on emotion from a dynamic systems perspective. *New directions for child development, 77,* 5–24.

Fox, N. A., & Calkins, S. D. (2000). Multiple-measure approaches to the study of infant emotion. In M. Lewis & J. M. Haviland-Jones (Eds.), *Handbook of emotions* (2nd ed., pp. 203–219). New York: Guilford.

Fox, N. A., Henderson, H. A., Rubin, K. H., Calkins, S. D., & Schmidt, L. A. (2001). Continuity and discontinuity of behavioral inhibition and exuberance: Psychophysiological and behavioral influences across the first four years of life. *Child Development, 72,* 1–21.

Fracasso, M. P., Busch-Rossnagel, N. A., & Fisher, C. B. (1993). The relationship of maternal behavior and acculturation in the quality of attachment in Hispanic infants living in New York City. *Hispanic Journal of Behavioral Sciences, 16,* 143–154.

Fraiberg, S. (1977). *Insights from the blind.* New York: Basic Books.

Frankel, K. A., & Bates, J. E. (1990). Mother–toddler problem solving: Antecedents in attachment, home behavior, and temperament. *Child Development, 61,* 810–819.

Fraser, A. M., & Brockert, J. E. (1995). Association of young maternal age with adverse reproductive outcomes. *New England Journal of Medicine, 332,* 1113–1117.

Freedman, D. (1974). *Human infancy: An evolutionary perspective.* Hillsdale, NJ: Lawrence Erlbaum Associates.

Fretts, R. C., Schmittdiel, J., McLean, F. H., Usher, R. H., & Goldman, M. B. (1995). Increased maternal age and the risk of fetal death. *The New England Journal of Medicine, 333,* 953–957.

Freud, S. (1965). *Normality and pathology in childhood.* New York: International Universities Press.(Original work published.)

Freud, S. (1949). *An outline of psycho-analysis.* Norton: New York.

Freud, S. (1962). Screen memories. In J. Strachey (Ed. & Trans.), *The standard edition of the complete psychological works of Sigmund Freud* (Vol. 3, pp. 303–322). London: Hogarth. (Original work published 1899.)

Freud, S. (1966). *Introductory lectures on psychoanalysis* (J. Strachey, Trans. & Ed.). New York: Norton. (Original work published 1916–1917.)

Fried, P. A. (1993). Prenatal exposure to tobacco and marijuana: Effects during pregnancy, infancy, and early childhood. *Clinical Obstetrics and Gynecology, 36,* 319–337.

Friedman, S. L., & Sigman, M. D. (1992). Past, present, and future directions in research on the development of low-birthweight children. In S. L. Friedman & M. D. Sigman (Eds.), *The psychological development of low-birthweight children. Annual Advances in Applied Developmental Psychology* (Vol. 6, pp. 3–22). Norwood, NJ: Ablex.

Frijda, N. H. (2000). The psychologists' point of view. In M. Lewis & J. M. Haviland-Jones (Eds.), *Handbook of emotions* (2nd ed., pp. 59–74). New York: Guilford.

Frodi, A. M. (1985). When empathy fails: Aversive infant crying and child abuse: In B. M. Lester & C. F. Z. Boukydis (Eds.), *Infant crying: Theoretical and research perspectives* (pp. 263–277). New York: Plenum.

Frodi, A. M., Lamb, M. E., & Wille, D. (1981). Mothers' responses to the cries of normal and premature infants as a function of the birth status of their child. *Journal of Research in Personality, 15,* 122–133.

Fullilove, M. T. (1993). Minority women: Ecological setting and intercultural dialogue. In D. E. Stewart & N. L. Stotland (Eds.), *Psychological aspects of women's health care: The interface between psychiatry and obstetrics and gynecology* (pp. 519–539). Washington, DC: American Psychiatry Press.

Furman, W., & Giberson, R. S. (1995). Identifying the links between parents and their children's sibling relationships. In S. Strauss (Series Ed.) & S. Shulman (Vol. Ed.), *Human development: Vol. 7. Close relationships and socioemotional development* (pp. 95–108). Norwood, NJ: Ablex.

Furrow, D., & Nelson, K. (1986). A further look at the motherese hypothesis: A reply to Gleitman, Newport, and Gleitman. *Journal of Child Language, 13,* 163–176.

Furrow, D., Nelson, K., & Benedict, H. (1979). Mothers' speech to children and syntactic development: Some simple relationships. *Journal of Child Language, 6,* 423–442.

Gaensbauer, T. J. (1980). Anaclitic depression in a three-and-a-half-month-old child. *American Journal of Psychiatry, 137,* 841–842.

Gaensbauer, T. J., & Hiatt, S. (1984). Facial communication of emotion in early infancy. In N. A. Fox & R. J. Davidson (Eds.), *The psychobiology of affective development.* Hillsdale, NJ: Lawrence Erlbaum Associates.

Galinsky, E., Howes, C., Kontos, S., & Shinn, M. (1994). *The study of children in family child care and relative care.* New York: Families and Work Institute.

Galper, A., Wigfield, A., & Seefeldt, C. (1997). Head Start parents' beliefs about their children's abilities, task values, and performances on different activities. *Child Development, 68,* 897–907.

Ganchrow, J. R., Steiner, J. E., & Daher, M. (1983). Neonatal facial expressions in response to different qualities and intensities of gustatory stimuli. *Infant Behavior and Development, 6,* 189–200.

Gandour, M. J. (1989). Activity level as a dimension of temperament in toddlers: Its relevance

for the organismic specificity hypothesis. *Child Development, 60,* 1092–1098.

Garmel, S. H., & D'Alton, M. E. (1994). Diagnostic ultrasound in pregnancy: An overview. *Seminars in Perinatology, 18,* 117–132.

Garcia, M. M., Shaw, D. S., Winslow, E. B., & Yaggi, K. E. (1997, April). Sibling conflict and the development of externalizing behavior problems in young children. In D. Teti (Chair), *Sibling relationships at risk.* Symposium conducted at the biennial meeting of the Society for Research in Child Development, Washington, DC.

Garnica, O. K. (1977). Some prosodic and paralinguistic features of speech to young children. In C. Snow & C. Ferguson (Eds.), *Talking to children: Language input and acquisition.* Cambridge, England: Cambridge University Press.

Garrett, P., Ng'andu, N., & Ferron, J. (1994). Poverty experiences of young children and the quality of their home environments. *Child Development, 65,* 331–345.

Gaskins, S. (1999). Children's daily lives in a Mayan village: A case study of culturally constructed roles and activities. In A. Goncu (Ed.), *Children's engagement in the world: Sociocultural perspectives* (pp. 25–60). New York: Cambridge University Press.

Gazzaniga, M. S. (1970). *The bisected brain.* New York: Appleton-Century-Crofts.

Geber, M. (1956). Developpement psychomoteur del'enfantafricain. *Courrier, 6,* 17–28.

Geber, M., & Dean, R. F. A. (1957a). Gesell tests on African children. *Pediatrics, 20,* 1055–1065.

Geber, M., & Dean, R. F. A. (1957b). The state of development of newborn African children. *Lancet, 272,* 1216–1219.

Gelfand, D. M., & Teti, D. M. (1990). The effects of maternal depression on children. *Clinical Psychology Review, 10,* 329–353.

Gelman, S. A., & Diesendruck, G. (1999a). A reconsideration of concepts: On the compatibility of psychological essentialism and context sensitivity. In E. K. Scholnick, K. Nelson, S. A. Gelman, & P. H. Miller (Eds.), *Conceptual development: Piaget's legacy* (pp. 79–102). Mahwah, NJ: Lawrence Erlbaum Associates.

Gelman, S. A., & Diesendruck, G. (1999b). What's in a concept? Context, variability, and psychological essentialism. In I. E. Sigel (Ed.), *Development of mental representation: Theories and applications* (pp. 87–111). Mahwah, NJ: Lawrence Erlbaum Associates.

Gentner, D. (1982). Why nouns are learned before verbs: Linguistic relativity versus natural partitioning. In S. S. Kuczaj II (Ed.), *Language development: Vol. 2. Language, thought, and culture.* Hillsdale, NJ: Lawrence Erlbaum Associates.

Gentner, D. (1978). What looks like a jiggy but acts like a zimbo? A study of early word meaning using artificial objects. *Paper and Reports on Child Language Development, 15,* 1–6.

George, C., Kaplan, N., & Main, M. (1985). *An adult attachment interview.* Unpublished manuscript, University of California at Berkeley, Department of Psychology.

Georgieff, M. K. (1994). Nutritional deficiencies as developmental risk factors: Commentary on Pollit and Gorman. In C. A. Nelson (Ed.), *Minnesota Symposia on Child Development* (Vol. 27, pp. 145–159). Hillsdale, NJ: Lawrence Erlbaum Associates.

Gesell, A. (1945). *The embryology of behavior.* New York: Harper & Row.

Gesell, A. (1954). The ontogenesis of infant behavior. In L. Carmichael (Ed.), *Manual of child psychology* (2nd ed.). New York: Wiley.

Gesell, A., & Ames, L. B. (1937). Early evidences of individuality. *Human Infant Scientific Monthly, 45,* 217–225.

Gesell, A. L., & Armatruda, C. S. (1945). *The embryology of behavior: The beginnings of the human mind.* New York: Harper.

Gesell, A. L., & Armatruda, C. S. (1962). *Developmental diagnosis: Normal and abnormal child development, clinical methods, and practical applications* (3rd ed.). New York: Harper.

Gewirtz, J. L., & Pelaez-Nogueras, M. (2000). Infant emotions under the positive-reinforcer control of caregiver attention and touch. In J. C. Leslie & D. Blackman (Eds.), *Experimental and applied analysis of human behavior* (pp. 271–291). Reno, NV: Context.

Ghim, H. R. (1990). Evidence for perceptual organization in infants: Perception of subjective contours by young infants. *Infant Behavior and Development, 13,* 221–248.

Gianino, A., & Tronick, E. (1988). The mutual regulation model: The infant's self and interactive regulation and coping and defensive capacities. In T. Field, P. McCabe, & N. Schneiderman (Eds.), *Stress and coping* (Vol. 2, pp. 47–68). Hillsdale, NJ: Lawrence Erlbaum Associates.

Gibson, E. J. (1969). *Principles of perceptual learning and development.* New York: Appleton-Century-Crofts.

Gibson, E. J., & Walk, R. D. (1960). The "visual cliff." *Scientific American, 202,* 64–71.

Gibson, E. J., Owsley, C. J., & Johnston, J. (1978). Perception of invariants by five-month-old infants: Differentiation of two types of motion. *Developmental Psychology, 14,* 407–415.

Gibson, J. J. (1979). *The ecological approach to visual perception.* Boston: Houghton Mifflin.

Gilbert, J. H. V. (1982). Babbling and deaf children: A commentary on Lenneberg et al. (1965) and Lenneberg (1967). *Journal of Child Language, 9,* 511–515.

Gjerde, P. F. (1996). Longitudinal research in a cultural context: reflections, prospects, challenges. In D. W. Shwalb & B. J. Shwalb (Eds.), *Japanese childrearing: Two generations of scholarship.*

Culture and human development (pp. 279–299). New York: Guilford.

Glanz, J. C., & Woods, J. R., Jr. (1993). Cocaine, heroin, and phencyclidine: Obstetric perspectives. *Clinical Obstetrics and Gynecology, 36,* 279–301.

Glaser, R., & Rosner, J. (1975). Adaptive environments for learning: Curriculum aspects. In H. Talmage (Ed.), *Systems of individualized education* (pp. 84–135). Berkeley, CA: McCutchoen.

Gleitman, L. R., & Gleitman, H. (1992). A picture is worth a thousand words, but that's the problem: The role of syntax in vocabulary acquisition. *Current Directions in Psychological Science, 1,* 31–35.

Gleitman, L. R., Newport, E. L., & Gleitman, H. (1984). The current status of motherese hypothesis. *Journal of Child Language, 11,* 43–80.

Glenn, S. M., & Cunningham, C. C. (1983). What do babies listen to most? A developmental study of auditory preferences in non-handicapped infants and infants with Down Syndrome. *Developmental Psychology, 19,* 332–337.

Gogate, L. J., Bahrick, L. E., & Watson, J. D. (2000). A study of multimodal motherese: The role of temporal synchrony between verbal labels and gestures. *Child Development, 71,* 878–894.

Goldberg, S. (1977). Infant development and mother–infant interaction in urban Zambia. In P. H. Leiderman, S. R. Tulkin, & A. Rosenfeld (Eds.), *Culture and infancy: Variations in the human experience* (pp. 211–243). New York: Academic.

Goldberg, S., & DiVitto, B. (1983). *Born too soon.* San Francisco: Freeman.

Goldberg, S., & DiVitto, B. (2002). Parenting children born preterm. In M. H. Bornstein (Ed.), *Handbook of parenting: Vol 1. Children and parenting* (2nd ed., pp. 329–354). Mahwah, NJ: Lawrence Erlbaum Associates.

Goldberg, S., MacKay-Soroka, S., & Rochester, M. (1994). Affect, attachment, and maternal responsiveness. *Infant Behavior and Development, 17,* 335–339.

Goldfield, B. A. (1987). The contributions of child and caregiver to referential and expressive language. *Applied Psycholinguistics, 8,* 267–280.

Goldfield, B. A. (in press). Pointing, naming, and talk about objects: Referential behavior in children and mothers. *First Language.*

Goldfield, B. A. (1985/1986). Referential and expressive language: A study of two mother–child dyads. *First Language, 6,* 119–131.

Goldfield, B. A. (1993). Noun bias in maternal speech in one-year-olds. *Journal of Child Language, 20,* 85–99.

Goldfield, B. A., & Snow, C. E. (1989). Individual differences in language acquisition. In J. B. Gleason (Ed.), *The development of language.* Columbus, OH: Merrill.

Goldin-Meadow, S., & Mylander, C. (1983). Gestural communication in deaf children: Noneffect of parental input on language development. *Science, 221,* 372–374.

Goldin-Meadow, S., & Mylander, C. (1984). Gestural communication in deaf children: The effects and noneffects of parental input on early language development. *Monographs of the Society for Research in Child Development, 49*(Serial, No. 207).

Goldman, P. S. (1974). An alternative to developmental plasticity: Heterology of CNS structures in infants and adults. In D. G. Stein, J. J. Rosen, & N. Butters (Eds.), *Plasticity and recovery from brain damage* (pp. 149–174). New York: Academic.

Goldman-Rakic, P. S., Bourgeois, J. P., & Rakic, P. (1997). Synaptic substrata of cognitive development: Life-span analysis of synaptogenesis in the prefrontal cortex of the nonhuman primate. In N. A. Krasnegor, G. R. Lyon, & P. S. Goldman-Rakic (Eds.), *Development of the prefrontal cortex: Evolution, neurobiology, and behavior* (pp. 27–47). Baltimore: Brookes.

Goldsmith, H. H., & Lemery, K. S. (2000). Linking temperamental fearfulness and anxiety symptoms: A behavior–genetic perspective. *Biological Psychiatry, 48,* 1199–1209.

Goldsmith, H. H., Lemery, K. S., Aksan, N., & Buss, K. A. (2000). Temperamental substrates of personality. In V. J. Molfese & D. L. Molfese (Eds.), *Temperament and personality development across the life span* (pp. 1–32). Mahwah, NJ: Lawrence Erlbaum Associates.

Goldsmith, H. H., Rieser-Danner, L. A., & Briggs, S. (1991). Evaluating convergent and discriminant validity of temperament questionnaires for preschoolers, toddlers, and infants. *Developmental Psychology, 27,* 566–579.

Goldstein, L. H., Diener, M. L., & Mangelsdorf, S. C. (1996). Maternal characteristics and social support across the transition to motherhood: Associations with maternal behavior. *Journal of Family Psychology, 10,* 60–71.

Golinkoff, R. M., Mervis, C. B., & Hirsh-Pasek, K. (1994). Early object labels: The case for a developmental lexical principles framework. *Journal of Child Language, 21,* 125–155.

Gonzales, N. M., & Campbell, M. (1994). Cocaine babies: Does prenatal exposure to cocaine affect development. *Journal of the American Academy of Child and Adolescent Psychiatry, 33,* 16–19.

Goodman, J. C., & Nusbaum, H. C. (Eds.). (1994). *The development of speech perception: The transition from speech sounds to spoken words.* Cambridge, MA: MIT Press.

Goodnow, J. J. (2002). Parents' knowledge and expectations: Using what we know. In M. H. Bornstein (Ed.), *Handbook of parenting: Vol. 3. Status and social conditions of parenting* (2nd ed., pp. 439–460). Mahwah, NJ: Lawrence Erlbaum Associates.

Goodnow, J. J., Cashmore, R., Cotton, S., & Knight, R. (1984). Mothers' developmental timetables in two cultural groups. *International Journal of Psychology, 19,* 193–205.

Goodsitt, J. V., Morgan, J. L., & Kuhl, P. K. (1993). Perceptual strategies in prelingual speech segmentation. *Journal of Child Language, 20,* 229–252.

Gopnik, A., & Meltzoff, A. (1987a). The development of categorization in the second year and its relation to other cognitive and linguistic developments. *Child Development, 58,* 1523–1531.

Gopnik, A., & Meltzoff, A. (1987b). Language and thought in the young child: Early semantic developments and their relationship to object permanence, means–ends understanding and categorization. In K. Nelson & A. van Kleeck (Eds.), *Children's language* (Vol. 6). Hillsdale, NJ: Lawrence Erlbaum Associates.

Gordon, J. (2000). Ecological influences on parenting and child development. *British Journal of Social Work, 30,* 703–720.

Gottfried, A. E., Fleming, J. S., & Gottfried, A. W. (1998). Role of cognitively stimulating home environment in children's academic intrinsic motivation: A longitudinal study. *Child Development, 69,* 1448–1460.

Gottfried, A. E., Gottfried, A. W., & Bathurst, K. (2002). Maternal and dual-earner employment status and parenting. In M. H. Bornstein (Ed.), *Handbook of parenting: Vol. 2. Biology and ecology of parenting* (2nd ed., pp. 207–229). Mahwah, NJ: Lawrence Erlbaum Associates.

Gottfried, A. W. (Ed.). (1984). *Home environment and early cognitive development.* New York: Academic.

Gottlieb, G. (1971a). *Development of species identification in birds: An inquiry into the prenatal determinants of perception.* Chicago: University of Chicago Press.

Gottlieb, G. (1971b). Ontogenesis of sensory function in birds and mammals. In E. Tobach, L. R. Aronson, & E. Shaw (Eds.), *Biopsychology of development* (pp. 67–128). New York: Academic.

Gottlieb, G. (1992). *Individual development and evolution.* New York: Oxford University Press.

Gottlieb, G. (1997). *Synthesizing nature–nurture: Prenatal roots of instinctive behavior.* Mahwah, NJ: Lawrence Erlbaum Associates.

Granrud, C. E. (1987). Size constancy in newborn human infants. *Investigative Ophthalmology and Visual Science, 28*(Suppl.), 5.

Granrud, C. E. (1993). *Visual perception and cognition in infancy.* Hillsdale, NJ: Lawrence Erlbaum Associates.

Granrud, C. E., & Yonas, A. (1984). Infants' perception of pictorially specified interposition. *Journal of Experimental Child Psychology, 37,* 500–511.

Greco, C., Hayne, H., & Rovee-Collier, C. (1990). Roles of function, reminding, and variability in categorization by 3-month-olds. *Journal of Experimental Psychology: Learning, Memory, and Cognition, 16,* 617–633.

Green, J. A., Gustafson, G. E., & West, M. J. (1980). Effects of infant development on mother–infant interactions. *Child Development, 51,* 199–207.

Green, J. A., & Statham, H. (1996). Psychosocial aspects of prenatal screening and diagnosis. In T. Marteau & M. Richards (Eds.), *The troubled helix: Social and psychological implications of the new human genetics* (pp. 140–163). Cambridge, England: Cambridge University Press.

Greenberg, D., Užgiris, I. C., & Hunt, J. M. (1968). Hastening the development of the blink response with looking. *Journal of Genetic Psychology, 113,* 167–176.

Greenough, W. T., Black, J. E., & Wallace, C. S. (1987). Experience and brain development. *Child Development, 58,* 539–559.

Griffiths, R. (1954). *The abilities of babies.* New York: McGraw-Hill.

Grolnick, W., Frodi, A., & Bridges, L. (1984). Maternal control style and the mastery motivation of one-year-olds. *Infant Mental Health Journal, 5,* 72–82.

Grolnick, W. S., Kurowski, C. O., McMenamh, J. M., Rivkin, I., & Bridges, L. J. (1998). Mothers' strategies for regulating their toddlers' distress. *Infant Behavior and Development, 21,* 437–450.

Groome, L. J., Loizou, P. C., Holland, S. B., Smith, L. A., & Hoff, C. (1999). High vagal tone is associated with more efficient regulation of homeostatis in low-risk human fetuses. *Developmental Psychobiology, 35,* 25–34.

Groome, L. J., Swiber, M. J., Holland, S. B., Bentz, L. S., Atterbury, J. L., & Trimm, R. F. (1999). Spontaneous motor activity in the perinatal infant before and after birth: Stability in individual differences. *Developmental Psychobiology, 35,* 15–24.

Grossmann, K., & Grossmann, K. E. (1986). Newborn behavior, early parenting quality and later toddler–parent relationships in a group of German infants. In J. K. Nugent, B. M. Lester, & T. B. Brazelton (Eds.), *The cultural context of infancy.* Norwood, NJ: Ablex.

Grossmann, K. E., & Grossmann, K. (1990). Preliminary observations on Japanese infants' behavior in Ainsworth's Strange Situation. (Annual Report No. 2, pp. 617). Sapporo, Japan: Hokkaido University, Research and Clinical Center for Child Development, Faculty of Education.

Grossmann, K. E., Grossmann, K., & Zimmermann, P. (1999). A wider view of attachment and exploration: Stability and change during the years of immaturity. In J. Cassidy & P. R. Shaver (Eds.), *Handbook of attachment: Theory, research, and clinical applications* (pp. 760–787). New York: Guilford.

Gubler, H., & Bischof, N. (1991). A systems' perspective on infant development. In M. E. Lamb & H. Keller (Eds.), *Infant development: Perspectives from German-speaking countries* (pp. 35–66). Hillsdale, NJ: Lawrence Erlbaum Associates.

Gunnar, M. R., & Stone, C. (1984). The effects of positive maternal affect on infant responses to pleasant, ambiguous, and fear-provoking toys. *Child Development, 55,* 1231–1236.

Gunnar, M., Mangelsdorf, S., Larson, M., & Hertsgaard, L. (1989). Attachment, temperament, and adrenocortical activity in infancy: A study of psychoendocrine regulation. *Developmental Psychology, 25,* 355–363.

Guralnick, M. J. (1997a). *The effectiveness of early intervention.* Baltimore: Brookes.

Guralnick, M. J. (1997b). Second-generation research in the field of early intervention. In M. J. Guralnick (Ed.), *The effectiveness of early intervention* (pp. 3–20). Baltimore: Brookes.

Hack, M., Flannery, D. J., Schluchter, M., Cartar, L., Borawski, E., & Klein, N. (2002). Outcomes in young adulthood for very-low-birth-weight infants. *The New England Journal of Medicine, 346,* 149–157.

Hack, M., Klein, N. K., & Taylor, H. G. (1995). Long-term developmental outcomes of low birth weight infants. *The future of children, 5,* 176–196.

Hainline, L., Riddell, P., Grose-Fifer, J., & Abramov, I. (1992). Development of accommodation and convergence in infancy: Normal and abnormal visual development in infants and children. *Behavioral Brain Research, 49,* 33–50.

Haith, M. M. (1980). *Rules that babies look by.* Hillsdale, NJ: Lawrence Erlbaum Associates.

Haith, M. M. (1991). Gratuity, perception-action integration and future orientation in infant vision. In F. Kessel, A. Sameroff, & M. Bornstein (Eds.), *Contemporary constructions of the child: Essays in honor of William Kessen.* Hillsdale, NJ: Lawrence Erlbaum Associates.

Haith, M. M. (1999). Some thoughts about claims for innate knowledge and infant physical reasoning. *Developmental Science, 2,* 153–156.

Haith, M. M., & Benson, J. B. (1998). Infant cognition. In W. Damon (Editor-in-Chief), D. Kuhn, & R. S. Siegler (Vol. Eds.), *Handbook of child psychology: Vol. 2. Cognition, perception, and language* (5th ed., 199–254). New York: Wiley.

Haith, M. M., & McCarty, M. E. (1990). Stability of visual expectations at 3.0 months of age. *Developmental Psychology, 26,* 68–74.

Hala, S. (1997). (Ed.). *The development of social cognition.* Hove, England: Psychology Press/ Lawrence Erlbaum Associates (UK)/Taylor & Francis.

Halford, G. (1999). The development of intelligence includes the capacity to process relations of greater complexity. In M. Anderson (Ed.), *The development of intelligence. Studies in developmental psychology* (pp. 193–213). Hove, England: Psychology Press.

Halliday, M. (1975). *Learning to mean.* London: Arnold.

Halpern, L. F., MacLean, W. E., Jr., & Baumeister, A. A. (1995). Infant sleep-wake characteristics: Relation to neurological status and the prediction of developmental outcome. *Developmental Review, 15,* 255–291.

Hardy-Brown, K. (1983). Universals in individual differences: Disentangling two approaches to the study of language acquisition. *Developmental Psychology, 19,* 610–624.

Hardy-Brown, K., & Plomin, R. (1985). Infant communicative development: Evidence from adoptive and biological families for genetic and environmental influences on rate differences. *Developmental Psychology, 21,* 378–385.

Hardy-Brown, K., Plomin, R., & DeFries, J. C. (1981). Genetic and environmental influences on rate of communicative development in the first year of life. *Developmental Psychology, 17,* 704–717.

Harkness, S., & Super, C. M. (1983). The cultural construction of child development: A framework for the socialization of affect. *Ethos, 11,* 221–231.

Harkness, S., & Super, C. M. (1985). Child–environment interactions in the socialization of affect. In M. Lewis & C. Saarni (Eds.), *The socialization of emotions* (pp. 21–36). New York: Plenum.

Harkness, S., & Super, C. M. (1996). *Parents' cultural belief systems: Their origins, expressions, and consequences.* New York: Guilford.

Harkness, S., & Super, C. M. (2002). Culture and parenting. In M. H. Bornstein (Ed.), *Handbook of parenting* Vol. 2. *Biology and ecology of parenting* (2nd ed., pp. 253–280). Mahwah, NJ: Lawrence Erlbaum Associates.

Harlow, H. F. (1958). The nature of love. *American Psychologist, 13,* 673–685.

Harlow, H. F. (1960). Primary affectional patterns in primates. *American Journal of Orthopsychiatry, 30,* 676–684.

Harlow, H. F., & Zimmermann, R. R. (1959). Affectional responses in the infant monkey. *Science, 130,* 421–432.

Harman, C., & Fox, N. A. (1997). Frontal and attentional mechanisms regulating distress experience and expression during infancy. In N. A. Krasnegor, G. R. Lyon, & P. A. Goldman-Rakic (Eds.), *Development of the prefrontal cortex: Evolution, neurobiology, and behavior* (pp. 191–208). Baltimore: Brookes.

Harmon, R. J., & Morgan, G. A. (1999). Research problems and variables. *Journal of the American Academy of Child and Adolescent Psychiatry, 38,* 784–785.

Harnad, S. (Ed.). (1987). *Categorical perception: The groundwork of cognition.* New York: Cambridge University Press.

Harris, G. (1997). Development of taste perception and appetite regulation. In G. Bremner, A. Slater, & G. Butterworth (Eds.), *Infant development: Recent advances* (pp. 9–30). Hove, England: Psychology Press.

Harris, S. R., & Langkamp, D. L. (1994). Predicative value of the Bayley mental scale in early detection of cognitive delays in high-risk infants. *Journal of Perinatology, 14,* 275–279.

Hart, B., & Risley, T. R. (1992). American parenting of language-learning children: Persisting differences in family–child interactions observed in natural home environments. *Developmental Psychology, 28,* 1096–1105.

Hart, B., & Risley, T. R. (1995). *Meaningful differences in the everyday experience of young American children.* Baltimore: Brookes.

Hartmann, D. P., & George, T. P. (1999). Design, measurement, and analysis in developmental research. In M. H. Bornstein & M. E. Lamb (Eds.), *Developmental psychology: An advanced textbook* (4th ed., pp. 125–195). Mahwah, NJ: Lawrence Erlbaum Associates.

Hartshorn, K., & Rovee-Collier, C. (1997). Infant learning and long-term memory at 6 months: A confirming analysis. *Developmental Psychobiology, 30,* 71–85.

Hartshorn, K., Rovee-Collier, C., Gerhardstein, P., Bhatt, R. S., Klein, P. J., Aaron, F., Wondoloski, T. L., & Wurtzel, N. (1998). Developmental changes in the specificity of memory over the first year of life. *Developmental Psychobiology, 33,* 61–78.

Harwood, R. L., Miller, J. G., & Irizarry, N. L. (1995). *Culture and attachment: Perceptions of the child in context.* New York: Guilford.

Harwood, R. L., Schölmerich, A., Schulze, P. A., & Gonzales, A. (1999). Cultural differences in maternal beliefs and behaviors: A study of middle-class Anglo and Puerto Rican mother–infant pairs in four everyday situations. *Child Development, 70,* 1005–1016.

Hastings, P. D., & Rubin, K. H. (1999). Predicting mothers' beliefs about preschool-aged children's social behavior: Evidence for maternal attitudes moderating child effects. *Child Development, 70,* 722–741.

Haviland, J. M., & Lelwica, M. (1987). The induced affect response: 10-week-old infants' responses to three emotion expressions. *Developmental Psychology, 23,* 97–104.

Hawley, T. L. (1994). The development of cocaine-exposed children. *Current Problems in Pediatrics, 24,* 259–266.

Hayes, A. (1984). Interaction, engagement, and the origins and growth of communication: Some constructive concerns. In L. Feagans, C. Garvey, & R. Golinkoff (Eds.), *The origins and growth of communications* (pp. 136–161). Norwood, NJ: Ablex.

Hayes, L. A., & Watson, J. S. (1981a). Facial orientation of parents and elicited smiling by infants. *Infant Behavior and Development, 4,* 333–340.

Hayes, L. A., & Watson, J. S. (1981b). Neonatal imitation: Fact or artifact? *Developmental Psychology, 17,* 655–660.

Hayne, H. (1996). Categorization in infancy. In C. Rovee-Collier & L. P. Lipsitt (Eds.), *Advances in infancy research* (Vol. 10, pp. 79–120). Norwood, NJ: Ablex.

Haynie, D. L., & Lamb, M. E. (1995). Positive and negative facial expressiveness in 7-, 10-, and 13-month-old infants. *Infant Behavior and Development, 18,* 257–259.

Healey, B. T., Fox, N. A., & Porges, S. W. (1988). *The heritability of autonomic patterns and social behavior in young twins.* Unpublished manuscript, University of Miami Medical School, Miami, FL.

Hebb, D. O. (1946). On the nature of fear. *Psychological Review, 53,* 259–276.

Hebb, D. O. (1949). *The organization of behavior: A neuropsychological theory.* New York: Wiley.

Hebb, D. O. (1953). Heredity and environment in mammalian behavior. *British Journal of Animal Behavior, 1,* 43–47.

Heibeck, T. H., & Markham, E. M. (1987). Word learning in children: An examination of fast mapping. *Child Development, 58,* 1021–1034.

Held, R. (1989). Perception and its neuronal mechanisms. *Cognition, 33,* 139–154.

Held, R. (1993). What can rates of development tell us about underlying mechanisms? In C. E. Granrud (Ed.), *Visual perception and cognition in infancy* (pp. 75–89). Hillsdale, NJ: Lawrence Erlbaum Associates.

Held, R., & Hein, A. (1963). Movement-produced stimulation in the development of visually guided behavior. *Journal of Comparative and Physiological Psychology, 56,* 872–876.

Hellige, J. B. (1993). *Hemispheric asymmetry: What's right and what's left.* Cambridge, MA: Harvard University Press.

Henriques, J. B., & Davidson, R. J. (1990). Regional brain electrical asymmetries discriminate between previously depressed subjects and healthy controls. *Journal of Abnormal Psychology, 99,* 22–31.

Henriques, J. B., & Davidson, R. J. (1991). Left frontal hypoactivation in depression. *Journal of Abnormal Psychology, 100,* 535–545.

Hepper, P. G., Shahidullah, S., & White, R. (1990). Origin of fetal handedness. *Nature, 345,* 431.

Herbert, J., & Hayne, H. (2000). Memory retrieval by 18-30-month-olds: Age-related changes in representational flexibility. *Developmental Psychology, 36,* 473–484.

Hernandez, D. J. (1997). Child development and the social demography of childhood. *Child Development, 68,* 149–169.

Hershenson, M. (1964). Visual discrimination in the human newborn. *Journal of Comparative and Physiological Psychology, 58,* 270–276.

Hertsgaard, L., Gunnar, M., Erickson, M. F., & Nachmias, M. (1995). Adrenocortical responses to the strange situation in infants with disorganized/disoriented attachment relationships. *Child Development, 66,* 1100–1106.

Hess, C. R. (in press). NICU-based interventions for high-risk infants. In D. M. Teti (Ed.), *Handbook of research methods in developmental psychology.* Malden, MA: Blackwell.

Hess, R. D., Azuma, H., Kashiwagi, K., Dickson, W. P., Nagano, S., Holloway, S., Miyake, K., Price, G., Hatano, G., & McDevitt, T. (1986). Family influences on school readiness and achievement in Japan and the United States: An overview of a longitudinal study. In H. W. Stevenson, H. Azuma, & H. Hakuta (Eds.), *Child development and education in Japan* (pp. 147–166). New York: Freeman.

Hesse, E. (1999). The Adult Attachment Interview: Historical and current perspectives. In J. Cassidy & P. R. Shaver (1999), *Handbook of attachment: Theory, research, and clinical applications* (pp. 395–433). New York: Guilford.

Hewlett, B. S., Lamb, M. E., Shannon, D., Leyendecker, B., & Schölmerich, A. (1998). Culture and early infancy among central African foragers and farmers. *Developmental Psychology, 334,* 653–661.

Higgins, S. T., & Katz, J. L. (Eds.). (1998). Cocaine abuse: Behavior, pharmacology, and clinical application. San Diego, CA: Academic.

Hillier, L., Hewitt, K. L., & Morrongiello, B. A. (1992). Infants' perception of illusions in sound localization: Reaching to sounds in the dark. *Journal of Experimental Child Psychology, 53,* 159–179.

Hiltunen, P., Moilanen, I., Szajnberg, N., & Gardner, N. (1999). The IFEEL pictures: Transcultural aspects of importing a new method. *Nordic Journal of Psychiatry, 53,* 231–235.

Hinde, R. A. (1997). The interpenetration of biology and culture. In D. Magnusson (Ed.), *The lifespan development of individuals: Behavioral, neurobiological, and psychosocial perspectives: A synthesis* (pp. 359–375). New York: Cambridge University Press.

Hines, M., & Kaufman, F. R. (1994). Androgen and the development of human sex-typical behavior: Rough-and-tumble play and sex of preferred playmates in children with congenital adrenal hyperplasia (CAH). *Child Development, 65,* 1042–1053.

Hirose, T., & Barnard, K. (1997). Interactions between depressed mothers and their infants: Maternal verbal joint attention and its effect on the infant's cognitive development. *Early Child Development and Care, 138,* 83–95.

Hirshberg, L. (1990). When infants look to their parents: II. Twelve-month-olds' response to conflicting parental emotional signals. *Child Development, 61,* 1187–1191.

Hirshberg, L. M., & Svejda, M. (1990). When infants look to their parents: I. Infants' social referencing of mothers compared to fathers. *Child Development, 61,* 1175–1186.

Hirsh-Pasek, K., Nelson, D. K., Jusczyk, P. W., Cassidy, K. W., Druss, B., & Kennedy, L. (1987). Clauses are perceptual units for young infants. *Cognition, 26,* 269–286.

Hochberg, J. E. (1962). Nativism and empiricism in perception. In L. Postman (Ed.), *Psychology in the making*. New York: Knopf.

Hoek, H. W., Brown, A. S., & Susser, E. S. (1999). The Dutch famine studies: Prenatal nutritional deficiency and schizophrenia. In E. S. Susser, A. S. Brown, & J. M. Gorman (Eds.), *Prenatal exposures in schizophrenia. Progress in Psychiatry* (pp. 135–161). Washington, DC: American Psychiatric Press.

Hoff, E. (2002). Causes and consequences of SES-related differences in parent-to-child speech adolescence. In M. H. Bornstein & R. H. Bradley (Eds.), *Socioeconomic status, parenting, and child development*. Mahwah, NJ: Lawrence Erlbaum Associates.

Hoff, E., Laursen, B., & Tardif, T. (2002). Socioeconomic status and parenting. In M. H. Bornstein (Ed.), *Handbook of parenting* (2nd ed.). Mahwah, NJ: Lawrence Erlbaum Associates.

Hoff-Ginsberg, E. (1985). Some contributions of mother-speech to their children's syntactic growth. *Journal of Child Language, 12,* 367–385.

Hoff-Ginsberg, E., & Shatz, M. (1982). Linguistic input and the child's acquisition of language. *Psychological Bulletin, 92,* 3–26.

Hoffman, H. S., Cohen, M. E., & DeVito, C. J. (1985). A comparison of classical eyelid conditioning in adults and infants. *Infant Behavior and Development, 8,* 247–254.

Holden, G. W., & Miller, P. C. (1999). Enduring and different: A meta-analysis of the similarity in parents' childrearing. *Psychological Bulletin, 125,* 223–254.

Hollenbeck, A. R., Gewirtz, J. L., Sebris, S. L., & Scanlon, J. W. (1984). Labor and delivery medication influences parent–infant interaction in the first post-partum month. *Infant Behavior and Development, 7,* 201–209.

Hollich, G. J., Hirsh-Pasek, K., Golinkoff, R. M., Brand, R. J., Brown, E., Chung, H. L., Hennon, E., & Rocroi, C. (2000). Breaking the language barrier: An emergentist coalition model for the origins of word learning. *Monographs of the Society for Research in Child Development, 65*(3).

Hollomon, H. A., & Scott, K. G. (1998). Influence of birth weight on educational outcomes at age 9: The Miami site of the Infant Health and Development Program. *Journal of Developmental and Behavioral Pediatrics, 19,* 404–410.

Hood, B. M., & Murray, L. (1996). Habituation changes in early infancy: Longitudinal measures from birth to 6 months. *Journal of Reproductive and Infant Psychology, 14,* 177–185.

Hopkins, B., & Westra, T. (1988). Maternal expectations of their infants' development: Some cultural differences. *Developmental Medicine and Child Neurology, 31,* 384–390.

Hopkins, B., & Westra, T. (1990). Motor development, maternal expectation, and the role of handling. *Infant Behavior and Development, 13,* 117–122.

Hornik, R., & Gunnar, M. R. (1988). A descriptive analysis of infant social referencing. *Child Development, 59,* 626–634.

Hornik, R., Risenhoover, N., & Gunnar, M. (1987). The effects of maternal positive, neutral, and negative affective communications on infant responses to new toys. *Child Development, 58,* 937–944.

Howes, C. (1997). Teacher sensitivity, children's attachment and play with peers. *Early Education and Development, 8,* 41–49.

Howes, C., & Smith, E. W. (1995). Children and their child care caregivers: Profiles of relationships. *Social Development, 4,* 44–61.

Howes, C., Galluzzo, D., Hamilton, C. E. Matheson, D., & Rodning, C. (1989, April). *Social relationships with adults and peers within childcare and families*. Paper presented to the Society for Research in Child Development, Kansas City, MO.

Hoyert, D. L. (1996). Fetal mortality by maternal education and prenatal care, 1990. *Vital and Health Statistics, Series 20*(30), 1–7.

Hubel, D. H., & Wiesel, T. N. (1959). Receptive fields of single neurons in the cat's striate cortex. *Journal of Physiology, 148,* 574–591.

Hudson, J. A., & Sheffield, E. G. (1998). Deja vu all over again: Effects of reenactment on toddlers' event memory. *Child Development, 69,* 51–67.

Huffman, L. C., Bryan, Y. E., del Carmen, R., Pedersen, F. A., Doussard-Roosevelt, J. A., & Porges, S. W. (1998). Infant temperament and cardiac vagal tone: Assessments at twelve weeks of age. *Child Development, 69,* 624–635.

Huston, A. C. (1983). Sex typing. In P. H. Mussen (Gen. Ed.), E. M. Hetherington (Ed.), *Handbook of child psychology: Vol. 4. Socialization, personality, and social development* (pp. 387–467). New York: Wiley.

Huttenlocher, P. R. (1979). Synaptic density in human frontal cortex–developmental changes and effects of aging. *Brain Research, 163,* 195–205.

Infant Health and Development Program. (1990). Enhancing the outcomes of low-birth-weight, premature infants: A multisite, randomized trial. *Journal of the American Medical Association, 263,* 3035–3042.

Ingersoll, E. W., & Thoman, E. B. (1999). Sleep/wake states of preterm infants: Stability, developmental change, diurnal variation, and relation with caregiving activity. *Child Development, 70,* 1–10.

Ivenskis, A., & Finlay, D. C. (1980). *Cardiac responses in four-month-old infants to stimuli moving at three different velocities.* Paper presented at the International Conference on Infant Studies, New Haven, CT.

Ivkovich, D., Collins, K. L., Eckerman, C. O., Krasnegor, N. A., & Stanton, M. E. (1999). Classical delay eyeblink conditioning in 4- and 5-month-old infants. *Psychological Science, 10,* 4–8.

Izard, C. E. (1979). *The maximally discriminative facial movement scoring system.* Unpublished manuscript, University of Delaware.

Izard, C. E., & Ackerman, B. P. (2000). Motivational, organizational, and regulatory functions of discrete emotions. In M. Lewis & J. M. Haviland-Jones (Eds.), *Handbook of emotions* (2nd ed., pp. 253–264). New York: Guilford.

Izard, C. E., & Dougherty, L. M. (1982). Two systems for measuring facial expressions. In C. E. Izard (Ed.), *Measuring emotions in infants and children* (pp. 97–126). New York: Cambridge University Press.

Izard, C. E., & Malatesta, C. Z. (1987). Perspectives on emotional development: I. Differential emotions theory of emotional development. In J. D. Osofsky (Ed.), *Handbook of infant development* (2nd ed., pp. 494–554). New York: Wiley.

Izard, C. E., Dougherty, L. M., & Hembree, E. A. (1983). *A system for identifying affect expressions by holistic judgments (AFFEX).* Newark: University of Delaware, Computer Network Services and University Media Services.

Izard, C. E., Fantauzzo, C. A., Castle, J. M., Haynes, O. M., Rayias, M. F., & Putnam, P. H. (1995). The ontogeny and significance of infants' facial expressions in the first 9 months of life. *Developmental Psychology, 31,* 997–1013.

Izard, C. E., Hembree, E. A., Dougherty, L. M., & Spizzirri, C. C. (1983). Changes in facial expressions of 2- to 19-month-old infants following acute pain. *Developmental Psychology, 19,* 418–426.

Izard, C. E., Hembree, E. A., & Huebner, R. R. (1987). Infants' emotional expressions to acute pain: Developmental change and stability of individual differences. *Developmental Psychology, 23,* 105–113.

Jacobsen, J. L., Wille, D. E., Tianen, R. L., & Aytch, D. M. (1983, April). *The influence of infant–mother attachment on toddler sociability with peers.* Paper presented at the biennial meetings of the Society for Research in Child Development, Detroit, MI.

Jacobson, J. L., & Jacobson, S. W. (1994). The effects of perinatal exposure to polychlorinated biphenyls and related contaminants. In H. L. Needleman & D. Bellinger (Eds.), *Prenatal exposure to toxicants: Developmental consequences* (pp. 130–147). Baltimore: Johns Hopkins University Press.

Jacobson, J. L., Boersma, D. C., Fields, R. B., & Olson, K. L. (1983). Paralinguistic features of adult speech to infants and small children. *Child Development, 54,* 436–442.

Jacobson, S. W. (1979). Matching behavior in the young infant. *Child Development, 50,* 425–430.

Jacobson, S. W., Jacobson, J. L., O'Neill, J. M., Padgett, R. J., Frankowski, J. J., & Bihun, J. T. (1992). Visual expectation and dimensions of infant information processing. *Child Development, 63,* 711–724.

Jacobson, S. W., Jacobson, J. L., Sokol, R. J., Martier, S. S., & Ager, J. W. (1993). Prenatal alcohol exposure and infant information processing ability. *Child Development, 64,* 1706–1721.

Jakobson, R. (1968). *Child language, aphasia and phonological universals.* New York: Humanities. (Original work published 1941.)

Jakobson, R. (1971). Why "Mama" and Papa"? In A. Bar-Adon & W. F. Leopold (Eds.), *Child language.* Englewood Cliffs, NJ: Prentice-Hall.

James, W. (1890). *The principles of psychology.* New York: Henry Holt.

Jasnow, M., & Feldstein, S. (1986). Adult-like temporal characteristics of mother–infant vocali interactions. *Child Development, 57,* 754–761.

Jensen, A. (1969). How much can we boost IQ and scholastic achievement? *Harvard Educational Review, 39,* 1–123.

Johnson, M. H. (1997a). Developing an attentive brain. In R. Parasuraman (Ed.), *The attentive brain* (pp. 427–443). Cambridge, MA: MIT Press.

Johnson, M. H. (1997b). *Developmental cognitive neuroscience.* Cambridge, MA: Blackwell.

Johnson, M. H. (1999). Developmental neuroscience. In M. H. Bornstein & M. E. Lamb (Ed.), *Developmental psychology: An advanced textbook* (pp. 199–230). Mahwah, NJ: Lawrence Erlbaum Associates.

Johnson, M. H., & Gilmore, R. O. (1996). Developmental cognitive neuroscience: A biological perspective on cognitive change. In E. Carterette, M. Friedman (Series Eds.), R. Gelman, & T. K.-F. Au (Eds.), *Handbook of perception and cognition: Perceptual and cognitive development* (2nd ed., pp. 333–372). San Diego, CA: Academic.

Johnson, M. H., & Morton, J. (1993). Authors' response. *Early Development and Parenting, 2,* 248–249.

Johnson, M., Dziurawiec, S., Ellis, H. D., & Morton, J. (1991). Newborns' preferential tracking of face-like stimuli and its subsequent decline. *Cognition, 40,* 1–19.

Johnson, S. P., & Aslin, R. N. (1995). Perception of object unity in 2-month-old infants. *Developmental Psychology, 31,* 739–745.

Johnstone, T., Van Reekum, C. M., & Scherer, K. R. (2001). Vocal expression correlates of appraisal processes. In R. K. Scherer, A. Schoor, & T. Johnstone (Eds.), *Appraisal processes in emotion: Theory, methods, research* (pp. 271–284). New York: Oxford University Press.

Johnson, W., Emde, R. N., Pannabecker, B., Stenberg, C., & Davis, M. (1982). Maternal perception of infant emotion from birth through 18 months. *Infant Behavior and Development, 5,* 313–322.

Jones, K. L., & Smith, D. W. (1973). Recognition of the fetal alcohol syndrome in early infancy. *Lancet, 2,* 999–1001.

Jones, K. L., Smith, D. W., Ulleland, C. N., & Streissguth, A. P. (1973). Pattern of malformation in offspring of chronic alcoholic mothers. *Lancet,* 1267–1271.

Jorde, L. B., Carey, J. C., & White, R. W. (1995). *Medical genetics.* St. Louis, MO: Mosby.

Jusczyk, P. W. (1994). Infant speech perception and the development of the mental lexicon. In J. C. Goodman & H. C. Nusbaum (Eds.), T*he development of speech perception: The transition from speech to spoken words* (pp. 227–270). Cambridge, MA: MIT Press.

Jusczyk, P. W. (1995). Language acquisition: Speech sounds and the beginning of phonology. In J. L. Miller & P. D. Eimas (Eds.), *Speech, language, and communication. Handbook of perception and cognition* (2nd ed., Vol. 11, pp. 263–301). San Diego: Academic Press.

Jusczyk, P. W., & Aslin, R. N. (1995). Infants' detection of the sound patterns of words in fluent speech. *Cognitive Psychology, 29,* 1–23.

Jusczyk, P. W., Friederici, A. D., Wessels, J. M., Svenkerud, V. Y., & Jusczyk, A. M. (1993). Infants' sensitivity to the sound patterns of native language words. *Journal of Memory and Language, 32,* 402–20.

Jusczyk, P. W., Houston, D. M., & Newsome, M. (1999). The beginnings of word segmentation in English-learning infants. *Cognitive Psychology, 39,* 159–207.

Kagan, J. (1974). Discrepancy, temperament and infant distress. In M. Lewis & L. A. Rosenblum (Eds.), *The origins of fear.* New York: Wiley.

Kagan, J. (1994a). *Galen's prophecy.* New York: Basic Books.

Kagan, J. (1994b). *The nature of the child.* New York: Basic Books.

Kagan, J. (1997). Temperament and the reactions to unfamiliarity. *Child Development, 68,* 139–143.

Kagan, J., & Arcus, D. (1994). Reactivity in infants: A cross-national comparison. *Developmental Psychology, 30,* 342–345.

Kagan, J., & Klein, R. (1973). Cross-cultural perspectives on early development. *American Psychologist, 28,* 947–961.

Kagan, J., & Moss, H. A. (1962). *Birth to maturity.* New York: Wiley.

Kagan, J., & Zentner, M. (1996). Early childhood predictors of adult psychopathology. *Harvard Review of Psychiatry, 3,* 341–350.

Kagan, J., Arcus, D., Snidman, N., Yufeng, W., Hendler, J., & Greene, S. (1994). Reactivity in infants: A cross-national comparison. *Developmental Psychology, 30,* 342–345.

Kagan, J., Kearsley, P., & Zelazo, P. (1978). *Infancy: Its place in human development.* Cambridge, MA: Harvard University Press.

Kagan, J., Reznick, J. S., & Snidman, N. (1999). Biological basis of childhood shyness. In A. Slater & D. Muir (Eds.), *The Blackwell reader in developmental psychology* (pp. 65–78). Malden, MA: Blackwell.

Kagan, J., Reznick, J. S., Snidman, N., Gibbons, J., & Johnson, M. O. (1988). Childhood derivatives of inhibition and lack of inhibition to the unfamiliar. *Child Development, 59,* 1580–1589.

Kagan, J., Snidman, N., & Arcus, D. (1998). Childhood derivatives of high and low reactivity in infancy. *Child Development, 69,* 1483–1493.

Kagan, J., Snidman, N., Zentner, M., & Peterson, E. (1999). Infant temperament and anxious symptoms in school age children. *Development and Psychopathology, 11,* 209–224.

Kamhi, A. (1986). The elusive first word: The importance of the naming insight for the development of referential speech. *Journal of Child Language, 13,* 155–161.

Kant, I. (1924). *Critique of pure reason* (F. M. Müller, Trans.). New York: Macmillan. (Original work published 1781.)

Kaplan, P. S., Goldstein, M. H., Huckeby, E. R., Owren, M. J., & Cooper, R. P. (1995). Dishabituation of visual attention by infant- versus adult-directed speech: Effects of frequency modulation and spectral composition. *Infant Behavior and Development, 18,* 209–223.

Karrer, J. H., Karrer, R., Bloom, D., Chaney, L., & Davis, R. (1998). Event-related brain potentials during an extended visual recognition memory task depict delayed development of cerebral inhibitory processes among 6-month-old infants with Down syndrome. *International Journal of Psychophysiology, 29,* 167–200.

Karzon, R. G. (1985). Discrimination of polysyllabic sequences by one- to four-month-old infants. *Journal of Experimental Child Psychology, 39,* 326–342.

Katz, L. C., & Schatz, C. J. (1996). Synaptic activity and the construction of cortical circuits. *Science, 274,* 1133–1138.

Kawasaki, C., Nugent, J. K., Miyashita, H., Miyahara, H., & Brazelton, T. B. (1994). The cultural organization of infants' sleep. *Children's Environments, 13,* 135–141.

Kaye, K. (1982). *The mental and social life of babies: How parents create persons.* Chicago: University of Chicago Press.

Keen, C. L., Bendich, A., & Willhite, C. C. (Eds.). (1993). *Maternal nutrition and pregnancy outcome*

(Annals of the New York Academy of Sciences, Vol. 678). New York: New York Academy of Sciences.

Keller, H., & Boigs, R. (1991). The development of exploratory behavior. In M. E. Lamb & H. Keller (Eds.), *Infant development: Perspectives from German-speaking countries* (pp. 270–290). Hillsdale, NJ: Lawrence Erlbaum Associates.

Keller, H., & Schölmerich, A. (1987). Infant vocalizations and parental reactions during the first 4 months of life. *Developmental Psychology, 23,* 62–67.

Kelley, S. A., & Brownell, C. A. (2000). Mastery motivation and self-evaluative affect in toddlers: Longitudinal relations with maternal behavior. *Child development, 71,* 1061–1071.

Kellman, P. J. (1993). Kinematic foundations of infant visual perception. In C. E. Granrud (Ed.), *Visual perception and cognition in infancy* (pp. 121–173). Hillsdale, NJ: Lawrence Erlbaum Associates.

Kellman, P. J. (1996). The origins of object perception. In R. Gelman & T. K.-F. Au (Eds.), *Handbook of perception and cognition: Perceptual and cognitive development* (2nd ed., pp. 3–48). San Diego, CA: Academic.

Kellman, P. J., & Banks, M. S. (1998). Infant visual perception. In W. Damon (Editor-in-Chief), D. Kuhn, & R. S. Siegler (Vol. Eds.), *Handbook of child psychology: Vol. 2. Cognition, perception, and language* (5th ed., pp. 103–146). New York: Wiley.

Kellman, P. J., & Spelke, E. S. (1983). Perception of partly occluded objects in infancy. *Cognitive Psychology, 15,* 483–524.

Kellman, P. J., Yin, C., & Shipley, T. F. (1995). A common mechanism for occluded and illusory contours: Evidence from hybrid displays. *Investigative Ophthalmology and Visual Science Supplements, 36,* S847.

Kelly, S. J., Day, N., & Streissguth, A. P. (2000). Effects of prenatal alcohol exposure on social behavior in humans and other species. *Neurotoxicology and Teratology, 22,* 143–149.

Kelly-Vance, L., Needelman, H., Troia, K., & Ryalls, B. O. (1999). Early childhood assessment: A comparison of the Bayley Scales of Infant Development and play-based assessment in two-year-old at-risk children. *Developmental Disabilities Bulletin, 27,* 1–15.

Kennard, M. A. (1936). Age and other factors in motor recovery from precentral lesions in monkeys. *Journal of Neurophysiology, 1,* 477–496.

Kennell, J. H., Voos, D. K., & Klaus, M. H. (1979). Parent–infant bonding. In J. D. Osofsky (Ed.), *Handbook of infant development* (pp. 786–798). New York: Wiley.

Kent, R. D. (1984). The psychobiology of speech development: Coemergence of language and a movement system. *American Journal of Physiology, 246,* R888–R894.

Kent, R. D., & Murray, A. D. (1982). Acoustic features of infant vocalic utterances at 3, 6, and 9 months. *Journal of the Acoustical Society of America, 72,* 353–365.

Kerns, K. A. (1996). Individual differences in friendship quality: Links to child–mother attachment. In W. M. Bukowski, A. F. Newcomb, & W. W. Hartup (Eds.), *The company they keep: Friendship in childhood and adolescence* (pp. 137–157). New York: Cambridge University Press.

Kessen, W. (1965). *The child.* London: Wiley.

Kessen, W., Haith, M. M., & Salapatek, P. H. (1970). Human infancy: A bibliography and guide. In P. Mussen (Ed.), *Carmichael's manual of child psychology.* New York: Wiley.

Ketterlinus, R. D., Lamb, M. E., & Nitz, K. (1991). Development and ecological sources of stress among adolescent parents. *Family Relations, 40,* 435–441.

Kier, C., & Lewis, C. (1998). Preschool–sibling interaction in separated and married families: Are same-sex pairs or older sisters more sociable? *Journal of Child Psychology and Psychiatry and Allied Disciplines, 39,* 191–201.

Klahr, D. (1999). The conceptual habitat: In what kind of system can concepts develop? In E. K. Scholnick, K. Nelson, S. A. Gelman, & P. H. Miller (Eds.), *Conceptual development: Piaget's legacy. The Jean Piaget Symposium Series* (pp. 131–161). Mahwah, NJ: Lawrence Erlbaum Associates.

Klaus, M. H., & Kennell, J. H. (1981). *Parent–infant bonding.* St. Louis, MO: Mosby.

Klein, P. (1988). Stability and change in interaction of Israeli mothers and infants. *Infant Behavior and Development, 11,* 55–70.

Kleiner, K. A. (1987). Amplitude and phase spectra as indices of infants' pattern preferences. *Infant Behavior and Development, 10,* 49–59.

Kleitman, N. (1963). *Sleep and wakefulness.* Chicago: University of Chicago Press.

Kline, M. W., Fletcher, C. V., Federici, M. E., Harris, A. T., Evands, K. D., Rutkiewicz, V. L., Shearer, W. T., & Dunkle, L. M. (1996). Combination therapy with stavudine and didanosine in children with advanced human immunodeficiency virus infection: Pharmacokinetic properties, safety, and immunologic and virologic effects. *Pediatrics, 97,* 886–890.

Klinnert, M. (1984). The regulation of infant behavior by maternal facial expression. *Infant Behavior and Development, 7,* 447–465.

Klinnert, M. D., Emde, R. N., Butterfield, P., & Campos, J. J. (1986). Social referencing: The infant's use of emotional signals from a friendly adult with mother present. *Developmental Psychology, 22,* 427–432.

Klinnert, M., Sorce, J., Emde, R. N., Stenberg, C., & Gaensbauer, T. (1984). Continuities and change in early affective life: Maternal perceptions of surprise, fear, and anger. In R. N. Emde

& R. J. Harmon (Eds.), *Continuities and disconti-nuities in development* (pp. 339–354). New York: Plenum.

Koffka, K. (1935). *Principles of Gestalt psychology.* New York: Harcourt Brace.

Kohn, M. L. (1987). Cross-national research as an analytic strategy. *American Sociological Review, 52,* 713–731.

Kojima, H. (1986a). Childrearing concepts as a belief-value system of the society and the in-dividual. In H. Stevenson, H. Azuma, & K. Hakuta (Eds.), *Child development and education in Japan* (pp. 39–54). New York: Freeman.

Kojima, H. (1986b). Japanese concepts of child development from the mid-17th to mid-19th century. *International Journal of Behavioral Devel-opment, 9,* 315–329.

Kolb, B. (1989). Brain development, plasticity, and behavior. *American Psychologist, 44,* 1203–1212.

Koocher, G. P., & Keith-Spiegel, P. C. (1990). *Child, ethics, & the law.* Lincoln: University of Nebraska Press.

Kopera-Frye, K., & Arendt, R. (1999). An alter-native path to exceptionality: Prenatal effects of teratogenic substances on developmental pro-cesses. In V. L. Schwean & D. H. Saklofske (Eds.), *Handbook of psychosocial characteristics of exceptional children* (pp. 347–376). New York: Kluwer.

Korenman, S., Miller, J., & Sjaastad, J. (1995). Long-term poverty and child development in the United States: Results from the NLSY. *Child and Youth Services Review, 17,* 127–155.

Kotch, J. B., Browne, D. C., Dufort, V., & Winsor, J. (1999). Predicting child maltreatment in the first 4 years of life from characteristics assessed in the neonatal period. *Child Abuse and Neglect, 23,* 305–319.

Kowal, A., & Kramer, A. (1997). Children's un-derstanding of differential parental treatment. *Child Development, 68,* 113–126.

Krasnegor, N. A., Lyon, G. R., & Goldman-Rakic, P. A. (Eds.). (1997). *Development of the prefrontal cortex.* Baltimore: Brookes.

Krishna, R. B., Levitz, M., & Dancis, J. (1993). Transfer of cocaine by the perfused human pla-centa: The effect of binding to serum proteins. *American Journal of Obstetrics and Gynecology, 169,* 1418–1423.

Kuchuk, A., Vibbert, M., & Bornstein, M. H. (1986). The perception of smiling and its expe-riential correlates in 3-month-old infants. *Child Development, 57,* 1054–1061.

Kugiumutzakis, G. (1993). Intersubjective vocal imitation in early mother–infant interaction. In J. Nadel & L. Camioni (Eds.), *New perspectives in early communicative development* (pp. 23–47). London & New York: Routledge.

Kuhl, P. K. (1993). Innate predispositions and the effects of experience in speech perception: The native language magnet theory. In B. de

Boysson-Bardies, S. de Schonen, P. Jusczyk, P. McNeilage, & J. Morton (Eds.), *Developmental neurocognition: Speech and face processing in the first year of life* (pp. 259–274). Dordrecht, the Netherlands: Kluwer Academic.

Kuhl, P. K., & Meltzoff, A. N. (1988). Speech as an intermodel object of perception. In A. Yonas (Ed.), *Perceptual development in infancy: The Minnesota Symposia on Child Psychology* (Vol. 20, pp. 235–266). Hillsdale, NJ: Lawrence Erlbaum Associates.

Kuljis, R. O., & Rakic, P. (1990). Hypercolumn in private visual cortex can develop in the ab-sence of cues from photoreceptors. *Proceedings of the National Academy of Science, 87,* 5303–5306.

Kuo, Z. Y. (1967). *The dynamics of behavior devel-opment: An epigenetic view.* New York: Random House.

Lamb, M. E. (1977a). The development of mother–infant and father–infant attachments in the sec-ond year of life. *Developmental Psychology, 13,* 637–648.

Lamb, M. E. (1977b). The development of parental preferences in the first two years of life. *Sex Roles, 3,* 495–497.

Lamb, M. E. (1977c). Father–infant and mother–infant interaction in the first year of life. *Child Development, 48,* 167–181.

Lamb, M. E. (1978a). The development of sibling relationships in infancy: A short-term longitu-dinal study. *Child Development, 49,* 1189–1196.

Lamb, M. E. (1978b). Interactions between 18-month-olds and their preschool-aged siblings. *Child Development, 49,* 51–59.

Lamb, M. E. (1978c). Qualitative aspects of mother– and father–infant attachments. *Infant Behavior and Development, 1,* 265–275.

Lamb, M. E. (1981a). Developing trust and per-ceived effectance in infancy. In L. P. Lipsitt (Ed.), *Advances in infancy research* (Vol. 1, pp. 101–127). Norwood, NJ: Ablex.

Lamb, M. E. (1981b). The development of father–infant relationships. In M. E. Lamb (Ed.), *The role of the father in child development* (Rev. ed., pp. 459–488). New York: Wiley.

Lamb, M. E. (1981c). The development of social ex-pectations in the first year of life. In M. E. Lamb & L. R. Sherrod (Eds.), *Infant social cognition* (pp. 155–175). Hillsdale, NJ: Lawrence Erlbaum Associates.

Lamb, M. E. (1981d). Fathers and child develop-ment: An integrative overview. In M. E. Lamb (Ed.), *The role of the father in child development* (Rev. ed., pp. 1–70). New York: Wiley.

Lamb, M. E. (1982a). The bonding phenomenon: Misinterpretations and their implications [Guest editorial]. *Journal of Pediatrics, 101,* 555–557.

Lamb, M. E. (1982b). Early contact and mother–infant bonding: One decade later. *Pediatrics, 70,* 763–768.

Lamb, M. E. (1982c). Individual differences in infant sociability: Their origins and implications for cognitive development. In H. W. Reese & L. P. Lipsitt (Eds.), *Advances in child development and Behavior* (Vol. 16, pp. 213–239). New York: Academic.

Lamb, M. E. (1986). The changing roles of fathers. In M. E. Lamb (Ed.), *The father's role: Applied perspectives* (pp. 3–27). New York: Wiley.

Lamb, M. E. (1987). Predictive implications of individual differences in attachment. *Journal of Consulting and Clinical Psychology, 55*, 817–824.

Lamb, M. E. (1996). Effects of nonparental child care on child development: An update. *Canadian Journal of Psychiatry, 41*, 330–342.

Lamb, M. E. (1997). The development of father–infant relationships. In M. E. Lamb (Ed.), *The role of the father in child development* (3rd ed., pp. 104–120). New York: Wiley.

Lamb, M. E. (1998). Nonparental child care: Context, quality, correlates, and consequences. In W. Damon (Series Ed.), I. Sigel, & K. A. Renninger (Eds.), *Handbook of child psychology: Child psychology in practice* (5th ed., pp. 73–133). New York: Wiley.

Lamb, M. E. (2000a). The effects of quality of care on child development. *Applied Developmental Science, 4*, 112–115.

Lamb, M. E. (2000b). The history of research on father involvement: An overview. *Marriage and Family Review, 29*, 23–42.

Lamb, M. E. (2002). The development of father–infant relationships. In C. Tamis-LeMonda & N. Cabrera (Eds.), *Handbook of father involvement* (pp. 93–117). Mahwah, NJ: Lawrence Erlbaum Associates.

Lamb, M. E., & Easterbrooks, M. A. (1981). Individual differences in parental sensitivity: Origins, components, and consequences. In M. E. Lamb & L. R. Sherrod (Eds.), *Infant social cognition: Empirical and theoretical considerations*. Hillsdale, NJ: Lawrence Erlbaum Associates.

Lamb, M. E. & Elster, A. B. (1985). Adolescent mother–infant–father relationships. *Developmental Psychology, 21*, 768–773.

Lamb, M. E., & Gilbride, K. (1985). Compatibility in parent–infant relationships: Origins and processes. In W. Ickes (Ed.), *Compatible and incompatible relationships* (pp. 33–60). New York: Springer.

Lamb, M. E., & Malkin, G. M. (1986). The development of social expectations in distress-relief sequences: A longitudinal study. *International Journal of Behavioral Development, 9*, 235–249.

Lamb, M. E., & Nash, A. (1989). Infant–mother attachment, sociability, and peer competence. In T. J. Berndt & G. W. Ladd (Eds.), *Peer relationships in child development* (pp. 219–245). New York: Wiley.

Lamb, M. E., & Sternberg, K. J. (1992). Sociocultural perspectives on nonparental childcare. In M. E. Lamb, K. J. Sternberg, C. P. Hwang, & A. Brober (Eds.), *Childcare in context: Cross-cultural perspectives*. Hillsdale, NJ: Lawrence Erlbaum Associates.

Lamb, M. E., Frodi, A. M., Frodi, M., & Hwang, C.-P. (1982a). Characteristics of maternal and paternal behavior in traditional and nontraditional Swedish families. *International Journal of Behavioral Development, 5*, 131–141.

Lamb, M. E., Frodi, A. M., Hwang, C.-P., Frodi, M., & Steinberg, J. (1982b). Mother– and father–infant interaction involving play and holding in traditional and nontraditional Swedish families. *Developmental Psychology, 18*, 215–221.

Lamb, M. E., Gaensbauer, T. J., Malkin, C. M., & Shultz, L. (1985). The effects of abuse and neglect on security of infant–adult attachment. *Infant Behavior and Development, 8*, 35–45.

Lamb, M. E., Hwang, C. P., Frodi, A., & Frodi, M. (1982). Security of mother– and father–infant attachment and its relation to sociability with strangers in traditional and non-traditional Swedish families. *Infant Behavior and Development, 5*, 355–367.

Lamb, M. E., Hwang, C. P., Ketterlinus, R. D., & Fracasso, M. (1999). Parent–child relationships: Development in the context of the family. In M. H. Bornstein & M. E. Lamb (Eds.), *Developmental psychology: An advanced textbook* (4th ed., pp. 411–450). Mahwah, NJ: Lawrence Erlbaum Associates.

Lamb, M. E., Thompson, R. A., Gardner, W. R., & Charnov, E. L. (1985). *Infant–mother attachment: The origins and developmental significance of individual differences in Strange Situation behavior*. Hillsdale, NJ: Lawrence Erlbaum Associates.

Lang, P., Simons, R. F., & Balaban, M. T. (Eds.). (1997). *Attention and orienting: Sensory and motivational processes*. Mahwah, NJ: Lawrence Erlbaum Associates.

Langer, J., & Killen, M. (1998). The comparative study of mental development. In J. Langer & M. Killen (Eds.), *Piaget, evolution, and development* (pp. 1–6). Mahwah, NJ: Lawrence Erlbaum Associates.

Langlois, J. H., Roggman, L. A., Casey, R. J., Ritter, J. M., Rieser-Danner, L. A., & Jenkins, V. Y. (1987). Infant preferences for attractive faces: Rudiments of a stereotype? *Developmental Psychology, 23*, 363–369.

Lansink, J. M., & Richards, J. E. (1997). Heart rate and behavioral measures of attention in six-, nine-, and twelve-month-old infants during object exploration. *Child Development, 68*, 610–620.

Largo, R. H., Molinari, L., Comendale-Pinto, L., Weber, M., & Duc, G. (1986). Language development of term and preterm children during the first five years of life. *Developmental Medicine and Child Neurology, 28*, 333–350.

Lashley, K. S. (1938). Factors limiting recovery after central nervous system lesions. *Journal of nervous and mental disorders, 88*, 733.

Laver, J. (1980). *The phonetic description of voice quality*. Cambridge, England: Cambridge University Press.

Leaper, C., Anderson, K. J., & Sanders, P. (1998). Moderators of gender effects on parents' talk to their children: A meta-analysis. *Developmental Psychology, 34*, 3–27.

Lecanuet, J. P., Fifer, W. P., Krasnegor, N. A., & Smotherman, W. P. (Eds.). (1995). *Fetal development: A psychobiological perspective*. Hillsdale, NJ: Lawrence Erlbaum Associates.

Lecanuet, J. P., & Granier-Deferre, C. (1993). Speech stimuli in the fetal environment. In B. de Boysson-Bardies & S. Schonen (Eds.), *Developmental neurocognition: Vol. 69. Speech and face processing in the first year of life. Nato ASI series D: Behavioural and social sciences* (pp. 247–248). Norwell, MA: Kluwer Academic Publishers.

Lee, C. L., & Bates, J. E. (1985). Mother–child interaction at age two years and perceived difficult temperament. *Child Development, 56*, 1314–1325.

Lemerise, E. A., & Dodge, K. A. (2000). The development of anger and hostile interactions. In M. Lewis & J. M. Haviland-Jones (Eds.), *Handbook of emotions* (2nd ed., pp. 594–606). New York: Guilford.

Lemery, K. S., & Goldsmith, H. H. (1999). Genetically informative designs for the study of behavioural development. *International Journal of Behavioral Development, 23*, 293–317.

Lempers, J. D. (1979). Young children's production and comprehension of nonverbal deictic behaviors. *Journal of Genetic Psychology, 135*, 93–102.

Lenneberg, E. H. (1967). *The biological foundations of language*. New York: Wiley.

Leopold, W. P. (1949). *Speech development of a bilingual child: A linguist's record: Vol. 3. Grammar and general problems in the first two years*. Evanston, IL: Northwestern University Press.

Lerner, J. V., & Lerner, R. M. (1994). Explorations of the goodness-of-fit model in early adolescence. In W. B. Carey & S. C. McDevitt (Eds.), *Prevention and early intervention: Individual differences as risk factors for the mental health of children: A festschrift for Stella Chess and Alexander Thomas* (pp. 161–169). Philadelphia: Brunner/Mazel.

Lerner, J. V., Hertzog, C., Hooker, K. A., Hassibi, M., & Thomas, A. (1988). A longitudinal study of negative emotional states and adjustment from early childhood through adolescence. *Child Development, 59*, 356–366.

Leslie, A. M. (1988a). The necessity of illusion: Perception and thought in infancy. In L. Weiskrantz (Ed.), *Thought without language* (pp. 185–210). Oxford, England: Clarendon.

Leslie, A. M. (1988b). Pretense and representation in infancy: The origins of "theory of mind." *Psychological Review, 94*, 412–426.

Lester, B. M., & Boukydis, C. F. Z. (1991). No language but a cry. In H. Papoušek, U. Jurgens, & M. Papoušek (Eds.), *Nonverbal vocal communication: Comparative and developmental approaches*. Cambridge, England: Cambridge University Press.

Lester, B. M., & Boukydis, C. F. Z. (Eds.). (1985). *Infant crying: Theoretical and research perspectives*. New York: Plenum.

Lester, B., LaGasse, L. L., & Brunner, S. (1997). Data base of studies on prenatal cocaine exposure and child outcome. *Journal of Drug Issues, 27*, 487–499.

Lester, B. M., LaGasse, L. L., & Seifer, R. (1998). Cocaine exposure and children: The meaning of subtle effects. *Science, 282*, 633–634.

Leung, E., & Rheingold, H. (1981). Development of pointing as a social gesture. *Developmental Psychology, 17*, 215–220.

Levi, S., & Chervenak, F. A. (Eds.). *Ultrasound screening for fetal anomalies: Is it worth it?* (Annals of the New York Academy of Sciences, No. 847). New York: New York Academy of Sciences.

LeVine, R. A. (1997). Mother–infant interaction in cross-cultural perspective. In N. L. Segal & G. E. Weisfeld (Eds.), *Uniting psychology and biology: Integrative perspectives on human development.* (pp. 339–354). Washington, DC: American Psychological Association.

Levy-Shiff, R., Dimitrovsky, L., Shulman, S., & Har-Even, D. (1998). Cognitive appraisals, coping strategies, and support resources as correlates of parenting and infant development. *Developmental Psychology, 34*, 1417–1427.

Lewis, M. (2000a). The emergence of human emotions. In M. Lewis & J. M. Haviland-Jones (Eds.), *Handbook of emotions* (2nd ed., pp. 265–280). New York: Guilford.

Lewis, M. (2000b). Self-conscious emotions: Embarrassment, pride, shame, and guilt. In M. Lewis & J. M. Haviland-Jones (Eds.), *Handbook of emotions* (2nd ed., pp. 623–636). New York: Guilford.

Lewis, M., & Ramsay, D. S. (1999). Effect of maternal soothing on infant stress response. *Child Development, 70*, 11–20.

Lewis, M., Alessandri, S. M., & Sullivan, M. W. (1990). Violation of expectancy, loss of control, and anger expressions in young infants. *Developmental Psychology, 26*, 745–751.

Lewis, M., Feiring, C., & Weinraub, M. (1981). The father as a member of the child's social network. In M. E. Lamb (Ed.), *The role of the father in child development* (2nd ed. pp. 259–294). New York: Wiley.

Lewis, M., Sullivan, M. W., Stanger, C., & Weiss, M. (1989). Self development and self-conscious emotions. *Child Development, 60*, 146–156.

Lewkowicz, D. J., & Lickliter, R. (Eds.). (1994). *The development of intersensory perception: Comparative perspectives*. Hillsdale, NJ: Lawrence Erlbaum Associates.

Leyendecker, B., & Lamb, M. E. (1999). Latino families. In M. E. Lamb (Ed.), *Non-traditional families: Parenting and child development* (pp. 247–262). Mahwah, NJ: Lawrence Erlbaum Associates.

Leyendecker, B., Lamb, M. E., & Schölmerich, A. (1997). Studying mother–infant interaction: The effects of context and length of observation in two subcultural groups. *Infant Behavior and Development, 20,* 325–337.

Leyendecker, B., Lamb, M. E., Schölmerich, A., & Fracasso, M. P. (1995). The social worlds of 8- and 12-month-old infants: Early experiences in two subcultural contexts. *Social Development, 4,* 194–207.

Leyendecker, B., Lamb, M. E., Schölmerich, A., & Fricke, D. M. (1997). Contexts as moderators of observed interactions: A study of Costa Rican mothers and infants from differing socioeconomic backgrounds. *International Journal of Behavioral Development, 21,* 15–34.

Lieven, E. V., Pine, J. M., & Barnes, H. D. (1992). Individual differences in early vocabulary development: Redefining the referential–expressive distinction. *Journal of Child Language, 19,* 287–310.

Lindahl, L. B., & Heimann, M. (1997). Social proximity in early mother–infant interactions: Implications for gender differences? *Early Development and Parenting, 6,* 83–88.

Linder, T. W. (1990). *Transdisciplinary play-based assessment: A functional approach to working with young children.* Baltimore: Paul H. Brookes.

Lloyd, P., & Fernyhough, C. (Eds.). (1999). *Lev Vygotsky: Critical assessments: The zone of proximal development* (Vol. 3). New York: Routledge.

Locke, J. L. (1983). *Phonological acquisition and change.* New York: Academic.

Locke, J. L. (1997). A theory of neurolinguistic development. *Brain and Language, 58,* 265–326.

Loehlin, J. C., Horn, J. M., & Willerman, L. (1997). Heredity, environment, and IQ in the Texas Adoption Project. In R. J. Sternberg & E. Grigorenko (Eds.), *Intelligence, heredity, and environment* (pp. 105–125). Cambridge, England: Cambridge University Press.

Lorenz, K. (1970). *Studies in animal and human behavior* (R. Martin, Trans.). London: Methuen. (Original work published 1935.)

Lounsbury, M. L., & Bates, J. E. (1982). The cries of infants and different levels of perceived temperamental difficultness: Acoustic properties and effects on listeners. *Child Development, 58,* 677–686.

Lucariello, J. (1987). Spinning fantasy: Theme, structure and knowledge base. *Child Development, 58,* 434–442.

Luck, S. J., & Girelli, M. (1998). Electrophysiological approaches to the study of selective attention in the human brain. In R. Parasuraman (Ed.), *The attentive brain* (pp. 71–94). Cambridge, MA: MIT Press.

Lusk, D., & Lewis, M. (1972). Mother–infant interaction and infant developing among the Wolof of Senegal. *Human Development, 15,* 58–69.

Lustig, R. H. (1998). Sex hormonal modulation of neural development in vitro: Implications for brain sex differentiation. In L. Ellis & L. Ebertz (Eds.), *Males, females, and behavior: Toward biological understanding* (pp. 13–25). Westport, CT: Praeger.

Lutz, D. J., & Sternberg, R. J. (1999). Cognitive development. In M. H. Bornstein & M. E. Lamb (Eds.), *Developmental psychology: An advanced textbook* (4th ed., pp. 275–311). Mahwah, NJ: Lawrence Erlbaum Associates.

Lynch, M. P., Eilers, R. E., Oller, K., & Urbano, R. C. (1990). Innateness, experience, and music perception. *Psychological Science, 1,* 272–276.

Lynch, M. P., Short, L. B., & Chua, R. (1996). Contributions of experience to the development of musical processing in infancy. *Developmental Psychobiology, 28,* 377–398.

Lyons-Ruth, K., Easterbrooks, M. A., Davidson, C. C. E., & Bronfman, E. (1995, April). *Predicting school-age externalizing symptoms from infancy: Contributions of disorganized attachment strategies and mild mental lag.* Paper presented at the biennial meeting of the Society for Research in Child Development, Indianapolis, IN.

Lyons-Ruth, K., & Jacobvitz, D. (1999). Attachment disorganization: Unresolved loss, relational violence, and lapses in behavioral and attentional strategies. In J. Cassidy & P. R. Shaver (Eds.), *Handbook of attachment: Theory, research, and clinical applications* (pp. 520–554). New York: Guilford.

Lyytinen, P., Laakso, M. L., Poikkeus, A. M., & Rita, N. (1999). The development and predictive relations of play and language across the second year. *Scandinavian Journal of Psychology, 40,* 177–186.

Maccoby, E. E., & Martin, J. A. (1983). Socialization in the context of the family: Parent–child interaction. In M. Hetherington (Ed.), *Handbook of child psychology* (Vol. 10, pp. 1–103). New York: Wiley.

MacKain, K. S., Studdert-Kennedy, M., Spieker, S., & Stern, D. (1983). Infant intermodal speech perception is a left-hemisphere function. *Science, 219,* 1347–1349.

Macken, M. A., & Barton, D. (1980). The acquisition of the voicing contrast in English. *Journal of Child Language, 7,* 41–74.

MacNeilage, P. F., & Davis, B. L. (1990). Acquisition of speech production: Frames, then content. In M. Jeannerod (Ed.), *Attention and performance: Vol. 13. Motor representation and control* (pp. 453–476). Mahwah, NJ: Lawrence Erlbaum Associates.

MacNeilage, P. F., & Davis, B. L. (2000). On the origin of internal structure of word forms. *Science, 288,* 527–531.

MacTurk, R. H., & Morgan, G. A. (Eds.). (1995). *Mastery motivation: Origins, conceptualizations, and applications.* Norwood, NJ: Ablex.

MacTurk, R. H., Morgan, G. A., & Jennings, K. D. (1995). The assessment of mastery motivation in infants and young children. In R. H. MacTurk & G. A. Morgan (Eds.), *Mastery motivation: Origins, conceptualizations, and applications* (pp. 19–56). Norwood, NJ: Ablex.

Maestripieri, D., & Carroll, K. A. (1998). Risk factors for infant abuse and neglect in group-living rhesus monkeys. *Psychological Science, 9,* 143–145.

Magnusson, K. A., & Duncan, G. J. (2002). Parents in poverty. In M. H. Bornstein (Ed.), *Handbook of parenting: Vol. 4. Applied parenting* (2nd ed., pp. 95–121). Mahwah, NJ: Lawrence Erlbaum Associates.

Mahler, M., Pine, A., & Bergman, F. (1975). *The psychological birth of the human infant.* New York: Basic Books.

Main, M., & Cassidy, J. (1988). Categories of response to reunion with a parent at age six: Predictable from infant attachment classifications and stable over a one-month period. *Developmental Psychology, 24,* 415–426.

Main, M., & Hesse, E. (1990). Parents' unresolved traumatic experiences are related to infant disorganized attachment status: Is frightened and/or frightening parental behavior the linking mechanism? In M. T. Greenberg, D. Cicchetti, & E. M. Cummings (Eds.), *Attachment in the preschool years: Theory, research, and intervention* (pp. 161–182). Chicago: University of Chicago Press.

Main, M., & Solomon, J. (1991). Procedure for identifying infants as disorganized/disoriented during the Ainsworth Strange Situation. In M. Greenberg, D. Cicchetti, & E. M. Cummings (Eds.), *Attachment during the preschool years: Theory, research, and intervention.* Chicago: University of Chicago Press.

Maital, S. L., Dromi, E., Sagi, A., & Bornstein, M. H. (2000). The Hebrew Communicative Development Inventory: Language specific properties and cross-linguistic generalizations. *Journal of Child Language, 27,* 43–67.

Malatesta, C. Z. (1985, April). *Facial expressions of infants and mothers during early interaction.* Paper presented to the Society for Research in Child Development, Toronto.

Malatesta, C. Z., & Haviland, J. M. (1982). Learning display rules: The socialization of emotion expression in infancy. *Child Development, 53,* 991–1003.

Malatesta, C. Z., & Haviland, J. M. (1985). Signals, symbols, and socialization: The modification of emotional expression in human development. In M. Lewis & C. Saarni (Eds.), *The socialization of emotions.* New York: Plenum.

Malatesta, C. Z., Culver, C., Tesman, J. R., & Shepard, B. (1989). The development of emotion expression during the first two years of life. *Monographs of the Society for Research in Child Development, 54*(1–2), (Serial No. 219).

Malatesta, C. Z., Grigoryev, P., Lamb, C., Albin, M., & Culver, C. (1986). Emotion socialization and expressive development in preterm and full term infants. *Child Development, 57,* 316–330.

Mandler, J. M. (1997). Development of categorization: Perceptual and conceptual categories. In G. Bremner, A. Slater, & G. Butterworth (Eds.), *Infant development: Recent advances* (pp. 163–188). Hove, England: Psychology Press.

Mandler, J. M. (1998). Representation. In W. Damon (Series Ed.) & D. Kuhn & R. Siegler (Vol. Eds.), *Handbook of child psychology: Vol. 2. Cognition, perception, and language* (pp. 255-308). New York: Wiley.

Mandler, J. M. (2000). What global-before-basic trend? Commentary of perceptually based approaches to early categorization. *Infancy, 1,* 99–110.

Mandler, J. M., & Bauer, P. J. (1988). The cradle of categorization: Is the basic level basic? *Cognitive Development, 3,* 247–264.

Mandler, J. M., & McDonough, L. (1998). On developing a knowledge base in infancy. *Developmental Psychology, 34,* 1274–1288.

Maratsos, O. (1998). Neonatal, early and later imitation: Same order phenomena? In F. Simion & G. Butterworth (Eds.), *The development of sensory, motor, and cognitive capacities in early infancy: From perception to cognition* (pp. 145–160). Hove, England: Psychology Press.

Marcos, H. (1987). Communicative functions of pitch range and pitch direction in infants. *Journal of Child Language, 14,* 255–268.

Mareschal, D., & French, R. (2000). Mechanisms of categorization in infancy. *Infancy, 1,* 59–76.

Markmam, E. M. (1989). *Categorization in children: Problems of induction.* Cambridge, MA: MIT Press, Bradford Books.

Markman, E. M., & Hutchinson, J. E. (1984). Children's sensitivity to constraints on word meaning: Taxonomic vs. thematic relations. *Cognitive Psychology, 16,* 1–27.

Markman, E. M., & Wachtel, G. F. (1988). Children's use of mutual exclusivity to constrain the meaning of words. *Cognitive Psychology, 20,* 121–152.

Marler, P. (1987). Sensitive periods and the roles of specific and general sensory stimulation in birdsong learning. In J. P. Rauschecker & P. Marler (Eds.), *Imprinting and cortical plasticity* (pp. 99–135). New York: Wiley.

Marler, P., & Peters, S. (1987). A sensitive period of song acquisition in the song sparrow, *Melospiza melodia*: A case of age-limited learning. *Ethology, 76,* 89–100.

Marler, P., & Peters, S. (1989). Species differences in auditory responsiveness in early vocal learning. In R. J. Dooling & S. H. Hulse (Eds.), *The comparative psychology of audition: Perceiving complex sounds* (pp. 243–273). Hillsdale, NJ: Lawrence Erlbaum Associates.

Marler, P., Peters, S., & Wingfield, J. (1987). Correlations between song acquisition, song production, and plasma levels of testosterone and estradiol in sparrows. *Journal of Neurobiology, 18,* 532–548.

Martin, R. P., Wisenbaker, J., Baker, J., & Huttunen, M. O. (1997). Gender differences in temperament at six months and five years. *Infant Behavior and Development, 20,* 339–347.

Marvin, R. S., & Britner, P. A. (1999). Normative development: The ontogeny of attachment. In J. Cassidy & P. R. Shaver (Eds.), *Handbook of attachment: Theory, research, and clinical applications* (pp. 44–67). New York: Guilford.

Masataka, N. (1999). Preference for infant-directed singing in 2-day-old hearing infants of deaf parents. *Developmental Psychology, 35,* 1001–1005.

Mascolo, M. F., & Fischer, K. W. (1999). The development of representation as the coordination of component systems of action. In I. E. Sigel (Ed.), *Development of mental representation: Theories and applications* (pp. 231–256). Mahwah, NJ: Lawrence Erlbaum Associates.

Masur, E. F. (1982). Mothers' responses to infants' object-related gestures: Influences on lexical development. *Journal of Child Language, 9,* 23–30.

Masur, E. F. (1983). Gestural development, dual-directional signaling, and the transition to words. *Journal of Psycholinguistic Research, 12,* 93–109.

Matas, L., Arend, R., & Sroufe, L. A. (1978). Continuity of adaptation in the second year: The relationship between quality of attachment and later competence. *Child Development, 49,* 547–556.

Mathiesen, K. S., & Tambs, K. (1999). The EAS Temperament Questionnaire—factor structure, age trends, reliability, and stability in a Norwegian sample. *Journal of Child Psychology and Psychiatry and Allied Disciplines, 40,* 431–439.

Matthews, A., Ellis, A. E., & Nelson, C. A. (1996). Development of preterm and full-term infant ability on AB, recall memory, transparent barrier detour, and means–end tasks. *Child Development, 67,* 2658–2676.

Maurer, D., & Maurer, C. (1988). *The world of the newborn.* New York: Basic Books.

Maurer, D., Lewis, T. L., Brent, H. P., & Levin, A. V. (1999). Rapid improvement in the acuity of infants after visual input. *Science, 286,* 108–110.

Mayes, L. C., & Bornstein, M. H. (1996). The context of development for young children from cocaine-abusing families. In P. M. Kato & T. Mann (Eds.), *Handbook of diversity issues in health psychology* (pp. 69–95). New York: Plenum Press.

Mayes, L. C., & Bornstein, M. H. (1997a). The development of children exposed to cocaine. In S. S. Luthar, J. A. Burak, D. Cicchetti, & J. R. Weisz (Eds.), *Developmental psychopathology: Perspectives on adjustment, risk, and disorder*

(pp. 166–188). New York: Cambridge University Press.

Mayes, L. C., & Bornstein, M. H. (1997b). Attention regulation in infants born at risk: Prematurity and prenatal cocaine exposure. In J. A. Burack & J. T. Enns (Eds.), *Attention, development, and psychopathology* (pp. 97–122). New York: Guilford.

Mayes, L. C., Bornstein, M. H., Chawarska, K., & Granger, R. H. (1995). Information processing and developmental assessments in three-month-old infants exposed prenatally to cocaine. *Pediatrics, 95,* 539–545.

Mayes, L. C., Bornstein, M. H., Chawarska, K., Haynes, O. M., & Granger, R. H. (1996). Impaired regulation of arousal in 3-month-old infants exposed prenatally to cocaine and other drugs. *Development and Psychopathology, 8,* 29–42.

Mayes, L. C., Feldman, R., Granger, R. H., Haynes, O. M., Bornstein, M. H., & Schottenfeld, R. (1997). The effects of polydrug use with and without cocaine on mother–infant interaction at 3 and 6 months. *Infant Behavior and Development, 20,* 489–502.

Mayes, L. C., Granger, R. H., Frank, M. A., Schottenfeld, R., & Bornstein, M. H. (1993). Neurobehavioral profiles of neonates exposed to cocaine prenatally. *Pediatrics, 91,* 778–783.

Mayes, L. C., & Truman, S. D. (2002). Substance abuse and parenting. In M. H. Bornstein (Ed.), *Handbook of parenting: Vol. 4. Applied parenting* (pp. 329–359). Mahwah, NJ: Lawrence Erlbaum Associates.

McCall, R. B. (1994). What process mediates predictions of childhood IQ from infant habituation and recognition memory? Speculations on the role of inhibition and rate of information processing. *Intelligence, 18,* 107–125.

McCall, R. B., & Carriger, M. S. (1993). A meta-analysis of infant habituation and recognition memory performance as predictors of later IQ. *Child Development, 54,* 57–79.

McCall, R. B., & Kagan, J. (1970). Individual differences in the infant's distribution of attention to stimulus discrepancy. *Developmental Psychology, 2,* 90–98.

McCall, R. B., & Mash, C. W. (1995). Infant cognition and its relation to mature intelligence. In R. Vasta (Ed.), *Annals of child development* (Vol. 10., pp. 27–56). London: Kinsley.

McCall, R. B., & McGhee, P. E. (1977). The discrepancy hypothesis of attention and affect in infants. In I. C. Uzgiris & F. Weizmann (Eds.), *The structuring of experience.* New York: Plenum.

McCall, R. B., Eichorn, D. H., & Hogarty, P. S. (1977). Transitions in early mental development. *Monographs of the Society for Research in Child Development, 42*(3, Serial No. 171).

McCall, R. B., Kennedy, C. B., & Appelbaum, M. I. (1977). Magnitude of discrepancy and the distribution of attention in infants. *Child Development, 48,* 772–785.

McCormick, M. C. (1992). Advances in neonatal intensive care technology, and their impact on the development of low-birthweight infants. In S. L. Friedman & M. D. Sigman (Eds.), *The psychological development of low-birthweight children* (Annual Advances in Applied Developmental Psychology, Vol. 6, pp. 37–60). Norwood, NJ: Ablex.

McCormick, M. C., McCarton, C., Brooks-Gunn, J., Belt, P., & Gross, R. T. (1998). The Infant Health and Development Program: Interim summary. *Journal of Developmental and Behavioral Pediatrics, 19,* 359–370.

McCormick, M. C., & Workman-Daniels, K. (1996). The behavioral and emotional well-being of school-aged children. *Pediatrics, 97,* 18–25.

McCune, L. (1995). A normative study of representational play at the transition to language. *Developmental Psychology, 31,* 198–208.

McCune-Nicolich, L. (1981a). The cognitive bases of relational words in a single word period. *Child Language, 8,* 15–34.

McCune-Nicolich, L. (1981b). *Correspondence and decalage in symbolic development: A multidimensional approach.* Paper presented at meetings of the Psycholinguistics Circle, New York University.

McCune-Nicolich, L. (1981c). Toward symbolic functioning: Structure of early pretend games and potential parallels with language. *Child Development, 52,* 785–797.

McFalls, J. A., Jr. (1990). The risks of reproductive impairment in the later years of childbearing. *Annual Review of Sociology, 16,* 491–519.

McGillicuddy-DeLisi, A. V. (1985). The relationship between parental beliefs and children's cognitive level. In I. E. Sigel (Ed.), *Parental beliefs systems: The psychological consequences for children* (pp. 7–24). Hillsdale, NJ: Lawrence Erlbaum Associates.

McGillicuddy-DeLisi, A. V., & Subramanian, S. (1996). How do children develop knowledge? Beliefs of Tanzanian and American mothers. In S. Harkness & C. M. Super (Eds.), *Parents' cultural belief systems: Their origins, expressions, and consequences* (pp. 143–168). New York: Guilford.

McHale, J. P., & Rasmussen, J. L. (1998). Coparental and family group-level dynamics during infancy: Early family precursors of child and family functioning during preschool. *Development and Psychopathology, 10,* 39–59.

McLaughlin, B., White, D., McDevitt, T., & Raskin, R. (1983). Mothers' and fathers' speech to their young children: Similar or different? *Journal of Child Language, 10,* 245–252.

McLoyd, V. C. (1998). Socioeconomic disadvantage and child development. *American Psychologist, 53,* 185–204.

McLoyd, V. C., Ceballo, R., & Mangelsdorf, S. (1996). The effects of poverty on children's socioemotional development. In (J. Noshpitz, Series Ed.) & N. Alessi (Ed.), *Handbook of child and adolescent psychiatry: Vol. 4. Variety of development* (pp. 189–206). New York: Wiley.

McShane, J. (1980). *Learning to talk.* New York: Cambridge University Press.

Mead, M., & MacGregor, F. C. (1951). *Growth and culture.* New York: Putnam.

Meadow-Orlans, K. P. (2002). Parenting with sensory or Physical disability. In M. H. Bornstein (Ed.), *Handbook of parenting: Vol. 4. Applied parenting* (2nd ed., pp. 259–293). Mahwah, NJ: Lawrence Erlbaum Associates.

Mebert, C. J. (1991). Dimensions of subjectivity in parents' ratings of infant temperament. *Child Development, 62,* 352–361.

Medoff-Cooper, B., Carey, W. B., & McDevitt, S. C. (1993). The Early Infancy Temperament Questionnaire. *Journal of Developmental and Behavioral Pediatrics, 14,* 230–235.

Melhuish, E. C. (1982). Visual attention to mother's and stranger's faces and facial contrast in 1-month-olds. *Developmental Psychology, 18,* 299–331.

Meltzoff, A. N. (1988a). Infant imitation after a 1-week delay: Long-term memory for novel acts and multiple stimuli. *Developmental Psychology, 24,* 470–476.

Meltzoff, A. N. (1988b). Infant imitation of televised models by infants. *Child Development, 59,* 1221–1229.

Meltzoff, A. N. (1993). Molyneux's babies: Cross-modal perception, imitation, and the mind of the preverbal infant. In N. Eilan, R. McCarthy, & B. Brewer (Eds.), *Spatial representation: Problems in philosophy and psychology* (pp. 219–235). Oxford, England: Blackwell.

Meltzoff, A. N., & Moore, M. K. (1997). Explaining facial imitation: A theoretical model. *Early Development and Parenting, 6,* 179–192.

Meltzoff, A. N., & Moore, M. K. (1998). Object representation, identity, and the paradox of early permanence: Steps toward a new framework. *Infant Behavior and Development, 21,* 201–235.

Meltzoff, A. N., & Moore, M. K. (1999). A new foundation for cognitive development in infancy: The birth of the representational infant. In E. K. Scholnick, K. Nelson, S. A. Gelman, & P. H. Miller (Eds.), *Conceptual development: Piaget's legacy. The Jean Piaget Symposium Series* (pp. 53–78). Mahwah, NJ: Lawrence Erlbaum Associates.

Menacker, S. J., & Batshaw, M. L. (1997). Vision: Our window to the world. In M. L. Batshaw (Ed.), *Children with disabilities* (4th ed., pp. 211–239). Baltimore: Brookes.

Mennella, J. A., & Beauchamp, G. K. (1996). The early development of human flavor preferences.

In E. D. Capaldi (Ed.), *Why we eat what we eat: The psychology of eating* (pp. 83–112). Washington, DC: American Psychological Association.

Mennella, J. A., & Beauchamp, G. K. (1997). The ontogeny of human flavor perception. In E. C. Carterette & M. P. Friedman (Series Eds.) & G. K. Beauchamp & L. Bartoshuk (Eds.), *Handbook of perception and cognition: Tasting and smelling* (2nd ed., pp. 199–221). San Diego, CA: Academic.

Menyuk, P. (1977). *Language and maturation.* Cambridge, MA: MIT Press.

Mercer, J. (1998). *Infant development: A multidisciplinary approach.* Pacific Grove, CA: Brooks/Cole.

Merriman, J., Rovee-Collier, C., & Wilk, A. (1997). Exemplar spacing and infants' memory for category information. *Infant Behavior and Development, 20,* 219–232.

Mervis, C. B. (1987). Child-basic object categories and early lexical development. In U. Neisser (Ed.), *Concepts and conceptual development: Ecological and intellectual bases of categorization* (pp. 201–233). Cambridge, England: Cambridge University Press.

Mervis, C. B., & Rosch, E. (1981). Categorization of natural objects. *Annual Review of Psychology, 32,* 89–115.

Messer, D. J. (1981). The identification of names in maternal speech to infants. *Journal of Psycholinguistic Research, 10,* 69–77.

Messinger, D. S., Fogel, A., & Dickson, K. L. (2001). All smiles are positive, but some smiles are more positive than others. *Developmental Psychology, 37,* 642–653.

Metcoff, J. (1994). Clinical assessment of nutritional status at birth: Fetal malnutrition and SGA are not synonymous. *Pediatric Clinics of North America, 41,* 875–891.

Miller, G. A. (1981). *Language and speech.* New York: Freeman.

Mills, D. L., Coffey-Corina, S. A., & Neville, H. J. (1993). Language acquisition and cerebral specialization in 20-month-old infants. *Journal of Cognitive Neuroscience, 5,* 317–334.

Mills, D. L., Coffey-Corina, S. A., & Neville, H. J. (1997). Language comprehension and cerebral specialization from 13 to 20 months. *Development Neuropsychology, 13,* 397–445.

Minde, K. (2000). Prematurity and serious medical conditions in infancy: Implications for development, behavior, and intervention. In C. H. Zeanah (Ed.), *Handbook of infant mental health* (2nd ed., pp. 176–194). New York: Guilford.

Miranda, S. B., & Fantz, R. L. (1974). Recognition memory in Down syndrome and normal infants. *Child Development, 45,* 651–660.

Mittendorf, R., Williams, M. A., Berkey, C. S., & Cotter, P. F. (1990). The length of uncomplicated human gestation. *Obstetrics and Gynecology, 75,* 929–932.

Molfese, D. L., & Molfese, V. J. (1994). Short-term and long-term developmental outcomes: The use of behavioral and electrophysiological measures in early infancy as predictors. In G. Dawson & K. W. Fischer (Eds.), *Human behavior and the developing brain* (pp. 493–517). New York: Guilford.

Molfese, V. J., & Acheson, S. (1997). Infant and preschool mental and verbal abilities: How are infant scores related to preschool scores? *International Journal of Behavioral Development, 20,* 595–607.

Mondloch, C. J., Lewis, T. L., Budreau, D. R., Maurer, D., Dannemiller, J. L., Stephens, B. R., Kleiner-Gathercoal, K. A. (1999). Face perception during early infancy. *Psychological Science, 10,* 419–422.

Mondschein, E. R., Adolph, K. E., & Tamis-LeMonda, C. S. (2000). Gender bias in mothers' expectations about infant crawling. *Journal of Experimental Child Psychology, 77,* 304–316.

Moore, K. L., & Persaud, T. V. N. (1993). *The developing human: Clinically oriented embryology* (5th ed.). Philadelphia: Saunders.

Moore, M. K., Borton, R., & Darby, B. L. (1978). Visual tracking in young infants: Evidence for object identity or object permanence? *Journal of Experimental Child Psychology, 25,* 183–198.

Moore, G. A., Cohn, J. F., & Campbell, S. B. (1998). Mothers' affective behavior with infant siblings: Stability and change. *Developmental Psychology, 33,* 856–860.

Moore, G. A., Cohn, J. F., & Campbell, S. B. (2001). Infant affective responses to mother's still-face at 6-months differentially predict externalizing and internalizing behaviors at 18 months. *Developmental Psychology, 37,* 706–714.

Morelli, G. A., Rogoff, B., Oppenheim, D., & Goldsmith, D. (1992). Cultural variation in infants' sleeping arrangements: Questions of independence. *Developmental Psychology, 28,* 604–613.

Morgan, G. A., MacTurk, R. H., & Hrncir, E. J. (1995). Mastery motivation: Overview, definitions, and conceptual issues. In R. H. MacTurk & G. A. Morgan (Eds.), *Mastery motivation: Origins, conceptualizations, and applications* (pp. 1–18). Norwood, NJ: Ablex.

Morgan, J. L., & Demuth, K. (Eds.). (1996). *Signal to syntax: Bootstrapping from speech to grammar in early acquisition.* Hillsdale, NJ: Lawrence Erlbaum Associates.

Morgan, J. L., & Travis, L. L. (1989). Limits of negative information in language input. *Journal of Child Language, 16,* 531–552.

Mumme, D. L., & Fernald, A. (1996). Infants' responses to facial and vocal emotional signals in a social referencing paradigm. *Child Development, 67,* 3219–3237.

Mumme, D. L., Fernald, A., & Herrera, C. (1996). Infants' responses to facial and vocal emotional signals in a social referencing paradigm. *Child Development, 67,* 3219–3237.

Mundy, P., Sigman, M., Ungerer, J. A., & Sherman, T. (1986). Defining the social deficits in autism: The contribution of nonverbal communication measures. *Journal of Child Psychology and Psychiatry, 27,* 657–669.

Munn, P., & Dunn, J. (1989). Temperament and the developing relationship between siblings. *International Journal of Behavioral Development, 12,* 433–451.

Murdock, G. P. (1959). Cross-language parallels in parental kin terms. *Anthropological Linguistics, 1*(9), 1–5.

Murray, A. D. (1979). Infant crying as an elicitor of parental behavior: An examination of two models. *Psychological Bulletin, 86,* 191–215.

Murray, A. D. (1985). Aversiveness in the mind of the beholder: Perception of infant crying by adults. In B. M. Lester & C. F. Z. Boukydis (Eds.), *Infant crying: Theoretical and research perspectives* (pp. 217–239). New York: Plenum.

Murray, L., Sinclair, D., Cooper, P., Ducournau, P., & Turner, P. (1999). The socioemotional development of 5-year-old children of postnatally depressed mothers. *Journal of Child Psychology and Psychiatry and Allied Disciplines, 40,* 1259–1271.

Nachmias, M., Gunnar, M. R., Mangelsdorf, S., Parritz, R. H., & Buss, K. (1996). Behavioral inhibition and stress reactivity: The moderating role of attachment security. *Child Development, 67,* 508–522.

Nakazima, S. (1975). Phonemicization and symbolization in language development. In E. H. Lenneberg & E. Lenneberg (Eds.), *Foundations of language development: A multidisciplinary approach* (Vol. 1). New York: Academic.

Nathanielsz, P. W. (1999). *Life in the womb: The origin of health and disease.* Ithaca, NY: Promethean.

National Institute of Child Health and Human Development. (1996). Characteristics of infant child care: Factors contributing to positive caregiving. *Early Childhood Research Quarterly, 11,* 269–306.

National Institute of Child Health and Human Development Early Child Care Research Network. (1997a). Child care in the first year of life. *Merrill–Palmer Quarterly, 43,* 340–360.

National Institute of Child Health and Development Early Child Care Research Network. (1997b). The effects of infant child care on infant–mother attachment security: Results of the NICHD study of early child care. *Child Development, 68,* 860–879.

National Institute of Child Health and Human Development Early Child Care Research Network. (1997c, April). *Mother–child interaction and cognitive outcome associated with early child care: Results of the NICHD study of early child care.* Paper presented at the biennial conference of the Society for Research in Child Development, Washington, DC.

National Institute of Child Health and Development Early Child Care Research Network. (2000). The relation of child care to cognitive and language development. *Child Development, 71,* 960–980.

Needleman, H. L., & Bellinger, D. (Eds.). (1994). *Prenatal exposure to toxicants: Developmental consequences.* Baltimore: Johns Hopkins University Press.

Nehlig, A., & Debry, G. (1997). Potential teratogenic and neurodevelopmental consequences of coffee and caffeine exposure: A review of human and animal data. *Neurotoxicology and Teratology, 16,* 531–543.

Nelson, C. A. (1987). The recognition of facial expressions in the first two years of life: Mechanisms of development. *Child Development, 58,* 889–909.

Nelson, C. A. (1997a). Electrophysiological correlates of memory development in the first year of life. In H. W. Reese & M. D. Franzen (Eds.), *Biological and neuropsychological mechanisms. Life-span developmental psychology* (pp. 95–131). Mahwah, NJ: Lawrence Erlbaum Associates.

Nelson, C. A. (1997b). The neurobiological basis of early memory development. In C. Hulme (Series Ed.) & N. Cowan (Ed.), *The development of memory in childhood. Studies in developmental psychology* (pp. 41–82). Hove, England: Psychology Press.

Nelson, C. A. (Ed.). (2000). *The effects of early adversity on neurobehavioral development.* Mahwah, NJ: Lawrence Erlbaum Associates.

Nelson, C. A., & Bloom, F. E. (1997). Child development and neuroscience. *Child Development, 68,* 970–987.

Nelson, K. (1973a). Some evidence for the cognitive primacy of categorization and its functional basis. *Merrill-Palmer Quarterly, 19,* 21–39.

Nelson, K. (1973b). Structure and strategy in learning to talk. *Monographs of the Society for Research in Child Development, 38*(Serial No. 149).

Nelson, K. (1981). Individual differences in language development: Implications for development and language. *Developmental Psychology, 17,* 170–187.

Neville, H. J. (1995). Developmental specificity in neurocognitive development in humans. In M. S. Gazzaniga (Editor-in-Chief) & P. Rakic (Section Ed.), *The cognitive neurosciences* (pp. 219–231). Cambridge, MA: MIT Press.

Newborg, J., Stock, J. R., Wnek, L., Guidubaldi, J., & Svinicki, J. (1984). *Battelle Developmental Inventory.* Allen, TX: DLM Teaching Resources.

Newman, C. G. (1985). Teratogen update: Clinical aspects of thalidomide embryopathy: A continuing preoccupation. *Teratology, 32,* 133–144.

Newport, E. L., Gleitman, H., & Gleitman, L. R. (1977). Mother, I'd rather do it myself: Some effects and non-effects of maternal speech style. In C. Snow & C. A. Ferguson (Eds.), *Talking to children: Language input and acquisition*. Cambridge, England: Cambridge University Press.

Nicely, P., Tamis-LeMonda, C. S., & Grolnick, W. S. (1999). Maternal responsiveness to infant affect: Stability and prediction. *Infant Behavior and Development, 22*, 103–117.

Ninio, A. (1980). Picture-book reading in mother–infant dyads belonging to two subgroups in Israel. *Child Development, 51*, 587–590.

Ninio, A. (1995). Expression of communicative intents in the single-word period and the vocabulary spurt. In K. E. Nelson & Z. Reger (Eds.), *Children's language* (Vol. 8, pp. 103–124). Hillsdale, NJ: Lawrence Erlbaum Associates.

Nowakowski, R. S. (1987). Basic concepts of CNS development. *Child Development, 58*, 568–595.

Nulman, I., Revet, J., Altmann, D., Bradley, C., Einarson, T., & Koren, G. (1994). Neurodevelopment of adopted children exposed in utero to cocaine. *Canadian Medical Association Journal, 151*, 1591–1597.

Oakes, L. M., & Tellinghuisen, D. J. (1994). Examining in infancy: Does it reflect active processing? *Developmental Psychology, 30*, 748–756.

Oakes, L. M., Coppage, D. J., & Dingel, A. (1997). By land or by sea: The role of perceptual similarity in infants' categorization of animals. *Developmental Psychology, 33*, 396–407.

O'Brien, M., & Huston, A. (1985a). Activity level and sex-stereotyped toy choice in toddler boys and girls. *The Journal of Genetic Psychology, 146*, 527–533.

O'Brien, M., & Huston, A. (1985b). Development of sex-typed play behavior in toddlers. *Developmental Psychology, 21*, 866–871.

O'Brien, M., Peyton, V., Mistry, R., Hruda, L., Jacobs, A., Caldera, Y., Huston, A., & Roy, C. (2000). Gender-role cognition in three-year-old boys and girls. *Sex Roles, 42*, 1007–1025.

Oller, D. K. (2000). *The emergence of the speech capacity*. Mahwah, NJ: Lawrence Erlbaum Associates.

Oller, D. K., & Eilers, R. E. (1982). Similarity of babbling in Spanish- and English-learning babies. *Journal of Child Language, 9*, 565–577.

Oller, D. K., & Eilers, R. E. (1988). The role of audition in infant babbling. *Child Development, 59*, 441–449.

Olsho, L. W., Schoon, C., Sakai, R., Turpin, R., & Sperduto, V. (1982a). Auditory frequency discrimination in infancy. *Developmental Psychology, 18*, 721–726.

Olsho, L. W., Schoon, C., Sakai, R., Turpin, R., & Sperduto, V. (1982b). Preliminary data on frequency discrimination. *Journal of the Acoustical Society of America, 71*, 509–511.

Olson, H. C. (1998). Maternal alcohol use and fetal development. In E. A. Blechman & K. D. Brownell (Eds.), *Behavioral medicine and women: A comprehensive handbook* (pp. 31–38). New York: Guilford.

Olson, S. L., Bates, J. E., & Bayles, K. (1984). Mother–infant interaction and the development of individual differences in children's cognitive competence. *Developmental Psychology, 20*, 166–179.

Olson, S. L., Bayles, K., & Bates, J. E. (1986). Mother–child interaction and children's speech progress: A longitudinal study of the first two years. *Merrill-Palmer Quarterly, 32*, 1–20.

Oppenheim, D., Sagi, A., & Lamb, M. E. (1988). Infant–adult attachments on the kibbutz and their relation to socioemotional development four years later. *Developmental Psychology, 24*, 427–433.

Orlian, E. K., & Rose, S. A. (1997). Speed vs. thoroughness in infant visual information processing. *Infant Behavior and Development, 20*, 371–381.

Ospreen, O., Risser, A. H., & Edgell, D. (1995). *Developmental neuropsychology*. New York: Oxford University Press.

Oster, H. (1981). "Recognition" of emotional expression in infancy? In M. E. Lamb & L. R. Sherrod (Eds.), *Infant social cognition: Empirical and theoretical considerations* (pp. 85–125). Hillsdale, NJ: Lawrence Erlbaum Associates.

Oster, H., Hegley, D., & Nagel, L. (1992). Adult judgments and fine-grained analysis of infant facial expressions: Testing the validity of a priori coding formulas. *Developmental Psychology, 28*, 1115–1131.

Paarlberg, K. M., Vingerhoets, A. J. J. M., Passchier, J., Dekker, G. A., & Van Geijn, H. P. (1995). Psychosocial factors and pregnancy outcome: A review with emphasis on methodological issues. *Journal of Psychosomatic Research, 39*, 563–595.

Palkovitz, R. (1985). Fathers' birth attendance, early contact, and extended contact with their newborns: A critical review. *Child Development, 56*, 392–406.

Palti, H., & Adler, B. (1994). Do infant and early childhood tests predict intelligence quotients better than maternal characteristics? *Public Health Review, 22*, 27–37.

Paneth, N. S. (1995). The problem of low birth weight. *The future of children, 19–34. Long-term developmental outcomes of low birth weight infants* (pp. 19–34). Los Angeles: David and Lucille Packard Foundation.

Papoušek, H. (1969). Individual variability in learned responses in human infants. In R. J. Robinson (Ed.), *Brain and early behavior*. London: Academic.

Papoušek, H., & Bernstein, P. (1969). The functions of conditioning stimulation in human neonates and infants. In A. Ambrose (Ed.), *Stimulation in early infancy*. London: Academic.

Papoušek, H., & Papoušek, M. (1978). Interdisciplinary parallels in studies of early human behavior: From physical to cognitive needs, from attachment to dyadic education. *International Journal of Behavioral Development, 1,* 37–49.

Papoušek, H., & Papoušek, M. (1991). Innate and cultural guidance of infants' integrative competencies: China, the United States, and Germany. In M. H. Bornstein (Ed.), *Cultural approaches to parenting* (pp. 23–44). Hillsdale, NJ: Lawrence Erlbaum Associates.

Papoušek, H., & Papoušek, M. (1995). Intuitive parenting. In M. H. Bornstein (Ed.), *Handbook of parenting: Vol. 2. Biology and ecology of parenting* (pp. 117–136). Mahwah, NJ: Lawrence Erlbaum Associates.

Papoušek, H., & Papoušek, M. (2002). Intuitive parenting. In M. H. Bornstein (Ed.), *Handbook of parenting Vol. 2 Biology and ecology of parenting* (pp. 183–203). Mahwah, NJ: Lawrence Erlbaum Associates.

Papoušek, M., & Papoušek, H. (1981). Musical elements in the infant's vocalization: Their significance for communication, cognition, and creativity. In L. P. Lipsitt (Ed.), *Advances in infancy research* (Vol. 1, pp. 164–224). Norwood, NJ: Ablex.

Papoušek, M., & Papoušek, H. (1991). Early verbalizations as precursors of language development. In M. E. Lamb & H. Keller (Eds.), *Infant development: Perspectives from German-speaking countries* (pp. 299–328). Hillsdale, NJ: Lawrence Erlbaum Associates.

Papoušek, M., & Papoušek, H. (1996). Infantile persistent crying, state regulation, and interaction with parents: A systems view. In M. H. Bornstein & J. L. Genevro (Eds.), *Child development and behavioral pediatrics* (pp. 11–33). Mahwah, NJ: Lawrence Erlbaum Associates.

Papoušek, M., Papoušek, H., & Bornstein, M. H. (1985). The naturalistic vocal environment of young infants: On the significance of homogeneity and variability in parental speech. In T. M. Field & N. Fox (Eds.), *Social perception in infants* (pp. 269–297). Norwood, NJ: Ablex.

Papoušek, M., Papoušek, H., & Haekel, M. (1987). Didactic adjustments in fathers' and mothers' speech to their 3-month-old infants. *Journal of Psycholinguistic Research, 16,* 491–516.

Parke, R. D. (1979). Perspectives on father–infant interaction. In J. D. Osofsky (Ed.), *Handbook of infant development* (pp. 549–590). New York: Wiley.

Parke, R. D. (1996). *Fatherhood.* Cambridge, MA: Harvard University Press.

Parke, R. D. (2002). Fathers and families. In M. H. Bornstein (Ed.), *Handbook of parenting* (2nd ed., Vol. 3), *Status and social conditions of parenting* (pp. 27–73). Mahwah, NJ: Lawrence Erlbaum Associates.

Parke, R. D., & Buriel, R. (1998). Socialization in the family: Ethnic and ecological perspectives. In W. Damon (Editor-in-Chief) & N. Eisenberg (Vol. Ed.), *Handbook of child psychology: Vol. 3. Social, emotional, and personality development* (pp. 463–552). New York: Wiley.

Parker, S. T. (1998). A social selection model for evolution and adaptive significance of self-conscious emotions. In M. D. Ferrari & R. J. Sternberg (Eds.), *Self-awareness: Its nature and development* (pp. 108–134). New York: Guilford.

Parkin, A. J. (1997). The development of procedural and declarative memory. In C. Hulme (Series Ed.) & N. Cowan (Ed.), *The development of memory in childhood. Studies in developmental psychology* (pp. 113–137). Hove, England: Psychology Press.

Parks, P. L., Lenz, E. R., & Jenkins, L. S. (1992). The role of social support and stressors for mothers and infants. *Care, Health, and Development, 18,* 151–171.

Pataansuu, J., & von Hofsten, C. (1991). Infants' sensitivity to differential luminance as information about depth. *Scandinavian Journal of Psychology, 32,* 144–153.

Pawlby, S. J. (1977). Imitative interaction. In H. R. Schaffer (Ed.), *Studies in mother–infant interaction* (pp. 203–224). London: Academic.

Pederson, D. R., & Moran, G. (1995). A categorical description of infant–mother relationships in the home and its relation to Q-sort measures of infant–mother interaction. In E. Waters, B. E. Vaughn, G. Posada, & K. Kondo-Ikemura (Eds.), *Caregiving, cultural, and cognitive perspectives on secure-base behavior and working models: New growing points of attachment theory and research. Monographs of the Society for Research in Child Development, 60*(2–3, Serial No. 244), 111–132.

Pederson, D. R., Rook-Green, A., & Elder J. L. (1981). The role of action in the development of pretend play in young children. *Developmental Psychology, 17,* 756–759.

Peeples, D. R., & Teller, D. Y. (1975). Color vision and brightness discrimination in two-month-old human infants. *Science, 189,* 1102–1103.

Pegg, J. E., Werker, J. F., & McLeod, P. J. (1992). Preference for infant-directed over adult-directed speech: Evidence from 7-week-old infants. *Infant Behavior and Development, 15,* 325–345.

Peipert, J. F., & Bracken, M. B. (1993). Maternal age: An independent risk factor for cesarean delivery. *Obstetrics and Gynecology, 81,* 200–205.

Pelligrini, A. D., & Smith, P. K. (1998). Physical activity play: The nature and function of a neglected aspect of play. *Child Development, 69,* 577–598.

Penman, R., Cross, T., Milgram-Friedman, J., & Meares, R. (1983). Mother's speech to prelingual infants: A pragmatic analysis. *Journal of Child Language, 10,* 17–34.

Peters, A. M. (1983). *The units of language acquisition.* Cambridge, England: Cambridge University Press.

Peters, A. M. (1997). Language-learning strategies: Does the whole equal the sum of its parts? *Language, 53,* 560–573.

Petersen, G. A., & Sherrod, K. B. (1982). Relationship of maternal language to language development and language delay of children. *American Journal of Mental Deficiency, 86,* 391–398.

Petitto, L. A., Holowka, S., Sergio, L. E., & Ostry, D. (2001). Language rhythms in baby hand movements. *Nature, 413,* 35–36.

Petitto, L. A., & Marentette, P. F. (1991). Babbling in the manual mode: Evidence for the ontogeny of language. *Science, 251,* 1493–1496.

Pettersen, L., Yonas, A., & Fisch, R. O. (1980). The development of blinking in response to impending collision in preterm, full term, and postterm infants. *Infant Behavior and Development, 3,* 155–165.

Pettit, G. S., & Bates, J. E. (1984). Continuity of individual differences in the mother–infant relationship from 6 to 13 months. *Child Development, 55,* 729–739.

Pettit, G. S., Bates, J. E., & Dodge, K. A. (1997). Supportive parenting, ecological context, and children's adjustment: A seven-year longitudinal study. *Child Development, 68,* 908–923.

Phillips, D. (1991). Day care for young children in the United States. In E. C. Melhuish & P. Moss (Eds.), *Day care for young children* (pp. 161–184).

Piaget, J. (1952). *The origins of intelligence in children.* New York: Norton.

Piaget, J. (1953). *The origins of intelligence in the child.* London: Routledge & Kegan Paul. (Original work published 1936.)

Piaget, J. (1954). *The construction of reality in the child.* New York: Basic Books. (Original work published 1937.)

Piaget, J. (1962). *Play, dreams and imitation in childhood.* New York: Norton.

Piaget, J. (1983). Piaget's theory. In P. H. Mussen (Series Ed.) & W. Kessen (Vol. Ed.), *Handbook of Child Psychology: Vol. 1. History, theory, and methods* (pp. 103–128). New York: Wiley.

Piaget, J., & Inhelder, B. (1967). *The child's conception of space* (F. J. Langdon & J. L. Lunzer, Trans.). New York: Norton. (Original work published 1948.)

Pine, J. M., Lieven, E. V. M., & Rowland, C. F. (1997). Stylistic variation at the "single-word" stage: Relations between maternal speech characteristics and children's vocabulary composition and usage. *Child Development, 68,* 807–819.

Pipp-Siegel, S., Robinson, J. L., Bridges, D., & Bartholomew, S. (1997). Sources of individual differences in infant social cognition: Cognitive and affective aspects of self and other. In R. J. Sternberg & E. Grigorenko (Eds.), *Intelligence, heredity, and environment* (pp. 505–528). Cambridge, England: Cambridge University Press.

Pisoni, D. B., Lively, S. E., & Logan, J. S. (1994). Perceptual learning of nonnative speech contrasts: Implications for theories of speech perception. In J. C. Goodman & H. C. Nusbaum (Eds.), *The development of speech perception: The transition from speech sounds to spoken words* (pp. 121–166). Cambridge, MA: The MIT Press.

Plomin, R. (1999). Behavioral genetics. In M. Bennett (Ed.), *Developmental psychology: Achievements and prospects* (pp. 231–252). Hove, England: Psychology Press.

Plomin, R. (2000). Behavioural genetics in the 21st century. *International Journal of Behavioral Development, 24,* 30–34.

Plomin, R., & DeFries, J. C. (1985). *The origins of individual differences in infancy: The Colorado Adoption Project.* New York: Academic.

Plomin, R., Emde, R. N., Braungart, J. M., Campos, J., Corley, R., Fulker, D. W., Kagan, J., Reznick, J. S., Robinson, J., Zahn-Waxler, C., & DeFries, J. C. (1993). Genetic change and continuity from fourteen to twenty months: The MacArthur Longitudinal Twin Study. *Child Development, 64,* 1354–1376.

Plomin, R., Kagan, J., Emde, R. N., Reznick, J. S., Braungart, J. M., Robinson, J., Campos, J., Zahn-Waxler, C., Corley, R., Fulker, D. W., & DeFries, J. C. (1993). Genetic change and continuity from fourteen to twenty months: The MacArthur Longitudinal Twin Study. *Child Development, 64,* 1354–1376.

Plunkett, K. (1993). Lexical segmentation and vocabulary growth in early language acquisition. *Journal of Child Language, 20,* 43–60.

Plunkett, K., & Schafer, G. E. (1999). Early speech perception and word learning. In M. Barrett (Ed.), *The development of language: Studies in developmental psychology* (pp. 51–71). Hove, England: Psychology Press.

Plutchik, R. (1980). *Emotion: A psychoevolutionary synthesis.* New York: Harper & Row.

Polka, L., & Werker, J. F. (1994). Developmental changes in perception of nonnative vowel contrasts. *Journal of Experimental Psychology: Human Perception and Performance, 20,* 421–435.

Polygenis, D., Warton, S., Malmberg, C., Sherman, N., Kennedy, D., Koren, G., & Einarson, T. P. (1998). Moderate alcohol consumption during pregnancy and the incidence of fetal malformations: A meta-analysis. *Neurotoxicology and Teratology, 20,* 61–67.

Porges, S. W. (1995). Cardiac vagal tone: A physiological index of stress. *Neuroscience and Biobehavioral Reviews, 19,* 225–233.

Porges, S. W. (1997). Emotion: An evolutionary by-product of the neural regulation of the autonomic nervous system. In C. S. Carter & I. I.

Lederhendler (Eds.), *The integrative neurobiology of affiliation. Annals of the New York Academy of Sciences, 807* (pp. 62–77). New York: New York Academy of Sciences.

Porges, S. W., Doussard-Roosevelt, J. A., Portales, A. L., & Greenspan, S. J. (1996). Infant regulation of the vagal "brake" predicts child behavior problems: A psychobiological model of social behavior. *Developmental Psychobiology, 29,* 697–712.

Porter, R. H., & Winberg, J. (1999). Unique salience of maternal breast odors for newborn infants. *Neuroscience and Biobehavioral Reviews, 23,* 439–449.

Porter, R. H., Bologh, R. D., & Makin, J. W. (1988). Olfactory influences on mother–infant interactions. In C. Rovee-Collier & L. P. Lipsitt (Eds.), *Advances in infancy research* (Vol. 5, pp. 39–69). Norwood, NJ: Ablex.

Posada, G., Jacobs, A., Carbonell, O. A., Alzate, G., Bustamante, M. R., & Arenas, A. (1999). Maternal care and attachment security in ordinary and emergency contexts. *Developmental Psychology, 35,* 1379–1388.

Porter, R. H., Makin, J. W., David, L. B., & Christensen, K. M. (1992). Breast-fed infants respond to olfactory cues from their own mother and unfamiliar lactating females. *Infant Behavior and Development, 15,* 85–93

Prader, A., Tanner, J. M., & von Harnack, G. A. (1963). Catch-up growth following illness or starvation. *Journal of Pediatrics, 62,* 646–659.

Prechtl, H. F. R. (1974). The behavioral states of the newborn infant. *Brain Research, 76,* 185–212.

Preyer, W. (1881). *Mind of the child* (H. W. Brown, Trans.). New York: Appleton, 1888–1889.

Price, T. S., Eley, T. C., Dale, P. S., Stevenson, J., Saudino, K., & Plomin, R. (2000). Genetic and environmental covariation between verbal and nonverbal cognitive development in infancy. *Child Development, 71,* 948–959.

Prochner, L., & Doyon, P. (1997). Researchers and their subjects in the history of child study: William Blatz and the Dionne quintuplets. *Canadian Psychology, 38,* 103–110.

Provine, R. R. (1988). On the uniqueness of embryos and the difference it makes. In W. P. Smotherman & S. R. Robinson (Eds.), *Behavior of the fetus* (pp. 259–282). New York: Cambridge University Press.

Punales-Morejon, D. (1997). Genetic counseling and prenatal diagnosis: A multicultural perspective. *Journal of the American Medical Womens Association, 52,* 30–32.

Putnam, S. P., Sanson, A. V., & Rothbart, M. K. (2002). Child temperament and parenting. In M. H. Bornstein (Ed.), *Handbook of parenting Vol. 1. Children and parenting* (2nd ed., pp. 255–277). Mahwah, NJ: Lawrence Erlbaum Associates.

Quine, W. V. O. (1960). *Word and object.* Cambridge, MA: MIT Press.

Quinn, P. C. (1999). Development of recognition and categorization of objects and their spatial relations in young infants. In L. Balter & C. S. Tamis-LeMonda (Eds.), *Child Psychology: A handbook of contemporary issues* (pp. 85–115). Hove, England: Psychology Press.

Quinn, P. C., & Bhatt, R. S. (1998). Visual pop-out in young infants: Convergent evidence and an extension. *Infant Behavior and Development, 21,* 273–288.

Quinn, P. C., & Eimas, P. D. (1996). On categorization in early infancy. *Merrill-Palmer Quarterly, 32,* 331–363.

Quinn, P. C., & Eimas, P. D. (1996). Perceptual organization and categorization in young infants. In C. Rovee-Collier & L. P. Lipsitt (Eds.), *Advances in infancy research* (Vol. 10, pp. 1–36). Stamford, CT: Ablex.

Quinn, P. C., & Johnson, M. H. (2000). Global-before-basic object categorization in connectionist networks and 2-month-old infants. *Infancy, 1,* 31–46.

Quinn, P. C., Johnson, M. H., Mareschal, D., Rakison, D. H., & Younger, B. A. (2000). Understanding early categorization: One process or two. *Infancy, 1,* 111–122.

Rakic, P. (1987). Intrinsic and extrinsic determinants of neocortical parcellation: A radial unit model. In P. Rakic & W. Singer (Eds.), *Neurobiology of neocortex* (pp. 5–27). New York: Wiley.

Rakison, D. H. (2000). When a rose is just a rose: The illusion of taxonomies in infant categorization. *Infancy, 1,* 77–90.

Rakison, D. H., & Butterworth, G. E. (1998a). Infants' attention to object structure in early categorization. *Developmental Psychology, 34,* 1310–1325.

Rakison, D. H., & Butterworth, G. E. (1998b). Infants' use of object parts in early categorization. *Developmental Psychology, 34,* 49–62.

Ramsay, D. (1980). Beginnings of bimanual handedness and speech in infants. *Infant Behavior and Development, 3,* 67–78.

Rebelsky, F. (1967). Infancy in two cultures. *Nederlands Tijdschrift voor de Psychologie, 22,* 379–385.

Recchia, S. L. (1997). Social communication and response to ambiguous stimuli in toddlers with visual impairments. *Journal of Applied Developmental Psychology, 18,* 297–316.

Reese, E., & Cox, A. (1999). Quality of adult book reading affects children's emergent literacy. *Developmental Psychology, 35,* 20–28.

Regan, D. (1986). *Evoked potentials in science and medicine.* London: Chapman & Hall; New York: Wiley.

Reinisch, J. M. (1981). Prenatal exposure to synthetic progestins increases potential for aggression in humans. *Science, 211,* 1171–1173.

Reznick, J. S. (1997). Intelligence, language, nature, and nurture in young twins. In R. J.

Sternberg & E. L., Grigorenko (Eds.). *Intelligence, heredity, and environment* (pp. 483–504). New York, NY, US: Cambridge University Press.

Reznick, J. S., Fueser, J. J., & Bosquet, M. (1998). Self-corrected reaching in a three-location delayed-response search task. *Psychological Science, 9,* 66–70.

Rheingold, H., Gewirtz, J., & Ross, H. (1959). Social conditioning of vocalizations in the infant. *Journal of Comparative and Physiological Psychology, 52,* 68–73.

Richards, J. E. (unpublished manuscript). Neurophysiological basis of eye movements, and the effect of attention on eye movements in the development of infant saccades, smooth pursuit, and visual tracking.

Richards, J. E. (1994). Baseline respiratory sinus arrhythmia and heart rate responses during sustained visual attention in preterm infants from 3 to 6 months of age. *Psychophysiology, 31,* 235–243.

Richards, J. E. (1997). Peripheral stimulus localization by infants: Attention, age, and individual differences in heart rate variability. *Journal of Experimental Psychology, 23,* 667–680.

Richards, J. E., & Holley, F. B. (1999). Infant attention and the development of smooth pursuit tracking. *Developmental Psychology, 35,* 856–867.

Riviere, V., Darcheville, J. C., & Clement, C. (2000). Rapid timing of transitions in inter-reinforcement interval duration in infants. *Behavioural Processes, 52,* 109–115.

Rizzi, L. (2000). Remarks on early null subjects. In M. Friedman & L. Rizzi (Eds.), *The acquisition of syntax* (pp. 269–292). Harlow, England: Pearson.

Robertson, S. S., & Bacher, L. F. (1992, May). *Coupling of spontaneous movement and visual attention in infants.* Paper presented at the Biennial International Conference on Infant Studies, Miami, FL.

Robertson, S. S., & Bacher, L. F. (1995). Oscillation and chaos in fetal motor activity. In J. P. Lecanuet, W. P. Fifer, N. A. Krasnegor, & W. P. Smotherman (Eds.), *Fetal development: A psychobiological perspective* (pp. 169–189). Hillsdale, NJ: Lawrence Erlbaum Associates.

Robinson, G. E., & Wisner, K. L. (1993). Fetal anomalies. In D. E. Stewart & N. L. Stotland (Eds.), *Psychological aspects of women's health care: The interface between psychiatry and obstetrics and gynecology* (pp. 37–54). Washington, DC: American Psychiatric Press.

Rochat, P. (1997). Early development of the ecological self. In C. Dent-Read & P. Zukow-Goldring (Eds.), *Evolving explanations of development* (pp. 91–121). Washington, DC: American Psychological Association.

Rochat, P., & Morgan, R. (1995). Spatial determinants in the perception of self-produced leg movements by 3- to 5-month-old infants. *Developmental Psychology, 31,* 626–636.

Rochat, P., Querido, J. G., & Striano, T. (1999). Emerging sensitivity in the timing and structure of protoconversation in early infancy. *Developmental Psychology, 35,* 950–957.

Rodning, C., Beckwith, L., & Howard, J. (1989). Characteristics of attachment organization and play organization in prenatally drug exposed toddlers. *Development and Psychopathology, 1,* 277–289.

Roe, K. V., McClure, A., & Roe, A. (1983). Infant Gesell scores vs. cognitive skills at age 12 years. *Journal of Genetic Psychology, 142,* 143–147.

Roebuck, T. M., Mattson, S. N., & Riley, E. P. (1999). Prenatal exposure to alcohol: Effects on brain structure and neurpsychological functioning. In J. H. Hannigan & L. P. Spear (Eds.), *Alcohol and alcoholism: Effects on brain and development* (pp. 1–16). Mahwah, NJ: Lawrence Erlbaum Associates.

Roggman, L. A. (1992). Fathers with mothers and infants at the mall: Parental sex differences. *Early Child Development and Care, 79,* 65–72.

Rogoff, B. (1993). Play, cognitive development, and the social world: Piaget, Vygotsky, and beyond: Commentary. *Human Development, 36,* 24–26.

Rogoff, B. (1996). Developmental transitions in children's participation in sociocultural activities. In A. J. Sameroff & M. M. Haith (Eds.), *The five to seven year shift: The age of reason and responsibility. The John D. and Catherine T. MacArthur Foundation series on mental health and development* (pp. 273–294). Chicago: University of Chicago Press.

Rogoff, B. (1997). Evaluating development in the process of participation: Theory, methods, and practice building on each other. In E. Asmel & K. A. Renninger (Eds.), *Change and development: Issues of theory, method, and application. The Jean Piaget symposium series* (pp. 265–285). Mahwah, NJ: Lawrence Erlbaum Associates.

Rogoff, B., Ellis, S., & Gardner W. (1999). Adjustment of adult–child instruction according to child's age and task. In P. Lloyd & C. Ferny Hough (Eds.), *Lev Vygotsky: Critical assessments: The zone of proximal development* (Vol. 3, pp. 180–191). New York: Routledge.

Rogoff, B., Matusov, E., & White, C. (1996). Models of teaching and learning: Participation in a community of learners. In D. R. Olson & N. Torrance (Eds.), *The handbook of education and human development: New models of learning, teaching, and schooling* (pp. 388–414). Oxford, England: Blackwell.

Rogoff, B., Mistry, J., Gonçu, A., & Mosier, C. (1993). Guided participation in cultural activity by toddlers and caregivers. *Monographs of the Society for Research in Child Development, 58* (Serial No. 8, pp. 1–179).

Roizen, N. J. (1997). Down syndrome. In M. L. Batshaw (Ed.), *Children with disabilities* (4th ed., pp. 361–376). Baltimore: Brookes.

Rondal, J. A. (1980). Fathers' and mothers' speech in early language development. *Journal of Child Language, 7,* 353–369.

Roopnarine, J. L. (1986). Mothers' and fathers' behaviors toward the toy play of their infant sons and daughters. *Sex Roles, 14,* 59–68.

Roopnarine, J. L., Lasker, J., Sacks, M., & Stores, M. (1998). The cultural contexts of children's play. In O. N. Saracho & B. Spodek (Eds.), *Multiple perspectives on play in early childhood education* (pp. 194–219). Albany: State University of New York Press.

Rosch, E., Mervis, C. B., Gray, W., Johnson, M., & Boyes-Braem, P. (1976). Basic objects in natural categories. *Cognitive Psychology, 8,* 382–439.

Rose, R. J., Boughman, J. A., Corey, L. A., Nance, W. E., Christian, J. C., & Kang, K. W. (1980). Data from kinships of monozygotic twins indicate maternal effects on verbal intelligence. *Nature, 283,* 375–377.

Rose, S. A. (1994). Relation between physical growth and information processing in infants born in India. *Child Development, 65,* 889–902.

Rose, S. A., & Feldman, J. F. (1995). Prediction of IQ and specific cognitive abilities at 11 years from infancy measures. *Developmental Psychology, 31,* 685–696.

Rose, S. A., & Feldman, J. F. (1996). Memory and processing speed in preterm children at 11 years: A comparison with full-terms. *Child Development, 67,* 2005–2021.

Rose, S. A., & Feldman, J. F. (1997). Memory and speed: Their role in the relation of infant information processing to 11-year IQ. *Child Development, 68,* 630–641.

Rose, S., & Tamis-LeMonda, C. S. (1999). Visual information processing in infancy: Reflections on underlying mechanisms. In L. Balter & C. S. Tamis-LeMonda (Eds.), *Child psychology: A handbook of contemporary issues* (pp. 64–84). East Sussex, England: Psychology Press.

Rose, S. A., Feldman, J. F., Futterweit, L. R., & Jankowski, J. J. (1998). Continuity in tactual-visual cross-modal transfer: Infancy to 11 years. *Developmental Psychology, 34,* 435–440.

Rose-Krasnor, L., Rubin, K. H., Booth, C. L., & Coplan, R. (1996). Maternal directiveness and child attachment security as predictors of social competence in preschoolers. *International Journal of Behavioral Development, 19,* 309–325.

Rosenblith, J. F. (1992). *In the beginning: Development in the first two years of life* (2nd ed.). Thousand Oaks, CA: Sage.

Rosenstein, D., & Oster, H. (1997). Differential facial responses to four basic tastes in newborns. In P. Ekman & E. L. Rosenberg (Eds.), *What the face reveals: Basic and applied studies of spontaneous expression using the Facial Action Coding System (FACS)* (pp. 302–327). New York: Oxford University Press.

Ross, G., & Lawson, K. (1997). Using the Bayley-II: Unresolved issues in assessing the development of prematurely born children. *Journal of Developmental and Behavioral Pediatrics, 18,* 109–111.

Ross, G., Tesman, J., Auld, P. A. M., & Nass, R. (1992). Effects of subependymal and mild intraventricular lesions on visual attention and memory in premature infants. *Developmental Psychology, 28,* 1067–1074.

Rothbart, M. K. (1981). Measurement of temperament in infancy. *Child Development, 52,* 569–578.

Rothbart, M. K. (1995). Concept and method in contemporary temperament research [Review of the book *Galen's prophecy*]. *Psychological Inquiry, 6,* 334–348.

Rothbart, M. K., & Ahadi, S. A. (1994). Temperament and the development of personality. *Journal of Abnormal Psychology, 103,* 55–66.

Rothbart, M. K., & Bates, J. E. (1998). In W. Damon (Editor-in-Chief) & N. Eisenberg (Vol. Ed.), *Handbook of child psychology: Vol. 3. Social, emotional, and personality development* (5th ed., pp. 105–176). New York: Wiley.

Rothbart, M. K., & Derryberry, P. (1981). Development of individual differences in temperament. In M. E. Lamb & A. Brown (Eds.), *Advances in developmental psychology* (Vol. 1, pp. 37–81). Hillsdale, NJ: Lawrence Erlbaum Associates.

Rothbart, M. K., Posner, M. I., & Hershey, K. L. (1995). Temperament, attention, and developmental psychopathology. In D. Cicchetti & D. J. Cohen (Eds.), *Manual of developmental psychopathology* (Vol. 1, pp. 315–340). New York: Wiley.

Rothbaum, F., Weisz, J., Pott, M., Miyaki, K., & Morelli, G. (2000). Attachment and culture: Security in the United States and Japan. *American Psychologist, 55,* 1093–1104.

Rousseau, J. J. ( ). *Emile.* New York: Barron's Educational Series. (Original work published 1762).

Rousseau, J. J. ( ). *Confessions.* New York: Dover. (Original work published 1781.)

Rovee-Collier, C. (1996a). Measuring infant memory: A critical commentary. *Developmental Review, 16,* 301–310.

Rovee-Collier, C. (1996b). Shifting the focus from what to why. *Infant Behavior and Development, 19,* 385–400.

Rovee-Collier, C., & Boller, K. (1995). Interference or facilitation in infant memory? In C. J. Brainerd & F. N. Dempster (Eds.), *Interference and inhibition in cognition* (pp. 61–104). San Diego, CA: Academic.

Rovee-Collier, C., & Gerhardstein, P. (1997). The development of infant memory. In C. Hulme (Series Ed.) & N. Cowan (Ed.), *The development of memory in childhood. Studies in developmental psychology* (pp. 5–39). Hove, England: Psychology Press.

Rovee-Collier, C., & Shyi, G. C. W. (1992). A functional and cognitive analysis of infant long-term memory. In M. Howe, C. Brainerd, & V. F. Reyna (Eds.), *Development of long-term retention* (pp. 3–55). New York: Springer-Verlag.

Rovee-Collier, C., Griesler, P. C., & Earley, L. A. (1985). Contextual determinants of retrieval in three-month-old infants. *Learning and Motivation, 16,* 139–157.

Rowe, D. C. (1997). Genetics, temperament, and personality. In R. Hogan, J. Johnson, & S. Briggs (Eds.), *Handbook of personality psychology* (pp. 367–386). San Diego, CA: Academic.

Rubenstein, A. J., Kalakanis, L., & Langlois, J. H. (1999). Infant preferences for attractive faces: A cognitive explanation. *Developmental Psychology, 35,* 848–855.

Rubin, J., Provenzano, F., & Luria, Z. (1974). The eye of the beholder: Parents' view of sex of newborns. *American Journal of Orthopsychiatry, 43,* 720–731.

Rubin, K. H., Coplan, R., Cheah, L. N., & Lagace-Sequin, D. G. (1999). Peer relationships in childhood. In M. H. Bornstein & M. E. Lamb (Eds.), *Developmental psychology: An advanced textbook* (pp. 451–501). Mahwah, NJ: Lawrence Erlbaum Associates.

Rubin, K., Fein, G. G., & Vandenberg, B. (1983). Play. In E. M. Hetherington (Ed.), *Carmichael's manual of child psychology: Social development* (pp. 693–774). New York: Wiley.

Ruble, D. N., & Martin, C. L. (1998). Gender development. In W. Damon (Editor-in-Chief) & N. Eisenberg (Vol. Ed.), *Handbook of child psychology: Vol. 3. Social, emotional, and personality development* (pp. 933–1016). New York: Wiley.

Ruff, H. A. (1982a). Effect of object movement on infants' detection of object structure. *Developmental Psychology, 18,* 462–472.

Ruff, H. A. (1982b). Infants' exploration of objects. *Infant Behavior and Development, 5,* 207.

Ruff, H. A. (1982c). The role of manipulation in infants' responses to invariant properties of objects. *Developmental Psychology, 18,* 682–691.

Ruff, H. A. (1985). Detection of information specifying the motion of objects by 3- and 5-month-old infants. *Developmental Psychology, 21,* 295–305.

Ruff, H. A. (1989). The infant's use of visual and haptic information in the perception and recognition of objects. *Canadian Journal of Psychology, 43,* 302–319.

Ruff, H. A. (1990). Individual differences in sustained attention during infancy. In J. Colombo & J. Fagan (Eds.), *Individual differences in infancy: Reliability, stability, prediction.* Hillsdale, NJ: Lawrence Erlbaum Associates.

Russell, A., & Russell, G. (1989). Warmth in mother-child and father-child relationships in middle childhood. *British Journal of Developmental Psychology, 7,* 219-235.

Russell, M. J., Mendelson, T., & Peeke, H. V. S. (1983). Mother's identification of their infant's odors. *Ethology and Sociobiology, 4,* 29–31.

Rutstein, R. M., Conlon, C. J., & Batshaw, M. L. (1997). HIV and AIDS: From mother to child. In M. L. Batshaw (Ed.), *Children with disabilities* (4th ed., pp. 163–181). Baltimore: Brookes.

Rutter, M. (1998). Developmental catch-up, and deficit, following adoption after severe global early privation. *Journal of Child Psychology and Psychiatry and Allied Disciplines, 39,* 466–476.

Rutter, M. (2002). Maternal deprivation. In M. H. Bornstein (Ed.), *Handbook of parenting Vol. 4 Applied parenting* (pp. 181–202). Mahwah, NJ: Lawrence Erlbaum Associates.

Saarni, C. (2000). The social context of emotional development. In M. Lewis & J. M. Haviland-Jones (Eds.), *Handbook of emotions* (2nd ed., pp. 306–322). New York: Guilford.

Saarni, C., Mumme, D. L., & Campos, J. J. (1998). Emotional development: Action, communication, and understanding. In W. Damon (Editor-in-Chief) & N. Eisenberg (Vol. Ed.), *Handbook of child psychology: Vol. 3. Social, emotional and personality development* (5th ed., pp. 237–309). New York: Wiley.

Sackett, G. P. (1966). Monkeys reared in isolation with pictures as visual input: Evidence for an innate releasing mechanism. *Science, 154,* 1468–1473.

Sagi, A. (1981). Mothers' and non-mothers' identification of infant cries. *Infant Behavior and Development, 4,* 37–40.

Sagi, A., van IJzendoorn, M. H., Scharf, M., Koren-Karie, N., Joels, T., & Mayseless, O. (1994). Stability and discriminant validity of the Adult Attachment Interview: A psychometric study in young Israeli adults. *Developmental Psychology, 30,* 771–777.

St. Augustine. (398/1961). *The confessions.* New York: Viking.

St. James-Roberts, I., & Plewis, I. (1996). Individual differences, daily fluctuations, and developmental changes in amounts of infant waking, fussing, crying, feeding, and sleeping. *Child Development, 67,* 2527–2540.

Sameroff, A. J. (1996, Fall). Presidential address: Democratic and Republican models of development: Paradigms or perspectives. *Division 7 Newsletter of the American Psychological Association,* 1–9.

Sameroff, A. J. (1975). Early influences on development: Fact or fancy? *Merrill-Palmer Quarterly, 21,* 267–294.

Sameroff, A. J. (1983). Developmental systems: Contexts and evolution. In P. H. Mussen (Series Ed.) & W. Kessen (Vol. Ed.), *Handbook of child psychology: Vol. 1. History, theory, and methods* (pp. 237–294). New York: Wiley.

Sameroff, A., & Chandler, M. J. (1975). Reproductive risk and the continuum of caretaking casualty. In F. D. Horowitz (Ed.), *Review of child development research* (Vol. 4, pp. 137–244). Chicago: University of Chicago Press.

Sameroff, A. J., & Feil, L. A. (1985). Parental concepts of development. In I. E. Sigel (Ed.), *Parental belief systems* (pp. 83–105). Hillsdale, NJ: Lawrence Erlbaum.

Sandall, S. R. (1997). Developmental assessment in early intervention. In A. H. Widerstrom, B. A. Mowder, & S. R. Sandall (Eds.), *Infant development and risk: An introduction* (2nd ed., pp. 211–235). Baltimore: Brookes.

Sandhofer, C. M., Smith, L. B., & Luo, J. (2000). Counting nouns and verbs in the input: Differential frequencies, different kinds of learning? *Journal of Child Language, 27,* 561–585.

Sanson, A., Prior, M., Smart, D., & Oberklaid, F. (1993). Gender differences in aggression in childhood: Implications for a peaceful world. *Australian Psychologist, 28,* 86–92.

Saudino, K. J., Gagne, J. R., Grant, J., Ibatoulina, A., Marytuina, T., Ravich-Scherbo, I., & Whitfield, K. (1999). Genetic and environmental influences on personality in adult Russian twins. *International Journal of Behavioral Development, 23,* 375–389.

Savage, S. L., & Gauvain, M. (1998). Parental beliefs and children's everyday planning in European-American and Latino families. *Journal of Applied Developmental Psychology, 19,* 319–340.

Saxon, T. F. (1997). A longitudinal study of early mother–infant interaction and later language competence. *First Language, 17,* 271–281.

Saxon, T. F., Frick, J. E., & Colombo, J. (1997). A longitudinal study of maternal interactional styles and infant visual attention. *Merrill-Palmer Quarterly, 43,* 48–66.

Scarr, S. (1993). Biological and cultural diversity: The legacy of Darwin for development. *Child Development, 64,* 1333–1353.

Scarr, S., & Kidd, K. K. (1983). Developmental behavior genetics. In P. H. Mussen (Gen. Ed.), M. M. Haith, & J. J. Campos (Vol. Eds.), *Handbook of child psychology: Vol. 2. Infancy and developmental psychobiology* (pp. 345–433). New York: Wiley.

Scarr, S., & McCartney, K. (1983). How people make their own environments: A theory of genotype–environment effects. *Child Development, 54,* 424–435.

Scarr, S., & Salapatek, P. (1970). Patterns of fear development during infancy. *Merrill-Palmer Quarterly, 16,* 53–90.

Scarr, S., & Weinberg, F. A. (1983). The Minnesota adoption studies: Genetic differences and malleability. *Child Development, 54,* 260–268.

Schafer, G. E., & Bernstein, I. L. (1996). Taste aversion learning. In E. D. Capaldi (Ed.), *Why we eat what we eat* (pp. 31–51). Washington, DC: American Psychological Association.

Schaffer, H. R. (1984). *The child's entry into a social world.* London: Academic.

Schaffer, H. R., & Crook, C. K. (1980). Child compliance and maternal control techniques. *Developmental Psychology, 16,* 54–61.

Schaffer, H. R., Hepburn, A., & Collis, G. M. (1983). Verbal and nonverbal aspects of mothers' directives. *Journal of Child Language, 10,* 337–355.

Schama, K. F., Howell, L. L., & Byrd, L. D. (1998). Prenatal exposure to cocaine. In S. T. Higgins & J. L. Katz (Eds.), *Cocaine abuse: Behavior, pharmacology, and clinical applications* (pp. 159–179). San Diego, CA: Academic.

Scheibel, A. B., Paul, L. A., Fried, I., Forsythe, A. B., Tomiyasu, U., Wechsler, A., Kao, A., & Slotnick, J. (1985). Dendritic organization of the anterior speech area. *Experimental Neurology, 87,* 109–117.

Scherer, K. R. (1999). Appraisal theory. In T. Dalgleish & J. J. Power (Eds.), *Handbook of cognition and emotion* (pp. 637–663). Chichester, England: Wiley.

Scherling, D. (1994). Prenatal cocaine exposure and childhood psychopathology: A developmental analysis. *American Journal of Orthopsychiatry, 64,* 9–19.

Schiff, W., Benasich, A., & Bornstein, M. H. (1989). Infant sensitivity to audiovisually coherent events. *Psychological Research, 51,* 102–106.

Schmitz, S., Fulker, D. W., Plomin, R., Zahn-Waxler, C., Emde, R. N., & DeFries, J. C. (1999). Temperament and problem behavior during early childhood. *International Journal of Behavioral Development, 23,* 333–555.

Schneider, M. L. (1992). The effect of mild stress during pregnancy on birthweight and neuromotor maturation in rhesus monkey infants (*Macaca mulatta*). *Infant Behavior and Development, 15,* 389–403.

Schölmerich, A., Broberg, & Lamb. M. E. (2000). Precursors of inhibition and shyness in the first year of life. In R. Crozier (Ed.), *Shyness* (pp. 47–63). London: Routledge.

Schölmerich, A., Lamb, M. E., Leyendecker, B., & Fracasso, M. P. (1997). Mother-infant teaching interactions and attachment security in Euro-American and Central-American immigrant families. *Infant Behavior and Development, 20,* 165–174.

Schroeder, D. B., Martorell, R., Rivera, J. A., Ruel, M. T., & Habicht, J. (1995). Age differences in the impact of nutritional supplementation on growth. *Journal of Nutrition, 125,* 1051S–1059S.

Schuengel, C., Bakermans-Kranenburg, M. J., van IJzendoorn, M. H., & Blom, M. (1999). Unresolved loss and infant disorganization: Links to frightening maternal behavior. In J. Solomon & C. George (Eds.), *Attachment disorganization* (pp. 71–94). New York: Guilford.

Schuetze, P., & Zeskind, P. S. (1998). Relation between reported maternal caffeine consumption during pregnancy and neonatal state and heart rate. *Infant Behavior and Development, 20,* 559–562.

Schnur, E., & Schatz, M. (1984). The role of maternal gesturing in conversations with one-year-olds. *Journal of Child Language, 11,* 29–41.

Schwartz, G. M., Izard, C. E., & Ansul, S. E. (1985). The 5-month-old's ability to discriminate facial expressions of emotion. *Infant Behavior and Development, 8,* 65–77.

Schwartz, R. G., & Camarata, S. (1985). Examining relationships between input and language development: Some statistical issues. *Journal of Child Language, 12,* 199–207.

Scott, G. & Richards, M. P. M. (1990). Night waking in infants: Effects of providing advice and support for parents. *Journal of Child Psychology and Psychiatry, 31,* 551–567.

Segal, N. L. (1997). Twin research perspective on human development. In N. L. Segal, G. E. Weisfeld, & C. C. Weisfeld (Eds.), *Uniting psychology and biology: Integrative perspectives on human development* (pp. 145–173). Washington, DC: American Psychological Association.

Seifer, R. (2000). Temperament and goodness of fit: Implications for developmental psychopathology. In A. J. Sameroff & M. Lewis (Eds.), *Handbook of developmental psychopathology* (2nd ed., pp. 257–276). New York: Kluwer Academic/Plenum.

Seifer, R., Sameroff, A. J., Barrett, L. C., & Krafchuk, E. (1994). Infant temperament measured by multiple observations and mother report. *Child Development, 65,* 1478–1490.

Self, P. A., & Horowitz, F. D. (1979). The behavioral assessment of the neonate: An overview. In J. D. Osofsky (Ed.), *The handbook of infant development* (pp. 126–164). New York: Wiley-Interscience.

Seligman, M. E. P. (1970). On the generality of the laws of learning. *Psychological Review, 77,* 406–418.

Seltenheim, K., Ahnert, L., Rickert, H., & Lamb, M. E. (1997, May). *The formation of attachments between infants and care providers in German daycare centers.* Paper presented to the American Psychological Society, Washington, DC.

Senghas, A., & Coppola, M. (2001). Children creating language: How Nicaraguan sign language acquired a spatial grammar. *Psychological Science, 12,* 323–328.

Shatz, M. (1982). On mechanisms of language acquisition: Can features of the communicative environment account for development? In E. Wanner & L. Gleitman (Eds.), *Language acquisition: The state of the art.* Cambridge, England: Cambridge University Press.

Shaw, D. S., Owens, E. B., Vondra, J. I., Keenan, K., & Winslow, E. B. (1997). Early risk factors and pathways in the development of early disruptive behavior problems. *Development and Psychopathology, 8,* 679–700.

Sheppard, J. J., & Mysak, E. D. (1984). Ontogeny of infantile oral reflexes and emergency chewing. *Child Development, 55,* 831–843.

Sherman, M., Sherman, I., & Flory, C. B. (1936). Infant behavior. *Comparative Psychology Monographs, 12*(Whole No. 79).

Sherrod, L. R. (1981). Issues in cognitive-perceptual development: The special case of social stimuli. In M. Lamb & L. Sherrod (Eds.), *Infant social cognition* (pp. 11–36). Hillsdale, NJ: Lawrence Erlbaum Associates.

Shirley, M. (1933). *The first two years. A study of twenty-five babies* (Vols. 1, 2, & 3). Minneapolis: University of Minnesota Press.

Shostak, M. (1981). *Nisa: The life and words of a !Kung woman.* Cambridge, England: Harvard University Press.

Siegel, L. S. (1982a). Early cognitive and environmental correlates of language development at 4 years. *International Journal of Behavioral Development, 5,* 433–444.

Siegel, L. S. (1982b). Reproductive, perinatal and environmental factors as predictors of the cognitive and language development of preterm and full-term babies. *Child Development, 53,* 963–973.

Siegel, L. S. (1983). Correction for prematurity and its consequences for the assessment of the very low birth weight infant. *Child Development, 54,* 1176–1188.

Siegel, L. S. (1989). A reconceptualization of prediction from infant test scores. In M. H. Bornstein & N. A. Krasnegor (Eds.), *Stability and continuity in mental development: Behavioral and biological perspectives.* Hillsdale, NJ: Lawrence Erlbaum Associates.

Sigel, I. E., McGillicuddy-DeLisi, A. V., & Goodnow, J. J. (Eds.). (1992). *Parental belief systems: The psychological consequences for children* (2nd ed.). Hillsdale, NJ: Lawrence Erlbaum Associates.

Sigman, M. D., Cohen, S. E., & Beckwith, L. (1997). Why does infant attention predict adolescent intelligence? *Infant Behavior and Development, 20,* 133–140.

Simion, F., Valenza, E., & Umilta, C. (1998). Mechanisms underlying face preference at birth. In F. Simion & G. Butterworth (Eds.), *The development of sensory, motor, and cognitive capacities in early infancy: From perception to cognition* (pp. 87–101). Hove, England: Psychology Press.

Singer, L. T., Yamashita, T. S., Hawkins, S., et al. (1994). Increased incidence of intraventricular hemorrhae and developmental delay in cocaine-exposed, very low-birthweight infants. *Journal of Pediatrics, 124,* 765–771.

Sireteanu, R. (1996). Development of the visual field: Results from human and animal studies. In F. Vital-Durand, J. Atkinson, & O. J. Braddick

(Eds.), *Infant vision* (pp. 19–31). Oxford, England: Oxford University Press.

Skinner, B. F. (1957). *Verbal behavior.* New York: Appleton.

Slade, A. (1987a). A longitudinal study of maternal involvement and symbolic play during the toddler period. *Child Development, 58,* 367–375.

Slade, A. (1987b). Quality of attachment and early symbolic play. *Developmental Psychology, 23,* 78–85.

Slater, A. M. (1993). Visual perceptual abilities at birth: Implications for face perception. In B. de Boysson-Bardies, S. de Schonen, P. Jusczyk, P. McNeilage, & J. Morton (Eds.), *Developmental neurocognition: Speech and face processing in the first year of life* (pp. 125–134). Dordrecht, the Netherlands/Boston/London: Kluwer Academic.

Slater, A. M. (1995). Visual perception and memory at birth. In C. Rovee-Collier & L. Lipsitt (Eds.), *Advances in infancy research* (Vol. 9, pp. 107–162). Norwood, NJ: Ablex.

Slater, A. M. (1997). Visual perception and its organisation in early infancy. In G. Bremner, A. Slater, & G. Butterworth (Eds.), *Infant development: Recent advances* (pp. 31–53). Hove, England: Psychology Press.

Slater, A. M., & Butterworth, G. (1997). Perception of social stimuli: Face perception and imitation. In G. Bremner, A. Slater, & G. Butterworth (Eds.), *Infant development: Recent advances* (pp. 223–245). Hove, England: Psychology Press.

Slater, A. M., & Johnson, S. P. (1998). Visual sensory and perceptual abilities of the newborn: Beyond the blooming, buzzing confusion. In F. Simion & G. Butterworth (Eds.), *The development of sensory, motor, and cognitive capacities in early infancy: From perception to cognition* (pp. 121–141). London: Psychology Press.

Slater, A. M., Brown, E., Mattock, A., & Bornstein, M. H. (1996). Continuity and change in habituation in the first 4 months from birth. *Journal of Reproductive and Infant Psychology, 14,* 187–194.

Slater, A. M., Mattock, A., & Brown, E. (1990). Size constancy at birth: Newborn infants' responses to retinal and real size. *Journal of Experimental Child Psychology, 49,* 314–322.

Slater, A. M., Mattock, A., Brown, E., Burnham, D., & Young, A. (1991a). Newborn infants' visual processing of stimulus compounds. *Perception,*

Slater, A. M., Mattock, A., Brown, E., Burnham, D., & Young, A. W. (1991b). Visual processing of stimulus compounds in newborn babies. *Perception, 20,* 29–33.

Slater, A. M., Morison, V., & Rose, D. (1983a). Locus of habituation in the human newborn. *Perception, 12,* 593–598.

Slater, A. M., Morison, V., & Rose, D. (1983b). Perception of shape by the new-born baby. *British Journal of Developmental Psychology, 1,* 135–142.

Slobin, D. I. (1982). Universal and particular in the acquisition of language. In E. Wanner & L. R. Gleitman (Eds.), *Language acquisition: The state of the art.* Cambridge, England: Cambridge University Press.

Smith, B. A., & Blass, E. M. (1996). Taste-mediated calming in premature, preterm, and full-term infants. *Developmental Psychology, 32,* 1084–1089.

Smith, C. M. (1947). Effects of maternal undernutrition upon the newborn infant in Holland (1944–45). *Journal of Pediatrics, 30,* 229–243.

Smith, D. V., & Vogt, M. B. (1997). The neural code and integrative processes of taste. In E. C. Carterette, M. P. Friedman (Series Eds.), G. K. Beauchamp, & L. Bartoshuk (Eds.), *Tasting and smelling. Handbook of perception and cognition* (2nd ed., pp. 25–76). San Diego, CA: Academic.

Smith, J. M. (1936). The relative brightness value for three hues for newborn infants. *University of Iowa Studies of Child Welfare, 12,* 91–140.

Smith, K. E., Landry, S. H., & Swank, P. R. (2000). The influence of early patterns of positive parenting on children's preschool outcomes. *Early Education and Development, 11,* 147–169.

Smolak, L. (1987). Child characteristics and maternal speech. *Journal of Child Language, 14,* 481–492.

Smolucha, L., & Smolucha, F. (1998). The social origins of mind: Post-Piagetian perspectives on pretend play. In O. N. Saracho & B. Spodek (Eds.), *Multiple perspectives on play in early childhood education* (pp. 34–58). Albany: State University of New York Press.

Smotherson, W. P., & Robinson, S. R. (1996). The development of behavior before birth. *Developmental Psychology, 32,* 425–434.

Snow, C. E. (1977a). The development of conversation between mothers and babies. *Journal of Child Language, 4,* 1–22.

Snow, C. E. (1977b). Mothers' speech research: From input to interactions. In C. E. Snow & C. A. Ferguson (Eds.), *Talking to children: Language input and acquisition.* Cambridge, England: Cambridge University Press.

Snyder, L. S., Bates, E., & Bretherton, I. (1981). Content and context in early lexical development. *Journal of Child Language, 8,* 565–582.

Soja, N. N., Carey, S., & Spelke, E. S. (1991). Ontological categories guide young children's inductions of word meaning: Object terms and subject terms. *Cognition, 38,* 179–211.

Solomon, J., & George, C. (1999). The measurement of attachment security in infancy and childhood. In J. Cassidy & P. R. Shaver (Eds.), *Handbook of attachment: Theory, research, and clinical applications* (pp. 287–316). New York: Guilford.

Solomon, R. C. (2000). The philosophy of emotions. In M. Lewis & J. M. Haviland-Jones

(Eds.), *Handbook of emotions* (2nd ed., pp. 3–15). New York: Guilford.

Sorce, J. F., & Emde, R. N. (1981). Mother's presence is not enough: The effect of emotional availability on infant exploration. *Developmental Psychology, 17,* 737–745.

Sorce, J. F., & Emde, R. N. (1982). The meaning of infant emotional expressions: Regularities in care giving responses in normal and Down syndrome infants. *Journal of Child Psychology and Psychiatry, 23,* 145–158.

Sorce, J. F., Emde, R. N., Campos, J. J., & Klinnert, M. D. (1985). Maternal emotional signaling: Its effect on the visual cliff behavior of 1-year-olds. *Developmental Psychology, 21,* 195–200.

Spelke, E. S. (1994). Initial knowledge: Six suggestions. *Cognition, 50,* 431–445.

Spelke, E. S., & Hermer, L. (1996). Early cognitive development: Objects and space. In E. Carterette, M. Friedman (Series Eds.), R. Gelman, & T. K. F. Au (Eds.), *Handbook of perception and cognition: Perceptual and cognitive development* (2nd ed., pp. 71–114). San Diego, CA: Academic.

Spelke, E. S., Breinlinger, K., Jacobson, K., & Phillips, A. (1993). Gestalt relations and object perception: A developmental study. *Perception, 22,* 1483–1501.

Spelke, E. S., Breinlinger, K., Macomber, J., & Jacobson, K. (1992). Origins of knowledge. *Psychological Review, 99,* 605–632.

Spelke, E. S., Gutheil, G., & Van de Walle, G. (1995). The development of object perception. In S. M. Kosslyn & D. N. Osherson (Eds.), *Visual cognition: An invitation to cognitive science* (2nd ed., Vol. 2, pp. 297–330). Cambridge, MA: MIT Press.

Spelt, D. K. (1948). The conditioning of the human fetus in utero. *Journal of Experimental Psychology, 38,* 375–376.

Spence, A. J., & De Casper, A. J. (1984). *Human fetuses perceive maternal speech.* Paper presented to the International Conference on Infant Studies.

Spence, M. J., & Freeman, M. S. (1996). Newborn infants prefer the maternal low-pass filtered voice, but not the maternal whispered voice. *Infant Behavior and Development, 19,* 199–212.

Spiro, M. (1958). *Children of the kibbutz.* Cambridge, MA: Harvard University Press.

Spitz, R. A. (1965). *The first year of life.* New York: International Universities Press.

Sroufe, L. A. (1979). Socioemotional development. In J. D. Osofsky (Ed.), *Handbook of infant development* (pp. 462–516). New York: Wiley.

Sroufe, L. A. (1983). Infant–caregiver attachment and patterns of adaptation in preschool: The roots of maladaptation and competence. In M. Perlmutter (Ed.), *Minnesota Symposia on Child Psychology: Vol. 16. Development and policy concerning children with special needs* (pp. 41–83). Hillsdale, NJ: Lawrence Erlbaum Associates.

Sroufe, L. A. (1996). *Emotional development.* Cambridge, England: Cambridge University Press.

Sroufe, L. A. (2000). Early relationships and the development of children. *Infant Mental Health Journal, 21,* 67–74.

Sroufe, L. A., & Fleeson, J. (1986). Attachment and the construction of relationships In W. W. Hartup & Z. Rubin (Eds.), *Relationships and development* (pp. 51–72). Hillsdale, NJ: Lawrence Erlbaum Associates.

Sroufe, L. A., & Waters, E. (1976). The ontogenesis of smiling and laughter: A perspective on the organization of development in infancy. *Psychological Review, 83,* 173–189.

Sroufe, L. A., & Wunsch, J. P. (1972). The development of laughter in the first year of life. *Child Development, 43,* 1326–1344.

Sroufe, L. A., Waters, E., & Matas, L. (1974). Contextual determinants of infant affective response. In M. Lewis & L. Rosenblum (Eds.), *The origins of fear.* New York: Wiley.

Stack, D. M., & Poulin-Dubois, D. (1998). Socioemotional and cognitive competence in infancy: Paradigms, assessment strategies, and implications for intervention. In D. Pushkar, & W. M. Bukowski (Eds.), *Improving competence across the lifespan: Building interventions based on theory and research* (pp. 37–57). New York: Plenum.

Stein, Z., Susser, M., Saenger, G., & Marolla, F. (1975). *Famine and human development: The Dutch hunger winter of 1944–1945.* New York: Oxford University Press.

Steinberg, A. G., & Knightly, C. A. (1997). Hearing: Sounds and silences. In M. L. Batshaw (Ed.), *Children with disabilities* (4th ed., pp. 241–274). Baltimore: Brookes.

Steiner, J. E. (1977). Facial expressions of the neonate infant indicating the hedonics of food-related chemical stimuli. In J. M. Weiffenbach (Ed.), *Taste and development.* Bethesda, MD: U.S. Department of Health, Education, and Welfare.

Steiner, J. E. (1979). Human facial expressions in response to taste and smell stimulation. In H. Reese & L. Lipsitt (Eds.), *Advances in child development and behavior* (Vol. 13). New York: Academic.

Stenberg, G., & Hagekull, B. (1997). Social referencing and mood modification in 1-year-olds. *Infant Behavior and Development, 20,* 209–217.

Sterman, M. B., & Hoppenbrouwens, T. (1971). The development of sleep–waking and rest activity patterns from fetus to adult in man. In M. B. Sterman, D. J. McVinty, & A. M. Adinolf (Eds.), *Brain development and behavior.* New York: Academic.

Stern, D. N. (1990). *Diary of a child.* New York: Basic Books.

Stern, D. N. (1998). The process of therapeutic change involving implicit knowledge: Some implications of developmental observations for adult psychotherapy. *Infant Mental Health Journal, 19,* 300–308.

Stern, D. N., Spieker, S., Barnett, R., K., MacKain, K. (1983). The prosody of maternal speech: Infant age and context related changes. *Journal of Child Language, 10,* 1–15.

Stern, D. N., Spieker, S., & MacKain, K. (1982). Intonation contours as signals in maternal speech to prelinguistic infants. *Developmental Psychology, 18,* 727–735.

Stern, M., Karraker, K. H., Sopko, A. M., & Norman, S. (2000). The prematurity stereotype revisited: Impact on mothers' interactions with premature and full-term infants. *Infant Mental Health Journal, 21,* 495–509.

Stevens, E., Blake, J., Vitale, G., & MacDonald, S. (1998). Mother–infant object involvement at 9 and 15 months: Relation to infant cognition and early vocabulary. *First Language, 18,* 203–222.

Stevenson, M. B., Leavitt, L. A., Roach, M. A., Chapman, R. S., & Miller, J. F. (1986). Mothers' speech to their 1-year-old infants in home and laboratory settings. *Journal of Psycholinguistic Research, 15,* 451–461.

Stevenson, M. B., Ver Hoeve, J. N., Roach, M. A., & Leavitt, L. A. (1986). The beginning of conversation: Early patterns of mother–infant vocal responsiveness. *Infant Behavior and Development, 9,* 423–440.

Stevenson-Hinde, J., & Marshall, P. J. (1999). Behavioral inhibition, heart period, and respiratory sinus arrhythmia: An attachment perspective. *Child Development, 70,* 805–816.

Stilson, S. R., & Harding, C. G. (1997). Early social context as it relates to symbolic play: A longitudinal investigation. *Merrill-Palmer Quarterly, 43,* 682–693.

Stoel-Gammon, C., & Cooper, J. A. (1984). Patterns of early lexical phonological development. *Journal of Child Language, 11,* 247–271.

Stoel-Gammon, C., & Otomo, K. (1986). Babbling development of hearing-impaired and normally hearing subjects. *Journal of Speech and Hearing Discord, 51,* 33–41.

Stormshak, E. A., Bellanti, C. J., & Bierman, K. L. (1996). The quality of sibling relationships and the development of social competence and behavioral control in aggressive children. *Developmental Psychology, 32,* 79–89.

Streissguth, A. P., Barr, H. M., & Sampson, P. D. (1990). Moderate prenatal alcohol exposure: Effects on child IQ and learning problems at age 7$\frac{1}{2}$ years. *Alcoholism: Clinical and Experimental Research, 14,* 662–669.

Streissguth, A. P., Bookstein, F. L., Sampson, P. D., & Barr, H. M. (1995). Attention: Prenatal alcohol and continuities of vigilance and attention problems from 4 through 14 years. *Development and Psychopathology, 7,* 419–446.

Suomi, S. J., & Ripp, C. (1983). A history of motherless mother monkey mothering at the University of Wisconsin Primate Laboratory. In *Child abuse: The nonhuman primate data.* New York: Liss.

Super, C. M. (1976). Environmental effects on motor development: The case of "African infant precocity." *Developmental Medicine and Child Neurology, 18,* 561–567.

Super, C. M., & Harkness, S. (1982). The development of affect in infancy and early childhood. In D. A. Wagner & H. W. Stevenson (Eds.), *Cultural perspectives on child development.* San Francisco: Freeman.

Super, C. M., & Harkness, S. (1986). Temperament, development, and culture. In R. Plomin & J. Dunn (Eds.), *The study of temperament: Continuities, change and challenge.*

Super, C. M., & Harkness, S. (1997). The cultural structuring of child development. In J. W. Berry, & P. R. Dasen (Eds.), *Handbook of cross-cultural psychology: Vol. 2. Basic processes and human development* (2nd ed., pp. 1–39). Needham Heights, MA: Allyn & Bacon.

Susman-Stillman, A., Kalkoske, M., Egeland, B., & Waldman, I. (1996). Infant temperament and maternal sensitivity as predictors of attachment security. *Infant Behavior and Development, 19,* 33–47.

Swingley, D. (1999). Conditional probability and word discovery: A corpus analysis of speech to infants. In M. Hahn & S. C. Stoness (Ed.), *Proceedings of the Twenty-first Annual Meeting of the Cognitive Science Society* (pp. 724–729). Mahwah, NJ: Lawrence Erlbaum Associates.

Taine, H. A. (1889). *On intelligence* (T. D. Haye, Trans., 2 Vols.), New York: Holt.

Tamis-LeMonda, C. S., & Bornstein, M. H. (1990). Language, play, and attention at one year. *Infant Behavior and Development, 13,* 85–98.

Tamis-LeMonda, C. S., & Bornstein, M. H. (1991). Individual variation, correspondence, stability, and change in mother and toddler play. *Infant Behavior and Development, 14,* 143–162.

Tamis-LeMonda, C. S., & Bornstein, M. H. (1993). Infant antecedents of toddlers' exploratory competence. *Infant Behavior and Development, 16,* 423–439.

Tamis-LeMonda, C. S., & Bornstein, M. H. (1994). Specificity in mother–toddler language–play relations across the second year. *Developmental Psychology, 30,* 283–292.

Tamis-LeMonda, C. S., & Bornstein, M. H. (1996). Variation in children's exploratory, nonsymbolic, and symbolic play: An explanatory multidimensional framework. In C. Rovee-Collier & L. P. Lipsitt (Eds.), *Advances in infancy research* (Vol. 10, pp. 37–78). Norwood, NJ: Ablex.

Tamis-LeMonda, C. S., & Bornstein, M. H. (2002). Maternal responsiveness and early language acquisition. In R. Kail & H. W. Reese (Eds.), *Advances in child development and behavior* (Vol. 29, pp. 89–127). New York: Academic Press.

Tamis-LeMonda, C. S., Bornstein, M. H., Baumwell, L., & Damast, A. M. (1996). Responsive parenting in the second year: Specific influences on children's language and play. *Early Development and Parenting, 5,* 173–183.

Tamis-LeMonda, C. S., Bornstein, M. H., & Baumwell, L. (2001). Maternal responsiveness and children's achievement of language milestones. *Child Development, 72,* 748–767.

Tamis-LeMonda, C. S., Bornstein, M. H., Cyphers, L., Toda, S., & Ogino, M. (1991). Language and play at one year: A comparison of toddlers and mothers in the United States and Japan. *International Journal of Behavioral Development, 15,* 19–42.

Tamis-LeMonda, C. S., Bornstein, M. H., Cyphers, L., Toda, S., & Ogino, M. (1992). Language and play at one year: A comparison of toddlers and mothers in the United States and Japan. *International Journal of Behavioural Development, 15,* 19–42.

Tamis-LeMonda, C. S., Bornstein, M. H., Kahana-Kalman, R., Baumwell, L., & Cyphers, L. (1998). Predicting variation in the timing of language milestones in the second year: an events history approach. *Journal of Child Language, 25,* 675–700.

Tamis-LeMonda, C. S., Damast, A. M., & Bornstein, M. H. (1994). What do mothers know about the developmental nature of play? *Infant Behavior and Development, 17,* 341–345.

Tamis-LeMonda, C. S., & McClure, J. (1994). Relations between expectation formation and feature learning. *Infant Behavior and Development, 18,* 427–434.

Tamis-LeMonda, C. S., Užgiris, I. C., & Bornstein, M. H. (2002). Play in Parent-Child Interactions. In M. H. Bornstein (Ed.), *Handbook of parenting Vol. 5. Practical parenting* (pp. 221–241). Mahwah, NJ: Lawrence Erlbaum Associates.

Tanner, J. M. (1970). Physical growth. In P. Mussen (Ed.), *Carmichael's manual of child psychology* (Vol. 1, pp. 77–155). New York: Wiley.

Tanner, J. M. (1978). *Foetus into man: Physical growth from conception to maturity.* London: Open Books.

Tanner, J. M. (1990). *Foetus into man* (2nd ed.). Cambridge, England: Harvard University Press.

Tatzer, E., Schubert, M. T., Timischl, W., & Simbrunger, G. (1985). Discrimination of taste and preference for sweet in premature babies. *Early Human Development, 12,* 23–30.

Teichner, G., Ames, E. W., & Kerig, P. K. (1997). The relation of infant crying and the sex of the infant to parents' perceptions of the infant and themselves. *Psychology: A Journal of Human Behavior, 34,* 59–60.

Teller, D. Y., & Bornstein, M. H. (1986). Infant color vision and color perception. In P. Salapatek & L. B. Cohen (Eds.), *Handbook of infant perception: Vol. 1. From sensation to perception* (pp. 185–236). Orlando, FL: Academic.

Teller, D. Y., & Lindsey, D. T. (1989). Motion nulls for white versus isochromatic gratings in infants and adults. *Journal of the Optical Society of America,* 1945–1954.

Tellinghuisen, D. J., & Oakes, L. M. (1997). Distractibility in infancy: The effects of distractor characteristics and type of attention. *Journal of Experimental Child Psychology, 64,* 232–254.

Terman, L. M. (1916). *The measurement of intelligence.* Boston, MA: Houghton Mifflin.

Termine, N. T., & Izard, C. E. (1988). Infants' responses to their mothers' expressions of joy and sadness. *Developmental Psychology, 24,* 223–229.

Teti, D. M. (1999). Conceptualization of disorganization in the preschool years: An integration. In J. Solomon & C. George (Eds.), *Attachment disorganization* (pp. 213–242). New York: Guilford.

Teti, D. M. (2001, April). Conceptualizing disorganization in the preschool years. In E. Moss (Chair), *New perspectives on disorganized attachment.* Symposium presented at the biennial meeting of the Society for Research on Child Development, Minneapolis, MN.

Teti, D. M. (2002). Sibling relationships. In J. McHale & W. Grolnick (Eds.), *Interiors: Retrospect and prospect in the psychological study of families* (pp. 193–224). Mahwah, NJ: Lawrence Erlbaum Associates.

Teti, D. M. (in press). Socioemotional risks in early childhood. In N. J. Smelser, P. B. Baltes (Editors-in-Chief), & N. Eisenberg (Ed.), *International encyclopedia of the social and behavioral sciences.* Amsterdam: Pergamon.

Teti, D. M., & Ablard, K. E. (1989). Security of attachment and infant–sibling relationships: A laboratory study. *Child Development, 60,* 1519–1528.

Teti, D. M., & Candelaria, M. (2002). Parenting competence. In M. H. Bornstein (Ed.), *Handbook of parenting: Vol. 4. Applied parenting* (2nd ed., pp. 149–180). Mahwah, NJ: Lawrence Erlbaum Associates.

Teti, D. M., & Gelfand, D. M. (1991). Behavioral competence among mothers of infants in the first year: The mediational role of maternal self-efficacy. *Child Development, 62,* 918–929.

Teti, D. M., & Gelfand, D. M. (1997). Maternal cognitions as mediators of child outcomes in the context of postpartum depression. In L. Murray & P. J. Cooper (Eds.), *Postpartum depression and child development* (pp. 136–164). New York: Guilford.

Teti, D. M., & Lamb, M. E. (1986, April). *Attachment and caregiving between infants and older siblings.* Paper presented at the International Conference on Infant Studies, Los Angeles.

Teti, D. M., & Teti, L. O. (1996). Infant–parent relationships. In N. Vanzetti & S. Duck (Eds.),

A lifetime of relationships (pp. 77–104). Pacific Grove, CA: Brooks/Cole.

Teti, D. M., Bond, L. A., & Gibbs, E. D. (1986). Sibling-created experiences: Relationships to birth-spacing and infant cognitive development. *Infant Behavior and Development, 9*, 27–42.

Teti, D. M., Bond, L. A., & Gibbs, E. D. (1988). Mothers, fathers, and siblings: A comparison of play styles and their influence upon infant cognitive level. *International Journal of Behavioral Development, 11*, 415–432.

Teti, D. M., Bradley, M. E., Hastings, P., & Zahn-Waxler, C. (1999). Sibling relationships among children at risk for disruptive behavior. *Developmental Psychology.*

Teti, D. M., Gelfand, D. M., Messinger, D., & Isabella, R. (1995). Maternal depression and the quality of early attachment: An examination of infants, preschoolers, and their mothers. *Developmental Psychology, 31*, 364–376.

Teti, D. M., O'Connell, M. A., & Reiner, C. D. (1996). Parenting sensitivity, parental depression and child health: The mediational role of parental self-efficacy. *Early Development and Parenting, 5*, 237–250.

Teti, D. M., Sakin, J., Kucera, E., Corns, K. M. , & Eiden, R. D. (1996). And baby makes four: Predictors of attachment security among preschool-aged firstborns during the transition to siblinghood. *Child Development, 67*, 579–596.

Thal, D., & Bates, E. (1988). Language and gesture in late talkers. *Journal of Speech and Hearing Research, 31*, 115–123.

Thatcher, R. W. (1994). Cyclic cortical reorganization: Origins of human cognitive development. In G. Dawson & K. W. Fischer (Eds.), *Human behavior and the developing brain* (pp. 232–266). New York: Guilford.

Thelen, E. (1984). Learning to walk: Ecological demands and phylogenetic constraints. In L. P. Lipsitt & C. Rovee-Collier (Eds.), *Advances in infancy research* (Vol. 3). Norwood, NJ: Ablex.

Thelen, E. (1993). Timing and developmental dynamics in the acquisition of early motor skills. In G. Turkewitz & D. A. Devenny (Eds.), *Developmental time and timing* (pp. 85–104). Hillsdale, NJ: Lawrence Erlbaum Associates.

Thelen, E. (2000). Motor development as foundation and future of developmental psychology. *International Journal of Behavioral Development, 24*, 385–397.

Thelen, E. (2001). Dynamic mechanisms of change in early perceptual–motor development. In J. L. McClelland & R. S. Siegler (Eds.), *Mechanisms of cognitive development: Behavioral and neural perspectives* (pp. 161–184). Mahwah, NJ: Lawrence Erlbaum Associates.

Thelen, E., & Smith, L. B. (1994). *A dynamic systems approach to the development of cognition and action.* Cambridge, MA: MIT Press.

Thelen, E., & Spencer, J. P. (1998). Postural control during reaching in young infants: A dynamic systems approach. *Neuroscience and Biobehavioral Reviews, 22*, 507–514.

Thelen, E., Schoner, G., Scheier, C., & Smith, L. (2001). The dynamics of embodiment: A field theory of infant perseverative reaching. *Behavioral and Brain Sciences, 24*, 1–86.

Thodén, C. J., & Järvenpää-Michelsson, K. (1985). Sound spectrographic cry analysis of pain cry in prematures. In B. M. Lester & C. F. Z. Boukydis (Eds.), *Infant crying: Theoretical and research perspectives.* New York: Plenum.

Thoman, E. B. (1990). Sleeping and waking states in infants: A functional perspective. *Neuroscience and Biobehavioral Review, 14*, 93–107.

Thoman, E. B., & Whitney, M. P. (1990). Behavioral states in infants: Individual differences and individual analyses. In J. Colombo & J. Fagen (Eds.), *Individual differences in infancy: Reliability, stability, prediction* (pp. 113–136). Hillsdale, NJ: Lawrence Erlbaum Associates.

Thoman, E. B., Acebo, C., & Becker, P. T. (1983). Infant crying and stability in the mother–infant relationship: A systems analysis. *Child Development, 54*, 653–659.

Thomas, A., & Chess, S. (1977). *Temperament and development.* New York: Brunner/Mazel.

Thomas, A., & Chess, S. (1980). *The dynamics of psychological development.* New York: Brunner/Mazel.

Thomas, A., Chess, S., & Birch, H. (1970). The origins of personality. *Scientific American, 223*, 102–109.

Thomas, A., Chess, S., Birch, H., Hertzig, M., & Korn, S. (1963). *Behavioral individuality in childhood.* New York: New York University Press.

Thomas, D. G., & Crow, C. D. (1994). Development of evoked electrical brain activity in infancy. In G. Dawson & K. W. Fischer (Eds.), *Human behavior and the developing brain* (pp. 207–231). New York: Guilford.

Thompson, L. A., & Plomin, R. (1988). The sequenced inventory of communication development: An adoption study of two- and three-year-olds. *International Journal of Behavioral Development, 11*, 219–231.

Thompson, R. A. (1988). The effects of infant day care through the prism of attachment theory: A critical appraisal. *Early Childhood Research Quarterly, 3*, 273–282.

Thompson, R. A. (1990a). Emotion and self-regulation. In R. A. Thompson (Ed.), *Socioemotional development. Nebraska Symposium on Motivation* (Vol. 36, pp. 367–467). Lincoln: University of Nebraska Press.

Thompson, R. A. (1990b). Vulnerability in research: A developmental perspective on research risk. *Child Development, 61*, 1–16.

Thompson, R. A. (1998). Early sociopersonality development. In W. Damon (Editor-in-Chief) & N. Eisenberg (Vol. Ed.), *Handbook of child psychology: Vol. 3. Social, emotional, and personality development* (pp. 25–104). New York: Wiley.

Thompson, R. A. (1999). Early attachment and later development. In J. Cassidy & P. R. Shaver (Eds.), *Handbook of attachment: Theory, research, and clinical applications* (pp. 265–286). New York: Guilford.

Thompson, R. A. (2000). Understanding the dynamics of child maltreatment: Child harm, family healing, and public policy [Discussant's commentary]. In R. A. Dienstbier (Series Ed.) & D. J. Hansen (Volume Ed.), *Motivation and child maltreatment* (Vol. 46 of the Nebraska Symposium on Motivation, pp. 245–262). Lincoln: University of Nebraska Press.

Thompson, R. A., & Lamb, M. E. (1982). Stranger sociability and its relationship to temperament and social experiences during the second year. *Infant Behavior and Development, 5,* 277–288.

Thompson, R. A., & Lamb, M. E. (1984). Assessing qualitative dimensions of emotional responsiveness in infants: Separation reactions in the Strange Situation. *Infant Behavior and Development, 7,* 423–445.

Thompson, R. A., & Leger, D. W. (in press). From squalls to calls: The cry as a developing socioemotional signal. In B. Lester, J. Newman, & F. Pedersen (Eds.), *Biological and social aspects of infant crying.* New York: Plenum.

Thompson, R. A., & Limber, S. (1990). "Social anxiety" in infancy: Stranger wariness and separation distress. In H. Leitenberg (Ed.), *Handbook of social and evaluation anxiety* (pp. 85–137). New York: Plenum

Thompson, R. A., Lamb, M. E., & Estes, D. (1982). Stability of infant–mother attachment and its relationship to changing life circumstances in an unselected middle class sample. *Child Development, 53,* 144–148.

Tiedemann, D. (1787). Beobachtungen über die Entwicklung der Seetenfähigkeiten bei Kindern, Hessischen Beiträge zur Gelehrsamkeit und Kunst, 2, 313–315 and 3, 486–488.

Tinbergen, N. (1951). *The study of instinct.* Oxford, England: Oxford University Press.

Tinbergen, N. (1963). On aims and methods of ethology. *Zeitschrif Tier Psychologie, 20,* 410–433.

Tincoff, R., & Jusczyk, P. W. (1999). Some beginnings of word comprehension in 6-month-olds. *Psychological Science, 10,* 172–175.

Tomasello, M., & Brooks, P. J. (1998). Young children's earliest transitive and intransitive constructions. *Cognitive Linguistics, 9,* 379–395.

Tomasello, M., & Cale Kruger, A. (1992). Joint attention on actions: Acquiring verbs in ostensive and non-ostensive contexts. *Journal of Child Language, 19,* 311–333.

Trehub, S. E., & Trainor, L. J. (1993). Listening strategies in infancy: The roots of music and language development. In S. McAdams & E. Bigand (Eds.), *Thinking in sound: The cognitive psychology of human audition* (pp. 278–327). New York: Clarendon Press/Oxford University Press.

Trevarthen, C. B. (1974). Behavioral embryology. In E. C. Carterette & M. P. Friedman (Eds.), *Handbook of perception* (Vol. 3). New York: Academic.

Trevarthen, C. B. (1979). Communication and co-operation in early infancy: A description of primary intersubjectivity. In M. Bullowa (Ed.), *Before speech: The beginning of interpersonal communication.* Cambridge, England: Cambridge University Press.

Trevarthen, C. B. (1988). Universal co-operative motives: How infants begin to know the language and culture of their parents. In G. Jahoda & I. M. Lewis (Eds.), *Acquiring culture: Cross cultural studies in child development* (pp. 37–90). New York: Croom Helm.

Tronick, E. Z., Cohn, J., & Shea, E. (1986). The transfer of affect between mothers and infants. In T. B. Brazelton & M. W. Yogman (Eds.), *Affective development in infancy* (pp. 11–25). Norwood, NJ: Ablex.

Tubman, J. G., & Lerner, R. M. (1992). Temperament and adjustment in young adulthood: A 15-year longitudinal analysis. *American Journal of Orthopsychiatry, 62,* 564–574.

Tucker, D. (1992). Developing emotions and cortical networks. In M. Gunnar & C. A. Nelson (Eds.), *Minnesota symposium on child psychology* (Vol. 24, pp. 75–128). Hillsdale, NJ: Lawrence Erlbaum Associates.

Tulkin, S. R. (1977). Social class differences in maternal and infant behavior. In P. H. Leiderman, S. R. Tulkin, & A. Rosenfield (Eds.), *Culture and infancy.* New York: Academic.

Tulving, E. (1985). Memory and consciousness. *Canadian Psychology, 26,* 1–112.

Turkheimer, E., & Waldron, M. (2000). Nonshared environment: A theoretical, methodological, and quantitative review. *Psychological Bulletin, 126,* 78–108.

Turkewitz, G., & Kenny, P. A. (1982). Limitations on input as a basis for neural organization and perceptual development: A preliminary theoretical statement. *Developmental Psychobiology, 15,* 357–368.

Tzuriel, D. (1999). Parent–child mediated learning interactions as determinants of cognitive modifiability: Recent research and future directions. *Genetic, Social, and General Psychology Monographs, 125,* 109–156.

Ungerer, J. A., Zelazo, P., Kearsley, K., & O'Leary, K. (1981). Developmental changes in the representation of objects in symbolic play from 18 to 34 months. *Child Development, 52,* 186–195.

U.S. Department of Health and Human Services. (1999, August). *HIV/AIDS surveillance report: U.S. HIV and AIDS cases reported through*

December 1998 (Year-end ed., Vol. 10, No. 2). Washington, DC: Author.

Užgiris, I. C. (1989). Transformations and continuities: Intellectual functioning in infancy and beyond. In M. H. Bornstein & N. A. Krasnegor (Eds.), *Stability and continuity in mental development: Behavioral and biological perspectives* (pp. 123–143). Hillsdale, NJ: Lawrence Erlbaum Associates.

Uzgiris, I. C., & Hunt, J. M. (1975). *Assessment in infancy: Ordinal scales of psychological development.* Urbana: University of Illinois Press.

Vaal, J., van Soest, A. J., & Hopkins, B. (2000). Spontaneous kicking behavior in infants: Age-related effects of unilateral weighting. *Developmental Psychobiology, 36,* 111–122.

Valentine, C. W. (1937). A study of the beginnings and significance of play in infancy (II). *British Journal of Educational Psychology, 8,* 285–292.

Van Baar, A. L., Soepatmi, S., Gunning, W. B., & Akkerhuis, G. W. (1994). Development after prenatal exposure to cocaine, heroin, and methadone. *Acta Paediatrica, 404*(Suppl.), 40–46.

Van den Boom, D. C. (1991). The influence of infant irritability on the development of the mother–infant relationship in the first six months of life. In J. K. Nugent, B. M. Lester, & T. B. Brazelton (Eds.), *The cultural context of infancy* (Vol. 2, pp. 63–89). Norwood, NJ: Ablex.

Van den Boom, D. C. (1994). The influence of temperament and mothering on attachment and exploration: An experimental manipulation of sensitive responsiveness among lower-class mothers with irritable infants. *Child Development, 65,* 1457–1477.

Van der Molen, M. W., & Molenaar, P. C. M. (1994). Cognitive psychophysiology: A window to cognitive development and brain maturation. In G. Dawson & K. W. Fischer (Eds.), *Human behavior and the developing brain* (pp. 456–490). New York: Guilford.

van IJzendoorn M., & Kroonenberg, P. (1988). Cross-cultural patterns of attachment: A meta-analysis of the strange situation. *Child Development, 59,* 147–156.

van IJzendoorn, M. H., & Kroonenberg, P. M. (1990). Cross-cultural consistency of coding the Strange Situation. *Infant Behavior and Development, 13,* 469–486.

Vanhatalo, A. M., Ekblad, H., Kero, P., & Erkkola, R. (1994). Incidence of bronchopulmonary dysplasia during an 11-year period in infants weighing less than 1500 grams at birth. *Annaless Chirurgiae et Gynaecologiae, 208*(Suppl.), 113–116.

Vaughn, B. E., & Bost, K. K. (1999). Attachment and temperament: Redundant, independent, or interacting influences on interpersonal adaptation and personality development? In J. Cassidy & P. R. Shaver (Eds.), *Handbook of attachment: Theory, research, and clinical applications* (pp. 198–225). New York: Guilford.

Vaughn, B. E., Lefever, G. B., Seifer, R., & Barglow, P. (1989). Attachment behavior, attachment security, and temperament during infancy. *Child Development, 60,* 728–737.

Vaughn, B. E., Egeland, B., Sroufe, L. A., & Waters, E. (1979). Individual differences in infant-mother attachment at twelve and eighteen months: Stability and chance in families under stress. *Child Development, 50,* 971–975.

Ventura, S. J., Martin, J. A., Curtin, S. C., & Matthews, T. J. (1995). Report of final natality statistics. *Monthly Vital Statistics Report, 45*(11), 1–19.

Verma, R. P. (1995). Respiratory distress syndrome of the newborn infant. *Obstetrical and Gynecological Survey, 50,* 542–555.

Vernon, P. E. (1980). *Intelligence: Heredity and environment.* San Francisco: Freeman.

Vibbert, M., & Bornstein, M. H. (1989). Specific associations between domains of mother–child interaction and toddler referential language and pretense play. *Infant Behavior and Development, 12,* 163–184.

Vihman, M. M. (1991). Early syllables and the construction of phonology. In C. A. Ferguson, L. Menn, & C. Stoel-Gammon (Eds.), *Phonological development: Models, research, implications* (pp. 69–84).

Vihman, M. M., & Miller, R. (1988). Words and babble at the threshold of language acquisition. In M. D. Smith & J. L. Locke (Eds.), *The emergent lexicon.* New York: Academic.

Vihman, M. M., Macken, M. A., Miller, R., Simmons, H., & Miller, J. (1985). From babbling to speech: A reassessment of the continuity issue. *Language, 61,* 395–443.

Vital-Durand, F., Ayzac, L., & Pinzaru, G. (1996). Acuity cards and the search for risk factors in infant visual development. In F. Vital-Durand, J. Atkinson, & O. J. Braddick (Eds.), *Infant vision* (pp. 185–200). Oxford, England: Oxford University Press.

Volling, B. L., & Belsky, J. (1993). The contribution of mother–child and father–child relationships to the quality of sibling interaction: A longitudinal study. *Child Development, 63,* 1209–1222.

Volling, B. L., & Feagans, L. V. (1995). Infant day care and children's social competence. *Infant Behavior and Development, 18,* 177–188.

Von Hofsten, C. (1984). Developmental changes in the organization of prereaching movements. *Developmental Psychology, 20,* 378–388.

Vygotsky, L. S. (1967). Play and its role in the mental development of the child. *Soviet Psychology, 5,* 6–18.

Vygotsky, L. S. (1978). *Mind in society.* Cambridge, MA: Harvard University Press.

Wachs, T. D. (1987). Specificity of environmental action as manifest in environmental correlates of infant's mastery motivation. *Developmental Psychology, 23,* 782–790.

Wachs, T. D. (1999). The what, why, and how of temperament: A piece of the action. In L. Balter & C. S. Tamis-LeMonda (Eds.), *Child psychology: A handbook of contemporary issues* (pp. 23–44). Hove, England: Psychology Press.

Wachs, T. D. (in press). Person–environment "fit" and individual development. In D. M. Teti (Ed.), *Handbook of research methods in developmental psychology*. London: Blackwell.

Wachs, T. D., & Chan, A. (1986). Specificity of environmental action, as seen in environmental correlates of infants' communication performance. *Child Development, 57,* 1464–1474.

Wachs, T. D., & Combs, T. T. (1995). The domains of infant mastery motivation. In R. H. MacTurk & G. A. Morgan (Eds.), *Mastery motivation: Origins, conceptualizations, and applications* (pp. 147–164). Norwood, NJ: Ablex.

Wachs, T. D., & Gandour, M. J. (1983). Temperament, environment, and six-month cognitive–intellectual development: A test of the organismic specificity hypothesis. *International Journal of Behavior Development, 6,* 135–152.

Wachs, T. D., & Gruen, G. E. (1982). *Early experience and human development.* New York: Plenum.

Waddington, C. H. (1962). *New patterns in genetics and development.* New York: Columbia University Press.

Waddington, C. H. (1972). Form and information. In C. H. Waddington (Ed.), *Towards a theoretical biology* (Vol. 4, pp. 109–145). Edinburgh, Scotland: Edinburgh University Press.

Wakschlag, L. S., Chase-Lansdale, P. L., & Brooks-Gunn, J. (1996). Not just "ghosts in the nursery": Contemporaneous intergenerational relationships and parenting in young African-American families. *Child Development, 67,* 2131–2149.

Walden, T. A., & Knieps, L. (1996). Reading and responding to social signals. In M. Lewis & M. W. Sullivan (Eds.), *Emotional development in atypical children* (pp. 29–42). Hillsdale, NJ: Lawrence Erlbaum Associates.

Walker-Andrews, A. S. (1997). Infants' perception of expressive behaviors; Differentiation of multimodal information. *Psychological Bulletin, 121,* 437–456.

Walker-Andrews, A. S., & Dickson, L. R. (1997). Infants' understanding of affect. In S. Hala (Ed.), *The development of social cognition. Studies in developmental psychology* (pp. 161–186). Hove, England: Psychology Press.

Wallace, D. B., Franklin, M. B., & Keegan, R. T. (1994). The observing eye: A century of baby diaries. *Human Development, 37,* 1–29.

Warren, N. (1972). African infant precocity. *Psychological Bulletin, 78,* 353–367.

Wasz-Hockert, O., Michelsson, K., & Lind, J. (1985). Twenty-five years of Scandinavian cry-research. In B. M. Lester & C. F. Z. Boukydis (Eds.), *Infant crying: Theoretical and research perspectives* (pp. 83–104). New York: Plenum.

Waters, E. (1978). The reliability and stability of individual differences in infant–mother attachment. *Child Development, 49,* 483–494.

Watson, J. B. (1924/1970). *Behaviorism.* New York: Norton.

Watson, J. B. (1927, March). What to do when your child is afraid [interview with Beatrice Black]. *Children,* 25–27.

Watson, J. B. (1928). *Psychological care of the infant and child.* New York: Arno.

Watson, J. E., Kirby, R. S., Kelleher, K. J., & Bradley, R. H. (1996). Effects of poverty on home environment: An analysis of three-year outcome data for low birthweight premature infants. *Journal of Pediatric Psychology, 21,* 419–431.

Watson, J. S. (1966a). The development and generalization of "contingency awareness" in early infancy: Some hypotheses. *Merrill-Palmer Quarterly, 12,* 123–135.

Watson, J. S. (1966b). Perception of object orientation in infants. *Merrill-Palmer Quarterly, 12,* 73–94.

Watson, J. S. (1985). Contingency perception in early social development. In T. M. Field & N. A. Fox (Eds.), *Social perception in infants.* Norwood, NJ: Ablex.

Waxman, S. R., & Gelman, R. (1986). Preschoolers' use of superordinate relations in classification and language. *Cognitive Development, 1,* 139–156.

Weigle, T. W., & Bauer, P. J. (2000). Deaf and hearing adults' recollections of childhood and beyond. *Memory, 8,* 293–309.

Weinfield, N. S., Sroufe, L. A., Egeland, B., & Carlson, E. A. (1999). The nature of individual differences in infant-caregiver attachment. In J. Cassidy & P. R. Shaver (Eds.), *Handbook of attachment: Theory, research, and clinical applications* (pp. 68–88). New York: Guilford.

Weinraub, M., Horvath, D. L., & Gringlas, M. B. (2002). Single parenthood. In M. H. Bornstein (Ed.), *Handbook of parenting: Vol. 3. Status and social conditions of parenting* (2nd ed., pp. 109–140). Mahwah, NJ: Lawrence Erlbaum Associates.

Weir, C., Soule, S., Bacchus, C., Rael, J., & Schneider, J. (2000). The influence of vicarious reinforcement and habituation in contingency learning in infants. *Merrill-Palmer Quarterly, 46,* 693–716.

Weir, R. H. (1962). *Language in the crib.* The Hague, the Netherlands: Mouton.

Weisberg, P., & Rovee-Coller, C. (1998). Behavioral processes of infants and young children. In K. A. Lattal & M. Perone (Eds.), *Handbook of research methods in human operant behavior* (pp. 325–370). New York: Plenum.

Weisler, A., & McCall, R. B. (1976). Exploration and play: Resume and redirection. *American Psychologist, 31,* 492–508.

Weiss, B. (1994). The developmental neurotoxicity of methyl mercury. In H. L. Needleman & D. Bellinger (Eds.), *Prenatal exposure to toxicants: Developmental consequences* (pp. 112–129). Baltimore: Johns Hopkins University Press.

Wells, G. (1979). Variation in child language. In P. Fletcher & M. Garman (Eds.), *Language acquisition.* Cambridge: Cambridge University Press.

Wentzel, K. R. (1998). Parents' aspirations for children's educational attainments: Relations to parental beliefs and social address variables. *Merrill-Palmer Quarterly, 44,* 20–37.

Werker, J. F. (1995). Exploring developmental changes in cross-language speech perception. In D. N. Osherson, L. R. Gleitman, & M. Liberman (Eds.), *An invitation to cognitive science: Vol. 1. Language* (2nd ed., pp. 87–106). Cambridge, MA: MIT Press.

Werker, J. F., & McLeod, P. J. (1989). Infant preference for both male and female infant-directed talk: A developmental study of attentional and affective responsiveness. *Canadian Journal of Psychology, 43,* 230–246.

Werker, J. F., Pegg, J. E., & McLeod, P. J. (1994). A cross-language investigation of infant preference for infant-directed communication. *Infant Behavior and Development, 17,* 323–333.

Werner, E. E. (1972). Infants around the world: Cross-cultural studies of psychomotor development from birth to two years. *Journal of Cross-Cultural Psychology, 3,* 111–134.

Werner, E. E. (1988). A cross-cultural perspective on infancy: Research and social issues. *Journal of Cross-Cultural Psychology, 19,* 96–113.

Werner, H., & Kaplan, B. (1963). *Symbol formation.* New York: Wiley.

Wexler, K., & Culicover, P. (1980). *Formal principles of language acquisition.* Cambridge, MA: MIT Press.

Wheeler, S. F. (1993). Substance abuse during pregnancy. *Primary Care Clinics in Office Practice, 20,* 191–207.

White, B. L., Castle, P., & Held, R. (1964). Observations on the development of visually directed reaching. *Child Development, 35,* 349–364.

White, M. I., & LeVine, R. A. (1986). What is an "ii ko" (good child)? In H. W. Stevenson & H. Azuma (Eds.), *Child development and education in Japan. A series of books in psychology* (pp. 55–62). New York: W. H. Freeman.

White, R. W. (1959). Motivation reconsidered: The concept of competence. *Psychological Review, 66,* 297–333.

Whitney, M. P., & Thoman, E. B. (1993). Early sleep patterns of premature infants are differentially related to later developmental disabilities. *Developmental and Behavioral Pediatrics, 14,* 71–80.

Widom, C. S. (2000). Motivation and mechanisms in the "cycle of violence." In R. A. Dienstbier (Series Ed.) & D. J. Hansen (Vol. Ed.), *Motivation and child maltreatment* (Vol. 46 of the Nebraska Symposium on Motivation, pp. 1–37). Lincoln: University of Nebraska Press.

Wiesel, T. N., & Hubel, D. H. (1974). Ordered arrangement of orientation columns in monkeys lacking visual experience. *Journal of Comparative Neurology, 158,* 307–318.

Willatts, P. (1997). Beyond the "couch potato" infant: How infants use their knowledge to regulate action, solve problems, and achieve goals. In G. Bremner & A. Slater (Eds.), *Infant development: Recent advances* (pp. 109–135). Hove, England: Psychology Press. Erlbaum (UK) Taylor & Francis.

Wilson, D. A., & Sullivan, R. M. (1994). Neurobiology of associative learning in the neonate: Early olfactory learning. *Behavioral and Neural Biology, 61,* 1–18.

Wilson, R. S. (1978). Synchronies in mental development: An epigenetic perspective. *Science, 202,* 939–948.

Wilson, R. S. (1983). The Louisville twin study: Development synchronies in behavior. *Child Development, 54,* 298–316.

Wilson, R. S. (1984). Twins and chronogenetics: Correlated pathways of development. *Acta Genetica Gemellologica, 33,* 149–157.

Wohlwill, J. F. (1973). *The study of behavioral development.* New York: Academic.

Wolf, D., & Gardner, H. (1981). On the structure of early symbolization. In R. Schiefelbusch & D. Bricker (Eds.), *Early language: Acquisition and intervention* (pp. 287–327). Baltimore: University Park Press.

Wolff, P. H. (1966). The causes, controls, and organization of behavior in the neonate. *Psychological Issues, 5* (Monograph No. 17).

Wood, N. S., Marlow, N., Costeloe, K., Chir, B., Gibson, A. T., & Wilkinson, A. R. (2000). Neurologic and developmental disability after extremely preterm birth. *The New England Journal of Medicine, 343,* 378–384.

Woolgar, M. (1999). Projective doll play methodologies for preschool children. *Child Psychology and Psychiatry Review, 4,* 126–134.

Wright, C. A., George, T. P., Burke, R., & Gelfand, D. M. & Teti, D. M. (2000). Early maternal depression and children's adjustment to school. *Child Study Journal, 30,* 153–168.

Wyly, M. V. (1997). *Infant assessment.* Boulder, CO: Westview.

Yogman, M. W. (1998). Male Paternal behavior in humans and nonhuman primates. In N. A. Krasnegor & R. S. Bridges (Eds.), *Mammalian parenting: Biochemical, neurobiological, and behavioral determinants* (pp. 461–481). New York: Oxford University Press.

Yonas, A. (1981). Infants' responses to optical information for collision. In R. N. Aslin, J. R. Alberts, & M. R. Peterson (Eds.), *Development of* *perception: Psychobiological perspectives* (Vol. 2). New York: Academic.

Yonas, A., Arterberry, M. E., & Granrud, C. E. (1987). Space perception in infancy. *Annals of Child Development, 4,* 1–34.

Youngblade, L. M., & Dunn, J. (1995). Individual differences in young children's pretend play with mother and sibling: Links to relationships and understanding of other people's feelings and beliefs. *Child Development, 66,* 1472–1492.

Younger, B. A., & Fearing, D. D. (1999). Parsing items into separate categories: Developmental change in infant categorization. *Child Development, 70,* 291–303.

Younger, B. A., & Fearing, D. D. (2000). A global-to-basic trend in early categorization: Evidence from a dual-category habituation task. *Infancy, 1,* 47–58.

Zajonc, R. B. (1983). Validating the confluence model. *Psychological Bulletin, 93,* 457–480.

Zecevic, N., Bourgeois, J. P., & Rakic, P. (1989). Changes in synaptic density in motor cortex of rhesus monkey during fetal and postnatal life. *Developmental Brain Research, 50,* 11–32.

Zeifman, D., Delaney, S., & Blass, E. M. (1996). Sweet taste, looking, and calm in 2- and 4-week-old infants: The eyes have it. *Developmental Psychology, 32,* 1090–1099.

Zelazo, P. R., & Stack, D. (1997). Attention and information processing in infants with Down syndrome. In J. A. Burack & J. T. Enns (Eds.), *Attention, development, and psychopathology* (pp. 123–146). New York: Guilford.

Zelazo, P. R., Zelazo, N. A., & Kolb, S. (1972). "Walking" in the newborn. *Science, 176,* 314–315.

Zeskind, P. S., & Lester, B. M. (1978). Acoustic features and auditory perceptions of the cries of newborns with prenatal and perinatal complications. *Child Development, 49,* 580–589.

Zeskind, P. S., & Ramey, C. T. (1981). Preventing intellectual and interactional sequelas of fetal malnutrition: A longitudinal, transactional, and synergistic approach to development. *Child Development, 52,* 213–218.

Zigler, E. F., & Finn-Stevenson, M. (1999). Applied developmental psychology. In M. H. Bornstein & M. E. Lamb (Eds.), *Developmental psychology: An advanced textbook* (pp. 555–598). Mahwah, NJ: Lawrence Erlbaum Associates.

Zola-Morgan, S., & Squire, L. R. (1993). Neuroanatomy of memory. *Annual Review of Neuroscience, 16,* 547–563.

Zukow-Goldring, P. (2002). Sibling caregiving. In M. H. Bornstein (Ed.), *Handbook of parenting: Vol. 3. Status and social conditions of parenting* (2nd ed., pp. 253–286). Mahwah, NJ: Lawrence Erlbaum Associates.

Photo Credits

Name Index

❖

Subject Index

❖